The Oxford Reference Guide to
ENGLISH MORPHOLOGY

The Oxford Reference Guide to

ENGLISH MORPHOLOGY

Laurie Bauer, Rochelle Lieber,
and Ingo Plag

OXFORD
UNIVERSITY·PRESS

OXFORD
UNIVERSITY PRESS

Great Clarendon Street, Oxford, OX2 6DP,
United Kingdom

Oxford University Press is a department of the University of Oxford.
It furthers the University's objective of excellence in research, scholarship,
and education by publishing worldwide. Oxford is a registered trade mark of
Oxford University Press in the UK and in certain other countries

British Library Cataloguing in Publication Data

Data available

ISBN 978-0-19-957926-6

Printed and bound by
CPI Group (UK) Ltd, Croydon, CR0 4YY

CONTENTS

Part V   Interaction

Part VI   Themes

ABBREVIATIONS AND NOTATION

The phonetic transcription system we use is basically that of Wells (2008).

{ }	enclosing morphemes
/ /	enclosing representations of pronunciation where phonetic detail is not important
[ ]	enclosing pronunciations; showing alterations to quotations
< >	enclosing spellings
" "	enclosing quotations
' '	enclosing glosses; enclosing quotations within quotations
SMALL CAPS	new technical terms; lexemes; a representation of a variable by its word class
Italics	cited words and morphs; titles; data sources
Bold	to mark matters of interest in examples and quotations.
*	unacceptable
?	of questionable acceptability
%	used by some people, variable
♦	is related morphologically to
✋	not attested
~	varies with
‖	divides British and American pronunciations or spellings
'	main stress
`	secondary stress
.	syllable boundary
A	adjective
arch.	archaic
Adv	adverb
AusE	Australian English
BNC	British National Corpus
BrE	British English
CanE	Canadian English
COCA	Corpus of Contemporary American English
dial.	dialect(al)
IrE	Irish English
N	noun

NAmE	North American English
NonSt	non-standard
NZE	New Zealand English
RP	Received Pronunciation
SAfE	South African English
ScE	Scottish English
sl.	slang
St	standard
V	verb
X	a variable form or meaning, usually representing the meaning of a base

PREFACE

This project began in 2007 over breakfast somewhere in Europe, we no longer remember where. Laurie observed to Shelly that there was need for a comprehensive reference volume covering the whole of contemporary English morphology. Although English is the most extensively described of the world's languages, no such volume existed; the closest to this kind of work was Marchand (1969), and that was over 40 years old and covered only word-formation. Shelly agreed that a comprehensive reference work would be useful, and we briefly considered how it might get written. It could not be a handbook with multiple authors contributing individual chapters, as it needed to have a consistent authorial voice. But we agreed that two people could not do it. Thus was Ingo recruited. We had no idea at the time how big a project it would become, how exciting a collaboration it would be, and how much fun we would have in the process. Nor did we realize how much new we would learn about a language whose morphology we thought we knew reasonably well.

This work is a true collaboration, with each of us contributing equally to the final product, and hence the order of authors on the title page is alphabetical. Each of us participated in some way in the drafting and revising of every chapter. The reader may be able to discern different voices in the writing at different points, but we have done our best to make the volume a seamless whole. We hope we have succeeded.

There are many individuals and groups we need to thank. Shelly wishes to acknowledge the support of the Provost's office of the University of New Hampshire for a Faculty Fellowship in the early stages of our work. Thanks also to students Josh Albair and Heather Froelich for help with gathering data.

Laurie wishes to thank the Royal Society of New Zealand for a grant through its Marsden Fund which supported the project. He would also like to thank Natalia Beliaeva and Liza Tarasova for their work in support of the project.

Ingo wishes to thank the Volkswagen-Stiftung and the Thyssen-Stiftung for his *Opus-Magnum* award, which allowed him to focus on this project for an entire year and to spend parts of this year working with Laurie in Wellington. Ingo is also grateful to his colleagues at his department in Siegen who supported him during his period of absence by keeping the home fires burning.

Many thanks also go to Ingo's student assistants at Siegen, who lent their support in various ways, for example by doing extensive corpus searches, proof-reading or providing other kinds of valuable service: Julia Homann, Lena Hüsch, Jennifer Matthes, and Ute Raffelsiefer.

All three authors wish to thank several people for providing comments on individual chapters at various stages of the manuscript. These are Sabine Arndt-Lappe, Natalia Beliaeva, Melanie Bell, Linda Hilkenbach, Julia Homann, Kristina Kösling, Gero Kunter, and Mareile Schramm.

Finally, we wish to thank our spouses and families for suffering our yearly meetings. We could not have completed this book without the support and hospitality of David, Yitzl, and Raoul; Claudia, Jonas, Hannah, and Leo; Winifred and Ingrid.

PART I

Introduction

....

CHAPTER 1

Aims and structures

1.1 AIMS

English is one of the best-described languages in the world: there are hundreds, if not thousands of books and articles on various aspects of its structure and semantics, from descriptive, historical, and theoretical perspectives. Nevertheless, there is no single-volume work that focuses on the current state of English morphology. This volume is intended to fill that gap by offering a comprehensive descriptive overview of English morphology and of the theoretical problems associated with it.

Major aspects of English morphology are covered in recent textbooks (Carstairs-McCarthy 2002; Plag 2003; Harley 2006), but these are written for pedagogical purposes, and their value as general reference works is limited. Marchand's milestone monograph *The Categories and Types of Present-day English Word-formation* (Marchand 1969) and Adams's concise *Complex Words in English* (Adams 2001) cover only English word-formation, but not inflection. Marchand (1969) is devoted to the historical development of English word-formation and is largely based on dictionary data. Written over forty years ago, it is inevitably dated: we would expect that there is much that is new to say about the state of English morphology in the second decade of the twenty-first century. Adams (2001) is more recent, of course, but it does not engage with theoretical issues. Finally Huddleston and Pullum's (2002) *Cambridge Grammar of the English Language* covers English morphology briefly, but as a small part of a general grammar of English without developing the theoretical discussion, and without relating to disciplines other than traditional structural linguistics.

Morphological theory has also made great strides in recent years. Certainly, since Marchand's time there has been an explosion of interest in word-formation and inflection, both in English and other languages, with the result that our understanding of the workings of the mental lexicon is far more sophisticated than it was fifty years ago. And as will be discussed in detail in Chapter 3, our ability to find and manipulate data has improved considerably with the development of vast computerized corpora.

In sum, we see a need for a comprehensive, up-to-date overview of contemporary English morphology that is based on large collections of data that reflect the usage of words by contemporary speakers of English. In our view, such an overview should be as theory-neutral as possible to allow access for the widest possible audience, but it should be theoretically

informed, combining recent findings in corpus linguistics, theoretical linguistics, psycholinguistics and computational linguistics. Furthermore, it is our aim to include different varieties of English. In general, differences between varieties seem to be rather minor, but there
are cases where they merit discussion.

The present book will offer a thorough, data-rich description of all phenomena of English
word-formation (derivation, compounding, conversion, and minor processes such as subtractive morphology) and inflection. Our focus in the description will be on structure and
use, to the exclusion of various other interesting topics (e.g. processing or acquisition). The
descriptive account will, however, be complemented by a consideration of the theoretical
challenges that these phenomena present.

1.2   STRUCTURE OF THE BOOK

As mentioned in Section 1.1, our goal is to offer a data-rich and relatively theory-neutral
description of English morphology, combined with a consideration of some of the theoretical issues raised by the phenomena we describe. We will cover not only areas of English
morphology that have been well-studied—nominalizations, agentive forms, comparatives,
root and synthetic compounds—but also areas that have been less well studied or hardly
studied at all: adjective-forming affixes like *-al* and *-ic*, abstract noun-forming suffixes like
-hood, *-dom*, and *-ship*, neoclassical compounds, the morphology of numbers, and the status
of irregularly inflected forms in contemporary English.

There are a number of phenomena that we have chosen not to include, however. Among
these we have chosen not to discuss the formation of verb-particle constructions, on the
grounds that they are better treated as a matter of syntax than of morphology, although we
will discuss cases of conversion from verb-particle constructions (Chapter 19.2.3). We have
not included cases like *forget-me-not* or *jack-in-the-box* because we consider them to be lexicalized phrases (Chapter 19.2.1.2). Readers will also find that we have not discussed affixes or
formatives that are productive only in highly scientific or technical fields, for example, the
endings *-ate* (*perchlorate*) and *-ose* (*glucose*) that occur in chemical terms, or the suffix *-mo*
(*twelvemo*) that occurs only in the language of printers. Finally, in deciding which affixes to
treat in detail, we have largely limited ourselves to affixes that are available to native speakers
for coining new words or to affixes for which there are sufficient examples that they might
become available, for example, in jocular contexts. We will therefore exclude consideration of
historical remnants like *-ric* (*bishopric*), *-ter* (*laughter*), and *-le* (*sparkle*), which are clearly no
longer available to native speakers.

As might be imagined, there are many conceivable ways that a work of this sort might be
organized, and deciding which one most suited our aims or the demands of our readers was
a daunting task. We decided against listing individual affixes alphabetically and treating each
one separately (as Marchand 1969 does), on the grounds that doing so would preclude

making comparisons concerning the formal and semantic characteristics of various cohorts of affixes and types of conversion and compounding. We decided to separate descriptive sections from more theoretical sections in the interest of making the book as useful as possible to the widest range of potential readers, including theoretical linguists, psycholinguists, computational linguists, English language teachers, and interested non-academics.

The book is divided into six parts. The remainder of this introductory part of the book is devoted to setting out clearly and in detail the terminology we use (Chapter 2) and the methods we have applied in obtaining, analysing, and citing data (Chapter 3). Chapter 4 concerns orthographic practices that overarch inflection and word-formation in English. The descriptive chapters of the book (in Parts II–V) contain a detailed account of word-formation and inflection in contemporary English, giving equal weight to formal considerations (phonology, orthography, selectional properties, productivity) and to semantic considerations. Part II is comprised of Chapters 5 to 8, which are devoted to the inflection of verbs, adjectives and adverbs, nouns, and function words respectively. In Part III, we treat derivation, under which we include affixation and conversion, but also, where relevant, minor processes like back-formation, clipping, and the formation of acronyms. Chapter 9 gives a general overview of phonological processes that recur in many processes of English derivation. Chapters 10 to 12 concern the derivation of nouns, Chapter 13 the derivation of verbs, Chapter 14 the derivation of adjectives, and Chapter 15 the derivation of adverbs. Chapters 16–18 take up other sorts of derivation, from locatives and negatives to evaluatives. Part IV is devoted to compounding, one chapter (Chapter 19) to formal properties and another (Chapter 20) to matters of semantic interpretation. In this part we include discussions of blends, as well as of neoclassical compounds. Part V is the final descriptive section of the book, and is devoted to the ways in which various morphological processes can interact with each other in English. Chapter 21 deals with combinations of affixes, including issues of affix-ordering. Chapter 22 concerns the ways in which complex forms (compounds and phrases) interact with affixation. Chapter 23 discusses paradigmatic processes in English word-formation.

Part VI of this volume is devoted to some of the many areas of theoretical concern that have been raised by the enormous amount of research on English morphology in recent decades. We do not argue from the standpoint of any extant theoretical framework, but rather survey the issues and show where the descriptive data we have set out in sections II–V bears on them.

Although the organization of the book allows for a clear placement of most affixes, there were nevertheless quite a few cases where we were forced to make assignments to one chapter or another that might seem odd or arbitrary. As an example, we chose to put *arch-* in the chapter on Locatives of Time and Space, even though *arch-* (*archfiend*) might not seem to be locative in the same sense as *pre-* or *post-*. But since *arch-* is at least metaphorically locational, and no other rubrics seemed obvious, we felt that that chapter was the best we could do. We preferred this solution to having a chapter that we would be forced to call 'Random Bits'.

A final problem concerned the decision whether to treat particular forms as prefixes or as first elements of compounds (either native or neoclassical); for example, were we to count *nano-* (*nanometric, nanostructure*) or *over-* (*overfly, overcoat*) as prefixes or the lefthand element of compounds? We made such decisions based on whether we could find signs of particularly affixal behaviour in such forms (as set out in Chapter 19.2.2) or where it seemed useful to be able to draw parallels with obvious affixes. Again, some readers will inevitably disagree with our judgements on given points.

This book is intended to be used as a reference work, of course, and readers can dip in and look for what we have to say about one phenomenon or another. But those readers who have the interest and stamina to read the book through systematically will sometimes be surprised, as we were in gathering the data and writing the book, at the phenomenal exuberance of the morphology of English and the range of resources speakers have at their disposal to create and use new words.

CHAPTER 2

Basic principles: terminology

2.1 PROSPECTUS

In this chapter we set forth the terminology that we will use in this book. Our intention here is not to create a new theoretical framework or to endorse a particular existing theoretical framework, but rather to provide a relatively theory-neutral terminology that is sufficient to fulfil the needs of this book, without doing violence to the core of commonly accepted terms. We seek as much as possible to choose terms that are widely accepted among morphologists of all stripes, and to avoid those that have developed specialized meanings within a particular framework. We have aimed at clear, simple, and (as much as possible) uncontroversial definitions of those terms. We start in Section 2.2 with a definition of 'word' and related terms, and of the various issues they raise. Subsequent sections look at terms that concern word-internal elements, word classes, the distinction between inflection and derivation, notions of lexicalization and productivity, native versus non-native morphology, and terminology concerning syntactico-semantic concepts such as 'argument' and 'adjunct'. In what follows we will use small capitals to mark terms for which we provide definitions.

2.2 'WORD' AND RELATED TERMS

Like so many fundamental notions in linguistics, 'word' has resisted definition. Even a good definition of 'word' in a particular language proves to be surprisingly elusive; a universal definition of the notion, in anything but the broadest terms, is apparently beyond the abilities of current linguistics (see Bauer 2000; Dixon and Aikhenvald 2002). Part of the difficulty is that, as an element of the English language, the word *word* can be used to denote things which are conceptually very different from each other, and that we need a better classification and a more precise terminology if we are to serve the needs of morphologists. Fortunately, most of this terminology is widely accepted, although there are some terms which have varying usages in different theoretical frameworks.

2.2.1 Word-form and lexeme

In a sentence like (1), there are two answers to 'How many different words are there in this sentence?'

(1)   Every time Fred sees violence on TV, he says seeing it destroys the soul.

In one answer, *sees* and *seeing* are forms of 'the same word', in the other, they are 'different words'. Where *sees* and *seeing* are 'different words', we will use the term WORD-FORM; where they are 'the same word' we will use the term 'lexeme'. In other words, 'word-form' refers to a phonological/ orthographic shape irrespective of meaning. LEXEME is an abstraction over one or more word-forms that convey the same lexical meaning. Making this distinction then allows us to retain the term WORD for occasions where the distinction between word-form and lexeme is not crucial to the discussion (Bauer 1983). Word-forms are generally marked by the use of italics, while there is less agreement on a notation for lexemes. We adopt here the notation of Lyons (1968) and use small capitals. Notationally, therefore, we can say that *sees* and *seeing* are forms of SEE.

While this distinction has been well canvassed in the recent literature, it leaves various questions unanswered. To begin with, it presupposes the distinction between inflection and derivation, which is not necessarily as clear-cut as we might wish (see below, Section 2.5, and Chapter 24). Derivational affixes create new lexemes from old lexemes, inflectional affixes create new word-forms from old word-forms. To the extent that there are questions about the distinction between inflection and derivation, the distinction between word-form and lexeme is equally in doubt.

Importantly, there is equivocation in the literature as to whether an item like *but* or *the* is or is not a lexeme. For some, perhaps deriving from the French tradition, grammatical words of this type (see Section 2.2.2 on the ambiguity of the term 'grammatical word') are not lexemes. For others, there is no reason why we should not see BUT as a lexeme invariably realized by the word-form *but*. Here we take the second position, and by doing so make two assumptions: first, that an item like *but* is part of the lexis of English and not simply part of the grammar, and second that a lexeme can have a paradigm which includes only one form. Taking this approach also allows us to avoid the issue of whether there is a lexeme THIS with the two forms *this* and *these*, even though these are grammatical words in the sense used just above: for us, there is a lexeme THIS.

An error often made by beginning students is to confuse the word-form which is used as the CITATION FORM for a lexeme with the lexeme itself. We name the lexeme HIT by using one of its word-forms (although in principle we could name it in some more random way, e.g. as lexeme # 3,762). In English, the form used as the citation form for a verb is the base form of the verb. In the case of HIT, because the plain non-past form, the preterite, and the past participle form are formally identical, it is difficult to tell which form is being used except by means of the more general parallel.

In general terms, since lexemes are tied to particular inflectional paradigms (each lexeme is realized by a set of word-forms), we take the position that no noun and verb can belong to the same lexeme, since they have different paradigms. This view is apparently not shared by some dictionaries, which list, for example, *butter* (noun) and *to butter* (verb) under the same headword. While we acknowledge the relationship between these two words (which we attribute to conversion, see Chapter 25), we take it that they are distinct lexemes.

While word-forms, by definition, include inflectional suffixes (if any), it is not clear whether they include clitics. Is *butcher'll* in *The butcher'll dice the meat for you* a word-form of BUTCHER? We take this not to be the case, and rather treat forms like *butcher'll* as consisting of two separate word-forms; that is, host and clitic each constitute a word-form.

Word-forms are generally said to be definable in terms of various criteria. In particular, they are supposed to be the smallest items which can stand alone as an utterance, be themselves movable, though the elements within them are not movable, and be uninterruptable. Thus, given a form such as *uncountable*, we find the results set out in (2).

(2) a. What kind of noun is this? Uncountable.

b. There were uncountable reasons for this. The reasons were uncountable.

c. uncountable, *unablecount, *countableun, *countunable

d. *un totally countable, *uncount reason able

However useful these criteria may be, there are problems with them if they are interpreted as necessary and sufficient conditions for word-form-hood. For example, apart from mentions (for example, in the sentence "'ran' is the past tense of 'run'") past tense forms typically do not occur alone. At the same time, (3) clearly does illustrate an acceptable utterance.

(3) Are you feeling cold?—Ish.

If *-ish* is not to be interpreted as a word-form, we need some mechanism for telling us precisely when the use in isolation criterion will or will not work.

The criterion of immovable elements is apparently broken by pairs such as *armchair / chair-arm, boathouse / houseboat, doghouse / housedog*, but here the meaning is different, while the criterion is really aimed at cases where there is no contrast of meaning. Extremely marginal cases are thus things like *horse-zebra*, which for some speakers is potentially synonymous with *zebra-horse* meaning 'a cross between a zebra and a horse', although for other speakers, for example those who have special knowledge of interspecies breeding, the two compounds might have distinct denotations. The interruptability criterion is apparently broken by the marginal process of expletive insertion that gives us *kanga-bloody-roo, Talla-fucking-hassee.*

2.2.2 Grammatical word

The term 'grammatical word' is used in two distinct ways in the literature (Bauer 2004b). The first, for which we will retain the term GRAMMATICAL WORD, contrasts with LEXICAL WORD. The former includes conjunctions, articles, prepositions, particles; the latter nouns, verbs and adjectives.

For the second meaning, consider again (4).

(4)   a. I will have to **tread** in your footsteps.

     b. *It was strange to walk on the ground where he had **tread**.

     c. The **sheep** is being shorn.

     d. The **sheep** are being shorn.

In all these cases the items shown in bold are the same orthographic words, realizing a single lexeme, but fulfilling different functions. The different functions are definable in terms of the place the word-form holds in the relevant paradigm. A word defined in terms of its place in the paradigm is sometimes termed a 'grammatical word', but, to keep the distinction clear, we will prefer the alternative term, MORPHOSYNTACTIC WORD. Note that regular -*ed* forms of English verbs will typically represent two morphosyntactic words: the past tense and past participle forms. Not all identity of word-forms is due to a question of morphosyntactic words. *Bound*, out of context, may be, among other things, the past participle of BIND or a noun meaning 'jump', but this is a matter of a single word-form belonging to two distinct lexemes.

Another issue arises with respect to the form *hit* in the sentences in (5).

(5)   a. I can never **hit** the bullseye.

     b. I **hit** the bullseye last night for the first time.

Hit in (5a) has a different function from *hit* in (5b); in traditional terms, the first is the infinitive, the second is the past tense of hit. Although these two are the same word-form, they constitute two distinct morphosyntactic words, as they realize two different sets of morphosyntactic features.

2.2.3 Orthographic word

An ORTHOGRAPHIC WORD is a word-form as defined by the spelling system. Thus, if we define spaces and punctuation marks such as commas, colons, and so on as boundary markers in the English spelling system, an orthographic word is an element in a written text surrounded by boundary markers. Next we have to ask whether apostrophes and hyphens are boundary markers or not. No matter which decision is taken, this decision does not affect the problem of whether they are one or two lexemes, word-forms, and so on.

There are other places where there is inconsistency in English as to how to write individual items: *all right* versus *alright*, *in so far as* versus *insofar as*. The standardization of English spelling is so great that such examples are rare, but the fact that they persist is in itself a noteworthy point.

The lay notion of 'word' is determined by the orthographic word; this is circular, since the orthographic word is derived from some more fundamental appreciation of what a word is (although, of course, there may be some confusion where historical change affects the basis for taking a decision). It is an open question how far the orthographic word corresponds to the more technical notion of 'word-form'. Even linguists tend to assume that there is a good match (perhaps with the exceptions mentioned above), but it might be possible to argue for clitic status for items like *the, a, an* and even for subject pronouns like *I, he, she*, which would make quite an important difference.

2.2.4 Phonological word

A number of scholars distinguish the notion of 'phonological' or 'prosodic word' from grammatical or orthographic word. The PHONOLOGICAL WORD is the domain within which certain phonological or prosodic rules apply, for example, rules of syllabification or stress placement. Phonological words may be smaller or larger than grammatical or orthographic words. For example, Raffelsiefen (1999) has argued that complex words containing vowel-initial suffixes like *-ish* consist of a single prosodic word, whereas complex words that contain consonant-initial suffixes like *-less* contain two prosodic words. Words like *fattish* containing the former suffix are syllabified as one unit with the base final consonant forming the onset of the second syllable, as in (6a). In contrast, with a word like *snackless*, the base final consonant forms the coda of the first syllable. The suffix *-less* constitutes its own phonological word as in (6b):

(6)   a. $((fæ)(tɪʃ))_{P\text{-word}}$

   b. $(snæk)_{P\text{-word}}(ləs)_{P\text{-word}}$

Others define the phonological word slightly differently, for instance in terms of phonotactics, so that *unnaturally* and *brokenness* are made up of more than one phonological word each, since English words do not (otherwise) allow geminates within them (Goldsmith 1990: 122). Some scholars do not include prefixes within the phonological word (Vogel 2006: 532). There is obviously a great deal more to be said about the distinction between the phonological word and the grammatical word, and the justification for this distinction in English. We will return to these matters in Chapter 9.

2.2.5 Lexical item

By LEXICAL ITEM we understand any item which, because of its lack of predictable semantics or form, must be listed in the mental lexicon. We prefer the term 'lexical item' (used by Carstairs-McCarthy 2002: 13) over Di Sciullo and Williams's (1987: ch. 1) 'listeme'. So lexical items form a superset that includes lexemes as a subset. Lexical items also include:

- Items formed by the lexicalization of syntactic structure (e.g. *forget-me-not, jack-in-the-box, house of God, Australian Capital Territory*).
- Idioms (e.g. *by and large, red herring, take* [ ]$_{NP[+human]}$ *to the cleaners* 'ruin [NP] financially', *the man on the Clapham omnibus* 'the average man on the street' (BrE), *come the raw prawn* 'attempt to deceive' (AusE).
- Phrasal verbs (*put up* 'accommodate', *put up with* 'tolerate', *run up* 'allow to accumulate', *do in* 'murder').
- Fixed figurative expressions (*be like a dog with two tails* 'show extreme happiness', *be between a rock and a hard place* 'have only two options, each of which is unpalatable', *better the devil you know (than the devil you don't know)*).
- Proverbs (*too many cooks spoil the broth, many hands make light work*).

Many lexical items are items which can be found in standard printed dictionaries, not so much because their meaning is totally unpredictable, but because they happen to be the way the notion is expressed in English. For example, the *Concise Oxford Dictionary* (2008) lists *open marriage* (not, for instance, *free marriage*), *open sandwich* (not, for instance, *topless sandwich*), *open secret* (not, for instance, *public secret*). So lexical items may be dictionary entries, and as such are probably represented in a speaker's mental lexicon.

2.2.6 Orthography and words

As mentioned in Section 2.2.3, the general assumption for English is that orthographic words correspond to word-forms, and that these are 'words' *par excellence*. Moreover, thanks to high levels of literacy in English, the lay notion of a word is determined by the orthographic word. In most cases this does not give rise to great theoretical problems for the study of English (though we will take up issues concerning the representation of compounds in Chapter 19). However, from a theoretical standpoint, this is the wrong way around. As pointed out above, we must assume that the orthographic word is based on the linguistic knowledge of speakers, and is the output of that unconscious knowledge (based, in all probability, on criteria such as uninterruptability). Thus it is that items are more likely to be written as single words the more item-familiar (Meys 1975) they are or the more lexicalized they are. For example, the *OED* gives the case of *altogether* written as two words in the earliest forms of English, but being written as a single word from an early period (and there is a comment on confusion between *altogether* and *all together* in more modern usage). The change from *all right* to *alright* is much more modern (first citation for *alright* in the *OED* is for 1893), but the process seems the same. Thus it seems that orthography is influenced by lexicalization and frequency, though the spelling seems to be a conservative representation. In principle, this could lead to a mismatch between the linguist's notion of a word and the lay notion as represented in the orthography.

2.3 WORD-ELEMENTS

In this section we look at the elements that make up words. The elements we will consider here are not purely phonological elements such as consonants, vowels, or syllables or their orthographic equivalents, but elements which are capable of carrying meaning. We also consider ways of forming words using processes which seem to be equivalent in function to the use of the elements to be discussed here.

This is an area where there is a great deal of controversy (overt or covert) in the literature on word-structure. The term 'morpheme' is one which has multiple definitions, many of them incompatible, in writings about morphology. Our aim is not to produce yet another definition or set of definitions, or to create a new way of considering morphological structure in general. Rather we want to provide a terminology which can be used relatively transparently in discussing word structure, without leading to internal contradiction.

2.3.1 Morph

By a MORPH we understand any phonological (or graphemic) element of a word-form which has function or meaning in the construction of a word. In (7) we illustrate some word-forms analysed into morphs.

(7) a. snow-blind, sport-s-man, wind-mill

  b. cat-s, hop-ing, lift-ed

  c. pre-view, re-enter

  d. Gandhi-ism, kill-er

  e. dis-interest-ed-ness, un-contain-abil-ity

Clearly, there are different kinds of morph, and we will provide a more detailed classification and nomenclature below.

Some morphs have the ability to stand alone as word-forms (whether or not they actually do so in the word-forms in which we find them). In (7), for example, *snow*, *cat*, and *contain* have this ability, while *re-*, *-ism*, and *-ic* do not. A morph which has the ability to be a word-form on its own is termed a POTENTIALLY FREE MORPH (or FREE MORPH for short); a morph that lacks this ability (except in cases of mention in linguistic discourse) is termed an OBLIGA-TORILY BOUND MORPH (or BOUND MORPH for short). When we mention obligatorily bound morphs in isolation, we mark them with a hyphen which indicates where the rest of the word-form would have to fall, as illustrated earlier in this paragraph.

Most of the potentially free morphs in (7) have lexical meaning, which we could look up in a dictionary. With the obligatorily bound morphs, it may be clear in some instances that there is a lexical meaning, while in others this is less clear. For instance, *pre-* has a meaning of 'earlier in time', but the 'meaning' of *-ing* is far less easy to express: rather it seems to have some function (or set of functions) in creating word-forms of various lexemes.

Every word-form can be exhaustively analysed into a sequence of morphs. There are no 'left over' items in (7) which are not morphs. Note that, as elements of word-forms (or in the case of potentially free morphs, potential word-forms), morphs are treated typographically like word-forms, and written in italics when mentioned. Where appropriate, morphs may also be presented in transcription.

2.3.2 Morpheme and allomorph

A MORPHEME is classically defined as the smallest meaningful unit of morphological analy-sis; however, in order to be more precise and to make clear the relationship of the term 'morpheme' to that of 'morph', we need first to introduce a third term, 'allomorph'. There are many occasions on which morphs, though phonologically not identical, are function-ally or semantically equivalent and are in complementary distribution. Consider a simple example in (8).

(8)   embark   endanger
      embed   ensnare
      embody   entomb
      emplane   entrain

Bark, *bed*, *body*, *plane*, *danger*, *snare*, *tomb*, and *train* are potentially free morphs, and they are preceded by an obligatorily bound morph which, in every case, has the same meaning, which we might gloss roughly as 'cause to be in'. In the examples in (8), sometimes this morph is *em-*, and sometimes it is *en-*. The two variants are in complementary distribution, and we can predict which of the two will occur in any given word-form: the version *em-* occurs before bilabial consonants, and the version *en-* occurs before alveolar consonants (we avoid other environments for ease of presentation). We say that these two morphs, *em-* and *en-* are ALLO-MORPHS of the same 'morpheme'. More generally, ALLOMORPHS are phonologically distinct variants that occur in complementary phonological environments. Groupings of allomorphs may be termed morphemes.

The implication here (just as with the corresponding phonological terms of 'allophone' and 'phoneme') is that morphs are forms which occur in the flow of speech/writing, while morphemes are abstract elements which derive from the linguist's analysis. We speak of allomorphs where there are two or more morphs which belong to the same morpheme and which are normally in complementary distribution. Each of the allomorphs is one possible realization of the morpheme. Of course, in cases where there is only ever one morph to represent a particular morpheme, the same relationship holds, so that the morph *dog* is the only morph to realize (or represent) the morpheme {dog}. Since allomorphs are morphs, they are treated in the same way as morphs in terms of notation: they are italicized, sometimes transcribed.

While the distinctions made above may seem relatively clear in the abstract, it has long been noted that it is not always clear how to apply them in particular cases. There are a number of recurrent cases where this causes disagreement. For example, we sometimes find cases in which morphs are in complementary distribution, although they are not phonologically related to each other. The classic example of this is the allomorphy of plurals in English (see Chapter 7). In regular cases, the allomorphs are /s/, /z/, and /ɪz/, where /ɪz/ occurs after sibilants, /s/ occurs after other voiceless consonants, and /z/ occurs elsewhere, as illustrated in (9). This allomorphy is easily understood in phonological terms (assimilation and epenthesis to break up illegal geminates), and is not controversial.

(9) horses   /hɔːsɪz ‖ hɔːrsɪz/   judges   /dʒʌdʒɪz/
     dogs   /dɒgz ‖ dɔːgz/   flies   /flaɪz/
     cats   /kæts/   strikes /straɪks/

However, what is controversial is the status of the -*en* that occurs—in standard varieties at least—only with the lexeme ox. Is this another allomorph of the same morpheme, or is it an allomorph of a synonymous morpheme altogether? As for our purposes nothing hinges on the answer to this question, we leave this decision open.

Another difficult case is where there is form in common, but no meaning in common. The classic example of this is English words borrowed from Latin, as illustrated in (10). We do not need to know about the analyses of these words in Latin, but we do need to know whether they are all analysable into two morphs in English.

(10) concur   incur   recur
             deduce   educe   induce   reduce
      confer defer   infer   refer
      commit demit   emit   remit

comport	deport	export	import	report
contend		extend	intend	
convert		evert	invert	revert

Those who argue for the one-morph solution claim that no element smaller than the entire word here has a constant meaning (in English). That is, a recurrent meaning for the elements *in-* and *-fer* that might be argued to occur in *infer* cannot be found except by an etymological analysis. Those who argue for the two-morph analysis (e.g. specifically, Aronoff 1976) accept this point, but claim that certain regularities of behaviour are lost here if these elements are not recognized. For example, the *-mit* that occurs in these words always leads to a nominalization in *-mission*. This particular argument goes to the heart of the definition of the morpheme, which for most scholars demands a semantic unity. We will thus not accept elements like *-mit* as morphs, but we will accept them as FORMATIVES, which we define as an overarching category that includes both morphemes and elements contributing to the construction of words whose semantic unity or function is obscure or dubious.

A third vexed case is where the morphs have no associated meaning at all. These are sometimes termed EMPTY MORPHS. An example is the <n> in the word *platonic*. This <n> has no meaning; it is merely there to allow the morph *Plato* to be attached to the morph *-ic*. Items like this can be analysed in a number of ways; it might be argued that the <n> is a matter of base allomorphy (*Platon-* alongside *Plato*) or affix allomorphy (*-nic* alongside *-ic*), or that it is entirely separate from either base or affix. For the purposes of this volume where nothing hinges on the specific analysis, we will take a rather agnostic stance here and refer to elements of this sort simply as EXTENDERS. We allow extenders as morphs because we defined 'morph', above, as having 'a function or meaning', and here it is the function which is paramount.

Another problematic case is where the contrastiveness of the morphemes is low. Just like phonemes, morphemes are contrastive units. Part of the reason we recognize two morphemes (and correspondingly, morphs) in *smiles* and *smiled* is that the two words contrast in meaning (that is, in their temporal reference) and that this contrast can be located at the difference between the <s> and the <d>, which must therefore belong to different morphemes. However, there are places where the notion of contrast is less clear-cut, and where the identification of morphemes is more a matter of the preference of the analysing linguist.

As an example, consider the case of *-er* and *-or* (see Chapter 11). In most cases these elements are in complementary distribution (although the factors which determine the distribution may be complex), and are synonymous. However, there are sometimes said to be cases like *sailer* and *sailor* (the first a ship, the second a person) where there appears to be a contrast. Should such an example inevitably lead to setting up *-er* and *-or* as belonging to different morphemes? Despite the contrast—the hallmark of the morpheme—most practitioners would seem to believe that this is not sufficient, as it applies in a single isolated case and does not occur in a larger group of words. Further, the contrast turns out to be spurious, as the *OED* cites *sailer* as the older spelling, and the *sailor* spelling as a relatively recent development.

Another related example comes from items like *diner* ('location, e.g. place where one eats on a train/particular kind of restaurant/person who dines'), *driver* ('golf club/person who drives'), *sleeper* ('place on a train in which one can sleep/person who sleeps/brace laid to support railway tracks'), *smoker* ('place where one may smoke/person who smokes/device which smokes food'). In this particular case, some might argue that we have homonymous forms, but since they contrast in meaning, we might conclude that there are two (or more) different morphs of the form *-er* belonging to two (or more) different morphemes. But most practitioners resist any such conclusion, preferring to say that such cases involve polysemy and that the semantics of the single morpheme is underspecified enough to cover all of these examples (see Chapter 10).

The types of example illustrated above show why individual practitioners may disagree on particular morphemic analyses without causing real damage to the notion of morpheme. Some scholars, however, argue that the notion of morpheme is inherently flawed (see e.g. Anderson 1992). They operate with the word-form as the basic unit, within which they identify morphs (defined rather less strictly than we have defined them here), but without the link between morph and morpheme that has been drawn in this section, with the result that they do not have a category of morpheme. While we accept that there are problematic instances where the number of formal elements and the number of semantic elements does not seem to match neatly (and a form like *was* in English might be just such a case, since the meanings of 'be', 'past tense', and 'singular' are all wrapped up in what might be seen as a single morph), we find the allomorphy relationship far too useful to discard out of hand, and allomorphy implies morphemes.

2.3.3 Root, base, and affix

Three terms which are indispensible in analysing words are 'root', 'base', and 'affix', although it is difficult to define them in a non-circular fashion; we therefore rely on examples to clarify these concepts. A ROOT is the centre of a word, a lexically contentful morph, either free or bound, which is not further analysable; it is what remains when all affixes are removed. For example, in (11), the roots are *contamin, member, warn, cut, align, smoke, judge, pay, standard, impose,* and *nature*. AFFIXES are obligatorily bound items which attach to roots. In English there are two kinds of affix: PREFIXES and SUFFIXES. Prefixes are obligatorily bound morphs attached before (to the left of) a root; suffixes are obligatorily bound morphs attached after (to the right of) a root, as illustrated in (11) and (12).

(11) *Prefixes in English*: de-contaminate, dis-member, fore-warn, inter-cut, mis-align, non-smoker, pre-judge, re-pay, sub-standard, super-impose, un-natural

(12) *Suffixes in English*: America-n, fair-ness, friend-ship, girl-hood, hospital-ize, man-ly, parent-al, prefer-s, pur-ify, relate-d, usher-ette, watch-er, wish-ing

Because English frequently allows affixation to forms already containing affixes, we will sometimes have reason to use the term BASE: a BASE is any morphological element to which other elements are added in the creation of words. So a base may consist only of a root, as in a word like *friend-ly*, of more than one root, as in a compound like *file cabinet*, of a phrase like *old maidish*, or of a root plus one or more affixes, such as when the suffix *-ness* attaches to *friend-ly* in *friend-li-ness*.

Although under normal circumstances affixes are obligatorily bound and roots are poten-tially free, this is not always the case. Consider the words in (13):

(13)   nomin-ee, neuro-jargon, robot-icide, neuro-logy

In all of these words, we have morphs that are bound. The morphs *neuro-*, *-(i)cide*, and *-(o)logy* do not occur independently, and they do recur in a number of words, as affixes do. Similar to affixes, some of them typically occur in initial position (e.g. *neuro-*) and others in final position (e.g. *-(i)cide*). Still, most morphologists would hesitate to call them affixes. For one thing, if we were to term them affixes, we would be left with the possibility of a word that consists entirely of affixes (for example, *neurology*), which goes against the definition of affix given above. For another, there are some items in this category which can occur either ini-tially or finally (e.g. *derm* in *dermatitis* or *endoderm*), which is never the case for affixes in English. We will therefore make a distinction between OBLIGATORILY BOUND ROOTS (or BOUND ROOTS for short) and affixes. Obligatorily bound roots can serve as bases for affixes or other obligatorily bound roots.

It now becomes necessary to clarify the difference between an obligatorily bound root and an affix. The distinction is usually based on the type of semantic information that the morph carries: bound roots are generally said to have more substantial lexical content than affixes do, or as Bauer (1998b: 407) terms it, a higher degree of lexical density. The distinction makes intuitive sense; the meaning of *neuro-* 'pertaining to the nervous system or brain' seems much more substantial than the meaning of *re-* 'again'. In practice, however, it is not always easy to determine which morphs have sufficient lexical content to be considered bound roots, and which fall below the threshhold. Most morphologists would agree that *nomin-*, *neuro-*, and *-(i)cide* are bound roots, and that *in-*, *pre-*, *-ize*, and *-ness* are affixes. But items like *mini-*, *mega-*, and *super-* seem to fall on the line between affixes and bound roots. They convey notions of size (and also evaluation) that are often in other languages conveyed by affixes. Inevitably the amount of lexical content is a gradient matter, and different morphologists might draw the dividing line between bound roots and affixes in a different place.

Bound roots of various sorts are very important in English morphology, perhaps particu-larly so in neoclassical compounds like *phytolith* or *neurogenic*, and we will have occasion to explore the properties of bound roots in many chapters of this work. We should therefore make clear at the outset our assumption that while obligatorily bound roots are like free roots in having lexical content, unlike free roots, they lack syntactic category (see also, for example,

Giegerich 1999). Items like *nomin-* in *nominate* or *nominee,* or *bapt-* in *baptize* or *baptism* or *neuro-* in *neurology* cannot be said to be nouns, adjectives, or verbs.

Another point we should clarify concerns cases like those in (14):

(14)   a. She wore a mini. (*viz. skirt/dress*)

      b. She drove a mini.

      c. That's super.

      d. Isms and ologies (*see e.g. Eskin 1995*)

      e. The concert was mega!

      f. 'Was it good?' 'Ish.'

In (14) we see a number of items that we might normally consider to be affixes apparently being used in such a way that they are free—so clearly not obligatorily bound. We could, of course, argue that items like *ism* have become lexemes (and for some of the items, like *super,* which has a rather different meaning when it is used in isolation than when it is used as a prefix in, for example, *super-cooler,* this would seem plausible). But on the whole speakers still feel most of these elements to be prefixes being used as something else. In the terminology of Hallidayan grammar (Halliday 1966: 111–18) they have undergone RANKSHIFT.

We will also make use of the term SPLINTER on occasion. A splinter is a portion of a word that is non-morphemic to begin with but has been split off and used recurrently on new bases (free or bound). Formally it may be an affix plus some portion of its original base (e.g. *-licious* as in *bootielicious,* *-rific* as in *splatterific*), part of an original compound (*-gate* as in *Monicagate,* *-scape* as in *deathscape*), or merely the end of an originally mono-morphemic word (*-rama* as in *cashorama*). Semantically, splinters usually carry some of the semantic content of the original word from which they split (*-licious* from *delicious,* *-scape* from *landscape,* etc.), and therefore are more contentful than typical affixes (see Chapter 23 for a more detailed discussion of splinters).

A term that we will not use in this work is STEM, as it is used in at least two different ways in the literature. The term is sometimes used in the sense that we have used OBLIGATORILY BOUND ROOT. But it is also used in the British tradition for the base to which an inflectional affix can be added (see Section 2.5 on inflection). We try to avoid confusion here by eschewing the term entirely, using instead the term OBLIGATORILY BOUND ROOT as we have defined it above, and when necessary referring to the base to which inflectional affixes attach as the INFLECTIONAL BASE.

Where we have need to refer to all words derived with the same affix or by the same morphological process, we will use the term MORPHOLOGICAL CATEGORY.

Finally we mention here two sorts of word-formation to which we will return in later chapters. Both can be discussed in terms of affixes and bases but are not straightforward affixation.

PARADIGMATIC morphological processes are processes that are based on form-meaning correspondences between words, instead of the concatenation of formatives. For example, sets of forms like *baptism* ⬩ *baptize* ⬩ *baptist* and *agonize* ⬩ *agonism* ⬩ *agonist* might be considered as related in a paradigmatic fashion. In a word-based morphology all morphology might be considered paradigmatic. In an approach that is agnostic as to the question of word-based versus morpheme-based morphology, the term is mostly used to refer to processes which do not lend themselves to a straightforward analysis in terms of a syntagmatic concatenation of linguistic forms (see Chapter 23).

One sort of word-formation that might be considered paradigmatic is BACK-FORMATION, which is traditionally defined as the deletion of a suffix or prefix in analogy to pairs of base and derivative that feature the affix in question (see Chapter 23 for discussion). A classic example is the verb *peddle*, which is derived from *peddler* (originally spelled *peddlar*) on the assumption the *-er* is the personal suffix occurring in *writer*, *freighter*, etc. Once back-formation has occurred, it becomes invisible to speakers; linguistically naïve contemporary speakers have no reason to think, for example, that *peddle* was derived from *peddler*, rather than the other way around.

2.3.4 Vowel, consonant, and stress alternations

There are some instances in English morphology where changes which in most parts of the system are marked with affixes are marked by changes to the phonological make-up of the base. In such cases we find two phonologically related bases for the same lexeme. Such bases may differ in vowels, in consonants, or in stress patterns. Where vowels are involved, this is sometimes referred to in the literature as APOPHONY; we will use the more transparent terms VOWEL ALTERNATION, CONSONANT ALTERNATION, and STRESS ALTERNATION (or STRESS SHIFT) here.

There are several areas in which we find vowel alternations. In one, singular and plural nouns exhibit different vowels. The relevant pairs are shown in (15) (see also Chapter 7). Historically known as UMLAUT, those changes were caused by assimilation of the vowel in the root to a high vowel in a suffix. In every case, the suffix vowel has subsequently disappeared, so that the cause is not visible in current English.

(15) foot   feet
      goose   geese
      louse   lice
      man   men
      mouse   mice
      tooth   teeth
      woman   women

Vowel alternations also sometimes characterize the inflectional parts of irregular verbs, distinguish causative verbs from their non-causative counterparts, or link a few verbs with their corresponding nouns. Historically such alternations have been known as ABLAUT. Some examples of each type are provided in (16).

(16)   a.   *vowel alternation in inflection*

        fall   fell   fallen

        ride   rode   ridden

        sing   sang   sung

    b.   *vowel alternation in non-causative/causative pairs*

        fall   fell

        lie   lay

        rise   raise

    c.   *vowel alternation between verbs and corresponding nouns*

        abide   abode

        shoot   shot

        sing   song

We also occasionally find consonant alternations distinguishing nouns and their corresponding verbs or singular and plural in a few irregular nouns. Most, but not all, such cases involve fricatives. Examples are presented in (17).

(17)   a.   *noun/verb pairs*

        belief   believe

        defence   defend

        house (*with final* /s/)   house (*with final* /z/)

        portent   portend

        sheath   sheathe

    b.   *singular/plural pairs*

        house (with /s/)   houses (with /z/) (but not always in ScE)

        path (with /θ/)   paths (with /ð/)

        wife   wives

There are innumerable cases of stress change brought about by morphological processes in English, but the one that is of concern here is one that links words belonging to different classes, as illustrated in (18) (for further details see Chapter 9).

(18)   ábstract_{N, A}   abstráct_V

(18)   ábstract_{N, A}   abstráct_V
       íncrease_N   incréase_V
       ímport_N   impórt_V
       wálk-out_N   walk óut_V

2.3.5 Suppletion

In origin, the term SUPPLETION is used for the situation where two (or more) lexical paradigms are merged and forms from each of the lexemes are taken into a new paradigm (Boyé
2006): this is the situation we find with English *go* ◆ *went*. From there, the term has been
generalized to any case where stems in a paradigm are formally unrelated.

There are some cases in English which are uncontroversially viewed as suppletion, and
they are listed in (19). However, the definition given above is not sufficiently restrictive to
determine precisely where the boundaries of suppletion lie, what we must see as multiple
bases and what we must view as lack of morphological relatedness.

(19)   bad/badly ◆ worse ◆ worst
       be ◆ am ◆ is ◆ are ◆ was ◆ were
       far ◆ further ◆ furthest
       go ◆ went
       good/well ◆ better ◆ best
       little ◆ less ◆ least
       much/many ◆ more ◆ most
       one ◆ first
       two ◆ second

It is quite clear that instances of allomorphy caused by regular phonological operations do
not count as suppletion. Thus alternations between the forms in *persuade* ◆ *persuasive* or
opaque ◆ *opacify* do not cause suppletion (see Chapter 9.3.1.5). It is less clear that vowel
apophony (whether umlaut or ablaut) does not: certainly *sing* and *sung*, *mouse* and *mice* are
usually perceived as different grammatical words in the paradigms of the relevant lexemes.
These are not normally considered suppletive, however. Even less are alternations such as *do*
◆ *does* /dʌz/, considered suppletive, despite the fact that they create unpredictably different
bases for morphological processes.

In (20) we present a series of potentially controversial instances (see also the discussion in
Dressler 1985). Each of the examples in (20) stands for an indefinitely large set of words in
English.

(20)   a. *formally unrelated words*
         Indiana ◆ Hoosier 'resident of Indiana'
         Liverpool ◆ Liverpuddlian
         dog ◆ canine
         moon ◆ lunar
         Manchester ◆ Mancunian

       b. *borrowing from different languages*
         hexagon ◆ sexennial
         sheep ◆ mutton

       c. *competing affixes*
         intensify ◆ verbalize

       d. *alternative bases*
         Manchester ◆ Mancunian
         mystify ◆ mystification

       e. *possibly suppletion*
         three ◆ third

The examples in (20) fall into distinguishable groups, some with borderline cases. There are those where there is, by some fluke of the history of English, an unrelated word which fulfils a function which, in some other instances, could be filled by a derivative (20a). We do not see these as instances of suppletion at all, but as instances of vocabulary expansion by means other than word-formation. These include the collateral adjectives like *lunar* and *canine*, where the vocabulary expansion comes in the first instance through borrowing (see Koshiishi 2002). *Liverpuddlian*, originating as a joke about pools and puddles, is another instance of this type. There are cases like (20b) where English happens to have borrowed synonymous elements from different languages, but again there seems little reason to see these as suppletion rather than as prolific borrowing. As for (20c), even if the affixes *-ify* and *-ize* are synonymous and in complementary distribution (which is not entirely the case, though very nearly), we view them as separate items rather than as unpredictable alternates in a paradigm. The case of the intrusive *-c-* in *mystification* (20d), we treat as an extender (see Chapter 9.3.3 and Chapter 10.2.1.3) rather than as an unpredictable base. This leaves only *third* (20e), and this is the most suppletion-like example (especially since *first* and *second* were listed in (19)). The reason it is perhaps less obvious than *first* and *second* is that historically it is derived from a regular form, even if there are no other parallel formations today.

In short, we can (and will, in what follows) take quite a restrictive view of what involves suppletion; others may take a less restrictive one, and include some of the types of relation illustrated in (20).

2.3.6 Compounds

The definition of COMPOUND and the process of distinguishing compounds from phrases on the one hand and derived words on the other is notoriously fraught with difficulty, and we will discuss these issues in detail in Chapters 19 and 20. For our purposes here, we will provide a provisional and relatively uncontroversial definition of COMPOUND: we understand a compound to be a lexeme that is composed of two or more bases, with the restriction that a phrase may not occur in the righthand position.

2.3.7 Non-morphological word-elements

If by 'morphology' we mean 'those bits of word structure which can be analysed into morphs and morphemes', there is some residue of elements that do not easily fit. Some of those are considered here merely to draw attention to their existence and marginal status, as we will have little or no occasion to refer to them in what follows.

2.3.7.1 *Phonesthemes and sound symbolism*

PHONESTHEMES are elements of a word which recur and where the sound of the element often seems to reflect the meaning in some way, but which do not allow for an exhaustive analysis of words into meaningful morphs (and morphemes) (Firth 1964: 184). Some examples are provided in (21).

> (21)   a. glare, gleam, glimmer, glimpse, glint, glisten, glitter, glossy
>
>   b. bump, dump, hump, slump, thump
>
>   c. sleazy, slime, slippery, slosh, slovenly, sludge, sluggard, slum, sly

Although there may be some room for personal opinion as to which of the words belong in particular lists, on the whole the words in (21a) have something to do with light (perhaps particularly reflected light and small amounts of light); those in (21b) have something to do with a dull sound; those in (21c) have to do with something unpleasant, especially unpleasant to the touch. The effect is felt to be connected with the recurrent phonological elements, /gl/, /ʌmp/, and /sl/. Note, however, that the remnant parts of the word are not necessarily recurrent (-*int*, -*isten*, -*itter*, and -*ossy* are not recurrent word-forming elements with a constant meaning), and so an analysis of these elements as morphs would imply the establishment of a large number of morphs which occur in only one word. Although there is some evidence that phonesthemes show similarity to morphemes in terms of mental processing (Bergen 2004), they will not be treated as a morphological phenomenon here. As we will discuss in Chapter 8, we will take a similar position on items like *th-ence* and *wh-ence* or *h-ither* and *th-ither*.

Beyond phonesthemes there are some claims for sound symbolism in the English vocabulary. Most of these claims are concerned with so-called onomatopoeic words, words that are supposed to reflect directly the sounds they represent or whose production they represent, or the sounds made by the entities they denote. Examples are given in (22).

(22)   bang, bark, bow-wow, bump, coo, crash, cuckoo, groan, gurgle, hiss, miaow, murmur, neigh, splash, squeak, squeal, twitter, whicker, whoosh

The degree of match with reality that is implied by such words is filtered through language history and cultural expectations: other languages' onomatopoeic words for the same sounds or entities would not necessarily sound anything like these. Even if these sounds are taken to represent real-world sound in some way, the words themselves are generally monomorphemic. There are no elements in them whose function is to represent a particular sound or sound-type.

The other main place where sound symbolism is sometimes claimed is with words denoting size, including diminutives. It is sometimes claimed that words denoting smallness or closeness are produced with a narrow passage between the front of the tongue and the hard palate (so high front vowels and palatal consonants), while words denoting largeness or distance are produced with the mouth wider open (low vowels, possibly velar consonants). *Here* has a higher vowel than *there*, and *little* has a higher vowel than *large*, illustrating the way in which these correlations are supposed to work. Of course, *distant* and *close*, *small* and *big* have the vowels precisely the wrong way round. In order to determine how far this supposed correlation fits, some kind of statistical survey of all relevant English words would have to be undertaken, although to our knowledge no such survey has been made. We note, though, that diminutive suffixes in English (see further Chapter 18) such as *-ling* and *-y* do fit with the general predictions to some extent.

2.3.7.2 *Subtractive and prosodic morphology*

English has a number of ways of forming new words that involve either the subtraction of elements or the manipulation of the prosodic structure of words. Some of these processes are more systematic than others, and it may be disputed whether they deserve to be treated as morphological, as these ways of making new words do not readily allow for analysis into morphs or morphemes and in some cases (initialisms and acronyms, not treated in this work) are based on orthography rather than on morphology.

One type of word-formation that is based on the prosodic structure of words is CLIPPING, that is, the shortening of a word by deletion of some of its phonological material. Some simple examples are given in (23).

(23)   a.   brill • brilliant, deli • delicatessen, jumbo • jumbo jet, lab • laboratory, photo • photograph

....

   b. jamas ◆ pyjamas (*BrE*), phone ◆ telephone, blog ◆ weblog

   c. tec ◆ detective (*BrE, archaic*), shrink ◆ headshrinker, flu ◆ influenza

As has been shown in Lappe (2007), there are several relatively systematic patterns that determine the phonological shape of the output, with the resulting word conforming to particular requirements on syllable structure, stress, and its relation to the base word. Clippings will be discussed in Chapter 18.

   Another type of prosodic morphology is the process of expletive insertion (McMillan 1980). This looks like a form of infixation, except that what is inserted into the middle of a word is not an affix, but an entire word. This process is illustrated in (24) and discussed in more detail in Chapter 18.

(24)   abso-bloody-lutely, guaran-frigging-tee, kanga-bloody-roo, propa-fucking-ganda

2.4 WORD CLASSES

WORD CLASSES, also traditionally called syntactic category, form-classes, or parts of speech, are classifications of the words of a language in accordance with their grammatical behaviour. Because school-grammar inherited a set of word classes from classical grammar, it sometimes comes as a surprise to the uninitiated to realize that these classes are creations of linguists, and not part of nature. Accordingly, the precise criteria used to delimit a particular class and the number of classes needed to classify the words found in any given language, are open questions, and there may be many solutions to the problem. Having said that, we will mainly be concerned with just four word classes here: nouns, verbs, adjectives, and adverbs. On the whole these are the least controversial classes, and they are the most critical in a description of the morphology of English. This is not to say that other word classes such as prepositions and demonstratives never participate in processes of word formation in English, but merely that this participation is infrequent and far more marginal than the inflection and derivation of nouns, verbs, adjectives, and adverbs.

2.4.1 Defining word classes

Typically, WORD CLASSES are defined in terms of a number of intersecting criteria, including phonological, morphological, syntactic, and semantic criteria. As there is substantial discussion of the criteria for determining word classes in both the theoretical and descriptive literature (Quirk *et al.* 1985; Huddleston and Pullum 2002), we will assume familiarity with the basic criteria and simply refer the reader to the relevant sources (for example, Baker 2003 or

Croft 1991 for theoretical treatments and Quirk *et al.* 1985, and Huddleston and Pullum 2002 for descriptive treatments).

One issue that we should mention at least briefly, though, is whether we need to assume the existence of distinct syntactic categories at all, given examples like those in (25) and (26):

(25) a. The bottle is empty.

b. We should empty the bottles down the sink.

c. What should I do with the empty?

(26) a. His clothes were dripping by the time the rain stopped.

b. Her dripping nose was a real embarrassment to her.

c. They ate dripping on stale bread.

We will not provide the details here, but will discuss such examples in Chapter 25, as a matter of CONVERSION, that is, a change from one word class to another with no concomitant change in form.

2.4.2 Lexical versus grammatical, open versus closed classes

The word classes noun, adjective, verb, and adverb are OPEN word classes; that is they can easily receive new members by the application of morphological processes. Ayto (1990), for example, a dictionary of newly registered words from the last years of the 1980s, lists many new adjectives, nouns, and verbs (e.g. *aspirational, biodiversity, anonymize*), a few adverbs (e.g. *futuristically*) but no other types. Classes like prepositions, conjunctions, modals, determiners, pronouns, and so on are so-called CLOSED classes: any changes to them are rare, frequently involving a change to a whole paradigm, and such changes do not usually arise through the use of morphological processes. These closed classes provide grammatical information, and are therefore termed 'grammatical words' (see Section 2.2.2.), while adjectives, nouns, verbs, and adverbs are termed 'lexical words'.

2.4.3 Transposition

The term TRANSPOSITION has been used in two ways in the morphological literature. One use designates as transposition morphological processes that cause a change of word class without concomitant semantic change other than what results from changing category. For example, *parent* is a noun, but *parental* is an adjective that just means 'pertaining to parents'; *amaze* is a verb, but *amazement* is a noun that denotes the 'process or result of amazing'. The other use of the term designates a change such as the one illustrated in *employ* and *employer* which involves both a category change from verb to noun, and also a specific semantic effect, which we can loosely gloss as 'one who VERBS (someone)'. Because of the ambiguity in the use of the term, we will avoid speaking of transposition, and where relevant, talk of category-change and accompanying semantic effects.

2.4.4 Headedness

There is a tradition in morphological studies (Marchand 1969; Williams 1981; Lieber 1992) of seeing the morpheme in a word which determines the word class of the word as the HEAD of the word. This is an extension of the syntactic notion of head, according to which the head of the noun phrase *big books* is the noun *books*, the head of the prepositional phrase *in the woods* is the preposition *in*, the head of the adjectival phrase *extremely poor* is the adjective *poor*, and so on. The head of the phrase is seen as characterizing the phrase in terms of word class and other grammatical and semantic properties. The difference between the syntactic notion of headedness and the morphological notion in this tradition is that the set of criteria used for determining headedness tends to be narrower in morphology (see Bauer 1990 for a review, and Matthews 2007 for a wider critique of the way in which the notion of head has been used). Moreover, it is not always clear how the notion of head is to be applied in morphology, especially within inflectional morphology, a subject to which we now turn.

2.5 INFLECTION VERSUS DERIVATION

Appeal has already been made to the distinction between inflection and derivation: INFLECTION creates word-forms from known lexemes, DERIVATION creates new lexemes from other lexemes. Thus, for example, the creation of a form *employs* from the lexeme EMPLOY would almost universally be accepted as inflection, and the creation of a lexeme AMAZEMENT from AMAZE would almost universally be accepted as derivation. There are, however, other instances which are far less clear-cut: both the creation of *caterpillars* from *caterpillar* and the creation of *usefully* from *useful* have, by different authorities, been assigned to both categories (see e.g. Beard 1982; Haspelmath 1996). Thus the notions of inflection and derivation must be given some independent content if a suitable definition is to be provided.

   This has been done in the recent literature by viewing inflection and derivation as canonical categories, and by providing a number of criteria which, in the canonical cases, distinguish the two, or tests which can be used to determine which kind of morphology is being used in individual cases. There is a great deal of discussion about the distinction in the literature (see for example, Scalise 1988; Dressler 1989; Anderson 1992; Plank 1994), but here we will simply list some criteria from Plank (1994), referring the reader to Chapter 24 for further discussion.

- Inflection is typically formally regular; derivation may not be.
- Inflection is typically semantically regular; derivation may not be.
- Inflection is typically fully productive; derivation typically shows (unmotivated) gaps in productivity.
- Inflection does not add significantly to the meaning of the base, but contextualizes that meaning; derivation adds to the meaning of the base.
- Inflection allows prediction that a form will exist to cover some notion; derivation does not allow the same security of prediction.
- Inflection does not change the major category (noun, verb, etc.), but derivation may.
- Inflection is what is relevant to the syntax; derivation is not syntactically relevant.
- You cannot replace an inflected form with an uninflected form in a sentence, but you can replace an inflectional base (which may have been created by derivational morphology) with a morphologically simple form (that is, one belonging to a different lexeme).
- Where both occur in the same word-form, derivational affixes are typically closer to the root than inflectional ones.

Plank (1994) argues that criteria like these provide a clear-cut distinction between inflection and derivation in English, and this is true for many affixes. But it is not true for all (see Beard 1982 on plurals; Haspelmath 1996 on *-ly* adverbs). In Chapter 24, we will return to the issue of how to distinguish inflection from derivation in English. In the meantime, however, we must make some sort of decision as to what to treat under inflection and what to treat under derivation in the descriptive sections of this work. For presentational purposes, we here stipulate that the following processes of English morphology are inflectional: plural and possessive marking on nouns, third-person singular marking on present-tense verbs, past tense and past participle marking on verbs, present participle marking on verbs, comparative and superlative marking on adjectives and adverbs. All other affixal processes in English are derivational.

2.6 Lexicalization and productivity

2.6.1 The historical development of individual words

If we trace a word through its own individual history, we find a number of distinguishable phases. Consider the word *incentivize*, listed by Ayto (1990) as originating in 1989. If we accept that date seriously (though it may only represent the first attested date of the word in print, not the first use of it), we can say that in 1988 there was no such word. However, there was a pattern available to speakers of English in 1988, based on words like *collectivize, computerize, editorialize, fossilize, revolutionize,* and dozens like them, where *-ize* is added to a noun with any one of a relatively small number of meanings (see Plag 1999; Lieber 2004; and Chapter 13 on the semantics of *-ize*). In 1988, therefore, *incentivize* was a possible or POTEN-TIAL WORD, one which the system had the ability to create, but for which there was as yet no perceived need.

We can rephrase that by saying that in 1988, *incentivize* was TYPE-FAMILIAR to speakers of English, but not ITEM-FAMILIAR. Speakers were aware of the general pattern (this is what we mean by the term TYPE-FAMILIAR), but did not know this particular word formed on the pattern. Not until the potentiality was taken up in 1989 did the word have the possibility of becoming ITEM-FAMILIAR (Meys 1975). In principle, the moment that *incentivize* was COINED, it moved from being a potential word to being an ACTUAL (or existing) WORD. Of course, the moment of coining (or the written or spoken record of it) is rarely observable, and the transition between a potential word and an actual word is impossible to capture precisely. In many cases, the same form may be coined several times before it becomes part of the usage of a community, at which time we can say that the word has become INSTITUTIONALIZED. For that reason, the notion of actual words is notoriously fraught with difficulty.

Lexicographers like to distinguish between NONCE WORDS (new words which are used but do not become institutionalized or widely established in community use) and NEOLO-GISMS which eventually become part of the community's norm. From a morphological point of view it is not clear that the two processes are distinct. Both deal with the creation of a new word using the available resources of the language of the community; the difference is merely a matter of whether speakers pick up the new word, something which is a sociological phenomenon as much as a linguistic one. We will therefore confine ourselves to the term 'neologism' in this work, and avoid the use of the term 'nonce'.

The moment a word is used any vagueness that there may be in its linguistic structure is removed. For example, *zinger* (Ayto 1990) could in the abstract be a person, an animal, or an object, and only after its first use does it become fixed as meaning 'a riposte'. This is the start of IDIOMATIZATION. Typically it occurs with the passage of time. Idiomatized words do not have a meaning that is compositionally retrievable from the elements (the morphemes) which make up the word. For instance, the word *driver*, when it denotes a human, not only denotes a person who makes a thing move forward, but denotes someone who drives a motor vehicle on land. It is not clear how much of this information should be considered part of the linguistic structure of the words concerned, and how much should be said to be part of usage; it is clear, though, that extra information can be added to the perceived meaning of the word that is not reflected in its morphological structure. Sometimes this extra information becomes more important than the morphological information. The transmission in a car may indeed transmit something from one part of the vehicle to another, but we think of it as a piece of machinery rather than in terms of its transmitting function. We should also note that although idiomatization typically occurs with the passage of time, it is nevertheless possible for words to be coined with meanings that are idiomatic from their inception; for example, according to the *OED*, the verb *cannibalize* was attested from the very beginning with the meaning 'to take parts from one machine to use in another'. It has never had the compositional meaning 'to act like a cannibal'.

It is also the case that a word can lose its connections with its base because of changes in the language or changes in society. To *solicit* can be a crime ('to offer one's services as a prostitute'), but a *solicitor* in the British legal system is a person of standing, who would not be expected to be involved in soliciting of this kind. *Solicit* has gained new meanings since *solicitor* was coined. On the other hand, the world has changed so that *fighter* can denote a plane as well as a person.

Words whose origins remain transparent change their phonological form in line with the changing pronunciation of their elements. As the pronunciation of *child* has changed, so the pronunciation of *childhood* has kept up. But where the semantic link is lost, a word may change its form independent of the form of its elements. The history of English is full of such cases: consider *lord* from *loaf ward*, *hussy* from *housewife*, *health* from *heal* (and ultimately from *whole*) and *forehead*, which was once /fɒrɪd/ and changed its pronunciation as a consequence of the spelling. Once phonological changes have occurred which divorce a morphologically complex word from its base (and/or its affixes), a word loses its status as a multi-morphemic unit, and becomes monomorphemic.

If the loss of motivation affects all the words formed with a particular affix or word-formation process, that process may be lost. At one stage in the history of English, there must have been a process of vowel change that linked verbs to their causatives. We have only a few such examples left (for example, *fall • fell, lie • lay*). Speakers today no longer perceive the derivational relationship here, and the process is, to all intents and purposes, dead.

Similarly, there used to be a set of verbs beginning with the form *to-*, just as we still have a set of verbs beginning with *with-* (*withdraw, withhold, withstand*). We can no longer see any constant meaning associated with the *with-* in these formations, but the *to*-formations (some listed in (27)) have vanished completely.

(27) to-hang   'append'
      to-hear   'listen to'
      to-lay   'put forward'
      to-set   'affix'
      to-stand   'assist'

The vanishing of the individual words here has meant that the entire pattern is lost: we can no longer make new words according to this pattern at all.

Having said that, it is often difficult to say whether a particular pattern has vanished or not. The process which gives *breadth, depth, length, warmth* and others is often cited as an example of a dead process, and it probably is. But *coolth* keeps getting reinvented (it has been around since the sixteenth century). Wentworth (1941) is a lengthy illustration of the fact that the suffix -*dom*, whose demise had been proclaimed repeatedly in the early twentieth century, was (and still is) alive and well (see Chapter 12).

2.6.2 Availability

Sometimes the history of a word is a description of the process of lexicalization. Words may move from being morphological complexes (sometimes, syntactic complexes), through reducing levels of transparency, affected by both semantic and phonological features, to the point of being unanalysable and monomorphemic or until they vanish completely. Processes which can still be exploited in the speech community for the creation of new words are said to be AVAILABLE (or, in less specific terms, PRODUCTIVE). The ablaut giving rise to causative verbs and verb-formation with *to-* are no longer available to speakers of current English. We cannot create a verb *say* meaning 'to cause to sigh' or a verb *to-sit* meaning, perhaps, 'to visit the sick' and expect to be understood in the current state of the language. On the other hand, *incentivize* is a relatively recent word which could be coined and understood in the language of the late 1980s. The process of -*ize* suffixation is available to speakers.

It is not always clear whether something is available or not. Bauer (2001: 9) suggests that -*ment* is no longer available in modern English, but we later (see Chapter 10) find some evidence that it is still used occasionally. Nevertheless, in principle the question of whether something is available is a yes/no decision. In general terms, when we speak of a process being 'unproductive' or of 'marginal productivity' we mean that as far as we are able to ascertain, the process cannot be freely used by members of the speech community of English.

2.6.3 Profitability

Processes which are available are not all available to the same degree. Although -*ness* and -*ity* are both available as suffixes in current English, we find that -*ness* is used to form neologisms more often than -*ity* is. The degree to which something can be used to create new words is termed the PROFITABILITY of that process. A great deal of the variation in profitability can be attributed to the number of domains in which a particular process can be used, but some of it is a matter of competition between processes, some of it is a matter of the meaning associated with a particular process and the corresponding value of the process to speakers, and some of it appears to be residual randomness.

By DOMAIN, we understand a linguistically defined set of bases that promote or permit the use of a particular morphological process. Another way of looking at the same idea is to say that there are constraints on when a particular process can be used. Consider some examples:

2.6 Lexicalization and productivity   33

The *-ly* suffix which creates adjectives like *friendly, stately, weekly, womanly* is, when it is used to coin new words, used most notably on bases which denote humans (perhaps rational beings). Examples from the British National Corpus (BNC) are given in (28).

(28)   actorly, auntly, dancerly, designerly, headmasterly, readerly, ruffianly, spinsterly, writerly

Thus the domain (possibly one of the domains) of this suffix is bases which are [+ human].

The suffix *-ity*, despite a very few minor exceptions like *oddity*, is added to words which are of non-native origin (see below, Section 2.7 and also Chapter 27). Typical examples include those in (29):

(29)   acidity, activity, chastity, circularity, fertility, feudality, mediocrity, obesity, orality, scarcity, scrupulosity

One of the ways in which the non-native character of the word in the base can be guaranteed is by having a non-native suffix. One of the suffixes which most obviously takes native words and turns them into suitable bases for *-ity* suffixation is *-able*. So one of the domains for *-ity* suffixation is words with the final suffix *-able*. Examples from Corpus of Contemporary American English (COCA) are given in (30).

(30)   absorbability, actability, ad-lib-ability, ageability, answerability, bendability, brushability, climbability, cryability, fakeability, foldability, garageability, guessability

The nominal *-al* which derives nouns from verbs applies only to verbs which have stress on the final syllable (some examples from BNC are given in (31)). The sole apparent exceptions are the word *burial* (which historically was not derived with this suffix, though the etymological difference is no longer visible) and *-al* nouns which have subsequent prefixation which changes the stress, for example *mistrial*. Note that this does not mean that all verbs which have final stress take *-al*; it only means that to take *-al*, there must be final stress, or, to phrase it differently, *-al* derivatives are stressed on the penult.

(31)   accrual, acquittal, appraisal, approval, arousal, arrival, betrayal, betrothal, carousal, committal, conferral, denial, dispersal, disposal

Finally, profitability is affected by COMPETITION between processes. Two processes compete when they both have the potential to be used in the coining of new synonymous forms from the same base. Usually, competition disappears over time, and processes become semantically or formally specialized. Thus, for instance, Plag (1999) argues that *-ify* and *-ize* are largely in complementary distribution, depending on the form of the base, and thus compete only with regard to a very small number of possible bases.

2.6.4 Blocking

Another factor which may limit the profitability of particular processes is BLOCKING (Aronoff 1976). Blocking may be defined as the failure of a particular word to become established in a community due to the fact that a word with the same base and the same meaning is already established in that community. The classic example is the lack of the word *gloriosity*, ostensibly blocked because there is an already established word *glory*. The basic argument is that the existence of a word already bearing a meaning precludes the coining of another word with the same meaning. We discuss the notion of blocking in detail in Chapter 26.

2.6.5 Notions of regularity and irregularity

The notion of productivity is tied in with the notion of regularity, but not in any direct manner. Processes which are productive are often regular, but processes that are regular need not be productive. In practice, the notion of regularity may mean any one of a number of things.

It may mean that something is rule-governed. The notion of rule-governedness itself is not entirely obvious, but refers to a pattern which is frequent enough and predictable enough that it seems feasible to give a set of statements which reflect the way in which words are coined using a particular process. Rule-governedness would involve stating domains, for example. At the other end of the scale, there would be cases that are clearly not rule-governed: this is certainly the case for the plural form *oxen*, since this precise affixation process without accompanying vowel change applies only to this word. This case must involve lexical listing, rather than formation by rule, which would imply availability.

Regularity may also mean that something is frequent. However, if regularity is frequency, it is not necessarily correlated with productivity. Something may be frequent in texts without being productive at all. The example of the suffix *-ment*, cited above, is relevant here. Conversely, rare morphological processes may be productive: it is difficult for *step-* to be added to much, because in general it is added to names of close relatives, and there are not many such potential bases. However, it is extended to words like *step-son-in-law* and *step-relations* (BNC), which suggest a certain degree of profitability and availability given appropriate circumstances.

Regularity may also mean that a formation is morphotactically and semantically transparent. Highly profitable processes are always semantically transparent (though not necessarily unambiguous), but the apparent continued availability of some vowel change processes for irregular past tenses suggests that availability is not always the same as transparency.

Accordingly, it is preferable to be more specific than calling any process 'regular', though we will talk of semantic regularity, meaning semantic constancy associated with a particular process.

It should also be noted that because it is possible for there to be processes which are available but which are not equally profitable, the output sets (and correspondingly, the frequency of the formation types in text) may differ considerably. It does not follow that only one (or some other small number) of these sets is 'regular'. Regularities may be statable over small numbers of words as well as over large numbers.

2.7 NATIVE AND NON-NATIVE

English is a language that has had a long history of contact with and borrowing from other languages, such that both its vocabulary and the processes by which new words are formed can be classed as NATIVE or NON-NATIVE (although not always perfectly neatly). Other terms used for the distinction are GERMANIC, for native, and LATINATE or LEARNED for non-native. To understand the distinction it is necessary to know at least a bit of the history of English.

The English language is derived from a West Germanic language originally spoken along the North Sea coast in modern Friesland. Various dialectally varied versions of this language were brought to England with the Anglo-Saxon invaders, who overran the Celts (of whom very few direct traces remain in the English vocabulary). With the Viking invasions, another layer of Germanic, but North Germanic, was added to the West Germanic fundaments. Words and word-formation processes from these Germanic origins are the ones that we call NATIVE.

In 1066, the Norman invasion brought French to England. French was mostly used by those with some kind of authority, not in everyday interaction in the villages, so that English remained remarkably free of French influence on the grammatical system. However, a large number of French words were added to the English vocabulary. With the Renaissance, in order to improve English and make it a language fit for modern usage, a huge number of Latin and Greek words were added to the Germanic and French ones. A large number of pairs and triplets still exist in modern English, distinguished by their etymological origin. Some of these are illustrated in Table 2.1.

Eventually, sufficient words containing particular affixes were borrowed so that a pattern could be perceived in English, and new words were coined in English containing these non-native affixes. At this point, those affixes become part of the English language. These patterns are the ones that we refer to as NON-NATIVE.

When undertaking an analysis of the non-native stratum of English word-formation, care is always required. Some words have been borrowed in their entirety, for example, *countess*, *hostess*, *princess*, and *prioress*; others such as *adulteress*, *ambassadress*, *authoress*, *heiress*, and *priestess* are genuine English formations, in the sense that the affix is attached to a base on which it could not be found in the source language. The latter cases are instances of English word-formation; the former set are instances where a particular suffix can now be analysed, but which were not instances of English word-formation. Of course, as far as native speakers of the language are concerned, the two sets of examples cannot be distinguished.

Table 2.1 Native and non–native triplets

Germanic	French	Latin/Greek
abide	endure	tolerate
adder, snake	serpent	viper
ask	enquire	interrogate
blue	azure	cerulean
bold	impudent	audacious
breach	infringement	violation
choice	preference	predilection
dear	precious	valuable
dwell	reside	inhabit
foretell	prophesy	predict
hallowed	sacred	consecrated
hire	payment	remuneration
lithe	pliant	flexible

From Earle (1890)

It is clear from Table 2.1 that not only were new roots introduced, but also words that were complex in their language of origin.

2.8 Lexical syntactico-semantic terminology

A major goal of this work is to describe the semantic range and scope of the word-formation processes of English. It is therefore necessary to have a vocabulary with which to discuss the lexical semantic properties of these processes. Some terms that we make use of should be familiar and will be used in the expected way. Among these are terms like: 'count' and 'mass'; 'gradable' and 'non-gradable'; 'event' and 'state'; 'agent', 'patient', 'theme', 'location', 'source', 'goal', 'instrument', and 'beneficiary'. What is especially problematic, however, is that there is no established terminology for describing the kinds of quasi-syntactic relations that we find in some types of derivation and compounding. By this we mean types of derivation or compounding where the interpretation of a word or part of a word can be likened to that of, for example, the subject or object of a sentence. We will therefore try to be especially clear about the terminology that we will employ.

2.8.1 Argument, adjunct, and verbal diathesis

Some of the terminology we will make use of is familiar from syntactic theory. The terms ARGUMENT and ADJUNCT are used in syntax to refer to phrases that stand in specific relations to the verb. Arguments are phrases that are semantically required by the verb. INTRANSITIVE verbs are verbs that require one argument, typically the subject (although see below). TRANSITIVE verbs require two arguments, subject plus either object or prepositional object. DITRANSITIVE verbs require two arguments in addition to the subject:

(32)   *Intransitive verbs:* yawn, sneeze, arrive, fall
        The chiropractor yawned.
        The guests have arrived.

(33)   *Transitive verbs*:
        a. *With object*: eat, cover, destroy, catch
            Our dog eats insects.
            The children destroyed the sandcastle.

        b. *With prepositional object*: suffer, adhere
            My mother-in-law suffers from insomnia.
            We will adhere to your rules.

(34)   *Ditransitive verbs*: show, put, give, tell
        We showed the painting to the expert.
        Someone put grease on the doorknob.

Note that although arguments are semantically necessary to the meaning of a verb, they may not always be obligatory syntactically; a verb like *eat* can have an implicit object, as we find, for example, in a sentence like *I am eating.* In referring to the range of arguments required by a given verb, we use the term VERBAL DIATHESIS.

One distinction that we will occasionally make reference to in this work is the distinction between two types of intransitive verbs, those that are termed 'unaccusative', and those that are termed 'unergative' (the terminology is admittedly awkward, but it is sufficiently standard at this point that we will not try to improve on it). UNACCUSATIVE verbs are those intransitive verbs whose single argument is interpreted as a theme or patient (for example, *arrive* or *fall*). UNERGATIVE verbs are those intransitive verbs whose single argument is agentive, even if involuntarily so (for example, *yawn* or *sneeze*). The former tend in English to be verbs of change of state or of directed motion, the latter verbs that denote movements or actions of the body, although there are some unaccusative and unergative verbs that do not belong to either of these categories. Typical diagnostics are available in the syntactic literature for distinguishing unergative and unaccusative verbs; for example, unergatives, but not unaccusatives, can be used in the so-called 'reflexive plus result' construction but not unaccusatives (e.g. *I yawned/*arrived myself tired*).

ADJUNCTS are phrases that are not semantically necessary to the meaning of a verb. For example, in the sentence in (35), the phrases in brackets express notions of location, time, and beneficiary that add optional information:

(35) Matilda played the sonata [in the drawing room] [last night] [for the countess].

So whereas the verb *play* requires only a subject and an object, it may optionally occur with phrases that express other semantic relations. The verb *put*, on the other hand, requires a subject, object, and location as part of its diathesis.

While the distinction between argument and adjunct is relatively clear in theory, it is notoriously difficult to deploy in practice. For English there are a number of standard tests that can be used to distinguish arguments from adjuncts (see, for example, Carnie 2006)—for example, an adverb can be inserted before an adjunct but not before an argument; the order of adjuncts can be changed, but not the order of arguments—but these tests sometimes give conflicting results. We will not attempt to solve this problem here, but will try to stick to cases where the distinction between argument and adjunct is relatively clear-cut.

Another issue with regard to arguments is the extent to which simplex items other than verbs can be said to allow (or require) arguments. That some adjectives (e.g. *fond*) take arguments is relatively uncontroversial. The ability of simple nouns to take arguments is somewhat more controversial. Here we will assume, following Löbner (1985), that nouns can indeed be said to have arguments. Nouns like *leg*, *mother*, or *author* will be termed RELATIONAL nouns here. These are nouns whose semantics presuppose another 'participant'; a *leg* must be a leg of something, a *mother* must be mother of someone, and so on. Nouns that do not presuppose other phrases (e.g. *book*, *wisdom*) in this way can be termed SORTAL.

2.8.2 Referencing

It is very often the case in word-formation that a derived word that is based on a verb or relational noun refers to one of the arguments of that verb or noun. For example, forms in English derived with the suffix *-er* generally denote participants in an event that would be expressed by the subject of a sentence, for example, agent (*writer*) or instrument (*copier*); that is, a *writer* is someone who writes, a *copier* something that copies. Similarly, in a compound like *city employee*, the first element of the compound denotes a participant that would be expressed by the subject in a sentence, the second a participant that would be expressed by an object; that is, the interpretation is that the city employs someone. We will have occasion in Chapter 11 to go into the complex polysemy exhibited by personal affixes in very great detail. We just point out briefly here that it would be inaccurate to refer to *-er* nouns as agent and *-ee* nouns as patient nouns, as each of these affixes can express a range of thematic relations compatible with the functions of subject and object in a sentence. We could, of course, call them 'subjective' and 'objective' affixes instead. However, the terms 'subjective' and 'objective' are already multiply polysemous and to use them in this specialized way is likely to lead to unnecessary confusion.

We therefore propose to use the terms SUBJECT-REFERENCING and OBJECT-REFERENCING instead. When derived words or parts of compounds denote a participant that would normally be expressed as the subject of a sentence, we will call those words SUBJECT-REFERENCING. Similarly, when derived words denote a participant that would normally be expressed by the object or prepositional object of a sentence, we will call them OBJECT-REFERENCING and PREPOSITIONAL-OBJECT-REFERENCING. A word like *driver* is subject-referencing. The word *truck* in the compound *truck driver* is object-referencing, although the compound as a whole is subject-referencing, as it is a hyponym of its head.

2.9 LAST WORD

We have tried in this chapter to clarify the main terms that will recur throughout this work. More specialized terms will inevitably be introduced in some chapters, and we will endeavour to define and exemplify them as we go along.

....

CHAPTER 3

Basic principles: methods

3.1 PROSPECTUS

A central aim of this reference volume is to present as broadly as possible the contemporary state of English morphology, comprising both inflection and word-formation. In the past, such wide coverage of contemporary data was difficult if not impossible to achieve. Marchand's monumental *Categories and Types of Present-Day English Word-Formation* (Marchand 1969) was mainly historical; his chief source of data was the *Oxford English Dictionary* (*OED*). Of course, as Marchand's intention was to trace the history of various word-formation processes, the enormous richness of the *OED* was quite suitable for his aims. Our intent is not to revisit Marchand's territory, however, but rather to look closely at the current state of English word-formation. In this chapter we discuss how we have generated the data on which this book is based, the methods we have used in analysing it, and the conventions we have used for presenting it.

3.2 SOURCES OF DATA

3.2.1 The corpora

We take up this project at an auspicious time, as sources of data and the methods of analysis have changed markedly in recent decades, allowing us to see the scope of English morphology in a way that would not have been possible just a decade ago. As in many sub-disciplines of linguistics, the advent of digital corpora and lexical databases has had an enormous impact on the study of morphology. The significant advances in both empirical and theoretical approaches to morphology over the past decade are largely due to these methodological tools. With the aid of corpus data, it is now possible to study English word-formation virtually in real time. Our most important electronic sources are listed below.

- *The Corpus of Contemporary American English* COCA (Davies 2008). This corpus, first released in 2008, is the largest freely-available corpus of English, with 425 million words at the time of writing. It is a balanced corpus with texts equally distributed over five

genres: spoken language, fiction, popular magazines, newspapers, and academic journals, and it represents American English from 1990 through 2011 with roughly 20 million
words for each year.

- *The British National Corpus* BNC (e.g. Burnard 2007). The BNC represents a wide cross-
section of British English from the late twentieth century (1980–94), both spoken (*c.* 10
million words) and written (*c.* 90 million words). The **written part** includes, for example,
texts from newspapers, periodicals, and journals, academic books and popular fiction,
published and unpublished letters, and memoranda, school and university essays. The
spoken part consists of informal conversations and spoken language collected in various
contexts such as business or government meetings, radio shows, and phone-ins.
- *CELEX* (Baayen *et al.* 1995). CELEX is a lexical database which contains data from
German, British English, and Dutch, and has been extensively employed in linguistic
and psycholinguistic research. Apart from orthographic features, the CELEX database
comprises representations of the phonological, morphological, syntactic, and frequency
properties of words. We use the English part of CELEX, which has been compiled on
the basis of dictionary data and text corpus data. The dictionary data come from the
Oxford Advanced Learner's Dictionary (1974, 41,000 entries) and from the *Longman
Dictionary of Contemporary English* (1978, 53,000 entries). The text corpus data come
from the COBUILD corpus (17.9 million words). Overall, CELEX contains lexical
information about 52,446 English lexemes, which are represented by 160,594 word
forms. Unlike the previously listed corpora, with CELEX all decisions concerning phonological, morphological, or other aspects of the words concerned were taken by the
compilers of this database.
- *Google Book Corpus*. The *Google Book Corpus* is a corpus of 155 billion words taken from
1.3 million books written in American English from 1810 through 2009. This corpus went
on line in 2011 (Davies 2011).
- Other corpora such as *The Corpus of Historical American English* (COHA) (Davies
2010), *The Wellington Corpora of Spoken and Written New Zealand English* (WSC and
WWC, respectively, Bauer 1993; Holmes *et al.* 1994), the *Morbocomp* corpus (Scalise
and Bisetto 2012), and the *Boston University Radio Speech Corpus* (Ostendorf *et al.*
1996).
- Dictionaries of neologisms, reverse dictionaries, and other dictionaries, for example
Lehnert (1971); Mish (1983); Ayto (1990); Barnhart *et al.* (1990); Green (1991); Tulloch
(1991); Knowles (1997).

Of these databases, we have relied most heavily on COCA, as it is the largest available corpus
and the one that is updated most often. As much of what we can learn about contemporary
English morphology comes from looking for neologisms and encountering infrequently-
occurring forms, this corpus gives us the most promising material to work with. We have
made use of the other corpora to compare results, to fill in details and to look for possible

cross-dialectal differences. COHA has allowed us to look for trends in word-formation over the last two centuries.

3.2.2 Methods of obtaining and treating data from the corpora

To obtain data from the corpora, we searched for pertinent words or patterns by using string searches. For example, to investigate words with a particular suffix, say, verb-forming-*ize* as in *randomize*, in COCA or the BNC, we would extract from the databases all orthographic words that end in the strings <ize>, <izes>, <ized>, <izing>, <ise>, <ises>, <ised>, or <ising>. The resulting lists of course still contained a large number of words that were either irrelevant or problematic, and we would therefore subject them to standard data-cleaning procedures. Obviously useless data—misspelled words, words with odd punctuation, words ending in the string which obviously did not contain the affix (*size, prize, bodywise*)—were first eliminated. This initial cleaning, however, inevitably left problematic forms that were more difficult to deal with. The thorniest task was to decide whether particular words could be considered to bear the affix in question.

There are a number of issues that arise with respect to such determinations. First, there is semantic diversity. Semantically diverse affixes pose the question as to whether they really represent a single morpheme or a number of different, homophonous ones. In those cases where there was a sufficiently clear semantic relationship between different meanings or readings, we opted for a polysemy approach, thus avoiding a proliferation of affixes. That is, in some cases we made a judgement call about the degree of semantic relatedness that led us to group certain affixes together as a single affix. Others might disagree with our decisions, but usually we were inclined to go in the direction of lumping rather than splitting.

Second, there are derivatives that are not formed on potentially free bases but on obligatorily bound bases. Some theorists might argue that forms like *baptize* or *propagate* are morphologically simplex, since they are not derived by the suffixation of -*ize* or -*ate* to an already existing base word. However, we decided to adopt the position that independent of the theoretical approach one might take, there is an undeniable non-arbitrary connection of derivatives like these two to other words featuring -*ize* and -*ate*, in that the two strings at least indicate the verbal status of the word. Thus, even in these cases one could argue for the presence of a suffix which indicates the verbal category of the word, if nothing else. If such an argument could be made, we did not eliminate these examples from consideration. In other words, we took the position of being inclusive so as not to preclude data that might add to our understanding.

The third problem is closely related to the previous one and concerns semantic and phonological opacity. While the focus of this book is on productive morphology, which is overwhelmingly transparent in nature, we inevitably encountered forms that were non-transparent, either in terms of meaning or phonology. Opacity is a gradient notion and decisions about morphological segmentability are difficult and often quite arbitrary. However, they in general concern only a rather small minority of words with particular affixes, such that the occasional arbitrary decision normally does not unduly influence the overall picture. Indeed, decisions on the inclusion or exclusion of words as members of a morphological category are most important in quantitative analyses (e.g. of productivity). Since this book is not primarily interested in quantification, but in patterns of structure and usage, we are confident that occasional arbitrary decisions did not have a significant impact on our overall results. In general, we have tried to document the potentially controversial data, as well as the uncontroversial.

A word is also necessary about how we made judgements about the novelty of words. It is obvious that claims about productivity are based on noticing the extent to which neologisms formed by a particular process can be found. Our practice in determining the novelty of forms was simply to check words against the *OED On Line*. Obviously this is an imperfect method, but we reasoned that the *OED On Line* is updated constantly and there was no other established source that would give us a better indication of whether words were established or how established they were. Judgements about novelty are, like judgements about opacity, difficult to make. Forms can be coined more than once, so we also used the *OED* to determine whether a word had a steady use over time or a use so intermittent (perhaps used only one or twice several centuries ago) that an appearance of that word in a contemporary source probably indicates a re-coinage.

For practical reasons, not all sources have been systematically used for the description of each of the phenomena to be dealt with. For example, some chapters rely more on exemplification with data taken from COCA, others more on the BNC, and yet others primarily make use of data not collected from corpora at all. The choice of a particular source often depended on whether we already had collections of cleaned data from one of the corpora, in other cases it was a matter of personal interest or taste. In many cases, we simply went for the largest corpus, that is, COCA, since new coinages of a particular morphological category are often so rare that they cannot be found in sufficient numbers even in a corpus as large as the BNC. In any case, the patterns described have been checked for their validity across varieties and corpora whenever possible.

3.2.3 Other sources of data

All of the sources described so far are well-established tools of linguistic research. In addition to these widely recognized sources we have also made use of other freely available resources (both print and internet) that were not designed as research tools for linguists but nevertheless provide very interesting and pertinent data. Indeed, we freely admit to being opportunistic scavengers, taking up whatever source of new words might be available. These non-scientifically oriented sources are especially useful in those cases where, due to the limitations of electronic searches and the properties of the pertinent morphological categories, it is not possible to systematically search for and extract relevant forms from corpora. Among these cases are back-formations, truncations, blends, and even compounds of various sorts, as none of these types can be accessed by the sort of string search that gives us data for affixes.

Two useful sources were *Urban dictionary* (http://www.urbandictionary.com/, last accessed 1 November 2012) and *Wordspy* (http://www.wordspy.com/, last accessed 1 November 2012), which are websites that collect neologisms and provide relevant citations for these new words. Other such sources were websites of specialized communities whose communicative needs make the coinage, or collection and documentation, of derived or compounded words necessary. For example, websites on dogbreeding (e.g. http://www.dogbreedinfo.com/hybridmain.htm, last accessed September 2012) provide lists of names of mixed-breed dogs that can be conveniently used to investigate patterns of blend-formation. Similarly, websites designed to support genealogical research can be used to collect nicknames derived by truncation and/or -*y*- suffixation (as, for example, done by Lappe 2007).

Finally we have also made use of data collected by pure happenstance: items we encountered in newspaper, radio, TV, or materials collected by our students for classes. We have on occasion used the internet to verify the existence of words or to examine popular usage. We have also occasionally used material elicited in production experiments that were carried out to test the properties of certain morphological categories for which corpus data are not easily available for the above-mentioned reasons. We have, however, been cautious about asking individual speakers for judgements on words. One thing that we have learned from this project is that our intuitions about whether *xyz* could possibly be a word are often not very good. We have frequently found novel words in our sources that seem completely unremarkable in context, but which seem weird or improbable out of context, and might strike some speakers as impossible. For this reason, our practice has been to be as non-judgemental as possible. We have not excluded words from consideration because we felt that they were somehow improbable or 'wrong'. Others might dispute our non-prescriptive stance, but we have chosen the path of inclusivity again in the hopes that such forms have something to tell us about how speakers of English actually create new words and extend the meanings of established words.

3.3 CITING DATA

Our intention in this volume is to make use of the data from the above-mentioned sources to provide rich exemplification for all patterns discussed. We must therefore say something about our conventions for listing examples and citing illustrative quotations from the data bases.

Examples are given in citation form, regardless of the inflectional form in which they were attested in the corpus. A reader wanting to check the corpus for the citation of a particular noun might therefore need to check the plural form as well as the singular to find the attestation. Similarly, to find the attestation of a verb, the reader might have to search the corpus for the past tense or the 3rd person singular forms. Where lists of examples are given, they are alphabetized. Further, where affixes have two or more allomorphs, forms with extenders (for example, *-ation, -cation, -sion, -tion, -ion, -ution*, and *-ition* or *-able* and *-ible*), we have chosen to refer to the affix in discussion using a single form, rather than listing all possible forms at each mention, except where specific allomorphs or forms with extenders are the direct topic of discussion.

In addition to giving extensive lists of forms that illustrate particular affixes or other types of word-formation, we attempt wherever possible to show how forms are used in context. This is, of course, absolutely critical where we are discussing the semantic properties of various word-formation processes. Where quotations are drawn from one of the corpora, we begin the quotation with the name of the book, newspaper, magazine, TV programme, or other source from which the quotation is drawn, followed by the year of publication or usage. We treat examples drawn from other written sources (our own reading of novels or newspapers, for example) similarly. This introductory material is always presented in italics. Where examples are drawn from internet sources other than the corpora, we give the URL in parentheses next to the example.

Where we discuss phonological properties of affixes or other word-formation processes, we transcribe forms using the IPA. Transcriptions are taken from the 3rd edition of the *Longman Pronunciation Dictionary* (Wells 2008), with certain simplifications (e.g. eliminating various diacritics) where fine phonetic detail is not needed. Where necessary we cite both standard British English pronunciation and standard North American English in that order, with the symbol ‖ separating the two.

3.4 Interpretation of data

There are innumerable places in the construction of such a comprehensive reference work as this one where we found it necessary to rely on fine judgements. In addition to the cases mentioned above concerning the polysemy of affixes, the treatment of opaque forms and the like, we constantly found it necessary to make judgements about the category of the base in a complex word or even the category of the output. With regard to the latter, we should mention that although COCA and the BNC are parsed for part of speech, we did not necessarily rely on the parsing given in the database, choosing rather to make our own judgements as to part of speech in a given syntactic context.

With regard to the former, there are numerous cases where the base of a complex form could theoretically be counted as either a noun or a verb for example, there being so many forms in contemporary English that have been subject to conversion. Determinations of the category of the base in cases such as these are notoriously tricky, and wherever we have needed to make such determinations we have attempted to justify our reasoning. In some cases we have left the decision open where we have not found sufficient evidence to support a choice one way or the other. Readers may of course choose to dispute our decisions.

....

CHAPTER 4

Orthography

4.1 PROSPECTUS

In this chapter we consider the way in which the morphological structure of words interacts with their spelling. We will first have a look at how vowel length is represented in English orthography, and the way in which this is affected by morphological processes of affixation. We then consider some other orthographic processes which influence the spelling of morphologically complex forms or the link between spelling and pronunciation.

Since it is of particular importance in this chapter, we will not talk of vowels and consonants but of vowel sounds and consonant sounds and of vowel letters and consonant letters. The vowel letters are <a, e, i, o, u> and sometimes <y> (though <y> is a consonant letter in some positions, e.g. initially in the word *yacht*). The letter <w> may form part of a sequence of letters that stand for a vowel sound (e.g. *show*).

4.2 THE REPRESENTATION OF VOWEL SOUND LENGTH

4.2.1 Basics

We start with a note on terminology. English vowel sounds have traditionally been divided into two groups, long and short, also analysed as tense and lax respectively. In this chapter, where we concentrate on orthography, we will stick to the traditional terms as these are typically used in discussions of spelling, but in Chapter 9 where we focus on morpho-phonological alternations, we use the terms 'tense' and 'lax', which have more currency among phonologists. Note also that much of what follows is informed by the discussion in Carney (1994).

Short vowel sounds differ from long vowel sounds phonologically in not occurring in word-final position in a stressed syllable. So a monosyllabic word cannot end in /æ/ (a short vowel), but can end in /u:/ (a long vowel). Monosyllabic words containing a short vowel must end in a consonant. The English spelling system represents, not entirely consistently, a much older stage of the language, and many vowels have changed from long to short or vice versa since the spelling system was established. In native vocabulary, one of the ways of marking the length of vowel sounds was to use two vowel letters. As can be seen in (1), today this is an untrustworthy guide. Some of the changes that lead to the forms illustrated in (1) give rise to unpredictable irregularities in the spelling system. The difference between <oo> representing /uː/, /ʊ/ or /ʌ/ (in, for example, *food*, *wood*, and *blood* respectively) is a matter of historical changes operating at different periods of history. Originally, all these words would have had the same vowel sound.

(1)	Letters	Short vowel sound	Long vowel sound
	<a>	cat	spa
	<e>	bed	he
	<i>	bit	I
	<o>	not	fro
	<u>	fuss	truth
	<ai>	plaid	faint
	<ea>	head	mead
	<ei>	foreign	feint
	<eo>	leopard	people
	<ey>	chimney	prey
	<oo>	blood	brood
	<ou>	touch	foul
	<ow>	knowledge	brow

From a phonetic point of view, long vowel sounds can be divided into MONOPHTHONGS and DIPHTHONGS, monophthongs being vowels of constant quality and diphthongs being vowels which change their quality within their syllable. Because of the number of phonetic changes that have affected the English vowel system since the spelling system was established, as well as scribal practice, the spelling system no longer reliably indicates a distinction between monophthongs and diphthongs. All that matters for the issues discussed in this chapter is whether the vowel sound is long or short. The spelling system pairs the vowel sounds as long and short sounds corresponding to the same vowel letter; this is not a phonetic correspondence, and only sporadically a phonological one. It is basically a historical set of correspondences. The correspondences are set out in (2).

(2)	Vowel letter	Short pronunciation	Example	Long pronunciation	Example
	<a>	æ	cat	eɪ	name
	<e>	e	bed	iː	me
	<i>	ɪ	pit	aɪ	hide
	<o>	ɒ ‖ ɑ	pot	əʊ ‖ oʊ	mode
	<u>	ʌ, ʊ	but, put	(j)uː	mute

It needs to be noted that the rules of English spelling are not the same for words of different etymological origins. Only in words of Greek origin does <ph> spell /f/, for instance (although the slang word *phat* extends this unpredictably). Only in words of French origin does <eau> spell /əʊ‖oʊ/. While the English spelling system has ways of spelling native words which reflect the distinctions between long and short vowel sounds, these same techniques are not consistently applied to non-native words (on the native and non-native distinction, see Chapter 2.7 and Chapter 27). Where the rules on double consonants and silent <e> fit words of French or classical origin, it must be taken that they do so either because the spelling has been interpreted in that way, or by accident.

4.2.2 Double consonants

One general rule for spelling native words in English is that when a stressed vowel sound is short, this is indicated in the spelling by having two consonant letters after the vowel letter. This is true even when the two consonant letters are not the same, as in *help, kiln, swamp*, whose spelling shows them to contain short vowel sounds (RP and related varieties have a long vowel in *ask, mast*, etc., but this is a late development). The interesting cases for our purposes are those where there is a double letter whose sole function is to indicate that the preceding vowel sound must be read as being short. Some examples are given in (3).

(3)   batter, cotton, cuddle, marry, minnow, offal, pillow, posset, rabbit, tissue, udder

There are some things which need to be understood about double consonant letters. The doubled versions of <c>, <ch>, and <ge> are <ck>, <tch>, and <dge> respectively. The letter <v> is rarely doubled (since a double <v> would be indistinguishable from a <w> in handwriting), so that words like *navvy* are exceptional (and modern) rather than the rule. Doubling does not occur with <x>, <sh>, or <th>.

We might expect double consonant letters to be used word-finally as well as word-medially, since long and short vowel sounds can be followed by a single consonant: *cut* with a short vowel sound and *coot* with a long vowel sound both end with a single consonant. While the two-vowel letter orthography helps here (and would once have helped more), it has been shown above that it is no longer a trustworthy indication. Double consonants on the ends of words are mainly restricted to <ck>, <dge>, <ff>, <ll>, <rr>, <ss>, <tch>, <tt>, <zz>, and are not consistent. *His* and *hiss, quiz* and *fizz, cut* and *butt* illustrate some variation. There are some extra double letters which arise because there is a preference in English for lexical words to be written with at least three letters, so *add, ebb, egg, inn, odd* provide unusual double letters on this principle (most words affected by the short-word rule provide double vowel letters rather than double consonants: *bee, pee, see, wee*—contrast *he* and *we* which are grammatical).

4.2.3 Silent

If a double consonant letter word-medially indicates a preceding short vowel pronunciation, then a single medial consonant letter must indicate a long vowel sound. This is true, as shown with monomorphemic words in (4). Note, however, that this rule works well only when the single letter occurs at the end of a stressed syllable: elsewhere, because the vowels are often reduced to /ə/ or /ɪ/, the number of consonants is not significant.

(4)   baby, chafer, even, holy, ivy, open, spider, Viking

Since a final single consonant letter can follow the representation of what must be interpreted as either a short vowel sound or a long vowel sound, some way is needed of distinguishing between these two readings. The answer is the 'silent <e>', which makes the single consonant letter orthographically intervocalic, and forces a long pronunciation. The history of this, though, is just the opposite: the final <e> letters were once pronounced, so these single consonant letters were intervocalic in phonological as well as in orthographic terms. This gives rise to the examples in (5), where the final, 'silent' <e> forces a long interpretation of the vowel sound.

(5)   bide, dole, hate, mete, mule

4.2.4 Consonant doubling

The implications of this for morphology arise when a suffix with an initial vowel letter is added to a base with a final stressed syllable containing a short vowel sound. If that base is spelled as ending with a single consonant letter, that consonant letter will need to be doubled to protect the short vowel sound of the base. Examples are given in (6).

(6)   dim   dimmed

hit   hitting

man   manned

sip   sipped

stop   stopping

sun   sunny

There is a certain amount of consonant doubling where the previous syllable is not stressed. In general North American English (NAmE) has the more regular form here, when it differs from British English (BrE). Some examples are given in (7).

(7)

	BrE	NAmE
benefited (*also* benefiting)		✓
benefitted (*also* benefitting)	✓	✓
biased (*also* biasing)	✓	✓
biassed (*also* biassing)	✓	
counsellor	✓	
counselor		✓
marvellous (*also* marvelled, marvelling)	✓	
marvelous (*also* marveled, marveling)		✓
traveler (*also* traveled, traveling)		✓
traveller (*also* travelled, travelling)	✓	
worshiper (*also* worshiped, worshiping)		✓
worshipper (*also* worshipped, worshipping)	✓	✓

Words which show similar variation between single and double letters in morphologically complex words include: *backlog, focus, grovel, handicap, hiccup, label, leapfrog, marshal, overlap, pummel, signal, snivel*, etc.

Note that only a few consonants double in this environment: we find <ll>, <pp>, <ss>, <tt>, and occasionally <gg> in this kind of doubling, but it is not general.

In some words with final stress, the same confused doubling can also be found, where the double letter in the BrE spelling is misleading after a stressed vowel, since it suggests a short pronunciation, as shown in (8).

(8)

	BrE	NAmE
control, controlled, controlling, controller	✓	✓
control, controled, controling, controler		✓
woolen		✓
woollen	✓	

Other words which show this variation between single and double letters in morphologically complex words include: *distil, appall, enthrall, extol, patrol*.

Note that although *woolen* and *wooly* both exist, they are not treated in an entirely parallel fashion, with *woolly* being preferred even in *woolen* areas.

Ironically, there are a few words which are spelled variably with a single or double final consonant, usually following a short vowel sound, and here the double consonant tends to be the NAmE spelling and the single consonant the BrE spelling.

(9)

	BrE	NAmE
appal	✓	
appall	✓	✓
distil	✓	
distill	✓	✓
fulfil	✓	
fulfill	✓	✓
enrol	✓	
enroll	✓	✓
instal	✓	
install	✓	✓

While CanE mostly follows the NAmE pattern, and AusE, NZE, and SAfE mostly follow the BrE pattern, there is variation in all of them; indeed, as illustrated above, BrE and NAmE are not monolithic in regard to their spelling conventions here.

4.2.5 Loss of silent <e>

Since, in the current system of English, silent <e> can be seen to be necessary to represent the long pronunciation of a vowel letter which appears before a single final consonant, its function is lost when a vowel initial suffix is added. Thus, since the final <e> in *hope* is there to ensure a long pronunciation for the <o>, there is no need for it in *hoping*, where the <i> now fulfils the same purpose. This gives rise to pairs such as those in (10), where consonant doubling maintains a short vowel sound.

(10)

copping	coping
fatted	fated
hatter	hater
hopping	hoping
matting	mating
mopping	moping
rapping	raping
ratting	rating
ripper	riper
sitting	siting
tilling	tiling

The rule is general enough that it is the exceptions which need attention.

- The rule applies only to a silent <e>; a final <e> which is part of some other grapheme is not affected. Thus *see* + *ing* gives <seeing> and not *<seing>.
- A final <e> can have other functions. One of these is to ensure the 'soft' pronunciations of <c> and <g> (/s/ and /ʤ/ respectively). Where the 'soft' pronunciation would be threatened by the loss of <e>, the <e> is retained: *charge* + *-able* is <chargeable>, *peace* + *-able* is <peaceable>, *trace* + *-able* is <traceable>. Despite this rule, *acknowledgment, fledgling, judgment,* and *knowledgable* are standard alternatives to *acknowledgement, fledgeling, judgement,* and *knowledgeable,* although sometimes with regional variation.
- When an adjectival *-y* is added to a noun base the final <e> may be retained or deleted, sometimes with variation between the two spellings. The spellings <stoney> and <stony> are alternatives (with the latter the more common), but <dopey> seems to be more common than <dopy>. Other relevant bases include *bone, game, horse, joke, rope, shake, tone* (but the standard form from *fire* is *fiery*).

4.3 THE LETTER <I> REPLACING <Y>

A word-final <y> is replaced by <i> when a plural, 3rd person singular present tense, past tense, past participle, comparative, or superlative affix is added, as illustrated in (11). The suffix in such cases begins with an <e>, even in instances like *skies* (below), where this might not be expected.

(11)		*plural*	*3rd sing*	*past tense*	*past participle*	*comparative*	*superlative*
	pry		pries	pried	pried		
	sky	skies					
	silly					sillier	silliest
	empty	empties	empties	emptied	emptied	emptier	emptiest

The general rule does not apply:

- when the <y> is part of a digraph with another vowel letter: *days, jockeys, toys, enjoyed, obeyed, stays* (but note irregular *laid, paid*);
- when the <y> is in *by*, as in *lay-bys*; in the abbreviation *poly • polytechnic* (BrE) (pl. *polys*);
- when the <y> is final in a proper name: *the four Marys, the two Germanys*.

This rule also applies less regularly before the agentive/instrumental suffix *-er* in *drier/dryer*, *flier/flyer*, but *carrier, crier, supplier*, and *pryer*.

The same <y> to <i> rule may apply before other suffixes as well, even where those suffixes are consonant-initial. It does not apply if the change would lead to a sequence of <ii>. It does not apply before a singular possessive <'s>. Some examples are given in (12), and some counter-examples in (13).

(12)   ally   alliance

           deny   denial

           hardy   hardily

           likely   likelihood

           marry   marriage

           merry   merriment

           pity   pitiless

           plenty   plentiful

           rely   reliable

(13)   baby   babyhood, babyish, baby's

           busy   busyness (*this is a modern coinage, contrasting with* business, *whose meaning is no longer transparent*)

           dry   dryness

           fairy   fairydom, fairyhood

           fly   flying, flyable

           lady   ladyship, lady's

           party   partyless

4.4   VELAR SOFTENING

Typically spelling differences in complex words are accompanied by pronunciation changes. In the case of forms like *electric • electricity*, however, we find an apparent phonological alternation between /k/ and /s/ with no accompanying difference in spelling. This particular phenomenon has come to be called VELAR SOFTENING. As this is a morpho-phonological alternation that does not affect spelling, we will not look further at it in this chapter, but will return to it in Chapter 9.

4.5 HYPHENATION

Hyphenation in English is subject to fashion and arbitrary prescription, some of which may appear to give differences between national varieties. Accordingly, this section is less concerned with giving rules than showing some of the ways in which hyphenation is used. We have nothing to say in this section about hyphenation at line-breaks, where it is often a function of syllable structure, though we note that morphology can be used for identifying appropriate breaks, even here: for example a line-break at *film-ing* is preferred to the purely phonological *fil-ming*. Nevertheless, we are concerned here with other hyphens which are used to mark morphological structure in some way.

4.5.1 Hyphens in derivatives

On the whole, hyphens are rarely used to mark off suffixes but can be found marking off prefixes. There are a number of cases where hyphenation can frequently be found:

- When the last letter of the prefix is the same as the first letter of the base. This is particularly likely when the two identical letters are vowel letters: *anti-inflammatory, co-ordinate, de-energize. Counter-revolutionary* and *dis-satisfied* are more likely to be found with no hyphens. Even those cases with two identical vowel letters are not always hyphenated. Also note the exceptional *ski-ing* (with the variant *skiing*), where a suffix may get a hyphen.
- When the last letter of the prefix is a vowel letter and the first letter of the base is a different vowel letter. This is less common than the last case, but may be useful to prevent sequences of vowel letters being perceived as digraphs: *anti-emetic, psycho-active, semi-automatic.*
- When more than one prefix is used, including sequences where the same prefix is repeated: *re-discover, mega-mega-rich* (but note *hemisemidemiquaver* (BrE) is usually not hyphenated).
- Where the use of a hyphen allows the disambiguation of otherwise homographic words: *dis-ease* (White 2002: 64) versus *disease*, *re-cover* versus *recover*, *re-form* versus *reform*, *re-mark* versus *remark*, *re-present* versus *represent*, *re-sign* versus *resign*.
- Where the derivative has a phrasal base. In these cases, the entire word is hyphenated, including the affix. An example is *finer-than-thou-ness* (Trevanian 1998: 201), or the established (NAmE) *stick-to-it-iveness*.
- Where the prefix is added to a numeral or a word beginning with a capital letter or any other typographically odd character: *pre-1990, un-American, un-"allowable".*
- Where prefixes are coordinated: *pre- and post-operatively, pro- and anti-government forces.*

- Where a prefix is felt to be particularly independent of its base. This usage is particularly variable, partly because the notion of independence may be speaker-specific, and partly because publishers may have conventions on these words. Prefixes such as *anti-*, *ex-*, *non-*, *over-*, *past-*, *semi-* seem particularly susceptible to this usage. The independence of the prefix may simply mean that the writer is aware of creating a neologism, so that the hyphen helps the reader parse an unfamiliar word.
- Where suffixes are felt to be unusual or unusually independent. An example is *science fiction-y* (Vittachi 2008: 183). The suffixes *-ish* and *-y* seem particularly susceptible to this use, perhaps because of their productivity.

Note that infixed expletives, though their status as affixes may be doubtful (see Chapter 18), are separated off by hyphens: *unbe-fucking-lievable, un-bloody-likely*.

4.5.2 Hyphens in compounds

When it comes to writing sequences of noun + noun, English orthography is notoriously variable. The two nouns may be written solid (with no space between them), they may be hyphenated, or they may be written as two separate orthographic words, apparently at random. Consider the data given in Table 4.1 where the spellings given in four different dictionaries are tabulated.

Not only do the dictionaries not agree with each other, they are not obviously internally consistent. While the four dictionaries given here represent different national varieties (*Chambers* (2006), BrE; *Webster's Third New International* (1993), NAmE; *Macquarie* (1997), AusE; *OED* on-line, BrE), the differences between them seem to depend more on house style (for example, a move to avoid the hyphen on the part of Webster's) than on national variety. There are,

Table 4.1 Spelling of some noun–noun sequences according to different dictionaries

Dictionary	Chambers	Webster's	Macquarie	OED
Elements				
night + bird	solid	separate	hyphen	solid
night + rider	solid	separate	solid	hyphen
night + walker	hyphen	solid	separate	hyphen
night + watchman	hyphen	separate	solid	solid
nut + gall	solid	solid	hyphen	solid
nut + grass	hyphen	separate	solid	separate

of course, many examples where the four works agree (*needlefish* and *night owl* are consistently spelled); but the fact that there is so much disagreement indicates that there is no universally accepted norm, and thus that the linguist cannot rely on the orthography of a given word to provide linguistic information in these instances (see Chapter 19 for a more detailed discussion of the variability of spaced versus non-spaced compound spellings).

Despite this inauspicious lack of systematicity, there are many other places where the use of a hyphen is much more systematic. A hyphen is regularly (though not necessarily always) used

- in compounds made of a letter and a word: *e-mail, U-turn*;
- in appositional compounds: *singer-songwriter, builder-teacher-lawyers* (Vittachi 2008: 88);
- in translative and co-participant coordinative compounds (see Chapter 20): *the* **London-Boston** *flight, a* **French-Greek** *dictionary, the* **Russian-Chinese** *talks*. In these cases an en-dash may be used rather than a hyphen, which may imply a distinct structure for these constructions;
- in compounds made up of a derivative and a particle: *a* **dressing-down**, *a* **passer-by**, *a* **put-down**, *a* **runner-up**, *a* **walk-through**;
- in phrasal compounds, where the phrasal first element of the compound is hyphenated: *The old* **manage-somehow-on-a-shoestring** *days were definitely gone* (Meynell 1978: 125); *He sat there with a* **think-of-me-as-one-of-the-guys** *smile* (Kernick 2003: 119);
- in compound verbs: *freeze-dry, trickle-irrigate*;
- in exocentric verb–noun compounds: *know-all, scare-crow*; some of these are written solid: *dreadnought, pickpocket*;
- in compound adjectives, especially when used attributively (see also below): **card-carrying** *member,* **fast-approaching** *train,* **ready-made** *clothing,* **sky-blue** *dress*;
- when hyphenated compounds are coordinated: *1,000* **short- and medium-range** *missiles* (BNC).

4.5.3 Other lexical and grammatical hyphens

Hyphens are also used within lexical items which are not formed by derivation or composition. For example, hyphens are used

- in noun + preposition + noun structures viewed as fixed lexical items: *lady-in-waiting, man-at-arms, mother-in-law*. The same is true of place-names built on the same pattern: *Weston-super-Mare, Newcastle-upon-Tyne*;
- in noun + adjective lexical items, whose structure is French: *court-martial, governor-general*. These may also be written separately, and in some instances are more usually written separately: *lie direct, sum total*;

- in numbers such as 37 or when written out in full: *thirty-seven, four-fifths* (see Chapter 18).

Hyphens may be used to resolve the ambiguity of written sentences by indicating constituency: one reading of *They sold twenty dollar items* can be indicated by the insertion of a hyphen. In morphology this becomes relevant in any two-word construction which is used in the structure ((X Y) N), where X and Y are variables over words of any word class, and may be the same word class. In such constructions, the X and Y may be hyphenated to show their constituency. Examples include *before-tax profits, day-care facility, roll-neck sweater, small-business operators, wrap-around skirt, yes-no question*. Note that the hyphen would not necessarily be used if these constructions were not used attributively. Whether (X Y) in this structure should count as a compound or as a syntactic structure is controversial; see Chapter 19.2.1.2 for further discussion of this point. We find a similar use of hyphenation of compound adjectives, such as *able-bodied, fast-paced, never-ending, pitch-black, space-borne*. In some cases this hyphen resolves a potential ambiguity, as in *30-odd students* versus *30 odd students*.

PART II

Inflection

CHAPTER 5

Verb inflection

5.1 PROSPECTUS

In this chapter we will be concerned with how the morphosyntactic categories of the verb are encoded in English. After a look at the distinction between lexical and auxiliary verbs we will deal with lexical verbs. Finally, we will turn to the inflection of the modal auxiliary verbs and to the incorporation of infinitival *to* into certain verbs.

5.2 LEXICAL VERSUS AUXILIARY VERBS

English distinguishes between two kinds of verbs, lexical and auxiliary. The distinction is based on a variety of diagnostic criteria, most of them syntactic in nature. Thus, auxiliary verbs precede lexical verbs in the same clause, have certain types of complement, and behave in a peculiar way in a number of syntactic constructions, such as negation, inversion, ellipsis, and emphasis. The particulars of the syntactic behaviour of this class of words are well described in the standard grammars and will not concern us here in great detail since we focus on the morphological side of the matter. It should be noted, however, that with regard to their syntactic behaviour, the auxiliaries do not show a completely uniform behaviour across all syntactic constructions, and we will see that their morphological behaviour is also not necessarily identical across different lexemes.

We will start our discussion of the morphological differences between the two major classes of verb with the lexical verbs as a reference point. The number of different forms in the inflectional paradigms of lexical verbs in standard varieties of English ranges from eight for a single verb (BE, with the forms *be, am, are, is, was, were, being, been*) to only three for some 40 verbs (e.g. PUT with *put, puts, putting*). The different paradigms of individual verbs show different kinds and numbers of syncretism, to be discussed more extensively in Section 5.3.5.1. If we implement an analysis that recognizes morphosyntactic contrasts in the system as soon as at least two verbs show this contrast (that is, we ignore some of the categories that are found only with BE), we can distinguish the six morphosyntactic categories given in Table 5.1, illustrated with three different verbs, with, five, four, and three

Table 5.1 Verbal inflectional paradigms

Morphosyntactic category	GIVE	TALK	PUT
past	gave	talked	put
non-past { *3rd sg*	gives	talks	puts
non-3rd sg	give	talk	put
infinitive/subjunctive/imperative	give	talk	put
present participle	giving	talking	putting
past participle	given	talked	put

different forms, respectively. We deal with BE more fully in Section 5.3.4.1: it has a formal person–number distinction within the past tense category (*was* versus *were*), one within the non-3rd singular non-past category (*am* versus *are*), and one between the past tense form and the counterfactual form for the 1st and 3rd person singular (*I was, she was* versus *I were, she were*).

The details of this analysis will be discussed in Section 5.3. What is important for the discussion of the dichotomy between auxiliary verbs and lexical verbs is the fact that we can safely posit six morphosyntactic categories for the English verb, with varying degrees of syncretism across different verbs. We have a distinction between past forms and non-past forms, there is a form that is used in infinitival, subjunctive, and imperative clauses, a present participle form and the past participle form. The present participle occurs in progressive constructions, the past participle in passive and perfect constructions. Both kinds of participle can also be used as adjectives (as in *a disturbing story, one of the invented alphabets*, see Chapter 14 for discussion), and the present participle can serve as an event nominal (as in *the teaching of the arts*, see Chapter 10).

There is variation in non-standard varieties of English as to the kinds of morphosyntactic category, the number of such categories and the ways they are encoded. The present-day standard system described here is historically derived from a much richer system of categories and realizations, and some contemporary conservative dialects of English tend to have more different verb forms than the standard, encoding more different categories. Some dialects of English have different or fewer morphosyntactic category distinctions in their system. Another parameter of variation is the distribution of the different forms across the different categories, which can differ across dialects. For example, northern dialects of Britain are known for their peculiar subject–verb agreement pattern (the 'northern subject rule', for example, Pietsch 2005; Wales 1996: 45) where what is called the 3rd singular non-past form in Table 5.1 is used variably in certain plural and non-3rd singular environments. Another well-known example is the use of habitual *be* in African-American English, some varieties of Caribbean English and IrE (e.g. Rickford 1986; Green 1998). A description of such dialectal systems is not attempted here. However, we will document variation with forms that express the same morphosyntactic category, such as preterite *spelled* • *spelt*, or participle *beat* • *beaten* • *bet* (ScE, NZE, IrE).

Let us now turn to the auxiliaries. The class of auxiliary verbs that emerges from syntactic analyses of verbal behaviour potentially has the members shown in (1).

(1)   a. CAN, COULD, DARE, MAY, MIGHT, MUST, NEED, OUGHT, SHALL, SHOULD, WILL, WOULD

   b. BE, DO, HAVE

   c. GET, GO, TO, USE

   d. BETTER

The items in (1a) are the traditionally acknowledged set of so-called modal auxiliary verbs. Perhaps controversially, we list COULD, MIGHT, SHOULD, WOULD as separate lexemes rather than as past tenses of CAN, MAY, SHALL, or WILL, since their semantics does not correspond simply to that of CAN, MAY, SHALL, and WILL with different time reference. Morphologically, the modals can be distinguished from lexical verbs in important respects. *Need* and *dare*, however, behave differently from the other modal verbs in (1a), and we will discuss their behaviour in detail in Section 5.4. The remaining modals, which we will call 'core modals' for ease of reference, have impoverished inflectional paradigms, lacking participles (**canning*, **maying*, **shoulding*) and 3rd person singular forms (**oughts*, **shalls*), and for some of them even past tense forms (**musted*, **oughted*, **shalled*, etc.). Core modals also share another morphological property, they generally do not serve as bases for further word-formation. The core modal WILL is also used as a lexical verb, with interesting morphological properties. This will be discussed in Section 5.3.6.

The auxiliaries in (1b) are non-modal auxiliaries, and they share much of their syntactic behaviour with the modal auxiliaries. They are, however, also used as lexical verbs, and their special status has earned them the name of 'primary verbs' (e.g. Quirk *et al.* 1985). In terms of morphology, they are characterized by the full paradigms that are typical of lexical verbs, and will therefore be treated together with the lexical verbs, but in a distinct section (Section 5.3.4).

The items in (1c) are controversial in their status. The aspect-marking verb USE, as in *She used to follow him to work every day*, partly behaves like an auxiliary in some varieties of English, but in others it does not (see Section 5.4.2 for further discussion). Finally, the infinitival marker *to* is of unclear grammatical status, with analyses ranging from conjunction to VP-subordinator (e.g. Huddleston *et al.* 2002: 1183–7) to non-finite modal auxiliary verb (e.g. Pullum 1982). Given its (almost) invariable morphological behaviour we can afford to remain agnostic as to its status and will consider it only in connection with its behaviour regarding certain verbs preceding it, as in, for example, *gonna*, *wanna* (see Section 5.5).

The lexical verb GET also occurs in passive constructions in the same syntactic position as BE, which, together with its lexical morphology, can be taken as an argument for its belonging to the set in (1b). Similarly, the verb GO, in its present participle form plus a preceding form of BE plus a following TO is in competition with *will*, and could therefore also be included in the auxiliary verbs. There are, however, strong syntactic arguments not to include them in the class of auxiliaries, as they behave like lexical verbs in crucial syntactic tests like question formation and negation. Morphologically, nothing unexpected happens with these verbs either. The future-oriented construction with GO can be seen as an idiomatic use of the present participle of this verb, and passive GET enjoys the same full paradigm as in other syntactic constructions. The two candidates GET and GO also lack a specific morphological property that all finite auxiliary verb forms share and that distinguishes auxiliaries from lexical verbs, namely that they can act as a morphological host for the suffixed negator *n't*. Future-marking GO and passive GET cannot. The two verbs are thus syntactically and morphologically not distinct from (other) lexical verbs and will not be treated as auxiliaries here. Similar arguments would hold for some apparent auxiliaries as used in certain dialects of English, such as ScE *want* (as in *This car wants washed*).

We are slightly controversial in adding the marginal example BETTER, which, in some varieties, occurs in sentences like *I better do it, bettern't I?* The fact that it can take reduced *n't* shows its status, but it is rare in writing or formal speech where the older and fuller form *had better* is preferred. We have little to say about this form beyond noting its existence.

Based on this brief overview of the two classes of verbs we will now turn to the details of the inflection of lexical verbs. Further intricacies of the morphology of auxiliary verbs will be discussed in Section 5.4.

5.3 LEXICAL VERBS

5.3.1 The verbal paradigm

In Table 5.1 we briefly introduced the paradigm of English lexical verbs with only minimal justification and discussion. In this section we will take a closer look at the morphosyntactic categories, their justification and realization across verbs. Table 5.2 recasts the paradigm, from a different perspective, focusing on the forms and their names instead of the morphosyntactic categories. We will treat the verb BE separately in Section 5.3.4.

Table 5.2 has only five rows in the first column, as it recognizes the fact that the traditional categories of infinitive, subjunctive, and imperative collapse formally with the non-3rd singular non-past tense form. We use the label PLAIN FORM to express the fact that this form is identical in form with the base form, that is the form to which affixes are attached. The difference between infinitive, subjunctive, and imperative is no longer morphologically marked in

Table 5.2 Verbal paradigms: terminology, forms and morphosyntactic categories

Name of form		Regular verb	Irregular verb	(Morpho-)syntactic category realized by the form
base form {	plain form	talk	give	*infinitive, subjunctive, imperative non-3rd singular non-past*
	plain non-past form	talk	give	*tense*
3rd singular non-past		talks	gives	*3rd singular non-past tense*
preterite		talked	gave	*past tense*
present participle		talking	giving	*present participle*
past participle		talked	given	*past participle*

English, but is syntactically realized. That is, in certain syntactic constructions or sentence types the plain form is used. There is thus only one morphosyntactic category involved, which we could label 'infinitive-subjunctive-imperative' (cf. Huddleston 2002b: 83). We will use the less clumsy, and well-established term 'plain form' instead. The reasons for recognizing the morphosyntactic category of non-3rd singular non-past tense in spite of its being also realized by a plain form is that this form contrasts with the 3rd singular form, given the same sentence type (*I want some cake* versus *She wants some cake*). We will use the shorthand PLAIN NON-PAST FORM for this use of the base form. The base form, printed in small capital letters, will also be used as the citation form of the respective lexeme.

The proposed analysis implies that the finite versus non-finite distinction is a syntactic rather than a morphological one, as the non-finite infinitival form is identical to the finite subjunctive, imperative, and plain non-past forms. This turns the distinction between these identical forms into one of clause types.

As already pointed out in Section 5.2, the number and kinds of syncretisms that different verbs show is variable and deserves further study. For example, from a comparison of the two sample verbs TALK and GIVE we see that TALK, like all regular verbs, has four different forms, while GIVE has five. However, if we also take into account the different vowel in the preterite we might as well state that there is a base form syncretism with five of the six forms, plus an additional base form (with a different vowel) as the preterite. The different patterns of syncretisms will be discussed in more detail in the discussion of irregular verbs in Section 5.3.5.1.

The semantics of the non-past and the past tense form require some comment. The non-past is used not only to refer to events which habitually happen at a time including the present (*Mary leaves for work at eight o'clock*) and for states which are currently in force (*Wellington is the capital of New Zealand, This coffee tastes wonderful*), but also for eternal truths (*The sun rises in the east*) and for ongoing events in the here-and-now, as in a running commentary (*Rooney scores for England!*) or stage directions (*Mrs Smith picks up her knitting*) and performatives (*I apologize for what I said*). In academic discourse, it may be used to discuss the content of any written text, whether modern or historical (*Austen depicts her heroines with great honesty*). It is also used for scheduled future events (*The plane arrives at noon tomorrow*), and in subordinate clauses more generally for future events (*He will tell you when he arrives*). Despite our label of 'non-past' it may be used to narrate a presumed past event, typically in colloquial language or in jokes (*A horse walks into a bar, and the barman says, 'Why the long face?'*).

The past tense is used as a narrative tense, to relate completed events in the past, but also to mark attitudinal distance from an event, for instance for reasons of politeness (*I wondered whether you had time to see me*) or to express a hypothesis or doubt (*If you left now, you could be in Edinburgh before dinner*). For further details see, for example, Quirk *et al.* (1985) or Huddleston (2002b).

We will now turn to the discussion of the distinction between regular and irregular verbs, a distinction that we have already used in our discussion without proper justification.

5.3.2 Regular versus irregular verbs

As shown in Tables 5.1 and 5.2, we can distinguish between six morphosyntactic categories that are morphologically encoded. Depending on how these categories are realized, grammarians have introduced the distinction between regular and irregular verbs. In spite of what the terminology suggests, this distinction is not unproblematic, as will become clear as we go along.

According to most analyses, regular verbs are those that form their past tense forms with the predictable allmorphs of the so-called regular suffix *-ed* (as in *showed*, *talked*, *ended*), while all other verbs are irregular. There is also some irregularity found in the marking of 3rd person singular non-past, but this irregularity is restricted to the three verbs in standard varieties: BE, DO, and SAY. The respective forms are *is*, *does* /dʌz/ and *says* /sez/ (~ regular /seɪz/ in some varieties), and do not provide a sensible basis for a general category distinction. The recent verb *text* has, in some varieties, irregular third persons, either as *texes* or as *textes*, with the /ɪz/ allomorph occurring in an unpredictable environment.

The irregular verbs as defined above may form their preterite and past participles by various other means, for example by ablaut (*sing* ◆ *sang* ◆ *sung*), by suppletion (*go* ◆ *went* ◆ *gone*), by partial suppletion and addition of an unexpected *-t* (*bring* ◆ *brought* ◆ *brought*), by having the suffix *-en* in the participle form (*show* ◆ *showed* ◆ *shown*), or some combination of these (*give* ◆ *gave* ◆ *given*). There is even a group where all three forms concerned are homophonous (*put* ◆ *put* ◆ *put*). Thus, there seems to be a clear dichotomy of a nicely predictable set of forms and a mixed bag of largely unpredictable miscellaneous forms.

One problem with such a view and the above definition of what is regular and irregular, is, however, that it is not always clear which verbs should be treated as irregular. Sometimes the right suffix allomorph is accompanied by some additional change in the base, as for example with *have* ◆ *had, do* ◆ *did, teach* ◆ *taught*, which makes the forms appear regular in terms of suffixation, but irregular in terms of base allomorphy. Another problem is that some verbs have variably regular and irregular past tense forms, for example *betted* ◆ *bet, knowed* ◆ *knew, learned* ◆ *learnt*, which would make them belong to both classes. Traditional wisdom also holds that irregular verb forms need to be stored in the mental lexicon, while the regular suffix is generally applied to new verbs, and the regular verb forms need not be stored (and mostly are not). However, as we will see in some of the discussions to follow, this is a rather simplistic view of the matter that is unable to account for a number of empirical facts. Finally, the terminology may suggest that the irregular verbs form their preterites and past participles in rather arbitrary ways. As we will see, however, there are a number of clear sub-patterns within the set of irregular verbs.

In spite of these problems we will use the established distinction here and treat all those forms as regular whose past tense is fully predictable as being marked exclusively by the expected allomorph of the *-ed* suffix, with no accompanying change of the base. All other verbs are treated as irregular. Those verbs that have both regular and irregular variants of the past tense will be treated with their irregular variants in the section on irregular verbs. The theoretical and psycholinguistic status of the distinction between regular and irregular will be discussed in more detail in Section 5.3.5.2.

One could of course ask the question whether regular verbs and irregular verbs might also differ in other respects, that is, whether the difference in inflectional patterning is accompanied by other, non-inflectional properties that distinguish the two kinds of verb. And indeed, such differences can be found.

For example, it has long been observed that, on average, irregular verbs tend to be of higher frequency than regular verbs. Empirical studies using corpus frequencies (e.g. Baayen and Moscoso del Prado Martín 2005) have shown that the probability of a verb being irregular dramatically increases with higher token frequencies. For illustration, we may look at the frequency of verbs in the BNC lemmatized word list (Killgariff 2006), which contains the 1,281 most frequent verbs as found in this corpus. The top 13 verbs in this list are all irregular, with the first regular verb, LOOK, occupying rank 14. In contrast, there are only two irregular verbs among the bottom 100 verbs, BET and BLEED. High frequency protects word forms from falling out of memory, and it therefore does not come as a surprise that the most irregular verb is also the most frequent one, BE, which is in fact the second most frequent word of English overall (after *the*), according to the BNC frequency list.

Apart from a frequency difference, there is also a difference between regulars and irregulars that concerns their morphological families. A morphological family of a given word consists of all morphologically complex words (i.e. types) in which that word occurs as a constituent. For example, the morphological family of *accept* would contain *accept, acceptable, acceptably, acceptability, acceptance, accepter/acceptor, accepting, acceptive* (based on the attested forms in COCA). Verbs with irregular preterites tend to have morphological family sizes that are significantly smaller than those of regular verbs, although the irregulars tend to have a higher token frequency and would therefore be expected to enter further derivation, all other things being equal (Baayen and Moscoso del Prado Martín 2005).

Finally, there is some debate about the role of semantics in verbal inflectional patterning. Contrary to standardly expressed views that the distinction between regular and irregular verbs is one of form only (e.g. Kim *et al.* 1991), there is robust empirical evidence that regular and irregular verbs may differ in their semantic properties. Evidence for semantic effects on verb inflection has emerged from production experiments, as documented in Bybee and Slobin (1982) and Ramscar (2002). Baayen and Moscoso del Prado Martín (2005) provided large-scale distributional evidence on the role of semantics in inflection. Controlling for frequency, the authors show that the number of synonyms is larger for irregular verbs. Furthermore, sets of synonyms for irregular verbs are much more likely to contain other irregular verbs than sets of synonyms of regular verbs are to contain other regular verbs. This means that irregulars tend to live in a semantically more densely populated space, having more semantic relations to other words and being more similar to each other than regulars. Incidentally, this may have contributed to the survival of the many irregular forms in the history of the language, as forms with stronger semantic ties to other words tend to have stronger lexical representations in memory.

In sum, it seems that the difference in the inflectional behaviour of verbs goes together with differences in other areas. We will return to some of these facts in the theoretical discussion in Chapter 23.

5.3.3 Regular verbs

Regular verbs have only four different forms, one of them being the plain form, already dealt with above. In the following we will discuss the three suffixed forms and some issues relating to the orthography of the suffixed forms.

5.3.3.1 *Preterite and past participle*

Regular verbs are characterized by the fact that their preterite and past participle are fully predictable and involve the suffixation of one of three allomorphs to the base form. The allomorph /ɪd/ or /əd/ occurs after base-final /d/ and /t/. All other bases take /d/ or /t/, depending on the voicing of the base-final segment. Bases with voiced final segments take /d/, bases with voiceless final segments take /t/. This is illustrated in (2). We transcribe the syllabic allomorph as /ɪd/, ignoring the considerable variation between /ɪd/ and /əd/.

(2)	/ɪd/	/d/	/t/
	added /ædɪd/	played /pleɪd/	shipped /ʃɪpt/
	faded /feɪdɪd/	dragged /drægd/	pushed /pʊʃt/
	knitted /nɪtɪd/	teased /tiːzd/	packed /pækt/

5.3.3.2 *3rd singular non-past*

The 3rd singular non-past form is derived from the base form by adding the pertinent allo-morph of the suffix *-s*. This allomorphy is similar to the allomorphy of the plural *-s* (from which it differs only by not being subject to haplology), and also similar to that of the past tense suffix (in the general pattern of variation). Verbs ending in a sibilant (i.e. one of the sounds /s, z, ʃ, ʒ, tʃ, dʒ/) take the allomorph /ɪz/ or /əz/, all other bases take either /z/ or /s/, depending on the final segment of the base. If the base ends in a voiced segment the voiced allomorph /z/ is chosen, if not, the unvoiced allomorph /s/ is chosen. Examples are presented in (3). As with the past tense suffix, the variation between the two epenthetic forms is ignored.

(3)

/ɪz/	/z/	/s/
passes /pɑːsɪz ‖ pæsɪz/	plays /pleɪz/	ships /ʃɪps/
eases /iːzɪz/	drags /drægz/	puffs /pʌfs/
wishes /wɪʃɪz/	moves /muːvz/	packs /pæks/
judges /dʒʌdʒɪz/		

5.3.3.3 *Present participle*

Apart from the plain forms, the present participle is the only form that is of the same struc-tural make-up for all lexical verbs, no matter whether regular or irregular. It is derived by adding the suffix *-ing* to the base form. The suffix has two allomorphs, /ɪŋ/ and /ɪn/, the lat-ter being prescriptively viewed as a non-standard form, though it may be heard from other-wise standard speakers. Variation between these two has been frequently subject to sociolinguistic investigation (e.g. Trudgill 1974).

5.3.3.4 *Orthographic issues*

The default spelling of the suffixes is <ed>, <s>, and <ing>, but the attachment of these strings to the orthographic representations of the verbal bases may bring with it some adjust-ment in the orthographic representations of certain verb forms. These adjustments concern the doubling of base-final consonant letters before <ed> and <ing>, the deletion of final mute <e> before the same suffixes, and the change of <y> to or <ie> before <ed> and <s>, respectively. These changes follow the general principles of morphology–orthography inter-action in morphology that are laid out and illustrated in Chapter 4.

In addition to what follows from these general principles, the following peculiarities should be noted with verbal inflected forms. First, the 3rd singular suffix *-s* has two spelling variants, <s> and <es>, with the latter occurring after bases ending in <s> (<kisses>), <z> (<buzzes>), <x> (<boxes>), <sh> (<pushes>), and <ch> (<matches>) and the relevant words ending in <o> (e.g. <vetoes>, see Chapter 7). The suffix *-ed* has also two spelling vari-ants, <ed> and <d>. The latter is used with words that end in <e> (*baked, created, dyed, hoed*), and after specific base allomorphs of certain verbs (e.g. *did*). The spellings <paid>, <laid>, and <said> (and the spellings of pertinent derivatives, such as <mislaid>) are lexical exceptions to the rule that base-final <y> is preserved after vowel letters if it is part of a vowel digraph (as in <employed> or <stays>). With regard to *-ing*, bases ending in <ie>, such as <die, lie, tie, vie>, have <y> instead of <ie> before *-ing*.

5.3.4 Irregular verbs I: The primary verbs BE, DO, and HAVE

5.3.4.1 *BE*

Apart from its being a lexical verb, specifically, a copula, BE is used as an auxiliary verb in progressive aspect constructions and in passive sentences. The full paradigm of BE is given in (4). This verb is the only one in standard English that distinguishes the three person categories in the singular. Instead of a distinction between 3rd singular and non-3rd singular, BE encodes all three persons in the singular differently in the non-past (*am • are • is*). In the past tense paradigm there is a distinction between 2nd singular and non-2nd singular (*were • was*). Furthermore, (4) has a column for the counterfactual. As already mentioned, this category is not formally marked with any other verb, and with all other verbs the preterite is used in the respective clauses, which means that the counterfactual in English is a syntactic, and not a morphosyntactic category. With BE, however, we find a morphological distinction between the counterfactual and the past tense encoded for the 1st and 3rd singular.

(4)

		non-past	*past*	*counterfactual*
singular	*1st*	am	was	were
	2nd	are	were	were
	3rd	is	was	were
plural	*1st*	are	were	were
	2nd	are	were	were
	3rd	are	were	were
imperative		be		
present participle		being		
past participle		been		

What is also striking with this verb is the degree of suppletion. One can differentiate between six different bases that are phonologically quite distinct (*am, is, are, was, were, be*).

Although BE is the most irregular verb of English with the highest number of different forms and morphosyntactic distinctions, the distribution of its forms has things in common with other irregular verbs and indeed with regular verbs. The non-finite forms are all derived from a single base, *be*, as is the case in regular verbs and many irregular ones. Furthermore, in standard varieties there is no person distinction in the plural forms, and the levelling of forms in the past tense goes beyond the levelling found in the non-past. Finally, the suffixes used for the participles are also used by other verbs (-*ing* by all verbs, -*en* by many irregular verbs).

The combination of negation and BE brings about some interesting forms and issues, which we will discuss in Section 5.4.4. There is also some variation in the forms of BE used in different dialects of English, as for example the number levelling of the preterite forms (*I was* • *we was*), the use of *been* as a preterite in many non-standard dialects, and the use of invariant *be* in African-American English.

5.3.4.2 *DO*

Like BE and HAVE, DO can be a lexical verb or an auxiliary. The auxiliary verb DO is used in all constructions requiring DO-support, namely in negated sentences, interrogatives, negative inversion, emphatic, and elliptical constructions. The paradigms of the lexical DO and the auxiliary verb DO differ, in that the auxiliary does not have participle forms and the auxiliary behaves differently in negative contraction. Negative contraction will be discussed with that of the other auxiliaries in Section 5.4.4. In some varieties of English, the auxiliary and the lexical verb display further morphological differences. For instance, the regional English speakers described in Cheshire (1982: 34–6) have a distinction between lexical *dos* /duːz/ and auxiliary *do*, both used for all persons in the non-past. Furthermore, there are varieties that have a paradigm *do* • *done* • *done* for the lexical verb, and *do* • *did* for the auxiliary (Anderwald 2009: 126). The form *done* is also used as a perfective aspect marking auxiliary in Southern U.S. English and African-American English (see Green 1998).

The paradigm for the lexical verb in standard English is given in (5):

(5)

		spelling	phonology
base form	plain form	do	/duː/
	plain non-past form	do	/duː/
3rd singular non-past		does	/dʌz/
preterite		did	/dɪd/
present participle		doing	/duːɪŋ/
past participle		done	/dʌn/

Like regular verbs, the verb DO has six forms in its paradigm, and it also shows the predictable allomorphs of the 3rd singular and past tense suffixes, the same syncretism of the two plain forms as regular verbs and the same suffix for the present participle. However, we find base allomorphy with the 3rd singular (/duː/ • /dʌ-z/), with the preterite (/duː/ • /dɪ-d/), and with the past participle (/duː/ • /dʌ-n/), and the past participle suffix is one that occurs with irregular verbs, not with regular verbs.

5.3.4.3   *HAVE*

The primary verb HAVE is similar to DO in that its paradigm also closely resembles that of regular verbs, with only some base allomorphy disturbing the otherwise regular picture. Consider (6).

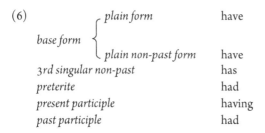

(6)			
	base form	*plain form*	have
		plain non-past form	have
	3rd singular non-past		has
	preterite		had
	present participle		having
	past participle		had

The 3rd singular, the preterite, and the past participle all show the predictable regular suffixes, but do not have the base-final /v/. Disregarding this base allomorphy, the formal distinctions and syncretisms are exactly the same as those of regular verbs.

5.3.5   Irregular verbs II: all others

In this section we take a closer look at the large number of remaining irregular verbs, all of which show some deviation from the regular paradigm discussed above. Their exact number is hard to determine, as it at least partially depends on how lexemes are treated that are putatively derived from irregular verbs (e.g. *misspell*). In many cases, these are no longer morphologically complex (e.g. *become*), but others certainly are (*deepfreeze, outswim*). Another problem is of course the sampling procedure itself. Some lists we find in the literature contain verbs that other lists do not, irrespective of morphological complexity. Due to these problems, the number of irregular verb lexemes given in the literature ranges, for example, between 167 (Anderwald 2009: 3) and 470 (listed by *englishpage.com*). Palmer *et al.* (2002: 1600–10) give 176, Quirk *et al.* (1985: 104) 261. Figures are of course lower in those sources that define the term 'irregular verb' in a more restrictive way, for example by reserving it for verbs that use vowel change to mark the past tense, or for verbs that do not use a suffix.

What is clear is that the class of irregular verbs seems much less open than the class of regular verbs. Claims that it is a closed class are certainly too strong, as new verbs can in principle enter the irregular class by compounding, derivation, or back-formation. For example, we found 126 such irregularly inflected forms at *englishpage.com* that were not listed by Quirk *et al.* (e.g. HAND-FEED, INTERWEAVE, OUTSWIM, OVERHANG, PRESHRINK, REGRIND, TELECAST, TEST-DRIVE, TYPEWRITE, UNDERBID, UNHANG). There are extremely rare cases where verbs move from the regular class into the irregular one. A well-known historical case involved TEACH, as a consequence of various sound changes that differentially affected different forms.

5.3.5.1 *The classification of irregular verbs*

The kinds of deviations from the regular pattern which we find with irregular verbs are manifold and have been the source of diverse attempts at categorizing the verbs into different classes. All classifications refer exclusively to properties of and relations between three forms—the plain form, the preterite, and the past participle—as the other two forms, the 3rd singular and the present participle, are nicely predictable for all lexical verbs, with the exception of BE, HAVE, DO, and SAY, as discussed above. Many irregular verbs have the suffix *-en*, which has the allomorph /n/ after base-final vowels (and base-final /r/ in rhotic varieties), and /ən/ elsewhere.

Turning now to existing descriptions and classifications of irregular verbs we can state that the number and nature of the proposed classes differ from researcher to researcher, depending on which particular feature or features are chosen as the basis for the classification. Most available classifications are based on the forms as spoken, which is an obvious road to take as changes in vowel quality across the different morphosyntactic categories are very frequent and important, and phonological vowel quality is not mapped straightforwardly onto the spelling (consider plain form <read> /riːd/ • preterite <read> /red/).

Quirk *et al.* (1985), to begin with, distinguish seven classes (sometimes with subclasses) on the basis of the combinations in the distribution of three properties: whether there is a suffix used, whether preterite and past participle is identical, and whether all three forms have the same vowel. Palmer *et al.* (2002: 1600–9) set up four classes (with various subclasses) based on four central criteria, that is whether there is some allomorph of the regular suffix discernible, whether there is only a vowel alternation, and whether the past participle is formed with the suffix *-en*. The fourth class is residual and contains 'other formations'. The theoretical basis of these two classifications is not very clear. Both taxonomies rely on formal similarities between different sets of forms, with some of the criteria being syntagmatic in nature (i.e. suffixation), some of them paradigmatic in nature (identity of vowels, or identity of certain forms, across the paradigm). Why it is exactly these similarities and not others that form the basis of the taxonomy seems to be partly arbitrary, partly a matter of frequency of particular similarities, and partly even a reflection of the historical strong verb classes as they survive in the modern system.

For further illustration of the problem of classification let us first look at a classification based on the presence and quality of vowel change from plain form to the preterite. On the basis of this feature, Baayen and Moscoso del Prado Martín (2005) end up with 32 classes (one of them containing all verbs with no vowel change). In their sample, which is based on CELEX, the number of verbs in each class ranges from only 1 to 38. Another classification based on vowel alternations is also possible, focusing on whether forms have the same or different vowels. We have classified the verbs from the Quirk *et al.* list accordingly and

Table 5.3 Kinds of vowel alternations

Class	Vowel pattern	Example
A (N=39)	a–b–c	sing • sang • sung
B (N=134)	a–b–b	keep • kept • kept
C (N=42)	a–b–a	give • gave • given
D (N=3)	a–a–b	shear • sheared • shorn
E (N=75)	a–a–a	hit • hit • hit

ended up with the classification in Table 5.3, listing the kinds of vowel patterns using the letters a, b, and c to denote different vowels, and using capital letters A to E to label the resulting verb classes. Note that there are many lexemes among the 261 irregular verbs given in Quirk *et al.* (1985) that have more than one irregular paradigm, which increases the number of paradigms discussed from 261 to 293. We also give the frequency of the pattern per class. We can see that the most frequent patterns are a–b–b and a–a–a, covering more than two thirds of the verbs.

Anderwald (2009) sets up five classes on the basis of whole form syncretism. Given three forms in the paradigm, and given that of these, none, two, or all three could be identical, one arrives at five logically possible syncretisms, which in fact are all attested and which constitute Anderwald's five irregular verb classes (with various subclasses). This is schematically represented in Table 5.4. All combinations occur, although with varying frequency. The type frequency of each pattern, based on the Quirk *et al.* (1985) list, is given in the first column, including more than one irregular pattern for a given verb if listed and pertinent.

This is an insightful classification as it allows us to relate the irregular patterns to the regular pattern. Thus all regular verbs and a large number of irregular verbs distinguish between the plain form and that for the preterite and the past participle (class 2, cf. regular TALK and irregular HOLD). One could therefore claim that this difference is a typical characteristic of the English verbal system, as was done by early authors such as Lowth (1762: 85–6, cited in Anderwald 2009: 98). The plain form and the preterite are the same for 46 verbs. Four of

Table 5.4 Syncretism of whole forms

Anderwald's class	Plain form	Preterite	Past participle	Example
1 (N=108)	a	b	c	give • gave • given
2 (N=129)	a	b	b	hold • held • held
3 (N=10)	a	b	a	come • came • come
4 (N=4)	a	a	b	beat • beat • beaten
5 (N=42)	a	a	a	hit • hit • hit

these verbs have different past participles (e.g. BET with its past participle variant *betted*, and BEAT with its past participle variant *beaten*), which makes them class 4 verbs, and 42 of them also have a past participle of the same form (class 5, e.g. COST, CUT, HIT, HURT, PUT). There are only ten verbs that have the same past participle form as the plain form but a different past tense form (class 3).

Another classificational approach based on syncretism could focus on different kinds of bases for one verb if there is a suffix present in at least one of the three forms. Thus, we could posit that some verbs have more than one base form and that these different bases have different combinatorial properties. For example, GIVE may be analysed as having one base form *give*, which is used as a plain form, as the base for the suffix -*s* and, crucially, also for the past participle suffix -*en*. This type of approach gives us another kind of syncretism, base syncretism. Table 5.5 summarizes base syncretism patterns for suffixed irregular verbs, assigning capital letters to the classes.

All of the five possible syncretism combinations are attested in the Quirk *et al.* list. Class A shows that even suffixed verbs can have three different base forms (cf. *drive • drove • driven*). Class B verbs take the same base for the participle as for the past tense (cf. also *awake •awoke • awoken*); in class C the plain form and participle bases are syncretic. The constellations labelled class D and class E are quite remarkable because each of them has only one verb, and in each case there are also competing regular participles available for these two verbs (*showed* and *sheared*). Hence, the table indicates that (apart from the two isolated verbs instantiating Classes D and E) irregular verbs that have a suffix come in only three patterns, excluding paradigms with syncretism between the plain form and the preterite.

Our overview has shown that there are very many conceivable properties and relations between forms that could be employed as a basis for classification, some of which have been used in the literature, some not. In (7) we list a number of features and their respective potential values. Most of these, sometimes in combination, have been used in the literature to set up classes or subclasses. Different authors have used different kinds of codings for the same kind of structural phenomenon, and we list the different codings separately. We also indicate some of the sources that have used the respective criterion for their classification.

Table 5.5 Syncretism of bases, verbs with suffixed forms

Class	Plain form base	Preterite base	Past participle base	Example
A (N=27)	a	b	c	ride • rode • ridden
B (N=55)	a	b	b	keep • kept • kept
C (N=33)	a	b	a	give • gave • given
D (N=2)	a	a	b	shear • sheared • shorn
E (N=34)	a	a	a	show • showed • shown

(7)   a. suffix
- presence of irregular suffix *-en* in the participle: yes, no (e.g. Palmer *et al.* 2002)
- presence of some form of *-ed* suffix: yes, no (e.g. Palmer *et al.* 2002)
- kind of suffix: regular *-ed* suffix, false allomorph of *-ed*, *-en*, none
- paradigm cell in which suffix occurs: only in preterite, only in participle, in both preterite and participle

   b. vowel
- change in base vowel (plain form versus preterite): none, many different changes (e.g. Baayen and Moscoso del Prado Martín 2005)
- change in base vowel (plain form versus preterite): yes, no (e.g. Quirk *et al.* 1985)
- co-occurrence of vowel change and suffixation: yes, no (e.g. Palmer *et al.* 2002)
- number of ablaut stages: none, two-stage, three-stage (e.g. Quirk *et al.* 1985)
- kind of ablaut series: seven different ones (e.g. Katamba 1993)

   c. syncretism
- kind of full form syncretism: five possible combinations (Anderwald 2009)
- kind of base syncretism: five possible combinations (see Table 5.5)
- vowel quality syncretism: five possible combinations (see Table 5.3)

Let us summarize our discussion of possible classifications of the similarities between different sets of verbs. There is a long (and potentially open-ended) list of criteria and their combinations that can be employed to group forms into classes that share certain properties, and the general absence of insightful pertinent methodological principles leads to classifications that may be intuitively plausible, but mostly seem to lack any theoretical or practical relevance. In particular, the whole question of productivity appears to have been ignored. This will be discussed in the next section.

5.3.5.2 *Productivity, variability, and irregularity*

There is a widespread opinion that only the regular way of past tense formation is productive, while irregular verb inflection is not. In order to see whether this is really the case we will first look at the variation that many irregular verbs show and then revisit the potential evidence that irregular past tense inflection is not totally unproductive.

Of the 261 verbs listed in Quirk *et al.* (1985), 72, that is, almost three out of ten, are listed with variant forms (some of them regular, some irregular). If one included the great many non-standard forms that can be found in colloquial usage (e.g. *knowed* with hundreds of attestations in COCA), this figure is even higher. This means that the system is in fact much more variable than is allowed for in theoretical accounts which claim that irregular forms block the formation of regular forms. Of the 72 verbs that have variable forms, 66 have only two competing patterns, but four verbs have three competing patterns and two verbs have four competitors in some of the cells of the paradigm. If we had widened the data set from that provided by Quirk *et al.*, we would have found even greater variability. The different sets of verbs are illustrated in (8), (9), and (10).

(8)   *Verbs with two competing patterns (N=66)*

abide • abided • abided

abide • abode • abode

(9)   *Verbs with three competing patterns (N=4)*

a. bestride • bestrode • bestridden

bestride • bestrode • bestrid

bestride • bestrode • bestrode

b. chide • chided • chided

chide • chid • chidden

chide • chid • chid

c. cleave • cleaved • cleaved

cleave • cleft • cleft

cleave • clove • cloven

d. stride • strode • strid

stride • strode • stridden

stride • strode • strode

(10)   *Verbs with four competing patterns (N=2) (The assumption is made that* bade *is pronounced* /beɪd/; *some speakers pronounce it* /bæd/.)

a. bid • bad • bade

bid • bade • bade

bid • bid • bid

bid • bade • bidden

b. forbid • forbad • forbid

forbid • forbade • forbid

forbid • forbad • forbidden

forbid • forbade • forbidden

What is remarkable with the verbs that have more than two competing patterns is that all competing patterns are irregular ones, which raises the question of whether in the set of verbs with only two competing forms it is always a regular pattern competing with an irregular one, as suggested by the example in (8). This is not the case, however. Of the 66 verbs that have two competing patterns, 19, that is almost one-third, have two irregular patterns competing with each other.

A closer inspection of this variability reveals that all forms with an a–b–c pattern (in the vowel or in the whole form) have a variant with an a–b–b pattern. Furthermore, those forms whose bases end in /t/ or /d/ have a tendency to develop a–a–a variants, either instead of a–a–b suffixed variants (e.g. *bit • bit • bit ~ bitten*), or instead of forms with different vowels (*shit • shat ~ shit*, or *spit • spit • spit ~ spit • spat • spat*). The recent usage of *text* as an invariable verb in some varieties of English illustrates this point perfectly. In sum, there are three patterns that seem to be able to attract new verbs, the regular verb pattern, the two-stage a–b–b ablaut pattern (in various instantiations) and the complete homophony pattern a–a–a.

If we go beyond the set of words from Quirk *et al.*, and also include, for example, the variable irregular verbs that Anderwald (2009) investigates as 'non-standard' verb forms, this picture is independently corroborated. Of these verbs, we find 16 attested in COCA with a frequency of more than five regular preterite and past participle forms per lexeme (BLOW, BURST, BUST, CATCH, COME, DIG, DRAW, GIVE, GROW, HEAR, KNOW, RUN, SEE, SHINE, SING, SINK, TEACH, TELL, THROW). In addition, three verbs show up with irregular competing past tenses, levelling the respective paradigms to an a–b–b ablaut pattern (*see • seen • seen, sing • sung • sung, sink • sunk • sunk*—and, indeed, all of the verbs which standardly have /ɪ/-/æ/-/ʌ/ ablaut). There are even places where verbs borrow forms from other lexemes, as with the confusion of *bought* and *brought* in several varieties of English.

Further evidence concerning the potential productivity of some of the irregular patterns can be gleaned from studies involving past tense formation with nonce verbs, such as Bybee and Moder (1983), Prasada and Pinker (1993), Marcus (1995, 1999), Xu and Pinker (1995), Albright and Hayes (2003) or Wagner (2010). These experiments have also shown that speakers create irregular past tense forms, and they do so especially if the nonce base form has certain phonological properties. For example, generalizing across different studies, ablaut forms (instead of regular preterites) seem most likely with nonce forms that are monosyllabic, have a complex, /s/-initial onset, have /ɪ/ as their base vowel, and end in a velar nasal (e.g. Bybee and Moder 1983; Albright and Hayes 2003; Wagner 2010: ch. 3.2.2). Thus, the data in these studies show that there are rather clear patterns, but these patterns cannot be generated by very general deterministic rules that produce a correct output from any given input form. Instead, one needs either highly constrained rules that are specified to apply to very small subsets of the data (as in Albright and Hayes 2003), or analogical models that can operate on the basis of similarity of forms to existing (cohorts of) forms in the lexicon (e.g. Keuleers 2008).

5.3.5.3 *Orthographic issues*

The regular spelling alternations, as discussed in Chapter 4 and in Section 5.3.3.4, apply, and there are not many orthographic idiosyncrasies to be noted in addition. The irregular suffix *-en* has three spelling variants, <en>, <n>, and <ne>. The variant <n> occurs after bases that end in <e>, <y>, <w>, <r> (<given>, <lain>, <shown>, <sworn>), the variant <ne> is restricted to two verbs (<borne>, <done>), and <en> occurs elsewhere.

5.3.6 Defective paradigms

As mentioned in Section 5.2, the core modals are characterized by the fact that they have defective paradigms, that is they lack certain forms. There are also, however, a few lexical verbs that are, at least to some extent, defective. In most instances, this means that speakers are unsure about what the relevant part of the verb might be, and avoid the issue whenever possible. This gives rise to a gradient notion of defectiveness: some forms of some verbs are less frequently used than might be expected, and in the limiting case are not used at all. Instances are the verbs STRIDE and BEWARE, the former of which, for some apparently arbitrary reason, does not have a generally agreed past participle (*strode, strid, stridden, strided*). The verb BEWARE is even more impoverished and has only the plain form, with the consequence that we only find it in infinitival, subjunctive, and imperative constructions.

There are also, however, less clear cases. REPUTE and RUMOUR, for example, have been said to be defective (Ward *et al.* 2002: 1435), as they are assumed not to occur outside passive constructions and therefore not to have the pertinent other forms. However, the example in (11), from COCA, implies that this is really a preference rather than a strict absence of forms, though it is less clear whether this is the case for *rumour*.

(11)   *AB4 1991*: Over his kindred he held a wary and chary care, which bountifully was expressed when occasion so required, **reputing** himself not only principal of the family but a general father to them all

Ward *et al.* (2002: 1435–6) also mention that the verb SAY cannot occur in an active verb + object + infinitive construction (**They say Kim to be a manic depressive*). This looks like a matter of verbal diathesis rather than defectiveness.

Another potential candidate for defectiveness is the lexical verb WILL 'wish, want', which behaves syntactically like the modal verb and could therefore be classified as another primary verb, together with BE, DO, and HAVE. Lexical WILL has the full set of forms we know from regular verbs (*will • wills • willed • willing*), and even an alternate preterite form *would*, but far-reaching restrictions on the usage of some of these forms make this verb appear to live on the verge of defectiveness. The first peculiarity concerns the 3rd singular non-past form. While *willed* is quite frequent as a preterite or past participle (with more than a hundred attestations in the BNC) with no apparent restriction as to its subject (apart from sentience), the 3rd singular form *wills* seems highly restricted, especially in BrE. In the BNC we find only 12 attestations of *wills*, nine of which have *God* as a subject, and such usage appears to be very formal. The same is apparently not true in NAmE. The form *wills* occurs in COCA more than 300 times with a wide variety of subjects. Some subjects denote power figures (God, Allah, the president) but others are attested (proper names, *a young Polish boy*, pronouns that do not refer to power figures). We frequently find *wills* followed by a reflexive (*she wills herself*). There is no particular formal flavour. Another peculiarity is the alternate preterite form, *would*. Historically, this form originated as a preterite and subjunctive form, but is now largely restricted to collocations with *rather*, as in (12).

> (12)   *FPK 1992:* I **would rather** he'd stayed at home with us, but it was his choice, and he's not a child any longer.

The analysis of potentially defective verbs suggests that defectiveness, outside the domain of the core modal auxiliaries, is best seen as a very rare, and perhaps gradient, phenomenon.

5.4 Auxiliary verbs

In this section we will look more closely at the morphological behaviour of auxiliary verbs. The auxiliary verbs BE, DO, and HAVE were treated in Section 5.3.4, and we will include them here only with regard to those aspects of auxiliary behaviour that were not discussed in that section, namely weak forms, clitics, and negation.

Potential candidates for auxiliary status are the verbs in (13), where (13a) gives the core modal auxiliaries and (13b) three auxiliaries whose morphological behaviour is, however, quite different from that of the core modals.

> (13)   a.   CAN, COULD, MAY, MIGHT, MUST, OUGHT, SHALL, SHOULD, WILL, WOULD
>
> b.   DARE, NEED, USE

We will deal with each group in turn in the following two subsections, and subsections 5.4.3 and 5.4.4 will then be devoted to clitics and weak forms, and to the negative forms of auxiliaries.

5.4.1 Core modal auxiliaries

5.4.1.1 *The semantics of modals*

The semantics of modals have been dealt with in many publications including Coates (1983), Quirk *et al.* (1985), Palmer (1974, 1990, 2001), Huddleston (2002b). These studies indicate that the whole question of the semantics of the English modals is far from simple and not easily summarized. We have no information to improve on the descriptions in such texts, and the complex semantics associated with the modals has little direct relevance to the forms. We should also note that there are many periphrastic expressions which carry modal meanings, but which are not usually listed as 'the modals': forms such as *be able to, be going to, be possible that, be willing to, better (not), have (got) to, maybe, perhaps*. We should also note that there is a great deal of dialectal variability in the form and meaning of modals in English. This ranges from the existence of 'double modals', such as *might could* in some varieties of English, to the fact that *haven't got to* may mean 'there is no obligation to' in some dialects and 'must not' in others, to the fact that in some varieties *shall* is never or very seldom used at all. Overall statements of precisely what the modals mean 'in English' are thus difficult. Rather than spend a great deal of space on this topic, we present Figure 5.1 (adapted from Coates 1983: 26) to illustrate the complexity of the meanings associated with the various modal verbs. While many readings are presented in Figure 5.1, and the mapping between forms and meanings is clearly complex (as Figure 5.1 illustrates), the meanings illustrated are closely related to one another, to the extent that a given modal in context may be ambiguous between readings.

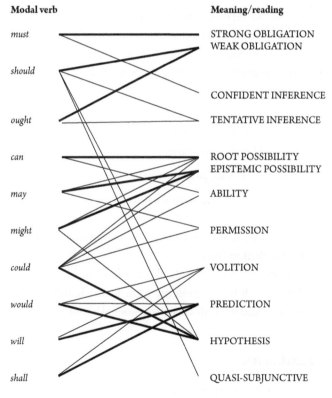

FIGURE 5.1 Modal verbs and their meanings/readings. Bold lines represent primary use, thin lines represent secondary or infrequent uses.

Adapted from Coates (1983: 26).

5.4.1.2 *The form of modals*

As mentioned in Section 5.2, the core modals can be morphologically characterized by their defective paradigms. They do not have non-finite forms that would allow them to occur in the respective non-finite syntactic constructions, and they also lack 3rd person singular non-past forms.

Since we have listed *could*, *might*, *should*, and *would* as separate modals on the basis of their meaning, we might argue that the core modals do not even have a preterite form. However, there are places where *could* (and the other forms listed here) can act as the preterite of CAN, etc. under sequence of tense rules in indirect speech. This is illustrated in (14).

(14)   a. He said, 'I will come.'

       b. He said he would come.

       c. Mary says that she can come.

       d. Mary said that she could come.

It thus seems that *could* and *would* have a dual function: one as a preterite form, and one as a separate modal verb with their own meanings. *Might* and *should* are awkward as past tense forms of *may* and *shall*, partly because of the restricted usage of *may* and *shall*, and partly because the meanings of the erstwhile preterites have diverged semantically from the original base to such a great extent.

(15)   a. The teacher said, 'Yes, you may leave early.'

       b. The teacher said I might leave early.

       c. My godmother says I shall go to the ball.

       d. My godmother said I should go to the ball.

While (15b) is clearly possible, it sounds pedantic or old-fashioned, while (15d) does not sound as though it is equivalent to (15c).

We might thus argue that we have modals like *must* and *ought* which have no preterite, modals like *can* and *will* which have a preterite form that is homophonous with another modal, and modals like *may* and *shall* which are transitional between the two.

5.4.2 Other auxiliaries

The three verbs given in (13b) are rather intricate cases, with NEED and DARE sharing some peculiarities. These two modals behave syntactically both as lexical verbs and as auxiliary verbs. For example, they can take both bare infinitives (a sign of being an auxiliary) and *to*-infinitives (a sign of being a lexical verb). Interestingly, this distinction has other correlates, syntactic and morphological. Huddleston (2002b: 111) implies for DARE that the auxiliary use goes together with a lack of 3rd person marking in the non-past. This is, however, not the case, as the many attestations to the contrary show, two of which, from COCA, are shown in (16).

(16) *Chicago Sun-Times 1999*: And yet he **dares think** about it, even though he knows he has a bull's-eye on his bumper

Symposium 1993: She is condemned because she **dares reject** the stereotype of the submissive woman

Given that the morphological and syntactic facts do not clearly map onto each other, it is not clear whether a lexical distinction between auxiliary DARE and lexical DARE is warranted at all. Rather, we find variant forms expressing the same morphosyntactic property (e.g. 3rd singular non-past).

With NEED, however, we do find a neat complementary distribution of structural properties. When NEED is used with a bare infinitive, that is as an auxiliary, its paradigm is defective and has only one form, the non-past *need*, and no preterite, thus aligning with MUST and OUGHT. This is illustrated in (17a–c), from COCA.

(17) a. *Sierra 1990*: None is so poor that **he need sit** on a pumpkin.

b. *Atlanta Journal Constitution 1996*: **He needs to write** what makes his heart sing.

c. *ABC_GMA 2007*: He **needed to win**, he needed the black vote.

The verb USE as an aspectual marker is also ambiguous in its status. For many speakers it always behaves syntactically like a lexical verb, for others it has some of the syntactic properties of auxiliaries. The construction is only used with anterior temporal reference, which has the morphological consequence that, independent of syntactic behaviour as a lexical or auxiliary verb, only the preterite and past participle forms occur. This has led to some variation in the spelling of the form too. Thus one can easily find attestations of <use to>, where standard orthography would have <used to>, as in (18), from COCA.

(18) *Houston Chronicle 1999*: he doesn't spend nearly as much time as he **use to** on the practice range.

Furthermore, the construction is incompatible with the present participle (**She was using to come by every day*) and the verb thus ends up with a highly defective paradigm.

5.4.3 Auxiliary clitics and weak forms

Being function words, auxiliaries occur most often unstressed, but must receive at least some degree of stress in certain syntactic positions, for example before the gap in stranded position (e.g. *We'll help you if we can*, see, for example, Palmer *et al.* (2002: 1613) for further discussion). Traditionally, we speak of 'strong' and 'weak' forms. In (19), we give these allomorphs for all pertinent auxiliaries. In general, the weak forms involve a more centralized vowel and sometimes the loss of a consonant in addition. The non-strong realizations of *are* are treated further below.

(19)	*spelling*	*strong form*	*weak form(s)*
	am	/æm/	/əm/
	be	/biː/	/bi/
	been	/biːn ‖ bɪn/	/bɪn/
	was	/wɒz ‖ wʌz ~ wɑːz/	/wəz/
	were	/wɜː ~ weə ‖ wɜː/	/wə ‖ wər/
	can	/kæn/	/kən/
	could	/kʊd/	/kəd/
	do	/duː/	/dʊ, də/
	does	/dʌz/	/dəz, dz/
	have	/hæv/	/həv, əv/
	had	/hæd/	/həd, əd/
	has	/hæz/	/həz, əz/
	must	/mʌst/	/məst, məs/
	shall	/ʃæl/	/ʃəl, ʃə, ʃ/
	should	/ʃʊd/	/ʃəd, ʃd, ʃt/
	will	/wɪl/	/wəl, əl/
	would	/wʊd/	/wəd, əd/

Some of the verbs listed in (19) have yet other forms, namely clitic forms that attach to the word immediately preceding them. There is also one verb, DO, that has a proclitic, that is /d/, for the forms *do* and *did*, which attaches to the following pronoun *you*, as in non-past *D'you need a hand?* and past *D'you have a good time?* (20) gives the clitic forms.

(20)	verb form	(host +) clitic spelling	host + clitic pronunciation
	am	I'm	/aɪm/
	are	you're	/jɔː ~ jʊə ~ jə ‖ jʊər ~ jər/
		we're	/wɪə ~ weə ~ wə ‖ wɪər ~ wər/
		they're	/ðeə ~ ðeɪə ‖ ðer ~ ðər/
	do	d'you	/djuː, djʊ, djə, dʒuː, dʒə/
	did	d'you	/djuː, djʊ, djə, dʒuː, dʒə/
		'd	/d/
	have	've	/v ~ f/
	had	'd	/d/
	has	's	/z ~ s/
	will	'll	/l/
	would	'd	/d/

The clitic forms are not simply to be seen as further reduced variants of weak forms for at least three reasons. First, not all verbs that have weak forms have enclitic forms, second, the syntactic distribution of the clitics is more restricted than that of the weak forms, and, third, some pronoun–clitic combinations have weak and strong forms themselves (e.g. *we're* and *did you* illustrated in (20)). Note however that, depending on the kind of environment, the distinction between some weak forms and the corresponding clitic is not always very clear. For example, the orthographic representation <'ll> after a consonant letter, as in *that'll do it*, may be realized with only the clitic /l/ or with the weak form /əl/. Furthermore, some sources list /ə ‖ ər/ as weak forms of *are*, and not, as we do, as clitics. We opt for a clitic analysis of *'re* on the grounds that a weak form analysis cannot account for the facts that the pronoun and the auxiliary form an indivisible phonological unit in /jɔː, jə, wə, ðeə, ðer, ðər/. Furthermore, there are weak and strong forms of the pronoun clitic combinations themselves, as shown in the last column of (20).

The distributional restrictions of the clitics are quite intricate and vary for different sets of forms. In general, the clitics attach to preceding NPs, but there are some systematic exceptions to this. The least restricted forms are the clitic forms of *has* and *is*. They attach to the widest range of preceding constituents, including NP subjects (*Jane's not at home*), some subordinators (*the book that's on the shelf*), interrogative words and phrases (*How's your mother?*; *How bad's your ear?*) and a few more constructions (see Palmer *et al.* 2002: 1614–16 for more discussion).

More restricted is the encliticized realization of *did*, *had*, and *would*, /d/. It only attaches to vowels and it occurs in fewer syntactic environments than the *has/is* clitic *'s*. Which environments are possible and which ones are not, is not entirely clear, however. Not all grammars also list *'d* as a clitic form of *did*, but the existing evidence strongly suggests its inclusion as such. Some examples from COCA are given in (21) (we have eliminated the spaces round clitics used in the corpora for tagging purposes)

(21)   a. *American Scholar 2010*: The phone rang. "**How'd** it go?" Lester asked. "With the murderer? Did you talk to him?"

   b. *Sporting News 2009*: Hey, **how'd** you like that? It was a pretty sweet catch, wasn't it?

As with the clitic forms of *has* and *is*, the use of the *'d* clitic may lead to ambiguities in specific contexts. For example, *I'd cut it* can mean 'I would cut it' or 'I had cut it', or *how'd they find us?* can mean 'how did they find us' or 'how would they find us'.

The most restricted clitics are *'ll*, *'m*, *'re* and *'ve*, for which it has been claimed that they attach only to NPs that are their own and sole subjects (e.g. Kaisse 1983: 98). This seems to be true for *'ve* and *'re* (and trivially for *'m*), as shown in (22) for *'ve*, taken from Kaisse, but not for *'ll*, as many attested examples like those in (23) show (taken from COCA).

(22)   a. I've got it.

   b. *John and I've got it.

(23)   a. *Batman Returns 1992*: **Josh and Jen'll** put a spin on this.

   b. *Faulkner 2007*: "**Jenny and I'll** bring your TV," said Martin.

One can also find spellings with two clitics attaching to one another, but in these cases the second clitic, which is usually *'ve*, is a weak form and realized with a schwa. Consider (24), from COCA.

(24)   *Ind_Oprah 2004*: I**'d've** been terrified if I thought anything like that

5.4.4 Negation

All of the auxiliaries, in contrast to all other verbs of English, have negative forms, in which the negative element /nt/, spelled <n't>, is suffixed to the auxiliary. In these cases, the negation has sentential scope. The negative form of the auxiliary is in free variation with constructions that have the affirmative auxiliary form and the free sentential negator *not*, as shown in (25) and (26), from the BNC. Examples like that in (26b) may be dialectal, being more common in northern British English.

(25)   a. *CD5 1992*: there **haven't been** any drugs here for ages.

   b. *Hansard extracts 1991–1992*: there **have not been** any previous accidents of this nature within the tunnel.

(26) a. *FSP 1989*: **Haven't** you been listening?

  b. *KCX 1992*: Mm **have** you **not** been working then?

In contrast to the free form negation, negative auxiliary forms can never be used to express VP-negation, that is a type of negation in which the negation has scope only over the VP, and not over the whole clause. This leads to a potential meaning contrast between the two constructions, at least in writing, as shown in (27).

(27) a. I **could not** pay attention.

   'What I could do is not pay attention' or 'I was unable to pay attention'

  b. I **couldn't** pay attention.

   'I was unable to pay attention'

The negative suffix can be attached to each of the (non-clitic) forms of the respective verbs' paradigms. The suffix integrates phonologically with the base, which, depending on its phonological structure, may or may not lead to the addition of a syllable (cf. monosyllabic *aren't* with disyllabic *couldn't*). If the addition of *n't* leads to an increased number of syllables, the nasal of the suffix is syllabic (e.g. /dɪdn̩t/). Bases with final /n/ do not have geminate nasals. Six of the negative auxiliary forms show deviant allomorphies or spellings, or both. They are listed in (28). Note that *shan't* listed in (28) is not NAmE, and is rare or non-existent in some other varieties as well.

(28)

verb form	negated verb form spelling	negated verb form pronunciation
can	\<can't>	/kɑːnt ‖ kæːnt/
do	\<don't>	/dəʊnt ‖ doʊnt/
must	\<mustn't>	/mʌsnt/
shall	\<shan't>	/ʃɑːnt/
used	%\<usedn't > ~ \<usen't>	/juːsnt/
will	\<won't>	/wəʊnt ‖ woʊnt/

A number of additional peculiarities of auxiliary negation are noteworthy. First, the aspectual verb USE cannot take the negative suffix in all dialects or with all speakers. This is expected, given its variable status as auxiliary or lexical verb discussed above. If the verb is lexical in status, it does not have a negative form. A possible negative for *used to* is *didn't use(d) to*, as illustrated in (29) from the BNC.

(29)   *Nottingham Oral History Project*: They **didn't use** to cut it in slices

   Bacons College lesson: What do we have that we **didn't used to** have?

Second, the verb CAN has an additional negative form, in which the free form negator is suf-fixed to the form *cannot*. This form has initial stress and, just like the negative form *can't*, cannot be used to express VP-negation. The form *cannot* is more formal in character than the form *can't*, but the syntactic distributions of *can't* and *cannot* seem to be equivalent (*pace* Palmer *et al.* 2002: 1611). This is illustrated in (30), with examples from the BNC (although Palmer *et al.* are right to the extent that the construction in (30a) is rare though found in both BNC and in COCA, usually spelled <can not>).

(30)   a. *HHV 1992*: **Cannot** we have a proper system of no-fault payments for medical injuries?

   b. *G1D 1993*: **Can't** we have a vodka?

   c. *Dancy, Johnathan. 1992*: **Can** we **not** then simply accept that justification continues ad infinitum?

Third, not all of the negative auxiliary forms that can be found in the language are uniformly considered part of the standard English system. Thus, *ain't* occurs as an additional suppletive negative form of *am, are, is, have*, and *has* in many varieties, and is described as being informal or non-standard. Another such form is *amn't*, which is especially frequent in IrE and ScE, but seems not to be restricted to these areas. Another variant form for the 1st singular non-past BE is *aren't*, which, again contrary to what Palmer *et al.* (2002: 1612) suggest, can be found in both interrogative and affirmative clauses, especially in spoken registers, and more especially in BrE, as shown by the examples from the BNC given in (31).

(31)   a. *KBW1992*: **Aren't I** hopeless?

   b. *KBD1992*: **I aren't** bothered for them.

5.5 INCORPORATION OF INFINITIVAL *TO*

The infinitive marker TO combines with seven verbs to form morphologically complex units that deserve special treatment. The verbs are WANT, GO, HAVE, USE, GOT, OUGHT, and SUP-POSE. The spellings for the respective forms of WANT TO and GOING TO, <wanna> and <gonna>, are established, for the other verbs we use <hafta>, <useta> , <gotta>, <oughta> and <supposeta> /s(ə)pəʊstə ‖ s(ə)poʊstə/. The phenomenon is also known as *to*-contrac-tion, a label that suggests that it is a phonological process of fusion. However, it can be argued that we are not dealing with on-line phonological reduction due to fast speech but are faced with complex forms in their own right, which all show some peculiarities in phonological shape and behaviour that are not readily described under the assumption of a syntactic and phonological concatenation process of the two words involved. For ease of reference, we will use the traditional term 'contraction' to refer to the phenomenon, but do so without commitment to the underlying analytical assumptions. We will discuss the facts in detail for WANT TO, but we find the same patterns of usage with the other forms. We therefore discuss the properties of the other verbs in more detail only if they differ from those of WANT TO.

The form *wanna* can be used in all contexts in which the verb form *want* and the infinitival marker TO, introducing the complement of WANT, are syntactically adjacent. Notably, the noun *want* adjacent to infinitival *to* does not contract (it virtually never occurs), nor do we find contraction if the *to* following *want* introduces an adjunct, or a complement of another verb. The examples of adjuncts in (32) are from Hudson (2006: 605).

(32)   How much paint do you want to finish the house?

I'll arrange for the books you want to be sent to your house.

The form *wanna* is only a possible realization of WANT TO in those contexts where the plain form or the plain non-past form of WANT, that is *want*, is possible, making incorporation with *wants, wanted, wanting* impossible. The form is phonetically realized as /wɒnə ‖ wɑːnə ~ wɔːnə ~ wʌnə/, with an additional alternation in the final vowel in some varieties, where schwa alternates with /ʊ/ if the following word starts with a vowel (see Hudson 2006: 606–8 for discussion). This variety-dependent alternation can also be found with the other verbs of this group.

The future-oriented progressive form *going to* has a variant with incorporated infinitival marker, *gonna*, which can be realized as /gənə, gɒnə, gʌnə ‖ gɔːnə, gɑːnə/. Contraction affects GO only in the pertinent idiomatic usage, the homophonous verb GO cannot contract if followed by *to* (**He's gonna jail* meaning 'He is going to jail').

The verb HAVE in its idiomatic obligation-expressing usage with an immediately adjacent *to*-infinitive can realize the two non-past forms *have to* and *has to* as /hæftə/ and /hæstə/. Notably, these forms show regressive devoicing that is not found across the board (cf. *li[v]e to, do[v]etail, li[v]etrapping, fi[v]e times*).

The aspect-marking construction with *used to* has already been described in Section 5.4.2. The contracted form of this construction *useta*, pronounced /juːstə/, is phonologically different from the non-aspect-marking form *used to*, as it does not normally alternate in stranded positions. In contrast, non-aspectual *used to*, as in *this is not what she is normally used to* cannot end in a schwa. In some dialects *useta* is used as a base form (as in *She didn't useta*).

The idiomatic construction (HAVE) GOT TO expresses an obligation or necessity and, in its contracted form is pronounced /gɒtə ‖ gɑːɾə/. In many varieties of English, including NAmE, *gotta* does not rhyme with *not to*, which is an indication of the lexical status this form enjoys. In some varieties of NAmE, and possible others as well, *gotta* can be a 3rd singular form. The form *gotsta* is found in NAmE and is used with all persons (contrary to what is suggested in Pullum 1997: 89), as in (33) from COCA.

(33)   *Outdoor Life 1997:* You **gots to** dig them deeper

The contracted variant for *ought to* is /ɔːtə ‖ ɔːɾə ~ ɑːɾə/. As pointed out by Pullum (1997), *oughta* does not ryhme with *thought to* (as in *you oughta be happy* versus *they are thought to be happy*), as the latter, at least in NAmE, cannot have a schwa. Thus, *oughta*, like the other verbs discussed, has its own lexically specified phonological peculiarities.

Finally, the contracted form of SUPPOSED TO, *supposeta*, shows the same kind of non-alternation of schwa and /ʊ/ as the previously discussed verbs. Pullum (1997: 89) provides the wonderful minimal pair of *supposed to* versus *host to* given in (34).

(34)   a.   You should pour the champagne, you're sposta

       b.   You shouldn't pour it, you should wait for the host [tʊ] / *host[ə]

At the syntactic level, *supposeta* co-occurs only with the clitic form of the copula, if there is a choice (*ʔYou are supposeta take out the garbage*).

APPENDIX

Irregular verbs in English

We provide below a list of 387 irregular verb forms in English derived from the various sources at our disposal. We make no claim about the status of the forms we list beyond that we believe that they are used. Specifically, some may be standard, others non-standard or dialectal, and we make no attempt to mark such matters; we simply list the forms alphabetically in each category. The lack of a form cannot definitely show that it does not exist, merely that we have not found it listed or used. Under each fundamental verb, we list verbs created from it by word-formation, provided that they too have irregular forms: such verbs are listed in italics. *Grandstanded* is not listed because it is regular. Where there are alternative forms existing side-by-side there may be, but need not be, a semantic difference between them. Forms which were originally past participles but which are now only adjectives (forms such as *drunken, sunken*) are ignored. Forms which are phonologically regular but orthographically irregular (*laid, paid*) are also ignored.

Base form	*Preterite*	*Past participle*	*Also regular*	*Notes*
abide	abode	abode	Yes	
be	was were	been		
bear	bore	borne		

Base form	Preterite	Past participle	Also regular	Notes
forbear	*forbore*	*forborne*		
overbear	*overbore*	*overborne*		
beat	beat bet	beat beaten bet		
browbeat	*browbeat*	*browbeat browbeaten*		
begin	began begun	begun		
bend	bent	bent		
unbend	*unbent*	*unbent*		
bereave	bereft	bereft	Yes	
beseech	besought	besought	Yes	
bet	bet	bet	Yes	
bid	bad bade bid	bade bid bidden		<bade> may be pronounced /bæd/ or /beɪd/
forbid	*forbad forbade*	*forbid forbidden*		
outbid	*outbid*	*outbid outbidden*		
overbid	*overbid*	*overbid*		
rebid	*rebid*	*rebid*		
underbid	*underbid*	*underbid underbidden*		
bind	bound	bound		
rebind	*rebound*	*rebound*		
unbind	*unbound*	*unbound*		
bite	bit	bit bitten		
frostbite	*frostbit*	*frostbitten*		
bleed	bled	bled		
blow	blew	blown	Yes	
break	broke	broken		
breed	bred	bred		
crossbreed	*crossbred*	*crossbred*		
inbreed	*inbred*	*inbred*		
interbreed	*interbred*	*interbred*		
outbreed	*outbred*	*outbred*		
overbreed	*overbred*	*overbred*		
bring	brought	brought		
build	built	built		
overbuild	*overbuilt*	*overbuilt*		

(*continued*)

Base form	Preterite	Past participle	Also regular	Notes
prebuild	*prebuilt*	*prebuilt*		
rebuild	*rebuilt*	*rebuilt*		
burn	burnt	burnt	Yes	
sunburn	*sunburnt*	*sunburnt*	Yes	
burst	burst	burst	Yes	
bust	bust	bust	Yes	
buy	bought	bought		
overbuy	*overbought*	*overbought*		
cast	cast	cast		
broadcast	*broadcast*	*broadcast*	Yes	
forecast	*forecast*	*forecast*		
miscast	*miscast*	*miscast*		
overcast	*overcast*	*overcast*		
rebroadcast	*rebroadcast*	*rebroadcast*	Yes	
recast	*recast*	*recast*		
roughcast	*roughcast*	*roughcast*		
sand-cast	*sand-cast*	*sand-cast*		
telecast	*telecast*	*telecast*		
typecast	*typecast*	*typecast*		
catch	caught	caught	Yes	
chide	chid	chid chidden	Yes	
choose	chose	chosen		
cleave	cleft clove	cleft cloven	Yes	
cling	clung	clung		
clothe	clad	clad	Yes	
come	came come	come	Yes	
become	*became*	*become*		
overcome	*overcame*	*overcome*		
cost	cost	cost		
creep	crept	crept	Yes	(regular in combination *creep out*)
crow	crew	crew	Yes	
cut	cut	cut		
recut	*recut*	*recut*		
undercut	*undercut*	*undercut*		
deal	dealt	dealt		

Base form	Preterite	Past participle	Also regular	Notes
misdeal	*misdealt*	*misdealt*		
redeal	*redealt*	*redealt*		
dig	dug	dug	Yes	
dive	dove	dived dove	Yes	
do	did done	done		
misdo	*misdid*	*misdone*		
outdo	*outdid*	*outdone*		
overdo	*overdid*	*overdone*		
predo	*predid*	*predone*		
redo	*redid*	*redone*		
undo	*undid*	*undone*		
drag	drug	drug	Yes	
draw	drew	drawn	Yes	
outdraw	*outdrew*	*outdrawn*		
overdraw	*overdrew*	*overdrawn*		
redraw	*redrew*	*redrawn*		
withdraw	*withdrew*	*withdrawn*		
dream	dreamt	dreamt	Yes	
daydream	*daydreamt*	*daydreamt*	Yes	
drink	drank drunk	drunk	Yes	
outdrink	*outdrank*	*outdrunk*		
overdrink	*overdrank*	*overdrunk*		
drive	drove	driven		
outdrive	*outdrove*	*outdriven*		
test-drive	*test-drove*	*test-driven*		
dwell	dwelt	dwelt	Yes	
earn	earnt	earnt	Yes	rarely in writing
eat	ate eat	eaten		
overeat	*overate*	*overeaten*		
fall	fell	fallen		
befall	*befell*	*befallen*		
feed	fed	fed		
hand-feed	*hand-fed*	*hand-fed*		
overfeed	*overfed*	*overfed*		

(*continued*)

Base form	Preterite	Past participle	Also regular	Notes
spoon-feed	*spoon-fed*	*spoon-fed*		
underfeed	*underfed*	*underfed*		
feel	felt	felt		
fight	fought	fought		
outfight	*outfought*	*outfought*		
find	found	found		
fit	fit	fit	Yes	
refit	*refit*	*refit*	Yes	
retrofit	*retrofit*	*retrofit*	Yes	
flee	fled	fled		
fling	flung	flung		
fly	flew	flown		
outfly	*outflew*	*outflown*		
test-fly	*test-flew*	*test-flown*		
forsake	forsook	forsaken		
freeze	froze	frozen		
deepfreeze	*deepfroze*	*deepfrozen*	Yes	
quick-freeze	*quick-froze*	*quick-frozen*		
unfreeze	*unfroze*	*unfrozen*		
get	got	got gotten		
beget	*begot*	*begotten*		
forget	*forgot*	*forgot forgotten*		
give	gave give	given	Yes	
forgive	*forgave*	*forgiven*		
misgive	*misgave*	*misgiven*		
go	went gone	gone went	Yes	
forgo	*forwent*	*forgone*		
undergo	*underwent*	*undergone*		
grind	ground	ground		
regrind	*reground*	*reground*		
grow	grew	grown	Yes	
regrow	*regrew*	*regrown*		
outgrow	*outgrew*	*outgrown*		

Base form	Preterite	Past participle	Also regular	Notes
hang	hung	hung	Yes	The regular verb *hang* is normatively taken to be a hyponym of *execute*, though colloquially the irregular form is used here as well.
overhang	*overhung*	*overhung*		
unhang	*unhung*	*unhung*		
rehang	*rehung*	*rehung*		
have	had	had		
hear	heard	heard	Yes	
mishear	*misheard*	*misheard*		
overhear	*overheard*	*overheard*		
rehear	*reheard*	*reheard*		
heave	hove	hove	Yes	
hew	hewed	hewn	Yes	
hide	hid	hid hidden		
unhide	*unhid*	*unhidden*		
hit	hit	hit		
hold	held	held		
behold	*beheld*	*beheld*		
uphold	*upheld*	*upheld*		
withhold	*withheld*	*withheld*		
hurt	hurt	hurt		
keep	kept	kept	Yes	
ken	kent	kent	Yes	esp. ScE
kneel	knelt	knelt	Yes	
knit	knit	knit	Yes	
reknit	*reknit*	*reknit*	*Yes*	
unknit	*unknit*	*unknit*	*Yes*	
know	knew	known	Yes	
lead	led	led		
mislead	*misled*	*misled*		
lean	leant	leant	Yes	
leap	leapt	leapt	Yes	

(continued)

Base form	Preterite	Past participle	Also regular	Notes
outleap	*outleapt*	*outleapt*	Yes	
learn	learnt	learnt	Yes	
mislearn	*mislearnt*	*mislearnt*	Yes	
relearn	*relearnt*	*relearnt*	Yes	
unlearn	*unlearnt*	*unlearnt*	Yes	
leave	left	left		
lend	lent	lent		
let	let	let		
sublet	*sublet*	*sublet*		
lie	lay	lain		
underlie	*underlay*	*underlain*		
light	lit	lit	Yes	
moonlight	*moonlit*	*moonlit*	Yes	
relight	*relit*	*relit*	Yes	
lose	lost	lost		
make	made	made	Yes	
premake	*premade*	*premade*		
remake	*remade*	*remade*		
unmake	*unmade*	*unmade*		
mean	meant	meant		
meet	met	met		
mow	mowed	mown	Yes	
plead	pled	pled	Yes	
prove	proved	proven	Yes	
disprove	*disproved*	*disproven*	Yes	
put	put	put		
input	*input*	*input*	Yes	
output	*output*	*output*	Yes	
quit	quit	quit	Yes	
read	read	read		
misread	*misread*	*misread*		
proofread	*proofread*	*proofread*		
reread	*reread*	*reread*		
sight-read	*sight-read*	*sight-read*		
rend	rent	rent		
rid	rid	rid	Yes	

Base form	Preterite	Past participle	Also regular	Notes
ride	rode	ridden rode		
outride	*outrode*	*outridden*		
override	*overrode*	*overriden*		
ring	rang rung	rung	Yes	The regular verb is denominal
rise	rose	risen		
arise	*arose*	*arisen*		
run	ran run	run		
outrun	*outran*	*outrun*		
overrun	*overran*	*overrun*		
rerun	*reran*	*rerun*		
saw	sawed	sawn	Yes	
say	said	said		
gainsay	*gainsaid*	*gainsaid*		
see	saw seen	seen	Yes	
oversee	*oversaw*	*overseen*		
seek	sought	sought		
sell	sellt sold	sellt sold	Yes	
outsell	*outsold*	*outsold*		
oversell	*oversold*	*oversold*		
presell	*presold*	*presold*		
resell	*resold*	*resold*		
undersell	*undersold*	*undersold*		
send	sent	sent		
resend	*resent*	*resent*		
set	set	set		
beset	*beset*	*beset*		
inset	*inset*	*inset*		
misset	*misset*	*misset*		
offset	*offset*	*offset*		
preset	*preset*	*preset*		
reset	*reset*	*reset*		
typeset	*typeset*	*typeset*		
upset	*upset*	*upset*		

(continued)

Base form	Preterite	Past participle	Also regular	Notes
sew	sewed	sewn	Yes	
oversew	*oversewed*	*oversewn*	Yes	
resew	*resewed*	*resewn*	Yes	
unsew	*unsewed*	*unsewn*	Yes	
shake	shook	shaken shook		
shave	shaved	shaven	Yes	
shear	shore	shorn	Yes	
shed	shed	shed		
shew	shewed	shewn		Now old-fashioned. See *show*.
shine	shone	shone	Yes	The transitive form is more likely to be regular
outshine	*outshone*	*outshone*		
shit	shat shit	shat shit	Yes	
shoe	shod	shod	Yes	
shoot	shot	shot		
outshoot	*outshot*	*outshot*		
overshoot	*overshot*	*overshot*		
show	showed	shown	Yes	See also *shew*.
shred	shred	shred	Yes	
shrink	shrank shrunk	shrunk		
preshrink	*preshrank*	*preshrunk*		
shrive	shrove	shriven	Yes	
shut	shut	shut		
sing	sang sung	sung		
outsing	*outsang*	*outsung*		
sink	sank sunk	sunk		
sit	sat	sat		
outsit	*outsat*	*outsat*		
resit	*resat*	*resat*		
slay	slew	slain	Yes	
sleep	slept	slept		
outsleep	*outslept*	*outslept*		
oversleep	*overslept*	*overslept*		
slide	slid	slid		
backslide	*backslid*	*backslid backslidden*		

Base form	Preterite	Past participle	Also regular	Notes
sling	slung	slung		
unsling	*unslung*	*unslung*		
slink	slunk	slunk	Yes	
slit	slit	slit		*slitted* is found, but is denominal
smell	smelt	smelt	Yes	
outsmell	*outsmelt*	*outsmelt*	Yes	
smite	smote	smitten		
sneak	sneak snuck	snuck	Yes	
sow	sowed	sown	Yes	
speak	spoke	spoken		
misspeak	*misspoke*	*misspoken*		
outspeak	*outspoke*	*outspoken*		
overspeak	*overspoke*	*overspoken*		
speed	sped	sped	Yes	
outspeed	*outsped*	*outsped*		
spell	spelt	spelt	Yes	
misspell	*misspelt*	*misspelt*	Yes	
spend	spent	spent		
misspend	*misspent*	*misspent*		
outspend	*outspent*	*outspent*		
overspend	*overspent*	*overspent*		
underspend	*underspent*	*underspent*		
spill	spilt	spilt	Yes	
overspill	*overspilt*	*overspilt*	Yes	
spin	span spun	spun		
unspin	*unspun*	*unspun*		
spit	spat spit	spat spit		*spitted* is denominal
spoil	spoilt	spoilt	Yes	
spread	spread	spread		
spring	sprang sprung	sprung		
stand	stood	stood		
misunderstand	*misunderstood*	*misunderstood*		
understand	*understood*	*understood*		
withstand	*withstood*	*withstood*		

(*continued*)

Base form	Preterite	Past participle	Also regular	Notes
steal	stole	stolen		
stick	stuck	stuck		
unstick	*unstuck*	*unstuck*		
sting	stung	stung		
stink	stank stunk	stunk		
stove, stave	stove	stove	Yes	
strew	strewed	strewn	Yes	
stride	strode	strid stridden strode		
bestride	*bestrode*	*bestrid bestridden bestrode*		
strike	struck	stricken struck		
string	strung	strung		
hamstring	*hamstrung*	*hamstrung*		
restring	*restrung*	*restrung*		
unstring	*unstrung*	*unstrung*		
strive	strove	striven	Yes	
swear	swore	sworn		
forswear	*forswore*	*forsworn*		
outswear	*outswore*	*outsworn*		
sweat	sweat	sweat	Yes	
sweep	swept	swept		
swell	swelled swole	swollen	Yes	
swim	swam swum	swam swum		
outswim	*outswam*	*outswum*		
swing	swung	swung		
take	took	taken		
betake	*betook*	*betaken*		
mistake	*mistook*	*mistaken*		
overtake	*overtook*	*overtaken*		
partake	*partook*	*partaken*		
retake	*retook*	*retaken*		
undertake	*undertook*	*undertaken*		
teach	taught	taught	Yes	
misteach	*mistaught*	*mistaught*		
reteach	*retaught*	*retaught*		
tear	tore	torn		

Base form	Preterite	Past participle	Also regular	Notes
retear	*retore*	*retorn*		
tell	tellt told	tellt told	Yes	
foretell	*foretold*	*foretold*		
retell	*retold*	*retold*		
text	text	text		
think	thought	thought		*Thunk* is sometimes used jocularly as a past participle.
outthink	*outthought*	*outthought*		
overthink	*overthought*	*overthought*		
rethink	*rethought*	*rethought*		
thrive	throve	thriven	Yes	
throw	threw	thrown	Yes	
outthrow	*outthrew*	*outthrown*		
overthrow	*overthrew*	*overthrown*		
thrust	thrust	thrust		
tread	tread trod	tread trod trodden	Yes	
retread	*retread retrod*	*retread retrodden*		
wake	woke	woken	Yes	
awake	*awoke*	*awoken*	Yes	
reawake	*reawoke*	*reawaken*		
rewake	*rewoke*	*rewaken*	Yes	
wear	wore	worn		
rewear	*rewore*	*reworn*		
weave	wove	woven	Yes	
interweave	*interwove*	*interwoven*	Yes	
reweave	*rewove*	*rewoven*	Yes	
unweave	*unwove*	*unwoven*	Yes	
wed	wed	wed	Yes	
rewed	*rewed*	*rewed*	Yes	
weep	wept	wept		
wet	wet	wet	Yes	
rewet	*rewet*	*rewet*	Yes	
win	won	won		
rewin	*rewon*	*rewon*		

(*continued*)

Base form	*Preterite*	*Past participle*	*Also regular*	*Notes*
wind	wound	wound		
interwind	*interwound*	*interwound*		
overwind	*overwound*	*overwound*		
rewind	*rewound*	*rewound*		
unwind	*unwound*	*unwound*		
wring	wrung	wrung		
write	wrote	written		
handwrite	*handwrote*	*handwritten*		
miswrite	*miswrote*	*miswritten*		
outwrite	*outwrote*	*outwritten*		
overwrite	*overwrote*	*overwritten*		
rewrite	*rewrote*	*rewritten*		
typewrite	*typewrote*	*typewritten*		
underwrite	*underwrote*	*underwritten*		

CHAPTER 6

....

Adjective and adverb inflection

6.1 PROSPECTUS

The inflection of adjectives and adverbs in English is confined to the marking of the morphosyntactic category 'degree' with positive, comparative, and superlative forms. This category also often
goes under the name of 'comparison' (e.g. Quirk *et al.* 1985), and we will use both terms interchangeably. Following standard treatments we consider comparison in English a case of inherent
inflection (e.g. Haspelmath 2002: 67, Booij 2007: 101, see Section 24.2 for discussion). Similar to
the genitive, comparison of adjectives and adverbs involves two different structural realizations
for the comparative and the superlative, respectively. One option is suffixation by *-er* (comparative) or *-est* (superlative), the other a syntactic construction with *more* (comparative) or *most*
(superlative) preceding the adjective or adverb. We will refer to the suffixed realizations using the
terms affixal, synthetic, or morphological, and the terms periphrastic, analytic, or syntactic for
the constructions involving the degree markers *more* and *most*. Unlike Quirk *et al.* (1985) and
Pullum and Huddleston (2002) we will not restrict the term 'inflectional' to the affixal realization, since we recognize degree as an inflectional category that, similar to the inflectional category
of genitive (see Chapter 7), is either expressed morphologically or syntactically.

   We will first discuss the semantic issues involved with comparison, then discuss the properties of affixal degree-formation, before turning to a detailed description of the comparison
of adverbs and adjectives, including a detailed treatment of the determinants of the choice
between synthetic and analytic forms of comparative and superlative with adjectives. Due to
our focus on morphological issues, we will not delve into the properties of various syntactic
comparative constructions.

6.2 SEMANTIC ISSUES: DEGREE AND GRADABILITY

The meaning conveyed by degree marking is one in which a comparison is made (implicitly
or explicitly) along a scale of values. The positive form denotes an unmarked given value (e.g.
wide), the comparative expresses a higher degree (*wider*), the superlative the highest degree

on the respective scale (*widest*). Note that the superlative form is sometimes used as an intensifier, in the sense of 'very', as in (1), from COCA. In attributive position this particular reading of the superlative is often recognizable through the indefinite article, as shown in (1b).

(1)   a. *Rule Book 2011*: "**Most impressive**," said Poppins. "Much creative effort…"

b. *Live event 8:00 PM EST 2010*: Daniel showed extraordinary poise at **a most** difficult moment.

Notably, a few *-er* suffixed forms may look like comparatives but do not express the meaning 'more' in these forms because they have taken on an extended meaning. They are listed in (2).

(2)   earlier   'before, previously'
       later   'subsequent(ly), afterwards'
       lesser   'insignificant'

In the appropriate context, these forms may, however, be interpreted as regular comparatives (as in, for example, *She arrived earlier than her sister*).

It is uncontroversial, and follows from the meanings conveyed by degree marking, that only those adjectives and adverbs that are gradable, or at least allow a gradable reading, can have comparative and superlative forms. For an adjective or adverb to be gradable, we must be able to conceive of it as denoting a quality that is not absolute, but rather present in greater or lesser amounts along a scale (Rusiecki 1985; Bierwisch 1988a, 1988b, 1989; Pullum and Huddleston 2002).

Adjectives (and the corresponding *-ly* adverbs) are also sometimes divided into those that are qualitative and those that are relational, as exemplified in (3):

(3)   a. *qualitative*: red, low, short, wide, fierce, intelligent, demanding, certain, private, normal, quiet, aware

b. *relational*: Dutch, architectural, analytic, geographic, coastal, rhomboid, Palestinian

Most qualitative adjectives are gradable, with alleged exceptions being adjectives like *dead*, *pregnant*, *prime* (as in numbers), *male/female*, *unique*. Relational adjectives are more frequently said to be non-gradable.

It seems, however, that nearly any adjective can be coerced into a gradable reading if it can be construed as picking out a set of qualities that can be present or absent in various degrees. So, although *herbal* typically means 'made from herbs' and seems solidly relational, under appropriate circumstances we can conceive of this adjective as being gradable:

(4)   *Jon Bonné SFC 2007*: It's subtle, showing a twinge of Pinot Gris ripeness but a **more herbal** nose: envision damp hay, ripe pear and celery.

Even adjectives like *dead* or *pregnant* are often coerced into gradability, with something more dead being further on in the process of dying or even more decomposed, and someone more pregnant being further on in a pregnancy, as shown in (5).

(5) *Brimstone 2005*: A sleeping man wouldn't have his torso scorched and caved in upon itself like a burned log. She had seen many dead people during her childhood in Colombia, and Mr. Jeremy looked **deader** than any of them.

Ind_Oprah 2003: The **more pregnant** that I got, the worse the beatings got.

As Pullum and Huddleston (2002) point out, prescriptivists often advise against comparative and superlative uses of absolute adjectives (*more unique, the most unique*), but contemporary English speakers generally find no difficulty in construing such adjectives as gradable.

6.3 THE AFFIXAL COMPARATIVE AND SUPERLATIVE

As already mentioned, many adjectives and adverbs can form the comparative by affixation of *-er* and the superlative by affixation of *-est*:

(6) | | | |
|---|---|---|
| red | redder | reddest |
| gentle | gentler | gentlest |
| hardy | hardier | hardiest |
| serene | serener | serenest |

The comparative suffix is pronounced as /ə/ in non-rhotic dialects and /ər/ in rhotic dialects. The superlative suffix is pronounced /ɪst/ or /əst/. In order not to unnecessarily crowd our phonetic transcriptions we will use only /ɪst/ when transcribing pertinent forms.

In bases ending in syllabic [l̩], the /l/ sometimes but not always loses its syllabicity and is resyllabified as the onset of the syllable formed by the affix. We find this loss of syllabicity with *gentle* and *simple*, see (7a), but only optionally with *little* (7b). This elision and resyllabification does not occur with bases ending in syllabic [r] or [n], see (7c). In non-rhotic dialects the final [r] of the base is pronounced in intervocalic position, that is, when followed by the suffix.

(7) a. gentle ◆ gentler ◆ gentlest
    [ʤentl̩ ◆ ʤentlə ‖ ʤentlər ◆ ʤentlɪst]
    simple ◆ simpler ◆ simplest
    [sɪmpl̩ ◆ sɪmplə ‖ sɪmplər ◆ sɪmplɪst]

b. little • littler • littlest
[lɪtl̩ • lɪtlə ~ lɪtl̩ə • lɪtl̩ɪst ~ lɪtl̩ɪst] (*non-rhotic varieties*)
[lɪtl̩ • lɪtlər ~ lɪtl̩ər • lɪtl̩ɪst ~ lɪtl̩ɪst] (*rhotic varieties*)

c. meager • meagerer • meagerest
[miːgə ‖ miːgər • miːgərə ‖ miːgərər • miːgərɪst]
often • oftener • oftenest
[ɒf(t)ən ‖ ɔːf(t)ən • ɒf(t)ənə ‖ ɔːf(t)ənər • ɒf(t)ənɪst ‖ ɔːf(t)ənɪst]

With some bases ending in /ŋ/ we find the addition of /g/ before the suffixes, as shown in (8):

(8)   long • longer • longest
[lɒŋ ‖ lɔːŋ ~ laːŋ • lɒŋgə ‖ laːŋgər • lɒŋgɪst ‖ laːŋgɪst]

Other bases that work this way are *strong, young,* and (for at least some speakers) *wrong.* For speakers who allow superlatives in *-ingest* (*winningest, sleepingest*) (see below), there is no addition of /g/ before the superlative suffix.

The affixes are consistently spelled <er> and <est>, respectively, with the expected doubling of a final base consonant following a lax vowel (9a), replacement of final <y> by <i> (9b), and elision of silent <e> before the suffixes (9c):

(9)   a. thin • thinner • thinnest
fat • fatter • fattest

b. dainty • daintier • daintiest
bumpy • bumpier • bumpiest

c. white • whiter • whitest
fine • finer • finest

6.4 Double comparison

Although prescriptivists frown on it, double comparison is widespread in colloquial varieties of English. In double comparison both the *more/most* and the *-er/-est* markers are present, as illustrated in the examples in (10) from COCA.

(10)   *ABC_GMA 2006*: Is it because pornographers are getting a little **more craftier** with the, with the, with the Internet

CBS_Early 2007: if you want to put, like, an ornament in there, like a brooch or something like that to make it look a little **more dressier.**

FantasySciFi 2009: Some of our **more brighter** engineers did this.

Rolling Stone 1996: I think when I'm **most happiest** is when I'm actually so tense, so angry, so mad and disgusted, and I can relieve all that and be happy.

Interestingly, some adjectives are found with *-er/-est* in this construction that would not normally occur in the affixal construction. Some examples from COCA are provided in (11). Such examples are rare, and it is not clear to what extent double comparison is subject to different constraints from simple comparison.

(11)   *ABC_Nightline 1997*: Who's the **most beautifulest** baby in the world?

     Associated Press News 1998: Most people probably would have thought of him as the **most wickedest** man in town.

Double comparison seems always to be variable, and the difference, if any, between double and simple comparison for those speakers who use both is not clear.

6.5 ADVERBS

Not only adjectives, but also adverbs can undergo degree inflection. Since adverb degree formation is different from adjectival degree formation in certain respects, we will treat it separately in this section.

Before doing so, some further clarification is needed as to which kinds of non-adjectival bases have comparative and superlative forms. Pullum and Huddleston (2002: 533), for example, state that some determiners and prepositions may also instantiate the morphological category of degree. The pertinent forms are given in (12), with (12a) showing the determiners, and (12b) the prepositions:

(12)   a. few ◆ fewer ◆ fewest
       little ◆ less ◆ least
       many/much ◆ more ◆ most

     b. close ◆ closer ◆ closest
       far ◆ farther ~ further ◆ farthest ~ furthest
       near ◆ nearer ◆ nearest

The syntactic category of the words in (12) is, however, controversial, and most dictionaries seem to list them as adjectives or adverbs or both. For the purposes of this chapter we will also treat them as adverbs or adjectives. All non-adjectival forms that show degree formation have in common that they meet the gradability requirement.

Adverbs in *-ly* differ from adjectives in that they generally do not take the synthetic degree variants (see Chapter 15 for further discussion of *-ly* adverbs). Thus, apart from rare exceptions, such as the archaic forms *boldlier, quicklier*, periphrastic comparative or superlative forms are obligatory. Two cases are illustrated in (13) with examples from COCA:

(13)   *Our Lady of the Forest 2003*: Tom moved **more boldly** into the doorway.

Time 2001: So it came along on a gold spoon, one from another, and I handed it to the Queen, and then she tried to tip it out on the Prime Minister's shoulder, **most gently**…

Some adverbs that are not formed from adjectives via *-ly* suffixation are attested with both analytic and synthetic degree forms. Palmer *et al.* (2002: 1584) list the ones in (14a) as pertinent, but even large corpora do not have the two variant forms for all of them. We found analytic as well as synthetic variants only for *fast, hard*, and *often* in COCA. The less expected variant of these words is exemplified in (14b), but it seems that in general variation in this group is very limited.

(14)   a.   early, fast, hard, late, long, often, soon

b.   BNC. *The Daily Mirror*: The way the English game is evolving it is becoming ever **more fast** and physical. We were lacking in that department last year.

CBS 48 Hours 10:00 PM EST 2010: And when you love that person, it makes it so much **more hard**.

Fort Clay, Louisiana 2010: I wish I could come ashore **oftener**.

There are some *-ly* adverbs that also have unsuffixed variant forms, such as *easy ~ easily, loud ~ loudly, quick ~ quickly, slow ~ slowly*. Palmer *et al.* (2002: 1584–5) remark that while the positive form of the unsuffixed variant (e.g. *loud*) seems less frequent than the positive of the suffixed form (e.g. *loudly*), the comparative and the superlative seem to prefer the synthetic variants based on the unsuffixed adverb (i.e. *louder, loudest*). This point can be nicely illustrated with data from COCA, where we find, for example, only four attestations of *talked loud* as against 19 of *talked loudly*, whereas for the comparative forms there are four instances of *talked louder* and only one of *talked more loudly*. This pattern may also occasionally extend to other adjectives and adverbs of high frequency, as evidenced in sentences such as *That's easier said than done* (instead of *more easily*), or *Speak clearer!* (instead of *more clearly*) (examples from Quirk *et al.* 1985: 465).

A small number of adverbs, some of which we have already mentioned, have suppletive forms for the comparative and the superlative. Notably, these suppletive forms are identical to the comparative and superlative forms of the corresponding adjectives.

(15) a. badly • worse • worse

       well • better • best

       little • less • least

       far • farther ~ further • farthest ~ furthest

       much • more • most

The difference between *further* and *farther* (and the corresponding superlatives) is not clear (but see Quirk *et al.* 1985: 459 for a different view), and deserves further study.

6.6 ADJECTIVES

6.6.1 Irregular paradigms

Among adjectives, there are several irregular paradigms, too. These involve unexpected vowel alternations or suppletion:

(16)

good	better	best
far	farther/further	farthest/furthest
bad	worse	worst
much, many	more	most
little	less	least

As indicated above, *little* has a regular paradigm in contemporary English as well. We also find the archaic comparative and superlative forms of *old*, that is, *elder* and *eldest*, surviving in a limited range of contexts. Thus, the form *elder* is most frequently used as a noun denoting a senior person in charge of a tribe, society, or church, but in its form as an attributive adjective it is most often used in designating familial relations (*the elder daughter/uncle/grandchild*, etc.) and in the collocation *elder statesman*. Note that the noun *elder* also serves as a base for adjectival derivation in *elderly*, which, given that inflectional suffixes do not typically occur inside derivational ones, is an additional piece of evidence that the form with this reading has lost its status as a comparative. The superlative *eldest* is almost always used in designating familial relations.

The adjective *bad* shows some additional peculiarities. There is a mix of suppletion and regular suffixation in the non-standard form *worser*, in which the comparative is thus doubly marked. We also find the regular forms *badder* and *baddest* along with *worse* and *worst*, but usually with a colloquial meaning of 'impressive' or 'formidable':

(17) *Washington Post 2002*: Rather like the Sex Pistols, the YBAs get their special status by virtue of what they aren't. There were proto-punks in the United States that the Pistols

took off from, just as there have been much **badder** bad boys in the American art world than Damien Hirst or Chris Ofili.

Denver Post 2009: Of golf's four major championships, the U.S. Open has long been the one most likely not only to puff out its chest, but, like the **baddest** kid on the playground, actually go out looking for a fight.

There are also adjectives with defective paradigms. For example, although the adverb *well* has a superlative form *best*, the adjective *well* 'in good health' is awkward under comparison: *weller* is attested in COCA, we have not attested ✋*wellest*, and *best* seems impossible.

6.6.2 Affixal versus periphrastic comparative and superlative

As mentioned at the beginning of this chapter, English provides two ways of forming the comparative and superlative of adjectives. The matter has been widely discussed in the literature (e.g. Quirk *et al.* 1985; Bauer 1994; Kytö and Romaine 1997; Huddleston and Pullum 2002; Dixon 2005; Hilpert 2008; Mondorf 2009a, to mention only a few), and it has been suggested that many different factors may play a role. What has to be stated at the outset is that more recent corpus-based studies have shown that the degree of variability is much greater than standardly assumed in both descriptively (Quirk *et al.* 1985; Huddleston and Pullum 2002) and theoretically oriented approaches (for example, Poser 1992; Kiparsky 2005; Dixon 2005; Embick 2007).

Much of the theoretical discussion of the comparative and superlative concerns the phenomenon of 'blocking', where the existence of the affixal forms of the comparative and superlative is said to preclude the existence of the periphrastic forms. Our study of the corpora (like others before) indicates, however, that while there may be a preference for one or the other form, there in fact is no such thing as blocking. This is in line with other inflectional categories we look at in this book (see Chapter 26 for discussion).

In the most extensive study of the phenomenon, Mondorf (2009a) provides large-scale empirical evidence for the significant influence of phonological, morphological, lexical, semantic, syntactic, and dialectal factors in the choice of comparatives. Multivariate studies such as Szmrecsanyi (2005) and Hilpert (2008) have yielded results along the same lines. We will discuss these factors in the following subsections. Unfortunately, no comparable studies have yet been undertaken for the superlative, but it is more than likely that one would find similar results. Peters (1999) shows for most adjectives in her investigation that comparative and superlative have similar distributions of analytic and synthetic forms across the two categories, but with a minority of adjectives, one finds opposite preferences for the two categories involved, with the superlative preferring synthetic forms and the comparative preferring analytic forms. For an explanation of these patterns a multivariate analysis of pertinent data would be necessary. In view of this situation we will focus on the comparative, but wherever possible we will complement the discussion of the comparative with some data and results of our own, or from the literature, if available, concerning the realization of the superlative.

6.6.2.1 *Phonological factors*

There are a number of phonological factors that have been shown to influence the choice of analytic and synthetic degree variants. The one that is most often mentioned in grammar books, and which is indeed also the factor emerging with the greatest predictive power in multivariate analyses (e.g. Hilpert 2008), is the number of syllables. Other phonological factors mentioned in the literature are the kinds of base-final segments, and the stress. We will discuss each in turn.

According to received wisdom, monosyllabic adjectives typically take the affixal forms (as in *red* ◆ *redder* ◆ *reddest*), disyllabic adjectives vary (e.g. *happy* ◆ *happier* ◆ *happiest* as against *defunct* ◆ *more defunct* ◆ *most defunct*), and trisyllabic and longer adjectives take only the periphrastic form (e.g. *horrible* ◆ *more horrible* ◆ *most horrible*). While the length of an adjective counted in number of syllables is generally a good predictor for the choice of the inflectional variant, it has to be stated that monosyllables can still show variable behaviour. Notably, it is often the case that both synthetic and analytic comparative and superlative forms are found with the same adjective, which means that there is considerable within-type variability. In (18) we give some examples that illustrate cases that go against the oft-cited generalization on monosyllabic adjectives.

(18) *Virginia Quarterly Review 2002*: I worried you would find a girl in the jungle **more brave** than I, more fierce and valiant.

NPR_Morning 2002: I would say that this is bad, no question about it. But it's only slightly **more bad** than the usual bad situation for flu vaccination.

New York Times 2005: If these people were similarly cute with F.B.I. agents and the grand jury, they've got an obstruction-of-justice problem possibly **more grave** than the hard-to-prosecute original charge of knowingly outing a covert agent.

Analog Science Fiction & Fact 2003: She wasn't ever going to get much **more smart** than she already was, but she was so sweet!

San Francisco Chronicle 1999: Of her goofy television persona, she says, "I actually am **more weird** than I am on the air, and I have to tone myself down."

Virtually all one-syllable adjectives have affixal forms, but Palmer *et al.* (2002: 1583) note the following as exceptions:

(19) cross, fake, ill, like, loath, prime, real, right, worth, wrong

However, all of the above (except *worth* and *loath*, both of which are syntactically anomalous in a number of ways) are attested at least occasionally in the affixal comparative. COCA yields the following examples:

(20) *Virginia Quarterly Review 2000*: They bulge with home-canned green beans, Christmas sugar cookies, and a butcher-papered chunk of tenderloin, **primest** part of the deer.

Friends for Life 1995: "Do you suppose she's all right? Or might she be **iller** than she realizes? More important, is there anything we can do? I feel so helpless...so responsible somehow."

Geographical Review 1998: "That may not be entirely right, but it is turning out to be **righter** than I would have thought."

Atlantic Monthly 1994: "Sounds like shy to me," my father said, brisk and certain. My father was certain about everything. "Better come in." "I'm not shy," I said again, **crosser**.

There are more exceptions to the generalizations concerning monosyllabic and polysyllabic adjectives, but these are morphologically determined and therefore treated in Section 6.6.2.2.

There is, however, another issue involved with the input-based generalization that trisyllabic bases favour the periphrastic realizations of degree. As argued by Mondorf (2003, 2009a), what may really count is not the length of the base form of the adjective, but rather the length of the inflected form, which may not exceed three syllables. Under this output-oriented formulation it is possible to predict correctly that trisyllabic bases with final syllabic consonants may take synthetic comparative and superlative suffixes if the final consonant is resyllabified as part of the onset of the final syllable. This can account for forms such as *incredibler* (COCA), and *sensibler*. However, it is not clear whether the output-oriented formulation is really more adequate, as it would predict the occurrence of many similar forms such as ✋*probabler* or ✋*suitabler*. There is of course the additional complication that morphologically complex adjectives tend to avoid the synthetic variants anyway (see Section 6.6.2.2 for discussion) and that, due to the scarcity of pertinent monomorphemic adjectives, the amount of data on which the output-based formulation could be tested against the traditional input-based formulation is vanishingly small.

The form *cartoonier* (attested in COCA) may even suggest that what is important is not the number of syllables but the prosodic shape, that is, that the base ends in a trochee, or, in output-based parlance, that the synthetic output needs to end in a dactyl. This would elegantly account for the fact that disyllabic iambs disprefer suffixal degree variants (see below), but, like so many other proposed rules, would leak considerably. Furthermore, forms like *absoluter* (COCA) do not conform to any of the rules we have considered so far.

Let us turn to the next phonological determinant, the final segments. Especially with disyllabic adjectives, the influence of the final segments of an adjectival base can be of two different kinds. There are effects that could be analysed as haplology effects, and there are other effects of the final segment(s) whose motivation is not so clear.

Let us first consider haplology. Bases ending in <st> hardly ever take a synthetic superlative. For example, none of the 122 instances of superlative *honest* in Mondorf's data has ✋*honestest*, and similar results hold for *just, moist, modest, robust,* and *unjust*. Another haplology effect can be observed especially, but not exclusively, in rhotic varieties of English with bases ending in /r/, such as *austere, bare, bitter, dire, mature, pure, sour, sure, slender*. They avoid the identical onset and coda in a potential synthetic comparative by preferring the analytic variants to a much greater extent than comparable bases with a phonologically different ending. In general terms, adjectives ending in /l/ also prefer the analytic comparative, which could be interpreted as another haplology effect, namely the avoidance of a liquid in both the onset and coda of the final syllable of the inflected form.

Other phonological material at the end of the base may also have an influence on the choice of synthetic or analytic variants. Thus, adjectives with final consonant clusters tend to have a higher ratio of analytic comparatives than comparable adjectives without final clusters. There have also been claims about adjectives with final high front vowels or /l/ plus a high front vowel (Hilpert 2008). It seems, however, that these particular phonological sequences are most often realizations of suffixes (i.e. -y and -ly, respectively), and we will therefore deal with these in the section on morphological determinants.

Finally, stress has an influence on the choice of degree realization. Adjectives that end in a stressed syllable are much more prone to analytic comparatives and superlatives than adjectives ending in an unstressed syllable (e.g. Leech and Culpeper 1997; Hilpert 2008). Another putative stress-related effect on the choice of degree variants is stress clash avoidance, as claimed by, for example, Kuryłowicz (1964: 15), or Mondorf (2009a: Section 4.1). In this view, synthetic variants are held to be overrepresented in environments with a stressed syllable following a finally-stressed adjectival base. However, Mondorf's own results are statistically inconclusive, and in multivariate studies this factor did not survive as influential (e.g. Hilpert 2008: 406).

6.6.2.2 *Morphological factors*

In this subsection we look at the role of the morphological make-up of the base in degree marking. There is a well-established general effect of morphological complexity at work (e.g. Mondorf 2003; Hilpert 2008), such that morphologically complex adjectives prefer the periphrastic degree variants. However, there are some more things to be said about particular kinds of morphological categories involved in this. We will discuss verbal participles, derived adjectives, and compound adjectives in turn.

Perhaps the clearest morphologically related effect concerns verbal participles as adjectives, which generally do not form synthetic comparatives. Cases in point are, for example, present participles like *stunning* or *winning*, and past participles such as *blessed* or *worn*. For illustration of the general pattern consider *stunning*, which has 66 periphrastic attestations of the comparative and 160 of the superlative in COCA, but no synthetic attestations at all. The past participle *worn* also has no synthetically formed degree forms in COCA.

However, exceptions to these kinds of pattern can be found, as, for example, in the behaviour of *winning* as attested in COCA. The synthetic superlative *winningest* has 272 attestations as against only 28 periphrastic ones. In contrast, there is no synthetic comparative attested for *winning*. Interestingly, the synthetic superlatives are all semantically restricted to sports contexts (21a), while all but one periphrastic superlative instantiate the figurative meaning, as shown in (21b). In (21c) we give an example of a periphrastic comparative.

(21)   a. *AP 2010*: Schlossnagle is already **winningest** coach in school history

b. *Arthas: the rise of the Lich King 2009*: Arthas gave the girl his **most winning** smile.

c. *Newsweek 1994*: Clinton will have to try to project a **more winning** image.

Violations such as the one in (21a) of the strong general trend towards periphrastic degree marking seem to be lexeme-specific. One of the more interesting points that emerges from a study of participles in *-ing* in COCA is that they show a marked tendency towards allowing the affixal forms in the superlative, at least in NAmE, but not in the comparative. This was noted by Montgomery (1999) for Appalachian English, but seems not to be restricted to that dialect of NAmE. Indeed, such forms are mentioned in Jespersen (1942: 353), and illustrated with literary examples.

Another frequently observed morphological effect is that adjectives containing the prefix *un-* prefer the synthetic degree forms, irrespective of how many syllables are involved, and they thus often violate the generalization that polysyllabic adjectives prefer periphrastic expression of degree. A particular striking example illustrating this fact is given in (22), from COCA (note that this example also shows coercion of a relational adjective into a gradable one, see Section 6.2 above):

(22)   *Basic 2003*: # STYLES # Then it's unofficial. He takes a hit from an ASTHMA INHALER, as a '71 PONTIAC GTO drives through the gate and pulls up. Hardy emerges. # OSBORNE # (re: his appearance) Doesn't get any **unofficialer** than that... The two old friends embrace.

Going against the general trend of morphologically complex adjectives, those derived with the suffixes *-y* or *-ly*, as in *guilty, hungry, handy, risky, friendly, lively, manly* have been found to (slightly) favour the synthetic variants (e.g. Leech and Culpeper 1997; Hilpert 2008), but there is massive type-dependent variation in the distributions. For example, in Mondorf's (2009a: 34) data set, *hungry* has less than 20 per cent analytic comparatives while *guilty* has 80 per cent analytic comparatives. However, among the violators of the trisyllabic-plus rule we find a preponderance of *-y*-suffixed adjectives. For *finicky, lemony, orangey, slippery, watery* we find attested comparatives like *finickier, lemonier, orangier, slipperier, waterier*.

Adjectives formed by the suffixation of ornative adjectival *-ed* to multi-word bases, such as *broad-minded, full-flavoured, low-priced* appear to be extremely variable across types with some preferring the analytic, others the synthetic variants. For example, while *full-flavoured* or *high-priced* strongly prefer the synthetic comparative in Mondorf's data set, *broad-minded* or *sure-footed* show the opposite tendency (Mondorf 2009a: 48).

With other adjectival suffixes there is a clear trend towards periphrastic comparatives and superlatives, with some variation in many of the categories. Using COCA, we tested the suffixes *-al, -an, -ant, -ate, -esque, -ful, -ic, -ile, -ish, -ist, -ive, -less, -ous, -some* with a pseudo-random selection of pertinent adjectives listed in (23) and (24), excluding adjectives from the sample with very low frequency, in order to avoid adjectives with no degree-marked forms attested at all. In (23) we list the frequencies of synthetic and analytic comparative variants separated by a slash, while (24) gives the respective figures for the superlative variants of these adjectives. All variants that occurred less than 50 times were checked individually and non-pertinent forms were manually weeded out. Variants with a frequency of 50 or more were not individually checked, so that these figures, indicated by '>50', '>100' or '>1000' in (23) and (24), may slightly overestimate the frequencies of these variants.

With the data in (23) we can first observe that all adjectives sampled are attested with periphrastic comparatives. Many of the pertinent adjectives also have the occasional synthetic comparatives in COCA, though of much less frequency than the corresponding periphrastic variant (*-ant, -ful, -ish, -ous, -some*). Some adjectives (for example, those in *-ant, -ate, -esque, -ist, -ive, -less*) are exclusively attested in COCA with periphrastic comparative forms, but this does not necessarily mean that synthetic forms of these adjectives are generally impossible.

(23)   *Comparative choice with selected complex adjectives (suffixal/analytic attestations in COCA)*

    a. global (0/ >100), mortal (0/4), racial (0/2), verbal (0/34)

    b. spartan (0/14), Tuscan (0/2), human (0/ >100), Balkan (0/1), terran (0/1), urban (0/ >100)

    c. brilliant (0/ >50), fragrant (0/17), buoyant (0/25), fluent (1/22), decent (1/29), stringent (0/ >100)

    d. ornate (0/27), prostrate (0/1), private (0/ >100)

    e. burlesque (0/4), grotesque (0/23)

    f. careful (1/ >100), thankful (1/19), doubtful (0/25), needful (0/2), playful (0/ >50), spiteful (0/4)

    g. cosmic (0/14), ethnic (0/6), gothic (0/3), mystic (0/3), psychic (0/2), scenic (0/30)

    h. foolish (1/40), bullish (0/25), hawkish (0/ >50), purplish (0/1), sluggish (0/24), youngish (0/1)

    i. centrist (0/ >50), racist (0/12), sexist (0/3)

    j. active (0/ >100), festive (0/38), fictive (0/1), massive (0/ >100), native (0/8), pensive (0/11)

    k. aimless (0/1), baseless (0/1), harmless (0/6), lifeless (0/1), pointless (0/1), wingless (0/1)

    l. famous (4/ >100), bulbous (0/6), gracious (0/ >50), heinous (0/24), spacious (0/ >100), wondrous (0/16)

    m. awesome (0/22), handsome (35/ >50), lonesome (1/11), fearsome (0/22), irksome (0/6), loathsome (0/10)

Almost all adjectives in the sample are also attested with superlative forms. Among the superlatives, synthetic superlatives are generally extremely rare, with only three of the morphological categories having adjectives using it at all (*-an, -ous, -some*). It is with the last suffix that we find a synthetic degree form variant that outnumbers the analytic ones (*handsome*) or that reaches at least the same frequency (*lonesome*).

(24)   *Superlative choice with selected complex adjectives (suffixal/analytic attestations in COCA)*

    a. global (0/10), mortal (0/4), racial (0/1), verbal (0/4)

    b. spartan (0/2), Tuscan (0/0), human (1/49), Balkan (0/0), terran (0/0), urban (0/9)

    c. brilliant (0/ >100), fragrant (0/23), buoyant (0/4), fluent (0/3), decent (0/43), stringent (0/ >100)

    d. ornate (0/15), prostrate (0/0), private (0/ >100)

    e. burlesque (0/0), grotesque (0/16)

    f. careful (0/>50), thankful (0/25), doubtful (0/9), needful (0/5), playful (0/12), spiteful (0/0)

    g. cosmic (0/2), ethnic (0/0), gothic (0/0), mystic (0/1), psychic (0/0), scenic (0/>100)

    h. foolish (0/18), bullish (0/6), hawkish (0/18), purplish (0/0), sluggish (0/8), youngish (0/0)

    i. centrist (0/5), racist (0/20), sexist (0/3)

    j. active (0/ >100), festive (0/18), fictive (0/0), massive (0/ >100), native (0/1), pensive (0/0)

    k. aimless (0/0), baseless (0/1), harmless (0/7), lifeless (0/2), pointless (0/5), wingless (0/0)

    l. famous (1/ >1000), bulbous (0/0), gracious (0/ >50), heinous (0/ >50), spacious (0/11), wondrous (0/30)

    m. awesome (1/49), handsome (94/75), lonesome (4/4), fearsome (0/>50), irksome (0/5), loathsome (0/11)

Let us now turn to compounds, which have been claimed to take only periphrastic degree expression (e.g. Bauer 1988: 134). This claim is problematic, however. Different cases can be distinguished, depending on the position of the adjective(s) involved. Adjectival compounds with a present participle as head and an adjective in the left position (e.g. *easy-going, fast-moving, long-standing*) can indeed take analytic degree forms on the adjective in first position (e.g. *more easy-going*) or show affixal inflection on the initial adjective (*easier-going*). Which pattern is preferred varies across compounds, with some compounds strongly preferring one variant, for example analytic for *easy-going*, others preferring the other variant, for example synthetic for *fast-moving* (see Mondorf 2009a: 45 for the distributions of individual adjectives).

A similar situation can be found with other compounds that have other adjectival heads. They seem to be able to take both kinds of variants, although our corpora attest this for only a minority, which is not surprising given the general very low frequency of such compounds. In (25a) we list some synthetic forms, in (25b) some periphrastic forms, all from COCA.

(25) a. bottom-heavier, bug-friendlier, butt-uglier, eye-easier, self-esteemier, sing-songier, smart-assier, squeaky-cleaner, sugar-plummier

b. more accident-prone, more broad-based, more environment-friendly, more sing-songy, more world-weary

There are also structures with adjectives in the first position and nouns in the second position that are sometimes analysed as compounds and which pose the question of how to grade the adjective in these structures, for example *hard-line, large-scale, left-wing, low-key,* or *short-term.* As shown by Mondorf (2006, 2009b), both types of variant are common in this group, very often attested on the same base, as illustrated for *hard-line* in (26), from COCA:

(26) a. *USA Today 1991*: these changes of command might instead be signalling a shift to an even **harder-line** administration

b. *CNN_Q&A 2003*: Can those settlers, the **more hard-line** settlers, remain where they are in places like Nablus and Hebron?

The comparison of compounds presents a serious challenge to stratal approaches to the lexicon in which compound-formation is ordered at a later derivational stage than affixation, and in which the insertion of an affix into a compound, as in (26a) is predicted to be impossible. Furthermore, with cases such as those in (25a) we are dealing with level ordering paradoxes, as the semantic scope of the comparative suffix is the whole compound, while comparative suffixation to such long polysyllabic adjectives should be impossible for prosodic reasons (see Booij and Rubach 1984; Kiparsky 1982c; Selkirk 1982: 101; Booij 1993: 36–41 for other level ordering paradoxes).

6.6.2.3 *Lexicalization*

The preceding discussion has already shown that preferences towards the respective variants are frequently lexeme-specific, and there are often no clear explanations available why one particular adjective would be more prone to periphrastic comparison, while another, quite similar adjective would prefer synthetic variants. Nevertheless, it is possible to find some patterning in this apparently confused picture, using the notion of lexicalization. The degree of lexicalization can be conceptualized as the strength of the lexical representation of a particular lexeme and its forms. Frequency of occurrence and spelling have been successfully used as correlates of this notion of lexicalization (e.g. Sepp 2006; Plag *et al.* 2007, 2008 for compounds, Mondorf 2000, 2009a, 2009b for the comparative).

Following up on earlier claims by many authors (e.g. Sweet 1891: 327; Bolinger 1968: 120; Gnutzmann *et al.* 1973: 425, 434; Quirk *et al.* 1985: 463), Mondorf (2009a) and Hilpert (2008) provide ample empirical evidence that frequency plays a role in the choice of the degree variants. Adjectives with higher frequency tend to have higher proportions of synthetic variants, and the same holds for adjectives with a higher ratio of comparative forms as against positive forms. Note that Hilpert's multivariate model proves that the observed frequency effect is not the consequence of the fact that more frequent adjectives also tend to be shorter, and hence more prone to synthetic comparison, but that it is an independent effect alongside the length effect.

Spelling can be used as an indicator of lexicalization as more fused spellings tend to indicate the writers' perception of the structure in question as a single lexical item (see again the references cited above for discussion). Mondorf (2009a, 2009b) now shows that with decreasing orthographic (i.e. lexical) fusion the proportion of synthetic comparatives increases for all types of pertinent compounds. That is, with two-word spellings such as *high risk, full flavoured* we find a higher proportion of the synthetic variant (*higher risk, fuller flavoured*) than with hyphenated or one-word spellings (*higher-risk, higherrisk, fuller-flavoured, fullerflavoured*).

6.6.2.4 *Semantic factors*

Semantics also acts as a determinant in comparison realization. Mondorf (2009a) provides data that show that with abstract readings of monosyllabic adjectives (as for *clean* in *a clean break*), the chances of periphrastic comparative formation increase dramatically, overriding the prosodic constraint against such forms.

Another semantic effect seems to be that adjectives that appear to be less easily construed as gradable appear to be more prone to choose periphrastic comparatives. The comparison of the adjective *right* is a case in point with 80 per cent of *more right* (as against 20 per cent of *righter*) in Mondorf's data (2009a: 12).

6.6.2.5 *Syntactic factors*

It has also been shown that certain syntactic environments may favour particular degree variants. Thus, the presence of *to*-infinitival complements, prepositional complements, premodification of the adjective, and predicative (as against attributive) position all increase the chances of a periphrastic comparative or superlative (e.g. Leech and Culpeper 1997; Lindquist 1998; Mondorf 2003; Hilpert 2008; Mondorf 2009a). Examples from COCA illustrate this with some monosyllabic adjectives, which might be expected to prefer the synthetic variant.

(27)   a. *Parenting 2010:* "Children are **more apt to** stay seated if the parent simulates a car trip," she says.

     b. *PBS_Newshour 2009:* We couldnt [sic] be **more proud of** her as a family.

     c. *Devil red 2011:* Leonard leaned over him. "Let me make it **even more clear**."

     d. *NBC_MeetPress 2010:* I have never been **more proud**.

Mondorf (2009a) also finds some evidence that there is a tendency for sentence-final as against sentence-medial positions to increase the likelihood of periphrastic comparison and attributes this to the fact that, being one word longer, this tendency is to do with creating end-weight in the pertinent sentences. It is unclear, however, how this effect relates to the attributive/predicative position effect and whether it would survive in a multivariate analysis.

Finally, Szmrecsanyi (2005) has found that the use of the word *more* in the discourse preceding the comparative choice context in question increases the chances of a periphrastic comparison, similar to what we see happening in the genitive alternation (see Chapter 7). An example from the BNC showing this effect is presented in (28), where *more friendly* is chosen instead of the competing *friendlier*.

(28) *Broadcast news*: the atmosphere was totally different, much **more** relaxed, much **more friendly**

6.6.2.6 *Dialectal factors*

There also seem to be differences in degree marking when it comes to different varieties of English. Several studies (e.g. Kytö and Romaine 2000; Mondorf 2009a) have found, for example, that NAmE is more prone to analytic comparison than BrE. The reasons for such differences are largely unclear, and, to our knowledge, other varieties have not been investigated systematically.

6.6.2.7 *Summary*

To summarize, a large number of factors have been found to be influential in the choice between analytic and synthetic forms of degree marking. Overall these factors generally do not lead to categorical contexts but rather increase the chances of the occurrence of one variant over the competing alternative realization. From a theoretical standpoint this is very interesting as it means that the realization of an inflectional category is probabilistic, instead of being grammatically or lexically strictly determined. While this situation is very similar to the genitive alternation (see Chapter 7), it seems typologically a rather rare phenomenon.

Another theoretical issue is whether there may be any more general mechanism that unites the different determinants. Applying Rohdenburg's (1996) Complexity Principle, Mondorf (2009a: 6) argues for such an overarching mechanism and states that '[i]n cognitively more demanding environments which require an increased processing load, language users tend to make up for the additional effort by resorting to the analytic (*more*) rather than the synthetic (*-er*) comparative.' Although this seems to be an appealing explanation for a number of the variables we have discussed, it also raises a number of problems that cast some doubt on the generality of this approach, or on its rationale.

The underlying assumption for making the Complexity Principle work with degree formation is that analytic forms are generally easier (or should we say *more easy*?) to process than synthetic forms, all other things being equal. If this were generally the case, it is, for example, unclear why certain rather complex adjectives (e.g. those prefixed by *un-*, see above) or certain more complex constructions with adjectives, for example those involving a complement introduced by *than* (see, for example, Hilpert 2008), would still prefer the synthetic variant. So, as far as we can see, there is no independent psycholinguistic evidence for the assumption that analytic degree structures are more easily processed than synthetic ones. And even if this assumption were correct, why would the synthetic variants persist as a stable feature of the language? A final problem is that it is unclear whether 'processing complexity' is the same in production and perception. In principle, what could be advantageous in production may be detrimental in perception, or the other way round. At present, there is only indirect support for the Complexity Principle operating in degree formation.

···

CHAPTER 7

Noun inflection

7.1 PROSPECTUS

In this chapter we discuss two morphological processes: the marking of plurals and the marking of possession. Plural marking shows a great deal of variation and irregularity, which contrasts with the relative regularity of possession marking. Some argue that possession marking is not strictly inflectional, but whether it is or not, it interacts with plural marking in ways which suggest that the two need to be dealt with together.

7.2 PLURAL

The English number system has two values, usually termed singular and plural, but more accurately termed unmarked and plural. The label 'unmarked' is preferable because there are several cases where the unmarked form is used even though there may be reference to several entities either implicitly or explicitly. Consider the examples in (1).

(1)   a. The tiger is a fierce animal.

        b. Tiger skins can fetch a great deal of money.

        c. More than one tiger was seen.

        d. Every tiger is carnivorous.

        e. *It is three mile long.

Typically the semantically unmarked form (the 'singular') is also morphologically unmarked, while the plural form is indicated in some way. We will first discuss the semantics of pluralization, then deal with the various formal ways of marking plural, starting with the regular suffix -s (variously pronounced). Then other ways of marking plurals and the less regular cases will be considered.

7.2.1 Semantics of pluralization

It might be thought that the semantics of pluralization is simple: plural forms denote 'more than one'. But there is more to be said: on the one hand, we can mean a number of things by 'more than one', and, on the other, plurals do not always denote 'more than one' in a straight-forward way.

English inflection being rather impoverished, the plural marking can be deployed to cover a number of different concepts that in other languages might be distinguished morphologically. For example, a plural noun like *poodles* is interpreted as generic, as in (2a) or equally well as collective or distributive in (2b):

(2) a. Poodles never shed.

b. The poodles ate the meat.

That is, (2b) can be interpreted as several poodles eating a piece of meat all together, or each of several poodles eating its own piece of meat sequentially. English leaves it to context to disambiguate such nuances.

We must also mention here several sorts of form–meaning mismatches that can be found in English. The first is collective nouns such as *people, police, folk, cattle, poultry, livestock, vermin*. There is psycholinguistic evidence (from agreement and pronominalization) that these are semantically plural in spite of lacking any morphological marking (e.g. Bock *et al.* 2006). Unlike forms like *sheep* or *fish* the collectives do not have a singular interpretation as well. However, with collectives there is a potential mismatch between notional and grammatical plural. The test case for this problem is subject–verb agreement, which shows whether the subject head noun is lexically specified for the morphosyntactic feature of singular or plural. Although there are a few collectives such as *people* that invariably trigger plural agreement (with determiners, verbs, and pronouns), there is a lot of variation with regard to these lexical specifications across speakers and varieties. In general, BrE tends to show more plural agreement than NAmE (e.g. Johansson 1979; Bock *et al.* 2006). Compare, for example, BrE (3a) with NAmE (3b), from COCA. Note, however, that more recently, BrE seems to be developing in the direction of NAmE (Bauer 1994).

(3) a. I don't think the Royal Family are known for their intelligence. (Bock *et al.* 2006: 64)

b. *CNN_LiveToday 2004*: The royal family is not too happy about the publicity.

Other nouns may be marked for plurality, but do not necessarily designate plurals. Among these are what Payne and Huddleston (2002: 340) call 'bipartites', that is, nouns that designate objects characteristically comprised of two parts. Among these are words denoting articles of clothing worn on the lower part of the body, utensils with two inter-working parts, and items associated with vision:

(4) a. *clothing*: bermudas, bloomers, boxers, breeches, briefs, BVDs, capris, chinos, corduroys, drawers, dungarees, flannels, galluses, jeans, khakis, knickers, leggings, long johns, overalls, pajamas, pants, pantaloons, panties, pedal pushers, plus fours, shorts, skivvies, slacks, suspenders, tights, tighty-whities, trousers, trunks, undies

b. *utensils*: bellows, callipers, clippers, cutters, forceps, pincers, pliers, scales, scissors, secateurs, shears, snippers, tongs, tweezers

c. *vision*: bifocals, binoculars, glasses, goggles, spectacles

It appears that at least some of these can also be used without the final -*s*. We find this especially when the word functions as a premodifier to another noun, as in *pant legs*, or *goggle lens*, but we also find the unmarked base in canonical head position of noun phrases:

(5) *Prevention 2009*: Comb brows upward using a brow brush; trim stragglers straight across with a cuticle **scissor**. Then, with a slant-edged **tweezer**, pull strays from in between eyebrows (the inner corner of your brow should line up with the inner corner of your eye).

NBC_Today 2007: Don't be afraid to layer it over a pretty blouse or a turtleneck, but whatever you're layering it over, make sure that's sort of thin. And we love it over a **legging** and a flat boot.

The question then arises how bipartites such as these are themselves pluralized. Payne and Huddleston (2002: 341–2) remark that, 'There is some uncertainty and variation among speakers as to how readily they [viz. the bipartites] can also be applied to a plurality of such objects', but we find some regularity in the corpus data. Normally, to pluralize the bipartites, it is necessary to use a partitive construction with a quantifier: *two pairs of jeans, a set of tweezers*. We do not seem to find phrases like *two leggings* or *three tweezers*. However, we do occasionally find these bipartite plurals used in lists of objects that suggest that a plural sense is intended:

(6) *Harpers Bazaar 2010*: The aesthetician used an array of products by Yon-Ka and Sonya Dakar—exfoliants and cleansers and masks—and all the regular tools: **tweezers**, lancets, cotton pads.

Atlanta Journal Constitution 2010: Small sharp objects such as **scissors**, **tweezers**, nail clippers and small tools may be carried onboard.

We turn now to other sets of nouns that might fall under the designation of pluralia tantum, that is, nouns that have a plural form but no corresponding singular. As Acquaviva (2008: ch. 2) points out this does not seem to be a single coherent designation. Looking first at formal criteria, we can identify one group of pluralia tantum that end in the plural -*s* but lack a corresponding singular base form without the -*s* (*doldrums, dregs, shenanigans, hustings*).

Then, there is also a second group of nouns in -*s* which do have corresponding singular forms, but where those forms have an entirely distinct meaning. These in turn can be divided into those whose base is another noun (*accommodations, damages, spirits*) and those whose base appears to be non-nominal (*amends, belongings, eats, linguistics, regards, greens*). Among the forms on non-nominal bases, we frequently find adjectival forms in -*ic* (see (7a) below) and -*able* (e.g. *adjustables, burnables, buyables, compostables, fashionables, floatables, gardenables, honorables, immovables*, see COCA for many more). In cases where the affixation of plural -*s* appears to be category-changing, we might begin to wonder whether what we have is a separate derivational affix, rather than the plural suffix.

We can also look at pluralia tantum from the point of view of semantics; that is, we find several coherent semantic fields in which pluralia tantum are relatively common, including names of academic fields (7a), diseases (7b), pseudo-diseases, or psychological states (7c), and names for games (7d). There are, however, many miscellaneous items that don't seem to fit into neat semantic categories (7e). Some of the items in (7) behave like plurals morphosyntactically, in that they trigger plural subject–verb agreement, or are pronominalized by plural pronouns. Examples are culled from Payne and Huddleston 2002, Quirk *et al.* 1985, and our own files:

(7) a. *Names for subjects*: academics, acoustics, acrobatics, classics, cybernetics, economics, ethics, genetics, gymnastics, informatics, linguistics, mathematics, phonetics, physics, politics, pragmatics, semantics, statistics

b. *Diseases*: bends, chills, hemorrhoids, hiccups, hives, measles, mumps, piles, rabies, rickets, shingles

c. *Pseudo-diseases or psychological states*: creeps, heebie-jeebies, jim-jams, jitters, runs, shakes, shits, squirts, willies

d. *Games:* billiards, checkers, craps, darts, dominoes, draughts

e. *Other pluralia tantum*: accommodations, amends, annals, archives, arms, arrears, arts, ashes, auspices, balls, bangs, banns, bowels, brains, civvies, clothes, confines, congratulations, contents, credentials, customs, damages, directions, doldrums, dregs, droppings, druthers, dues, eats, entrails, environs, fatigues, funds, goods, grassroots, greens, grits, groceries, grounds, guts, hots, humanities, hustings, innards, intestines, irons, letters, lodgings, looks, manners, minutes, news, nuptials, odds, outskirts, pains, particulars, premises, quarters, regards, relations, remains, rights, roots, savings, shenanigans, smarts, spirits, stairs, stays, surroundings, talks, teachings, thanks, trappings, trimmings, troops, tropics, valuables, victuals, vittles, wages, wits, woods, writings

In some cases we have items that are just part of fixed idioms: *to be in the doldrums, to have one's druthers, to have the hots for*, etc.

A final topic we might raise here is the pluralization of non-count nouns. Non-count nouns typically designate substances treated as undifferentiated (*milk, oxygen*), abstractions (*truth*), or aggregates of items, either uniform (*rice*) or variable (*furniture*), whose boundaries are not conceptually salient. Just about any non-count noun can, however, be pluralized if it can be reconceptualized as a bounded entity, as happens, for example, when we conceive of *milk* in a container, or different types of rice; in cases such as these it is perfectly natural to think of *milks* or *rices*.

(8)   *New Yorker 2006*: He tossed one of the **milks** in the air and tried to shoot it on the wing,…

      Vegetarian Times 1998: Rice comes in the familiar brown and white varieties, but now numerous aromatic **rices** are also sold in grocery stores.

There are very few non-count nouns that are not amenable to this sort of reconceptualization, although Acquaviva (2008: 15) cites the word *fun* as one that is highly resistant.

7.2.2 Regular marking of the plural

In this section, we look at the regular marking of the plural from the point of view of orthography (see also Chapter 4) and pronunciation (see also Chapter 9).

7.2.2.1 *Spelling*

The regular plural suffix is <-s> added to the default form (9a). However, if the default form ends in any one of the letters/letter sequences <ch, s, sh, x, z> then the suffix takes the form <-es> (9b).

(9)   a. car ◆ cars
        hat ◆ hats
        translator ◆ translators

    b. church ◆ churches
        dish ◆ dishes
        fox ◆ foxes
        mass ◆ masses
        waltz ◆ waltzes

If the suffix is <-es> by this rule and the default form ends in a single <z>, then that <z> may be doubled according to the normal rules of consonant doubling.

(10)   fez ◆ fezzes
      quiz ◆ quizzes

With final <s> there is some variation, in that one can find forms that show doubling of the <s>. In most cases the spellings showing doubling are clearly minority choices (e.g. <busses>, <gasses> as against the much more common <buses>, <gases>). Most of the words with final <s> have the final <s> in an unstressed syllable, where consonant doubling is less likely anyway.

(11)   alias • aliases
       atlas • atlases
       bus • buses, busses
       canvas • canvases, canvasses
       dais • daises
       f(o)etus • f(o)etuses
       gas • gases, gasses
       ibis • ibises
       iris • irises
       pancreas • pancreases
       plus • pluses, plusses
       rhinoceros • rhinoceroses

Where the default form ends in <y> immediately preceded by a consonant letter, the plural is normally made by replacing the <y> with <i> and then adding <es>.

(12)   academy • academies
       buggy • buggies
       fancy • fancies
       hierarchy • hierarchies
       ideology • ideologies
       lullaby • lullabies
       mummy • mummies
       policy • policies
       sky • skies
       spy • spies
       sympathy • sympathies
       tabby • tabbies

Where <y> is part of a vowel digraph, it is normally retained, and the plural with <s> is formed:

(13)   buoy ◆ buoys
       convoy ◆ convoys
       day ◆ days
       guy ◆ guys
       railway ◆ railways
       Thursday ◆Thursdays
       X-ray ◆ X-rays

Where the <u> preceding the <y> is part of a <qu>, because the <y> is not part of a vowel
digraph, the plural with <ies> is still used:

(14)   obloquy ◆ obloquies
       soliloquy ◆ soliloquies

Proper nouns ending in <y> usually retain the <y> in plural forms.

(15)   the four Marys
       the two Germanys ~ the two Germanies
       Say five Hail Marys.
       How many Bettys do you know?
       Of all the Februarys I remember, this has been the coldest.

There are no general rules for determining the plural form of words ending in single <o>
(words ending in <oo> like *igloo*, *kangaroo*, *zoo*, etc. make their plural regularly by adding
<s>). Some such words have an <s> plural (16a), others have an <es> plural (16b), and yet
others allow both (16c). Note that the (16a) words include those which have a vowel letter
before the <o>, abbreviations, and the names of peoples.

(16)   a.   albinos, avocados, bimbos, boleros, bonobos, boyos, cameos, casinos, cellos (*also*
            celli), Chicanos, combos, curios, dos ('parties'), dynamos, egos, embryos, Eskimos,
            Filipinos, garbos (AusE), gigolos, gizmos, hairdos, impresarios, journos (AusE),
            jumbos, kilos, memos, merinos, milkos (AusE), photos, placebos, pros, radios,
            ratios, Romeos, silos, solos (*also* soli), sopranos (*also* soprani), stilettos, studios,
            tangelos, tempos (*also* tempi), torsos, trios, turbos, vaqueros, videos, weirdos,
            winos

       b.   buboes, dominoes, echoes, goes, heroes, negroes, noes, potatoes, tomatoes,
            torpedoes, vetoes

       c.   archipelagos/archipelagoes, banjos/banjoes, buffalos/buffaloes (*also* buffalo, *see
            below*), cargos/cargoes, desperados/desperadoes, flamingos/flamingoes, frescos/

frescoes, grottos/grottoes, halos/haloes, hobos/hoboes, innuendo/innuendoes, mangos/mangoes, mottos/mottoes, peccadillos/peccadilloes, salvos/salvoes, volcanos/volcanoes, zeros/zeroes

The words in (16b) are all from the seventeenth century or earlier, while nineteenth-century or later Italian and Spanish loans are in category (16a).

While there are many sub-cases of the words listed in (16a) which can be accounted for by assigning them to particular categories, it seems that in the twenty-first century the default is simply to use an <s> plural, and that learning spellers or learners of EFL need to learn the list of exceptional items in (16b). The existence of so many <es> plurals here (or at least potential cases) suggests that this has not always been the case, and that the <es> plural was once the default on nouns ending in <o>.

There have been, and to a lesser extent continue to be, various fashions for using <'s> rather than just <s> to mark the plural. Various subtypes can be recognized here. These vary in how common they are. The ones listed in (17) and (18) can be found quite frequently in our sources.

(17)   *Things which are not thought of as being proper words (symbols, numbers, letters, abbreviations)*:

Mind your p's and q's.

Her academic record was full of A's.

He has several β+'s; the 1960's.

They all have M.A.'s.

I always use &'s in references.

My 1's are just like my 7's.

(18)   *Words which are being used as nouns because they are being mentioned*:

If if's and but's were apples and nuts.

There are too many and's in this sentence.

Note that the linguist's usage of italicizing instances of mention does not do away with the possibility of using apostrophes in these cases.

(19)   *Things which are perceived as being marginal words*:

I've been to too many of these do's.

(20)   *Foreign words which end in a vowel letter other than <e>*:

pizza's, toga's, wadi's, piano's, guru's, ju-ju's

(21)   *Occasionally with proper names ending in <s>*:

keeping up with the Jones's (or Joneses)

In twenty-first-century usage all of these are rare in standard usage, though the apostrophe is sometimes maintained to distinguish *a's* from *as*, *i's* from *is*. In non-standard usage, the type illustrated in (20) persists, and is often extended to words which do not end in a vowel at all. This is often termed the greengrocer's apostrophe, since it is seen on market stalls and in shops advertising wares such as *pear's*, *apple's*, and even, notoriously, *golden deliciou's*. Such apostrophes are simply considered wrong by prescriptivists.

7.2.2.2 *Pronunciation*

The regular sibilant suffix has three allomorphs: /s/, /z/, and /ɪz/ or /əz/ (depending on the variety of English—we will use the transcription with /ɪ/ here). The allomorph /ɪz/ follows base-final sibilant consonants (/s, z, ʃ, ʒ, tʃ, dʒ/), the /s/ follows any other base-final voiceless consonants (/p, t, k, f, θ/), and the /z/ variant is the elsewhere variant, following all other base-final voiced obstruents, all sonorant consonants and all vowels.

(22)	base	base final segment + allomorphy	base	base final segment + allomorphy	base	allomorphy
	gas	/s+ɪz/	cap	/p + s/	home	/m + z/
	topaz	/z+ɪz/	cat	/t + s/	gun	/n + z/
	dish	/ʃ + ɪz/	track	/k + s/	song	/ŋ + z/
	rouge	/ʒ + ɪz/	chief	/f + s/	bottle	/l + z/
	church	/tʃ + ɪz/	wreath	/θ + s/	dog	/g + z/
	judge	/dʒ + ɪz/			spa	/ɑː + z/
					war	/ɔː + z ‖ r + z/

This system is problematic for some nouns that show base allomorphy with the plural, as in *thieves*, *paths*, and *houses*. This type is dealt with in the next section.

7.2.3 Regular suffix plus change in the base

Some nouns which end in voiceless fricatives make their plural form not only with the relevant allomorph of the regular suffix, but with an additional change to a stem-final voiced fricative. Thus the plural of *thief* with a final /f/ is *thieves*, with a /v/ and consequently a final /z/. There are no instances of this happening with a final /ʃ/, so there are three sets here: final /s/, final /f/, and final /θ/. They are all slightly different.

There is only one noun which shows a base alternation between /s/ and /z/ in the plural, and that is *house* /haʊs/, *houses* /haʊzɪz/. Even this is not universal: in ScE the plural is regular: /haʊsɪz/.

Plurals for nouns ending in /f/ fall into three categories: (a) those that always change to /v/, (b) those that variably change to /v/, and (c) those that never change to /v/. In most cases, any phonetic change is reflected in an orthographic change.

(23) *Always /v/*   *Variably /v/*   *Never /v/*

      calves   behalfs, behalves   briefs

      elves   dwarfs, dwarves   chiefs

      knives   halfs, halves   fifes

      lives   hoofs, hooves   oafs

      loaves   roofs, rooves   proofs

      sheaves   scarfs, scarves   reefs

      shelves   wharfs, wharves   reliefs

      thieves   safes

      wives   serfs

      wolves   waifs

In addition to the examples in (23) note *beef ⬥ beeves* (old-fashioned, poetic, or dialectal for 'cattle'). Also note, *staves*, now considered the plural of *stave*, and thus a regular form, is etymologically the plural of *staff*. *Turves* as the plural of *turf* is now extremely uncommon, since *turf* is usually taken as an non-count noun. The form *halfs* is more likely to occur in the term *%centre halfs* or in *%three halfs of bitter* than in the expression *a game of two halves*. Some of these forms are prescribed as part of the standard, for example *roofs*, though there is still a great deal of variation.

The origin of this alternation is that the voiced fricatives were once allophones of the voiceless fricatives which occurred intervocalically. When the voiced fricatives took on phonemic status as a result of the influence of French on Middle English, the alternation arose. However, since the voiced fricatives were only found intervocalically and in vocabulary which predated the relevant period, words which end in <ff> were not affected, and later loan words were not affected. Thus words like *bluff, duff, gaff, huff, mastiff, midriff, puff, riff, whiff* all take regular plurals, as do *aperitif, calif ‖ caliph, chef, clef, graph, leitmotif, serif, shadoof*.

Note that in general it is the common words that undergo fricative voicing. The plurals in the first column of (23) have an average frequency of over 1300 in the BNC, while those in the third column have an average frequency of under 200, with the middle column showing intermediate values. That is, high frequency often has the effect of protecting morphological irregularity. However, one word which does not fit into the general run of the irregulars and is of low frequency in this range is sometimes heard with a /v/-plural: it is the word *giraffe*, which may have higher frequency in the language of children than in the language of adults.

Where /θ/ is voiced to /ð/ in the formation of the plural, there is no reflection of the difference in the spelling. Accordingly, there is little normative pressure on these words. Again we find words which have the voiced plural, words which fluctuate between the voiced and the regular plural, and words which show the regular /θ/ plural.

(24) a. *plurals in /ðz/*: booth (*for those who pronounce it with final /θ/*), mouth, youth ('young man')

b. *both plurals found*: lath, oath, path, sheath, truth, wreath

c. *plurals in /θs/*: berth, birth, breath, cloth, death, depth, earth, faith, growth, heath, length, month, moth, smith, strength, tenth (*and all similar fractions*), youth ('young days'), *and foreign words in* -lith, -path, hyacinth, myth, shibboleth, zenith, etc.

The word *bath* has in BrE the plural /bɑːðz/ when it refers to a public swimming pool, but /bɑːθs/ when it refers to domestic installations. Notice that *clothes* /kləʊðz, kləʊz ‖ kloʊðz, kloʊz/ derives historically from *cloth*, though the relationship is now opaque.

The comment is often made that the regular plural is found when nouns such as *leaf* are the heads in exocentric compounds such as *the Toronto Maple Leafs* (a sports team). Pinker (1999) claims that this happens exclusively in names. Certainly this is not consistently true of all exocentrics, as can be seen in (25).

(25)

singular form	final segments of pluralized form
broadleaf (*plant*)	/fs/
cloverleaf (*junction*)	/fs/, /vz/
cottonmouth (*snake*)	/ðz/
frogmouth (*owl*)	/θs/, /ðz/
loudmouth (*person*)	/θs/, /ðz/
low-life (*person*)	/fs/, /vz/
waterleaf (*plant*)	/fs/

Many of the /θs/ and /ðz/ clusters are variably simplified in all but the most formal styles with the omission of the dental fricatives (and perhaps some compensatory lengthening of the alveolar fricative), so that *clothes*, for example, is regularly /kləʊz ‖ kloʊz/. The /fs/, /vz/ clusters are not subject to the same simplification, but word-final clusters /kst/ and /kt/, as in *text* or *effect*, are: *texts* and *effects* are frequently pronounced [teks] and [ɪfeks], respectively.

7.2.4 Plurals with vowel alternation

A small number of nouns have inherited from Germanic some plural forms that are created by changing the vowel in the base. These cases are a remnant class of nouns which, at one stage in their history, had a plural suffix containing [j] or [i], which had the effect of fronting a back vowel in the base. The process is traditionally referred to as umlaut, and the plurals, accordingly, as umlaut plurals, although all phonetic motivation for the alternations has long since vanished.

The relevant nouns in English are

(26)   foot /fʊt/ • feet /fiːt/
       goose /ɡuːs/ • geese /ɡiːs/
       louse /laʊs/ • lice /laɪs/
       mouse /maʊs/ • mice /maɪs/
       tooth /tuːθ/, */tʊθ/ • teeth /tiːθ/
       man /mæn/ • men /men/
       woman /wumən/ • women /wɪmɪn/

Although there is some regularity in spelling here (with <oo> in the base form correspond-ing to <ee> in the plural and <ou> in the base form corresponding to <i> in the plural), there is far less of a pattern in the pronunciation. In any case, these are patterns that are not prone to extension, except in facetious contexts.

   Although there is no sign of loss of these irregular plurals in standard literal usage, there are some places where there is variation in usage. *Mouse* denoting a piece of computing equipment, for example, has either *mice* or *mouses* as its plural. Consider, too, the following examples where *Mickey Mouse* is made plural. Here, the regular plural is more frequent than the umlaut plural (e.g. with the regular plural having 214 as against 125 irregular plurals in the 155 billion word American English Google Books corpus).

(27)   I have never seen so many Daffy Ducks and Mickey **Mouses** in one place. (*McNab 2008: 477*)

(28)   One specialized in dreadful plastic kitsch; another toys, ten thousand Mickey **Mice**. (*Rathbone 2001: 26*)

Goose in the literal sense usually has the plural *geese* (and where it does not, we would prob-ably suspect a slip of the tongue), but note (29) where *goose* is not used literally.

(29)   Todd didn't need…wilder **gooses** to chase. (*Anderson & Benson 1995: 381*)
       If it turns out that Qatar is innocent…our **gooses** could be cooked. (*Sandford 2001: 300*)

Similarly, where *louse* is not used literally (and for the purposes of humour and poetry), we can find a regular plural:

(30)   And that's when those **louses** / Go back to their spouses / Diamonds are a girl's best friend (Jule Styne, from *Gentlemen Prefer Blondes*, 1953)

The plural of *sabre-tooth* ‖ *saber-tooth*, which is an exocentric compound, is generally agreed to be *sabre-tooths* ‖ *saber-tooths* rather than ʔ*sabre-teeth* ‖ ʔ*saber-teeth*, but there does not seem to be a regular pattern here, as can be seen from the other exocentrics in (31), where the forms are as listed in the *OED* and *Webster's* (*W*). All are so rare that they fail to occur in the BNC.

(31)   coltsfoot • coltsfoots (*W*)

flat-foot (*sl*) • flatfoots (*also W and COCA*), flatfeet (*also COCA*)

goosefoot • goosefoots (*'plant'*), goosefeet (*'hinge, junction etc.'*)

pussyfoot • pussyfoots (*also W and COCA*)

tenderfoot • tenderfoots, tenderfeet (*both in W and in COCA*)

The other way round, *spice* is occasionally heard as the plural of *spouse* and *hice* as the plural of *house* in joking contexts. *Mongoose* is sometimes erroneously thought of as containing *goose*, and is pluralized as *mongeese*.

Note that where *man* is unstressed as the second member of a compound (or something which was formed as a compound), the spelling of the plural remains <men>, but the pronunciation of the plural is the same as the singular:

(32)   postman /pəʊsmən ‖ poʊsmən/ • postmen /pəʊsmən ‖ poʊsmən/

Scotsman /skɒtsmən ‖ skɑːtsmən/ • Scotsmen /skɒtsmən ‖ skɑːtsmən/

7.2.5   Plurals in <n>

There are a few nouns which form their plurals in <n>, remnants of a much larger Middle English group. The relevant nouns are *ox, oxen; brother* ('monk'), *brethren; child, children.* *Brother* ('male sibling') has a regular plural in <s>, and even *brother* 'monk' may have a regular plural.

A very few <n> plurals beyond the standard ones are sometimes heard, usually as jokes. *Vax* (the name of a brand of computer) is sometimes pluralized as *Vaxen* by initiates, a similar case is *boxen* (for Unix hardware); *sistren* is sometimes used in parallel with *brethren* and occasionally used in isolation. See the COCA examples in (33).

(33)   a.   *Southern Review 1994*: Oh, I was transported, **sistren** and brethren. What was I, nineteen? And I had a splendid love, and I had a splendid city, and I had a splendid life

b.   *Every dark desire 2007*: The girl cut her eyes at Naomi and brushed past her. Or at least tried to. 'Good evening, **sistren**,' Naomi greeted in a new purring voice. The woman inhaled deeply as if smelling something particularly sweet; then she smiled. People moved in, ebbing around them, some looking at Naomi with interest, others with sneers.

7.2.6 Unmarked plurals

Unmarked plurals are those where the plural form is the same as the base form. Some authorities refer to these as 'zero plurals' (see e.g. Quirk *et al.* 1985), a term which we avoid since it raises all the theoretical problems associated with affixes of zero form contrasting with a lack of an affix. There are several distinguishable types of unmarked plural, which will be treated separately below, though the classification is not a neat one.

In this treatment we ignore the fact that a noun like *cattle* is always treated as a plural, which we assume is a matter of lexis, and we also ignore a structure like *six foot three* where we assume that the syntactic construction takes a singular form rather than that *foot* is an unmarked plural.

First there are very few nouns which always have a plural form indistinguishable from the base form, but which do not fit easily into the major categories of unmarked plurals. These are *bob* (obsolete BrE sl. 'shilling'), *craft* (in the 'vehicle' sense), *offspring*, *quid* (BrE sl. 'pound'), *sheep*, and their compound forms like *aircraft*. In modern usage, *dice* belongs in this category, though Caesar's *Alea jacta est* is still often quoted in the form *the die is cast*, and speakers for whom this is a living singular–plural alternation have a totally irregular plural here. *Swine* also belongs here when being used metaphorically to refer to a person or people: *He is such a swine/They are such swine*. When referring to pigs, *swine* (like *cattle*) is always plural.

Second, there are forms which show no change in pronunciation, but do show a change in the written form. These include forms with reduced *-man* (like *postman, Scotsman*). In NZE *woman* increasingly belongs to this class.

Next there are some semantic classes. The first of these includes the word *fish* (and its compounds) and the names of specific fish such as *cod, salmon, snapper, trout*. There are several factors that seem to contribute to whether or not the plural is marked with words for fish: semantic, formal, lexical. There are, though, no hard and fast rules apparent in usage in this area.

Semantic factors include the type of sea creature being referred to: words referring to cetaceans, sharks, and shellfish (unless captured under some other generalization) tend to have regular plurals (with, for example, *lobster* and *shrimp* showing variability), even when they are being hunted or seen as a source of food: *whales, dolphins, hammerheads, mussels, clams, oysters, scallops* etc. The word *fish* itself is usually used with an unmarked plural, a tendency that becomes even stronger when it is compounded: *blackfish, crayfish, dogfish, lemonfish*, etc. There is a large lexical component as to whether individual fish names take an unmarked plural or a marked plural: *cod, salmon, trout* are clearly used most often with the unmarked plural, while *anchovies, bloaters, eels, herrings, sardines, soles* are more likely to have regular plurals. Even here, though, there is enormous variation. Fish that are named with hypocoristic forms, whether these arise formally from suffixation or from clipping, always take regular plurals: *crays, kingies, spotties*, etc. (Bauer 2009a).

Where birds are concerned, there are a number of bird names which can have an unmarked plural: *capercaillie, duck, grouse, partridge, pheasant, pigeon, ptarmigan, quail*. The regular plural here seems to be more likely when several different species are referred to, as in (34), or when individual birds are referred to.

(34)   Determining the age of pinnated and sharp-tailed grouses (*Amman 1944*)

There is still a lexical element to the choice of plural here. In the expression *a brace of ~*, the regular plural is preferred for *partridges, pheasants*, and *pigeons*, but the unmarked plural preferred for *grouse* and *quail* (American English Google Books corpus). *Grouse* when it means 'complaint' always takes the regular plural.

Where animals are concerned, the traditional description says that an unmarked plural is used when wild animals are hunted for food (*antelope*) or for their hides/skins (*mink*), not when they are hunted as vermin (see Sweet 1898: 44–5). If this was the rule, it is not clear to what extent it still is, though unmarked plurals of many animal names seem more usual in hunting contexts. This class might account for *deer*, which is rarely used in the regular plural. Again, *antelopes* or *elands* often mean 'types of X', but there is a lot of variation from one lexeme to another. *Bison, elk*, and *moose* seem particularly rare in the regular plural form, but take regular plural forms when these words are appropriated as names for human organizations or teams. Again, this could be the regularization of names.

There is a set of inhabitant words, most of which end in *-ese*, which are generally plural when they are nouns but which can occasionally still be found used as singular forms as well. The words include *Chinese, Genovese, Japanese, Javanese, Maltese, Milanese, Portuguese, Swiss, Viennese, Vietnamese*, and some more. The most normal use of these words is in a phrase like *the Vietnamese* to refer to the set of people who are Vietnamese, and these forms take plural concord:

(35)   Her support for the Vietnamese continued all her life. (*Dekker 2007*)

   The Viennese were regarded abroad as a good-natured, easygoing, and highly cultured people. (*Waugh 2008*)

However, these words can occasionally also be used as singulars, making them part of the unmarked plural class:

(36)   A Vietnamese has stolen 'Cambodian' ID in this manner (http://www.mail-archive. com/camdisc@googlegroups.com/msg08303.html)

   The inquiry came from a Japanese called Masami Tobari (http://www.memorial.krsk. ru/eng/Dokument/Public/20030618.htm)

Such singulars are, though, extremely rare from native speakers of English at the current period, and are often viewed as deprecatory in some way. The same is true to an even greater extent of the old, non-standard forms where *Chinese, Portuguese*, etc. was reinterpreted as having a plural marker, so that the singular was *Chinee, Portuguee*, etc.

Other ethnic names can be found either with regular plurals or with unmarked plurals: *Apache(s), Bantu(s), Bedouin(s), Inuit(s)* (*Inuit* is the plural form in the donor language), *Maori(s), Navajo(s), Shona(s)*. *Sioux* is spelled the same in the singular and the plural, and pronounced /suː/ in the singular and /suː/ or /suːz/ in the plural. In Australia, tribal names usually do not have plural marked, so that the singular and plural forms are homophonous, for example *Eora, Wiradjuri, Yolngu*. Exceptions are the *Koori(s)* and *Noongar(s)*, which have both marked and unmarked plural forms, for reasons that are not quite clear.

In New Zealand there is an extra set of unmarked plurals, since words borrowed from the Maori language are often left unmarked. For most nouns, plural is not marked on the noun in the Maori language, and many Maori people feel strongly that, as a matter of respect for the Maori language, these nouns should also be left unmarked when they are borrowed into English. Thus nouns such as *kaka, kea, tui* (which denote birds) or *kauri, pohutukawa, rimu* (which denote trees), and the word *Maori* itself, when denoting people, are often left unmarked in the plural. A phrase such as *the kauri* can thus be ambiguous as to whether it is singular or plural, even though it would not be ambiguous in Maori (where number would be marked on the determiner). Although there is a strong prescriptive movement toward unmarked plurals of Maori nouns in NZE (which may spread to nouns borrowed from other non-European languages), the use of regular plurals is widespread in informal usage.

7.2.7 Foreign plurals

With a handful of languages, nouns borrowed from those languages come with their foreign plural forms attached. However, not all nouns from the relevant languages necessarily retain the plural from the foreign language concerned, and there is a certain amount of variation about usage. While it is true that there are some nouns which almost always retain the foreign plural, and others which virtually never use the foreign plural in English, this does not lead to a useful classification for foreign learners (since the classes are random) or for native speakers (since even the potentially relevant grouping cannot be discerned from the form of the singular). The vast majority of foreign nouns can be used with regular English plurals (even nouns like *datum* which rarely occurs in the singular), and competing foreign plurals often survive in specialized discourses. In the following we will discuss a number of donor languages and the plural forms that words from these languages take in English.

7.2.7.1 *Greek*

Where words from Greek are concerned, there are two major patterns of concern, illustrated in (37). The first pattern comprises words ending in <on> that form their plural by replacing <on> by <a>. The second of these patterns picks up some words which are actually Latin in origin, and some of the Greek words make their way into English via Latin, so 'Greek' here is more of a mnemonic than a strict etymological comment. These words form their plural by replacing the word-final rhyme by /iːz/.

(37) a. criterion • criteria

automaton, anacoluthon, criterion, *and variably:* ganglion, phenomenon, prolegomenon

b. crisis • crises

acropolis, amanuensis, amniocentesis, anacrusis, analysis, antithesis, apotheosis, arsis, axis, basis, crisis, diærisis, dieresis, diagnosis, dialysis, emphasis, hypothesis, metamorphosis, metathesis, nemesis, neurosis, paralysis, parenthesis, periphrasis, psychosis, syllepsis, symbiosis, synopsis, synthesis, taxis, testis, thesis, thrombosis

A small number of Greek words belong to a slightly different pattern: *apsis* • *apsides*, *iris* (in the eye) • *irides* (or a regular plural). *Ibis, iris* (a flower), *mantis, metropolis, necropolis, trellis* have regular plurals. *Pelvis, penis* may have a word-based regular plural, or a stem-based *-es* plural. *Dais, loris* are not Greek words, and have regular plurals.

The spellings <axes> and <bases> are ambiguous, either providing the regular plural of *axe* and *base* or providing the Greek plural of *axis* and *basis*. The pronunciations are distinct, however: /æksɪs/ versus /æksiːz/; /beɪsɪs/ versus /beɪsiːz/.

7.2.7.2 *Latin*

With Latin words there are four regular patterns, and some exceptional patterns. The regular patterns are illustrated in (38) to (41). Words like (38) are Latin masculine nouns in *-us*, which regularly show such plurals in English, especially in technical uses. The pronunciation of the plural <i> varies between /iː/ and /aɪ/ depending on whether the traditional English pronunciation of Latin is used or the classical pronunciation of Latin, and not all words vary in the same way. *Octopus* is not a Latin noun of the appropriate form, so that *octopi*, while extremely common as a plural form, albeit a non-standard one, is etymologically fallacious. The Greek plural would be *octopodes*, but the regular English plural *octopuses* is standard.

(38) alumnus • alumni

bacillus, cactus, focus, fungus, hippopotamus, locus, nucleus, stimulus, stylus, terminus

There are some Latin nouns, such as *census, coitus, flatus, prospectus, quercus* which belong to a different declension class in Latin and thus do not take an *-i* plural. These normally take a regular plural in English, if they are used in the plural at all.

Words like (39) are Latin neuter nouns in *-um*.

(39)   bacterium • bacteria

addendum, curriculum, datum, desideratum, erratum, forum, labium, millennium, ovum, referendum, spectrum, stratum, symposium

Words like (40) are Latin feminine nouns in *-a*. Words from this set regularly show the Latin plural in English, especially in technical uses. There are four different pronunciations of the suffix attested, and speakers seem to vary a great deal in which word can take each of the four realizations: /ə ~ eɪ ~ iː ~ aɪ/. There are many foreign words borrowed into English which do not belong to this class because they are not Latin: *algebra* is Arabic, *drama* is Greek, *guerrilla* is Spanish, *pizza* is Italian, and so on. *Genera* and *opera* are Latin, but are already irregular plurals (see (43) below).

(40)   larva • larvae

alga, alumna, amoeba, antenna, formula, vertebra

Words like (41) are Latin third declension nouns in *-x*. Of these, *appendix* and *index* frequently also show the regular plural, often semantically distinguished from the Latin plural: *appendixes* are parts of the body, not additions at the ends of books, and *indexes* are parts of books rather than mathematical signs. These distinctions, however, are not rigorously maintained, and the plural of *appendix* in particular is more variable than this simple statement suggests.

(41)   matrix • matrices

appendix, codex, cortex, index, matrix, vortex (*and words ending in the suffix* -trix, *as in* animatrix, Madonnatrix)

Media, as in *news media*, is strictly speaking a plural of the kind in (39), the plural of *medium*. It is often used as a singular in non-technical English, as shown in the BNC example in (42).

(42)   *New Internationalist n.d.*: The **media** has added another dimension to racism by accusing Africans of importing AIDS.

Note the contrast with *mediums*, which is the plural of *medium* in the sense of 'person who claims to converse with spirits'. Although the artistic term is *mixed media*, in most other sense, the two plurals are interchangeable.

There are also a number of Latin plurals which, as far as the grammar of English is concerned, are irregular. Some common ones are listed in (43).

(43)   a. corpus • corpora

b. genus • genera

    c. larynx • larynges

    d. opus • opera

    e. pharynx • pharynges

    f. species • species

7.2.7.3 *French*

The majority of plurals in French are marked with an *-s*, and thus indistinguishable in writing from English plurals. Those that require comment, therefore, are those that diverge from this pattern in some way. There are two main types here, as illustrated in (44).

(44) a. plateau /plætəʊ ‖ plætoʊ/ • plateaux ~ plateaus /plætəʊz ‖ plætoʊz/

      b. rendezvous /rɒndeɪvuː ‖ rɑːndeɪvuː/ • rendezvous /rɒndeɪvuːz ‖ rɑːndeɪvuːz/

Words which work like (44a) include *adieu, bureau, chapeau, chateau* (in French: *château*), *milieu, tableau, trousseau*. Words which work like (44b) and show no change in the spelling but a change in the pronunciation include *chamois, chassis, corps, faux pas, patois*, where the final <s> is not pronounced in the singular.

7.2.7.4 *Hebrew*

A handful of nouns can take Hebrew plurals in *-im*. The main nouns for which this is found in English are *cherub, goy, kibbutz, seraph*. *Cherubim* and *seraphim* are often restricted to use where a biblical reference is intended, while *cherubs* would be the only possible plural of *cherub* meaning 'small, delightful child'.

7.2.7.5 *Italian*

There are some apparent Italian plurals in English, but their presence is to some extent misleading. The first set of Italian plural forms are those belonging to musical terms, for example *alti, bassi, castrati, celli, concerti, contralti, libretti, mezzi, soprani, tempi, virtuosi*. These are used exclusively by musicians or people with a close connection to classical music, and the form *celli* rarely appears except in musical scores. Such forms are probably better viewed as cases of code-switching than as genuine English plurals. The regular English plural is always a possibility here.

    The next set are food terms such as *macaroni, penne, ravioli, spaghetti, tagliatelli, tortellini*. While these forms are Italian plural forms, they act as singular non-count nouns in English, like *rice* or *porridge*. That is, English has *Here's your spaghetti, eat it* and not, as would be said in Italian, *eat them*. Equally, English has *How much spaghetti would you like?*, and not *How many spaghetti would you like?*. *Lasagna* and *lasagne* (singular and plural respectively in Italian) are used apparently randomly in English as the name of the dish. *Confetti* and *graffiti*, while not food terms, are used in much the same way as *spaghetti* etc., though *graffito* is available as a technical term in art history or archaeology. *Putti* seems to be more used than *putto*, and *one of the putti* seems more common than *a putto*. Again, this might be a case of code-switching. The use of the term *paparazzi* is very confused in English: it may be used as a singular, as a plural, and in plural use may add a regular plural. *Panini* and *zucchini* are the most surprising since, though they are Italian plural forms, they are used in English as singular forms (with regular plural marking added as required).

7.2.7.6 *Others*

The use of other foreign plurals (*as / æsir* from Norwegian, *Festschrift / Festschriften* from German, *hafiz / huffaz* from Arabic) seems to depend on the bilingual competence of the individual speaker/writer (and their willingness to show this competence). While unmarked plurals are often possible in these cases, the regular English plural is clearly the norm. The use of unmarked plurals in New Zealand usage of Maori words was discussed in Section 7.2.5.

7.2.8 Plurals of some complex lexical items

The general rule for complex lexical items is that they take the plural marker on the righthand edge of the word: *drop-outs, forget-me-nots, hardships, inputs, singer-songwriters, windmills*. This section is concerned with the exceptions, or potential exceptions (since there is some variability here), to this general rule. There are several sub-types.

First there are long-established phrases borrowed from French, where the French structure has a noun followed by an adjective: *attorney general, court martial, governor general, heir apparent, knight errant, letter patent,* and so on. Normatively, these take the plural marking on the first element, but there is a widespread tendency to put the plural marking on the righthand edge in the regular manner. Many of these expressions are extremely rare or specialized legal terms, which means they are treated as regular by those who are not familiar with them.

Next we have hyphenated expressions made up of a noun followed by a prepositional phrase: *coat-of-arms, commander-in-chief, daughter-in-law* (and other parallel expressions with *-in-law*), *grant-in-aid, maid-of-honour ‖ maid-of-honor, man-of-war*. Parallel to these are some expressions with noun-*and*-noun rather than a prepositional phrase: *coach-and-six, gin-and-tonic* (and other drinks). Some of these take the kind of plural that the corresponding syntactic phrase would take (e.g. *commanders-in-chief*, parallel to *agreements in principle*), and a few can take only this kind of plural (*coats-of-arms, men-of-war*). The corpus evidence suggests that the plural on the right edge is especially prevalent in spoken language. This is perhaps particularly true of the *-in-law* series.

There are some compound titles which used to be inflected on both elements (Sweet 1898) or on the first (Jespersen 1914: 23). Many of these are little used today, and where they are used, may be inflected regularly: *knight templar, lord chancellor, lord justice, lord lieutenant, lord mayor, major-general*.

Agent nouns coined from phrasal verbs with the structure V-*er*-Prep have the plural mark on the first element: *hangers-on, passers-by, runners-up.* However, even here, right edge plural forms can be found: *passer-bys, runner-ups.* These are regarded as incorrect, and are still minority forms, but they can be found even in edited text. Some people avoid the issue by repeating the -*er*, and then marking the plural at the right edge: *blower-uppers* (cf. Bauer 1983: 71). See also example (45) from COCA.

(45) *San Francisco Chronicle*, 1997: HUD owns homes, which are sold as-is without warranty. These **fixer-uppers** can be real bargains because the asking price will reflect the money needed to be invested to improve the home.

Colloquially, the extra -*er* may even be doubled, as in (46).

(46) As you'll recall he was a **rule looker upperer** in the first outing. (*http://web.me.com/ nataliendpeter/Site/Orders_of_the_day/Entries/2010/1/24_Including_Black_Powder,_ part_2.html*)

...allow only 5 seconds or something to eliminate the **looker upperers** amongst us (*http://www.wildaboutbritain.co.uk/forums/general-wildlife/49633-british-wildlife-quiz- anybody-got-1-a.html#post446844*)

A few appositional compounds with *man* or *woman* in the first element make both elements plural: *gentlemen-farmers, journeymen carpenters, menservants, women drivers, women doctors, women teachers.* This construction appears to be found only with *man* and *woman* (not, for instance, with *child*), and with *man*, at least, is occasionally replaced by the regular right edge marking.

7.3 POSSESSIVE/GENITIVE

Historically, English had a genitive case, and its markers were part of the inflectional system. What remains of that system is something written as <'s> or <'>, which we will refer to as S-GENITIVE. The genitive has among its functions to mark possession (hence the competing label 'possessive') but this kind of marking does not behave entirely like typical inflectional morphology since the marker also attaches to phrases. This phenomenon is known as the 'group genitive' (Quirk *et al.* 1985: 328) or 'phrasal genitive' (Payne and Huddleston 2002: 479). In contrast, the so-called 'head genitive' shows the marking on the head noun of the NP. Consider the examples in (47).

(47) The kitten's tail
The kitten I saw's tail

The kitten I was telling you about's tail

Somebody important's idea

Somebody else's idea

Here we see that the <'s> is added not necessarily to a noun (which would be what we would expect if it were inflectional) but to the entire phrase, and that its host may be of any word class. Such cases are generally considered to be clitics rather than inflections, and many scholars take this point of view (e.g. Carstairs-McCarthy 2002: 37). Payne (2011), however, argues on the basis of the behaviour of coordinated single genitives in which a pronoun is the second coordinate (e.g. *[*Kim and you*]'s children*, as against the acceptable [*Kim and her husband*]'s or [*the woman next to you*]'s children) that the interaction of head genitive marking and phrasal genitive marking in such structures is impossible to accommodate under a clitic analysis. A clitic analysis entails that the clitic be blind to the morphological makeup of the second coordinate (e.g. Anderson 2005), which is, however, not the case. In a similar vein, Payne and Huddleston (2002: 480–1) hold that the possessive in modern English is still inflectional, on the grounds that it is so tightly enmeshed with plural marking (see below).

In view of this situation, one might want to avoid the term 'genitive' and use 'possessive' instead. The label 'genitive' runs counter to some expectations concerning inflectional endings, and the term 'possessive' suggests a certain meaning of these constructions, which, as shown in the next subsection, in many cases is not there. We will therefore use the grammatically inspired term, that is 'genitive' and we will concentrate on those cases where it looks most inflectional, that is, where the possessive marking is added directly to the noun.

We will also discuss the periphrastic alternative to the <'s>/<'> marker, namely the use of the preposition *of* (OF-GENITIVE) since the two constructions are interdependent and can be taken as two alternant realizations of the same underlying morphosyntactic category. However, we will not discuss further intricacies of the syntax of genitives, such as the role of definiteness, event nominalizations involving genitives, or oblique genitives (as in *a friend of Laurie's*). The reader is referred to general reference grammars for a treatment of these syntactic aspects of genitive usage.

7.3.1 Semantics

As well as marking possession, the genitive is used to show a number of other semantic relationships between two nouns. In (48) we present one possible classification of meanings, others can be found, for example, in Payne and Huddleston (2002: Sec 16.5.2), or Quirk *et al.* (1985: 321–2).

(48) *meaning*	*s-genitive*	*of-genitive*
locative	New Zealand's scenery	peace of mind

source	mother's love	smell of bourbon
time/location	winter's day	first day of Lent
causative	the war's roots	the roots of the war
purpose	wolf's bane	day of rest
cause	*Zest 2011*: an allegorical response to the **war's** devastation	the devastation of war
partitive	an hour's delay	lump of cheese
named after	Hodgkin's lymphoma	bridge of sighs
essive	Dublin's fair city	sign of the cross
topic	season's greetings	book of birds

Part of the difficulty in dealing with the meanings of the genitive is that it is not clear that all post-modifying *of*-phrases are genitive: *That clown of a boy* does not permit of an alternative with <'s>, but uses markers which also mark possession. This introduces a certain random quality into what is covered in this section.

There are also grammatical readings of the genitive, particularly when the noun modified by the genitive is a deverbal nominalization. Then we find both subject-referencing genitives (49) and object-referencing genitives (50):

(49) a. the train's arrival, the arrival of the train

b. *Newsweek 1995*: **Yigal Amir's assassination of** Prime Minister Yitzhak Rabin ('Amir assassinated Rabin').

c. *CNN_Politics 2000*: The **senator's criticism of** gratuitous sex and violence ('The senator criticized gratuitous sex and violence').

(50) the prisoner's release, the release of the prisoner ('someone released the prisoner'), John's painting ('John painted something', *or* 'someone painted John'), Lincoln's assassination ('someone assassinated Lincoln', *or* 'Lincoln assassinated someone')

The examples show that there is a certain amount of pragmatic interpretation of the genitives in such cases, but the preference seems to be for s-genitives to be subject-referencing and for of-genitives to be object-referencing where that interpretation is not blocked by the context. Where both s- and of-genitives are present, the s-genitive must be subject-referencing and the of-genitive object-referencing.

As is pointed out by Payne and Huddleston (2002: 475), it is possible to treat genitives associated with nominalizations just like genitives associated with any other noun, so that, for instance, if each student in the class had been assigned an assassination to write about, *Lincoln's assassination* could be the assassination studied by the student called Lincoln, even if it involved the assassination of Martin Luther King.

7.3.2 Spelling

The major pattern for singular possessives is to add <'s> to the base form of the noun.

(51)   car ⬩ car's   hero ⬩ hero's
      cat ⬩ cat's   house ⬩ house's
      child ⬩ child's   mummy ⬩ mummy's
      cox ⬩ cox's   waltz ⬩ waltz's
      dog ⬩ dog's   wife ⬩ wife's
      fish ⬩ fish's   wolf ⬩ wolf's

Note that the rule applies independent of the last letter of the base to which the <'s> is added, and that there are no changes to the form of the bases as there are with the plurals (see Section 7.2): *wolf's* must be possessive and *wolves* must be plural. There are very few exceptions to this general principle, though *for goodness' sake* is one of them.

Where the base is a proper noun and ends in <s> there is generally a choice. Either the main rule can be followed (as in (51)), or a simple <'> can be added to the <s>. Note that irrespective of which spelling is chosen (e.g. <Dickens'> or <Dickens's>), speakers may read out the form employing the [ɪz] allomorph.

(52)   Aristoteles ⬩ Aristoteles' ⬩ Aristoteles's
      Burns ⬩ Burns' ⬩ Burns's
      Dickens ⬩ Dickens' ⬩ Dickens's
      Euripides ⬩ Euripides' ⬩ Euripides's
      James ⬩ James' ⬩ James's
      Jesus ⬩ Jesus' ⬩ Jesus's
      Matthews ⬩ Matthews' ⬩ Matthews's

Which form is preferred is variable. Greek names are perhaps most likely to be marked simply with <'>, while English names, especially given names, are most likely to have <'s>. With hypocoristic names like *Bas, Bess, Les*, the <'s> version (and the corresponding /ɪz/ pronunciation) is virtually obligatory. Names like *Clausewitz* and *Fritz*, which end with the letter <z> but the sound /s/ take the <'s> variant.

Where a plural possessive is required, if the plural form does not end in <s>, then <'s> is added.

(53)   children ⬩ children's
      men ⬩ men's
      mice ⬩ mice's

oxen ◆ oxen's

teeth ◆ teeth's

women ◆ women's

Where the plural form ends in <s>, then a simple <'> is added.

(54)   aviatrices ◆ aviatrices'

cats ◆ cats'

dogs ◆ dogs'

indices ◆ indices'

mummies ◆ mummies'

wives ◆ wives'

wolves ◆ wolves'

7.3.3 Pronunciation

The pronunciation of genitive <'s> is generally the same as the pronunciation of the regular plural, as shown in (55a) (see also Section 7.2.2.2), with two groups of systematic exceptions concerning bases ending in an alveolar fricative. In both of these groups we observe a haplology effect (see Chapter 9 for a discussion of the notion of haplology). In the case of the genitive <'s>, this effect is that only one alveolar fricative surfaces. One group of haplological genitive forms are words ending in morphemic -s, that is regular plural nouns, as in (55b), or other kinds of morphemic -s, as in (55c) and (55d), both taken from Stemberger (1981: 793). Another group is proper nouns and abbreviations, at least in some dialects, as shown in (55d–f), examples from COCA, where we find variable pronunciations with final /ɪz/ or simply final /z/ or /s/.

(55)   a. cat's ◆ cats ◆ cats'   /kæts/

dog's ◆ dogs ◆ dogs'   /dɒgz ‖ dɔːgz/

horse's ◆ horses ◆ horses'   /hɔːsɪz ‖ hɔːrsɪz/

church's ◆ churches ◆ churches'   /ʧɜːʧɪz ‖ ʧɜːrʧɪz/

b. for politics' sake

c. linguistics' contribution to the study of language

d. *The song reader (2003): a novel*: We'd moved into our apartment on the second floor of **Agnes' house** when I was just a baby.

e. *CNN_Event 1999*: Yes, the diary was found in **Harris' house**.

f. *Agricultural Research 1999*: Sharpley was recently appointed to coordinate **ARS'**
contribution to a new national program with NRCS

7.3.4 s-genitive versus of-genitive

7.3.4.1 *Variability and non-variability*

The use of s-genitives is often in variation with the use of periphrastic genitives with the
preposition *of*, so that we can find both of the alternatives in (56), both from the BNC.

(56)   *Mitcham: Age Concern England, 1989*: As far as possible, the daily **lives of people** should
be determined by their own decisions

British Journal of Social Work, 1991: a final section considers the quality of **people's lives**
as perceived by their relatives and others

This raises the obvious question on which basis speakers decide which variant to take. First of
all there seem to be constructions where no variation can be observed (when trying to hold the
meaning constant). This holds for partitive genitives, that is those in which the possessum narrows down the quantity or number of the referent(s) of the non-head, as in (57a) and (57b).

(57)   a. *a cake's piece   a piece of cake

*a bread's slice   a slice of bread

*a beer's barrel   a barrel of beer

*a book's copy   a copy of a/the book

*a chicken's half   a half (of a) chicken

*(an) advice's word   a word of advice

*(a) garlic's clove   a clove of garlic

*(a) jam's jar   a jar of jam

b. *my students' some   some of my students

* my childrens' one   one of my children

*his players' three   three of his players

Equally, no variation is observable with personal pronouns as possessors. Thus *the house of
me* is impossible, and where a pronoun combines with *of*, the construction is not necessarily
synonymous with a genitive involving the possessive determiner, as in examples like *the
thought of me* versus *my thought*, or *the picture of me* versus *my picture*.

Other non-variable genitives are the s-genitives called 'post-genitive' (58a), 'local genitive'
(58b), and 'independent genitive' (58c) by Kreyer (2003), and the *of*-phrases that modify a
pronominal head (58d) or complement a non-nominal non-head (58e).

(58) a. a friend of mine
        a student of hers

    b. We meet at Laurie's.
        She is staying at Frank's.

    c. Your house is bigger than Fred's.
        My car is smaller than the doctor's.

    e. My house is as big as that of the mayor.
        *My house is as big as the mayor's that.

    f. the idea of providing the food
        *providing the food's idea

Turning to those constructions in which both variants are possible and synonymous, the choice of the synthetic versus the analytic genitive is probabilistic. There are many different factors which tend to influence the preference of one form over another, but no single factor which can guarantee a particular form. Among the most important determining factors we find animacy of possessor, meaning relationship, semantic category of the possessor, length of possessor, length of possessum, sentence length, final segment of the possessor, and previous mention. In the following we will briefly review these factors, as they have emerged in studies such as Kreyer (2003), Hinrichs and Szmrecsanyi (2007), Rosenbach (2005), or Szmrecsanyi (2006).

7.3.4.2 *Animacy*

The higher up the animacy hierarchy the possessor is, the more likely it is that the synthetic possessive will be used (e.g. Rosenbach 2005). This tendency is illustrated with the examples in (59), with number of occurrences in the BNC given for comparison. The data are ordered according to the proportion of s-genitives.

(59) *s-genitive*	*N*	*of-genitive*	*N*	*proportion of s-genitive*
the house's	56	of the house	3299	0.02
the idea's	15	of the idea	296	0.05
the committee's	314	of the committee	629	0.5
the nation's	630	of the nation	681	0.93
the ant's	8	of the ant	6	1.33
the frog's	14	of the frog	10	1.4
the teacher's	352	of the teacher	195	1.81
the dog's	210	of the dog	113	1.86

7.3.4.3 *The meaning relationship*

As already mentioned, object-referencing relationships tend more to be encoded by the of-genitive, while the subject-referencing meaning has a greater proportion of the synthetic construction. Where both subject-referencing and object-referencing genitives are found in a single NP, the subject-referencing is marked with the synthetic possessive, and the object-referencing is marked with the of-genitive, as in *The newspaper's publication of the story*.

7.3.4.4 *Semantic category of the modifier*

The synthetic genitive is particularly frequent where the possessively-marked noun denotes time or place: *the country's population, summer's end, tomorrow's dinner, the university's science building, a week's pay* (see e.g. Sweet 1898: 52; Quirk *et al.* 1985: 324). For example, we find 147 attestations in COCA of *the country's population*, but only 30 of the corresponding of-genitive construction.

7.3.4.5 *Length effects*

There are two kinds of length effects, one observable in the NP itself, and one emerging from the discourse context. The context effect is straightforward. The longer the sentence in which we find the pertinent NP, the more speakers or writers prefer the of-genitive. This suggests a processing advantage for the of-genitive. Processing constraints are also most likely responsible for the fact that longer possessor phrases have a tendency towards the of-genitive whereas length in other parts of the noun phrase (prenominal modifiers, nominal complements) makes the s-genitive more likely. In both cases, the longer constituent is placed towards the end of the NP, which follows the principle of end-weight and facilitates processing (e.g. Hawkins 1994). Consider the data in (60) for illustration.

(60)   a. *Long possessor*
            the analysis of [the full data set]
            the phone number of [the guy who lives next door]
        b. *Length elsewhere*
            Germany's [first two very successful attempts]
            the committee's [decision to withdraw the proposal]

7.3.4.6 *Final segment*

If the final segment of the possessor is a sibilant, the chances rise that the of-genitive is used. This might appear to be functionally motivated by the avoidance of ambiguity in examples such as /ðə skuːlz dɔː(r)z/, which could be *the school's doors* or *the schools' doors*. To choose *the doors of the schools* to make clear what the message is. However, only a minority of these cases involve regular plural nouns, and the effect also holds for other sibilants, that is for /ʃ, ʒ, tʃ, dʒ/. This suggests that we may be dealing not with ambiguity avoidance but with a phono-logical-articulatory planning difficulty.

7.3.4.7 *Previous mention*

Following up on a claim by Altenberg (1982), Szmrecsanyi (2006) has shown that previous mention of a particular construction favours the use of the same construction in the next genitive choice context. This can be explained as an on-line priming effect.

7.3.4.8 *Other factors*

Genitive choice is also susceptible to stylistic or textual variation. Thus, texts with a higher lexical density (as measured by type–token ratio) have more s-genitives than texts with lower lexical density (Szmrecsanyi 2006: 97).

Another factor is nestedness. Sequences of synthetic possessives, such as *His wife's cousin's son's award* are rare, whereas strings of *of*-modifiers are not. Where possible, therefore, multiple modifiers in nested genitives are usually distributed so that there will be at most one synthetic possessive in the set.

There are also preferences linked to specific lexical items. Some phrases with genitives are more or less fixed lexical items and show preferences which cannot be explained by the determinants just discussed. Some examples are given in (61), with figures showing occurrence in COCA.

(61)	decency's sake	5	the sake of decency	0
	France's republic	0	the republic of France	5
	kings' king	0	king of kings	71
	life's love	2	love of [poss. pronoun] life	451
	sun's rays	242	rays of the sun	127

Finally, there are differences between varieties of English. Szmrecsanyi (2006) finds that within the British Isles speakers from the Hebrides, the Midlands, or Wales have a preference for of-genitives, in contrast to speakers from the southeast of Britain. Differences between NAmE and BrE have also been noted, to the effect that the synthetic variant is more frequent in NAmE, but the strength of the effect varies in interaction with other variables. There is also ongoing change, such that the s-genitive is being more widely used (Ainsworth 1992; Rosenbach 2002).

....

CHAPTER 8

Function words: pronouns, determiners, wh-forms, deictics

8.1 PROSPECTUS

In this chapter we will consider all other English word classes that might conceivably be subjected to morphological analysis, among them pronouns, determiners of various sorts, wh-words, and deictics. We will not be concerned with the way in which the particular forms are used except where this impacts on our analysis: for example, the fact that *we* can be used as a royal or authorial plural as in (1) and (2) is not relevant to the general pattern of pronouns in English, and is not part of our remit. Similarly, the use of *they* as a singular, as in (3), while of great prescriptive and descriptive interest, does not impact on the way in which the system is structured. Nor does the use of feminine pronouns to refer to ships or machines, or the variable use of *she* or *he* as an impersonal pronoun in place of *it* in some varieties of English (for the latter see Pawley 2002, 2008; Siemund 2007).

(1) We are not amused.

(2) In this paper we will illustrate … [*in a paper with a single author*]

(3) Everybody$_i$ is hoping that they$_i$ will win.

We begin with pronouns and then look at determiners, wh-words, and deictics.

8.2 PRONOUNS

8.2.1 Personal

The first set of personal pronouns is laid out in (4). The major difficulty here is a matter of nomenclature. Traditionally these are referred to as nominative and accusative pronouns (Payne and Huddleston 2002: 426) or subjective and objective pronouns (Quirk *et al.* 1985: 346). But if, following Hudson (1995), we query the whole notion of case for English, such nomenclature seems misleading (though see Quinn 2005 for a more nuanced view). We here propose the labels SOLE SUBJECT form (for pronouns like *I*) and the DEFAULT form, on the grounds that for many speakers the only place where pronouns like *I* occur regularly is when they are uncoordinated subjects of finite verbs, and the pronouns like *me* occur unless there is some reason to have a pronoun from the other series.

In (4) we present both standard and alternative forms of the personal pronouns. The forms occurring in the column marked 'alternatives' are dialectal (archaic, sometimes) or register-specific forms of differing degrees of generalization. See, for example, Wright (1905), Wentworth (1944), Orton *et al.* (1978) and the *OED*, and for a wider look which includes creoles, see Wales (1996: 90). IrE is notable for allowing reflexive forms (see Section 8.2.3) to be used without antecedent in place of the standard forms (Filppula 2004: 93).

(4)			Sole subject		Default	
			Standard	*Alternatives*	*Standard*	*Alternatives*
1st person singular			I	ch, ich, he, her	me	us, I
2nd person singular			you	thou	you	thee
3rd person singular	masculine		he		him	(ə)n
	feminine		she	shoo, hoo	her	
	neuter		it		it	(ə)n
1st person plural			we		us	/ʌs/ ~ /ʌz/
2nd person plural			you	ye, yous, yes /jiːz/, y'all, you-all(s), you guys, yous guys, you 'uns	you	ye, yous, yes /jiːz/, y'all, you-all(s), you guys, yous guys, you 'uns
3rd person plural			they		them	

Although various forms are recorded in (4), there can be a lot of phonetic variation, for example in the form of the pronoun *I*, and many of the pronouns have a distinct form in unstressed position, where pronouns are often found (see, for example, Wales 1996: 14).

In addition to the pronouns in (4), we should add the paradoxically named impersonal personal pronoun, *one*, usually denoting some unspecified person, but in a socially very narrow dialect of BrE indicating the first person singular.

8.2.2 Possessive pronouns

The possessive pronouns are set out in (5). Again nomenclature is a problem. Payne and Huddleston (2002: 426) talk about dependent and independent possessives (for *my* and *mine* respectively), but many syntactic theories see the possessive as the head of the construction, so that the label 'dependent' seems contradictory. Quirk *et al.'s* (1985) determinative function and independent function is better. Wright (1905) uses conjunctive and disjunctive (respectively), Kruisinga (1932) uses attributive and independent, Poutsma (1916) uses conjoint and absolute. An alternative terminology would see these as possessive adjectives and possessive pronouns respectively, or as prosodically weak and strong. We will use the terms DETERMINATIVE for those possessives like *my* that behave syntactically as determiners and ABSOLUTE for those like *mine* that can occur in predicative contexts. The possessive pronouns are presented in (5):

(5)

		Determinative		*Absolute*	
		Standard	*Alternatives*	*Standard*	*Alternatives*
1st person singular		my	me	mine	mines, my
2nd person singular		your	thy, thee	yours	thine, yourn
3rd person singular	masculine	his	he	his	hisn
	feminine	her		hers	hern, hersn
	neuter	its	it, his	its	
1st person plural		our	wə(r), us, we	ours	ourn
2nd person plural		your	ye, you	yours	yourn, you-all's, y'all's, your-all's, yous guys', your guys'
3rd person plural		their		theirs	theirn

The forms that are available allow for greater regularity than is present in standard varieties, and some dialects actually exploit this. In particular, some dialects have consistent -*n* forms in the absolute forms, others have consistent -*s* forms, while standard Englishes have a mixture. Note also that absolute forms that contain apparently determinative forms (e.g. *you all's*) are sometimes disfavoured; a double possessive (*your-all's*) is a relatively frequent outcome.

8.2.3 Reflexive and emphatic pronouns

The reflexive pronouns are given in (6).

(6) *Standard*   *Alternative*
  myself
  yourself   thyself
  himself   hisself
  herself
  itself

ourselves	usselves
yourselves	
themselves	theirselves

Apart from the variation illustrated above, there is variation in the phonetic form of the *-self* element: often the /f/ or /v/ is elided or the /l/ is elided. Sometimes the /l/ is replaced by /n/ when there is no /f/ or /v/. In some contexts there may not be a separate set of reflexive pronouns, the default pronoun illustrated in (4) being used instead.

8.3 DETERMINERS

The demonstrative determiners (or 'determinatives', using the terminology of Payne and Huddleston 2002) are laid out in (7). *Yon* is old-fashioned or dialectal; it is no longer part of the standard language. It appears to be used to point out objects which are within sight but further away than those covered by *that*.

(7)		*proximal*	*distal*	*super-distal*
	singular	this	that	yon
	plural	these	those	yon

Yon may take on the form *yond* or *yonder* (though *yonder* is also an adjective and an adverb). Some dialects use *this here* and *that there* in place of simple *this* and *that*. *This* may be replaced in some dialects by *thick(y)* or some derived form, *that* may be replaced by *thack(y)*, *thon*. In ScE *those* is replaced by *they*.

8.4 WH-WORDS

Wh-forms are used in English both as the initial element in relative clauses and in wh-questions; traditionally this set of forms is referred to in the former case as 'relative pronouns' and in the latter as 'interrogative pronouns'. Also included in the traditional designation of relative pronouns is the form *that*, which is better analysed as a conjunction (e.g. van der Auwera 1985; Huddleston *et al.* 2002: 1056–7) or complementizer (Carnie 2006). As this form is generally morphologically invariant in relative clauses, we do not discuss it here, although note that in ScE *that's* is possible in possessive contexts.

In both relative and interrogative contexts there is a great deal of variation in usage in the contemporary language, as well as regional and diachronic variation. In (8) and (9) we present a rather full, conservative, and standard set of wh-words, on which we add comments below. The data in (8) are divided up according to whether the wh-form occurs in a restrictive (defining) or non-restrictive (parenthetical) relative clause.

(8)   Relative clauses

	Restrictive		*Non-restrictive*	
	rational beings, higher animals	*other referents*	*rational beings, higher animals*	*other referents*
Subject	who	which, when, where, why	who	which, when, where, why
Non-subject	whom, who		whom, who	
Possessive		whose		

(9)   Interrogatives

	rational beings, higher animals	*other referents*
Subject	who	which
	which	what
Non-subject	who	which
	whom	what, when, where, why, how
	which	
Possessive		whose

Whom as direct object is infrequent, perhaps more so in interrogative than in relative contexts, especially in spoken English. It is often replaced by *who* when referring to a direct object. *Whom* is used more consistently in both relative clauses and interrogatives as a non-preposed object of a preposition (e.g. *to whom*), although in some varieties (e.g. NZE) *which* can be used following a preposition even for an animate referent.

(10)   60,000 refugees, of which half could die (*Radio New Zealand 1994*)

Nonetheless, *whom* remains part of the system in non-subject contexts, especially in very conservative or formal written style.

8.5 Compound determinatives

Here we consider a set of non-canonical compound forms (see Chapter 19.2.3) which denote indefinites. It is again difficult to decide what to call these items. They consist of a quantifier as first element and a semantically light noun (*thing*, *body*) or pronoun (*one*) as second element. For lack of a better term, we adopt the terminology of Payne and Huddleston (2002: 423) and call them 'compound determinatives'. They are set out in (11).

(11)   *Rational beings*   *Non-personals*

         nobody   no one, no-one   nothing /nʌθɪŋ/

         somebody   someone   something

         everybody   everyone   everything

         anybody   anyone   anything

8.6 DEICTIC PRO-FORMS

We include here the set of forms which might be viewed as pro-adverbs referring to a particular temporal or locative space. The relevant simple forms are set out in (12).

(12)		Spatial location			Temporal location		
		proximal	*distal*	*interrogative*	*proximal*	*distal*	*interrogative*
	location	here	there	where	now	then	when
	source	hence	thence	whence			
	goal	hither	thither	whither			

Note that *hence* is frequently used with a meaning equivalent to 'therefore' rather than a specifically spatial meaning. *Thence* and *whence* have similar functions.

Here and *there* also enter into several non-canonical compound forms, some of which are illustrated in (13).

(13)   elsewhere, henceforth, hereabout(s), hereafter, hereby, hereto, hereupon, herewith, hitherto, thenceforth, thereabout(s), thereafter, thereby, therefore, thereupon

Note that many of these compounds which are built on the spatial locatives set out in (12) nevertheless make reference to temporal location. *Therefore* is used as a conjunction rather than as an adverb; *hereafter* and *thereafter* have uses as nouns.

8.7 ANALYSIS OF THE FORMS

However we try to analyse the various forms collected together here, we have to recognize that there is little in English function words to signal their morphological relatedness. *My* and *his* have little in common to demonstrate their possessiveness, for instance.

Furthermore, although we can see various tendencies in the formal and semantic analysis of these forms (and generative syntactic theory sometimes tries to exploit these tendencies; see for example Di Sciullo 2005; Klinge 2005b), it seems unlikely that most of them are actively parsed by contemporary speakers. The exceptions are the compound forms, and even there, there is often little semantic connection between the second element when it occurs in the compound and when it occurs as an independent form. For example, *therefore* does not have any obvious semantic link with *for/fore*. With a form like *hence* there is a certain amount of evidence from usage that the force of the word is not appreciated by speakers, since many of them say *from hence*, and *from whence*, even though *hence* and *whence* include a 'from' meaning.

(14)   BNC. *Pamela, or the Reform Rake 1987*: Pamela shall not stir **from hence**

COCA. *Analog Science Fiction & Fact 2006*: They will be taken up to the stars **from whence** we came

BNC. *The Dyke & the Dybbuk 1993*: it sends me back, in some discomfort, to the place **from whence** I came

We also need to consider the frequency of the elements dealt with in this chapter. The basic forms are all so frequent that they no longer require specific parsing for appropriate use or for understanding.

8.7.1 Initial <th>, <h>, and <wh>

A number of the forms have an initial <th> (phonologically /ð/), something they share with the definite article *the*. Indeed, we could see *the* as the minimal form here, with only (in most instances) the minimal vowel /ə/ supporting the /ð/ while words such as *thou, thee, thy, thine, they, them, their, theirs, this, that, these, those, there, thence, thither, then* all have some supporting material. Historically, the analysis of this initial /ð/ as being an indication of deixis seems valid. It is also notable that the only words of English with initial /ð/ are in this set (if *though* can be added). However, *thither*, now a rather rare member of the set and often occurring in the phrase *hither and thither* (more than a third of the uses attested in COCA), is pronounced with an initial /θ/ (and thus removed from the set) in some varieties of ScE and NAmE.

Initial /h/ in the deictic set of *here, hither, hence* seems to indicate proximity, especially where it contrasts with initial /ð/ and <wh>. However, the initial /h/ in *him* and *her*, and in *who* cannot belong to the same grouping, since these words are not used for proximal objects.

The initial <wh> (more usually these days pronounced as simply /w/, though the <wh> spelling persists) is a regular concomitant of interrogativity in *why, when, what, which, whither, whence, where*. However, some of these forms are also used to introduce relative clauses where there is no longer any trace of interrogativity. At some level this is explained historically by the fact that the relative use developed from the interrogative one in the late Middle English period, possibly with some influence from French (Fischer 1992: 301; Fischer and Van der Wurff 2006: 128). In *who, whom, whose* the <wh> spelling persists, but the pronunciation as /h/ masks any relationship.

Although there is thus little empirical synchronic evidence for morphological complexity, both Di Sciullo (2005) and Klinge (2005a) have tried to make an argument for analysing the wh-forms and deictics as complex; the former, for example, claims that *wh-* in wh-words is a quantifier and the *th-* in words like *this* and *that* a determiner. What remains (e.g. *-o* in *who*, *-at* in *what* or *that*) is analysed in terms of features like [+/–human] or [+/–proximate]. Whatever the benefits of such analyses, it is nonetheless clear that these elements are not morphemes in the classic sense of the term, and it is uncertain what is to be gained by analysing them as complex.

8.7.2 Oblique <m>

The final <m> in *him, them, whom* is historically a dative inflection which by the end of the Middle English period indicated any oblique case, rather than strictly a dative. Given that we have avoided an analysis in terms of case, the precise meaning of this /m/ becomes difficult to specify, and must be obscured by the loss of *whom* in most environments.

8.7.3 Final <n>, <r>, <s>, and <t>

A final /n/ indicates possession in *mine, thine,* and is generalized to the absolute forms in some dialectal forms. However, the final /n/ of *then, when, yon* has no such correlation.

A final historical /r/ (variously treated in non-rhotic varieties of English) indicates possession in *her, their, your.* Again, this is historically correct, but there are too few forms for a pattern to emerge in contemporary English.

A final <s>, usually pronounced /z/, but sometimes /s/ depending on the phonotactic environment in which it is found, indicates possession in *his, its* and in the absolute possessive forms (e.g. *yours, hers,* etc; see (5)). This is supported by the possessive marker on nouns, and is probably robust and recognizable.

Historically, the final <t> in *it* and *what* indicates neuter gender, but that pattern is not recuperable in the modern forms.

8.7.4 Thou and you

The spelling <ou> in *thou* and *you* might appear to show a relationship (despite the different pronunciation in modern English), but since, historically speaking, *thou* is nominative while *you* is accusative, *thee* is accusative while *ye* is nominative, there is no usable pattern here.

8.7.5 Analysability and morphemic status

In principle, therefore, forms like *h-ence, th-i-ne, th-ither, wh-o-m, you-r-s* are analysable as shown into partly helpful elements. It would, though, be a mistake to assume that these elements are morphemes, available to the introspection of the modern speaker. Rather, what we have here are sub-morphemic elements which may set up what Hockett (1987) calls resonances. While there may be some value in drawing some of the generalizations to the attention of sophisticated second language learners at a suitable level of expertise, fundamentally, all the non-compound forms are best treated as morphologically unrelated members of their sets.

PART III

Derivation

....

CHAPTER 9

Derivation: phonological considerations

9.1 PROSPECTUS

This chapter gives an overview of phenomena in derivation where morphology and phonology interact. While such phenomena will also be dealt with in some detail in the chapters to follow, the present chapter provides a general introduction to the role of phonology in English derivation and the principles that govern the morpho-phonological behaviour of many of the morphological categories to be described in the upcoming chapters.

There are some rather isolated cases of derivation in which the relevant meaning is solely expressed through a manipulation of the base-internal phonological structure. This is, for example, the case with some umlauted causative verbs (*fall* ⋄ *fell, lie* ⋄ *lay, rise* ⋄ *raise, sit* ⋄ *set*) or with certain very rare nominalizations (e.g. *abide* ⋄ *abode, sing* ⋄ *song*). We do not consider these cases of unproductive morphology in this chapter.

After a general discussion of the role of phonology in English derivation in the next section, we will deal with the problem of allomorphy in Section 9.3, and with particular kinds of phonology–morphology interactions in Section 9.4 (on the role of prosody), Section 9.5 (on haplology), Section 9.6 (on prosodic morphology) and Section 9.7 (on phonological selectional restrictions).

9.2 PHONOLOGY IN DERIVATIONAL MORPHOLOGY

English derived words are related to their bases in at least two respects, semantically and phonologically. In other words, a derived word normally shares both a meaning component and parts (or all) of its form with its base. A look at a sample of derived words reveals, however, that the formal relation, that is the phonetic or phonological relation between base and derivative, is not necessarily straightforward. The issue is how faithful the derivative is to the phonological structure of the base. The words in (1) illustrate different cases:

(1)   a. help • helpless, blue • blueness, test • test-wise, assess • assessment

b. govern • government, rest • restless, exact • exactly

c. cónjugàte • cònjugátion, cólony • colónial

d. feminine • feminize, mercury • mercurate

e. cylinder • cylindric, enter • entrance

f. serene • serenity, meter • metrical

g. endocentric • endocentricity, erase • erasure

h. Jacob • Jake, Alfred • Freddy, celebrity • celeb, professor • prof, beer + nirvana • beervana, Japanese + English • Japlish

The words in (1a) give examples of affixation in which the base is phonologically fully recoverable from the derivative. The suffixes in the derivatives form syllables of their own, and the suffix is phonologically not integrated into the base, which means that the morphological boundary and the phonological boundary (i.e. the syllable boundary) coincide. This is an interesting fact, as in many cases, the first consonant of the consonant-initial suffix could in principle be syllabified as the second consonant of an onset that starts with the base-final consonant, as in *hel.pless or *tes.twise. But this does not happen; the suffix does not form a phonological unit with its host. Affixes that display this kind of inert behaviour have been called 'non-cohering' (e.g. Dixon 1977: 93; Kaisse 2005: 28) and are generally consonant-initial.

The cases in (1b) present base-derivative pairs where, phonetically, the bases are not straightforwardly recognizable in the derived word, that is, the derivatives are phonologically not fully transparent. For example, *government* is mostly pronounced /gʌvmənt/ or /gʌvəmənt ‖ gʌvərmənt/, and *restless* and *exactly* are often pronounced without a /t/. Quite frequently such phonological opacity goes together with semantic opacity, as, for example, in the case of *government*, which does not denote 'action of VERBing' (as is standardly the case with *-ment* derivatives), but rather denotes the people who govern, or, more generally, 'political authorities'. Notably, these particular cases of phonological opacity are idiosyncratic, that is, they reflect the history of individual words, or they concern phonetic simplifications that are highly dependent on the frequency of individual words. For example, while *exactly* is rather frequent and easily loses its /t/, *conjunctly* is of low frequency and is unlikely to occur without its /t/. In what follows we will not dwell on such idiosyncrasies but focus on the more systematic patterns of phonological opacity.

We should note that phonological variation as a result of morphological contiguity varies from the categorical to the extremely variable. In the literature, such matters are sometimes dealt with as a distinction between lexical and post-lexical phonology (see e.g. Mohanan 1986). Unfortunately, a distinction is very often difficult to draw, especially when the same process (say, for example, the assimilation of a nasal to the place of articulation of a following consonant) may be involved in both lexical and post-lexical phonology. The deletion of /t/ mentioned above may not be strictly morphological in the sense that it might occur in the syntactic phrase *the exact lenition* as well, and be subject to factors such as the speed of speech, the formality of the occasion, the audience for the speech event and so on, but it does have the effect of masking the transparency of morphological processes. We will not discuss such matters further here, but our focus is on those processes which affect phonemic structure rather than, for instance, degrees of nasality or aspiration. This is in line with the notion of morpho-phonemic variation being involved. We take this slightly further than normal in that we do consider some instances which are not categorical but variable.

Examples (1c) to (1h) show morpho-phonological alternations that affect words of the same morphological category and that are systematic in nature; (1c) gives examples of stress shift, (1d) shows the truncation of the base under suffixation, (1e) illustrates some extreme cases of resyllabification, (1f) contains instances of vowel alternations, and (1g) of consonant alternations. In these instances the phonology takes the morphological strings and treats them as single units; affixes which are or can be involved in such strings have been termed 'cohering affixes'. Which affixes are classified as cohering and which ones as non-cohering is not always clear, however. Some authors (e.g. Kaisse 2005) use the possibility of stress shifts as a criterion, but if syllabification is used as a criterion, all vowel-initial suffixes are cohering. And even consonant-initial suffixes are capable of causing phonological alternations (*deep* ◆ *depth, marked* ◆ *mark*[ə]*dness*) or of showing syllabic integration with the base. For example, adverbial *-ly* does not geminate in *frailly* but coalesces with base-final syllabic /l/ to form an onset, something which also occurs in *gently*, and the suffix could therefore be classified as cohering.

Returning to our different kinds of phonology–morphology interaction in (1), we see an extreme case of phonology–morphology interaction in (1h), often referred to as 'prosodic morphology'. Here, a morphological category is primarily or exclusively characterized by a manipulation of the prosodic structure (instead of by affixation or conversion), for example by deleting phonological material to create derived words of a certain prosodic structure.

To summarize, the examples in (1b–h) illustrate patterns in which a given base stands in a phonologically non-trivial relationship to its derivative. As we will see, individual morphological categories often display a kind of relationship that is peculiar to this category. These relationships will be further investigated in Sections 9.3 to 9.6.

Phonology may also play another role in word-formation patterns. For example, affixes may have different phonetic realizations on a systematic basis, that is allomorphs, and the distribution of these allomorphs may be phonologically governed, as shown for *-al* and *in-* in (2). Such cases of affix allomorphy will be discussed in more detail in Section 9.3.2.

(2)   a. -al: polar / *polal *versus* *labiar / labial,

b. in-: inaccessible ◆ illegal ◆ improbable

Finally, phonology may have a say in imposing selectional restrictions on combinations of bases and affixes. For example, the nominal suffix *-al* (as in *refusal*) can be found only on bases that are stressed on the final syllable (consider *arríval, bestówal, renéwal*). Section 9.7 will take a closer look at the kinds of restrictions that can be observed with different derivational categories.

Before turning to the discussion of the individual morpho-phonological patterns, a word is in order as to the kind of approach we are taking here. Phonological alternations in derivational morphology, such as stress shifts (e.g. *prodúctive* ◆ *productívity*) or base truncations (e.g. *feminine* ◆ *feminize*), have attracted a lot of attention in the theoretical literature, mostly under the label of 'Lexical Phonology'. In much of this literature, a serial derivational approach is predominant, which is also reflected in the terminology that is widely used to talk about the pertinent phenomena. For example, the term 'stress shift' implies that a given stress is shifted from the position it occupies in the base to another position in the derivative when an affix is added to that base. More recent work in morpho-phonology has shown, however, that such a serial-derivational approach is by no means the only possible one and that, for example, output-oriented approaches, or approaches taking into account other related words apart from the base, may often be able to provide a more insightful account of the empirical facts.

In this chapter, we will continue using the established terminology, but without a commitment to the derivational approaches that underlie this terminology. We will also approach the phonological facts from a morphological perspective. Thus, we will conceptualize morpho-phonological alternations as kinds of base allomorphies and affix allomorphies.

Lexical Phonology has also capitalized on the idea of lexical strata with two (or sometimes three) levels of affixation, with the affixes of each level assumed to show the same kind of behaviour concerning, for example, stress shift, syllabification, trisyllabic laxing, velar softening, etc. More recent work (e.g. Plag 1999; Raffelsiefen 1999, 2004, see also the chapters to follow in this volume) has shown, however, that each derivational category comes with its own set of phonological restrictions and properties, and that the stratal division of the lexicon is at best a gradient in psycholinguistic or statistical terms (Hay 2002; Plag and Baayen 2009) and at worst non-existent in structural terms (see Chapter 27). We will therefore not frame our discussion in stratal terms.

9.3 ALLOMORPHY

As defined in Chapter 2, allomorphs are phonologically distinct variants of a morpheme that occur in complementary phonological environments. The cases in (1b) show, however, that under a wider definition, allomorphs may also occur in free variation. Furthermore, we will see that different allomorphs of the same affix may also be morphologically conditioned.

The examples in (1c) to (1g) illustrate that allomorphy in English derivation is often observable with bases, but affixal allomorphy may also occur, as shown in (2). In the following we will first deal with base allomorphy, then turn to affix allomorphy. As mentioned in Chapter 2, there are also elements, what we have called extenders, whose status as part of the affix, or as part of the base, or as part of neither, is not entirely clear. In the former case, we would treat these cases as base allomorphy, in the second as affix allomorphy, and in the third we would need a new kind of category, probably similar to what has been called a 'linking element' with German and Dutch compounds. We will discuss extenders in Section 9.3.3.

9.3.1 Base allomorphy

Different kinds of more or less systematic base allomorphy can be distinguished. We will briefly introduce them here and discuss the more intricate ones in greater detail in the sections to follow.

9.3.1.1 *Prosodic restrictions and adjustments*

Prosody becomes relevant when morphological categories impose prosodic restrictions on their derivatives. These restrictions can have two kinds of consequences. First, the restrictions may be satisfied by choosing only those bases which meet the relevant criteria. For example, for nominalizations in *-al* only those verbs that end in a stressed syllable can be bases, such that *-al* derivatives end in a trochee (*arríval, refúsal*). Simplifying somewhat, the suffix *-ize* allows only bases that end in a trochee, or, under specific circumstances, end in a dactyl (*rándomize, hóspitalize*). This kind of selectional restriction will be dealt with in Section 9.7.

The second possible consequence of prosodic restrictions may be that in order to satisfy the restrictions, certain adjustments are made, so that the derivative fits the restrictions, but does so at the cost of a loss of phonological transparency, that is by sacrificing some of the phonological identity of the base. The most widely discussed adjustment comes under the label of stress shift and concerns patterns in which base and derivative differ concerning which syllable(s) carry stress. Stress shift is thus basically a consequence of some stress-related prosodic restriction imposed on the derivatives of a particular morphological category and generally happens only in those cases where the restriction is not trivially satisfied anyway. For example, *-ity* is said to be stress-shifting, but in fact shifts stress only in those cases where the stress does not end up on the antepenult syllable of the derivative anyway (cf. *prodúctive • productívity* versus *inténse • inténsity*).

Another way of satisfying prosodic constraints is the insertion of phonological material, or the deletion of phonological material. Both types of solution can be found in English derivational morphology. For example, we find prosodically conditioned epenthesis with adverbial *-ly* (*amaz[ə]dly, suppos[ə]dly*), and prosodically conditioned truncation with *-ize* (*patina* • *patinize, summary* • *summarize*). Truncation and epenthesis will be discussed in more detail in the sections on truncation (Section 9.3.1.2) and on vowel alternations (Section 9.3.1.4).

The problems involved with morphologically-induced stress shift are quite intricate and we will discuss them in greater detail in Section 9.4. In this section we only lay out the most basic properties of this type of alternation. The examples in (3) illustrate stress shift for a number of suffixes. In general, stress shift is restricted to suffixation and is found only with non-native suffixes (but not all non-native suffixes show it). There are instances of stress shift with prefixes, too, such as *ímpious, ímpotent, préface, préfix, prémature* (BrE), *réplicate*, but these are individually lexicalized, and in many cases the sense of the prefix is lost, or the status of the forms as morphologically complex is questionable anyway, as in *ímpetus, préfect, rémedy*. Because these are so unpredictable, we do not deal with them in any detail in this chapter. As we can see in (3), there are suffixes that attract the main stress of the derivative to themselves (such as *-ee* or *-ese*), and suffixes that require a certain syllable of the derivative to carry the main stress.

(3)   a.   -ation: persónifỳ • persònificátion, rándomìze • ràndomìzátion

       b.   -al$_A$: président • presidéntial, súicide • sùicídal

       c.   -ese: jóurnal • jòurnalése, Japán • Jàpanése

       d.   -ity: mónstrous • mònstrósity, prodúctive • pròductívity

Of necessity, imposing a particular main stress position on a different syllable involves the creation of a different prominence pattern as a whole, which raises the question of how the stress distribution in the base relates to the distribution of stresses in the derivative. This is the problem known as 'stress preservation'. In (3c), for example, *journalese* preserves the main stress of the base as a secondary stress in the derivative, while *Japanese* completely destresses the syllable that carries the main stress in the base.

Quite often, the stress pattern imposed on the derived word leads to vowel qualities different from those of the corresponding vowels of the base. For ease of discussion, we will talk about vowel qualities in terms of 'tense' and 'lax', following the terminology of Jakobson *et al.* (1951). The terminology is phonetically obscure (Lass 1976), but no more awkward to use than the alternatives (long/short, checked/unchecked, [±ATR]) and it allows us to keep well-known terms such as 'trisyllabic laxing'. Using this terminology, the schwa in the last syllable of *president* corresponds to a full vowel under *-al* suffixation (*presidential*), and the tense vowel of *explain* corresponds to a schwa in *explanation*, and to the lax vowel /æ/ in *explanatory*. Note also that it is not always possible to assign a given affix unambiguously to the class of stress-shifting suffixes, as the pertinent derivatives may show variable behaviour, as is shown later in this chapter. Table 9.1 summarizes the basic patterns involved in prosodic adjustments.

Table 9.1 Prosodic adjustments: overview

Type of adjustment	Selected affixes concerned	Example
none	-ful, -less, -wise	resourceful, hopeless, cornerwise
selectional restrictions	-al$_N$, -er, -ize	arrival, electioneer, randomize
truncation	-able, -al, -ize	manipulable, liberal, feminize
epenthesis	-ly, -ness	supposedly, markedness
stress shift	-al$_A$, -ation, -ese, -ity	parental, computation, Japanese, partiality

9.3.1.2 *Base truncation*

Base truncation is the name of a phenomenon in which final segments of bases are no longer present in the derivative. Consider the examples in (4).

(4) a. demonstrate ◆ demonstrable, navigate ◆ navigable

   b. philosophy ◆ philosopher, astronomy ◆ astronomer

   c. emphasis ◆ emphasize, summary ◆ summarize

   d. chlorine ◆ chloral, ventriloquy ◆ ventriloqual

   e. Malta ◆ Maltese, China ◆ Chinese

It has been claimed (e.g. by Aronoff 1976) that base truncation concerns the deletion of morphemes, as seems to be the case in (4a), where the suffixation of -*able* seems to trigger the deletion of the verbal suffix -*ate*. Similarly, data such as (4b) suggest the deletion of a suffix -*y*. The facts can, however, also be explained in a generative type of approach by considering both -*ate* and -*able* derivatives, as well as the -*er* formations in (4b), as being derived from bound bases (e.g. Raffelsiefen 2004: 121). Such bound bases could then also be used to account for other kinds of formations (e.g. *toler-ate*, *toler-able*, *toler-ant*, etc.).

A similar analysis applies to cases where inflectional endings from the classical languages are deleted before the addition of derivational endings. Etymologically speaking, this is probably the result of patterns in classical morphology, but it leaves apparently unmotivated truncation in English where the deleted material is neither inflectional nor affixal. Examples are *cerebellum-ar, genera-ic, nebula-ous, nucleus-ar, phenomenon-al, scrotum-al*.

The data in (4c) to (4e) demonstrate that the rhymes of final unstressed syllables can undergo deletion with the suffixes -*ize*, -*al*, and -*ese*. Deletion in (4c) may be analysed as a prosodic optimization strategy, avoiding a stress lapse, that is a sequence of two unstressed syllables, before -*ize*. The exact conditions under which the truncations illustrated in (4c) to (4e) occur are laid out in the chapters where these suffixes are described in detail.

The examples in (4c) to (4e) also nicely show that stress shift is independent of other kinds of morphology–phonology interactions, as all three suffixes can induce base trunca-tion, but they differ in their stress-shifting capacity: *-ize* is generally not stress-shifting, while adjectival *-al* often causes stress to move to the antepenult syllable of the derivative, and *-ese* is auto-stressed.

9.3.1.3 *Syllabification, gemination, and degemination*

As already mentioned in Section 9.2, cohering suffixes form a phonological unit with their host, which entails that syllabification can work across the morpheme boundary, especially if the suffix is vowel-initial. The whole question of syllabification is particularly controversial in English, with disputes in the literature as to where syllable boundaries go and what the proper techniques for discovering them are. Moreover, there is a certain amount of evidence that syllabification and resyllabification may be variable in some words, either from dialect to dialect or from speech-style to speech-style. Claims about resyllabification therefore have to be made with appropriate care and hedging. Nevertheless, there seems to be some degree of agreement, which we will try to exploit in what we say. One such point of agreement is that resyllabification in English derivation is restricted to vowel-initial suffixes. Consonant-initial suffixes generally do not induce resyllabification (but note what was said concerning the behaviour of *-ly* just above), and prefixes generally do not cause resyllabification either, as can be seen with *dis.please* or *mis.teach* that have base-initial aspiration of the plosive, an indi-cation of a preceding syllable boundary. However, some individual prefixed forms, such as *mi.stake, su.burbia* do show resyllabification, but such phonological opacity is often accompa-nied by semantic opacity. In those cases where we do find resyllabification with a prefix and semantic opacity is not involved, resyllabification seems to be favoured in foot-medial envi-ronments, as in $(dì.sa)_{\text{FOOT}}llów$, $(ì.nex)_{\text{FOOT}}périenced$ (Giegerich 1999: 279–80).

In spite of all controversies, it is relatively clear that there are some suffixes where many speakers syllabify a derived word in such a way that a base-final segment then forms the onset of the final syllable of the derived word, as shown in (5).

(5)   irri.t-ate, adver.t-ize, coura.ge-ous, esca.p-ee, ea.t-er, mea.t-y

Where there is a final <er> pronounced /ə ‖ ər/, the /r/ always surfaces as the onset to the next syllable when a vowel-initial suffix follows, whether the support vowel for the /r/ is written and pronounced (as in (6a)) or not (as in (6b)).

(6)   a. cylinderish, disasterish, entering, metering

      b. cylindric, disastrous, entrance, metrical

A related matter is whether base-final sonorants are syllabic in the derivative. As a general tendency, it is the native suffixes that favour the syllabic treatment. What complicates matters further, however, is the fact that even within a given morphological category, syllabification of base-final sonorants is often not uniform. For example, with -*ess*, we find non-syllabic *tigress*, but also syllabic *pantheress*, we find non-syllabic *huntress, paintress, waitress*, but also syllabic *farmeress, speakeress, teacheress*. Formations in -*er* also seem variable, with non-syllabic *fiddler* and *smuggler*, and variably syllabic *bottler* and *meddler*. For -*ous*, we find *disastrous* and *monstrous* alongside syllabic *murderous* and *feverous*. Adjectival derivatives in -*y* also show variability, sometimes even with the same word (*angry, buttery, leathery, wintery/wintry, wriggly*). In sum, it is hard to establish larger generalizations across and within morphological categories beyond those stated above. Most of the alternations are simply lexically governed, with similar words showing a tendency to undergo the same kinds of alternation.

With final nasals, there are other problems. Looking first at examples with a sequence of two nasals, the sequence may be present only in a subset of derivatives with vowel-initial suffixes and not in the base form. Examples are given in (7).

(7) *with* /n/: autumnal, columnar, *columnist, condemnable, condemnatory, condemnation, damnable, damnation, hymnal, *limner, limnology, solemnity, *solemnize

   without /n/: autumn, column, condemn, condemning, damn, damning, hymn, limn, limning, solemn

Final syllabic /m/ is usually resyllabified into the next syllable when the affix begins with a vowel, as in *baptismal, chasmic, orgasmic, phantasmagorical, rhythmic*. According to the *OED* this happens with native adjectival -*y* as in *chasmy* and *phlegmy*. This does not happen, however, before -*ing* (*orgasming*).

Another problem concerning syllabification is gemination and degemination. This problem emerges, for instance, with /l/-final bases that take /l/-initial suffixes. Here we can observe non-uniform behaviour of different suffixes and even of the same suffix with different speakers or at different levels of formality, speech tempo, and so on. In the style represented in pronouncing dictionaries, adverbial -*ly*, for example, geminates with *stalely* and *vilely*, but not with *fully* and *really*, nor with all suffixed bases ending in -*al* (*federally, globally, spiritually*), and variably with, for example *dully* and *wholly* (see Bauer 2001: 82 for more data). If the base ends in a syllabic /l/, no gemination occurs, as shown in *gently, idly, singly*. The suffix -*less*, on the other hand, hardly ever degeminates in this style, substantiating its status as non-cohering (*petalless, pupilless, sealless, soulless*).

9.3.1.4 *Vowel alternations*

There are many derivatives in which one vowel has a quality different from that of the corresponding vowel in the base. We can distinguish different types of phenomena, with the traditional terminology labelling the respective phenomenon being based on what happens to the base vowel when the suffix is added: vowel strengthening, vowel laxing, trisyllabic laxing, trochaic laxing, and vowel epenthesis. We will discuss each in turn.

Example (8) illustrates vowel strengthening, which is a term that refers to a pattern where a reduced vowel of the base corresponds to a full vowel in the derivative. This kind of alternation is usually the consequence of a stress shift to the vowel in question.

(8) at[ə]m • at[ɒ]mic ‖ at[ɑː]mic, tot[ə]m • tot[e]mic, Milt[ə]n • Milt[ɒ]nic ‖ Milt[ɑː]nic
     • Milt[əʊ]nian ‖ Milt[oʊ]nian, aut[ə]mn • aut[ʌ]mnal, manag[ə]r • manag[ɪə]rial ‖
     manag[ɪ]rial, r[ˈɪə]l ‖ r[iːə]l • r[iˈæ]lity

An obvious problem in a derivational approach is to understand which full vowel is chosen, given that the schwa in the base is a vowel that does not contain any information as to which vowel it might turn into under suffixation. The generative literature has proposed many different solutions to the problem, none of them being satisfactory (see Giegerich 1999: ch. 5 for a summary and discussion). The most adequate account seems to be one that makes crucial reference to the orthographic form (see Raffelsiefen 1993: 73–4, Giegerich 1999: ch. 5). In such an approach, the full vowel is realized as suggested by the normal spelling-to-pronunciation mapping of the respective letter, given the prosodic structure of the derivative. This analysis also entails the correct prediction that illiterate speakers have no way of predicting the right quality of the stressed vowel of *atomic* if they only know *atom*. Furthermore, it makes the correct prediction that there will be variation as to the pronunciation of some of the vowels given in (8). Giegerich (1999: 163) reports the results of an experiment in which speakers indeed produced variant forms that satisfied both the constraints of the spelling–pronunciation relation and of the morphological category in question. For example, *Handelian* came out with [iː], [e] or [eɪ] as its stressed vowel.

Let us turn to vowel reduction, which can be viewed as something like the reverse of the vowel strengthening pattern in that the tense vowel or diphthong of the base corresponds to a lax vowel in the derivative. However, the vowel in question is stressed in both base and derivative. This is illustrated in (9):

(9) a. convene • convention, deceive • deception, describe • description, produce • production, retain • retention

     b. destroy • destructive, receive • recipient, reside • residual

     c. deep • depth, five • fifty, thief • theft, wide • width

In (9a) and (9b) we find non-native bases, in (9c) native bases. Although the historical roots of the two patterns are completely different, the analysis for both sets of words can be the same. The phonological alternations are not productive with the kinds of words under discussion, and vowel laxing is therefore best viewed as morphologically and lexically conditioned base allomorphy. Note also that the quality of the lax vowel cannot be straight-forwardly derived from the quality of the tense vowel. Morphological or lexical conditioning is also supported by the fact that the laxing of the vowel is often accompanied by unpredictable behaviour of some of the consonants, as in *width* (where the <d> is variably voiced), and in *deception* and *production* (with an etymologically, but not phonologically, motivated base-final unvoiced plosive in the derivative).

Trisyllabic laxing is the name of a generalization according to which certain classes of derived words require that vowels that are three syllables or more from the end of the word be lax, provided the syllable following the pertinent vowel is unstressed.

(10) a. ser[iː]ne • ser[e]nity, vain • v[æ]nity

b. expl[eɪ]n • expl[æ]natory, comp[iː]te • comp[e]titive

Although trisyllabic laxing has been ascribed the status of a rule in Lexical Phonology and in Chomsky and Halle (1968), its status is somewhat obscure. Thus, it is not clear when it actually applies. Part of the problem is that even within morphological categories that frequently show it, we find variability. This is illustrated in (11) for the suffixes *-ity*, *-cy*, and *-al*.

(11) a. -ity: serene • ser[e]nity, *but* obese • ob[iː]sity, obscene • obsc[e]nity ~ obsc[iː]nity (Wells 2008)

b. -cy: private • pr[ɪ]vacy ‖ pr[aɪ]vacy, *but* pirate • p[aɪ]racy, diplomat • dipl[əʊ]macy ‖ dipl[oʊ]macy

c. -al: nation • n[æ]tional, *but* ceremony • cerem[əʊ]nial ‖ cerem[oʊ]nial

A related phenomenon is trochaic laxing. The observable vowel quality alternations are the same as with trisyllabic laxing, but the environment is different. It concerns the formation of trochaic disyllables, as in *cone* /kəʊn ‖ koʊn/ • c[ɒ]*nic* ‖ c[ɑː]*nic* or *cycle* /saɪkl/ • c[ɪ]*clic*. Again we find that this alternation is lexically specified and highly variable even for single lexical items (see, for example, Collie (2008) on c[aɪ]*clic* ~ c[ɪ]*clic*).

We turn finally to a type of vowel alternation in which zero alternates with schwa, a phenomenon that can be conceptualized as either vowel epenthesis or as allomorph selection. This phenomenon can be observed with *-ness* and with *-ly* (see Miner 1975; Wiese 1996b for details and more data).

(12) a. absorbed • absorb[ə]dness, marked • mark[ə]dness, well-formed • well-form[ə]dness

b. amazed • amaz[ə]dly, marked • mark[ə]dly, supposed • suppos[ə]dly

Table 9.2 Vowel alternations: overview

Type of adjustment	Selected affixes concerned	Examples
vowel strengthening	-an, -ic, -ity	Devonian, satanic, majority
vowel laxing	-ation, -ent, -th	observation, prevalent, depth
trisyllabic laxing	-al , -ory, -ity	criminal, explanatory, profanity
trochaic laxing	-ic	conic
vowel epenthesis	-ly, -ness	markedly, markedness

The pertinent mechanism that triggers epenthesis, or the selection of a different allomorph of the participle ending, makes reference to the foot structure of the base. Derivatives ending in *-ness* and *-ly* are apparently subject to a restriction for bases of more than one syllable to have a trochee before the suffix. This restriction is trivially satisfied in words such as *developedness, polishedness, astonishedly*, or *hurriedly*, and is satisfied in words such as *markedly* through the selection of a particular allomorph of the verbal participle that would not be licensed by the phonology of the verbal base (*mark*[ə]*d-*).

Table 9.2 summarizes the vowel alternations.

Table 9.3 presents a different view of vowel alternations, concentrating on the particular vowels which alternate rather than on the types of morphological process involved. The vowels /ɪə/, /eə/ and /ʊə/ are not included in Table 9.3 because they can all be seen as variants on sequences of vowel and /r/, from which they derive historically. Similarly /ɜː/ is not listed.

9.3.1.5 *Consonant alternations*

There are many kinds of consonant alternation, with some of them being given their own labels, such as velar softening or spirantization. The examples in (13) illustrate velar softening with the suffixes *-ity, -ify, -ize*, and *-ism*.

(13) a. atomic ♦ atomicity, iambic ♦ iambicity, opaque ♦ opacity

b. opaque ♦ opacify, silica ♦ silicify

c. classic ♦ classicize, erotic ♦ eroticize, historic ♦ historicize

d. classic ♦ classicism, historic ♦ historicism, romantic ♦ romanticism

The alternation has been described as a rule according to which a base-final /k/ is realized as /s/ before certain suffixes. It may appear that this rule is basically an assimilation rule, as the suffixes all seem to start with a front vowel. This does, however, not hold for *-ize*. The idea of a neat phonological rule is also called into question by the fact that not all words with base-final /k/ undergo velar softening. Some that do not are listed in (14).

Table 9.3 Alternations between vowels

	ɪ	e	æ	ʌ	ɒ‖ɑː	ʊ	iː	ɑː‖æ	ɔː	uː	eɪ	aɪ	ɔɪ	aʊ	əʊ
ɪ							**Elizabeth** Elizabethan								
e															
æ															
ʌ	**thumb** thimble	**compel** compulsion													
ɒ‖ɑː		**long** length	**coffee** caffeine												
ʊ															
iː	**receive** recipient	**succeed** success	**peace** pacifist	**bleed** blood	**heat** hot										
ɑː‖æ	**master** mistress	**France** French	**class** classify												
ɔː	**think** thought	**broad** breadth	**Gaul** Gallic		**war** warrior; **author** authority			**psalm** psalter							
uː			**root** radical	**moon** month	**school** scholar	**tutorial** tutor									
eɪ	**explain** explicable	**retain** retention	**table** tabular					**glass** glazier	**slay** slaughter	**two** twain					
aɪ	**wide** width						**see** sight								
ɔɪ				**destroy** destruction					**law** lawyer	**choose** choice					
aʊ	**foul** filth								**flower** floral	**doubt** dubious					
əʊ	**gold** gild		**holy** halloween	**no** none	**globe** globular		**Aberdeen** Aberdonian	**ghastly** ghost					**vocal** voice	**vocal** vowel	
ə		**telegraph** telegraphy	**acid** acidic					**particle** particular		**statute** statutory	**able** ability	**shire** Cheshire		**mouth** Portsmouth	**custody** custodian

....

(14)   zinc ♦ zin[k]ify, anarch(y) ♦ anarchism, monarch ♦ monarchism, Masoch ♦ masochism

Plag (2003: 210–12) discusses possible analyses and demonstrates that no principled phono-logical or orthography-based account of these facts is possible. This is because the whole set is etymologically motivated, and the rule does not apply in etymologically irrelevant envi-ronments. As was the case with other alternations discussed above, which words participate is ultimately lexically specified, but one regularity persists into English, namely that bases ending in *-ic*, consistently show the alternation (pace Ohala (1974), who claims that in experi-mental conditions, native speakers do not consistently use velar softening in relevant items that are unfamiliar).

Another consonantal alternation that is quite frequent in English derivation is spirantiza-tion. It is a pattern where base-final /t/ and /d/ in the free base correspond to /s/, /ʃ/ or /ʒ/ in the derivative, and base-final (underlying) /r/ corresponds to /ʒ/. Example (15) illustrates this for some of the morphological categories where the alternation can be found.

(15)   a.   /t/ ~ /s/: diplomat ♦ diplomacy, pirate ♦ piracy, president ♦ presidency

b.   /t/ ~ /ʃ/: equate ♦ *equation, erupt ♦ eruption, president ♦ presidential, protect ♦ protection, radiate ♦ radiation

c.   /t/ ~ /ʒ/: equate ♦ *equation

d.   /d/ ~ /s/: conclude ♦ *conclusive, corrode ♦ *corrosive, persuade ♦ *persuasive

e.   /d/ ~ /ʒ/: conclude ♦ conclusion, erode ♦ erosion, persuade ♦ persuasion

f.   /d/ ~ /z/: corrode ♦ *corrosive, divide ♦ *divisive, divisible, persuade ♦ *persuasive

g.   /r/ ~ /ʒ/: adhere ♦ adhesion, cohere ♦ cohesion

h.   /r/ ~ /s/: adhere ♦ *adhesive, cohere ♦ *cohesive

i.   /r/ ~ /z/: adhere ♦ *adhesion, cohere ♦ *cohesion

j.   /s/ ~ /z/: spouse ♦ *spousal

Note that with /t/, the voicing specification of the segment in question is normally the same in both forms, but not always, as shown by the example in (15c). *Equation* has a voiced frica-tive in some varieties instead of the expected unvoiced one. The reverse voicing patterns are also attested. Voiced /d/ regularly alternates with unvoiced /s/ in *-ive* derivatives, but *persua-sive* is also attested with a voiced base-final fricative, as shown in (15f). As far as we know there is no good description of the variation which clearly exists here, let alone any insight into whether there is any patterning to the variation.

Another alternation concerns suffixes, or allomorphs of suffixes, that have an initial front vowel or glide, such as *-ial*, *-ion*, or *-ure*. They trigger palatalization of the base-final segment, sometimes accompanied by voicing, as shown in (16).

Table 9.4 Velar softening, spirantization and palatalization: overview

Alternation	(Selected) affixes concerned	Examples
velar softening		
/k/ ~ /s/	-ify, -ism, -ity, -ize	silicify, classicism, elasticity, eroticize
spirantization		
/t/ ~ /s/	-y	piracy
/t/ ~ /ʃ/	-ation	eruption
/t/ ~ /ʒ/	-ation	%equation
/d/ ~ /s/	-ive	%conclusive
/d/ ~ /ʒ/	-ation	conclusion
/d/ ~ /z/	-ive	%persuasive
/r/ ~ /ʒ/	-ation	adhesion
/r/ ~ /s/	-ive	%adhesive
/r/ ~ /z/	-ive	%adhesive
/s/ ~ /z/	-al	%spousal
palatalization		
/s/ ~ /ʃ/	-al, -ion	circumstantial, convulsion
/s/ ~ /ʒ/	-ation	precision
/z/ ~ /ʒ/	-ation, -ure	confusion, composure
/t/ ~ /tʃ/	-ure	departure, implicature
/g/ ~ /dʒ/	-y, -ize	analogy, apologize

(16) a. /s/ ~ /ʃ/: circumstance • circumstantial, %erase ~ erasure

b. /s/ ~ /ʒ/: concise • concision, precise • precision

c. /z/ ~ /ʒ/: confuse • confusion, excise • excision, %erase • erasure, expose • exposure

d. /t/ ~ /tʃ/: depart • departure, implicate • implicature, moist • moisture

e. /g/ ~ /dʒ/: analogue • analogy, monologue • monologic

Note that the set of pairs that show a certain alternation can be extremely small and even within the small set there may be variation. For example, *monologize* is attested with both of the alternating sounds. A summary of the alternations discussed so far is given in Table 9.4. The inclusion of a suffix in the table does not mean that all potentially pertinent forms show the respective alternation, but that at least one or two do so.

We should also note the rather unusual alternation between <w> and <v>, which extends to <f(f)> and <v> in proper names: *Shaw • Shavian, Aronoff • Aronovian.*

A quite peculiar set of consonantal phenomena concern certain combinations of nasals with one other consonant. These combinations appear as combinations in certain derived words, but that other consonant is missing from the free base, or from other kinds of derivatives. The phenomenon is restricted to very few words, and is illustrated in (17) through (19). Item (17) concerns the clusters <gn> and <gm>, (18) shows <mn>, and (19) <mb>.

(17)	/n/ or /m/	/n/ or /m/	/gn/ or /gm/
	assign	assignment	assignation
	design	designer	designate
	paradigm	paradigmer	paradigmatic
	sign	signing	signal

(18)	/m/	/m/	/mn/
	autumn	autumnish	autumnal
	hymn	hymnless	hymnic
	solemn	solemnly	solemnize

(19)	/m/	/m/	/mb/
	bomb	bomber	bombastic, bombard
	crumb	crumby	crumbly

A final set of consonantal alternations concerns cases where we find singleton consonants in the derivative that do not surface in the base, as in *Plato* ◆ *Platonic*, *aroma* ◆ *aromatic*. Such extenders raise the question of whether they belong morphologically to the base or to the affix, and they will therefore be dealt with, together with similar pertinent cases in Section 9.3.3.

9.3.1.6 *Classically motivated allomorphy*

There is a set of irregular instances of stem allomorphy inherited from Latin, but apparently used morphologically in English. From the English point of view, these variants are only partly predictable in terms of patterns in the lexicon, some of which have been discussed above. Some examples of such alternations are provided in (20).

(20)	assume	assumption
	conceive	conception
	conjoin	conjunction
	deduce	deduction
	evolve	evolution
	move	motion

To the extent that they involve vowel alternations, these can be seen as special cases of what we might term 'classical ablaut' in English. Here we have instances of vowel change (not infrequently accompanied by consonant change) which reflect the apophony of inflectional systems in the classical languages (mainly Latin), and sometimes the changes between Latin and French. The variation is not motivated in English, and it is probable that these patterns should be seen as part of English etymology rather than as part of English morphology. What we find is that the same historical element arises in several different forms, either because of the phonological changes which have affected it in the transition between the various donor languages, or because of the patterns of apophony in the individual languages. Some examples are provided in (21), with the common etymological elements marked in bold font.

(21)   *Greek* 'bear, carry': sema**phor**e, peri**phery**

       Greek 'work': erg**on**omics, or**gan**, metall**urgy**

       Latin 'sit': **sess**ion, pre**side**, **sed**entary, super**sede**

       Latin 'act': **ag**ent, **ac**tion, intrans**ig**ent

       Latin 'fall': cas**cade**, ac**cid**ent, de**cad**ence

       Latin 'law': **leg**al, **loy**al, privi**lege**

       Latin 'rule': **reg**ular, **rig**orous, di**rect**, **ru**le

       Latin 'take': **cap**ture, con**ceive**, con**cep**tion, re**cup**erate

       Latin 'throw': pro**ject**, e**ja**culate

       Latin 'tip': **apex**, **apic**al

       Latin 'touch': **tac**tile, con**tig**uous, con**tam**inate, **tang**ible

       Latin 'vessel': **vase**, **ves**sel

       Latin 'year': **ann**ual, bi**enn**ial

9.3.1.7 *Base allomorphy: a summary*

In this overview of base allomorphy in English derivation we have seen that there are recurrent patterns of morpho-phonological alternations. Each of these patterns is regular in the sense that it can be described in terms of a systematic correspondence between basic and derived phonological representations. However, it has also become clear that the domains in which the respective alternations can be observed are not easily predictable. Certain groups of affixes may show a particular type of alternation, but the next type of alternation one looks at is unlikely to be found with exactly the same set of affixes. Furthermore, even within a given morphological category, the alternation does not consistently apply to all words that it could apply to, and even individual words may vary across or within speakers. The following chapters will provide much more empirical evidence for these conclusions, when each derivational morphological category is described in detail.

9.3.2 Affix allomorphy

When talking about affix allomorphy in derivational morphology, one faces the general problem of distinguishing allomorphs from morphemes. In other words, a primary consideration is whether two formatives express the same meaning. If that is the case, the two formatives can be considered as two potential allomorphs. Unfortunately, the semantics of many affixes is quite intricate and it is often not straightforward to tell whether one is dealing with two allormorphs of one affix, or with two different affixes. Our decisions are based on large-scale empirical evidence and are as theory-independent as possible.

9.3.2.1 *Suffix allomorphy*

There are many derived words in which the derivative seems to feature a variant of the suffix in question, or where, under an alternative analysis, the base shows a variant form. In many cases, the decision about which analysis is preferable is unclear or even impossible to make. In this section we discuss only the clear cases, that is those suffixes where we can make a case for suffix allomorphy.

Some suffixes have only distinct orthographic variants that do not show any phonetic–phonological distinctness: <able> ~ <ible>, <er> ~ <or>, <ant> ~ <ent>. Their distribution will be discussed solely in the respective chapters. With regard to the real allomorphies, we will see in this general overview that phonological and morphological restrictions are mostly responsible for the distribution of the allomorphs. For full discussion of the details involved in the respective allomorphy, the reader is referred to the individual chapters where these suffixes are treated at length. We first discuss some examples of suffixes whose realization is subject to phonological constraints. These constraints may involve restrictions on the segmental or on the prosodic level.

The suffix *-al* surfaces variably as <ar> or <al>, depending on the phonology of the base. In general, bases that end in an /l/ (or /l/ plus schwa, the latter being truncated) prefer the rhotic variant, as shown in (22). The restriction may also be expressed in prosodic terms as one against identical syllabic constituents filled by a liquid not in a cluster in the derived word. This would also account for the allomorph selection shown in (22b), but this restriction is only variably satisfied (see Raffelsiefen 1999 and Chapter 14 for details).

(22) a. arteriole • arteriolar, corolla • corollar, enamel • enamelar, fibrilla • fibrillar, nodule • nodular, protocol • protocolar

   b. alga • algal versus column • columnal ~ columnar, lamin • laminal ~ laminar

The nominal suffix *-ery* has two variants, <ery> and <ry>. The distribution is prosodically governed, with *-ry* attaching to disyllabic feet, and *-ery* to monosyllabic feet, as shown in (23a) and (23b), respectively. Counterexamples exist, however, as in (23c).

(23)   a. chíckenry, phéasantry, rábbitry

        b. hénnery, píggery, róokery

        c. mónastery, láundry

The nominal suffix *-ation* has the allomorphs *-ation* (*industrialization*), *-cation* (*personifica-tion*), *-ion* (*hyphenation*), *-sion* (*recursion*), and *-tion* (*absorption*). The allomorphs *-ation*, *-cation*, and *-ion* are productive and they exemplify morphologically conditioned allomor-phy: *-ation* attaches to *-ize*, *-cation* to *-ify* (with concomitant vowel laxing), *-ion* to *-ate* (with concomitant palatalization). This is illustrated in (24).

(24)   a. randomize • randomization, verbalize • verbalization

        b. personify • personification, magnify • magnification

        c. carbonate • carbonation, concentrate • concentration

There are also cases in which suffix allomorphy is induced by the suffixation of already suf-fixed words. For example, *-ic* has allomorphs that only emerge if the *-ic* derivative undergoes suffixation by *-ity* or *-an* (in the allomorph *-ian*), following the rules of velar softening and palatalization, respectively, as in *electricity* and *electrician*. The suffix *-ify* has an allomorph /ɪfɪ/ if combined with the pertinent allomorph of *-ation*, as in *magnification, personification*.

9.3.2.2 *Prefix allomorphy*

There are two fundamental types of prefixal allomorphy in English, a type which is based on allomorphy in the classical languages and a type which is based on assimilation which func-tions as a part of English word-formation. This second type has two sub-types (although the phonetic facts are not well described): they are commonly termed obligatory and optional assimilation (e.g. Weber 2002).

    The classical type works with a very few non-native prefixes whose allomorphs are origi-nally borrowed from the donor languages. Typically, these involve prefixes which vary between a final vowel and a final consonant, with the consonant-final prefix occurring prevo-calically (sometimes also before /h/). Some examples are given in (25). (See Chapter 19 for discussion of the instances with *-o-* in neoclassical formations.)

(25)			
	a-sexual	an-hydrous	an-aerobic
		a-historical	
	anti-body	ant-helion	ant-acid
		anti-hero	
	bi-labial		bin-ocular
	dia-chronic		di-optre ‖ di-opter

endo-cardium   end-arteritis
exo-cellular   ex-arteritis
                                exo-arteritis
hypo-dermic   hyp-aesthesia ‖ hyp-esthesia
                                hypo-allergenic

With the prefix *in-* we have a case of so-called 'obligatory' assimilation. The negative prefix *in-* displays assimilation with a following labial consonant (*impossible, immature, imbalance*). With a following /r/ or /l/, the writing system sees an assimilation of the final nasal of the prefix to the following sonorant, but phonetically the nasal is deleted: *irrelevant* /ɪreləvənt/, *illegal* /ɪliːgəl/. Before a vowel, /h/, or any other alveolar consonant, the form of the prefix is *in-* /ɪn/. This is usually seen to be the limit of the obligatory assimilation, but this takes no account of the fact that the prefix can also occur before a labio-dental (*infrequent*), before a post-alveolar (*injudicious*), before a velar (*incautious*). The *in-* prefix appears not to occur before a dental ([θ, ð]). In these cases, the facts of variation are unfortunately unclear, except that it is clear that there is variation. Either the nasal can stay unassimilated as [n], or it can become assimilated to the point of articulation of the following consonant ([ɱ], [ɲ], [ŋ]), or there can be a double articulation.

The instances of so-called obligatory assimilation are 'obligatory' largely in as much as the assimilation is expected to be marked in the orthography. However, in COCA we find examples like *inbelief* (see discussion in Chapter 17) which suggest that the orthographic obligatoriness may not be automatic.

The kind of assimilation before labiodentals, post-alveolars, and velars is like the optional assimilation we find with *un-*. There is no orthographically sanctioned assimilation of the final <n> of *un-*, but the /n/ may be assimilated to the place of articulation of any following consonant, as in *unbelievable, unfavourable, unthinking, unjust, unusual, unconscious, unwanted*. Whether the rates of assimilation and the factors influencing assimilation (formality, speech tempo, regional dialect, etc.) are the same for *incautious* and *unconscious* is not clear.

The prefix *en-* and the neoclassical element *syn-* both show orthographically-licensed assimilation before bilabials (*emplane, symbiosis*), but *en-* does not before /r/ or /l/ (*enlist, enroll*), and *syn-* does not seem to be found in relevant environments. The historical Latin prefix *con-* in words of Latin origin behaves like negative *in-* (*condemn, compel, collate, correct*), but is no longer recognizable as an English prefix. The Latin prefix *ad-*, no longer a prefix in English, has an even wider range of forms.

There are a few other cases of assimilation involving prefixes, but they are not systematic, and are variable, and can be found in places where there is no morphological boundary or a word boundary. They include *mi[z]*anthropy,* *mi[ʃ]*chance,* *mi[ʃ]*shapen*.

9.3.3 Extenders

Many derived words are characterized by seemingly meaningless formatives that occur between bases and particular suffix allomorphs. We have introduced the term extender for these elements (see Chapter 2.3.2). Some examples are collected in (26). The examples in (26a) show extenders directly on a base, those in (26b) extenders on what might be analysed as other extenders. This is done merely for the sake of clarity, rather than to make a strong morphological claim. The sequences of extenders in (26b) could just as easily have been analysed as single, longer extenders.

(26) a.	*extender*	*suffixes affected*	*examples*
	-at-	-ic, -ism, -ure	phlegmatic, lymphatism, signature
	-c-	-able, -ation, -ism, -y	applicable, justification, witticism, chieftaincy
	-e-	-an, -ous	Caesarean, gaseous
	-i-	-al, -an, -ary, -ation, -er	tutorial, grammarian, presidentiary, distanciation, hosier
	-in-	-al, -ation	attitudinal, pagination
	-it-	-ation, -ive, -ize, -or, -ure	competition, sensitive, sensitize, competitor, divestiture
	-l-	-ese	Congolese
	-n-	-ese, -ic, -ism, -ist, -ize	Balinese, Platonic, Platonism, tobacconist, Platonize
	-od-	-ic	spasmodic
	-s-	-ation	recursion
	-t-	-eer, -ic, -ism, -ist, -ize, -ure	muleteer, dramatic, egotism, dramatist, dramatize, mixture
	-u-	-al, -ous	processual, sensuous
	-ul-	-ar	cellular
b.	*extender*	*extender*	*examples*
	-c-	-at-	sensificatory
	-it-	-i-	dietitian
	-n-	-i-	Torontonian
	-v-	-i-	Peruvian

Two main questions emerge from such data: where does the extender belong, and what kinds of generalizations are possible as to when which extender occurs? We will deal with each question in turn.

Especially in the early generative literature (e.g. Chomsky and Halle 1968; Aronoff 1976), there are attempts to solve the segmentation problem by treating the extender as part of the base and devising a number of deletion or truncation rules to derive the attested shape of the derivatives. As pointed out, for example, by Szymanek (1985), such attempts fail to provide an accepted methodology to arrive at a convincing theory-independent account of the allomorphy. For example, the postulation of a stem *presidenti-* may nicely give us *presidential* when *-al* is attached, but this solution necessitates the deletion of the extender in other formations (e.g. *presidentship*). Even worse, the base *sense* takes an extender *-it-* in *sensitive* but *-u-* in *sensual*, so the bases are not necessarily consistent in which extender they take. Similar arguments hold for other extenders in other morphological categories. In the chapters that follow we discuss for each morphological category the status of potential extenders. In most cases, it is impossible to come up with a clear answer to the segmentation question, but sometimes distributional patterns can be used to justify a particular analysis independently.

Let us turn to the second question, the predictability of occurrence. Very often, extenders are found with forms borrowed from Latin or Greek, and as such, English has inherited only a limited number of extenders, often recurrent across morphological categories. Also due to these historical roots in loan words, the appearance of extenders is largely lexically governed and not predictable. For example, it is not evident from a present-day English perspective why *aroma* takes an extender when suffixed by *-ize* (*aromatize*), while *patina* does not (*patinize*). There are, however, certain pockets of regularity that can be either phonologically or morphologically characterized. Thus, with the exception of *doctor* and *pastor*, agent nouns in *-or* generally take the extender *-i-* when suffixed with *-al* (*ambassadorial, appressorial, directorial, editorial, fornicatorial, narratorial, professorial, procuratorial, proprietorial, senatorial*). Such patterns, where existent, will be identified in the descriptions of individual morphological categories in the chapters to follow.

9.4   PROSODY

As already mentioned, many suffixes impose a particular prosodic structure on their derivatives. In other words, many morphological categories are characterized not only by their members sharing a specific affix, but also by sharing a specific prosodic structure. In order to satisfy the restrictions imposed by such structural templates, derivatives often show phonological characteristics that differ from that of their bases. In the previous sections we have already seen that these characteristics may concern stress shifts, truncation, vowel alternations, or consonant alternations. In this section we will have a closer look at allomorphies that have their roots in prosodic adjustments. As mentioned above, prosodic adjustments can be made through stress shift, or through truncation or epenthesis. We have already discussed the latter two by way of examples from *-ize, -ness*, and adverbial *-ly*, and will concentrate on stress adjustments in this section.

9.4.1 Auto-stressed affixes

Auto-stressed affixes are characterized by the fact that each of them carries a specific stress: either primary or secondary. This can happen with prefixes and suffixes. As follows from general English stress rules, tense vowels and diphthongs carry stress by default (at least secondary stress). Affixes with such vowels predictably carry secondary stress, as is the case with, for example, the suffixes *-ate, -ite, -oid*, and *-ize*, or the prefixes *de-, post-*, and *pre-*. In other words, there is nothing morphological about this stress-behaviour. However, there are also affixes that may carry secondary or primary stress without there being a purely phonological reason. We will first discuss the pertinent prefixes, then the suffixes.

9.4.1.1 *Prefixes*

A closer look at prefixes such as *dis-, in-*, or *mis-* reveals that their stress behaviour is variable and seems to be influenced by the base to which they attach. Thus, for all three prefixes we find unstressed, secondarily stressed, and main stressed attestations. This is shown in (27):

(27) a. *unstressed*: disown, ingenious, immobile, mistake, misanthropist

b. *secondary stress*: disallow, disendow, illegitimate, inconsistent, mispronounce, missell, misname

c. *main stress*: disparate, indolent, infamous, misfit

All three prefixes have secondary stress as their default, but two patterns emerge with regard to the unstressed and secondarily stressed variants. The prefixes *dis-* and *in-* are unstressed when adjacent to a main stress, which can be interpreted as a stress clash effect. Words with main stress on these two prefixes are very rare and involve words with bound bases. The prefix *mis-*, in contrast, rarely occurs unstressed or main stressed, and if so, only in words with bound bases. Thus, *mis-* is not subject to stress clash repair.

The polysyllabic prefixes, such as *anti-, hyper-, mini-*, or *semi-* seem to variably occur either with a primary stress (*ánticline, hýpertext, mínivan, sémigloss*) or with a secondary stress (*ànticlóckwise, hỳperáctive, mìni-róundabout, sèmifínal*). If they occur with primary stress, the stressed positions of the base are preserved (as secondary stresses).

9.4.1.2 *Suffixes*

Apart from suffixes that are secondarily stressed due to their segmental phonological makeup, there are some suffixes that are main-stressed. The list of pertinent suffixes is rather short:

-*ana*, -*ee*, -*eer*, -*ese*, -*esque*, -*ette*, -*teen*. In Caribbean and IrE, the suffix -*ize* is also main-stressed. The suffix -*ess* may be stressed in some words, for example (variably) in *stewardess*, but is usually not stressed (*goddess*, *tigress*). Another candidate for the status of main-stressed suffix is the suffix -*ation*, particularly with its allomorphs -*ation* and -*cation*, but if we take all its allomorphs into consideration, that is, including -*ion*, which attaches, for example, productively to verbs in -*ate*, the best analysis seems to be the one that says that -*ation* derivatives have their stress on the penultimate syllable (*hyphenátion*, *convérsion*). The suffix is therefore better classified as stress-shifting, and will be treated in Section 9.4.2.

The obvious question with the auto-stressed suffixes, phrased in procedural terms, is what happens to the stresses of the bases when the stress shifts to the suffix. In general, we can observe stress preservation, that is, what is a stressed syllable in the base is also a stressed syllable in the derivative, with the complication that primary stress is demoted to secondary. This is illustrated in (28a). However, we also observe (sometimes variably) non-preservation of stress with at least some of the suffixes, as shown in (28b) for -*ana*, -*ee*, and -*ese*.

(28) a. Hóllingworth ◆ Hòllingworthiána, cóntact ◆ còntactée, áuction ◆ àuctionéer, Américan ◆ Amèricanése, Chómsky ◆ Chòmskyésque, lémon ◆ lèmonétte

b. Níxon ◆ Nixòniána, Thómpson ◆ Thompsòniána, invést ◆ ìnvestée, emplóy ◆ employée ~ èmployée, Japán ◆ Jàpanése, Táiwán ◆ Tàiwanése

In Section 9.4.3 we will have a closer look at stress-preservation and the principles that govern it.

9.4.2 Stress-shifting affixes

There are quite a number of morphological categories that produce a relatively fixed prosodic output in their derivatives. Affixation with these categories then necessarily involves a complex relationship between the base and the derivative in all those cases where the base, as part of the derivative, does not satisfy the prosodic restrictions imposed by the affix. From a procedural perspective, the affixes in question are capable of shifting the stress as found in the base to a position different from where the stress is in the base. It is only the suffixes that productively induce such prosodic adjustments in English.

We can distinguish between different kinds of stress-shifting suffixes, sometimes referred to as strong, weak, and long retractors (Liberman and Prince 1977; Hayes 1982). In this terminology, 'retraction' refers to the movement of stress away from the end of the word. The term is not restricted to morphologically complex words, but, as we will see, it is evident that retraction is often dependent on the morphological structure. We restrict our discussion to morphologically complex words, where strong retractors are suffixes that force the stress of the derivative always to end up on the same syllable counting from the word end, that is either on the antepenultimate, or on the penultimate syllable, irrespective of the syllabic structure of the syllables involved. For example, -*ation* derivatives all have stress on the penultimate syllable, irrespective of the syllabic structure. Examples of strong retraction, including -*ation* derivatives, are given in (29).

(29) a. -ation: cohésion, conventionalizátion, expectátion, personificátion, starvátion

      b. -ity: absúrdity, acceptabílity, obésity, productívity

Weak retraction is a pattern that is characterized by the stress position being co-determined by the weight of the penultimate syllable. In weak retraction, if the penult is heavy, stress falls on the penult, and if the penult is light, stress falls on the antepenult. In (30) we provide examples with suffixes that are supposedly weak retractors, among which we often find bound bases whose stress pattern is hard to discern independently anyway. In such cases the notion of stress shift is somewhat inappropriate. Furthermore, counterexamples to the proposed patterns can be found, as demonstrated for -*oid* in (30d). Other productive suffixes that show weak retraction (often variably, though) are the adjectival ones, -*ary*, -*ate*, -*ative*, -*atory*, -*ile*, -*ory*, and -*ose* (see further Chapter 14), and nominal -*ary*, -*ory*, -*ose*. Note that with polysyllabic suffixes the picture becomes more complicated, as the syllable whose weight is assumed to be decisive for stress assignment may no longer be the penultimate, but the antepenultimate, see (30e).

(30) a. -ide: cýanide peróxide

      b. -ine: elephántine, ívorine, labyrínthine, víctorine

      c. -ite: ánnamite, archimándrite, molýbdenite, sélenite

      d. -oid: archándroid, méteoroid, *but* bénz[iː]oid, Cáledonoid

      e. -ary: eleméntary, probátionary, státionary

Long retraction refers to words whose stress ends up on the third syllable before the suffix. This is illustrated in (31) for the adjectival suffix -*ory*. It seems, however, that such cases are best analysed as simple cases of stress preservation (see also Liberman and Prince 1977: 277).

(31) antícipatory, artículatory, hallúcinatory, manípulatory, stípulatory

Also with long retraction, the same suffix is able to show different kinds of behaviour, sometimes even with the same word, for example *compénsatory* (weak retraction) ~ *cómpensatory* (long retraction), *respíratory* (weak retraction) ~ *réspiratory* (long retraction), *eleméntary* (weak retraction, see (30e)) ~ *dísciplinary* (long retraction). Such data call into question the neat classification of suffixes into the various classes.

A particularly intricate case of stress-shift behaviour is the suffix *-able*, which nicely show-cases the complexities of the matter, as illustrated in (32) and (33). In (32a) and (32b) we find cases of the most prevalent pattern, which is for there to be no stress shift, no matter whether we have iamb-final bases (32a) or trochee-final bases (32b). In (32c) we illustrate cases of lexicalized stress shifts with bases that normally would not undergo stress shift.

(32)   a.   abrídge • abrídgeable, abúse • abúsable, besmírch • besmírchable, desíre • desírable, decláre • declárable

       b.   álter • álterable, ánswer • ánswerable, búdget • búdgetable, bálance • bálanceable, chállenge • chállengeable

       c.   *admíre • ádmirable, *compáre • cómparable, *prefér • préferable

Only with bases of three or more syllables that do not end in an iamb or a trochee do we find more regular stress shifts with *-able*. There are three different patterns, given in (33). The first set of words has bases that end in a dactyl. These words do not show stress shift. If, in contrast, the antepenultimate syllable of the derivative is heavy, we find two different patterns. One subset of words seems to stress shift categorically (33b), the other variably (33c).

(33)   a.   jét.ti.so.na.ble, mó.ni.to.ra.ble, ré.gis.te.ra.ble

       b.   al.lo.cá.ta.ble, a.ro.ma.tí.za.ble, ar.ti.cu.lá.ta.ble, ca.te.go.rí.za.ble, com.mer.cia.lí.za.ble, cul.ti.vá.ta.ble, do.cu.mén.ta.ble, ex.tra.dí.table, ma.ni.pu.lá.ta.ble, pre.di.cá.ta.ble

       c.   á.na.ly.za.ble ~ a.na.lý.za.ble, cér.ti.fy.a.ble ~ cer.ti.fý.a.ble, drá.ma.ti.za.ble ~ dra.ma.tí.za.ble, i.dén.ti.fi.a.ble ~ i.den.ti.fí.a.ble, í.te.mi.za.ble ~ i.te.mí.za.ble, ló.ca.li.za.ble ~ lo.ca.lí.za.ble, per.só.ni.fy.able ~ per.so.ni.fý.able, ré.cog.ni.za.ble ~ re.cog.ní.za.ble

Very often, the stress-shifted derivatives in productive morphological categories are lexicalized exceptions, as we saw with *-able*. Another example of this is *-ate*, which has been claimed to be a strong retractor in spite of the many exceptions (e.g. Liberman and Prince 1977: 275), but the evidence from neologisms strongly suggests that stress shift is generally not productive (Plag 1999). The same holds for *-ify*, and *-ize* (Plag 1999), which have sometimes been treated as stress-shifting (e.g. Zamma 2003). Kettemann's (1988) results demonstrate, however, that even those suffixes that do not productively shift the stress may induce stress shifts for very narrowly defined subsets of similar words, as shown by an experiment in which subjects had to attach *-ify* to bases ending in /ɪd/, and frequently created stress-shifted forms in obvious analogy to the stress-shifted lexicalized forms *humídify* or *solídify*.

As the above examples have shown, in spite of the many claims to the contrary, it is often not clear which suffixes belong to which of the four classes, non-stress-shifting, weak retractor, strong retractor, long retractor. Many suffixes show stress shift for a subset of words, and no stress shift, or a different kind of stress shift, for other words even though the differently treated bases have the same prosodic structure. Thus, Liberman and Prince's (1977: 276) statement still holds that 'the emerging picture is that retraction in complex words is largely controlled by suffix type, but admits of considerable lexical variation, particularly among the less productive morphological categories'.

This leads us to another source of apparent irregularities in the prosodic behaviour of derivatives, the relationship of derivatives to other derivatives. Traditional analyses of prosodic alternations have concentrated on the relationship between the less complex form, that is, the base, and the more complex form, the derivative. However, if we also take other complex forms into consideration as potential bases, many apparent exceptions turn out to be in regular correspondence with patterns in those other potential bases. Thus, stress is not shifted in *humídify* if, instead of the base *húmid*, we take the corresponding *-ity* derivative to be the relevant related form: *humídify • humídity* (cf. *solídify • solídity*). Similarly, the variable stress of *démonstrable ~ demónstrable* may be a consequence of the competing related forms *démonstrate* and *demónstrative*. This kind of approach, or the phenomenon that it tries to capture, has come under various names in the literature (with variant underlying theoretical assumptions), namely 'stem selection' (Raffelsiefen 2004: 95, with many more such examples and explicit analyses), 'paradigm uniformity' (e.g. Steriade 2000), 'multiple correspondence' (e.g. Burzio 1998), or the 'split-base' effect (Steriade 1999).

9.4.3 Stress preservation

As mentioned earlier, prosodic alternations not only pose the question of whether the derived word is stressed on the same syllable as the base, but also raise the problem of where the derivative is main stressed. There is also the problem of what happens to the main stressed syllable of the base when main stress is shifted to another syllable under suffixation. This problem has been given the name of stress preservation, but we will see that this derivational terminology and perspective is not always helpful, as it narrowly focuses on the relationship between the less complex base and its more complex derivative. In contrast, one can approach the problem from a more general perspective of lexical relatedness, according to which there are constraints on how the prosody of derived words must correspond to the prosodies of different kinds of related word (see also Chapter 23.2).

In cases of stress shift, we frequently find a pattern according to which the primary stress of the base corresponds to a secondary stress in the derivative. Such cases are illustrated in (34) for *-ation* and *-ity*.

(34)   a. -ation: ábdicate • àbdicátion, mágnify • màgnificátion, rándomìze • ràndomizátion

      b. -ity: degrádable • degràdability, sensátional • sensàtionálity, táciturn • tàcitúrnity

However, we also find patterns in which stress preservation is systematically absent, as in (35). Failure to preserve stress can be generally observed if the syllable in question is immediately adjacent to the derivative's main stress. The examples in (35) show both preservation and lack of preservation.

(35)   a. -ese: Cantón ‖ Cánton ◆ Càntonése versus Japán ◆ Jàp[ə]nése

      b. -ity: degrádable ◆ degràdabílity versus canónic ◆ càn[ə]nícity, cómplex ◆ c[ə]mpléxity

      c. -an: Ámazon ◆ Àmazónian versus phonétic ◆ phòn[ə]tícian, Apóllo ◆ Àpp[ə]lónian

As noted by many authors, there is also a third pattern, comprising forms that do not conform to either of the above two patterns. Such forms preserve stresses (at least variably) in spite of the fact that these stresses are adjacent to a main stress in the derivative. This is shown in (36). In accordance with perhaps most of the literature, we see reduction to schwa as evidence for unstressedness, a full vowel as evidence for at least some degree of stress. Those analysts who would not assign stress to the vowels in question have to deal with the question of variable vowel qualities instead. The problem remains essentially the same.

(36)   auth[e]ntícity, cre[eɪ]tívity, exp[e]ctátion, exp[ɔ:]rtátion, f[æ]scístic, impl[ɑ: ‖ æ]ntation

Notably there is no aberrant behaviour in the opposite direction, that is, there is no complete loss of stress when not adjacent to a main stress. This fact, among many others, shows that prosodic faithfulness is an important principle in English derivational morphology that is overwritten only by specific requirements of morphological categories, or by strong intervening phonological principles, such as the avoidance of stress clashes (see, e.g. Pater 2000).

The many lexical exceptions to stress preservation can be understood better if we take frequency into account. Collie (2008) investigates a corpus of 198 five- and six-syllable complex words with three pre-tonic syllables and various suffixes (taken from Jones 2003), in which regular stress preservation would have been expected to occur on the second syllable counting from the left, as in *anticipation* or *sensationality*. The majority of the forms indeed show the predicted behaviour, but about one-quarter have variable stress preservation (*authórity* ◆ *àuthoritárian* ~ *authòritárian*), and an additional 4 per cent are listed with stress on the first syllable (*repátriate* ◆ *rèpatriátion*). An investigation of the frequencies of the bases and derivatives involved reveals that a higher frequency of the base and a lower frequency of the derivative favour stress preservation. In other words, stress preservation is the default for productive derivation, and failure to preserve stress correlates with lexicalization.

9.5 HAPLOLOGY

In this section we discuss a family of rather widespread suffixal phenomena that are all characterizable by haplology, that is by the avoidance of identical phonological structure in morphologically complex words, usually coming about by the addition of a suffix. Where we find haplology it typically arises in a particular morphological environment, not just a phonological environment: that is, the particular affixes involved are important for the application (or non-application) of haplology. We have already discussed one pertinent case, the allomorphy of the suffix *-al*, but the phenomenon is much more common, as the data in (37) to (39) show. There are three different sorts of haplological effect, the first of which is the choice of a particular allomorph as in (37). The only suffix that has this possibility in store to handle a haplology effect seems to be adjectival *-al*, which we have already discussed in Section 9.3.2.1. We repeat the pertinent data in (37) for convenience.

(37) arteriole ◆ arteriolar, corolla ◆ corollar, enamel ◆ enamelar, fibrilla ◆ fibrillar, nodule ◆ nodular, protocol ◆ protocolar

The second type of effect is the phonological adjustment of the base, which is much more common, as shown in (38a). The constraint against identical onsets leads to truncation with *-ess* and *-ize*. This constraint may interact with other prosodic constraints, for example with those on foot structure. A comparison of the data in (38a) with those in (38b) shows, for example, that identical onsets in *-ize*-formations are not repaired with trochaic bases, but only with dactylic ones (see Plag 1998, 1999 for a full analysis).

(38) a. adventure ◆ adventuress (*adventu.re.ress), murderer ◆ murderess (*murde.re.ress), sorcerer ◆ sorceress (*sorce.re.ress), feminine ◆ feminize (*femi.ni.nize), metathesis ◆ metathesize (*metathe.si.size)

    b. classicize, canonize, candidize, mirrorize, potentize, strychninize

Finally, there is the simple impossibility of attaching the respective suffix if the morphological category does not allow the kinds of adjustments that would be necessary to avoid the offending sound sequence. This is illustrated in (39) for *-age*, nominal *-al*, *-ee*, *-eer*, *-ish*, and *-ity*. Of these, the suffixes *-age*, nominal *-al*, *-eer*, *-ette*, *-ish* do not allow their derivative to end in a syllable with the same onset and coda, which leads to lexical gaps (39a). Derivatives in *-ity* do not allow the same onsets in the antepenult and penult (39b), and derivatives in *-ee* may not have a high front vowel immediately preceding the suffix (39c).

(39) a. *lar.geage, *we.dgage, *con.cea.lal, *in.ha.lal, *in.stil.lal, *rebe.lal, *re.vea.lal, *re.vol.ve.reer, *mor.ta.reer, *close.tette, *carpe.tette, *fi.shish, *mu.shish, *rub.bi.shish

b. *can.di.di.ty, *sor.di.di.ty, *splen.di.di.ty versus flo.ri.di.ty, hu.mi.di.ty, ra.pi.di.ty

c. *carryee, *freeee, *pityee, *seeee

Obviously, the force of an argument based on apparently non-existent forms depends largely on the assumed productivity of the respective suffix and the size of the sample, but it seems that for the categories mentioned a convincing case for lexical gaps can be made. At the other end of the scale, many of the attested forms showing haplology effects may be lexicalized, but the evidence from low frequency forms and neologisms shows that haplology is a pervasive and complex phenomenon, since it undoubtedly occurs productively in a number of morphological categories.

9.6 PROSODIC MORPHOLOGY

The term 'prosodic morphology' is used for morphological categories that are expressed predominantly or exclusively through prosody, that is by manipulations of, or restrictions on, the metrical or syllabic structure of the potential derivatives. This is, for example, the case with clippings, with certain types of hypocoristics, with blends, and with expletive insertion. We will briefly discuss each of these; for more detailed analyses the reader is referred to Chapters 18, 19, and 20.

9.6.1 Clippings

With clippings the relationship between a derived word and its base is expressed not by adding material (for example in the form of a suffix or prefix), but by the conspicuous and significant absence of phonetic material in the derived word. In (40a) this is illustrated for first names, in (40b) for common nouns.

(40) a. Pat ◆ Patricia, Pete ◆ Peter, Lon ◆ Alonzo, Trish ◆ Patricia

b. fab ◆ fabulous, fax ◆ facsimile, exec ◆ executive, lab ◆ laboratory, pro ◆ professional, ump ◆ umpire

Clippings have often been claimed to be irregular and highly idiosyncratic (for example, Dressler and Merlini Barbaresi 1994; Dressler 2000), but more recent work, for example Lappe (2007), has shown that such claims are ill-founded. Lappe's analysis of large sets of data reveals that there are severe restrictions on both the prosodic shape of clippings and the phonological relationship between the clipping and its base.

Thus, most clippings are exactly one syllable long, no matter how long the base word is. Furthermore, there is a strong tendency to have both onset and coda filled, and an obligatory requirement to have a heavy rhyme, with the effect that forms with only a consonant and lax vowel, or with only a long vowel or diphthong are ungrammatical (for example (*M[e] ♦ *Melanie*, or *I ♦ *Ida*).

The specific restrictions concerning the faithfulness of the clipping to its base allow for some variation, a fact that has undoubtedly contributed to the impression that clippings are idiosyncratic in their behaviour. For instance, the phonological material for name clippings may come from, or 'anchor to', either the first syllable or from a stressed syllable (cf. *Pat* ♦ *Trish* ♦ *Patrícia*, *Gail* ♦ *Ábigàil*). The surviving material in common noun clippings, in contrast, is overwhelmingly taken from the first syllable. If a common noun base starts with an unstressed syllable followed by a stressed syllable, two syllables (instead of only one) can make it into the clipping, with no stress shift (*celéb* ♦ *celébrity*, *exéc* ♦ *exécutive*).

Exceptions to these prosodic patterns are extremely rare (e.g. *Ron* ♦ *Aaron*), but these cases often involve clippings that are homophonous to regular clippings of other bases (cf. *Ron* ♦ *Ronald*). The surviving material consists of contiguous segments starting from the left edge of the relevant syllable. The heavy rhyme constraint explains why, especially with lax vowels, the first consonant of the following syllable also survives (as in *Pat* ♦ *Pa.tri.cia*): it makes the syllable of the derivative heavy. The segmental contiguity requirement is sometimes violated, as shown in forms such as in *Ike* ♦ *Isaac* or *Floss* ♦ *Florence*, where segments are skipped. Notably, skipping is systematic with derivatives that would otherwise end in /r/ (*Flor*).

9.6.2 Hypocoristics in *-ie*

This suffix is variably spelled <ie> or <y>, sometimes even <ey> and <ee>, and we use *-ie* as shorthand for all orthographic variants. Derivatives with this suffix are mostly disyllabic with stress on the first syllable, followed by an unstressed syllable (*Ándie*, *Jénny*, *Láurie*). This means that there must be serious prosodic and segmental adjustments with very many potential base words. As was the case with clippings of proper names, in *-ie* derivatives, material from the first syllable (*Australian* ♦ *Aussie*) or from a stressed syllable can survive (*umbrella* ♦ *brollie*, *tobacco* ♦ *baccie*). We also find similar segmental alternations as with clipped names (e.g. *Nathaniel* ♦ *Natty*), which, together with the anchoring facts, suggests that clippings may serve, and frequently do serve, as bases to hypocoristics in *-ie*, instantiating the same constraints and inheriting the same structures, modulo the additional complications that come with the suffixation of *-ie*. One such complication is that there is never a complex onset preceding *-ie*, even if the base has a complex onset in its second syllable (*Andrew* ♦ *Andy*, not *Andry*).

9.6.3 Expletive insertion

The final case of morphology where prosodic units and prosodic restrictions are chiefly responsible for the shape of the derived word is expletive insertion. Its status as a morphological (as against a potentially syntactic) process is somewhat controversial and will be discussed together with its semantics in more detail in Chapter 18.2.7. Here we concentrate on the prosody of the process (see also Hammond 1999: 161–4; Plag 2003: ch. 4 sec. 6). In this type of formation, an expletive is inserted into the base, as shown in (41).

(41)   èco-fucking-nómics
       àtmos-fucking-phére
       emàscu-bloody-láted
       pròpa-fucking-gánda
       hàndy-bloody-cáp
       trànsconti-bloody-néntal
       V̀-bloody-IṔ
       àny-fucking-thíng
       dìm-fucking-wít
       kùng-fucking-fú
       mìd-fucking-wést
       ùr-fucking-báne

The point of insertion of the expletive is governed by the prosodic structure of the base, such that the expletive must be inserted between two feet. This restriction excludes, for example, trochaic disyllables or dactylic trisyllables as potential bases (cf. *Áspen* ◆ **Às-fucking-pen*, *énemy* ◆ **éne-fucking-my* ◆ **é-fucking-nemy*), as the expletive would not have two feet surrounding it. Similarly, the expletive may not appear between an unstressed syllable and a following stressed syllable, as *benígn* ◆ **be-fucking-nígn* or *agénda* ◆ **a-fucking-génda*.

9.7 PHONOLOGICAL SELECTIONAL RESTRICTIONS

There are many suffixes in English that are subject to constraints concerning the kinds of phonological structures possible bases may exhibit. By way of illustration, we look at nominal *-al*, *-eer*, *-en*, and *-ify*. The examples in (42) illustrate a selection of forms in *-al* that are attested in COCA (those that start in one of the first four letters of the alphabet). Apart from *burial* (which, etymologically speaking, contains a different affix), all bases obey the constraint that the suffix only attaches to bases that have their main stress on the final syllable.

(42)   accrual, acquittal, appraisal, approval, arousal, arrival, avowal, bequeathal, bestowal, betrayal, betrothal, burial, carousal, committal, conferral, construal, deferral, demurral, denial, deposal, disbursal

Derivatives in *-eer* that are based on free bases (instead of bound roots) are all derived from bases that end in a trochaic foot, as shown in (43).

(43) allotmenteer, budgeteer, cameleer, canyoneer, concessioneer, conventioneer, envisioneer, imagineer, leafleteer, planeteer, summiteer

The suffix *-en* shows a segmental as well as a prosodic restriction. It only attaches to bases that are monosyllabic (or else end in an iamb) most of them also ending in an obstruent. Consider (44).

(44) awaken, blacken, brisken, broaden, crispen, deepen, lengthen, outen, quicken, ripen, strengthen, swiften, toughen

Finally, the verbal suffix *-ify* is sensitive to foot structure. Derivatives need to end in a dactyl, and given the inability to shift stress or to truncate, this restricts the suffix to three types of bases: those that are monosyllabic (45a), those that end in an iambic foot (45b), and those that end in a trochee that itself ends in /i/ so that the final vowel and the suffix-initial vowel can coalesce (45c).

(45) a. artify, massify, jazzify, sinify, trustify, tubify, youthify

b. bourgeoisify, opacify

c. gentrify, nazify, yuppify

One general question that such phonological restrictions raise is whether they should be formulated in an input-oriented or output-oriented fashion. This question has been discussed in a number of publications (e.g. Plag 1999; Raffelsiefen 1999; Pater 2004), with the general conclusion that there are at least some phenomena where output restrictions are better able to capture the empirical facts, while it seems that all input restrictions can be satisfactorily reformulated as output restrictions.

9.8 SUMMARY

In this chapter we have taken a bird's eye view of a plethora of instances of morphology–phonology interaction and tried to illustrate some general principles that are at work in these interactions. As became clear, semi-regularity or lexical government prevails in this area and variation is all-pervasive. This calls into question the theoretical and psycholinguistic status of many of the generalizations that can be found in the literature and raises the question of how the variability can be accounted for.

Overall, it seems that, very generally speaking, there are conflicting demands that have to be met by derived words in the mental lexicon. On the one hand (and abstracting away from conversion), derivatives, being new or different words, must be different in shape and in meaning from their base, but not too different, so that the relationship between base and derivative is still recoverable. Affixation seems to be a way to achieve this compromise. On the other hand, the words of a morphological category must be sufficiently similar to each other in shape and meaning in order to count as members of the same morphological category; this is already achieved by simply adding an affix, but quite frequently it also involves more intricate relationships between the words, or subsets of the words, of a given morphological category.

The similarity space between bases and their derivatives, and between derivatives of the same category is potentially vast, but not unconstrained, as increasing phonological dissimilarity leads to decreasing cohesion within a category, and to a loss of the consistent pairing of form and meaning that is at the heart of any morphology. Within this similarity space, derived words enter into similarity relationships not only with their respective bases and other members of their own category, but also with members of other categories. This is a crucial mechanism by which much of the variation and semi-regularity emerges that we find in the morpho-phonology of derived words in English.

Other sources of variation are the many lexical idiosyncrasies that come with large-scale borrowing of complex words from other languages, and the diachronic phonological and lexical developments that may affect the relation between form and meaning in complex words.

CHAPTER 10

....

Derived nouns: event, state, result

10.1 PROSPECTUS

In this chapter we discuss derived nouns denoting events, states, results, as well as related semantic categories such as products and means, specifically nouns formed with the suffixes *-ing*, *-ation* (and its variants *-cation*, *-ition*, *-ion*, *-sion*, *-ution*, *-tion*), *-ment*, *-al*, *-ure*, *-ance* (and its variants *-ence*, *-ancy*, *-ency*) and nouns formed by conversion. For ease of exposition in what follows, we will refer to these as event/state/result nouns, although it should be kept in mind that such nouns do sometimes have readings that go beyond events, states, and results. Nouns whose primary function lies in denoting participants in events (e.g. agent, patient) or qualities, collectives, and other abstracts will be treated in subsequent chapters. We begin with the formal properties of the processes in question, including the kinds of bases that undergo affixation or conversion, their syntactic category, their status as native or non-native, free or bound, as well as phonological or prosodic restrictions on bases. We then move on to the range of semantic interpretations available for the different kinds of formation. All examples in this chapter are taken from COCA, unless otherwise specified.

There is, of course, a vast amount of literature on the syntax of English nominalizations, much of it treating deverbal nouns in *-ing* (Lees 1960; Chomsky 1970; Pullum 1991; Yoon 1996), but also other event, state, and result nouns (Grimshaw 1990; Alexiadou 2001; Baker 2003; Heyvaert 2003, among many others). In this volume we are primarily concerned with the phonological and morphological properties of English nominalizations as derived words. We treat their syntactic properties only insofar as we are interested in their potential to reference one or another argument of their base when it is a verb. This largely syntactic literature will therefore not be the subject of further discussion.

10.2 FORMAL CONSIDERATIONS

Derived event/state/result nouns are formed both by affixation and conversion. The vast majority are formed on non-auxiliary verbal bases, although we find occasional formations on adjectives, and even nouns. Non-native verbs are by and large nominalized through affixation processes of varying levels of productivity, while native verbs tend to favour nominalization by conversion. There is, however, some overlap in base type between the two processes. All non-auxiliary verbs, whether of native or non-native origin, have at least a nominalization in *-ing*, and most verbs have one or more other nominalizations as well.

10.2.1 Non-native affixation

The principal non-native affixes for deriving event/state/result nouns are *-al*, *-ance*, *-ment*, *-ation*, and *-ure*. Of these only *-ation* displays a substantial degree of productivity in contemporary English, and this by virtue of prior affixation. We discuss nominalization by *-al*, *-ance*, *-ure*, and *-ment* first, and then look more closely at the more productive *-ation*.

10.2.1.1 *Minimally productive suffixes:* -al, -ance, -ment, *and* -ure

The suffixes *-al*, *-ance*, *-ure*, and *-ment* are largely exemplified by established words in contemporary English and show little productivity. We first discuss the combinatorial properties of these suffixes and then their phonology.

The suffix *-al* attaches to verbs only, a vast majority of them being non-native, with only occasional native bases being attested (e.g. *bequeathal*, *betrothal*). Examples like the following are found in COCA.

(1)   accrual, acquittal, appraisal, approval, betrothal, burial, carousal, committal, construal, deferral, demurral, denial, deposal, disbursal, espousal, observal, portrayal, proposal, rebuttal, recital, recusal, redressal, referral, refusal, rehearsal, removal, renewal, revisal, submittal, survival, transferral, transmittal, traversal, trial, upheaval, withdrawal

The suffix is found in the occasional novel form (e.g. *overthrowal*, COCA). What we cite as the suffix *-ance* covers six different variants, *-ance*, *-ence*, *-ancy*, *-ency*, *-ce* and *-cy*. The distribution is either heavily dependent on the morphology of the base, or else not entirely predictable. The first problem with these variants is the spelling with either <a> or <e>, as in *dependence* versus *resonance*. We consider this largely dependent on etymology and as rather random from the perspective of present-day English, and therefore we use the more frequent <a> in the citation form for this suffix.

The second problem is the variation between the presence or absence of a final *-y*, as in *consistence* versus *consistency*. In general, there seems to be little or no difference between *-y*-full and *-y*-less variants (cf. the synonymous pairs *abundance • abundancy, ascendence • ascendency, consistence • consistency, dependence • dependency, relevance • relevancy*), but some lexicalized pairs do exist that have different meanings (*emergence • emergency, residence • residency*).

The final problem is the presence or absence of *-an-* in the suffix, or, in other words, whether the suffix is realized as *-ce/-cy* or rather *-ance/-ancy/-ence/-ency*. In general, adjectives ending in *-ant* or *-ent* take *-ce/-cy*, while other bases take one (or more) of the other set.

This situation can be analysed in different ways. Apart from an analysis in terms of suffix allomorphy (e.g. *-ance* versus *-ce*), one could also posit bound roots as bases (e.g. *redundancy*). Alternatively we could analyse the alternation as a case of haplology (see Chapter 9.5), such that the non-appearance of *-ant-ance* is accounted for by the avoidance of the repetition of the same phonological string at the end of the nominalized form. Finally, in a paradigmatic approach (see Chapter 23.4) no reference is necessary to where potential morpheme boundaries are. Instead there is the regular correspondence relationship between the morphological categories of *-ant* adjectives with *-ate* verbs and with *-ance* nominalizations.

What confuses matters further is the fact that, perhaps in analogy to the deadjectival formations, the suffix *-y*, if attached to certain words ending in <t>, leads to a final string <cy>. These formations are dealt with in Section 10.2.5 below (see also Chapter 12.2.5 for discussion).

The examples in (2) and (3) illustrate the use of the suffix *-ance*, with the forms in (2) showing *y*-less formations, the ones in (4) the *y*-full formations.

(2)   -ance/-ence: abettance, abhorrence, abidance, ascendance, clearance, compellance, compliance, condolence, disobeyance, divergence, effervescence, endurance, entrance, exfoliance, guidance, hesitance, hindrance, illuminance, impedence, nurturance, observance, occupance, occurrence, performance, quittance, reactance, reminiscence, securance, severance, tolerance, transmittance, utterance, variance, vengeance

(3)   -ancy/-ency: absorbency, ascendency, claimancy, coherency, compliancy, concordancy, concurrency, dependency, deviancy, divergency, dominancy, expectancy, exultancy, hesitancy, inhabitancy, inherency, insistency, irritancy, luxuriancy, occupancy, pendency, persistency, precedency, radiancy, recurrency, repellency, residency, resistancy, retardancy, stagnancy, sufficiency, tendency, transcendency, vacancy

The suffix attaches to adjectives and verbs and, due to the regular correspondence of the pertinent derivatives just discussed, it is often unclear what the base for a given form actually is. Thus, sometimes, a triad of forms in *-ate*, *-ant*, and *-ance/-ancy* is attested (*hesitate, hesitant, hesitancy; alternate, alternant, alternance; participate, participant, participance*), which makes it impossible to decide whether the base of the *-ance* nominal is the verb in *-ate* or the corresponding adjective in *-ant* (or, in fact, a bound root). While most bases are non-native, *-ance* shows a small number of formations on native bases, mostly established forms (*hindrance, riddance*) with only the occasional apparent novel form (*believance, coming outtance*).

The suffix *-ure* attaches to verbs (see (4a)), but is found frequently on bound roots (4b), as well as occasionally on nominal bases (4c). It is occasionally attested with extenders, as in *-at-ure* (*signature, curvature, entablature*), *-it-ure* (*divestiture, penditure*), and *-t-ure* (*mixture*).

(4)   a. -ure *on verbs*: accenture, annexture, closure, composure, contracture, creature, curvature, departure, disclosure, erasure, expenditure, exposure, failure, fixture, flexure, gravure, implicature, jointure, licensure, mixture, orature, pleasure, pressure, procedure, sculpture, seizure, signature, vesture

    b. *-ure on bound roots*: comfiture, culture, embrasure, fissure, furniture, garniture, gesture, investiture, lecture, puncture, rupture, structure

    c. *-ure on nouns*: candidature, architecture, magistrature, portraiture

The suffix *-ment* is primarily deverbal (5a), but appears occasionally on bound bases (5b). Only a few forms are found based on adjectives (5c), or nouns (5d). There is a large majority of non-native bases, but native bases are by no means unusual (e.g. *hangment, hatchment, oddment, settlement, shipment, startlement, unfoldment, upliftment, upsetment, wonderment, worriment, worsenment*).

(5)   a. *-ment on verbs*: abandonment, abasement, abatement, assemblement, assessment, changement, chastisement, citement, commandment, development, disadvantagement, embitterment, emboxment, embracement, englobement, engulfment, evolvement, excitement, extinguishment, fakement, feignment, lodgement, lopment, malignment, management, statement, tracement, trapment, treatment, unfoldment

    b. *-ment on bound roots*: compartment, ornament, rudiment

    c. *-ment on adjectives*: embeddedment, hardyment, insensiblement, oddment, scarcement, surement

    d. *-ment on nouns*: illusionment

As the examples in (1)–(5) illustrate, these non-native nominalizing suffixes appear to have a preference for disyllabic bases, and among the disyllabic bases, for those that consist of an iambic foot. Whether this phonological pattern is actually a restriction on these suffixes, or merely an artefact of the tendency of non-native verbs to display this iambic pattern is difficult to determine.

    The suffix *-ment* can perhaps be taken as illustrative in this regard. The vast majority of its bases consist of an iambic foot: *abatement, abutment, allotment, appeasement, bombardment, enticement, equipment, investment, procurement, regalement, resentment*. Trochaic bases are attested, but far less frequently: *banishment, bafflement, languishment, punishment, ravagement, settlement*. Where it attaches to bases that are longer than two syllables, the first syllable has a tendency to belong to a prefix like *en-* or *dis-*: *entanglement, encouragement, disappointment*. In addition, *-ment* attaches to a number of monosyllabic bases: *movement, pavement, payment, placement, statement*. Interestingly, where it attaches to native bases (see Section 10.2.1.2), they display a variety of prosodic forms, including iambs (*uplíft, upsét*), trochees (*wónder, wórry*), and monosyllabic bases (*hang, ship*), thus suggesting that the overwhelming preponderance of iambic disyllables as bases might be seen as an artefact of the typical stress pattern of non-native verbs.

    Similarly, the suffix *-al* is frequently reported as selecting bases with final stress (e.g. Plag 2003); the sole counterexample to the generalization is the word *burial*, which etymologically speaking does not have the same suffix as, say, *arrival, refusal*. Synchronically, however, this difference is invisible, and *burial* is an exceptional word in the series.

Although the vast majority of forms with these suffixes are established, there are nevertheless some low frequency and novel forms that appear in corpus data. Low frequency formations that are attested with the suffixes *-al, -ance*, and *-ure*, either duplicate the meaning of an existing form (6), or display a nuance of meaning that differs from an established nominalization (7).

(6) a. *Jennifer Eight, 1992*: I don't know nothing about this "Jenn-ifer" girl, cept what some of the guys told me—but principal feature of the case was a gruesome **displayal** of the body.

  b. *Journal of Church and State, 1991*: Even if applied to civil courts, it has been said that such rules extend only to "real material jurisdiction in its strict meaning." (…) not extending to **disregardance** of the law (…) nor even to denial of natural justice (…).

  c. *Twentieth century British history. Oxford: OUP, 1991*: "The internal dissension [...] would be ludicrous if it were not a sinister symptom of the decadent **disrupture** of British public opinion, owing to lack of faith either in the present order or in any consistent and comprehensive principles of reconstruction."

(7) a. *Ear, Nose, and Throat Journal, 2005*: A diagnosis of bilateral peritonsillar abscess was suspected when **fluctuance** was elicited on finger palpation.

  b. *Denver Post, 2009*: Get with the lingo. There's a new word in the theater glossary— "**revisal**." That'what they're calling the revised "Molly Brown" musical. The book has been overhauled.

The *OED* cites both *disrupture* and *revisal*, with last dates of occurrence in the late nineteenth century, but it appears that they were never frequent or established forms. Thus their occurrence in contemporary corpora might be taken as a sign of marginal productivity. Although some of these forms have older citations in the *OED*, it is nevertheless unlikely that speakers have been exposed to them and more likely that they occur as spontaneous coinages in the texts captured in COCA.

Unlike *-al, -ance*, and *-ure*, where the number of new forms is negligible, we find more novel or low-frequency forms for *-ment* in COCA and BNC:

(8) *COCA*: accruement, addressment, alertment, ambushment, approvement, assemblement, assurement, attirement, ceasement, completement, conjoinment, contestment, dischargement, divorcement, fakement, financement, jugglement, lancement, omitment, razement, renouncement, revealment, unfoldment, worriment

  BNC: humblement, intendment, regardment

Although quite a few of these forms are attested in the *OED*, none were ever in wide use, and we might again consider them as sporadic and spontaneous creations where they occur in the corpora.

We find that these forms rarely differ in meaning from the more established nominalization for a given verb, as the examples below suggest:

(9) a. *ABC Good Morning America 1999*: In light of recent race-related crimes across the United States and movements to eliminate affirmative action, what is your stand on that as far as the continuation or the **ceasement**, I guess, of affirmative action?

b. *ABC Nightline 1990*: And I think an indication of that is the fact that Minister de Klerk, in his historic speech, made the **omitment** of not mentioning anything about black education.

c. *CBS Face the Nation 1993*: I want 10 years in prison without parole for possessing a firearm during the commission of a violent crime or a drug felony. I want 20 years for **dischargement** with the intent to do bodily harm.

d. *NPR 2000*: It's because we really start from scratch with no capital. It's hard to find **financement**.

There are rare cases, however, in which the nominalization in *-ment* is clearly intended to be distinguished semantically from the more commonly occurring nominalization of a particular verb.

(10) a. *Dateline NBC 2008*: Doctors wanted to give the babies a chance to grow and get stronger and give surgeons a chance to run tests to see if the rare separation surgery would be possible. This type of **conjoinment** is one of the most complicated to separate.

b. *Symposium, 1994*: **Revealment** in relation to the detective story is the moment of the unravelling of the mystery plot: the little old lady is shown to be a vile poisoner, the composed butler is a fiendish gambler with a propensity for murder.

In these examples, the nominalization *conjoinment* is clearly intended as a technical term for a medical condition, and *revealment* is coined as a literary term in distinction to the more usual nominal *revelation*.

To the very small extent that new forms can be created with the prefix *en-* (see Chapter 13), nominalization in *-ment* is likely, unless the derivation also ends in the suffixes *-ate*, *-ize*, or *-ify*. We find in COCA forms like *envotement* and *emplotment* which may be novel forms; neither the form in *-ment* nor the corresponding verb is attested in the *OED*. COCA also attests several verbs in *en-* that are not recorded in the *OED* and might be likely candidates for nominalization in *-ment*, although the forms are not attested: *enchamber, enchange, enclod, encloth, enflood, enfog, enmagick, enpool, enspirit, entragick, envoice, enweb.*

10.2.1.2 *Productive affixal nominalization: -ation*

The suffix *-ation* has a number of different variants (*-ation, -cation, -ion, -ition, -iation, -sion, -ution, -tion*), and we select the form *-ation* as the citation form as this string is common to all productive variants.

The suffix is the only one of the non-native nominalizing affixes that displays clear productivity in modern English. It is mostly found on verbs (see (16) and (17) below), although occasional forms do appear on bound bases (11):

(11)   -ation *on bound bases*: ambition, aspersion, benediction, benefaction, companion, compassion, constellation, contagion, contraption, contusion, diction, dimension, dominion, duration, ebullition, excursion, jurisdiction, monition, munition, nutrition, perdition, sedition, vocation, volition

There are also occasional forms on adjectives (12) and nouns (13). Some of these are loans rather than English formations, but have to be analysed as having a nominal base in synchronic structure; others are genuine English formations on a noun.

(12)   -ation *on adjectives*: adequation, contrition, discretion, distinction, erudition, explicitation, extinction, festivation, humanation, inanition, inchoation, palmation, precision

(13)   -ation *on nouns*: artefaction, concretion, intellection, metalation, ozonation, placentation

The vast majority of words in *-ation* are formed on non-native bases, but occasional forms on native bases can be found, as illustrated in (14):

(14)   -ation *on native bases*: backwardation, blackalation, bolsteration, botheration, flirtation, flotation, gatheration, harvestation, hateration, holleration, starvation

Occasionally we see extenders in these forms, as in *blackalation* or *hateration*. Some of these are clearly meant to be humorous, clever, or jocular formations.

(15)   *Rolling Stone 2002:* The queen of hip-hop soul hits Number One with "Family Affair," denouncing **holleration** and **hateration.**

The derivatives of this morphological category all have their main stress on the penultimate syllable, the suffix thus belongs to the set of stress-shifting suffixes (see Chapter 9 for more discussion).

The main area of productivity for this affix lies in its status as the default nominalizer of verbs formed with the suffixes -*ize* and -*ify*. As these are the predominant affixal means of forming new verbs in contemporary English, they provide a source of new bases for -*ation*. Any verb that is created with the suffix -*ize* will be nominalized using the variant -*ation*, while any verb created with the suffix -*ify* will be nominalized with -*cation* (and vowel change in the verbal suffix). The forms in (16) and (17) are only a few of the forms from COCA that we could cite.

(16)   *Nominalizations on -ize:* aerosolization, aristocratization, bilingualization, christmasization, corporativization, cyclomidization, dollarization, emblematization, figuralization, geometrization, hausaization, laicization, micralization, numinization, povertization, protestantization, reflectorization, skeletonization, solubilization, teddy-bearization, vascularization

(17)   *Nominalizations on -ify:* adultification, aridification, celebrification, crechification, dignification, disneyfication, etherification, floridification, glassification, humidification, jazzification, mall-ification, mississippification, parentification, rarification, sandification, sportification, spaghettification, townification, uglification, zombification

COCA does, however, also attest a handful of apparently novel forms on other sorts of bases including *bolsteration, complexation, distanciation, effemination, endorsation, expection, expendition, festivation, harvestation, hateration, judgitation,* and *ozonation*. There are a mere handful of forms in -*izement* (*advertizement, aggrandizement, enfranchisement*) or -*izance* (*cognizance* and its various derivatives), all of them item-familiar and of relatively high frequency. Of these, only *enfranchisement* is an English formation. The contemporary data culled from COCA thus corroborate the results of Bauer (2001) which assessed the productivity of nominalizing affixes in English on the basis of data from the *OED* (2nd edn) and the Wellington Corpus of New Zealand English and found -*ation* to be the only productive suffix. There are no examples with the suffix -*ify* plus other nominalizing affixes.

There are some nominalizations in -*age* which also belong semantically to this chapter (for example, *dosage, drainage, slippage, spillage, stoppage*), but which are treated in Chapter 12 with other words taking the same suffix.

10.2.2 Nominalizations with -*ing*

All non-auxiliary verbs in English, regardless of their origin or other means of nominalization, have nominal forms in -*ing*. We are chiefly concerned here with the -*ing* form that can occur with a determiner, and that takes its complement in the form of a prepositional phrase, typically with the preposition *of*, for example *the closing of the Suez Canal* or *the teaching of the arts*. What we call the nominal -*ing* form therefore has the external syntax of the other forms of nominalization that we discuss here, albeit a more active and typically less lexicalized semantics, a subject we will take up in Section 10.3.

What is perhaps more interesting is that while all verbs have a nominalization in *-ing*, a significant number of verbs have only a nominalization in *-ing*, having neither a nominalization formed with one of the affixes discussed above, nor a nominalization formed by conversion (at least according to standard dictionaries). Among these are the majority of verbs that are themselves derived from nouns, either by conversion (18) or by affixation of *de-*, *un-*, *inter-*, or *over-* (19).

(18)   *denominal*: antique, apprentice, bandage, bargain, bicycle, boss, bridge, bully, calve, can, chauffeur, coach, dust, escort, eye, ferret, garrotte, glue, group, gut, hammer, hay, host, joke, journey, ladle, lash, log, manicure, mark, network, package, paint, parachute, peel, picnic, pilot, pocket, quiz, referee, rhyme, rivet, robe, shepherd, shingle, smudge, snack, splinter, star, tape, thatch, tree, vacation, wallpaper, widow, witness, yoke

(19)   a. *prefix de-*: debone, debug, defog, defraud, defrost, defuzz, degas, degerm, deglaze, degrease, degrit, degum, dehair, dehead, dehorn, dehull, dehusk, deice, deink, demast, denude, desex, desprout, destarch, destress, detassle, detusk, devenom, dewater, dewax, deworm

   b. *prefix un-*: unbolt, unbosom, unbuckle, unbutton, unchain, unclamp, unclasp, unclip, unfasten, unfold, unglue, unhinge, unhitch, unhook, unlace, unlatch, unleash, unlock, unnerve, unpeg, unpin, unscrew, unshackle, unstaple, unstitch, untie, unzip

   c. *prefix inter-*: interlard, interleave, interlink, interlock, intermingle, intertwine, interweave

In addition, there are a significant number of both native and non-native underived verbs (20), (21) that seem not to have a nominalization other than the *-ing* form:

(20)   *native underived*: ask, bake, clean, clip, draw, drench, dwell, earn, flit, follow, forbid, gather, hang, hear, learn, mean, mourn, open, spell, teach, wed, write

(21)   *non-native underived*: blanch, board, broil, cavort, char, covet, crochet, curry, daunt, devour, extoll, fester, gloat, hurtle, lurk, perish, pierce, quit, quiver, rankle, render, squash, stuff, suffer, thrive, tremble, waver

10.2.3 Conversion

In addition to nominalization with the affixes discussed above, English frequently uses conversion to derive nouns from verbs. Indeed, the majority of native verbs have a conversion nominalization. A selection of verbs which form nominalizations using the process of conversion is given in (22).

(22)   answer, bark, beat, bend, bet, bid, boast, break, breed, build, burn, bust, cough, creep, cut, dare, deal, dig, do, dream, drink, drive, drop, end, fall, fart, feed, fling, flight, fold, forecast, freeze, grind, grip, heap, help, hit, hold, hope, kick, kill, knock, laugh, lead, leap, leave, like, life, need, neigh, nip, play, proof, pull, raise, reach, rest, ride, ring, rise, run, sail, say, sale, set, shake, shave, span, spare, speed, spill, spin, spit, split, spread, spring, sprout(s), stand, stick, sting, stink, sweep, swell, swim, swing, take, talk, tear, thank(s), throw, thrust, tread, trust, turn, wait, walk, want, wash, watch, weave, win, wish, wonder, work, worry, yawn

A non-negligible number of non-native verbs nominalize by conversion as well, as the examples in (23) illustrate. For verbs among the non-native portion of the English lexicon, nominalization by conversion is not nearly as frequent as by suffixation of *-ation*, but is somewhat more frequent than affixation with *-ment, -al, -ance, -ure*, and the other affixes mentioned in Section 10.2.1.1. Many of the words in (23) have parallel nominalizations with affixes, sometimes with the same meaning, sometimes with a different meaning.

(23)   acclaim, accord, act, advance, affront, blame, canter, capture, caress, cascade, collapse, comfort, cruise, decline, delay, design, desire, effect, elapse, embrace, escape, esteem, exchange, finish, haunt, lament, laud, marvel, measure, mount, move, notice, offer, order, preserve, press, pretend, process, profit, regard, regress, regret, reign, relapse, remark, reserve, respect, rest, result, return, reverse, review, revolt, reward, rhyme, sense, sojourn, study, supply, support, surge, surmise, surprise, surrender, touch, trace, travel, visit, warrant

Conversion has clearly been productive in both the native and the non-native sectors of the lexicon in earlier stages of English, but its status in contemporary English is harder to establish. Whether it continues to be productive depends largely on the creation of new verbs that are neither formed with the suffixes *-ize* and *-ify*, nor are themselves formed by conversion from adjectives or nouns. The creation of nouns by conversion is far less productive in current English than the creation of verbs. Nevertheless examples such as *a commute, a hijack, a work-to-rule* (BrE) (all twentieth-century examples) indicate that verb to noun conversion is available.

10.2.4 Nominalization by stress shift

There are quite a few disyllabic verbs, almost all non-native, that form their nominalizations by stress shift, changing from an iambic pattern to a trochaic one. Examples are given in (24).

(24)   accent, addict, address (*NAmE*), affect, affix, alloy, ally, annex, augment, combat, combine, commune, compress, console, consort, construct, contest, contract, contrast, converse, convert, convict, decrease, defect, discharge, discount, discourse, escort,

essay, excerpt, excise, exploit, export, extract, ferment, finance, indent, insert, insult, intern, intrigue, invite, mandate, object, permit, pervert, proceed, process, produce, progress, project, prolapse, prospect, recess, recoil, record, redress, refill, refund, refuse, research, retard, rewrite, segment, subject, surmise, survey, suspect, torment, transfer, transport, update, upgrade, uplift, upset

It is assumed in these cases that the noun is derived from the verb, rather than the opposite. As Kiparsky (1982b: 13) points out, for nominalizations that have lexicalized meanings, a semantically distinct verb can be derived from the derived noun, which then maintains the stress pattern of the noun: so *protést*$_V$ • *prótest*$_N$ • *prótest*$_V$.

Several trisyllabic or longer verbs exhibit nominalization with stress shift as well, as in (25).

(25)   álternàte (*BrE*), attríbute, envélope, réprimand

Note that in BrE, *alternate* has first syllable stress for the verb and second syllable stress for the noun, which is not what we might normally expect. The other examples do not show a consistent position of stress for the verb.

Sometimes the main stress in the noun and the verb do correspond, but the secondary stress changes. This happens not only with noun–verb pairs, but also with adjective–verb pairs, which are added here to give a fuller picture of the phenomenon. The last syllable in these words takes a secondary stress when the word is a verb, but is unstressed when it is a noun or an adjective. Examples are given in (26).

(26)   advocate (N, V), affricate (N, V), aggregate (A, N, V), appropriate (A, V), aspirate (N, V), associate (N, V), certificate (N, V), complement (N, V), compliment (N, V), confederate (A, N, V), consummate (A, V), coordinate (A, N, V), deliberate (A, V), desolate (A, V), document (N, V), duplicate (A, N, V), elaborate (A, V), estimate (N, V), experiment (N, V), geminate (A, N, V), graduate (N, V), implement (N, V), increment (N, V), intercept (N, V), moderate (A, V), numerate (A, V), ornament (N, V), prophesy (N, V), regiment (N, V), supplement (N, V), triplicate (A, V) (*and others similar*)

The phenomena illustrated in (24)–(26) are variable in contemporary English. Not all speakers show the stress differences on the same set of words, and there is also a diachronic shift with words both being added to and deleted from the sets. Some of the deletions occur when the nominal or verbal use of the word vanishes; in other cases both the nominal and the verbal forms come to take the same stress pattern.

Another phenomenon that might be discussed under the topic of stress change is the group of nominalizations formed from particle verbs like *put down, blow up, burn out, fuck up,* and so on. Whereas particle verbs can display various stress patterns in sentential contexts depending on whether the particle appears adjacent or non-adjacent to the verb, the nominalizations always display a trochaic stress pattern: *pút down, blów up*, etc. A similar stress pattern occurs in the examples in (27), which have particles or prepositions in initial position (and whose derivational history is not always clear).

(27)   bypass, download, income, inlay, input, outlay, output, overcharge, overlap, overlay, overload, overlook, override, overrun, overturn, throughput, underlay, underline, underscore, upgrade

10.2.5 Miscellaneous

A few nominalizations, predominantly from non-native verbs, exhibit devoicing of a final consonant: *abuse, excuse, extent, descent, belief*. For fuller treatment of this pattern see Chapter 25. Several nominal forms corresponding to Latinate verbs are based on different stem forms of the original Latin verbs: *defend • defense, expend • expense, respond • response, suspend • suspense, transcribe • transcript, exceed • excess, perceive • percept*. Some of these also exhibit stress shift (e.g. *percéive • pércept, transcríbe • tránscript*).

The suffix -*y* derives a limited number of pertinent nominalizations (e.g. *advocacy, assembly, burglary, beggary, conspiracy, delivery, determinacy, entry, felony, gluttony, inquiry*), but also abstract nouns of various types, treated in Chapter 19.2.5. That chapter also contains a discussion of the allomorphy patterns involved with this suffix and of its relation to other suffixes such as -*ery*, and -*ity*.

A handful of event nominalizations in -*th* still exist, among them: *birth, growth, health, stealth, tilth, troth, wealth* (for deadjectival formations with this suffix, see Chapter 12). This suffix is clearly unproductive, and has been so for several centuries (Marchand 1969). Finally, a number of verbs also display nominalizations with lexicalized plurals, for example, forms like *amends, arms, congratulations, creeps, digs, droppings, earnings, eats, lodgings, looks, regards, savings, staggers, surroundings, works, writings* (see Chapter 8.2.1). None of these processes, probably except for those on bases in -*ing*, exhibit productivity in contemporary English.

10.3 Semantic considerations

In what follows, we will assume that nominalizations typically display a range of meanings, with particular nuances determined by the semantic characteristics of the base combined with the syntactic context in which the nominalization is used. We will therefore typically discuss what we will refer to as 'readings' or 'interpretations', rather than 'meanings' or 'denotations', and give, wherever possible, specific citations in which the reading in question is displayed.

10.3.1 Range of readings

The basic division that is normally made is between eventive readings and result readings (e.g. Grimshaw 1990). All -*ing* nominals have an eventive reading, as do many, if not most, affixal nominalizations. As has been pointed out frequently, the eventive reading of non-*ing* nominalizations is most easily available when the nominalization displays the full argument structure of the corresponding verb,: as in *the professor's demonstration of the technique*.

Some theorists (e.g. Grimshaw 1990) distinguish between what they call 'complex event' and 'simple event' readings, the former being a syntactic context in which all verbal arguments are maintained in the phrase headed by the nominalization (e.g. *the Romans' destruction of the city*) and the latter a syntactic context in which one or more of the expected verbal arguments are absent (e.g. *the quick destruction of the city*). It is unclear whether there is any real distinction here, there being no independent way to identify the complex event reading from the simple except by determining how many arguments are present. So we will simply distinguish eventive from non-eventive interpretations in what follows.

Syntactic context plays the key role in the precise interpretation of any nominalization. For example a nominalization like *demonstration* clearly denotes an action in a sentence like (28a). But (28b) has what is usually termed a 'factive' reading (that is, 'the fact that the professor demonstrated the technique …'), and in (28c), what is in question is the manner in which the action is performed.

(28) a. The professor's demonstration of the technique proceeded smoothly.

b. The professor's demonstration of the technique was a scandal.

c. The professor's demonstration of the technique was deft.

All non-modal verbs exhibit -*ing* nominalizations. Nominalizations in -*ing* characteristically display eventive readings and are less prone to lexicalization or semantic drift, although there are a few that exhibit result, product, or means interpretations, as examples given below will suggest. Where there is lexicalization, it often involves narrowing of the verbal denotation to a specific context. So, for example, *mouldings* are specific sorts of things that are moulded, namely decorations on walls, *kindling* is small pieces of wood that help to kindle a fire, a *finding* is something that is found as an outcome of scientific research or a legal proceeding.

For native verbs whose only other nominalization is by conversion, the -*ing* nominalization is usually the only eventive nominalization, the conversion nominalization being more likely to display aspectual or result readings (see below), but not an eventive interpretation. Systematic exceptions here are verbs denoting emotions (*love, hate, fear, hope, trust, dislike*). These are stative verbs, and stative verbs are usually said to be awkward with eventive readings. However, when an eventive reading is needed, there is no problem with using the -*ing* nominalization:

(29)   *COCA. CNN_King 2004*: We have a lot more **loving** of our neighbor to do

   BNC. Cole, the Ladykiller, 1993: I make you feel suffocated, do I, with my **loving**?

Otherwise, the conversion nominal is more usual:

(30)   Her **love** of music; my **fear** of snakes

The general principle with conversion nominalizations is that they may exhibit any of the readings generally associated with nominalizations (see below). Nevertheless, there are some verbs whose conversion nominalizations appear to resist an eventive interpretation: e.g. *her drive of the car*, **the sailor's heave of the rope*. The examples in (31) are interpreted as eventive because they display full argument structure, and those in (32) because of the presence of the temporal adjectives *constant* or *frequent*.

(31)   *Denver Post 2004*: Last year, just before the 50th anniversary of Sir Edmund Hillary**'s climb of** Mount Everest, the Sherpas wanted to put up an Internet cafe at 18,500 feet, base camp on Everest.

   PBS Newshour 1995: Technically, in Pennsylvania, you only have to have one license plate on your car, so the officer was improper on **his stop of** this car, but while he stopped the car, he observed in the back seat over 200 pounds of cocaine.

   Ind_Geraldo 1992: But, of course, the fact that he was involved or may have been involved in that robbery two weeks before the crime doesn't really support **his murder of** your mom two weeks later.

   Environment 1990: Bolivia**'s swap of** $650,000 is tiny in comparison to the overall commercial debt of $500 million.

(32)   *American Heritage 1998*: We need to learn to understand our technological behavior as a **constant blend of** these very different modes of consciousness.

   Consumer Reports 2007: […] Bouts of coughing unrelated to colds or the **frequent spread of** any symptoms to the chest when you do have a cold.

   San Francisco Chronicle 1991: "[…] I can smell a skunk that was killed, and I know how many hours before it was killed," he said, in a conversation punctuated by the **frequent crash of** beer empties in a trash can behind the bar.

Interestingly, it seems easier to find non-native conversion forms in eventive contexts. Forms such as *report, surrender, review, catch, chase, appeal* and others occur easily with an eventive reading, as the examples in (33) suggest.

(33)   *American Spectator 2008*: When it was adopted, **his report of** events to the governor of Virginia placed it after fairly trivial matters, such as the authorization of some lighthouses.

ABC Primetime 1993: Tim's role in all of this didn't end with **his surrender of** those videotapes.

Driftless 2008: The dark foliage above him seemed to draw nearer and a spirit of fatigue invaded his senses, disrupting **his review of** recent events.

Sports Illustrated 2008: Even then, it took the replay official to determine that the ball had crossed the plane of the goal line on wideout Santonio Holmes**'s catch of** Ben Roethlisberger's four-yard pass.

Entertainment Weekly 2006: Clay gave up **his chase of** the Mister Softee truck and stood with one foot on the sidewalk and the other planted in the gutter, watching as it swerved into the center lane of Boylston Street, still tinkling.

Washington Post 2008: Fu […] said Bush**'s appeal to** Chinese officials on religious freedom and human rights was mostly for the benefit of his domestic critics.

Non-eventive interpretations can take a number of forms, among them results (the outcome of VERB-ing), products (the thing or stuff that is created or comes into being by VERB-ing), instrument (the thing that VERB-s, a way of VERB-ing), locations (the place of VERB-ing), agents (people or person who VERB-s), measure terms (how much is VERB-ed), paths (the direction of VERB-ing), patients (thing VERB-ed, thing affected or moved but not created by VERB-ing), states (the state of VERB-ing or being VERB-ed), and what might be called 'instances' (an instance of VERB-ing). We provide a few examples of each of these in (34)–(43). The (a) examples are lexical items with the potential to display the reading in question, given the right context. The (b) examples are attested citations from COCA illustrating that reading. It should be kept in mind that these same nominalizations can exhibit other readings, given other syntactic contexts.

(34) RESULT: *the outcome of VERB-ing*

    a. acceptance, acquittal, addition, adherence, adjunction, aggravation, agitation, alteration, amelioration, americanization, arousal, arrival, articulation, assassination, assessment, canonization, captivation, castigation, certification, collision, communication, completion, compression, computation, cooperation, correlation, degradation, evaluation, exertion, hesitation, impeachment, improvement, inflation, integration, movement, omission, operation, ordainment, ossification, procurement, reaction, reclamation, recognition, recurrence, repulsion, retrieval, revilement, revolution, rotation, satisfaction, stabilization, stimulation, stratification, submergence, surrender, transformation, understanding, unification, unionization, upset, veneration, vindication

    b. *USA Today 2009*: Still, most population specialists contend that the most likely long-term result will be the "browning of America," with the different races meeting and mingling joyfully as such groups always have done—but perhaps not without some lingering acrimony before complete **acceptance** is achieved.

New Yorker 2006: His aunt had lived to be ninety, and he was sixty-six. His son was twenty-four, which, he quickly computed, was the difference in age between his aunt and him. The **computation** meant nothing.

Time 2009: By that time, she was also married to a high school sweetheart, Kevin Edward Noonan—a marriage that ended in **divorce** in 1983.

African Arts 2009: For the Oromo, the lower body is connected to the past through its link to the ground, to birthing, and to **containment**.

Harpers Bazaar 2009: The result was the biggest **seizure** ever in New York City: 19 tractor trailers filled with counterfeit clothing and footwear with an approximate street value of $10 million.

(35)   PRODUCT: *the thing or stuff that is created or comes into being by* VERB-*ing*

    a. allotment, allowance, appendage, blot, brew, bruise, building, creation, description, drawing, embroidery, etching, gouge, growth, jumble, knowledge, pavement, puke, saute, scrape, slit, smear, spatter, spill, splatter, supply, tear, thought, wound

    b. *Southwest Review 2009*: Running my hand over that cold **carving** was like touching the new contours of my sister's face.

       USA Today 2009: The sticky-sweet **concoction** combines gin, cherry brandy, pineapple juice, Cointreau, grenadine and other ingredients.

       Southwest Review 2005: Back on the couch he fingered the stuffing the cat had clawed out, making the **tear** measurably worse.

(36)   INSTRUMENT: *the thing that* VERBs, *a way of* VERB-*ing*

    a. accompaniment, adornment, advertisement, clog, conveyance, cure, decoration, distraction, entertainment, feed, flattery, greeting, imagination, kindling, leavening, refreshment, tie, wrap

    b. *Men's Health 1994*: He sends you to a cardiologist, who confirms your worst fears: An artery that feeds the heart is blocked; you may be in danger of a heart attack. # It's obviously a scary diagnosis, but the doctor recommends angioplasty, a relatively simple and painless procedure to pinpoint and clear the **clog**.

       Happiness Key 2009: For **decoration**, three turquoise seahorses descended the wall at a forty-five-degree angle.

       Fantasy & Science Fiction 2009: "There's not much out here in the way of **refreshment**, Mister Lawyer. Your drivers could each use a plate of cookies."

(37)   LOCATION: *the place of* VERB-*ing*

    a. camp, dump, dwelling, exhibition, haunt, mooring, perch, residence, rise, roost, seat, wallow

    b. *New Yorker 2006*: But she did open the door at last, and beckoned him inside. They stood in the **entry**, quite close.

American Spectator 2009: It is in the same building as the **dwelling** of Irving Kristol and Gertrude Himmelfarb.

Life is Short But Wide 2009: Now he had a sizable sum to purchase a house for his new wife; she did not want to live on a **reservation**.

(38) AGENT: *people or person who* VERB-*s*

    a. administration, cheat, congregation, consort, cook, delegation, federation, flirt, following, prosecution, sneak, stray, help, snoop, sweep, tease

    b. *New York Times 2009*: He said the **administration** had determined that it could not stop the bonuses.

    c. *Washington Post 2008*: The **cook** melts chocolate over a warm-water bath, mixes water in, places the bowl over an ice bath and then whisks energetically until the mixture firms up.

    d. *Triquarterly 1997*: She was the girl dancing on the table at the party, the **tease** with the gleam in her eye.

(39) MEASURE: *how much is* VERB-*ed*

    a. deceleration, decrease, pinch, weight

    b. *Fantasy & Science Fiction 2009*: He took a **pinch** of some sort of crumbled herb from it and sprinkled it over the threshhold.

(40) PATH: *the direction of* VERB-*ing*

    a. ascent, ascendence, continuation, decline, descent, direction

    b. *Fantasy & Science Fiction 2009*: The road, after several bends and a gradual **ascent**, leveled off so suddenly he nearly lost his balance, caught by a forceful gust sweeping up along mountain gulches from the unseen plains below.

    Journal of International Affairs 2008: In 1924, the United States claimed the North Pole was an underwater **continuation** of Alaska.

(41) PATIENT/THEME: *the thing* VERB-*ed, thing affected or moved (but not created) by* VERB-*ing*

    a. catch, nosh, assignment, convention, jam (paper), offer, pick, exhibit, buy, choice, mount (horse), want, waste, purchase, washing, advance (money), acquisition, appropriation (money), discovery, donation, inheritance, learning, reading, closure, allocation, inclusion, investment, projection, repetition, submission, substitution, teaching(s), hire, kill, tip, allowance, appendage, cull, eats, grant, hoard, imprint, knowledge, marvel, belief, bequest, find, gain, payment, preference, yield, suspect

    b. *Good Housekeeping 2009*: The Good Housekeeping Research Institute had a panel of seniors test products that can help keep your parents safe; a small **purchase** now might avoid a major medical expense later.

    Triquarterly 2009: He was gobbling a fresh **kill**; his mouth and jaw were covered in blood.

(42) STATE: *the state of* VERB-*ing or being* VERB-*ed*

    a. admiration, alienation, annoyance, coexistence, comfort, contentment, dejection, delight, disappointment, discombobulation, disdain, dislike, disquiet, existence, exultation, fascination, fear, grief, hate, hope, perplexity, preoccupation, regret, reverence, suffering, thriving, trust, wonder, worship

    b. *Newsweek 2009*: The verse was written in the time of the shah, in the 1950s, when Khamenei was a young, idealistic Shia cleric who shared with its hard-drinking author a sense of claustrophobic **alienation** and deep frustration.

      USA Today 2009: It's a sly cautionary tag on a character study that reflects a collective **regret** and despair in today's uneasy world.

(43) INSTANCE: *an instance of* VERB-*ing*

    a. balk, bang, bark, beep, belch, bite, blast, blink, bounce, bump, climb, clunk, conflict, cough, crack, crawl, cuddle, dip, dive, glint, grab, groan, guess, halt, heave, hit, howl, hug, jab, jeer, jolt, jump, peek, ping, pitch, plop, prance, pucker, punch, push, rap, rebuke, shiver, shriek, shrug, shudder, sip, slap, slurp, smirk, snooze, sob, throb, throw, tickle, toss, try, twist, wag, wail, wait, win, yank

    b. *Houston Chronicle 1993*: There had been four errors—all by the Rockies—and three wild pitches. For good measure (or bad), there also were six walks and **a balk**.

      U.S. Catholic 2006: Claretian Father Cyrus Banque is a jovial host, with warm greetings for everyone and an engaging smile. But when the topic of conversation turns to justice and reconciliation for the new nation of East Timor, the Filipino missionary's smile breaks into **a frown** and his brow wrinkles.

Among the non-eventive interpretations, the result interpretation is by far the most frequent one exhibited, and should perhaps be considered the default non-eventive interpretation.

10.3.2 Referencing of arguments or aspect

Key to the interpretation of the non-eventive nominalizations is the referencing of arguments or aspectual characteristics (see Chapter 2.8.2).

In PRODUCT or PATIENT/THEME nominalizations (35), (41) it is the object that is referenced, albeit in slightly different ways. *Embroidery* is a product, the material thing that is brought into existence by the action of embroidering. A *purchase*, in contrast, is not created per se, but is rather the theme, that is, what is transferred by the action. Much less frequent is the referencing of the subject of the verbal base, which is what we find in the AGENT nominalizations in (38). Some of these forms are what Melloni (2007) calls 'agent collectives': the *administration*, for example, can be the people who administer something, and a *following* can denote the people who follow someone (usually someone prominent). Conversion forms like *flirt, cook, tease* tend to denote non-collective agents. In addition to forms that are clearly agentive, there are forms that are not directly agentive, but that nevertheless reference the subject, frequently because the verbal base is intransitive. Among these are nominalizations like: *bloom, decay, decomposition, deterioration, drift, effervescence, emanation, precipitation, ulceration, divergence, illumination, temptation, overhang, remains, sprout, spurt, affliction, amazement, disturbance, flop, indication, occurrence*. We will return to these forms in Chapter 11, where we look more closely at personal nouns.

Also relatively infrequent is the referencing of adjuncts like location, path, or measure. LOCATION nominalizations of course denote the place where the action of a verb occurs: an *enclosure* is the place where things are enclosed, and a *dwelling* the place where one dwells. There are only a few nominalizations that might be classed as MEASURE or PATH forms. A *pinch* (as in *a pinch of salt*) is the amount which is pinched, the *ascent* is the trajectory of ascending.

It should be noted that for agents, the suffix *-er* is far more typically used (see Chapter 11), so it is not surprising that there are so few agent or instrument forms derived by conversion or by affixes like *-ation* or *-ment*. On the other hand, although there is a dedicated affix *-ee* in English for sentient patients, there exist no specific affixes in English that derive non-sentient patients, either products or things transferred or affected, nor are there specific affixes denoting location, means, measure, or path nouns. It is therefore not surprising that affixes like *-ation, -ment, -al*, and conversion are sometimes enlisted to derive such forms. We will return to this issue in Chapter 11.

Non-eventive nominalizations do not always reference an argument of the verb. With certain classes of verb (see Section 10.2.2) they may reference specific aspectual characteristics of the verbal base, either a resulting state (*admiration, depression, bewilderment, hate*) or a punctual instance of the action (*yawn, kick, crack, chirp*).

10.3.3 Predictability of nominal semantics

There is frequently a relationship between the semantic class of the base verb and the interpretation of the nominalization of that verb. This is especially clear in the case of nominalizations that have either an instance or a state aspectual reading. The former nominalizations derive from verbs of instantaneous contact (44), verbs of bodily motion (45), and verbs of sound or light emission (46). State nominalizations most frequently derive from verbs of psychological state (47). Verbs with inherently spatial denotations give rise to location nominalizations (48). Means nominalizations derive from verbs that denote actions that require instruments of various sorts (49).

(44)   *verbs of instantaneous contact*: beat, hit, bump, chop

(45)   *verbs of bodily motion*: blink, chew, hop, lurch

(46) *verbs of sound or light emission*: howl, click, groan, mew, gleam, glint

(47) *verbs of psychological state*: excite, exasperate, disgruntle, alienate

(48) *inherently spatial verbs*: rise, enter, surround, enclose

(49) *verbs requiring instruments*: swaddle, season, remunerate, equip

It is not always possible, however, to characterize the verbs that give rise to particular sorts of nominalization.

10.3.4 Count versus mass interpretation

As Huddleston and Pullum (2002: 337) note, most nominalizations are not count or non-count per se, but can have count and non-count readings, given specific contexts. So *celebration* or *change* are possible on either interpretation:

(50) a. Some **celebration** is clearly called for.
          They did not believe that there had been enough **change**.

      b. We held two separate **celebrations** last week.
          The committee recommended three **changes**.

Some nominalizations tend to favour one reading or the other, however. Although it is not clear how systematic this phenomenon is, at least a few patterns can be discerned. For example, conversion nominalizations that express instantaneous aspect always have count readings, and typically do not also allow non-count readings.

(51) a. The monks began a chant.
          We heard two burps.

      b. *We want to hear some (/səm/) chant.
          *We expected to hear some burp.

      c. We wanted to hear some chanting.
          We expected to hear some burping.

A non-count reading is frequently preferred for the corresponding *-ing* nominalization, as the examples in (50c) illustrate.

  We also observe that forms with lexicalized meanings are somewhat likelier than non-lexicalized forms to have only the count reading. For example, semantically specialized nominalizations like *assignation* ('meeting'), *assignment* ('assigned task'), *fixture* ('attached piece of equipment'), *proposal* ('a plan'), *recital* ('musical performance'), or *variance* ('official dispensation') exhibit only the count reading, while less (or un-)lexicalized counterparts favour the non-count reading (*attention, composure, embitterment, importance, survival*), or allow either (*accommodation, assessment, closure, disposal, disturbance, renewal*).

CHAPTER 11

Derived nouns: personal and participant

11.1 PROSPECTUS

In this chapter we discuss morphological processes which derive personal or participant nouns, that is, nouns denoting agents, patients, themes, instruments, inhabitants, locations, and gendered forms. These are formed primarily by affixation in contemporary English, specifically by the suffixes *-an*, *-ant* (and its spelling variant <ent>), *-arian*, *-ee*, *-eer*, *-er* (and its variant <or>), *-ese*, *-ess*, *-ette*, *-i*, *-ish*, *-ist*, *-ite*, *-meister*, *-nik*, *-ster*, and *-trix*, as well as by the prefixes *grand-*, *great-*, *step-*, and *vice-*. We will also revisit some of the nominalizing processes discussed in Chapter 10, looking at the ways in which they overlap with the function of the primary personal and participant affixes discussed here. Similarly, we will touch on a few of the affixes that will be given a more detailed treatment in Chapter 12 as forming collective or abstract nouns, but which double to some extent in creating participant nouns.

It should also be noted that some sets of the person noun derivatives to be discussed in the present chapter are formally identical with pertinent adjectival derivatives. A majority of the nominal derivatives in *-an*, *-ant*, *-ist*, and *-arian* can also be found as adjectives (e.g. *American*, *modernist*, *vegetarian*), but the nature of the relationship between the nominal and adjectival forms is not entirely straightforward. Thus, there are nominal cases that are not also adjectives (e.g. *accountant*, *applicant*, *informant*) and adjective cases that are not also nouns (e.g. *aberrant*, *pleasant*, *hesitant*). While the fact that English allows prenominal modification by nouns may explain the categorial variation, a theoretical account is nevertheless a challenge, and there are in principle at least two different solutions available. The categorial variation could be considered either a case of suffixal homophony or a case of conversion. We remain agnostic with regard to the theoretical analysis and treat the pertinent derivatives in this chapter and in the chapter on adjectival derivation (Chapter 14). The suffix *-arian* is dealt with exclusively in this chapter, since the adjectives correspond straightforwardly to the nouns.

The examples in this chapter are taken either from BNC or COCA, unless otherwise specified.

11.2 FORMAL CONSIDERATIONS

In this section we consider such formal characteristics of personal and participant affixes as their selection of base types—whether they attach to native or non-native bases, bound or free bases, what syntactic categories they select, whether they take compound or phrasal bases, and so on—as well as their specific phonological restrictions and the extent to which they display argument structure. In order to organize this section, a rough first pass at semantic categories seems necessary, even though we will put off a close semantic analysis until Section 11.3. We will use five rough rubrics here, dividing affixes into those whose primary readings are typically subject-referencing readings (*-an, -ant, -arian, -eer, -er, -ist, -meister, -ster*), those which are typically object-referencing (*-ee*), those which denote inhabitants or languages (*-ite, -ese, -i, -ish*), and those which denote feminine gender (*-ess, -ette, -trix*). We stress at the outset that these are only rough categories and that they pertain to primary readings; a great many of the affixes that we discuss in this chapter have multiple readings, a point which will be taken up in detail in Section 11.3.

11.2.1 Subject-referencing affixes: *-er, -ant, -an, -ist, -meister, -ster, -nik, -arian*

We divide this group up into those that attach primarily to verbs (*-er, -or*, and *-ant*), those that attach primarily to nouns (*-an, -ist*), and the minor suffixes (*-meister, -ster, -eer, -nik*, and *-arian*).

11.2.1.1 -er *and* -ant

Of this group of suffixes, by far the most productive is *-er*, which attaches to a wide array of base types. It attaches indiscriminately to either native or non-native bases. It seems safe to say that *-er* can be used on just about any transitive verb in English, and on a wide variety of other verb types as well, as the examples in (1) illustrate.

(1)   a. *on transitive verbs*: writer, owner, eater, attacker, employer

b. *on di-transitive verbs*: comparer, confounder, giver, trader, seller, offerer, placer, sender

c. *on prepositional object verbs*: clinger, consulter, defaulter, disposer, escaper, harmonizer, listener, looker, moocher

d. *on unergative verbs*: beeper, belcher, blinker, dancer, buzzer, cougher, drifter, fencer, fiddler, sleeper, prancer, ranter, shrugger, skulker, womanizer

e. *on unaccusative verbs*: comer, descender, faller, perisher, riser, sloper

f. *on causative/inchoative verbs*: broiler, breaker, dropper, frier, hurter, leaker, rattler, roller, suckler, increaser

g. *on verbs taking sentential complements*: boaster, hoper, proclaimer, realizer, reckoner, resolver, swearer, theorizer, thinker, reasoner, venturer, wonderer

It is also worthy of note that *-er* forms can be derived from particle verbs (*pick up, punch out,* etc.) In NAmE this is generally done by adding *-er* to both elements, as shown in the COCA examples given in (2). For these forms, only four competing forms with only one *-er* are attested (*putter-in, fixer-up, picker-up, loosen-upper*). In BrE such *-er* derivatives of phrasal verbs seem to be avoided: of the sample of bases shown in (2), only one has a derivative attested in the BNC (*cleaner-up*). We find in the BNC, however, four words that do not occur in COCA (*roller-upper, washer-upper, roper-inner, stopper-inner*).

(2)   bringer-downer, cheerer-upper, cleaner-outer, cleaner-upper, cutter-upper, exciter upper, filler-outer, filler-upper, fixer-upper, leaver-outer, loosener upper, patcher-upper, pepper-upper, perker-upper, picker-upper, plane-checker-outer, puncher outer, pusher-upper, putter-inner, roller-upper, roper-inner, setter-upper, sniffer-arounder, sopper-upper, starter-upper, stopper-inner, taker-outer, thinker-upper, waker-upper, warmer-upper, washer-upper, wire-puller-upper

Although some of the examples in (2) are intended to be humorous, not all are, presumably as there is no plausible productive alternative that can be used to derive an agent noun for this class of verb.

The suffix also appears on a wide variety of other categories. It is commonly found on nouns, both proper and common.

(3)   a. *proper*: Afrikaaner, Aucklander, Berliner, Dusseldorfer, Dubliner, Icelander, Londoner, Lubavitcher, Montrealer

      b. *common*: birder, bondager, caver, churcher, confectioner, falconer, forker, freighter, islander, lifer, magicker, nutter, porker, ratter, roader, snouter, stoner

It can be found attached to nominal compounds and entire phrases as well.

(4)   a. *on nominal compounds*: shirtwaister, wildcatter, backbencher, backpacker, freestyler, householder, lowlander, outfielder, peasouper

      b. *on phrases*: do-gooder, no hoper, hardliner, naked-heeler, spoken-worder, main-chancer, all-nighter

And it is found at least occasionally on adverbial/prepositional bases and on cardinal numbers.

(5)   a. *on adverbial/prepositional bases*: insider, downer, outsider, southwester, uptowner

      b. *on cardinal numbers*: fiver, niner, tenner, thousander

For the most part, -*er* attaches to free bases, although there are a number of neoclassical compounds and other forms which end in -*y* when unsuffixed, but where we find loss of the final -*y* before -*er*:

(6) biographer, astronomer, philosopher, necromancer, adulterer, sorcerer, usurer

There are also several native forms (*chandler, vintner, glazer*) whose meaning suggests that they are formed with these suffixes, but where there is no existing free base. There are several others where an extending -*i*- exists, but which should probably be grouped with the previous three: *glazier, hosier.* And the form *collier* features both an unusual base allomorph and the extender -*i*-. It seems safe to say, however, that -*er* does not typically appear with bound bases.

The variant -*or* has a rather different formal profile. It attaches almost exclusively to non-native bases, the vast majority of them verbs, and many of them verbs in -*ate*.

(7) a. *on verbs in* -ate: abdicator, accommodator, agglomerator, annihilator, captivator, cremator, dehydrator, educator, humiliator, inseminator

b. *on other non-native verbs*: adjustor, assessor, attractor, circumcisor, condensor, corrector, creditor, detector, enactor, governor, infector, licensor

The only form on a native base is *sailor*, which according to the *OED* is a nineteenth-century respelling of earlier *sailer*.

Unlike -*er*, -*or* is found not infrequently on bound bases:

(8) -or *on bound bases*: acquisitor, admonitor, capacitor, cognitor, defensor, divisor, guarantor, interventor, lector, mentor, seductor

As with the suffix -*er*, -*or* is possible with verbs of most types, although transitive verbs predominate.

(9) a. *on transitive verbs*: actuator, advisor, condensor, dedicator, emancipator, irrigator, perpetrator

b. *on verbs with prepositional objects*: assimilator, commiserator, cooperator, interactor, intervenor, participator

c. *on unergative verbs*: brachiator, hibernator, introspector, prevaricator

d. *on unaccusative verbs*: decelerator, mutator, regressor

e. *on transitive/inchoative verbs*: alternator, evaporator, levitator

f. *on verbs taking sentential complements*: postulator, prognosticator

Only a small handful of forms are found on nominal bases:

(10) debtor, senator, suitor, cryptor, duplexor

Although it appears as *-or* in most forms, the suffix does occasionally exhibit the extenders *-at-* and *-it-*, with the extender *-c-* showing up in verbs formed with the suffix *-ify*:

(11) a. *-ator*: declarator, continuator, conservator, configurator, citator, respirator, comparator, conspirator, preparator, inhalator

b. *-itor*: competitor, servitor, conformitor, compositor

c. *-cator*: scarificator, purificator

The suffix *-er* is clearly productive on verbal and nominal bases. It attaches to just about any newly formed verb to create the corresponding agent/instrument noun (*googler, emailer*), and it appears on nouns as well (*birther*). Its non-native counterpart *-or* shows some degree of productivity on non-native verbal bases as well, as evidenced by forms that appear in COCA, but which are unattested in the *OED*:

(12) acculturator, adaptor, attributor, commentor, conformitor, cryptor, curruptor, debator, deductor, depictor, discussor, duplexor, emanator, enculturator, exacerbator, fractionator, frustrator, gestator, hereditator, implementor, improvisor, inflator, inflictor, intervenor, iterator, manifestor, obviator, palpator, repulsor, requestor

Deverbal forms in *-er* are typically able to project the object argument of the base verb in the form of a prepositional phrase headed by *of*: for example, *the reader of the book; the writer of the novel*. Projection of prepositional objects is possible, as attested in formations like *a listener to classical music*. Ditransitive verbs allow projection of the theme argument with the preposition *of* (*a seller of mangos*), and less easily the goal argument with *to* (*a seller to the US*), but simultaneous projection of both arguments appears to be unattested in the corpus (e.g. *a seller of mangos to the US*). And with verbal bases taking sentential complements, projection of the sentential complement seems impossible: **the realizer that the car was out of gas; *a boaster that she could swim ten miles*. A similar pattern obtains for the suffix *-or*.

The suffix *-ant* and its variant *-ent* are more restricted in their base types than *-er* and *-or*. They attach predominantly to transitive verbs, with very few items in other verbal categories. The formative *-ant* is found not only with nominal formations, but also with adjectival ones. There is some overlap, in the sense that some forms (*mutant, attendant, repellant*) can be construed as either nominal or adjectival in category depending on the syntactic context. Not every adjectival form in *-ant* has a nominal correlate and vice versa, however; forms like *luxuriant, malignant, nurturant, abundant* are used chiefly as adjectives, and forms like *defendant* or *discussant* as nouns.

(13) a. *on transitive verbs*: combatant, decongestant, defendant, deterrent, discussant, inhabitant, protectant, suppressant

    b. *on prepositional object verbs*: accountant, confidant, reactant, respondent

    c. *on causative/inchoative verbs*: floatant

    d. *on unergative verbs*: exhalant

    e. *on unaccusative verbs*: descendant

Adams (2001: 31) notes that *euphoriant* is formed on an adjectival base, and to this we can add *sterilant*. We know of no other examples in which -*ant* attaches to bases other than verbs or bound bases.

This suffix occurs frequently on bound bases that have corresponding forms ending in verbal -*ate*, or in other suffixes (-*ation*, -*able*, or -*ee*, for example).

(14)   a. *on bound bases of verbs in* -ate: asphyxiant, desiccant, fumigant, lubricant, migrant, officiant, replicant

    b. *on other bound bases*: applicant, appellant, occupant, reductant, surfactant

The suffix -*ant* attaches almost exclusively to non-native bases, the only apparent exceptions being *coolant, floatant,* and *healant.*

The suffix exhibits a small degree of productivity in contemporary English, as evidenced by the following examples, which can be found in BNC or COCA, but which do not appear in the *OED*.

(15)   actant, arrestant, calibrant, clonant, commutant, comparant, conductant, degreasant, encapsulant, floatant, healant, innoculant, titrant

Forms derived with the suffix -*ant* seem to be more resistant to projecting the argument structure of their verbal bases than are forms in -*er*. Phrases like *an inhabitant of Canada* or *the occupant of the White House* seem natural enough, *a discussant of issues* somewhat less so, although all three are attested in COCA. But many -*ant* forms derived from transitive verbs sound odd with a projected argument, and are not attested in this pattern in the corpora.

11.2.1.2 -ist *and* -an

Although -*ist* and -*an* overlap in function with each other and with the suffixes in the previous section, their formal profiles exhibit significant differences. The suffixes -*ist* and -*an* attach primarily to non-verbal categories, in contrast to -*er*, -*or*, and -*ant*, which take verbs as their bases far more often than nouns or adjectives. We consider each in turn.

The suffix -*ist* attaches to a wide range of nouns, both common and proper, as well as to adjectives; it can be found only infrequently on verbs.

(16)   a. -ist *on common nouns*: ageist, alarmist, artist, balloonist, banjoist, druggist, novelist, racist, rockist, sexist, tourist

b. -ist *on proper nouns*: Baathist, Dadaist, Darwinist, Decembrist, Francoist, Mitterrandist, Stalinist, Zionist

c. -ist *on adjectives*: ableist, absurdist, dualist, extremist, leftist, modernist, purist, realist

d. -ist *on verbs*: accompanist, conformist, shootist, splittist, transformist

The suffix also appears attached to bound bases.

(17)   -ist *on bound bases*: agonist, altruist, animist, aphorist, baptist, catechist, chemist, deist, dentist, evangelist, jurist, linguist

In some, but not all of these cases, the same bound base is also found with either *-ize* or *-ism* or both (*altruism ◆ altruist; agonism ◆ agonize ◆ agonist; baptism ◆ baptize ◆ baptist*), suggesting a pocket of English derivation with a paradigmatic flavour (see also Chapter 23).

Of all the agentive suffixes, *-ist* has the greatest propensity to appear on already derived bases, both nominal (18) and adjectival (19). Interestingly, it appears at least sporadically on other affixes that derive agents or instruments, as the examples in (18d–e) illustrate:

(18)   *-ist on other noun-forming suffixes*

a. *on* -ion: abolitionist, adoptionist

b. *on* -age: assemblagist, marriagist

c. *on* -ment: movementist

d. *on* -an: Africanist, Algerianist

e. *on* -er/-or: consumerist, redemptorist, detectorist, scooterist, settlerist, workerist

(19)   *-ist on adjective-forming suffixes*

a. *on* -al: ambientalist, accidentalist

b. *on* -ic: aerodynamicist, aestheticist, historicist

c. *on* -ive: collectivist, objectivist, positivist, relativist

d. *on* -able (*in its variant* -ible): impossibilist, infallibilist

e. *on* -ant (*and its variant* -ent): indifferentist, obscurantist

It is not unusual to find *-ist* on multiply-affixed bases, as in examples like *falsificationist, constitutionalist, congregationalist*. Indeed, we sometimes find *-ist* in doublets like those in (20). In some cases, such as (20a), there is no discernable semantic difference between the form derived on the complex adjectival base and that on the complex nominal base. More often than not, however, there is a distinction, as the examples in (20b) illustrate:

(20)   a.   *Daily Telegraph 1992*: Based on the teachings of A. S. Neill, the Scottish **educationalist** and founder of Summerhill, Kinokuni is offering pupils an "alternative to the production-line techniques" of the Japanese education system.

   Parliamentary Affairs 1991: Two generations later one **educationist**, Geoff Whitty, questioned the value of the political education movement precisely because of the official support it had received.

   b.   *The Art Newspaper 1992*: Throughout his career at the library, James constantly blocked efforts to improve security and cataloguing procedures, in particular those proposed by the director, **Islamicist** Wilfrid Lockwood, who had formerly worked with British Intelligence.

   The Economist 1985–1994: It is trying to assert itself politically, offering money the PLO can not match to young, educated Gazans to join the **Islamist** movement.

In the first example in (20b), we have a form that denotes someone who studies Islam, in the second a form that refers to an advocate of a political system that is based on Islam.

   In addition to appearing on bases formed by derivation, *-ist* can be found on compounds, and occasionally on phrases.

(21)   a.   *-ist on compounds*: foot fetishist, folklorist, keyboardist, morphologist, touch-typist, trade-unionist, watercolorist

   b.   *-ist on phrases*: gold-medalist, raw foodist, short-termist, white-supremacist

We find *-ist* predominantly on non-native bases and suffixes, including bases from outside the classical languages or French (*banjoist, Daoist, novelettist, Sikhist, tattooist*). However, it does occasionally take native bases and suffixes, as the examples in (22) illustrate.

(22)   *-ist on native bases*: duckist, fattist, folklorist, harpist, hornist, keyboardist, landscapist, leftist, rightist, scooterist, settlerist, shootist, splittist, stockist, welfarist, womanist

The suffix *-ist* does not generally affect base stress patterns (though note **obscurántist*, cited above) but it does sometimes induce elision of a root-final vowel, as illustrated in (23).

(23)   a.   *elision of root-final* /əʊ ‖ oʊ/: cellist, librettist, pianist, scenarist

   b.   *elision of root-final* /ə/: Buddhist, propagandist, Spinozist

Vowel elision tends, however, to be avoided when the result would be to reduce the base to a single syllable. So we find hiatus in forms like *copyist, Dadaist, flunkyist, hobbyist, lobbyist, oboist, soloist, stuccoist, zeroist*. Hiatus is also occasionally found in trisyllabic bases (*Nkrumahist, Pyreneeist*). Forms with hiatus seem generally acceptable if their base-final vowel is /uː/: *fujitsuist, tatooist*. An extender can be occasionally found (*attitudinist, lutenist, platonist, tobacconist; egotist, programmatist, suprematist*), but the appearance of these extenders does not appear to be in any way systematic. The suffix *-ist* triggers velar softening, as in cases like *lyric • lyricist, physics • physicist*.

The suffix *-an* forms agent nouns, nouns that denote inhabitants of a place or followers of a person, among other things. We will return to its semantic properties in Section 11.3. Formally *-an*, like *-ist*, attaches freely to nouns, both common and proper, and to bound bases.

(24) a. -an *on common nouns*: clinician, comedian, grammarian, guardian, logician, madrigalean, magician, musician, republican, vaudevillean

   b. -an *on proper nouns*: Bolivian, Chicagoan, European, Fijian, Friedmanian, Gaussian, Indonesian, Jungian, Leibnizian, Mozartian

   c. -an *on bound bases*: amphibian, crustacean, equestrian, mortician, patrician, quotidian, urban

We do not find *-an* on compounds or phrases.

Unlike *-ist*, *-an* rarely attaches to adjectives. There are no examples of this suffix attaching to underived adjectives, and although there are a number of apparent forms that appear to be derived on adjectives in *-ic* and *-ary*, it is unclear on semantic grounds whether these should be analysed as true derivations from the adjectives. In forms like *electrician* or *diagnostician*, derivation from the adjective seems plausible, but such an analysis seems less plausible for *theoretician* (a *theoretician* is someone who does theory), for example. Also unclear is whether forms like *parliamentarian* and *disciplinarian* are derived from adjectives *parliamentary* and *disciplinary* or from the corresponding nouns *parliament* and *discipline*. To complicate matters further, there is also the suffix *-arian*, which we will discuss further below.

Except when attached to proper nouns, *-an* takes almost exclusively non-native bases (but see the exception *elvan*). It characteristically induces stress shift and palatalization of /t/, /s/, /k/, in the appropriate environments, with primary stress appearing on the syllable preceding the suffix—either the penultimate or antepenultimate, depending on whether the suffix is *-an* or has an extender *-i-* or *-e-*. For a more detailed discussion of the stress patterns of *-an* derivatives the reader is referred to the chapter on derived adjectives (Chapter 14), where the pertinent properties are dealt with in the context of intricacies of related adjectival stress shifts.

The affix appears mostly as *-ian*, with *-an* occuring only rarely on common nouns (*protozoan*), bound bases (*vegan*), and personal names (*Augustan, Copernican, Elizabethan, Malartan, Petrarchan, Paulan*). The variant without extender appears with some frequency on place names, especially those ending in vowels to begin with (*African, American, Anjouan, Antiguan, Calcuttan, Chicagoan, Roman*). Base-final schwa often coalesces with the schwa-initial suffix, but it is not systematic where we find *-an* and where we find *-ian* on place names ending in <a> or <o>; compare forms like *Barcelonian* and *Canadian* to *American* and *Calcuttan*. Consonant-final place names tend to take *-ian* (*Brazilian, Brightonian, Chaddian,*

Egyptian, Palestinian), although forms like *Roman* also exist. Truncation of final segments can also be seen in cases like *Barbadian, Belgian,* and *Athenian.*

Of the two suffixes *-ist* and *-an, -ist* is clearly the more productive one on common nouns, with both suffixes displaying productivity on proper nouns. Humorous forms like *fattist* or *duckist* (see example (22)) suggest that *-ist* is productive to some extent on the pattern of 'person bearing a prejudice against X', but it also seems likely that given a new activity, *-ist* would be available simply for naming a practitioner of that activity; so someone engaging in the relatively novel fitness activity called *zumba* might very likely be referred to as a *zumbaist*, far less likely as a *zumbian*. On the other hand, it seems possible to attach *-ist* and *-ian* to just about any personal name, deriving a noun denoting an adherent or follower: *Bauerist, Bauerian, Lieberist, Lieberian, Plagist, Plagian* all seem likely creations, given the right circumstances.

11.2.1.3 *Minor suffixes:* -eer, -ster, -meister, -nik, -arian

It should be said at the outset that *-eer, -ster,* and *-meister* are all surprisingly productive, per-haps more so in NAmE than BrE (*-meister* seems to be NAmE only), although they are far more limited in terms of register and pragmatics than the previously discussed agentives. That is, the number of types to be found in the corpora is relatively small, but there are nev-ertheless quite a few low frequency and unfamiliar items among them that do not appear in the *OED*. These suffixes are all agentive in flavour, but unlike the affixes discussed above, each has an extra evaluative nuance along with agentivity. We will return to their semantic proper-ties in Section 11.3.1.

All three attach primarily to nouns, both simple and complex, although all three can also be found occasionally on verbal bases, and *-meister* and *-ster* appear on a few adjectival bases. Only *-eer* appears on bound bases, all of these being established examples borrowed directly from French. In NAmE, *-ster* also attaches to proper names, where it is always accompanied by the determiner *the* (that is, *the Bingster, the Newtster*):

(25) *-eer*

    a. *on simple nouns:* budgeteer, cameleer, canyoneer, planeteer, summiteer

    b. *on complex nouns:* allotmenteer, concessioneer, conventioneer, leafleteer

    c. *on phrases:* free-marketeer

    d. *on verbs:* envisioneer, imagineer, orienteer

    e. *on bound bases:* buccaneer, pioneer, volunteer

(26) *-ster*

    a. *on simple nouns:* anorakster, corkster, dealster, fraudster, funster, soupster, twerpster

    b. *on compounds:* junk-bondster

    c. *on proper nouns*: Binkster, Budster, Chuckster, Newtster

    d. *on adjectives*: hepster, oldster, swankster, youngster

    e. *on verbs*: dumpster, dunkster, spinster, strumster

(27) *-meister*

    a. *on simple nouns*: bagelmeister, cafemeister, peatmeister, ragemeister, trashmeister

    b. *on complex nouns*: action-meister, blockbuster-meister, coalition-meister, licemeister, mega-hitmeister

    c. *on adjectives*: glibmeister

    d. *on verbs*: boinkmeister, carvemeister, drill-meister, skimeister, talkmeister

These suffixes display no allomorphy, although apparent extenders appear in a few cases with *-eer*: *funkateer, muleteer, mouseketeer*, the latter clearly on analogy to *musketeer*. Although *-eer* favours non-native bases, all three can be found on either native or non-native bases.

The suffix *-nik* was productive primarily in the 1960s and 1970s (see Bauer 1983: 256–66), with denominal, deverbal, and deadjectival forms such as *citynik, failnik*, but also derivatives based on phrases (e.g. *holdupnik, no-goodnik, nuclear-freezenik, way-outnik*). In COCA and the BNC we also find very few more recent formations such as *flopnik*.

In many cases derivatives ending in the string <arian> can be analysed as containing the adjectival or nominal suffix *-ary* followed by the nominal suffix *-an* (e.g. *contr-ary-an, document-ary-an, libr-ary-an*). The reason for treating *-arian* as a suffix in its own right is that it attaches (moderately productively) to many bases where no corresponding form in *-ary* (or *-ar* form) is attested (e.g. *conservatarian, fruitarian, trinitarian, vegetarian* versus ✋*conservat-ary*, ✋*fruit-ary*, ✋*trinit-ary*, ✋*veget-ary*). In these cases, the derivatives in *-arian* regularly denote persons who follow a doctrine or frame of thought related to the base. The suffix is auto-stressed with main stress on the antepenultimate syllable (*authoritárian, communitárian, uniformitárian*). In COCA as well as the BNC we find the suffix exclusively on non-native bases.

11.2.2 Object-referencing affixes: *-ee*

The suffix *-ee* is the only suffix in contemporary English that is primarily object-referencing, although as we will see in Section 11.3.1, its semantics is fairly complex. It can be found on a wide variety of verbal bases, and occasionally on nominal bases:

(28) *-ee on verbs*

    a. *on transitive verbs*: arrestee, batteree, clonee, crushee, infectee, offendee, penetratee, producee, spankee

b. *on ditransitive verbs*: addressee, allotee, assignee, consignee, dedicatee, givee, issuee, offeree

c. *on verbs with prepositional objects*: complainee, conferee, insistee, lookee

d. *on unergative verbs*: bowlee, enlistee, snoree

e. *on unaccusative verbs*: fallee, standee

(29) -ee *on nouns*: bargee, biographee, executionee, haircutee, mastectomee, migrainee, refugee

Among the verbal bases, forms derived on transitives and ditransitives are most common, as would be expected for a suffix that is primarily object-referencing. It is interesting, however, that intransitive verbs—both unaccusative and unergative—are also attested. The reasons for this will be clarified in Section 11.3.1. Forms on nominal bases are rare, but they do occur.

The suffix *-ee* can be found on both native and non-native bases:

(30) a. -ee *on native bases:* askee, callee, chokee, cuddleee, drawee, fuckee, gossippee, helpee, standee, tellee, washee, wishee

b. -ee *on non-native bases*: complainee, contactee, expellee, indictee, interpretee, monitoree, observee, seducee

The suffix *-ee* prefers underived bases, but does occasionally appear on complex bases, as in *blackmailee, optionee, overlappee*. For verbal bases in *-ate*, the suffix is sometimes truncated (*amelioree, nominee, rehabilitee, separee*) and sometimes not (*appropriatee, delegatee, enunciatee*). Like *-arian*, *-ee* itself bears primary stress, with the usual stress alternation effects auto-stressed suffixes bring with them (*emplóy*, but *èmployée*; see Chapter 9.4.3).

It is unclear whether argument structure can be projected with deverbal derivations in *-ee*. It is easy enough to find phrases like *the company's employee* attested, but more difficult to argue that *the company* is a projection of the subject argument of the verb, as opposed to a simple possessor. In the example from COCA in (31), however, the presence of the adjective *recent* forces the subjective reading of the possessive phrase:

(31) *Arab Studies Quarterly 2002:* It is no surprise that both interim Afghan President Hamid Karzai and Zalmay Khalilzad, Bush's recent **appointee** as special envoy to Afghanistan, were former consultants to UNOCAL, the United States oil company that has sought to build an oil pipeline through Afghanistan.

Other convincing examples that are suggestive of the projection of argument structure come from ditransitive verbs, where the *-ee* form is construed as goal, and the theme argument appears in a prepositional phrase headed by *of*. Examples like the following can be found in COCA.

(32)   *Style 2002:* The "gentle friend," however, seems to disappear from the poem at its conclusion, frozen out of the scene as the speaker turns definitively toward her disembodied lover, the **addressee** of her final series of speech acts: "shall not I, too, be, /My spirit-love! upborne to dwell with thee?"

The Salzburg Years 1991: Meanwhile Queen Charlotte had asked to be the **dedicatee** of some of Mozart's works which Leopold duly had engraved at his own expense.

Such examples are relatively infrequent, however, and we must conclude that at this point the evidence in favour of projection of argument structure is suggestive but not conclusive.

11.2.3 Inhabitant and language: *-ite, -ese, -ish, -i*

The suffixes *-ite, -ese, -ish, -i,* and *-an* all form inhabitant and/or language nouns. We have already discussed the formal characteristics of *-an* in Section 11.2.1. Here we will take up *-ite, -ese, -ish,* and *-i.* These four have in common their propensity to attach to proper nouns, especially place names, and to designate inhabitants associated with those places, among other things. We will go into their semantic characteristics in Section 11.3.2.

The suffix *-ite* occurs with some productivity on names of cities, counties, and states, as well as on personal names, in which case it means 'follower of', see Section 11.3.2.

(33)   a. *-ite on place names:* Berkeleyite, Bethlehemite, Bombayite, Boulderite, Bronxite, Brooklynite, Cannes-ite, Dallasite, Hampshireite, Hamptonite, Harlemite, Hebronite, Houston-ite, Jerusalemite, Labradorite, Manhattanite, Memphisite, Muscovite, Seattleite, Wisconsinite, Wyomingite

   b. *-ite on personal names:* Austenite, Bakuninite, Benjaminite, Benthamite, Brezhnevite, Buchananite, Carterite, Clarkite, Clintonite, Friedmanite, Mengele-ite, Naderite, Paulite, Reaganite, Saddamite, Thatcherite

Interestingly, it is infrequent on names of countries, although we do find *Yemenite* alongside *Yemeni.* Some of the formations we find are Biblical in reference, among them *Canaanite, Gileadite, Israelite, Nazarite.*

The suffix is rarely found on common nouns or adjectives, although there are a few well-established forms like *anchorite, laborite, socialite, stylite,* and *urbanite.* More frequently we find *-ite* on bound bases, where it forms chemical, geological, or biological terms.

(34)   coprolite, hydrosulfite, merozoite, nitrite, stalagtite, trilobite

According to the *OED,* the chemical use is actually not the same suffix as *-ite* in the other cases, but was created as 'the systematic termination of the names of the salts of acids denominated by adjectives in *-ous*', to differentiate such substances from salts corresponding to adjectives in *-ic,* which receive the ending *-ate.*

The suffix *-ese* occurs frequently and productively on place names, on proper nouns other than place names, and on common nouns. With place names it can designate either the inhabitant noun or the noun naming the language, or both. With other bases, it designates something pertaining to language; we will go into its nuances in such cases more deeply in Section 11.3.2.

(35) a. -ese *on place names*: Burmese, Cantonese, Lebanese, Sudanese

   b. -ese *on proper nouns other than place names*: Australopithese, Clintonese, Greenspanese, Newsweek-ese, Starbucks-ese, Swinburnese, Whitehallese

   c. -ese *on common nouns*: aboriginese, cat-ese, computerese, dissertation-ese, doctor-ese, funeralese, headlinese, motherese, servicese

   d. -ese *on adjectives or nouns*: Americanese, evangelicalese, institutionalese, legalese, medicalese, mid-Victorianese

On common nouns it does not discriminate between native and non-native bases.

On place names it frequently results in elision of a base final /ə/ (*Burmese, Chinese, Guyanese*), and occasionally other segments (*Lebanese, Portuguese*), or insertion of an extender which avoids vowel hiatus (*Balinese, Congolese, Javanese, Rwandanese, Shanghainese, Togolese*), but examples like *Faroese* and *Chicagoese* suggest that this phenomenon is not systematic. The suffix bears primary stress, so when it is attached to a base with stress on the final syllable, stress shift occurs: *Sudán ~ Sùdanése, Taiwán ~ Tàiwanése*.

Neither the suffix *-ish* nor the suffix *-i* are productive in forming names of nationalities (*-ish* is productive elsewhere, see Chapter 14). Each is used in just a handful of cases to form the noun referring to the inhabitants and/or language of a country or other geographic designation.

(36) a. *inhabitant names in* -i: Adeni, Azerbaijani, Azeri, Baluchi, Bangladeshi, Bengali, Bhutani, Bihari, Gujarati, Iraqi, Israeli, Kashmiri, Kuwaiti, Nepali, Pakistani, Panjabi, Somali, Tajiki, Yemeni, Zanzibari

   b. *inhabitant names in* -ish: Danish, English, Finnish, Flemish, Frankish, Gaulish, Irish, Kentish, Kurdish, Pictish, Polish, Spanish, Swedish, Turkish

The suffix *-i* seems to be confined to inhabitant names in parts of the Middle and Far East. Bauer (1983: 253–5) raises the question whether it makes sense even to call *-i* a bona fide English suffix, as many of the items in (36a) are borrowed, and limitations on available bases make the creation of new forms unlikely. The suffix *-ish* seems to occur only on monosyllabic bases.

With regard to inhabitant names, it is generally hard to find clear patterns. Two potential patterns are that place names ending in *ton* take *-ian* (*Bostonian, Wellingtonian*), and those ending in *-land* tend to take *-er* (e.g. *Aucklander, Icelander*), but there are many instances of unpredictable bases (*Scotland • Scot, Monaco • Monegasque, Uzbekistan • Uszbek*).

11.2.4 Gender: *-ess, -ette, -trix*

Of the three contemporary feminizing suffixes, *-ess* and *-ette* display modest productivity, whereas few new forms in *-trix* can be found in the corpora. All three are confined to nominal bases, either native or non-native:

(37)   a. *-ess*: bartendress, bumess, composeress, dictatress, falconress, folkstress, funkstress, hauntress, huckstress, kidnapperess, maestress, mentoress, monstress, punkstress, vampiress, witchess

   b. *-ette*: astronette, bumette, chefette, columnistette, conductorette, disciplette, dudette, goblinette, gothette, hustlerette, idolette, nerdette, professorette, raiderette, reporterette, santa-ette, wenchette

   c. *-trix*: auctionatrix, auxiliatrix, coredemptrix, punditrix, robotrixes

The only base allomorphy we find with *-ess* and *-ette* is the frequent elision of /ə/ in bases ending with the suffix *-er* or *-or*. The form *governess* may be analysed as having base-final *-or* elided, or as a rare case of *-ess* attached to a verb. The form *governess* could, however, also be analysed as a case of (lexicalized) haplology, analogous to *murderess* and *sorceress* (Chapter 9.5, Plag 1998: 206).

11.2.5 Prefixes

There are also four person noun-forming prefixes *grand-, great-, step-,* and *vice-,* which all attach exclusively to nouns (e.g. *grandmother, grand-niece, step-daddy, stepfather, stepnephew, vice-chair, vice-chancellor, vice-regent*). The *grand-* and *step-* formations are main-stressed on the prefix, while *great-* and *vice-* formations are regularly secondarily stressed on the prefix, with occasional, lexicalized exceptions (e.g. *víceroy*).

11.3 SEMANTIC CONSIDERATIONS

What is most striking about the affixes discussed in this chapter is the degree of polysemy that they exhibit, and the extent to which their domains overlap with one another. Although one might expect that affixes would exhibit distinct and specialized semantic domains, this is certainly not the case in contemporary English. At best we can speak of the predominant semantic domains or functions of an affix, but virtually all the affixes we discuss in this chapter also have secondary domains or functions. Indeed, they overlap in some cases with the noun-forming affixes discussed in Chapters 10 and 12.

Table 11.1 illustrates these points by giving an overview of the semantic domains in which the personal/participant suffixes overlap with the event/state/result suffixes. The overlaps are restricted to those semantic domains that might be characterized as thematic domains, that is, domains like agent, experiencer, instrument, patient, theme, goal, location, measure, and means. Athematic domains (e.g. 'follower', 'inhabitant', or 'chemical') show no rivalry between the suffixes of the two sets.

Table 11.1 shows that each of the event/state/result suffixes has a secondary usage as a personal noun-forming suffix, and that these formations cover the whole range of the meanings that are conveyed by the personal suffixes, apart from the instrumental meaning, which is reserved for the two suffixes *-er* and *-ant*. The suffix *-er* has the widest distribution and the largest number of rival suffixes.

In what follows the semantic behaviour of the personal suffixes in Table 11.1 will be discussed in more detail, beginning with the thematic domain, in which all derivatives denote participants in events. We then go on to look at non-thematic domains including affixes that form nouns denoting followers, inhabitants, names of languages, chemical, biological, or geological terms, kinship terms, or terms denoting gender.

11.3.1 Thematic domains

The thematic domains we will explore here are those of agent (also experiencer, stimulus), instrument, patient/theme, goal, location, measure, and means (see Chapter 2). English is

Table 11.1 Overlapping semantic domains: thematic readings of nominal suffixes

	Agent/ exper./ stimul.	Instrument	Patient/ theme	Location	Measure	Means
Personal/ participant						
-er	prim	prim	sec	sec	sec	sec
-ant	prim	prim				
-ist	prim					
-ee	sec		prim			
-an	prim					
-ster	eval					
-eer	eval					
-meister	eval					
Event/ state/ result						
-ing	sec		sec	sec		sec
-ation	sec		sec	sec	sec	sec
-ment			sec	sec		sec
-ure			sec	sec		
-ance			sec	sec	sec	sec
-age			sec	sec		
-ery			sec	sec		
conversion			sec	sec	sec	sec

Note: prim = primary use, sec = secondary use, eval = with evaluative flavour

rich in derivational affixes that form agent nouns, with agent-forming affixes frequently also deriving instrument nouns. Interestingly, the language is far less rich in affixes that derive other thematic domains. Indeed, what we find is that thematic domains other than agent and instrument are generally covered by a number of affixes, with those affixes in turn often being used primarily or partially for other purposes.

11.3.1.1 *Agent, experiencer, instrument:* -er

The primary affixes in English for deriving agent, experiencer, and instrument nouns are *-er*, *-ant*, *-ist*, and *-an*, with *-er* being by far the most productive. Although agent nouns formed with the suffixes discussed in this section can denote professionals (e.g. *accountant, acupuncturist, biologist, breeder, clarinettist, consultant, grammarian, librettist, mortician, photographer, pianist, taxidermist, trader, writer*), they certainly need not; whether they do or not depends to some extent on whether the verbal base involves an activity that can be done as an occupation. Certainly, for example, *mortician* denotes a professional, but only because preparation of the dead for burial is not something that is done casually. Similarly with *acupuncturist*. But for *clarinettist* or *photographer*, the non-professional reading is certainly possible.

The vast majority of agent terms are derived with the suffix *-er*; indeed *-er* is probably the default for novel agentive formations, as the low-frequency items below suggest.

(38) a. *New England Review 2007*: She didn't remember him being such an inveterate **shrugger**.

   b. *NPR Science 2009*: That's more straightforward. One of our Twitter commenters, I guess a **tweeter**, did note that the promise of this is much better math ability.

   c. *Teaching Spelling 1988*: Because the error often produces a different word altogether the **misspeller** ought to recognise his mistake: so this again suggests poor visual memory.

Whether these are novel forms or not is probably impossible to determine, as the suffix is so productive that new forms derived with it are likely to go entirely unnoticed and therefore uncaptured in dictionaries; none of these three appears in the *OED* as of the writing of this chapter (*tweeter* occurs, but with an older instrumental reading).

Given the right kind of verbal base, forms in *-er* like *hearer, seer, smeller* or *pleaser, screamer, puzzler* may be interpreted as experiencers or stimuli, rather than as agents per se:

(39) a. *Odour nuisances and their control 1984*: A higher test, namely that "nothing in the way of smells was a nuisance to public health unless it so nauseated the **smeller** that he vomited" was rejected.

   b. *Harvard Journal of Law and Public Policy 2005*: The question whether identity is a limitation or starting point for freedom may be a **puzzler** for twenty-first century man, but it is an easier question when tossed the way of Publius.

c. *Entertainment Weekly 2001*: An atypically slapsticky episode, but it works: Perry and Schwimmer do the girlyman thing to spastic perfection, and the final diner scene with Monica dancing to "YMCA" while wearing flame-retardant boobs is a **howler**.

In other words, to the extent that thematic roles other than agent are subject-referencing, *-er* can form participant nouns expressing those roles as well (see Rappaport Hovav and Levin 1992; Booij 1986; Lieber 2004).

Instrument nouns are also subject-referencing, and not surprisingly *-er* is used productively in their derivation. We find forms like *amplifier, atomizer, beeper, blender, coaster, converter, cruiser, freighter, mailer, recliner, revolver, sparkler* which are lexicalized as instruments, but also cases like *browser, camper, kneeler, knocker, rocker, server, slaver, tumbler, walker, whaler* which can occur as agents or instruments depending on the animacy of the referent and on specific context.

Where we find *-er* on nominal, adjectival, or adverbial bases, such forms can denote agents or instruments, just as deverbal *-er* forms can. In such cases, the verbal relation is implied by context or can be inferred from the nature of the non-verbal base. So for example, a *confectioner* is someone who makes or sells confections, a *cricketer* someone who plays cricket, and a *freighter* something that carries freight. Such interpretations follow from the sort of activities that the base nouns could conceivably be involved in.

11.3.1.2 *Agent, experiencer, instrument: -ant*

The suffix *-ant* has also formed a significant number of agent forms in English, but it appears rarely to be productive in this function any more. Of the few apparent novel forms we find in the corpora, only two – *actant* and *commutant* – are agents.

(40) a. *Style 1994*: Stanzel's category, it will be remembered, is based on a binary opposition of the (non) coincidence of "realms of existence," whereas in Genette's model the defining criterion is whether or not the narrator is an **actant** on the story level of the narrative.

b. *Atlanta Journal Constitution 2005*: Compared to my colleagues who struggle with more challenging commutes, I'm a lucky man.... Trim 8-hour commute, then let's talk # You can learn a lot being a "**commutant**."

This suffix has frequently derived instrument nouns, specifically those denoting chemical agents: *accelerant, adulterant, asphyxiant, coagulant, colorant, concealant, contaminant, defoliant, denaturant, deodorant, depressant, desiccant, fumigant, inhalant, intoxicant, lubricant, oxidant, pollutant, propellant, relaxant, sealant, sterilant, stimulant*. Among the apparently novel instrument forms found in the corpora, we find *encapsulant, floatant*, and *healant*.

11.3.1.3 *Agent, experiencer, instrument: -ist*

There are many forms in *-ist* that have a truly agentive flavour, but there are also many that denote followers of a prominent person or doctrine rather than participants in an event. The two readings shade off into each other with no distinct line between them; whether we find a thematic agentive reading or an athematic non-agentive reading depends largely on the nature of the base noun. Given a base noun that can be construed as a participant in an event, the agentive reading becomes more plausible. So a *picturist* can be someone who makes or does something with pictures (see (41d)). On bases that denote modes of thought, political or social movements, and the like, the athematic reading is more likely to surface; a *consumption-ist* therefore need not be someone who consumes, but can rather be someone who believes in some theory concerning consumption. Further, as Marchand (1969: 309) points out, any noun designating a doctrine that can be formed using the suffix *-ism* can also have a corresponding noun in *-ist*, denoting a proponent of that doctrine (see also Chapter 12 on *-ism*).

We will return to the athematic use of *-ist*, including some rather specialized ones, in Section 11.3.2. In (41) we give some of the novel agentive forms in *-ist* from our data.

(41) a. affairist, aggressionist, ameliorist, assemblagist, batonist, celebrologist, concubinist, confrontationist, dietologist, explorationist, expressivist, installationist, picturist

b. *Innocent III 1993*: The priest had to be denounced by his parishioners; many with concubines would have escaped challenge. The married priest might be more obvious to the archdeacon on his visitation or inspection and to the rural deans in charge of the groups of parishes; the unmarried **concubinist** could well escape justice.

c. *The Art Newspaper (1985–1994)*: There he assisted him in the preparation of an installation called "La Salle Blanche". Broodthaers, who was an **installationist** in the days when such work was still rather uncommon, became a guru to a select handful of French and later American artists.

d. *Conversation 1991*: In the all play category the word card is shown to the **picturist** of each team. The all play word is sketched simultaneously by picturists in their respective teams at the start…

Unlike the other agent-forming suffixes we have discussed so far, *-ist* does not also form instrument nouns.

It does have two more specialized functions, however. It is standardly used on names of musical instruments to denote someone who plays that instrument (*banjoist*, *hornist*). Its competitor *-er* in this domain seems restricted to only a handful of forms (e.g. *drummer*, *trumpeter*). In at least one case, both can occur, with a potential for a semantic distinction concerning the type of music or type of harp that they play (*harper* versus *harpist*). And in recent years on the model of words like *racist* and *sexist*, it has come to attach to adjectives or nouns to designate someone with a prejudice against whatever the base denotes (*ableist*, *ageist, lookist*). Some of the latter formations are intended as humorous or ironic (*duckist, fattist*).

11.3.1.4 *Agent, experiencer, instrument:* -an

As with *-ist*, the suffix *-an* exhibits both thematic and athematic uses, deriving agent nouns, but also nouns denoting inhabitants, followers or proponents of an individual or doctrine, as well as several more specialized uses. And as with forms in *-ist*, the predominant reading of forms in *-an* is to some extent determined by the nature of the bases to which it attaches. Agentive forms in *-an* are generally established and relatively high frequency items (e.g., *arithmetician, comedian, grammarian, historian, librarian, mortician, musician, physician, politician, technician, theologian*). We find few if any novel agentive forms in the corpora. This suffix does not form instrument nouns. We will return to the athematic forms in *-an* in Section 11.3.2. As Bauer (2002) points out, forms in *-ician* (as opposed to *-ian*) are sometimes created as a means of elevating the status of an occupation (e.g., *aesthetician, beautician, mortician*).

11.3.1.5 *Agent, experiencer, instrument:* -eer, -ster, -meister

The derivational patterns we have described thus far are all evaluatively neutral. We turn now to the suffixes *-eer, -ster,* and *-meister*, which in contemporary English are agentive, but which also convey special evaluative nuances. Perhaps because of already existing forms like *musketeer, buccaneer,* and *cannoneer, -eer* has sometimes come to suggest someone who not only performs an action, but does so in a warrior-like way:

(42) *New York Times 1992:* There is indeed a larger issue at work here, but it is not the one Mr. O'Keefe mentioned. Mr. O'Keefe, a **budgeteer** who has yet to sit for Senate confirmation of his post and who has never served in the military, decided after conferring with Defense Secretary Dick Cheney, who likewise has never served, that he has the moral authority to discredit the cultural ethos of the entire Navy based on the conduct of a group of drunken aviators in a hotel suite.

   Christian Science Monitor 2003: May 29, 1953 The first successful ascent, by New Zealander Sir Edmund Hillary and Nepali Tenzing Norgay. # May 1, 1963 The first American **summiteer**, Jim Whittaker. # May 20, 1965 The first person to summit twice, Nawang Gombu Sherpa.

The suffix *-ster* is more colloquial than *-er*. It appears frequently in journalistic writing, often with a jocular tone. In novel forms it often carries an undertone of admiration or approval.

(43) *Forbes 1996:* The remaining stake is owned by **dealster** Michael Dingman, now a taxpatriate in the Bahamas (FORBES, Nov. 18), and by Unexim Bank, one of Russia's homegrown merchant banks.

   Ebony 1995: Shaquille O'Neal, the 23-year-old Orlando Magic megastar center and master **dunkster**, is tossing a miniature basketball through one of the many hoops positioned throughout his sprawling, two-story, $7 million home in an exclusive Orlando, Fla., suburb.

The second use of *-ster* in contemporary NAmE is somewhat more complex in its semantics. The suffix is found not infrequently in both colloquial written and spoken English attached to a person's name and preceded by the determiner *the*.

(44) a. *Houston Chronicle 1997*: You need to start hanging out with the **Chuckster** more. # Somebody in the media crowd mentioned that by buddying up with the **Chuckster**, Maloney could have had a guaranteed 6-for-18 shooting night, like Barkley had in Game.

b. *San Francisco Chronicle 1996*: In the business world no self-respecting Republican would buy the stock of a corporation whose execs were jumping ship. And why this sudden flight? Could it have anything to do with the thoroughly inhospitable and unproductive stance taken by the **Newtster** and his gang(sters)?

This use always conveys familiarity, and often approval of the person named, as is apparently the case in (44a), but it can have a slightly derisive tone, as (44b) illustrates.

A third evaluative agentive is *-meister*, which also conveys both agency and a clear evaluative note.

(45) *Atlanta Constitution 2005*: Are we to believe that **coalitionmeister** Ralph Reed expects Georgians to entrust him with the office of lieutenant governor? When swine take flight!

San Francisco Chronicle 1990: Bay Area **gossipmeister** Herb Caen said, "I guess the best gossip item of all time was the one about Adam and Eve and the apple, and it's been downhill every since. Maybe before I pass on, I'll come up with something half as good. [...]"

PBS_Newshour 1996: Sullivan was just the latest in a string of dieting cheerleaders. We've had bouncy exercising, eating gurus like Richard Simmons and, of course, our chief **dietmeister** these days, Oprah Winfrey, whose gains and losses we've tracked as if they were our very own.

As with the forms in *-ster*, these derivations are most often found in an informal register, sometimes conveying pure approval, but also sometimes slightly derisive or self-deprecating.

11.3.1.6 *Agent, experiencer, instrument: others*

In addition to the suffixes that typically derive agents and instruments, we must also mention other means of derivation that only occasionally give rise to agent nouns. Among these are the rare cases of agent-nouns formed by suffixes like *-ation* or by conversion, both of which more typically are deployed in event/state/result derivations (see Chapter 10):

administration, cheat, congregation, consort, cook, delegation, federation, flirt, following, help, prosecution, sneak, snoop, stray, sweep, tease. We also occasionally find agentive nouns derived with the suffix *-ee*, which generally derives patient or goal nouns. We will return to the primary use of *-ee* in the next section, but before we do, we briefly look at cases in which *-ee* has an agentive flavour. COCA and BNC yield the examples in (46).

(46) a. attendee, bargee, departee, devotee, enlistee, enrollee, escapee, fallee, retiree, returnee, standee

b. *Houston Chronicle 1995*: Center Ray Donaldson—a capable fill-in for free-agent **departee** Mark Stepnoski—went down with a broken leg, leaving the job to an overweight, out-of-shape Derek Kennard.

Outdoor Life 2007: For the observer, it may seem as if the falling person arrives at his landing spot in a mere fraction of a second. For the **fallee**, however, there is a great deal of time to think.

Christian Science Monitor 2009: "[…] There is a recently arrived group of excellent scholars of international caliber and international standards who returned to China because they saw its promise, and who are greatly improving academic standards," he wrote. # One such **returnee** is Rao Yi, who taught at Northwestern University in Chicago before becoming dean of the College of Life Sciences at Peking University just as Stearns began teaching there.

The Hudson Review 2005: Ann never left a choice place at the rail during intermission from a conviction that another **standee** would take possession by the time she returned.

While occasionally agentive forms in *-ee* are strongly agentive (*bargee*, for example, refers to someone who works on a barge, *devotee* to someone who is devoted to someone else), forms like *departee, returnee, fallee,* and *standee* convey a special nuance of weak agentivity, as opposed to the perfectly conceivable, and actually attested *departer, faller, returner,* and *stander* (indeed, all but *departer* are attested in COCA with far greater frequency than the *-ee* forms; *departer* is also attested in the *OED*). That is, the *-ee* forms convey a nuance of non-volitionality—a *departee, fallee, returnee,* or *standee* is not necessarily performing those actions willingly, so the use of the normally patient-forming suffix *-ee* rather than *-er* serves to convey that the doer of the action is less than fully agentive (e.g. Barker 1998).

11.3.1.7 *Patient, theme, goal*

The main affix that derives patient, theme, and goal nouns is *-ee*, although many of the nominalization processes discussed in Chapter 10 also secondarily produce patient or theme nouns, for reasons that will become apparent shortly. In the most thorough analysis of the semantics of this suffix to date, Barker (1998) shows that *-ee* produces patient and goal nouns that are sentient but lacking in volitionality, typically animate nouns, and more often than not nouns which refer to humans. For transitive verbs whose object is potentially animate, affixation results in patient nouns. For ditransitives in which the object is generally inanimate, the *-ee* form designates the goal:

(47) a. *on transitives*:

Houston Chronicle 1995: Blame it on child abuse from a cruel father. And, trust again, even long before this misbegotten mystery flight lands in Bangor, you'll figure for yourself who was the **abusee**.

Today's Parent 2000: Whether your child is the snubber or the "**snubbee**," your discreet guidance now is going to go a long way toward laying the groundwork for the turbulent teens.

b. *on ditransitives*

ABC Nightline 1994: I have definitely been a '**leakee**' on more occasion than one. I won't ask you whether you have been a 'leaker', but in principle, what is the advantage to an attorney of getting things out in the media before it shows up in court?

Boston College Environmental Affairs Law Review 1997: To be an intended beneficiary of the agreement, a person would have to meet two requirements: she would have to show that 1) "recognition of a right to performance in the beneficiary is appropriate to effectuate the intention of the parties"; and 2) "the circumstances indicate that the **promisee** intends to give the beneficiary the benefit of the promised performance."

Other derivational processes tend not to give rise to animate patient/theme terms; we find examples like *catch* (as in *he's a real catch*), or *suspect*, but few others. On the other hand, the suffix *-ee* only rarely forms inanimate patient nouns:

(48) *inanimate patient*

Horticulture 1991: When a host shrub is not furnished with branches to the ground, or when the chosen tree branch is out of easy reach, the gap between the climber and the **climbee** must be artificially but unobtrusively bridged.

In the passage above, the word *climbee* apparently refers to a tree. Other inanimates in *-ee* appear in specialized genres, such as linguistics or computer science, where forms such as *raisee* and *controlee* have been coined for grammatical constituents that undergo processes called 'raising' or 'control'.

As was the case with denominal forms in *-er*, denominal forms in *-ee* can carry thematic readings, even in the absence of an explicitly eventive or verbal base. In forms like *biographee* or *mastectomee* the nature of the relevant event can be inferred from the nominal base itself, with the *-ee* word denoting the patient/theme of that implied event. So a *biographee* is someone about whom a biography is written, and a *mastectomee* someone who has undergone a mastectomy.

There are also several deverbal cases where an animate or sentient patient is not a direct argument of the verb, but instead must be inferred from the nature of the event denoted by the verb. Barker gives the example of *amputee*, where the theme argument of the verbal base *amputate* is a limb, but the *-ee* form denotes the person whose limb has been removed. To this we can add a form like *snoree*. Indeed, the verb *snore* is intransitive, and does not have a grammatical patient argument at all, but the word *snoree* can nevertheless be created to denote someone who suffers from the noise of the *snorer*:

(49)   *Redbook 1999*: Buy Breathe Right nasal strips for the snorer and earplugs for the **snoree**, or just reach over and pinch his nostrils shut when the rumbles begin.

While English has a specific affix that derives animate patient/theme nouns, it is quite striking that it lacks specific affixal means to derive inanimate patient or theme nouns. What we find, instead, is that a variety of affixes or derivational processes whose primary uses are elsewhere are deployed to produce such nouns. As noted in Chapter 10, we find forms in *-ation*, *-ment*, *-al*, *-ing*, etc. as well as forms derived by conversion that receive an inanimate patient or theme interpretation, among them those in (50).

(50)   acquisition, advance ('money advanced'), allocation, allowance, appendage, appropriation ('money appropriated'), assignment, belief, bequest, buy, choice, closure, convention, cull, discovery, donation, exhibit, find, gain, grant, hire, hoard, imprint, inclusion, inheritance, investment, jam, kill, knowledge, learning, marvel, mount ('horse'), nosh, offer, payment, pick, preference, projection, purchase, reading, repetition, submission, substitution, teaching(s), tip, want, washing, waste, yield

We also find the affix *-er* extended to form patient/theme nouns. As pointed out by Rappaport Hovav and Levin (1992), this is not unusual on the assumption mentioned in the previous section that *-er* typically derives subject-referencing nouns, rather than specifically agent nouns. In other words, verbs whose subjects are usually patients or themes would actually be predicted to have patient forms in *-er*; examples would be the unaccusatives *fall* and *sink*, which give rise to the patient nouns *faller* and *sinker*, two forms that exist alongside the corresponding *-ee* formations. Similarly, we would expect *-er* to form patient nouns from verbs that can occur in a middle construction, where the subject also bears the theme or patient role; examples would be a verb like *milk* (*this cow milks well* • *a good milker*) or *look* (*she looks lovely* ~ *a real looker*).

   Not all cases of *-er* patient nouns can be accommodated by this analysis, however. We find cases like *loaner*, which designates not the person lending, but the thing (a car or a piece of equipment) that has been loaned; here we have a verb that does not take a patient/theme subject and is not used in the middle construction, so the appearance of *-er* on the inanimate patient noun can only be attributed to semantic extension. Similarly with the use of *shooter* like the one in (51), where *shooter* clearly refers to the animal shot at, rather than the person doing the shooting.

(51)   *Outdoor Life 2005*: I had taken bears before and had been hunting for several years for a truly outstanding bear, and here one was standing broadside at 20 yards. I didn't have to think twice about this bear. It was a **shooter**.

Rolling Stone 2006: Black Thought sounds fierce on this **banger** about the world going to hell in a handbasket

The word *banger* in the passage quoted above apparently refers to a song that is banged out, rather than the person singing. Ryder (1999: 276) gives several other examples that have a patient reading derived from verbs that do not take patient/theme subjects, among them *scratcher* ('a lottery ticket that is scratched to reveal the potentially winning patterns') and *keeper* ('something that should be or will be kept'). To this we can add the word *reader* which can refer not only to one who reads, but to a particular sort of thing that is read (a book of stories or essays that is used for pedagogical purposes).

11.3.1.8 *Location, measure, and means*

English also lacks productive processes which systematically derive location, measure, or means nouns, and therefore we also see extensions of various other derivational processes to these domains. Location nouns are occasionally derived with suffixes like *-er*, *-ery*, *-age*, as well as with the affixes and derivational processes discussed in Chapter 10.

(52)   a. *Location nouns in* -er: diner, smoker, crapper (*etymologically not an* -er *word to begin with, but certainly perceived by native speakers as one now*)

   b. *Location nouns in* -ery: bakery, beanery, bootery, brewery, cannery, eatery, fishery, grocery, hatchery, nunnery, nursery, refinery, rockery, swannery, tannery

   c. *Location nouns in* -age: hermitage, moorage, orphanage, parsonage, vicarage

   d. *Location nouns in* -ation, -ment, -al, *etc*.: camp, dump, dwelling, enclosure, entrance, entry, establishment, exhibition, exit, haunt, lodge, mooring, perch, reservation, residence, rise, roost, seat, store, surroundings, wallow

It is difficult to tell the extent to which these affixes are used productively in contemporary English to form new location nouns.

An interesting development is the occasional borrowing or extension of the Spanish ending *-ería* which forms place nouns as one of its functions (*carnicería* 'butcher shop', *papelería* 'stationery store') to form English place-nouns. The word *cafeteria* has been attested at least since 1839, according to the *OED*, which analyses the suffix as *-teria*. Some novel forms in COCA and BNC still follow this pattern as examples like *washateria, Caviarteria, Danceteria*, suggest. But it also appears that some recent creations are formed directly on analogy to the Spanish affix: *Condomeria, fruiteria, groceria*.

Measure nouns are more often than not derived with the suffix *-er*, although, as we have seen in Chapter 10, there are a few forms from *-ation*, *-ance*, and conversion (*abundance*, *deceleration, decrease, pinch, weight*). Sometimes it is the number itself that is affixed, as we find in the example in (53).

(53) *I remember, I remember 1990*: Should the strings become entwined then the first protagonist to shout "Strings!" had strike and so the conker bashing went on until one split. The winner's conker was then a **oner**, when it had disposed of two it became a **twoer**, but if it should then beat a **threeer** it then became a **fiver**.

More frequently we find a number plus measure word affixed with *-er*, as in a *four pounder*, a *thirty-five footer*, a *twelve-reeler*, and so on.

There is a fine line between a noun that expresses means and one that denotes an instrument. The distinction can be illustrated by comparing the words *beeper* and *stroller*. Whereas a *beeper* is something that beeps, a *stroller* is not something that strolls, but something by means of which one strolls (with a baby or toddler). There are a few nouns in *-er* that have this sort of interpretation (*stroller, walker, viewer*), and it is no surprise that where such nouns occur, the suffix *-er* is extended to them.

11.3.2 Athematic domains

Here we discuss derivational affixes that form nouns denoting inhabitants, followers of a person, names of languages, biological, chemical, geological terms, feminine gendered terms, or kinship terms. In other words, we cover here derivations that denote neither events nor participants in events, but are also not purely abstract (the latter are covered in Chapter 12). What we find in these domains is again a cluster of affixes with overlapping uses.

Nouns denoting inhabitants of a place may be formed with *-er, -an, -ite, -ese, -i,* and *-ish*. Forms in *-er* and *-ite* refer exclusively to inhabitants, not languages. In contrast, the suffix *-an* refers to language as well as inhabitant, wherever there is a language corresponding to the place in question (for example, *Italian* or *German*), although in many cases there is no corresponding language name (e.g. *Salvadorean, Nigerian*). The suffix *-ese* refers to both inhabitant and language as well, but it has also been extended beyond bases that denote place names to other kinds of proper and common nouns, where it denotes kinds of language or ways of speaking, often meant pejoratively: *Americanese, cat-ese, Clintonese, computerese, funeralese, Greenspanese, Swinburnese*. We also find a few corresponding inhabitant and language names in *-i* and *-ish*, but as mentioned in Section 11.2.3, these are not productive. In a few cases, language names do not have inhabitant names of the same form, for example, *Icelandic* versus *Icelander, Finnish* versus *Finn*.

The suffixes *-ist, -an, -arian,* and *-ite* all designate names for followers of people or adherents of doctrines or cultural practices. They are often interchangeable:

(54) a. *-ist*: Buddhist, immersionist, inspirationalist, jihadist, Leninist, loyalist, Marxist, Peronist, Trotskyist

b. *-an*: Chomskian, Freudian, Friedmanian, Keynesian, Marxian, republican, utopian, unitarian

c. *-arian*: conservatarian, fruitarian, realitarian

d. *-ite*: Gorbachevite, Friedmanite, Paulite, transvestite, Trotskyite, urbanite

Although individuals may on occasion try to assign different readings to the various affixes, it is unclear whether there is a systematic distinction to be made. Cases are easily found where there is no apparent difference in meaning, as in (55).

(55)   *Foreign Affairs 2009*: During the nineteenth and twentieth centuries, a **Marxist** theory of modernization proclaimed that the abolition of private property would put an end to exploitation, inequality, and conflict.

Studies in Latin American Popular Culture 1996: A second reason for the crisis in the theory of popular culture was its historic dependence on **Marxian** theory, even if that theory was Gramscian and therefore suspect in much of the Marxist world.

Although *Marxist* may be used more frequently for a follower of Marx the person and *Marxian* for a proponent of Marx's doctrine, this is not necessarily the case, and therefore the distinction is not to be attributed to the semantics of the suffixes.

In this cohort of suffixes, only *-ite* extends to scientific terminology, often forming terms for chemical substances, geological formations, fossil forms, and the like.

(56)   a. -ite *forming chemical terms*: hydrosulfite, nitrite, phosphite, phosphoramidite, polysacrulite

b. -ite *forming geological terms*: meteorite, pegmatite, perlite, stalactite, stalagmite

c. -ite *forming biological or paleontological terms*: circumsporozoite, dendrite, merozoite, trilobite

We turn finally to the suffixes which create feminine gendered terms in contemporary English. As mentioned in Section 11.2.4, the suffixes *-ess* and *-ette* display modest productivity, a fact which should be of some interest in the post-feminist world of the twenty-first century. However, perhaps precisely because of strides in gender equality, such terms have now sometimes come to have an evaluative nuance that they previously lacked. That is, where new forms arise, they may sometimes be used either jocularly or pejoratively to call attention to gender where their bases would typically not be taken as gendered (that is, to refer exclusively to men).

(57)   a. -ess

Paris Review 1995: Certainly, in an attaching-a-philosopher-to-a-radiator situation, the handcuffs win; they are the supreme rhetorical device for attaining juxtaposition.

If you must do this, I do endorse an attractive young woman as a **kidnapperess**, though preferably one that doesn't want you to write a book.

The Doors 1992: In the front of these three monoliths are about twenty beer bottles, numerous Jack Daniels bottles emptied and a lesbian **BARTENDRESS** pouring up a breakfast shot of bloody Marys…

b. -ette

Time 1990: "Some of the girls say I'm a nerd," said smiling fifth-grader LaDonna Wright, proudly wearing her jumper and blouse, "but I say, 'I'm a radical **dudette.**'"

Ind_Limbaugh 1992: It doesn't matter! We're doing it the way the **professorette** in Philadelphia wants and you need to learn affirmative action.

Sleepless in Seattle 1993: This kid calls up and says my dad needs a wife and I'm talking to myself in the car saying, this is completely disgusting, you're taking advantage of a child, and then the father gets on and this **shrinkette** says, do you want to talk about it?

The forms in *-ess* and *-ette* above range in connotation from self-deprecating and humorous to downright nasty. These suffixes are rarely used in an evaluatively neutral fashion in contemporary English. The suffix *-ette* of course also figures as a diminutive, where it is not always pejorative. We return to this use in Chapter 18.

Let us turn to the prefixes. The prefixes *great-*, *grand-*, and *step-* all indicate specific types of family relationships (and semantic extensions of this), which clearly differentiates them semantically from the homophonous adjectives *great* and *grand*, and from the noun *step*. The prefix *grand-* indicates a degree of ancestral or descendant relationship of two generations, as in *grand-child* ('the child of the child') or *grand-parents* ('the parents of parents or of one parent'). More forms are given in (58), from COCA.

(58)   granddad, grandmummy, grammy, grandfather, grand-poppa, grand-uberbabies, grand-sire

The semantics of this prefix requires the selection of kinship terms as bases, but one can find occasional examples that violate this restriction. However, these cases could be accounted for by coercion or metonymy, as in the example given in (59).

(59)   *Commentary 2009*: This open-ended definition of refugees applies for generations to come. It bestows housing, utilities, health care, education, cash allowances, emergency cash, credit, public works, and social services from cradle to grave, with many cradles and **grand-cradles** along the way, to its beneficiaries.

The prefix *great-* indicates one degree of ancestral or descendant relationship more than already indicated by its base. The prefix attaches to two kinds of bases, as shown in the COCA examples in (60a) through (60c). The first kind of base denotes an ancestral or descendant relationship of two generations and thus usually involves bases that already have the prefix *grand-* (60a), but words like *ancestors* seem to be able to be coerced into this meaning as well (60b). The second kind of base is kinship terms that straddle only one generation but involve a sibling on the next generation, as in (60c). The meaning 'one generation in addition' is, however, constant across all derivatives, such that a great-grandfather is the father of a grand-father, and a great-aunt is the aunt of a parent. Kinship terms that straddle only one genera-tion with no sibling relationship involved, such as *father* or *child* are not eligible as bases (**great-father*, **great-child*) and take *grand-* instead. Given its semantics of adding one genera-tion, it is not surprising to find derivatives with recursive use of *great-*, as shown in (60d).

(60)   a. great-grandfather, great-grandma, great-grandkid, greatgranny

       b. *Mother Jones 2001:* And you could see in all these graveyard sites, all the bodies have turned to dust. Our **great-ancestors**' dust is right here.

       c. great-aunt, great-auntie, great-nephew great-niece, great-uncle

       d. great-greatgranddaddy, great-great-nephew, great-great-grandparents, great-great-grandson, great-great-great-uncle

In present-day usage, formations with the prefix *step-* denote for the most part relatives obtained through a later marriage. The prefix normally attaches to kinship terms (e.g. *step-dad, stepfamily, stepmother, stepniece*), but it is sometimes extended to nouns denoting ani-mate beings or groups, or even inanimate things, as in *stepboss, step-dog, stepfriend*, and *stepcar*. In such cases the reading is often extended to mean 'X as taken over from an earlier relation-ship', or 'X as taken over from someone else'.

(61)   Congrats on the apartment and your new **stepdog**! (http://petoftheday.com/talk/archive/index.php/t-82025.html, 21 June 2011)

       stepboss: Your spouse's supervisor (http://www.urbandictionary.com/define.php?term=stepboss, 21 June 2011)

       stepcar: A vehicle owned by your spouse before you were married (http://www.urbandictionary.com/define.php?term=stepcar)

The prefix *vice-* derives person nouns denoting someone who acts regularly in place of the person denoted by the base. Bases generally refer to titles of offices, as in *vice-governor, vice-mayor, vice-prefect, vice-president, vice-speaker*.

....

CHAPTER 12

Derived nouns: quality, collective, and other abstracts

12.1 PROSPECTUS

In this chapter we look at affixes whose primary purpose is to derive nouns other than event/ state/result nouns or personal/participant nouns. Among the affixes we have in mind here are those that create abstract and collective nouns of various sorts, including *-ness, -ity, -dom, -ship, -hood, -ery, -ia, -y, -ana,* and *-age.* We will also look at the suffix *-ism,* which has a more specific meaning than the purely abstract or collective-forming affixes, but which nevertheless forms nouns that denote neither events nor participants in events. Again, we begin with formal considerations, and then move on to semantic considerations.

12.2 FORMAL CONSIDERATIONS

The affixes listed above fall into four natural cohorts, which we will take up in turn. The suffixes *-ness* and *-ity* fall together as affixes that prefer (but are not confined to) adjectival bases. The remaining suffixes, apart from *-y,* prefer (but again are often not confined to) nominal bases. We will divide the latter group into those that typically form abstract nouns (*-dom, -ship, -hood*), those that typically form collectives (*-ery, -age, -ana*), and those that typically denote fields of study or forms of doctrine (*-ism*). The suffix *-y* will be treated separately.

12.2.1 *-ness* and *-ity*

The vast majority of nouns in *-ness* and *-ity* are formed on adjectival bases. The suffix *-ness* takes as its base both simple and derived native and non-native adjectives, and even adjectival compounds, as the COCA examples in (1)–(3) illustrate:

(1)   -ness *on native adjectives:* afraidness, aliveness, awakeness, badness, belovedness, bigness, childishness, cleanness, closedness, coolness, deadness, deepness, fatherliness, gloominess, largeness, lewdness, newness, wakefulness

(2) -ness *on non-native adjectives:* abjectness, abrasiveness, benignness, bizarreness, ceremoniousness, combativeness, felicitousness, festiveness, globalness, inhibitedness, massiveness, obtuseness, perfectness, ubiquitousness

(3) -ness *on adjectival compounds:* airheadedness, airtightness, bloodymindedness, bond-indebtedness, boredom-proneness, choiceworthiness, church-relatedness, earth-embeddedness, five-sidedness, practical-mindedness, running-friendliness, thong-readiness

This suffix is not confined to adjectival bases, however, as it is also found not infrequently on nouns and nominal compounds, on phrases of various types, and on other categories as well, as the following examples from COCA show (see also Williams 1965).

(4) -ness *on nouns and nominal compounds:* ageness, airness, appleness, babeness, baseballness, birdness, celeb-ness, classness, cityness, cousin-ness, event-ness, factness, fadness, goatness, nation-ness, Ohioness, couch-potatoness, cross-borderness, holy-warness, homebodyness, hot-button-ness

(5) -ness *on phrases:* at-homeness, day-to-dayness, don't-know-nothingness, down-to-earthness, every-girlness, getting-on-ness, never-give-upness, not-quite-myselfness, out-of-bodyness, in-chargeness, I-can-do-it-too-ness, take-it-for-grantedness, to-be-looked-at-ness, you-are-thereness

(6) -ness *on other categories:* aboveness, aboutness, afterwardness, alwaysness, beforeness, beingness, comingness, itness, there-ness

Indeed we would be hard-pressed to find any category with the exception of verbs and bound bases to which *-ness* could not attach; *-ness* seems in effect to serve as a sort of default way of forming abstract nouns from non-verbal categories in contemporary English.

The suffix *-ity* is also apparently productive, but more restricted in its application. It occurs frequently on bound bases and adjectives of non-native origin, and as pointed out by Marchand (1969), among others, it is frequent on bases that end in adjective-forming affixes like *-al, -ic, -ive, -ous,* and especially *-able.*

(7) a. *underived bases:* aridity, density, gentility, liquidity, nullity, profanity, solidity, virility, chastity, crudity

　　b. *bound bases:* disparity, dexterity, congruity, mendacity, sagacity, temerity, amenity, celerity

(8) a. *on* -able: addressability, arousability, catchability, changeability, damageability, fishability, flexibility, impeccability, maintainability, merchantability, perceptibility, runability, schmoozability, understandability, vulnerability

　　b. *on* -ive: aggressivity, ascriptivity, attractivity, captivity, collectivity, commutativity, competitivity, conservativity, expansivity, inclusivity, massivity, predictivity, reclusivity, successivity, transitivity

c. *on* -ic: analyticity, apostolicity, authenticity, canonicity, causticity, crypticity, domesticity, endemicity, episodicity, formulaicity, hermeticity, messianicity, rhetoricity, symbolicity, vorticity

d. *on* -al: cardinality, causality, centrality, centrifugality, comicality, communality, conjugality, corpuscularity, figurality, filiality, historicality, ocularity, sentimentality, structurality, verbality

e. *on* -ous: anfractuosity, curiousity, fabulosity, generosity, hideosity, homozygosity, impetuosity, luminosity, miraculosity, preciosity, pomposity, religiosity, scrupulosity, tuberosity, virtuosity

As Marchand and others have pointed out, *-able* attaches to native as well as to non-native bases, and those *-able* derivatives that are formed on native bases can in turn be nominalized with *-ity* just as any other *-able* adjective can.

The suffix *-ity* appears only infrequently on nominal bases. We find the following examples in COCA.

(9)   -ity *on nouns*: imbecility, moronity, nerdity, rascality, scholarity, spherity

Oddly, we also find one novel *-ity* noun in COCA formed on the Greek prefix/combining form *pseudo-*. This could also have been coined on the basis of BrE *pseud*, but this is unlikely for the form in (10).

(10)   *Style: 1996*: Velickovic's pseudo-diary thus triggers off yet another intertextual dialogue, one with the growing number of "true" or "documentary" war-stories. Its "**pseudity**" implies an inborn inability in the museum refugees to discern clear and unambiguous facts, to opt for a single cultural or ethnic notion or adhere to any strong-thought ideology.

An indication of the continued vitality of this suffix is the appearance of forms that are item-unfamiliar and either unrecorded in the *OED*, or listed there as rare or obsolete. Among the forms of this sort in COCA are those in (11).

(11)   Algerianity, Angolanity, Caribbeanity, cosmopolitanity, creolity, crypticity, expansivity, miraculosity, nerdity, symbolicity, structurality, slackity

Also suggestive of the productivity of this suffix are forms that take *-ity* plus some part of a preceding adjective-forming suffix (e.g. *-osity, -ability, -ianity, -ativity*) to derive mock learned nouns. Some examples from COCA are given in (12).

(12)   Americanosity, babe-osity, craposity, fatassability, heaviosity, hornosity, inspirationosity, kitschianity, spinosity, stickativity, suavosity, waterosity

The items in (12) are used in a jocular way, suggesting that *-ity* is often perceived as belonging to a more formal register of English than *-ness*, and therefore that it carries a nuance of pomposity. But the examples in (11) show that when it is used by itself, new derivations in *-ity* may still be neutral in tone.

Note that *-al* before *-ity* is pronounced /æl/ (*normality, principality*), which is not what happens before some other affixes such as *-ia*.

The suffix *-ness* is not sensitive to the phonological or prosodic structure of its bases, nor does it affect either the segmental phonology or stress patterns of the bases it attaches to. The suffix *-ity*, on the other hand shows both segmental and stress effects on its bases. Thus, bases with the adjectival suffixes *-able, -ous, -ic* undergo phonological changes (and corresponding orthographic changes) when suffixed with *-ity*. Derivatives in *-ity* are obligatorily stressed on the antepenultimate syllable, no matter where the base is stressed (cf. *ácid • acídity, círcular • circulárity, límpid • limpídity*). The usual process of secondary stress preservation applies (or vowel reduction and distressing when adjacent to the derivative's main stress—see Chapter 9 for details: *ìnstruméntal • ìnstrumentálity*). Vocalic strengthening of schwa syllables in the base, with corresponding orthographic changes occurs with *-able* and *-ous* (*-able • -abílity, -ous • -ósity*). Trisyllabic laxing also applies.

(13)   a.   *with trisyllabic laxing*

      obscene /əbˈsiːn/   • obscenity /əbˈsenɪti/

      divine /dəˈvaɪn/   • divinity /dəˈvɪnɪti/

      profane /prəˈfeɪn/   • profanity /prəˈfænɪti/

      profound /prəˈfaʊnd/ • profundity /prəˈfʌndɪti/

   b.   *without trisyllabic laxing*

      obese • obesity

Finally, we find the effects of velar softening (see also Chapter 9) with this suffix: a base-final /k/ becomes /s/ before *-ity*, so we find pairs like *electric* /əlektɹɪk/ • *electricity* /eləktɹɪsɪti/, *opaque* /əʊpeɪk ‖ oʊpeɪk/ • *opacity* /əʊpæsɪti ‖ oʊpæsɪti/.

12.2.2   *-dom*, *-ship*, and *-hood*

These suffixes form various sorts of abstract nouns, and formally they are quite similar. All prefer nominal bases, and among the nominal bases those that denote persons (and sometimes animals), although many other types of nominal bases are attested:

(14)   -dom *on nouns*

    a.   *persons and animals:* afficionadodom, beardom, crackpotdom, daddydom, geekdom, girldom, pariahdom, pheasantdom, squirreldom, stakeholderdom

b. *other concrete nouns*: autodom, bagdom, bananadom, breakfastdom, diaperdom, entreedom, moviedom, muscledom, pre-fabdom, tacodom, twigdom, yachtdom

c. *abstract nouns*: cultdom, feardom, hackdom, marveldom, numberdom, slothdom, symboldom, thriftdom

(15) -ship *on nouns*

a. *persons*: advisorship, beginnership, buddyship, caretakership, cockneyship, consulship, fathership, guruship, inventorship, payeeship, queenship, roommateship, speakership

b. *other concrete nouns*: bagship, braidship, carpetship, latticeship, laurelship, seedship, shieldship

c. *abstract nouns*: camaraderieship, hateship, licenceship, loveship, tenureship, titleship

(16) -hood *on nouns*

a. *persons and animals*: anthood, babehood, buddyhood, daddyhood, geniushood, girlhood, gorillahood, insiderhood, poethood, princesshood, wimphood

b. *other concrete nouns*: fountainhood, mountainhood, objecthood, planethood, potatohood, shithood, thinghood

c. *abstract nouns*: articlehood, egohood, eventhood, genderhood, hellhood, narrativehood, one-step-behindhood, legendhood, powerhood, spherehood, storyhood, truthhood, unexistencehood

We also find these suffixes on bases other than nouns, although these forms are relatively infrequent.

(17) -dom *on non-nominal bases*

a. *on verbs:* boredom, rubdom, scrubdom, weepdom

b. *on adjectives:* elvendom, hipdom, nicedom, preppydom, singledom

(18) -ship *on non-nominal bases*

a. *on verbs:* courtship, settleship, viewship

b. *on adjectives:* hardship, entrepreneurialship

(19) -hood *on non-nominal bases*

a. *on verbs:* danglehood

b. *on adjectives*: foulhood, teenagehood, tribalhood, deafhood, falsehood, singlehood

All three of these suffixes can appear on compound and complex bases (*crackpotdom, stake-holderdom, roommateship, insiderhood, unexistencehood*). We have even found one instance of a dephrasal formation, with *-hood*: *low fathood*. All three can take either native or non-native bases, and do not appear on bound bases. They neither display allomorphy themselves, nor induce allomorphy on their bases.

The suffixes *-dom*, *-ship*, and *-hood* all appear to be highly productive in contemporary English. Their productivity is most apparent on nominal bases, but we do find the occasional novel forms on verbal or adjectival bases, as well. Indeed, among the forms cited in (14)–(19), only a few are item-familiar and of high frequency (*boredom*, *courtship*, *hardship*, *falsehood*); the vast majority are not recorded in the *OED*, and are apparently novel forms. We repeat the apparently novel forms in (20):

(20) a. afficionadodom, autodom, bagdoom, bananadom, breakfastdom, crackpotdom, cultdom, daddydom, diaperdom, elvendom, entreedom, feardom, hackdom, hipdom, marveldom, newdom, nicedom, numberdom, pheasantdom, pre-fabdom, preppydom, rubdom, scrubdom, singledom, slothdom, squirreldom, stakeholderdom, symboldom, tacodom, thriftdom, twigdom, weepdom

 b. advisorship, bagship, beginnership, blendship, braidship, buddyship, camaraderieship, caretakership, carpetship, entrepreneurialship, hateship, inventorship, latticeship, licenceship, payeeship, roommateship, seedship, settleship, tenrueship, viewship

 c. articlehood, babehood, buddyhood, daddyhood, danglehood, deafhood, eventhood, fathood, flathood, foulhood, fountainhood, genderhood, geniushood, gorillahood, insiderhood, legendhood, mountainhood, narrativehood, objecthood, potatohood, powerhood, princesshood, shithood, spherehood, storyhood, teenagehood, tribalhood, truthhood, unexistencehood, wimphood

Forms like these are sometimes meant to be playful, facetious, or humorous, but for the most part they are evaluatively neutral.

12.2.3 *-ery, -age, -ana*, and *-ia*

The suffixes *-ery* and *-age* both form nouns that denote collectives, locations, and nouns denoting aspects of behaviour. The suffix *-ana* has a more specific meaning, with its derivatives denoting collections of items associated with the denotation of the base. The suffix *-ia* also primarily denotes collectives and locations but diverse other meanings can also be found. We will return to their range of polysemy in Section 12.3. Here we concentrate on their formal properties, which are similar, although not identical.

The suffixes *-ery* and *-age* attach predominantly to nouns and verbs, although for many forms derived with these suffixes, it is difficult to tell whether their bases are nominal or verbal, as they frequently attach to bases that have both nominal and verbal forms related by conversion (Marchand 1969: 236 makes a similar observation).

(21) a. -age *on nominal bases:* antage, baronage, boobage, brokerage, clientage, cordage, footage, gooseage, herbage, mileage, parsonage, patronage, porterage, porkage, stumpage, symbolage, teacherage, veinage

b. -age *on verbal bases:* assemblage, cleavage, creepage, dilatage, eatage, fosterage, hurlage, pilferage, readage, reapage, shrinkage, spoilage, stowage, tillage, windage

c. -age *on indeterminate (N/V) bases:* awardage, blockage, chattage, dosage, reportage, coverage, cuttage, drippage, leakage, linkage, pumpage, sparkage, wrappage

(22) a. -ery *on nominal bases:* cakery, cheesery, crockery, duncery, geekery, grainery, knavery, midwifery, museumery, nitwittery, nunnery, prudery, riflery, slavery, speechery, webbery, wifery

b. -ery *on verbal bases:* begrudgery, cajolery, cookery, dazzlery, distillery, eatery, forgery, forgettery, gawkery, hatchery, mockery, mopery, refinery, waggery

c. -ery *on indeterminate (N/V) bases:* boozery, cannery, dockery, drudgery, foolery, bribery, fakery, framery, jokery, puffery, trimmery

Both suffixes appear infrequently on adjectival bases. In COCA we find *commonage, roughage, shortage; bravery, finery, drollery, greenery, slackery, snuggery,* and only a few others. The suffix -*age* also occurs on two prepositions (*outage, overage*), but these seem to be isolated cases.

We do not encounter -*age* on bound bases. With -*ery*, on the other hand, we very occasionally find bound bases (*electrocautery, monastery, lepidoptery, presbytery*). One question that arises is how to analyse forms like those in (23).

(23) a. butchery, butlery, grocery, mummery, sorcery,

b. delivery, discovery, flattery, pilfery

Here it would seem that we must choose between an analysis in which -*ery* is attached to bases like *groc-* or *butch-*, or one in which we have nominal or verbal bases that happen to end with <er> to which a suffix -*y* has been added. Neither of these options seems appealing. As for the first, the agentive suffix -*er* typically does not take bound bases, and such an analysis would not work in any case for the examples in (23b), where the bases are clearly simplex. The second option seems unlikely on semantic grounds, as these word show the same range of polysemy as the other -*ery* forms, rather than the semantics of -*y*, which is either an adjective forming suffix (e.g. *meaty, sweaty*; see Chapter 14), or a suffix forming diminutives (e.g. *doggy*; see Chapter 18), or an abstract-noun forming suffix that also derives event nouns. A third possibility seems to be more promising, namely that we have a case of haplology where the output forms lose one syllable if the base ends in /ə(r)/. This is similar to other cases of haplology involving final /ə(r)/, for example with the suffix -*ess*, as in *murderer • murderess, sorcerer • sorceress* (e.g. Plag 1998; Raffelsiefen 1999; see Chapter 9 for a more general discussion of haplology).

The suffix *-age* does not display allomorphy, nor does it induce allomorphy in its bases. The suffix *-ery* induces the haplology effect just discussed and variation between two forms, orthographically represented as <ry> and <ery>. In general, if the final letter of the base is <e>, the suffix surfaces as <ry> (e.g. *riflery, slavery, wifery*). However, there are also words for which this generalization does not hold, and the <ry> variant occurs in spite of the lack of a base-final <e> (e.g. *fetishry, mimicry, rivalry, victimry*, all from COCA). The conditions for this variation are not entirely clear, but it seems that the variation reflects the general tendency of this morphological category towards a dactyl-final output pattern.

Both *-age* and *-ery* accept either native or non-native bases. They prefer simplex bases, although we do occasionally find *-ery* on compounds or phrases (*asskickery, crackpottery, head-squishery, tightwaddery, wedding-cakery, dogoodery, old-fartery, Pink Sugar Cupcakery*) and very occasionally on already affixed bases (*confectionery, witchessery, interlacery* are among the very few we find in COCA).

Both *-age* and *-ery* display a reasonable degree of productivity in contemporary English. Among the forms attested in COCA, we find quite a few forms that are not listed in the *OED*, among them the ones in (24).

(24)   a.   antage, awardage, bonerage, boobage, brickage, bummage, chattage, derrickage, dilatage, dupage, fillage, garterage, gooseage, hurlage, nappage, peakage, peonage, pilferage, pissage, porkage, pupilage, readage, sandage, sleepage, smileage, sparkage, stemmage, stumpage, womanage

   b.   ass-kickery, auntery, barkery, benchery, boozery, brickery, bunnery, crushery, dazzlery, dishwashery, dockery, feedery, forgettery, gasbaggery, geekery, head-squishery, juicery, kookery, meatery, museumery, pimpery, ragtaggery, roastery, savery, signery, slackery, snittery, tightwaddery, tomcattery, vaguery, wedding-cakery, white-trashery

The suffix *-ana* seems to be attached mostly to proper nouns (*Americana, Africana, Nixoniana, Shakespeariana, Victoriana*), but forms based on common nouns can also be found, for example *cricketana* (*OED*), *hooliganiana, railwayana* (both BNC), *tobacciana*). The suffix carries the main stress of the derivative and thus belongs to the group of auto-stressed suffixes (see Chapter 9). In most forms we find the extender *-i-*, but it is unclear under what circumstances it occurs. The low frequency forms attested in COCA all seem to have the extender, while only a small minority of forms, all of them listed in the *OED*, occur without it (e.g. *Americana, Africana*). Forms with the extender show variably a secondary stress and the full vowel /əʊ ‖ oʊ/ on the pre-antepenultimate syllable (e.g. *Nìxoniána ~ Nixòniána*), especially if the base ends in <on>, probably in analogy with pertinent *-an* derivatives (e.g. *Thompsòniána, Washingtòniána*).

We find quite a few low frequency and new formations in corpora, which suggests that the suffix is productive (*Arizoniana, Hollingworthiana, hooliganiana, Houdiniana, Lincolniana, Nixoniana, railwayana, Thompsoniana, Washingtoniana*).

The suffix *-ia* denotes two seemingly distant types of concept. On the one hand we find clear collectives and locatives, on the other hand the suffix is used to create words with a scientific appeal and many different potential readings, two of which seem to be especially prominent. One of these readings is shown by the set of words ending in *-ia* that refer to a disease or condition, the other reading concerns names of flowers and other plants. Apart from a few established formations such as *encyclopedia, fossilia, genitalia, marginalia, memorabilia, suburbia*, the collective and locative suffix occurs productively only in derivatives based on nouns with the final element *land*, as in *Fordlandia* (the title of a book about Henry Ford), *gringolandia, Swamplandia* (a novel title), *New Zealandia, Radiolandia, TacoLandia* (the name of a taco stand). Other productive formations are much rarer, but can be found, and they may also be based on adjectives (e.g. *Americania, Bob-Dylan-Musicia, bizzaria, devotionalia*, all from COCA). Note that *-al* before *-ia* is pronounced /eɪl/ (*marginalia, regalia*), which does not happen elsewhere (e.g. before *-ity*).

Names of diseases and conditions are usually based on bound bases (as in *anorgasmia, homophobia, hypochondria, insomnia*), but occasionally other formations can be found, for example *disorientia*. Floral names are based on proper nouns, as in *Cooksonia, Dieffenbachia, Jeffersonia, Mertensia, Stewartia, Sinningia* (and many more). No matter which meaning is expressed, stress is always found on the penultimate syllable of the derivative, with the usual side-effects for the prosody of the base.

12.2.4 *-ism*

This suffix is highly productive, forming nouns referring to doctrines, kinds of speech, and scientific (or pseudo-scientific or mock scientific) fields of study.

The suffix *-ism* is formally much like *-ist* (see Chapter 11). This abstract noun suffix attaches to nouns, both proper and common, to adjectives, and to bound bases but only rarely to other categories such as verbs and adverbs. Among nouns and adjectives it attaches to both simple and complex forms, if anything taking an even wider range of already-suffixed bases than *-ist* does.

(25)   -ism *on underived nouns*

    a.   *on proper nouns:* Baathism, Bartokism, Bushism, Cezannism, Daltonism, Darwinism, Freudism

    b.   *on common nouns:* ageism, alcoholism, tourism, bossism, boyism, careerism, clanism, cougarism, dwarfism, faddism, foodism, motherism, salaryism

(26)   -ism *on complex nouns*

    a.   *on* -ion: abnegationism, citationism, compressionism, diffusionism, inflationism

    b.   *on* -ite: Jacobitism, Mennonitism

c. *on* -ment: employmentism (http://wikibin.org/articles/employmentism.html)

d. *on* -an: Africanism, authoritarianism, centenarianism, Hegelianism, Heideggerianism

e. *on* -er: believerism, boosterism, computerism, consumerism, founderism, haterism, insiderism, producerism, sleeperism, stakeholderism, strugglerism

f. *on* -ee: absenteeism, presenteeism, refugeeism, returneeism

g. *on* -ster: doomsterism, hipsterism, pranksterism, tricksterism

h. *on* -y: leftyism

i. *on* -ity: securityism

(27) -ism *on simple adjectives:* ableism, absurdism, evilism, goodism, mutism, oralism, purism, realism, rowdyism, truism

(28) -ism *on complex adjectives*

a. *on* -al: accidentalism, bestialism, biologicalism, compartmentalism, herbalism

b. *on* -ic: academicism, aceticism, crypticism, didacticism, hermeticism, heroicism

c. *on* -ive: abstractivism, cognitivism, collectivism, comparativism, electivism

d. *on* -ate: corporatism, separatism

e. *on* -able: fallibilism, infallibilism, possibilism

f. *on* -ant: decadentism, emergentism, indifferentism, militantism, protestantism

g. *on* -ine: alpinism, Byzantinism, femininism

h. *on* -ish: Britishism, Irishism, Yiddishism

i. *on* -ile: infantilism

(29) -ism *on bound bases:* ameliorism, amorphism, aphorism, baptism, fascism, exterminism, illuminism, judaism, Olympism, pessimism, scientism, theism

This suffix seems equally at home on native and non-native bases, although non-native predominate. It is found only infrequently on verbs (*donatism, splittism, distributism*) and adverbs (*beyondism, evenism*), but quite frequently on compounds, both neoclassical and native, and on whole (largely lexicalized) phrases.

(30) -ism *on compounds:*

a. *native compounds:* bandwagonism, big-shotism, blue-bloodism, copycatism, deaf–mutism, foot-ballism, highbrowism, landlordism, meatballism

b. *neoclassical compounds:* autobiographism, cryovolcanism, diaheliotropism

(31) -*ism on phrases:* can-doism, clean-shavenism, come-outerism, do-goodism, don't-give-a-damnism, get-even-with-themism, good-governmentism, hotshitism, me-tooism, not-in-my-backyardism, one-worldism, red-tapism

As with -*ist*, it is not unusual to find -*ism* on multiply affixed bases, as we see in forms like *configurationalism, establishmentarianism,* and *gigantificationism.*

The range of allomorphy we find with -*ism* is similar to that we find with -*ist*. We frequently find elision of a base final /i/, /əʊ ‖ oʊ/, or /ə/.

(32) a. *elision of* /i/: allegorism, conciliarism, exemplarism, Gandhism, peyotism, planetarism, therapism, zombism

b. *elision of* /əʊ ‖ oʊ/: albinism, caravaggism, pianism

c. *elision of* /ə/: Buddhism, Spinozism

Elision is by no means obligatory, however, especially where the final segment of the base is stressed, or if elision would result in an inability to identify the base. In such cases, we find vowel hiatus.

(33) a. *hiatus with base-final* /i/ *or* /iː/: absenteeism, Bennyism, flunkeyism, celebrityism

b. *hiatus with base-final* /əʊ ‖ oʊ/: Averroism, machoism, sopranoism, desperadoism, jingoism

c. *hiatus with base-final* /ə/: Bera-ism, Cassandraism, Pollyannaism, Sinatraism

The phenomenon is by no means systematic, however, as evidenced by the existence of occasional doublets in COCA: *tantrism ~ tantraism, vigilantism ~ vigilanteism, voluntarism ~ voluntaryism, yuppism ~ yuppieism.* And as with -*ist*, we occasionally find stem extenders: *egotism, miasmatism, Platonism, rabbinism, conservatism, witticism, comparatism.* The suffix -*ism* does not trigger stress shift in the base, but it does result in velar softening with bases ending in -*ic*: *agnosticism, athleticism, criticism.*

12.2.5 -*y*

The suffix -*y* derives event nominals (*burglary, beggary, felony, gluttony*) and abstract nouns of various semantic types. For the event nominalizations see Chapter 10, we will deal here with the abstract nouns, the reader should note, however that the distinction between the two categories is not always easy to draw (cf. *cruelty,* which is paraphrased in the *OED* as '[t]he quality of being cruel' and as 'a cruel deed').

For a number of reasons, the suffix is somewhat elusive. First, many words of English end in <y>, but their status as complex words may be doubtful (cf. *amnesty, family, industry, therapy*). Second, there is unclear overlap in distribution, meaning and form with other suffixes, such as *-ery*, and *-ity*. Third, the range of meanings is vast, covering practically the whole range of nominal meanings discussed in this book, from event to abstract to more specialized meanings. Fourth, for certain types of meaning, it is unclear whether they emerge in interaction with their base or whether the pertinent reading should be considered to be a property of the suffix. Finally, due to *-y*'s roots in Latin, Greek, and French very many pertinent forms are either semantically lexicalized and somewhat opaque, or they are based on bound roots whose meaning independent of the suffix is hard to determine. This generally makes it hard to discern the semantic contribution of the suffix. Our treatment of this suffix is therefore quite tentative.

One group among these are abstract nouns derived from adjectives (*difficulty, honesty, modesty*), but this usage is largely unproductive. It is also not clear whether, for this type of *-y* formation, one should also postulate another, separate suffix *-ty* (in cases like *certainty, loyalty, entirety, safety*), whether the *-t-* is an extender, whether *-ty* is an allomorph of *-y*, or whether both *-y* and *-ty* are allomorphs of *-ity*. In view of forms such as *bankruptcy* one might even posit another allomorph, *-cy*. Given the non-productivity of the de-adjectival pattern, these potential problems will be of no further concern.

There are also a lot of formations on the basis of nouns, such as *autarchy, baronetcy, barony, bastardy, chaplaincy, chieftaincy, idiocy, matriarchy*. Some of these have an extender *-c-*, whose distribution seems lexically governed. Even more numerous are derivatives involving neoclassical formations (e.g. *androgyny, endoscopy, isochrony, optometry, philosophy, photography, polygamy, telepathy*), many of them having a bound base.

What is remarkable about the neoclassical forms is the fact that they show stress shift (where necessary) to ensure a dactylic pattern at the right edge of the word (e.g. *phótograph • photógraphy*). Other morpho-phonological alternations occurring with *-y* derivatives concern final consonants, with the regular alternation of *-ate •-acy*, as in *diplomat • diplomacy, adequate • adequacy*.

Bound bases are also frequent among bases that are not neoclassical, as in *family, therapy*, with some sets of forms inviting analyses in terms of base truncation, for example of the base suffixes *-ous* or *-ic*, as in *lunatic • lunacy, anomalous • anomaly*.

12.3 SEMANTIC CONSIDERATIONS

Here we look at the complex web of polysemy displayed by the suffixes *-ness, -ity, -dom, -ship, -hood, -ery, -age, -ism*, and *-y*. Of the suffixes discussed in this chapter, the majority—*-ness, -ity, -dom, -ship, -hood, -y*—form abstract nouns, although we will need to unpack what we mean by 'abstract' here, as the concept is not as straightforward as it may seem. The suffixes *-ery, -age*, and *-y* cover a constellation of meanings that include collectives, locations, and modes of behaviour, but to some extent these can also overlap with the other five suffixes that form abstracts. Our last suffix *-ism* forms nouns that denote modes of belief or action, forms of speech, and fields of study.

12.3.1 Abstracts

English has a number of ways of forming abstract nouns depending on the sort of base preferred by particular suffixes. As mentioned in Section 12.2, *-ness* and *-ity* are most often found on adjectival bases, and *-dom*, *-hood*, and *-ship* on nominal bases. Interestingly, however, since it appears that we also find *-ness* on nouns with some frequency, and at least occasionally find *-dom* and *-hood* on adjectives, we will explore here whether the semantic contributions of these affixes are basically the same, with differences following from the category of the base, or if their contributions are actually somewhat different in nature. We will begin with the case of *-ness*, *-ity*, and *-y* on adjectives, next look at *-dom*, *-hood*, *-ship*, and *-y* on nouns, and finally look at the cases where we find the sort of cross-over in base type mentioned above.

The first question to be settled is what *-ness* and *-ity* mean, and whether they mean the same thing. Broadly speaking, forms in *-ity* and *-ness* denote the abstract quality or state conveyed by the base adjective. So *happiness* is the abstract quality or state of being *happy*, *purity* the abstract quality or state of being *pure*. Riddle (1985), however, argues for a subtle difference between the two suffixes: according to her, whereas *-ness* attaches to an adjective that denotes an 'embodied trait', *-ity* creates forms denoting abstract or concrete entities. What she means by the distinction is not entirely clear, but it seems to hinge on the degree of reification of the quality in question: *-ness* forms abstract nouns with a lower degree of reification than *-ity*. Riddle (1985: 437–8) cites a number of reasonably persuasive minimal pairs to support this hypothesis. For example, whereas *hyperactivity* names a diagnosable condition, *hyperactiveness* denotes only a property or set of properties that can be displayed by a particular individual at a particular moment. Similarly, *ethnicity* is a reified state of belonging to a particular group, whereas *ethnicness* denotes only a quality or property that describes a particular group or location (Riddle 1985: 440).

Persuasive though these specific examples are, not all possible *-ness* and *-ity* pairs seem to display a clear difference. *Purity* and *pureness*, for example, are used interchangeably, as are *exclusivity* and *exclusiveness*, *passivity* and *passiveness*, and many forms ending in *-able-ity* and *-able-ness*. Consider the examples from COCA in (34).

(34) a. purity *versus* pureness

> *Bicycling 2009*: The **purity** of having climbed Galibier is almost too much to bear—so raw, so honest that we need to step away, walk off and again convince ourselves that our jobs are important and our world depends, after all, on paying our phone bills and washing our cars and answering our e-mails.

> *New York Times 1998*: And when the show is over, even if some of us think it maybe isn't so hot that night, there is Harvey clapping and cheering like a fan. He is a fan, and it is the **pureness** and passion of his enthusiasm that has defined his accomplishment.

b. passivity *versus* passiveness

Commentary 2009: His father cleared his throat and Dan realized that the subject at hand was painful for him. Dan's **passivity** was no surprise to himself, but seemed to be hurting his father.

The Untamed One 2006: The woman's **passiveness** angered him. Where were her instincts for survival? Where was her rage that she had been given a life different from everyone else's? Why did she offer him her throat when she should be fighting him to the bitter end?

c. exclusivity *versus* exclusiveness

Denver Post 2009: And, for a few years anyway, filmmakers passionate about telling stories, true ones, held their collective breath and wondered whether they were going to push outside the **exclusivity** of the film-festival circuit and the Sundance or Discovery Channel into the mainstream movie-watching world.

Journal of International Affairs 2006: This would mean acknowledging the limits of pluralism by accepting the fact that all differences can not be accepted and through devising criteria to determine what is admissible and what is not. Mostly, it means sapping the cultural **exclusiveness** of our schools, offices, clubs, associations and political parties.

It would seem that either the *-ness* or the *-ity* form could be used in the contexts above with no apparent difference in meaning.

To the extent that Riddle's observation seems correct with respect to her own examples, we attribute it to the greater propensity of forms in *-ity* to be high frequency established forms and to have lexicalized meanings. Lexicalized forms can denote reified concepts or concrete objects. And indeed many *-ity* forms have such reified denotations. Indicative of this reification is the fact that some *-ity* nouns have become count nouns on specific readings, among them the examples in (35).

(35)   activity, atrocity, authority, capacity, community, curiosity, deformity, disability, eccentricity, enormity, facility, falsity, familiarity, festivity, formality, generality, imbecility, immunity, liability, locality, majority, mediocrity, minority, monstrosity, nationality, necessity, obscenity, oddity, particularity, peculiarity, personality, possibility, principality, probability, profanity, profundity, rarity, publicity, regularity, responsibility, triviality, utility, vulgarity

In addition we find other readings, and often one form can have more than one lexicalized reading. There are eventive readings (*activity, atrocity, festivity*), collectives (*Christianity, humanity, laity, majority, minority, nationality, nobility, security*), many forms denote concrete things (*curiosity, deformity, extremity, humidity, monstrosity*), people (*fatality*), or places (*locality, principality*). A few have specialized to refer to types of speech (*imbecility, obscenity, profanity, vulgarity*) or have an otherwise not fully transparent meaning, as in *publicity*. In all cases, the bases of these words can be suffixed with *-ness* to form nouns with the non-lexical-ized quality or state meaning. We should point out, however, that although *-ity* forms are far more prone to lexicalization than forms in *-ness*, it nevertheless appears that the vast majority of *-ity* forms attested in COCA are in fact not idiomatized. Adjectives suffixed with *-ness*, on the other hand, are only occasionally prone to idiomatization (as in *highness* or *illness*), seem-ingly always conveying the quality or state reading.

De-adjectival formations in *-y* are quality nouns very similar in sense to derivatives in *-ness* and *-ity*, as in *certainty, difficulty, entirety, honesty, loyalty, modesty,* or *safety*. Many *-y* forma-tions based on nouns express abstract meanings that denote various kinds of abstract notions related to the respective base (e.g. *anarchy, allergy, dynasty, epilepsy, lethargy, philosophy*). With pertinent bases, *-y* formations can also denote a kind of behaviour, an action or the result of action (e.g. *burglary, beggary*). The reader is referred to Chapter 10 for the latter formations.

The suffixes *-y, -dom, -ship,* and *-hood* can also form abstracts many of which can be roughly characterized as meaning 'the state or condition of being X'. As we have seen, their bases are typically nouns, rather than adjectives. So we have forms like *geekdom, buddyship, poethood,* or *baronetcy* that mean 'the condition or state of being a *geek, buddy, poet, baronet*'.

The suffixes *-dom, -ship,* and *-hood* are native in origin, and as Trips (2009) shows, all three started out in Old English (or pre-Old English) as free bases that entered frequently into compounds, gradually becoming grammaticalized to suffixes. The process of grammaticaliza-tion has largely bleached them of any original independent meaning, however, and as Lieber (2010) argues, any subtle differences in meaning between forms with the three suffixes appear to be attributable to the semantics of their bases rather than to the affixes themselves. Given specific kinds of bases, we can find extended meanings for all three. So with a base denoting a kind of ruler, forms in *-dom* can be extended to mean 'territory governed by X', as we find in *kingdom* or *sheikhdom*. And given a base that denotes an activity requiring a specialized skill, we find forms in *-ship* denoting the skill itself (e.g. *musicianship, sportsmanship*). We will see that these suffixes can also be extended to form collectives, but we will return to that aspect of their polysemy in Section 12.3.2.

Nevertheless, in many cases we find doublets or triplets on the same base which appear to be virtually indistinguishable in meaning, as the examples in (36) from COCA illustrate.

(36) a. *base*: guru

> *Newsweek 2003*: But despite the lure of full-time **gurudom**, Christensen says he finds B-school life too invigorating to give up.

> *People 1996*: Now the doc is approaching **guruhood** as another chubster, Bill Clinton, signed on, and Hillary asked him to rework the White House menu.

> *Atlanta Journal Constitution 1993*: That's Charles. He'll go out of his way to do something for a friend, even a stranger. Still, a busy life and impending **guruship** do have a downside.

b. *base*: student

Atlanta Journal Constitution 1991: I re-evaluate my situation in the fall, rather than the New Year. It's that mind frame of perpetual **studentdom.**

Commentary 2005: On the surface, Hyde Park appeared to be just another Chicago neighborhood, maybe a little more varied in its architecture—fewer bungalows, almost no two-flats–but the spirit of the place was conferred by the abundance of graduate students and the many hangers-on who, long after departing the university, remained in this enclave in a state of suspended **studenthood**.

Physical Educator 2003: **Studentship** can consist of an array of behaviours (Oleson & Whittaker, 1968). An example might be to tailor their journal entries to what they feel the teacher educator wanted to hear.

A similar case can be made for *-y*, where synonymous doublets like *baronetcy, baronetship, baronethood* can be easily found. We conclude that for the most part these suffixes serve to create abstract nouns from concrete bases, with little or no semantic distinction among the four suffixes.

Interestingly, we sometimes find these suffixes attaching to nominal bases that themselves already denote abstract nouns, and we might wonder why this would happen. Indeed, in some cases, it appears that the suffix is gratuitous, adding nothing to the base in terms of meaning.

(37)   *Fox_HC 2007*: Well, when I saw the movie at the Washington premier a couple weeks, there was nothing new there for me because all of the same myths that he is peddling have been peddled for years by the advocates of single-payer healthcare here in the United States. So there was nothing really new there. As far as **truthhood** [...], it is kind of hard to find there in this film.

Christian Science Monitor 1991: Of the 28,000 ejidos, only 3,000 communities have legal titles. # Even critics long to see the **titleship** problem resolved.

Prevention 2006: Whether your locale has frigid winters or simmering summers, the weather needn't be a one-way ticket to **slothdom**.

It is unclear whether there is any meaningful difference between *truth* and *truthhood, title* and *titleship*, or *sloth* and *slothdom* in these examples. None of the three examples in (37) appears to be used in a jocular fashion or to convey mock pomposity—they seem quite neutral in tone. It is possible that the suffixes enforce a mass or collective reading in these cases.

Having looked at the semantic range of the affixes *-ness, -ity, -dom, -ship*, and *-hood* when they occur on their preferred category of bases, we can now look at what these suffixes do on atypical categories of bases, that is, nouns for *-ness* and *-ity*, adjectives for *-dom, -ship*, and *-hood*. In doing so, we can get a clue as to the similarities and differences in the actual semantic contribution of the affixes.

It appears that when *-ness* attaches to nouns, the derived forms are actually rather different in meaning than the same nominal base with *-dom*, *-hood*, or *-ship*. In its capacity to attach to nouns or to whole phrases or sentences, *-ness* does not so much denote the state or condition of being the kind of entity denoted by the noun; rather it highlights or picks out the significant characteristics that make that entity what it is, denoting the abstract quality or state of those characteristics.

(38) a. *Cosmopolitan 2007*: With that goal in mind, Cosmo asked a variety of different experts to offer simple tips for making the most of four common physiques. Just ID your body type, discover the best ways to work your quirks, and then get ready to radiate some major **babeness.**

b. *Raritan 1995*: Directing a "sorrowful" look towards her potential killer, the bird is, in fact, mimicking, playing her own **birdness**, at least the kind of **birdness** Audubon wants for his lifelike, life-sized paintings.

c. *Christian Science Monitor 2005*: Darrah challenges stereotypes that portray working women as doing all the household chores while husbands lounge on the sofa watching football games. "We found very few occasions of true **couch-potato-ness**," he says.

d. *Houston Chronicle 1998*: This is what it's all about—this sense of empowerment, of **I-can-do-it-too-ness**. # "It's really important to me that these kids, these individuals, get the opportunity to be all they can be, to go out into the community and be useful," she says.

So *babeness* highlights the qualities of whatever it is that makes one a *babe*, *birdness* the essence of *birds*, and *couch-potato-ness* the essential qualities that define a person as a *couch potato*, and so on. In effect, *-ness* homes in on quintessential properties of its bases, whether they are adjectives or nouns. The suffixes *-dom*, *-ship*, and *-hood*, in contrast, have a more holistic denotation; so *babedom* or *babehood* denotes a status rather than a set of qualities. Although there are only a few cases of *-ity* attached to nouns (*imbecility*, *nerdity* see above, Section 12.2.1), we find that this suffix has the same propensity as *-ness* to highlight qualities that define the nominal base.

In contrast, when we find *-hood* or *-dom* on adjectives, the derived forms seem all but identical in meaning to forms derived with *-ness*.

(39) a. *Rolling Stone 2000:* I'm not trying to profess **nicedom** to the world, but we're nice guys.

b. *Radical Society 2003:* This whole time I let my life revolve around a secret **foulhood**, and liked it and let it make me think I was a special person, when really I was just a person who let her life revolve around a secret **foulhood**.

In other words, were we to substitute *niceness* or *foulness* for *nicedom* and *foulhood* in these examples it seems unlikely that any meaning would be lost or changed.

12.3.2 Collectives and location nouns

Our second broad category comprises *-age, -ery, -ana*, and *-ia*. The suffixes *-age* and *-ery* are most frequently used to form collective and location nouns. These suffixes are only partially overlapping, however, as *-age* also sometimes forms event, state, or result nouns, whereas *-ery* sometimes forms nouns that designate a kind of behaviour associated with a collective or group. Some forms with these suffixes are lexicalized with one or another of the various meanings (e.g. *nunnery* is a place noun, rather than a collective or behaviour noun; *buffoonery* is a behaviour noun, but not a place or collective), others can vary in reading depending on context, as can be seen with the examples of *rockery* and *fernery* below.

(40) *collective or measure*

a. -age

Atlanta Journal Constitution 2009: Smith, the UGA economist, expects Georgia farmers to plant 20 percent less **acreage** in peanuts this year and prices to be down 40 percent.

American Craft 1998: Although Di Mare rejected the fisherman's occupation, he reenacts his father's activities daiLy [sic] in art making—tying, knotting, twisting elements into **cordage**, carving small Lures, casting a sheet of paper, working with the materials of wood, bone, horn, feathers and thread.

Town and Country 2009: The shop is stocked with kitchen and tabletop accessories, furniture, gifts, wine and foodstuffs, all hand selected—and exuberantly described in accompanying **signage**—by the telegenic Emmy Award-winning chef and author Michael Chiarello.

NPR_ATC: When hurricanes pass fairly close here, you get enough water **dumpage** where I've seen a three-foot wall of water come down and just take trees and everything out and throw them all in the water here.

b. -ery

Analogue Science Fiction & Fact 2004: Charlie arose, brushed off rusty sand, and surveyed the broken **rockery** stretching to the horizon, listening to the wind keen as Phobos and Deimos gleamed in a navy blue sky.

New England Review 2002: On either side were banks knee-deep in lush **fernery**. At the top of the ridge, the road followed cleared pastures—mathers wondered who farmed them now—to more woods, even thicker.

Smithsonian 1993: In the fairly new, immense underground-entrance space below I. M. Pei's celebrated glass Pyramid (p. 53), dedicated shoppers roamed through boutiques crammed with expensive **knickknackery** and shawls priced at $300.

(41) *location*

    a. -age

        Smithsonian 1990: The architects will be further discouraged to learn that the addition provides **harborage** for other pests besides my family: to wit, starlings.

        Motor Boating 2005: Not far away, a Carlos 'n Charlies restaurant (the first in the U.S.) is perched on the shoreline, providing convenient **dockage** as well as a point where non-boaters can join in the fun.

        Enlightenment for Idiots 2008: The student of hatha yoga should practice in a solitary place, in a temple or a **hermitage**, an arrow-shot away from rocks, water, and fire. The **hermitage** should have a small door and no windows.

    b. -ery

        USA Today 2009: Loren bagged dried milk and ran a forklift at Lake Norden's **creamery** but moved to Willow Lake to farm so work didn't conflict with his daughters activities.

        The Crow 1994: MICKEY is the grease-aproned entrepreneur of MAXI DOGS, a steamy open-front **fast foodery.**

        Country Living 2008: A fern jungle thrives within the moist glass walls of a restored circa-1870 Scottish **fernery**. The Victorians embraced ferns for their exoticism, but also because their reproductive process is strictly behind the scenes. A **fernery** (a conservatory filled with ferns) was the ultimate jolly green indulgence.

        Houston Chronicle 1996: When using stone in a garden, it's important to understand the relationship between rocks and plants—especially if you are going to create a **rockery** or a garden in which plants are interspersed among rocks.

(42) *behaviour* (-*ery only*)

    Fortune 1992: Got a sneaking suspicion that your own company, or boss, may be reverting? Think you may see a few bristles erupting on his or her forehead, reminiscent of Lon Chaney Jr. in the grip of **werewolfery** as the moon waxes full?

    American Spectator 1991: So, while the questions of the appropriate size of government, the appropriate reach of U.S. foreign policy, and the appropriate rate of change in the ethnocultural character of the United States all matter, the question that matters most in the recurring Buchanan controversies is an easier one: How deeply into **kookery** can a man who claims to speak for conservatism go before other conservatives are obliged to repudiate him?

    San Francisco Chronicle 1999: Robin Williams is perfectly cast in this story based on a real doctor who uses **clownery** to reach out to patients.

    Military History 2009: One only has to read accounts of the Royal Navy's efforts to defend its ships from attacking Argentine aircraft during the Falklands War to see how feeble shipboard **gunnery** has become.

(43)   *event/state/result* (-age *only; see Chapter 11 for* -ery)

> *Cross Currents 1993*: Local communities in the biblical tradition can only achieve their
> fullest identity through deep **rootage** in this historical community of pilgrim people;
> otherwise they become isolated, quirky, self-indulgent, and anxious seekers after
> continual emotional highs from groovy worship or instant gurus.

> *Theological Studies 2008*: Among the consummationists, for instance, a serious problem
> proved to be how to distinguish marriage from **concubinage**, which was lawful in
> Roman jurisprudence and had been tolerated in the church for centuries.

> *International Journal of African Historical Studies 2005*: The bonds between grandparents
> and grandchildren within the context of clans persisted even under colonialism,
> enhanced by clans' ongoing resilience as social networks in crises, renewed on a regular
> basis by norms of inheritance and **fosterage**.

In many cases the readings that we find with these suffixes follow from the types of base they attach to. Where they attach to concrete count nouns, the collective reading is frequently available (*jewelry, signage*); similarly, with -*age*, a collective reading is predominant for bases that denote measures (*mileage, kilowattage*). There are also other meaning extensions such as 'payment for' (*postage, stampage, tonnage*). The location reading seems productive with bases denoting food items (*creamery, meatery*) or types of animals or people (*swannery, hermitage*). Behaviour nouns in -*ery* tend to be formed on bases that can denote agents or instruments (*clownery, gunnery*). And event/result/state nouns in -*age* are frequently formed on bases that themselves imply events or activities of some sort (*fosterage, rootage*).

The constellation of collective, measure, location, and behaviour readings seems to be quite a natural one. If we take the collective meaning as central, it is a logical extension from a collective of people or things to the place where those people or things are located, and the modes of behaviour that they exhibit. Lieber (2004) points out that it is a simple metonymy to go from a collective to a description of the behaviour of the collective (thus *midwifery* is what the collective of midwives do). And others have pointed out that place names are often extended to mean the group of people living in that place (e.g. *Seattle voted Democratic*), so the extension in the opposite direction from the collective to the location noun would be perfectly natural as well.

We might speculate, however, on why -*age* can derive event/result/state nouns, in addition to collective or place nouns, as this does not seem to be a simple logical extension of the cluster of meanings discussed in the previous paragraph. As we saw in Chapter 10, the majority of affixes that form event/state/result nouns take verbs as their bases. The suffix -*age* can also take verbs as its base, as well as nouns or bases that are indeterminate between the two, and we find it forming event/state/result nouns where alternatives with -*ation*, -*ment*, etc. do not exist: *coinage, coverage, fillage, linkage*, among others. As we saw in Chapter 10, of the typical affixes that create nominalizations from verbs, only -*ation* displays any degree of productivity, and that only on non-native verbs, mostly those formed with the suffixes -*ize* and -*ify*.

We might speculate that -*age* is marginally able to produce event/state/result nominalizations on verbs for which none of the other affixal means of creating nominalizations are available. Similarly, we have few options for creating event/state/result nouns from other nouns, and -*age* seems to provide a marginally productive means of doing so. As we saw above, the affixes -*dom*, -*hood*, and -*ship*, which take nominal bases, make a somewhat different semantic contribution to their bases: so *concubinedom* or *concubinehood* would profile the status of being a concubine rather than the activity of a concubine.

Interestingly, although -*dom*, -*hood*, and -*ship* do not form eventive nouns, they do sometimes form nouns denoting groups or collectives. Forms such as *brotherhood* and *membership* are often used as collectives, and quite a few -*dom* forms can have the collective interpretation as well.

(44) *Mother Jones 1990*: McNeilly's favorite example of well-executed peacetime conversion is taking place in St. Paul, Minnesota, where the International **Brotherhood** of Electrical Workers has taken the lead in planning for conversion of a Pentagon-dependent Unisys plant.

American Heritage 1990: The Longmeadow Country Club is the most prestigious, and its **membership** is mostly WASP.

MSNBC_Carlson 2006: Surely they may be the envy of mere mortals, but when **celebritydom**'s worshipped couples have a nasty falling out, few of us would ever wish to bask in their limelight.

The extension from an abstract specifically denoting a status to a collective of individuals holding that status seems a natural one, and often it is unclear in context whether the status or collective reading is intended.

The suffix -*ana* is more specific in meaning and less polysemous. Pertinent derivatives denote collections of items that are associated with the denotation of the base. The kinds of items referred to are often anecdotes, sayings, or quotations (as in *Shakesperiana*), but may refer to all kinds of (often memorable) things or activities connected with the base (e.g. *Arizoniana*, *Hollingworthiana*, *Houdiniana*).

The suffix -*ia* is quite diverse in its potential meanings. The interpretation of many derivatives is not very clear. For example, the *OED* gives the meaning of *suburbia* as 'A quasi-proper name for: The suburbs (*esp.* of London)'. This suggests a collective reading, which we take to be the core meaning of the suffix in present-day English, as we find it in *fossilia*, *genitalia*, *marginalia*, *memorabilia*, or *militia*. Pertinent forms that lend themselves to a locative interpretation (often alongside a collective interpretation) can also easily be found, especially with bases ending in -*land* (*Fordlandia*, *Dalilandia*, *Disneylandia*, *gringolandia*, *sugarlandia*). Established names of countries or regions could also be included in this category (*Australia*, *Melanesia*, *Polynesia*, *Rhodesia*). Apart from collectives and locatives, names of diseases and conditions are quite common (*anorgasmia*, *disorientia*, *homophobia*, *hypochondria*, *insomnia*, *mania*), and other areas of application are names of flowers (*Cooksonia, Dieffenbachia, Jeffersonia, Mertensia, Stewartia*) and alkaloids (*ammonia, strychnia*).

12.3.3 System of belief, action, or scientific study

The suffix *-ism* forms abstract nouns, specifically ones that designate systems of belief or action, but it has also given rise to several sense extensions from its core meaning.

For the most part, nouns formed with *-ism* denote systems of belief or doctrine, but they also sometimes denote patterns of action associated with a base. So whereas *Confucianism* is the system of belief or doctrine associated with Confucians, *cannibalism* is not, however, a doctrine or system of belief associated with cannibals, but rather is a pattern of action attributed to cannibals: cannibalism is the eating of one's own kind. Further examples of *-ism* nouns that exemplify the belief and action readings are given in (45):

(45) a. *system of belief or doctrine*: abolitionism, Anglicanism, atheism, Baathism, bandwagonism, Chassidism, creationism, egotism, essentialism, wiccanism

b. *pattern of action*: absenteeism, tourism, athleticism, barbarianism, boosterism, carnivorism, charlatanism, despotism, escapism, hooliganism, mesmerism, nudism

In some cases, a word can be interpreted indifferently either as a system of belief or as a pattern of action; *fanaticism* and *extremism*, for example, could be read either way, depending on context.

The suffix *-ism* has three extended meanings as well, forming nouns denoting peculiarities of language, kinds of prejudicial belief, or types of disease.

(46) a. *peculiarities of language*: aphorism, archaism, Britishism, Bushism, colloquialism, neologism, malapropism, witticism, Yiddishism

b. *kinds of prejudice*: ableism, ageism, heightism, looksism, racism, sexism, speciesism, weightism

c. *types of disease*: alcoholism, astigmatism, autism, dwarfism, mutism, parkinsonism, retrognathism

Use of *-ism* is relatively productive in creating words referring to peculiarities of language, as it can be attached to proper nouns for people or places to denote kinds of language peculiar to that person or place. An *Obamaism*, for example, would be a turn of phrase characteristic of Barack Obama. In forming names for kinds of prejudice, *-ism* is productive only to a small degree, probably because the range of bases that would be appropriate for this kind of derivation is somewhat limited. As for types of disease, *-ism* seems not to be productive in this domain.

....

CHAPTER 13

Derived verbs

13.1 Prospectus

The derivation of verbs is treated not only in this chapter, but also in other chapters through-out this book. The reason for this somewhat scattered discussion of complex verbs is, first, that a number of prefixes derive words of various syntactic categories, including verbs. These prefixes are treated in Chapters 16 through 18, that is, the chapters focusing on the expression of locatives of time and space, of negation, and of size, attitude, and quantity. The verb-deriving prefixes are, for example, *de-* (*dethrone*), *dis-* (*disrobe*), *down-* (*downsize*), *fore-* (*forewarn*), *hyper-* (*hyperventilate*), *out-* (*outdo*), *re-* (*retry*), *up-* (*upgrade*), or *un-* (*unsaddle*), and the reader is referred to the pertinent chapters for discussion. Second, complex verbs may arise through clipping or blending, and these processes are discussed in Chapters 18, 19, and 20.

In this chapter we will concentrate on those morphological categories that are not dealt with in one of the abovementioned chapters. Section 13.2 will explore formal characteristics, and Section 13.3 the semantic properties of these affixes.

13.2 Formal considerations

In this section we will first discuss the verb-forming prefixes that are not covered in other chapters. This is followed by a description of verbal suffixation, conversion into verbs and the treatment of back-formation, and other processes. In the final subsection we discuss the competition among the different verb-deriving processes.

13.2.1 Prefixation

Apart from the prefixes dealt with in the chapters mentioned above, there are three other prefixes that derive verbs: *a-*, *be-*, *for-*, *en-*. They are all unstressed and none of them is of noteworthy productivity in the present-day language; we will therefore not go into very much detail. Some examples of verbs derived with these prefixes are given in (1).

(1)   a. aggrieve, allay, amend, arise, ascend, aspire, awake

b. bebless, beblood, beglamour, befoul, bejewel, belabor, beleper, bepraise, beseech, bespeak, bestill, bethank, betrench

c. encash, encircle, encode, encrypt, endistance, enfeeble, enhat, enlarge, enqueue, entomb, envision

There are not many derivatives in *a-* and the *OED* lists no new formations since the year 1900. Further, where we do find existing verbs prefixed with *a-* it is not clear that the examples even constitute a single morphological category. Verbs that begin with *a-* have different historical origins, some being native (*awake*) and others non-native (*ascend*), and the meanings conveyed by the prefix are disparate, ranging from, for example, expressing upward movement (*ascend*) to bringing into a particular state (*allay*).

The prefix *be-* occurs on nouns (*beblood*), adjectives (*befoul*), and verbs (*bebless*) of native provenance. According to the *OED*, the prefix *be-* enjoyed its last neologism in 1926 (*beglamour*). However, COCA gives evidence of a small amount of continued productivity in the past participle form expressing an ornative meaning; novel formations based on nouns (*bedenimed, bejowled, besmogged, bestuccoed*) are not difficult to find; in such forms no distinction seems to be made between native and non-native bases (see also Chapter 21). It does not appear, however, that other verb forms are being produced in the contemporary language.

The prefix *en-* occurs on nominal (*enhat*), adjectival (*enfeeble*), and verbal (*encapsulate*) bases of both native and non-native origins, as well as on bases whose category is indeterminate between noun and verb (*encash, enqueue*). It has an allomorph with a bilabial nasal /ɪm/ (spelled) before bases with initial /b/,/p/, or /m/ (*embroil, empower, emmesh*), although this allomorphy appears not to be strict (for example, both *emmesh* and *enmesh* are attested in the *OED*). There are also spelling variants <in> or <im>, which can sometimes even occur with the same base, as in <enwrap> ~ <inwrap> providing synonymous outputs in most cases (though note lexicalized non-synonymous *ensure* versus *insure*).

The prefix gives rise to occasional neologisms, with six of them having been recorded in the *OED* for the past 100 years (*encode, encrypt, endistance, enhat, enqueue, envision*). The BNC adds *enmire* to this list. COCA has several forms not found in the *OED*: *encapture, enchamber, enchange, enclod, encloth, enculturate, enculture, enfield, enflood, enfog, enmagick, enmire, enpool, ensorcer, enspirit, entextualize, entragick, envenomate, envoice, enweb*. Notably, many of these more recent formations are denominal in origin, which may count as an argument that this prefix is category-changing, similar to *de-* (see Chapter 17), but unlike the majority of prefixes in English.

Finally, the prefix *for-* occurs in a handful of verbs, mostly inherited from Old English (*forbear* with a spelling variant <forebear>, *forbid, forbode, forget, forgive, forsake, forswear*). These forms are all lexicalized, and the semantic contribution of the prefix is unclear.

13.2.2 Suffixation

13.2.2.1 *The suffixes -ize and -ify*

We will treat the suffixes *-ize* and *-ify* together as they are intricately related. Their meanings, which we will discuss in Section 13.3.2, are very similar, if not identical, and their phonological restrictions lead to an almost complementary distribution with regard to the kinds of bases the two suffixes can attach to.

Bases may be either native or non-native, although non-native predominate.

(2)   a. *on non-native bases*
          alphabetize, dynamize, elasticize, opinionize
          classify, diversify, humidify, pacify

      b. *on native bases*
          awfulize, glitterize, leatherize, womanize
          falsify, prettify, webify, youthify

The two suffixes attach to nouns, adjectives, and bound bases, as the examples in (3)–(5) illustrate.

(3)   *on nouns*
      a. alphabetize, Beethovenize, cannibalize, dieselize, hospitalize, idolize, magnetize, opinionize, paganize, routinize, satirize, sectorize, sloganize, standardize, terrorize, tokenize, vaporize, victimize, womanize
      b. artify, bourgeoisify, classify, codify, citify, countrify, gasify, gentrify, karstify, mythify, nazify, notify, plastify, tubify, youthify, yuppify, zombify

(4)   *on adjectives*
      a. elasticize, equalize, eroticize, fertilize, glottalize, laminarize, nativize, passivize, paternalize, radicalize, randomize, reflexivize, rigidize, virilize
      b. aridify, densify, diversify, falsify, humidify, justify, purify, prettify, scarify, simplify, solidify

(5)   *on bound bases*
      a. baptize, dynamize, exorcize, erotize, feminize, harmonize, maximize, mathematize, mechanize, monetize, ostracize, pancreatize, quantize, temporize
      b. calcify, certify, crucify, deify, electrify, gratify, horrify, identify, magnify, mortify, pacify, quantify, ramify, ratify, reify, rectify, specify, technify, terrify

The analysis of the cases in (5a) as involving bound bases may sometimes compete with an analysis that posits predictable phonological adjustments, as in the case of *feminize* ◆ *feminine* or *harmonize* ◆ *harmony* (see below for discussion, and Chapter 9).

Very occasionally, one can even find phrases as bases as shown in (6). Note that the final element of the phrase is a phonologically legitimitate base for *-ify* (see below).

(6)   *American Spectator 1998*: After all, in today's **Ben-and-Jerrified** Vermont, the only Republicans you ever see on bumper stickers are confined to sentiments like "Newt Happens."

Forms based on verbs are also rare (*schmoozify, blackenize*) as are those on compounds (*hip-hopify*). Proper nouns are well-attested as bases (*Bobbitize, Finlandize, Haussmannize, Chuckify, Kurdify, Lilliputify*).

Quite often, we also find the presence of extenders, as shown in (7), where examples are taken both from COCA and from the *OED*. With some of the forms the morphological analysis involving an extender may be controversial and depends on what is regarded as the base. For example, *mediocritize* could be argued to be either derived from the adjective *mediocre*, with extender, or from the noun *mediocrity*, with regular deletion of the final vowel (see below).

(7)   AnnKleinicize, attitudinize, cinematize, dogmatize, fetishicize, lemmatize, mediocritize, negritize, platitudinize, problematized, rhematize, thematize

Although the overall number of verbs formed with these suffixes might be low in comparison to that of productive adjectival or, especially, nominal suffixes (e.g. Baayen and Lieber 1991), the suffixes *-ize* and *-ify* can nevertheless be considered highly productive, as can be seen from three kinds of evidence. First, there are many recent neologisms in COCA, as well as in the *OED*. Plag (1999: 115) found 346 new *-ize* formations and 30 new *-ify* formations for the twentieth century in the second edition of the *OED* (with the most recent online version of the third edition of the *OED* having even more, e.g. *therapize*). This productivity is corroborated by the corpus data, where we find a large proportion of low frequency forms. For example, the 20-million-word Cobuild corpus (Sinclair 1987) investigated by Plag (1999: 115) contains 80 *-ize* hapaxes and 18 *-ify* hapaxes. Data from COCA reveal even stronger productivity: a check of 200 item-unfamiliar *-ize* words turns up over 100 that are not recorded in the *OED*. Similarly, of 77 item-unfamiliar words in *-ify*, 52 are not listed in the *OED*. The examples in (8) illustrates neologisms that can be found in COCA and the BNC, as well as in *Wordspy*.

(8)   a.   *COCA*

-ize: algebraicize, batteryize, blenderize, clientelize, Enronize, felonize, gadgetize, glitterize, imagize, lichenize, margarinize, mestizoize

-ify: blottify, bumify, bumpify, Chuckify, dizzify, extensify, freakify, gourmetify, hippify, Kurdify, Lilliputify, silkify, startify, utopify

b. *BNC*

-ize: awfulize, Beethovenize, corpusized, Dylanize, Haydnize, Hawaiianize, Marleyize, Ohmannize, otherize, productize, Rwandaize, saxophonize, serverize, Tanalize, taslanize, Tillerize, Wymanize

-ify: fuzzify, geriatrify, gypsify, faintify, Jessify, Lewisify, moodify, sickify

c. *Wordspy*

-ize: dollarize, velocitize

-ify: gamify, sonify, wikify

Both suffixes are subject to strong phonological restrictions. Neither suffix can justifiably be characterized as stress-shifting, but there are other prosodic constraints at work. The suffix *-ize* generally selects bases that consist of a trochee (e.g. *rándomize*) or a dactyl (*hóspitalize*), while *-ify* selects monosyllabic bases or bases that consist of an iambic foot (*ártify, bourgéoisify*). In output-oriented terms, *-ify* derivatives must have a trochee before the last syllable of the derivative, while *-ize* words allow both trochees and dactyls (and under certain conditions even secondarily-stressed syllables, see below).

A systematic overlap of the domains of the two suffixes concerns trochaic bases ending in a high front vowel, such as *dandy, Dolby, Disney, orgy, Nazi, Turkey, wiki*. These forms can take both suffixes, as the base-final vowel and the initial vowel of *-ify* coalesce in these cases, such that forms like *dandify, Nazify, wikify* fulfil the output-restrictions on *-ify* derivatives. COCA gives us *Dolbyize, Disneyize, orgyize*, and *Turkeyize* as examples of pertinent *-ize* derivatives. Where different base forms are available that may satisfy the respective constraints, one can find doublets, as with *Russianize* (with trochaic base) and *Russify* (with a monosyllabic base).

But things are much more complicated than that. Let us first look at stress shift and stress reduction, then at other cases of base allomorphy. Although both suffixes typically satisfy the prosodic output conditions of their category by selecting the right kind of base instead of effecting a stress shift upon their bases (cf. **randómify, *ídentize*) there are quite a few forms that appear to go against this generalization. These forms are of at least four kinds.

The first group of violators consists of cases of long established formations which do not necessarily conform to the present-day restrictions, such as *baptize* (first attestation: 1297).

Second, there are formations that are most probably based on other complex words (instead of a simplex base) and preserve the foot structure of the complex base words they are derived from (e.g. *Jàpanése • Jápanìze, subjéctive • subjéctify* 'make subjective'); we might cite these as examples of analogical or paradigmatic word-formation (see Chapter 23). A subgroup of this set consists of *-ify* words whose bases are adjectives ending in *-id* (e.g. *arídify, humídify, solídify, valídify*). All of these have related *-ity* derivatives with the same main-stressed syllable (e.g. *humídity*), and these *-ity* forms are all attested much earlier than the corresponding *-ify* derivatives (see the respective entries in the *OED*). Given the uniform behaviour of this set of words, this creates another domain of overlap between *-ize* and *-ify*, as we would expect that, without stress shift, these trochaic bases would also take *-ize*. And indeed, such doublets can be found (e.g. *flúidize • fluídify, rígidize • rigídify*), but there are also cases where only one of the two possible formations are attested, for example, *líquidize •* ᵂ*liquídify* and ᵂ*húmidize • humídify*.

Third, very occasionally there are formations that simply fail to follow the clear trend set by the vast majority of more recent forms, as the examples from COCA in (9) illustrate:

(9)   a. *-ize*: blandize, cartoonize, cementize, discretize, event-ize, Francize, Iraqize, McKeachize

b. *-ify*: devil-ify, hip-hopify, Lewisify (BNC), lichenify, parentify

A few of the forms in (9b) (*devilify, Lewisify, parentify*), in order to have the normal stress pattern of *-ify* derivatives, would have to be stressed on the antepenult, inducing a stress shift. One reason for such aberrant behaviour may be that these forms usually occur in the written mode and it appears that the prosodic restrictions are not as forceful in the written as in the spoken language (cf. Raffelsiefen 2004; see Hanssen *et al.* to appear for empirical evidence for such an effect).

Finally, in the remaining cases, the English forms are modelled on similar words from other languages (e.g. *stylize* coined on German *stilisieren*, OED s.v. *stylize*, first attestation 1904).

Overall, however, our discussion of potential stress-shift violators should not obscure the fact that both the newly derived forms, as collected in (8), and the large set of existing derivatives appear to overwhelmingly observe the prosodic restrictions set out above (see also Plag 1999: ch. 6.2; Raffelsiefen 2004: 111).

Another stress-related phenomenon is stress reduction, with concomitant vowel reduction. This alternation generally occurs with bases that end in a main-stressed syllable followed by a secondarily-stressed syllable. Plag (1999: 166) gives the following list of examples.

(10)	ánòde • ánodìze	/əʊ/ ~ /ə/
	pódzòl • pódzolìze	/ɒ/ ~ /ə/
	sílàne • sílanìze	/eɪ/ ~ /ə/
	strýchnìne • strýchninìze	(/i/ ~ /ɪ/) ~ /ɪ/

Note that such words would not satisfy the input-oriented restriction formulated above that *-ize* attaches to trochees and dactyls. From an output-oriented perspective, however, the stress reduction makes these derivatives fit the general rhythmic pattern of *-ize* derivatives.

As observed by Raffelsiefen (2004: 138–9), stress- and vowel-reduction is restricted to the environment with two adjacent stresses and generally does not occur with bases where an unstressed syllable intervenes between main stress and secondary stress. Some of Raffelsiefen's examples are listed in (11).

(11)   áerosòlize, cátalòguìze, épidòtìze, prótocòlìze, vágabòndìze

We note, however, that *láterìte* • *láteritìze* (/aɪ/ ~ /ɪ/) is an exception.

Apart from stress-related effects, derivatives in *-ize* are subject to further phonological restrictions that manifest themselves in intricate allomorphy patterns. To begin with, we have to distinguish between dactylic bases that end in a consonant and those that end in a vowel. Those that end in a consonant show no phonological effects (see (12a)) unless the attachment of *-ize* leads to the repetition of identical phonological constituents. These haplology effects occur either with bases whose final syllable starts and ends with the same consonant, as in (12b), or with bases that end in a sibilant (12c). In all these cases, we see the loss of the base-final rhyme, which can be either interpreted as phonological adjustment or stem selection (see also Chapter 9).

(12)   a. hospital • hospitalize • ☝hospitize
             federal • federalize • ☝federize
             relative • relativize • ☝relatize

         b. ☝femininize • feminize
             ☝minimumize • minimize
             ☝metathesisize • metathesize

         c. ☝Socratesize • Socratize
             ☝syphilisize • syphilize
             ☝tetanusize • tetanize

Curiously enough, disyllabic bases are subject to haplology to a lesser extent, as they allow bases to stay intact even when their final syllable starts and ends with the same consonant, as in (13a). No forms with disyllabic bases can be found, however, if the two consonants are both alveolar sibilants (13b).

(13)   a. mirrorize, strychninize, terrorize

         b. ☝crisisize, ☝oasisize

The absence of forms such as those in (12c) and (13b) has led to claims that there are lexical gaps that arise in those cases where it is impossible to observe important conflicting

In cases such as these, given the existence of established verbs without the suffix, it may appear synchronically that *-ate* has attached to a verb (e.g. *imagine* with *-ate*, *pronounce* with *-ate*). Forms such as these are sometimes frowned upon by prescriptivists, but as the examples in (19) suggest, novel forms are not uncommon.

In some cases, due to the prevalence of base truncation (see below) and non-suffixal mechanisms of deriving verbs in *-ate*, it may not be clear whether a given derivative is noun-based or adjective-based. For example, *federate* may have been coined on the basis of *federation* or on the basis of *federal* (or both).

As with the suffixes *-ize* and *-ify*, it is not always obvious how to differentiate base truncation from suffixation to bound roots, that is the selection of a particular base allomorph. For example, *fraternate* may be analysed as being coined on the basis of the adjective *fraternal* under loss of the final rhyme, or directly on the bound base *fratern-*, which is found also with other derivatives (*fraternize, fraternism, fraternity*). Extenders may also be present in some forms, as in *affect**u**ate, algin**ate, author**ic**ate, different**i**ate, patho**stic**ate*.

The suffix was extremely productive in the nineteenth century with hundreds of forms listed in the *OED*, but, as shown in Plag (1999), it is less productive than *-ize* and *-ify* in contemporary English.

Phonologically, *-ate* derivatives are very similar to *-ize* derivatives in that the suffix normally does not induce a stress shift and prefers bases that end in a trochee. Thus, there seems to be a clear output restriction to derivatives that end in a trochee followed by the secondarily stressed final syllable (e.g. *artículàte, cávitàte, mótivàte*). To enforce this prosodic pattern, more severe phonological adjustments are observable with *-ate* than with *-ize*. Thus, *-ate* is generally intolerant concerning dactylic bases and induces truncation across the board, that is with both vowel-final and consonant-final bases. The examples in (20) illustrate this.

(20)   a.   *Vowel-final dactylic bases*: cavity ♦ cavitate, mercury ♦ mercurate

      b.   *Consonant-final dactylic bases*: alluvium ♦ alluviate ♦ ☝alluviumate, nitrosyl ♦ nitrosate ♦ ☝nitrosylate, residual ♦ residuate ♦ ☝residualate

One finds, however, many exceptions to the pattern just proposed. Apart from idiosyncratic formations (see Plag 1999: 216 for discussion), there are two kinds of systematic exception. First, there is a group of forms whose phonology is a direct reflection of their morphological relatedness, that is, they are prosodically faithful to their base word. For example, Plag (1999: 217) lists the forms shown in (21) as *-ate* derivatives that show the same stress patterns as the action nouns in *-ation* from which they are back-derived.

(21)   formáte, geláte, lènáte, notáte (*BrE*), oláte, predáte, soláte, solváte

The second class of exceptions contains derivatives with main stress on the penultimate syllable. These are formed on the basis of nouns ending in the nominal suffix *-ate* (which denotes particular kinds of salt). As noted by Plag (1999: 217) the corresponding *-ate* verbs are derived by conversion, as evidenced by *cítràte, hýdròbóràte, phósphàte,* and *xánthàte.*

13.2.3 Conversion

For ease of reference in this section we will use the term 'converted verb' for verbs derived by conversion. For a discussion of the theoretical problems involved with conversion as a morphological process, see Chapter 25.

Conversion into verbs is a highly productive process in English, although it is not as easy to document productivity for conversion as it is for affixal derivation, since it is difficult to extract pertinent forms from corpora using automatic or semi-automatic procedures. Nevertheless, we have made an attempt to do so. Plag (1999) uses dictionary-based quantitative measures, and finds that conversion is the most productive process deriving verbs from bases of other categories. Our results generally support this conclusion, but it is difficult to compare the productivity of conversion with that of the suffixes *-ize* and *-ify*, as the methods used for obtaining data are necessarily quite different.

Here, we describe the procedure we followed. We first extracted the 1000 most frequent singular common nouns from the 500,000 word COCA frequency-list. We counted all forms with item-familiar converted verbs (N = 473), and then checked the remaining nouns against both COCA and the *OED* for corresponding converted verbs. To make sure that we had only genuine cases of conversion we searched in COCA for forms in *-ing* or *-ed* that were attested in clearly verbal contexts (that is, when following auxiliary *be*, but not when prenominal). This procedure is quite conservative, and if anything leads us to undercount cases of conversion.

Using this procedure, we found a further 229 converted verbs that were attested either in the *OED* or in COCA or both, and that were not item-familiar. There were 24 verbs that were attested only in COCA that we can safely assume to be neologisms. We list them together with some of their contexts in (22) to illustrate their usage.

(22)   a. animal, army, baseball, bathroom, career 'to have a career', category, chest (*attested in* OED, *but with different meaning*), computer, crisis, decision, direction, door, driver, furniture, governor, manager, prayer, presence, response, song, theme, therapy, version, youth

   b. *CNN_Presents 2006*: There's times that he doesn't remember, but when I was racing, and I was probably more of a no-name, he **doored** me and knocked me out of the way.

   African American Review 2004: You'll be preparing our meals, **bathrooming** us, doing laundry, lifting if needed.

   Sports Illustrated 1992: When Holmes **decisioned** Ray Mercer recently, it took a trained eye to locate Smith amid the assemblage.

   New Yorker 2004: Buck would come **chesting** in, he would give us all a cobra smile with real white teeth.

Conversion into verbs allows a great diversity of bases, including simplex, derived, or compound nouns and adjectives, onomatopoeic expressions, and phrases. This is illustrated in (23) to (28) with a subset of the 488 twentieth-century neologisms in Plag (1999: Appendix 1) gleaned from the *OED*, and additional examples from *Wordspy*. The data in (23) and (24) clearly demonstrate that suffixed nouns and adjectives can indeed be bases of conversion into verbs, contrary to claims by Marchand (1969: 372), Gussmann (1987: 82), and Nagano (2008: 13). Examples in (25) and (26) show converted verbs based on onomatopoeic expressions and phrases, and (27) contains examples based on prepositions or adverbs, all of which predate the twentieth century. This last class of words shows many lexical gaps (e.g. 🖑*above*, 🖑*below*, 🖑*from*), which, together with the lack of more recent neologisms and the fact that many of the attested de-adverbial converted verbs are obsolete (e.g. *about*, *below*, *under*, see *OED*), may suggest that it is an unproductive class.

(23)   *Nouns as bases*

    a. *simplex*: angel, apex, archive, ball, caddy, dingo, doll, eel, fountain, garage, gel, goal, ham, jazz, lagoon, marmalade, matrix, muscle, nanny, napalm, orbit, petal, radio, vacuum, video, weasel, witch

    b. *derived*: birdie, clipper, interface, junction, larder, option, racketeer, sleeper, zipper

    c. *compound*: blockhouse, catfoot, eyeball, filmset, finger-post, highlight, keyboard, limehouse, newspaper, phagocyte, postcard, pot-hole, time-table

    d. *proper*: Amazon, Dell, MacGyver, Nasdaq

    e. *acronym*: RIF

(24)   *Adjectives as bases*

    a. *simplex*: camp, cruel, dual, hip, main, multiple, phoney, pretty, young

    b. *derived*: filthy, lethal, premature, romantic, skinny

    c. *compound*: polychrome, rustproof

(25)   *Onomatopoeic expressions as bases*

    burp, chuff, clink-clank, oink, ooh, plink, poof, pong, pring, quiff, razz, tick-tock, whomp, wham, whooom, zizz, zonk

(26)   *Phrases as bases*

    blind-side, cold-call, cold-cream, hands-up, wrong-foot, wrong-slot

(27)   *Adverbs or prepositions as bases*

    backward, down, in, out, up

Finally, other types of expression such as interjections or conjunctions can be converted into verbs, too, as shown in (28).

(28)   *Other expressions*

    but, oh, no, oh-oh, yes

It is possible to find conversion to verb from a suffixed noun even where the base noun is not semantically opaque, contrary to the claim by Marchand (1969: 372–3), Bauer (1983: 226), and Nagano (2008: 13) on the basis of examples like *birth, conference, motion, pleasure, pressure, question*. Where this happens, the new verb is not always synonymous with the base noun, though it may be, as is illustrated by the following examples from COCA.

(29)   *Christian Science Monitor 1993*: By this week's end we will have **dinnered** eight guests, two at a time.

    CBS_Morning 1993: Britain has something like 3,000 troops on the ground in central Bosnia and we have **drivered**, I think, 40,000 tons of food.

    PBS Newshour 1997: But what we find is that it's a virus that does not match any strain of influenza virus isolated since, but it is most related to the kind of influenzas that infect swine, suggesting that this influenza entered the human population after being **passaged** through pigs.

In the first case, it does not seem strange to find the verb *dinner* with the meaning 'provide dinner to', as this is clearly distinct from the meaning of *dine*. However, the two following converted verbs are more surprising, since the base verbs *drive* and *pass* would seem to fit the contexts above just as well as the converted verbs.

    Given a homophonous pair of words, one of them being a verb, and the other of some other category, it is not always clear whether the verb should be analysed as the derived word, but it seems that in most cases it is possible to take that decision based on a number of criteria (e.g. semantic complexity, semantic relatedness, frequency, age, etc.). This problem is more generally discussed in Chapter 25 (see also Nagano 2008 for a recent treatment and Bram 2011 for some empirical investigation into the degree of correlation between the different criteria).

    There is a very large group of noun–verb pairs in English in which the two words differ in their stress pattern, but which are otherwise (apart from stress-induced differences in vowel quality) segmentally identical (e.g. *dígest* • *digést, pérmit* • *permít, tórment* • *tormént*, see Chapter 10 for many more examples). Independent of the decision whether these pairs should be considered cases of conversion or not (see Chapter 25 for discussion), a closer look at the data reveals that in the vast majority of cases the verb is the base and the noun is derived. For this reason this set of forms is discussed in the chapter on event nominalizations (Chapter 10). However, sometimes we find competing stress patterns with pertinent verbs and it is those cases that are of interest in the context of this chapter. For example, the verbs *protest* or *refund* can be found with main stress on the first or on the second syllable. In such cases, the verb with the initial main stress is most probably derived by conversion from the derived noun and thus maintains the stress pattern of the noun, as all other converted verbs do (*protést*$_V$ • *prótest*$_N$ • *prótest*$_V$).

Converted verbs may be transitive or intransitive (with transitive usages being slightly more common, see Nagano 2008: 126), but it has frequently been observed (e.g. by Jespersen 1942: 108) that the intransitive converted verbs are sometimes used in quasi-transitive constructions with a semantically empty object *it*, as exemplified in (30), from COCA (see, for example, Nagano 2008, for a collection of pertinent examples). It is unclear, however, whether converted verbs are more susceptible to this kind of behaviour than other verbs.

> (30)   *ABA Journal 2004*: In the midst of this, I get a call from another client who wants me to grab the next plane to Ohio to take a look at three Midwestern industrial plants, located about four hours' drive from one another. Afterwards, I'll have to **hot foot it** to Chicago to give some talks at the ABA's headquarters.

Quite often, we find a base noun being converted to a verb in the presence of a particle, as shown in (31), from COCA.

> (31)   *Walk to the Full Moon 2002*: Yes, we could **fool about** with bits and pieces of the genome and clone the occasional sheep in the 1990s, but not create a new race—or should I say re-create an old one.
>
> *Mens Health 1995*: Don't expect to appreciate the flavor of a good, home-cooked meal if you're going to **wolf** it **down**.
>
> *A week in Texas 2010*: I could tell she thought I'd **chicken out.**

13.2.4   Back-formation and other processes

We have already seen in Section 13.2.2.2 that some verbs in *-ate* appear to be formed by back-formation. There are a great many other verbs that are derived by back-formation as well. Nagano (2008: ch. 6) lists some recent examples, a selection of which are given in (32), with those in (32b) representing examples of technical terms in linguistics.

> (32)   a. attrition ◆ attrit, breathalyzer ◆ breathalyze, demerger ◆ demerge, emotion ◆ emote, hijacker ◆ hijack, television ◆ televise
>
>   b. affix-hopping ◆ affix-hop, antecedent-government ◆ antecedent-govern, back-formation ◆ back-form, Chomsky-adjunction ◆ Chomsky-adjoin, pied-piping ◆ pied-pipe

Varying evidence can be brought to support the analysis of such verbs as back-formations. The most obvious sort of evidence comes from date of attestation, with the noun being attested before the verb. As Nagano (2008: 162) points out, however, sometimes the evidence is semantic, in that the meaning of the noun is included in the meaning of the verb (for example, *attrit* means 'to undergo attrition'). Sometimes evidence can come from frequency, with the longer form having a higher frequency than the back-formed one. And sometimes the evidence comes from allomorphy. Bauer (1983) gives the example of the verb *contracept* from *contraception*; nouns with the formative *cept + ion* generally correspond to verbs with the Latinate formative *ceive* (*reception* ◆ *receive*, *perception* ◆ *perceive*), so *cept* in a verb suggests back-formation from the noun.

The kinds of expressions that can serve as bases of back-formed verbs are quite diverse. Complex nouns as in (32a) are very common, as are compounds, as in (32b). The back-formed verbs arising from compounds are discussed in more detail in the chapters on compounding (see Chapters 19 and 20). Interestingly, bases for the back-formation of verbs need not be morphologically complex, as the examples in (33), taken from Nagano (2008: 172, originally from the *OED*) and our own collection, show.

(33)   Bolshevik ◆ bolsh, liason ◆ liase, lysis ◆ lyse, propaganda ◆ propagand, rotisserie ◆ rotisse, tiffin ◆ tiff, jacuzzi ◆ jacuze

Such forms seriously challenge the traditional definition of back-formation as the deletion of an affix, and indeed it seems that analogy at various levels of abstraction can make better sense of how these verbs are derived. For example, Nagano lists numerous nouns ending in *-is* that have a back-formed corresponding verb without this ending (e.g. *lysis* ◆ *lyse*, *phagocytosis* ◆ *phagocytose*, *pinocycosis* ◆ *pynocycose*, *sonolysis* ◆ *sonolyse*, *symbiosis* ◆ *symbiose*, *thrombosis* ◆ *thrombose*). These formations can be accounted for by analogy with the pair *analysis* ◆ *analyze*, or by making reference to the fact that even if final <is> may not be a suffix, it is segmentable from the bound roots that can be found with words ending in *-is*, as in *emphasis* ◆ *emphasize*, *hypothesis* ◆ *hypothesize*.

Some forms look like clippings that have not preserved the syntactic category of their nominal bases, that is, *bolsh* is presumed to be a verb clipped from the noun *Bolshevik*.

(34)   bolsh ◆ Bolshevik, hush ◆ husht, lap ◆ lapcock, loll ◆ Lollard, rattle ◆ ratline, tiff ◆ tiffin

However, the *OED* also lists the verbs *bolshevize*, *husht*, *ratline*, and *tiffin*, which suggests to us that the derivatives in (34) are more convincingly analysed as clipped from verbs. The verbs *lap* (first attestation 1839) and *loll* (given as obsolete by the *OED*, first attestation 1394) would also be structurally regular clippings, but their potential bases are not attested as verbs.

13.3 SEMANTIC CONSIDERATIONS

There is a great deal of overlap in the semantic categories exhibited in derived verbs, with conversion showing the widest range of available readings and the prefixes the narrowest range. The range of meanings generally correlates with the degree of productivity of the verb-deriving process: the more productive the process, the wider the range of readings that seems to be available. We begin with prefixes in Section 13.3.1, then treat suffixes (in Section 13.3.2), conversion (in Section 13.3.3) and back-formation (in Section 13.3.4).

13.3.1 Prefixes

The dubious status of *a-* as a verb-forming prefix makes it nearly impossible to say anything coherent about its semantics and we will not attempt to do so here. A similar case is *for-*. Verbs with this prefix are mostly opaque and it is not clear what the semantic contribution of *for-* is. The prefix *be-* is easier, although very many of the item-familiar forms in *be-* have highly lexicalized meanings (for example, *befall, beget, beseech, beset, bestow*). Where meanings are transparent we see several prominent senses. Many of the transparent forms are ornative (that is, 'provide with X') as with *beblood, beglamour, bejewel, beleper*, although interestingly, there is at least one verb in *be-* that is privative (*behead*). Frequently the ornative forms carry a nuance of intensification or wide coverage ('provide with X all over', as in *beshit, bethank*), especially where they occur as past participles (*bejowled, bespeckled*). Some forms are causative (*befoul, bestill*) and a few simply transitive (*belabor, bespeak, bemoan*).

The prefix *en-* is most frequently found with a locative or directional sense (that is 'put something into X'), as in *encoffin, encapsule, entomb*. In other cases it can be paraphrased as, for example, 'turn into' (*encash, encode, encrypt*) or 'provide with' (*encrust, enhat, enshroud*). On adjectival bases *en-* has a causative meaning (*enable, enfeeble, endear, enlarge, ensure*).

13.3.2 Suffixes

The semantics of *-ize* and *-ify* has been explored in considerable depth in Lieber (1998, 2004) and Plag (1999). The two suffixes are generally considered to share the same range of polysemy. This range is large but not unrestricted. Table 13.1 summarizes the different meanings proposed in the aforementioned literature.

In general, any given derivative is potentially ambiguous within the range of meanings that can reasonably be construed on the basis of the semantic potential of the two suffixes and the meaning of the base.

As shown in Plag (1999) and Lieber (2004) the different readings can be accounted for by rather straightforward meaning extensions of a basic causative/locative meaning. For example, inchoative and causative/resultative interpretations depend on the transitivity of the verb, that is on the presence of an additional argument. The ornative and locative meanings are reverse images of each other (that is, 'cause X to go into/onto something' or 'cause something to go into/onto X') that can even occur with the same base word. Thus, *computerize* may refer to an event in which data are put into a computer (ornative), or it can refer to an event in which

Table 13.1 The semantics of –*ize* and –*ify*

Category label	Paraphrase	Examples
inchoative	'become X'	oxidize, aerosolize, acidify, calcify
causative	'make X, cause to become X',	standardize, velarize, diversify, acidify
resultative	'make into X'	crystallize, unionize, teddify, yuppify
ornative	'make X go to/in/on something, provide with'	accessorize, texturize, glorify, youthify
locative	'make something go to/in/on X'	hospitalize, containerize, syllabify, codify
similative	'do/act/make/ in the manner of or like X'	Boswellize, despotize, (Lewisify)
performative	'do X'	philosophize, economize speechify, boozify

computers are put somewhere (locative), for example into an office. Furthermore, the inchoative/causative/resultative meanings on the one hand and the ornative/locative on the other are related to each other as the latter can be analysed as change-of-place verbs, while the former are change-of-state verbs. A change of state can thus be interpreted as a metaphorical change of place (see Plag 1999: ch. 6 and Lieber 2004: ch. 3 for discussion and formal modelling).

The similative and performative meanings arise with nominal bases denoting types of persons (*hooligan, despot*) or with proper names (*Boswell, Marx*), although not all derivatives with proper names show similative or performative meanings. Consider, for example, (35) from the BNC, in which the derivative shows an ornative meaning.

(35)   CBC W_newsp_other_social 1992: Agh! Get away from her! You'll be **Wymanised**! I never knew what they meant until I read Bill Wyman's story about his failed marriage to child bride Mandy Smith. To be **Wymanised** is to be overcome by a feeling of nausea when an excess of Wyman is forced upon you.

Metonymic readings of names may also lead to non-similative and non-performative readings. The verb *Marxize*, for example, can have an ornative meaning in the attested example *The socialists Marxize the West*, once the base *Marx* is interpreted metonymically as 'the ideas of Marx' (Plag 1999: 139).

For each of the meaning categories, we can find comparable numbers of examples with both -*ize* and -*ify* derivatives, which speaks strongly for the synonymy of the two suffixes. The only meaning that seems largely restricted to -*ize* is the similative one. Even with -*ize* there are not many examples with this meaning, but with -*ify* they seem not to exist at all. The only example that we were able to find in the corpora as a potential candidate for this category is given in (36).

(36)   *A7C W_biography* 1990: It brings together Lewis the scholar, Lewis the voracious
reader…Lewis the failed Romantic poet.…It is the story of a philologist (said to be
loosely based on Tolkien, but in fact fairly unlike him: Tolkien recognized some of his
own opinions and ideas **Lewisified** in the character) who, by a series of mishaps on a
walking tour, comes to a house where two sinister scientists, Weston and Devine, are
planning a visit to outer space.

Perhaps we should not be surprised, however, that examples of similatives are rare or non-
existent for *-ize* and *-ify*, as the core senses of these suffixes are clearly causative, with similatives and performatives being sense extensions. As we will see below, it is more common for
non-causative verbal meanings to be expressed through conversion.

Semantically, verbal derivatives in *-ate* are also quite heterogeneous, and much of that
heterogeneity can be attributed to various mechanisms that may lead to new verbs in *-ate*.
Based on the analysis of twentieth-century neologisms, Plag (1999: ch. 7) arrives at the conclusion that only one-third of the neologisms display the expected ornative or resultative
meanings, chiefly with bases denoting chemical substances. We repeat some of his examples
from these two categories in (37a) and (37b).

(37)   a. *ornative*

alluviate, fluorinate, fluoridate, formylate, iodinate, mercurate, nitrogenate,
phosphate, protonate

b. *resultative*

gelate, methanate, pupariate, phosphate, sulphonylate

De-adjectival derivatives typically show causative readings but, as mentioned earlier,
de-adjectival derivation seems not to be a productive pattern apart from isolated analogical
formations such as the twentieth-century coinage *passivate* (on the basis of *activate*), listed in
the *OED*.

Derivatives that arise through back-formation typically exhibit a reading dependent on
the meaning of the respective base word. As shown by Plag (1999: 207), a large proportion of
twentieth-century neologisms in *-ate* are back-derived from complex nouns and their meaning reflects that of their nominal base. An illustrative example is *escalate*, which is ambiguous
between two readings that directly reflect the respective derivational history. One reading is
paraphrased as 'To climb or reach by means of an escalator…To travel on an escalator' by the
OED, and is thus obviously modelled on the noun *escalator*. The other reading is synonymous with 'increase in intensity', which is derived from *escalation* (see Plag 1999 for more
examples and discussion).

There are, in addition, very many derivatives whose meaning appears to be highly idiosyncratic and heavily dependent on the context, as in *dissonate* 'be dissonant', *fidate* 'to give
immunity from capture', or *vagulate* 'to wander in a vague manner' (all from the *OED*).

13.3.3 Conversion

The range of readings exhibited by converted verbs is larger than that of the verbs derived by affixation and we find semantic patterns that are quite different from the other verb-deriving categories.

As Plag (1999) and Lieber (2004) show, quite a few verbs converted from nouns or adjectives fall into the semantic categories described in the preceding sections. Plag's examples (all twentieth-century neologisms from the *OED*) include locative *archive*, ornative *marmalade*, causative *rustproof*, resultative *package*, inchoative *gel*, performative *tango*, and similative *chauffeur*. However, we can find many other examples, for example the highly frequent instrumental 'use X, perform an action usually performed with X' (*hammer, glue, staple*), privative 'remove X' (*bark, skin*), stative 'be X' (*bay, landmark*). As observed by Lieber (2004), among converted verbs, but not among affixed verbs, one finds many with different motional meanings as in *cartwheel, fishtail* ('move in X manner'), *jet, lorry, jeep* ('move using X'), *quarterdeck* ('move at X location'). There are no stative or motional affixed forms, while among the conversion verbs there are far more performative and similative verbs than in any of the other categories. Furthermore, there are the many converted verbs that are motivated onomatopoeically and which mostly denote the making of the sound which the pronounced base is supposed to stand for (e.g. *plink, zizz*). In addition, one can find many highly idiosyncratic meanings that are largely dependent on the surrounding discourse context. Such formations have even been awarded special terminological status as 'contextuals' (Clark and Clark 1979; Aronoff 1980, see also Chapter 25).

Given this large variety of meanings and readings, it seems that the interpretation of newly converted verbs is highly underdetermined. The best we can say is that these verbs generally denote an event that is conventionally or contextually associated with the base. As might be expected, this underspecified semantics can lead to widely differing readings for a single verb. Example (38) illustrates this for *summer*, and there is an abundance of such cases. The paraphrases are quoted from the *OED*.

(38) summer
'To pass or spend the summer'
'To keep or maintain during summer'
'To sun oneself'
'To make summer-like'

With some verbs, one can even find completely opposite interpretations, depending on the context. For instance, the verbs *bark* and *bug* are each attested with both privative and ornative meanings, as shown in (39), with paraphrases from the *OED*.

(39) bark
'To strip off the bark from (a tree)'
'To enclose with or as with bark'

bug

'To clear (plants, etc.) of insects'

'To equip with an alarm system or a concealed microphone'

This extreme semantic flexibility raises the question whether there are any restrictions as to the semantic well-formedness of potential converted verbs. The answer to this question seems to be a qualified 'yes'. It follows from our above description of the semantics of conversion into verbs that readings seem unlikely which do not arise from a conventional association of the denotation of the base and some event. Thus, one can skin an animal, but legging a table, that is removing a leg from a table, is something we normally do not do, and this leads to problems in the interpretation of the potential verb *leg* as a privative verb in the absence of strong contextual cues. This, however, is more a fact about the world than about the English language.

Nagano (2008: 77–8) makes another claim with regard to restrictions on the semantic range of conversion, suggesting that only those converted verbs seem possible as privative verbs whose interpretation involves a part–whole relationship (for example, *bone, husk, juice, milk, pit*); in contexts where such a relationship is not given, the privative relation needs to be expressed through affixation (for example *debug, disarm, unmask*). However, although Nagano lists many illustrative examples of either kind, it is not too hard to find counterexamples to her claim. Thus, the verb *fish* is privative, even though fish are not a part of the water from which they are removed, and even *bug* can, according to the *OED*, mean 'remove bugs (from plants)', although there is no part–whole relation between the bugs and the plants from which the bugs are removed. Given that very many privative events involve part–whole relations anyway, further empirical research seems necessary to firmly establish this potential restriction.

13.3.4 Back-formation

Like converted verbs, verbs derived by back-formation are dependent on the meaning of their respective base word and denote the event conventionally associated with the base. One illustrative example already cited in Section 13.3.2. is *escalate*, which has two different readings, each of which can be straightforwardly related to the respective base (*escalator* or *escalation*). Nagano (2008: 163) gives many examples that suggest that an especially prominent meaning associated with back-formed verbs is the performative one: for example, to *burgle* is 'to do what a burglar does', to *buttle* is 'to do what a butler does'. Also prominent are instrumental readings: to *breathalyze* is 'to use a breathalyzer', to *jacuze* is 'to use the jacuzzi' (the last is from our own examples).

13.4 COMPETITION AMONG VERB-DERIVING PROCESSES

The wealth of different morphological mechanisms available to derive verbs calls for an analysis of their potential competition, and we have already hinted at potential competition in various places throughout this chapter.

Some of the restrictions we mentioned have the consequence of a rather neat distribution of labour in some domains. For example, we saw for *-ize* and *-ify* that the two suffixes are almost in complementary distribution due to their phonological restrictions. Or the fact that the verbal suffixes do not normally allow compounds or phrases as bases restricts such forms to conversion, back-formation, or clipping. Furthermore, since the semantics of the affixes is not identical to that of conversion, it should be expected that some processes are not eligible if a certain meaning is to be conveyed by the verb. Thus, of the 488 converted verbs in Plag's study, 409 express meanings that could not be denoted by the suffixation of *-ize*, *-ify*, or *-ate* (Plag 1999: 232).

But what about those domains where the categorial, morphological, or phonological restrictions, as well as the semantics, allow for more than one morphological process to derive a verb from a given base? A systematic look at such cases reveals that, given these circumstances, one can indeed often find doublets.

Plag (1999), for example, lists a fair number of synonymous pairs of converted verbs and suffixed or back-derived verbs, such as *carbon* • *carbonize, dual* • *dualize, indemn* • *indemnify, gel* • *gelate, pressure* • *pressurize.* In Nagano's (2008: 98) collection of derived verbs, roughly every seventh verb derived with the suffix *-ify* or *-ize* has a converted verb counterpart. This is similar to what we found with other rival processes (see Chapters 9 through 18) and can be taken as another indication that blocking is not a categorical mechanism (see Chapter 26).

CHAPTER 14

Derived adjectives

14.1 PROSPECTUS

In this chapter we consider the full range of affixes that derive adjectives in contemporary English, looking at both their formal characteristics and their semantic range. Of all the areas of English derivation, it seems safe to say that adjectival derivation has received the least scholarly attention, although there are several interesting descriptive and theoretical questions that arise with respect to the pertinent derivatives. We will take up the issue of stress placement with this cohort of affixes, the extent to which the various affixes are productive, and the extent to which some of them are semantically interchangeable. We will also consider whether such categories as gradable versus non-gradable or relational versus qualitative are a function of the specific affix, the base, or the context in which individual items appear. The examples in this chapter are taken from COCA, unless otherwise specified.

Some of the adjectival morphological categories to be discussed in the present chapter have numerous members that are formally identical with homophonous nominal derivatives. A great many adjectival derivatives in *-an, -ant, -ist, -arian,* and *-oid* have nominal counterparts (e.g. *American, pollutant, modernist, vegetarian, humanoid*). The relationship between the nominal and the adjectival categories is not entirely straightforward. There are nominal derivatives that have no adjectival counterpart (e.g. *accountant, applicant, informant, prefixoid*) and adjectival derivatives that are without nominal counterparts (e.g. *aberrant, pleasant, hesitant, Picassoid*). The fact that English allows prenominal modification by nouns may explain the categorial variation. A theoretical account is nevertheless a challenge, and there are in principle at least two different solutions available. The categorial variation could be considered a case of affix homophony or a case of conversion (see Chapter 25 for a general discussion of these notions). We remain agnostic with regard to the theoretical analysis and treat the pertinent derivatives in this chapter and, if also relevant, in the chapter on the derivation of person nouns (Chapter 11). The suffix *-arian* is dealt with exclusively in the noun chapter, since the nouns involved have a very specific meaning and the adjectives largely correspond in meaning. The suffix *-oid* is treated only in this chapter as the nominal derivatives seem to be dependent on the similative meaning that seems to be extended from the adjectival suffix.

Note that there is also a class of Latinate adjectives, so-called 'collateral' adjectives, which are semantically, but crucially not phonologically, closely related to corresponding nouns (e.g. *brachial* to *arm*, *canine* to *dog*, *paternal* to *father*, *vernal* to *spring*, *lupine* to *wolf*). We consider these relationships lexical and not morphological (cf. Koshiishi 2002).

14.2 FORMAL CONSIDERATIONS

We begin with an overview of the formal characteristics of the adjective-forming affixes, which are summarized in Table 14.1. In this table we list in the top row the kinds of bases the suffixes attach to and, in the final column, whether base allomorphy is observed with the respective suffix.

Adjective-forming affixes can be grouped according to their etymology, those that are of non-native origin, which are frequently associated with both base allomorphy and stress shift, and which often attach to bound bases, and those of native origin, which attach to free bases of any provenance, are inert with respect to stress, and are not associated with base allomorphy. The vast majority of adjective-forming affixes in English are non-native, specifically *-able, -al, -ant, -ary, -esque, -an, -ible, -ic, -ical, -ine, -ive, -oid, -ory, -ous*. Native affixes are *-ful, -ing, -ish, -ly, -some, -y*. The privative adjective-forming suffix *-less* is also native, but it will be dealt with in Chapter 16 with the other negative and privative affixes. We begin our discussion with the non-native affixes.

Before we do so, three remarks are necessary. We have chosen to treat *-ical* as a single suffix, rather than as a sequence of *-ic* and *-al* for two reasons. First, there are a fair number of forms in *-ical* that do not have corresponding bases in *-ic*, for example, *practical, vertical, biblical, commonsensical, indexical, quizzical*, and especially medical terms like *colovesical, surgical*, and the like. Second, for many forms in *-ical*, even where there is a corresponding *-ic* form attested, there is no sense in which the two suffixes are semantically additive. We will take up the relationship between *-ic* and *-ical* in more detail in Section 14.3.3. Some forms in *-ist-ic* may suggest a similar analysis as one suffix. See Section 14.3.4 for discussion.

A second point to be made at the outset is that we will treat the suffixes *-able* and *-ible* as distinct for the purposes of formal considerations, as they pattern somewhat differently, but will treat them as one suffix from the point of view of semantics, where there is no reason to distinguish them.

Third, there is the status of the element *-like*. In Chapter 16 we argue with Dalton-Puffer and Plag (2000) that a bound formative that is homophonous to a free form should only be considered to be an affix (as opposed to an element of a compound) if it shows a different semantic behaviour than the free form. This is not the case with *-like*, which should therefore be considered a compound element (and not even a 'semi-suffix', as in Marchand 1969: 356). We nevertheless treat *-like* here on a par with suffixes for practical reasons. Together with *-ish*, *-y, -esque*, and *-oid* it forms a set of closely related rival formatives that all derive words expressing a similative meaning. It is therefore useful to investigate this set together, irrespective of the categorial status one of the formatives might have or not have.

Table 14.1 Formal characteristics of adjective–forming suffixes

Suffix	N	A	V	bb	Compound	Phrase	Native	Non-native	Stress shift	Base allomorphy
-able	(✓)	✓	✓	✓	(✓)		*	✓	✓	(✓)
-al	✓	✓	(✓)	✓			*	✓	✓	(✓)
-ant	✓	(✓)	✓	✓			*	✓		
-ary	✓²	(✓)	(✓)	✓	(✓)		✓	✓	✓	(✓)
-esque	✓²	✓	✓	✓*			✓	✓		
-ful	✓²	(✓)		✓	*		✓	✓		
-an	✓		✓	✓			*	✓		(✓)
-ible	✓		(✓)	✓				✓	✓	✓
-ic	✓¹	*		✓	*			✓		✓
-ical	✓			✓	*			✓		✓
-ine	✓¹							✓		
-ing	✓¹		✓	✓	✓	✓	✓	✓		✓
-ish³	✓¹	✓	(✓)		✓	✓	✓	✓		
-ive	(✓)	(✓)	✓	✓			*	✓	✓	✓
-like⁴	✓¹	(✓)					✓	✓		
-ly	✓¹			✓			✓	✓	✓	
-oid	*	(✓)	(✓)	✓			✓	✓		
-ory	✓	(✓)	✓	✓			✓	✓	✓	✓
-ous	✓	(✓)	✓	✓			*	✓		
-some	✓	(✓)	✓	(✓)	✓		✓	✓		
-y	✓		✓		✓		✓	✓		
past pple							✓	✓		(✓)

✓ well-attested, (✓) infrequently attested, * isolated examples
¹ includes proper nouns,
² mostly proper nouns,
³ also occasionally pronouns and numbers,
⁴ also occasionally pronouns

14.2.1 Non-native affixes

14.2.1.1 *Kinds of bases*

We can divide the non-native affixes into two cohorts, those that attach primarily to nouns and those that attach primarily to verbs.

(1) a. *Attaching primarily to nouns*: -al, -ary, -esque, -ian, -ic, -ical, -ine, -oid, -ous

      b. *Attaching primarily to verbs*: -able, -ant, -ive, -ory

We give examples of words derived with these affixes in (2) and (3).

(2) a. -al: adenoidal, behavioral, chromosomal, deicidal, elemental, familial, germicidal, hexagonal, incestual, junctural, lectoral, manorial, natural, obituarial, paroxysmal, quadrupedal, referential, sacrificial, textual, urethral, verbal, zonal

      b. -ary: alimentary, budgetary, customary, dietary, evidentiary, fusionary, insurrectionary, legendary, momentary, nobiliary, originary, planetary, revisionary, supplementary, transitionary, urinary, visionary

      c. -esque: ayatollaesque, bimboesque, cougar-esque, divaesque, futuresque, gazeboesque, hippie-esque, island-esque, kindergartenesque, lionesque, minivanesque, novelesque, onionesque, painteresque, rubble-esque, shamanesque, traveloguesque, violinesque, zoo-esque

      d. -an: animalian, brontosaurian, centaurian, diocesan, equatorian, herbivorean, jackassian, mammalian, oceanian, piscivorian, republican, suburban, tragedian, utopian, zootopian

      e. -ic: alcoholic, basaltic, cyclonic, diadic, ectomorphic, fumarolic, genomic, halalic, imbecilic, jihadic, kleptocratic, lethargic, melancholic, nomadic, ozonic, palindromic, quietistic, rhapsodic, satiric, thoracic, urologic, vampiric, warrioristic, xerographic, yogic, zoophilic

      f. -ical: alphabetical, brahminical, charlatanical, demiurgical, farcical, indexical, nonsensical, paradoxical, theatrical, typical, whimsical

      g. -ine: alkaline, alpine, crystalline, dinosaurine, elephantine, estuarine, infantine, insectine, labyrinthine, pantherine, riverine, serpentine, tridentine, vulturine

      h. -oid: albinoid, beastoid, bungaloid, ellipsoid, fibrinoid, orchidoid, parasitoid, plasmacytoid, reptiloid, rubberoid, salmonoid, suffixoid, targetoid, walrusoid

      i. -ous: acronymous, bulbous, cadaverous, dolorous, eczematous, feverous, gelatinous, hazardous, injurious, lecherous, mountainous, nervous, penurious, rancorous, scandalous, tempestuous, usurious, victorious, wondrous, zealous

(3)   a. -able: abradable, blendable, cancelable, deployable, enactable, feelable, grazable, holdable, imbibable, jumpable, kneadable, listenable, matchable, networkable, ordainable, parsable, quashable, registerable, settleable, throwable, utterable, visitable, wadeable, zoomable

b. -ant: ascendant, combinant, defiant, excitant, floatant, guidant, inhalant, manifestant, nurturant, observant, pollutant, relaxant, securant, transformant

c. -ible: admissible, combustible, defensible, extensible, perceptible, recognizable

d. -ive: adaptive, coercive, decisive, emanative, formulative, gestative, immersive, mitigative, negotiative, oppressive, pervasive, receptive, seductive, transgressive, ulcerative, vituperative

e. -ory: applicatory, combinatory, defecatory, executory, facilitatory, genuflectory, hallucinatory, illusory, justificatory, legitimatory, mediatory, obfuscatory, possessory, redemptory, satisfactory, titillatory, undulatory, ventilatory

While the vast majority of deverbal adjectives of this type have transitive verbs as bases, all of them show some variety in the types of verbal bases they select. The suffix *-able*, for example, shows a marked preference for transitive bases, although it does occur to some extent on ditransitive bases and base verbs that take prepositional objects. There are only a few plausible examples on unergative or unaccusative bases.

(4)   a. -able *on ditransitive bases*: addable, addressable, equatable, faxable, placeable, tellable

b. -able *on bases with prepositional objects*: accountable, atoneable, commentable, conformable, listenable, panderable, wishable

c. -able *on unergative bases*: stutterable

d. -able *on unaccusative bases*: abateable, eruptable, flowable, perishable, rottable

We can find *-ant* on transitive verbs and verbs with prepositional objects, but there are almost no formations on other types of verb.

(5)   a. -ant *on transitive verbs*: arrestant, combinant, considerant, excitant, executant, expectant, observant, presentant, recombinant, transcendant

b. -ant *on bases with prepositional objects*: accordant, actant, aspirant, convergant, conversant

c. -ant *on unergative bases*: respirant

d. -ant *on unaccusative bases*: ascendant

The suffixes *-ive* and *-ory* are similar to *-ant*.

(6)   a. -ive *on ditransitive bases*: ascriptive, associative, donative, inductive

   b. -ive *on bases with prepositional objects*: collaborative, commiserative, elaborative, reactive

   c. -ive *on unergative bases*: genuflective, gesticulative, perseverative

   d. -ive *on unaccusative bases*: accelerative, degenerative, putrefactive, regressive

(7)   a. -ory *on ditransitive bases*: applicatory, compensatory, explanatory

   b. -ory *on bases with prepositional objects*: collaboratory, contributory, discriminatory, participatory

   c. -ory *on unergative bases*: genuflectory, hallucinatory, ovulatory, vomitory

   d. -ory *on unaccusative bases*: acceleratory, escalatory

Many of these affixes attach to bound bases, and to varying extents to other categories.

(8)   *Adjective-forming affixes on bound bases*

   a. -able: communicable, educable, isolable, regulable

   b. -al: apical, carnal, decimal, fluvial, mortal

   c. -ant: clairvoyant, distant, malfeasant, renaissant, spirant

   d. -ary: ancilliary, binary, culinary, liminary, pulmonary

   e. -an: circadian, equestrian, median, metropolitan, sylvan

   f. -ic: aquatic, barbaric, eclectic, hedonic, memetic

   g. -ical: amical, identical, practical, radical, surgical

   h. -ine: calcarine, equine, saline, uterine, vulpine

   i. -ive: amative, captive, diminutive, fictive, native

   j. -oid: android, asteroid, benzoid, Caucasoid, silicoid

   k. -ory: amatory, gustatory, nugatory, perfunctory, valedictory

   l. -ous: abstemious, bibulous, copious, fastidious, hydrous

The suffix -*able* shows the peculiarity that it frequently prefers to be attached to the bound base on which a verb in -*ate* is formed rather than to the full form of the verb, although both are possible (for example, *aggregatable*, *activatable*). The suffix -*esque* can be found in only a few cases on bound bases (*grotesque*, *picaresque*), although these are clearly early borrowings from French (see below) and not English derivations. The suffix -*oid* seems to be at least as often found on bound bases as on free bases.

   Of the affixes that typically attach to nouns, the following can also be found on verbal bases.

(9) a. -al: configural, continual, deferral, excretal, survival

b. -ary: deputary, expeditiary, imaginary

c. -ic: beatific, beautific, encryptic, integratic

d. -ous: continuous, covetous, infectious, prosperous, usurpatious

And similarly, some of the affixes that typically take verbal bases can also be found on nominal bases.

(10) a. -able: avalanchable, braillable, PBRFable (*Middleton 2006*), deskable, knowledgeable, merchantable

b. -ive: agentive, contemptive, qualitative, quantitative, sportive

c. -ory: statutory, preceptory

A surprising number of these affixes can be found at least occasionally on adjectival bases.

(11) a. -al: accusatorial, inclemental, monetarial

b. -ant: benignant, contrariant, malignant

c. -ary: mobiliary, sanguinary

d. -esque: africanesque, brutalesque, globalesque, lunaresque, suburbanesque

e. -ic: astralic, civilic, sanguinic

f. -ive: abruptive, distinctive, diversive, profusive

g. -oid: fantastic-oid, modernoid, pinkoid, simploid

h. -ous: complicitous, duplicitous, sanguineous, triumphalous

The non-native adjective-forming affixes attach almost exclusively to non-native bases, although there are isolated examples of attachment to native bases for a few of them. In (12) we present a relatively exhaustive list of the pertinent examples from COCA. Some of these are clearly intended as jocular (*crotchital, freshmanic, raspberrical, walkative*), but the majority are well-established and item-familiar.

(12) a. -al: bridal, tidal, crotchital, queerial

b. -ant: floatant

c. -an: elvan

d. -ic: apostolic, councilmanic, folkloric, freshmanic, runic, skaldic, Icelandic, Greenlandic (*and other forms ending in* -landic)

e. -ical: churchical, coxcombical, folklorical, raspberrical

f. -ive: talkative, walkative

g. -ous: heathenous, lumpous, plunderous, righteous, scabrous, slaughterous, slumberous, thunderous, wondrous

The three non-native affixes that attach freely to native bases are *-oid*, *-esque*, and *-able*. That *-esque* attaches to native bases is not altogether surprising considering that this suffix has a rather different history than the others; it is a borrowing from French, rather than Latin, and comes into English a bit later than the others (Marchand 1969 cites the first borrowings from the late sixteenth century). Why *-able* has taken so readily to native bases is less clear, although we might speculate that it has filled a semantic niche that is not covered by any native adjective-forming affix (see Section 14.2.2.1 below). The suffix *-oid*, while of Greek origin, also attaches quite freely to native bases.

(13) a. -esque *on native bases*: girlesque, hell-esque, holly-esque, hood-esque, island-esque, rubble-esque, slackeresque, snowbirdesque, wagonesque

b. -able *on native bases*: bakeable, bearable, bite-able, doable, feedable, fishable, hangable, meltable, nameable, paintable, ringable, settable, singable

c. -oid: bluesoid, craboid, flintoid, freakoid, rubberoid, walrusoid

The suffixes *-esque* and *-oid* are also interesting in that they attach also to names and other proper nouns, and indeed *-esque* shows a marked preference for them.

(14) -esque *on proper nouns*: Aspen-esque, Barbieesque, Brokeback-esque, Coplandesque, Dadaesque, Gatsbyesque, Halloweenesque, Nazi-esque, Pygmalianesque, Vegas-esque

(15) -oid *on proper nouns*: Dawkins-oid, Jacksonoid, Kuiperoid, Plutoid, Tayloroid

Also showing a marked preference for proper nouns is the suffix *-an*.

(16) -an *on proper nouns*: Alaskan, Aristotelian, Beethovenian, Burgundian, Caddoan, Djiboutian, Godzillian, Kazakhstanian

There is no doubt a connection between these adjectival forms and the personal nouns in *-an* discussed in Chapter 11.

Of the non-native adjective-forming affixes, *-esque* is also the only one that attaches with some frequency to compounds. Occasional examples on compound bases can be found for *-an*, *-ic*, and *-ical*, and somewhat more than occasional for *-able*, as the examples in (17) illustrate, but *-esque* seems quite productive on compound bases (18).

(17)   a. -able: backpackable, bushwackable, copyrightable, downloadable, lockoutable, networkable, spinoffable

   b. -an: fisticuffian, jackassian

   c. -ic: aldermanic, folkloric, freshmanic, freemasonic, councilmanic

   d. -ical: coxcombical, folklorical, raspberrical

(18)   -esque *on compound bases*: appleseed-esque, Coldplay-esque, dot-comesque, hummingbird-esque, merchant-ivoryesque, prom-queenesque, ragtime-esque, snowboard-esque, strobe-lightesque

None of the non-native adjective-forming affixes in English can be found on phrasal bases.

The suffixes -*ive* and -*ory* are selective about the phonological form of their bases. Specifically, they prefer bases that end in /t/ or /s/, often requiring a /t/ or /s/-final allomorph where the base shows allomorphy (see Section 14.2.1.2). So, for example, we find many forms like *impressive, dismissive, conductive, associative, assistive*, or *promissory, dispossessory, locomotory, vomitory*, where verbal bases already end in /t/ or /s/, as well as forms like *ascriptive, abrasive, repulsive*, and *conjunctive, intercessory, delusory*, where base allomorphs ending in /t/ or /s/ are available. Where there are no such allomorphs, the suffix shows up with the extenders -*at*- or -*it*- that allow the phonological requirement to be met, as we find in examples like *informative, determinative, definitive, explorative, purgative, punitive, condolatory, applicatory*.

Adjectival suffixes frequently attach to bases that are already suffixed, and the reader is referred to Chapter 26 for some discussion.

14.2.1.2 *Base and affixal allomorphy*

As is well-known from the literature on generative phonology (Chomsky and Halle 1968), Metrical Phonology (Hayes 1982), and Lexical Phonology and Morphology (Siegel 1974; Allen 1978; Kiparsky 1982a; Mohanan 1982; Giegerich 1999; among many others), some of the non-native affixes that form adjectives trigger allomorphy or stress shift or both on their bases. We can divide suffixes into those that do not affect stress, those that themselves bear stress, and those that can trigger stress shift. As we will show below, the patterns involving stress shift can be quite intricate and are sometimes variable.

It is clear that stress assignment to derived words in English in general often depends on the structure of the syllables involved. One crucial distinction to be made here is the one between heavy and light syllables. Another important aspect of our description is that we will focus on output patterns rather than rule-based input-oriented generalizations, as such an output-oriented approach has been shown often to be more adequate for the description of morpho-phonological alternations (e.g. Plag 1999; Lappe 2007, see also Chapter 9).

The group of non-stress-shifting adjectival suffixes can be illustrated with the non-native suffix -*ine*. This suffix has secondary stress, but is associated with neither stress shift nor base allomorphy (although *elephántine* might be an exception in BrE). The suffix -*esque* is an example of a suffix that bears primary stress; affixation of *-esque* does not change the underlying stress contour of the base except to reduce a primary stress to a secondary one. Most adjective-forming suffixes in English do, however, trigger some changes to the stress patterns of bases and are associated with some degree of base allomorphy.

The suffix *-able* typically does not alter the stress pattern of its bases if they are only one or two syllables. It can be found without stress shift on monosyllabic bases, iambic and trochaic bases, as well as disyllabic bases that end in a secondarily stressed syllable.

(19) a. *monosyllabic*: askable, bakeable, wantable

   b. *iambic*: abridgeable, abusable, besmirchable

   c. *trochaic*: alterable, answerable, budgetable, balanceable, challengeable

   d. *base ending in a secondarily stressed syllable*: archivable

The only exceptions we find are isolated forms that are highly lexicalized (*ádmirable, préferable, révocable*) or the rare monosyllabic bound base to which *-ize* has attached (*baptízable*).

Words in *-able* on bases that are longer than two syllables show three patterns. If the antepenultimate syllable of the derivative is heavy, the stress falls on the antepenultimate syllable, which consistently leads to stress shift with one subset of these forms, illustrated in (20a). Another subset of derivatives with heavy antepenult show variable stress shift. Some forms of this group are given in (20b). If, in contrast, the antepenult is light (i.e. contains only a short vowel or syllabic consonant), the stress is not shifted, as shown in (20c).

(20) a. *heavy antepenultimate syllable, non-variable*: al.lo.cá.ta.ble, a.ro.ma.tí.za.ble, ar.ti.cu.lá. ta.ble, ca.te.go.rí.za.ble, com.mer.cia.lí.za.ble, cul.ti.vá.ta.ble, di.ver.si.fí.a.ble, do.cu.mén. ta.ble, e.xe.cú.ta.ble, ex.tra.dí.table, ma.ni.pu.lá.ta.ble, per.so.ni.fý.able, pre.di.cá.ta.ble,

   b. *heavy antepenultimate syllable, variable*: á.na.ly.za.ble ~ a.na.lý.za.ble, cér.ti.fy.a.ble ~ cer.ti.fý.a.ble, drá.ma.ti.za.ble ~ dra.ma.tí.za.ble, i.dén.ti.fi.a.ble ~ i.den.ti.fí.a.ble, í.te. mi.za.ble ~ i.te.mì.za.ble, ló.ca.li.za.ble ~ lo.ca.lí.za.ble

   c. *light antepenultimate syllable*: jét.ti.so.na.ble, mó.ni.to.ra.ble, ré.gis.te.ra.ble

The suffix *-able* is not associated with base allomorphy, but its orthographic variant *-ible* frequently is, as is illustrated by examples like *admissible, permissible, transmissible, responsible, comprehensible, defensible, divisible, extensible, perceptible, destructible, submersible,* and *offensible*.

The suffix *-al* also occurs in the forms *-ial, -ual,* and *-ar*. The choice among *-al, -ial,* and *-ual* seems not to be rule-governed, but largely based on the respective Latin allomorphy patterns. For example, we find doublets in COCA like *factoral* alongside *factorial* or *monarchal* alongside *monarchial,* and near doublets and triplets like *accentual/agential/cliental, baronial/cantonal, habitual/digital*. The extender *-u-* is typically found on bases ending in clusters of obstruents (*aspect-**u**-al*, *concept-**u**-al*, *context-**u**-al*) or /n/ + obstruent (*consens-**u**-al*, *accent-**u**-al*), but at least in the latter case, it is not the only possibility (cf. *agent-**i**-al* and *cliental*).

On the other hand, the choice of the allomorph *-ar* seems to be more or less rule-governed. We find it with some consistency on bases that end in /l/ (*tonsillar*, *polar*, *capsular*) or a consonant cluster containing /l/ (*bulbar*, *vulgar*), and rarely on cases in which there is an /l/ in a preceding syllable (*linear*, *lumbar*, *lunar*, *columnar*, *plantar*, *planar* are the examples to be found in COCA). The single form *laminar* is notable in that the /l/ is in fact not even in a syllable adjacent to the suffix. But /l/ in a preceding syllable does not automatically trigger the *-ar* allomorph, as we also find forms like *clausal*, *colonial*, *influential*, *larval*, *millennial*, and the like. When a base ends in syllabic [l̩], the suffix appears as *-ular* (*clavicular*, *carbuncular*, *vehicular*). As Bauer and Huddleston (2002: 1708) point out, there are a few bases in which we find semantically distinct forms in both *-ar* and *-al* (*linear* versus *lineal*; *familiar* versus *familial*).

With *-al*, we observe that the suffix is prosodically highly integrated in that it triggers resyllabification, and stress shifts where necessary to achieve a certain output pattern that characterizes this morphological category. The words of this category are generally stressed like English monomorphemic nouns, imposing a stress shift on the base where necessary. Thus, if the penultimate syllable is light, we find stress on the antepenult, as shown in (21a). If the penult is heavy, the penult is stressed, illustrated in (21b). The stress shift cases are among those in (21b).

(21)   a. *penult is light*: aboríginal, áctional, clósural, dígital, épochal, fáctoral, lúmenal, márginal, monárchial

     b. *penult is heavy*: affínal, ancéstral, archíval, collóidal, collégial, concéptual, decádal, embryónal, ethérial, fragméntal, hormónal, mollúscal, monsóonal

There are, however, also (apparently rare) cases of derivatives that show variable stress behavior, such as *cómmunal* versus *commúnal*, where both stress patterns are in use.

The suffix *-al* and its variants involving extenders occasionally trigger allomorphy on their bases. We find frequent deletion of a base-final schwa vowel (*aortal*, *malarial*), which may be an instance of a more general constraint against identical vowels across morpheme boundaries. Only occasionally do we find the avoidance of vowel hiatus by means of the insertion of an extending consonant (*embryo-**n**-al*). Palatalization or spirantization of a base-final consonant is frequent (*agential*, *appendiceal*, *consensual*, *facial*, *laryngeal*), but voicing of a base-final consonant without palatalization is rare, perhaps confined to the example *basal*. We also find occasional examples in which trisyllabic laxing has occurred (*residual*, *criminal*).

With the suffix *-ant*, we again observe the strong tendency toward an output pattern in which the penult is stressed if heavy, and the antepenult is stressed if the penult is light. Thus, with bases like *triumph* or *dilate* we find stress shift (*tri.úm.phant*, *di.lá.tant*), while *có.lo.rant* and *núrtu.rant* show no stress shift. Longer base words also behave in accordance with the general output condition (*a.na.lý.sant*, *e.xé.cu.tant*, *ma.ni.fés.tant*). This suffix only occasionally results in base allomorphy. For verbal bases in *-ate*, the *-ant* adjective is invariably formed on the bound base without -*ate* rather than on the full form of the verb (*congreg-ant, devi-ant,* etc.). Otherwise, we find *divisant* from *divide*, and where a final /n/ is resyllabified with the suffix and underlying /g/ surfaces (*benignant, malignant*).

With respect to stress, the suffix -*ary* shows variable behaviour. The majority of the forms do not show stress shift, so that we get derivatives that stress the pre-antepenult or even the fifth syllable from the right, as in *de.pó.si.ta.ry, dí.sci.pli.na.ry* (NAmE), and *ac.cré.tio.na.ry*. The few forms that do show stress shift have stress on the antepenult or pre-antepenult: *a.li.mén.ta.ry, di.sci.plí.na.ry* (BrE, with /ɪ/ in the antepenult), *e.vi.dén.cia.ry, ves.tí.bu.la.ry*. We find only small amounts of segmental base allomorphy with forms in -*ary*: occasional cases of palatalization of base-final consonants (*beneficiary, evidenciary*) and deletion of base-final vowels (*medullary*).

The suffix -*an* has variants with extenders -*e*- and -*i*-. There seems to be no principled reason for the appearance of either variant, but forms with extenders and forms without seem to be numerically quite similar. We find occasional doublets like *Arizónan/Arizónian*. The suffix is capable of shifting the stress to ensure penultimate or ante-penultimate stress. Derivatives with the variant -*an* are variably stressed on the penult or antepenult (e.g. *Arizónan, carnivóran, diócesan*), while -*ean* and -*ian* derivatives are consistently stressed on the antepenult (see, for example, *actórian, bacchanálian, barónian, Baudeláirian, discórdian, equatórian, micróbian, animálian, avesáurian, cantelóupean, repúblican*, and the examples in the next paragraph).

We find only a small amount of segmental base allomorphy with -*an*. There is occasional palatalization of final /t/, as in *Aleutian*, but this is not a regular phonological process, especially where -*an* is attached to proper nouns (e.g. *Beckéttian*). Base-final vowels are often deleted (*ambrósian, volcánean*), but not always. With final /əʊ ‖ oʊ/ we sometimes find vowel hiatus (*Chicágoan, Cáddoan, Chácoan*) and sometimes the addition of an extender like /n/ (*Apollónian, Buffalónian*). Base-final /s/ sometimes deletes before -*an* (*Ándean, Athénian, Azórean, Cervántean*) but again not always (compare *Bráhmsian* with the previous examples).

The suffixes -*ic* and -*ical* appear to be textbook cases of stress shift: whatever the stress pattern of the base, we find stress on the syllable before the suffix. Thus, words in -*ic* almost invariably end in a trochee (*agéntic, ballétic, halálic, jihádic, occúltic, pirátic, poetic*; exceptions are, for example, the lexicalized forms *árabic, cátholic, chívalric*). Derivatives in -*ical* invariably stress the antepenult, also inducing stress shifts where necessary (*apocalýptical, eléctrical, meteorítical, rádical, theátrical*).

This suffix also exhibits various sorts of base allomorphy that we have seen with other non-native adjective-forming suffixes. We find deletion of base-final vowels (*historic, allergic, aortic, tornadic*), although we also find insertion of extenders -*t*- or -*n*-, which prevents vowel hiatus (*aromatic, asthmatic, empathetic; draconic, embryonic, messianic*). There does not seem to be anything systematic that determines which we find; indeed in COCA we find doublets like *empathic* versus *empathetic* or *diarrheic* versus *diarrhetic*. For a few cases, we find addition of -*at*- or -*et*- before the suffix (*axiomatic, emblematic, enzymatic, genetic*). Only in the case of *heroic* do we find vowel hiatus. Bases that end in /s/ exhibit /t/ before the suffix, as in *apocalyptic, chaotic, pelvic, synaptic, syntactic, syphilitic*. Base-final sonorants resyllabify with the suffix as in *cyclic, calendric, chasmic, rhythmic*. Cases of trisyllabic laxing can be found (*meteoritical*).

The suffix *-ive* has three additional variants with extenders, *-at-ive*, *-it-ive*, and *-ut-ive*. The last of these appears only on verbs containing the formatives *solve* and *volve* (*dissolutive*, *evolutive*), and *-itive* on verbs with the formatives *quire* (*inquisitive*, *acquisitive*), *pos* (*oppositive*), or *pet* (*competitive*, *repetitive*). Otherwise we find it only in the forms *additive* and *sensitive*. The variant *-ative* is found more frequently, but it is not clear that there is anything systematic about its appearance, as opposed to the appearance of the simple *-ive* variant. Indeed, in COCA we find at least a few doublets like *augmentative/augmentive* and *adaptative/adaptive*, and many near doublets like *revulsive* versus *pulsative*. That said, verbal bases that end in /r/ or non-coronal consonants like /m/ or /k/ appear to prefer the *-ative* variant (*comparative*, *explorative*, *confirmative*, *informative*, *evocative*). The string *-ative* also arises through the combination of the verbal suffix *-ate* with our adjectival suffix *-ive*. In the vast majority of cases this leads to destressing and vowel reduction to schwa of the secondarily stressed verbal suffix (cf. *íteràte* versus *íter*[ə]*tive*). Very rarely, we find two forms alongside each other (*íntegràtive* and *íntegr*[ə]*tive*, *íllustràtive* and *illústr*[ə]*tive*).

With regard to stress placement, *-ive* rarely has any effect on its base. Consider the many non-stress-shifting examples with penultimate stress (*extrospéctive*, *apprehénsive*, *corréctive*, *creátive*), with antepenultimate stress (*dónative*, *attríbutive*, *depósitive*), and even pre-antepenultimate stress (*dédicative*, *íntegrative*, *íterative*, *spéculative*). There are several highly lexicalized derivatives in *-ive* that show stress shift, in which case stress is placed on the antepenultimate syllable (*contémplative*, *corrélative*, *demónstrative*, *exécutive*, *négative*, *rélative*, *sédative*, *remónstrative*). Notably, to achieve stress on the antepenult, the stress is sometimes moved forward (*córrelàte* • *corrélative*), sometimes backward (*reláte* • *rélative*). If stress is shifted in a verbal base ending in *-ate*, vowel reduction in the verbal suffix is obligatory, as shown in the variably shifting adjective *illustrative*. In case of shift, this word does not secondarily stress the verbal suffix (e.g. *illústr*[ə]*tive*), thus avoiding a stress clash.

As *-ive* favours non-native verbal bases, it displays the full range of base allomorphy that we find in Latinate verbs. The range of base allomorphy that we find is illustrated in (22).

(22)

adhere	•	adhesive
appeal	•	appellative
ascribe	•	ascriptive
assume	•	assumptive
cohere	•	cohesive
compel	•	compulsive
conjoin	•	conjunctive
induce	•	inductive
inquire	•	inquisitive
perceive	•	perceptive
submit	•	submissive
succeed	•	successive

Note that with some of the forms involving <s> before the suffix, we find variation between voiced and voiceless realizations. In addition, we find occasional vowel laxing (*interventive*) and trisyllabic laxing (*definitive, declarative, competitive*), as well as occasional devoicing of a base-final obstruent (*infusive, attentive, disclosive*). Base-final /d/ sometimes becomes /s/, or sometimes /z/, in the derived form (*obtrusive, responsive, abrasive, conclusive*).

The suffix *-oid* does not induce stress shifts, but often attaches to bound bases that, given the denominal character of the suffix, could be analysed as truncated nouns, for example *bungalow* ◆ *bungaloid, magma* ◆ *magmoid, negro* ◆ *negroid, Picasso* ◆ *Picassoid, Pluto* ◆ *plutoid* (sic), *rhombus* ◆ *rhomboid, sigma* ◆ *sigmoid, volcano* ◆ *vulcanoid*. Such base truncation seems to be especially frequent when base-final vowel and suffix-initial vowel are the same.

The profile of *-ory* is very similar to that of *-ive*. It exhibits two variants with extenders, *-it-ory* and *-at-ory*, which appear under circumstances similar to the allomorphs of *-ive*. The variant *-itory* is infrequent, appearing on bases with the Latinate formatives *pos* and *pet* (*expository, competitory*) as well as in rare cases like *definitory* and *divinitory*. The *-atory* variant appears in words like *applicatory, comparatory, perspiratory, condolatory, amendatory*, and *combinatory*, with no particular pattern discernable. Again, at least one doublet *improvisatory/improvisory* can be found in COCA.

As with *-ive*, the stress pattern of the base is almost always maintained with *-ory*. On disyllabic bases, this seems invariably to be the case for trochees (*mandatory, gyratory, migratory, vibratory, commendatory*), and typically the case for iambs (*conclusory, advisory, observatory, amendatory*) although there are a few high frequency or lexicalized cases where stress shifts to the initial syllable of the base (*respiratory, combinatory, preparatory, revelatory*). For trisyllabic bases, amphibrachs and anapests exhibit maintenance of base stress (*contributory, interjectory, locomotory*). Dactylic bases typically maintain stress (*postulatory, dedicatory, copulatory*) except in a few cases where their penultimate syllables are heavy (*compensatory, obfuscatory, satisfactory*). For bases with more than four syllables, we only occasionally find stress retraction (compare for example, *prognosticatory* versus *interrogatory*).

With regard to base allomorphy, *-ory* triggers allomorphy on Latinate verbs, as *-ive* does, so we find forms like *compulsory, introductory, redemptory, satisfactory*, and *intercessory*. Base-final /d/ becomes /s/ before *-ory*, as in *conclusory, delusory, derisory*. We also find frequent laxing of a vowel in the final syllable of the base (*declamatory, declaratory, definatory, divinatory, explanatory*).

The suffix *-ous* appears with a wide variety of extenders: *-iti-ous* (*excrementitious*), *-ati-ous* (*flirtatious, usurpatious, vexatious*), *-t-ous* (*edematous, eczematous*), *-in-ous* (*altitudinous, cartilaginous, leguminous, voluminous*), *-u-ous* (*contempuous, sensuous, spirituous*), *-i-ous* (*capricious, censorious, felonious*), and *-e-ous* (*consanguineous, nectareous*). The last two variants are probably just spelling variants. As for the rest, it is hard to tell if there are any regularities to be found. We find doublets in COCA like *carbonous* and *carbonious, spiritous* and *spirituous*, as well as near doublets like *treasonous* versus *felonious, humorous* versus *censorious*.

The words with the suffix *-ous* are generally stressed on the penult if the penult is heavy, and on the antepenult if the penult is light. The suffix triggers stress shift where it is necessary to achieve the pertinent stress pattern. The former pattern is shown by *fi.la.mén.tous, ca.ta.rác.tous, ca.prí.cious, de.sí.rous, in.féc.tious*, the latter pattern by *a.cró.ny.mous, béau.te.ous, ca.dá.ve.rous, cár.bo.nous, ce.re.mó.ni.ous, com.plí.ci.tous, co.ní.fe.rous, con.tí.nu.ous, có.ve.tous, he.te.ró.ny.mous, me.ló.di.ous*. The highly lexicalized forms *ad.van.tá.geous, cou.rá.geous, out.rá.geous* are peculiar in their behaviour. They totally conform to the antepenult stress pattern with heavy penult, but they do so by showing stress shift and vowel tensing. This is somewhat strange, however, since there is no necessity for this. The unattested, non-shifting potential derivative, for example **advántageous*, would be in accordance with the required prosody for penultimate stress.

We find a modest amount of segmental base allomorphy with forms in *-ous*. There is occasional vowel laxing (*capricious, gangrenous, zealous*) and variety-dependent palatalization of a base-final /s/ (*capricious, gaseous, gracious, sensuous*). There is also sporadic resyllabification of base-final schwa syllables with loss of the schwa (*disastrous, lustrous*), but this seems not to be obligatory as we find *monsterous* alongside and synonymous with *monstrous*.

14.2.1.3 *Productivity*

The non-native adjective-forming suffixes show a range of productivity, varying from the fully productive to the nearly unproductive. Among them, it seems clear that *-able* and *-esque* are the most productive; indeed they appear to be completely productive. The suffix *-able* can be found on just about any transitive verb (and some intransitives, as we have seen), and *-esque* on any personal name. Since transitive verbs can be formed productively (see Chapter 13), and proper nouns are virtually inexhaustible, we seem to have an ever-expanding pool of bases to which these affixes can attach. The suffix *-oid* is also highly productive, even if somewhat restricted due to its scientific flavour.

At the other end of the scale we find the suffixes *-ant, -ary*, and *-ine* all of which exhibit relatively few types in COCA with almost no forms that appear to be novel (although possible novel forms for *-ant* and *-ary* are *averrant* and *testimonary*, neither of which are found in the *OED*). The suffix *-ary* is found on quite a few forms in *-ion*, but never on bases derived with the productive variant of the suffix, *-ation*.

The suffixes *-ine* and *-ive* also exhibit few apparently novel forms. With *-ine* we find *dinosaurine, cervantine, sigmodontine* none of which are attested in the *OED*. For *-ive* we find *assortive, contestive, precessive, situative*, and *walkative*, the last of which is clearly intended to be jocular. It is of course not surprising that we should find so few novel forms with *-ive*, since as we have seen above this suffix places fairly strict phonological conditions on its bases.

The other non-native adjective-forming suffixes fall somewhere in between these two poles. The suffix *-al*, for example, attaches quite productively to a base ending in the suffixes *-oid, -ation, -or*, or *-ure*, or neo-classical combining forms like *-cide* or *-some* (as in *chromosome*). There are occasional novel forms on underived bases, as for example, *altazimuthal, appendiceal, pelletal, silical, summital, tapestrial*, and *trombonal*, all attested in COCA.

The suffix *-ic* also shows some productivity. In addition to attaching to a wide range of neo-classical combining elements like *meter, naut, phile, phobe, logy, graph, path, gen, morph, scope, crat, nym, phage, soph, sphere, bot, cyt,* and so on, it also attaches quite freely to forms derived on the suffixes *-ite* and *-ist*. To the extent then that neoclassical compounds and derived forms in *-ist* are themselves productive, *-ic* is as well. The suffix *-ic* also appears on proper nouns where it is potentially productive, although it is not clear how many adjectivalizations of names are formed this way (*Saddamic* is surely a recent example though). And it is not difficult to find low frequency, apparently novel forms in COCA, among which are the forms in (23).

(23)   civilic, agentic, anodynic, armageddonic, aureolic, banjoic, bimbonic, boronic, bosonic, Boswellic, codic, dharmic, dolphinic, golemic, halalic, hurricanic, hybridic, koanic, legerdemainic, pheromonic, potentatic, rosemarinic, schadenfreudic, strychninic, tantrumic, tortic, tsunamic

The suffix *-ical* also attaches to neoclassical combining forms (especially those ending in *-ology*) and derived words in *-ist* but otherwise seems not to be nearly as productive as *-ic*. A few apparent neologisms can be found (*chessical, churchical, existorical*), but these seem to convey a self-conscious or ironic nuance that the neologisms in *-ic* generally lack.

The suffixes *-ory* and *-ous* are modestly productive. The former appears frequently on verbs in *-ate*. COCA yields apparently novel forms like *cavitatory, comparatory, congregatory, contestatory, defecatory, divinatory, enduratory, immolatory, incarnatory, inhalatory, isulatory, litigatory, productory,* and *tonsilory*. The suffix *-ous* is partial to neoclassical combining forms like *vore, nym, mat, morph, phone, phage, phil,* etc., and frequently gives rise to jocular or mockscholarly forms like *ginormous, grandilomentitudinous, redunculous, rumbustious, up-tighteous, mind-bendous, bimbocious,* and *crapulous*. In COCA we find other novel forms as well, including: *attitudinous, curtainous, debaucherous, desertous, exotendinous, fidelitous, gargantuous, hirsutulous, inquirious, razorous, revengeous, rippulous, rosivorous, squanderous, theonomous, tonerous, usurpatious,* and *vibrous*.

14.2.2 Native affixes

English has a wealth of native adjective-forming affixes alongside the non-native ones we have treated above. We will begin with the clearly derivational suffixes *-ed, -en, -ern, -ful, -ish, -ly, -some,* and *-y*, followed by the prefix *a-* and take up the participial adjectives in Section 14.2.3.

14.2.2.1 *Kinds of bases*

The adjective-forming suffixes *-ful, -ish, -like, -some,* and *-y* attach to a range of categories (24)–(27).

(24)   a. -ful *on nouns*: deceitful, faithful, gleeful, lawful, mindful, purposeful, slothful

       b. -ful *on verbs*: reflectful, resentful, vengeful, wakeful, watchful

       c. -ful *on adjectives*: gladful, proudful, rightful, wrongful

(25)   a. -ish *on nouns*: babyish, clannish, doggish, gluish, iconish, lardish, nannyish

       b. -ish *on verbs*: skitterish, sloggish, snappish, ticklish, whimperish

       c. -ish *on adjectives*: angry-ish, brownish, freeish, goodish, modernish, narrowish, roughish

       d. -ish *on numerals*: fivish, twentyish

(26)   a. -some *on nouns*: adventuresome, fruitsome, healthsome, joysome, mirthsome, riddlesome

       b. -some *on verbs*: frolicsome, irksome, meddlesome, vexsome, wrigglesome

       c. -some *on adjectives*: blithesome, darksome, lithesome, lonesome, wearisome

(27)   a. -y *on nouns*: arty, bitchy, coppery, feathery, girly, houndy, nebbishy, perfumy, rusty

       b. -y *on verbs*: blowy, choosey, droopy, grabby, moochy, picky, scrabbly, teetery, wilty

       c. -y *on adjectives*: crispy, dreary, greeny, moderny, swanky, yellowy

The suffix *-ly* occurs on nouns and noun phrases (28a), and *-ed* can be found on nouns (including nominal compounds) and noun phrases (28b).

(28)   a. -ly: actorly, beggarly, comradely, innerworldly, fleshly, laggardly, nightly, readerly

       b. -ed: bearded, blue-eyed, broad-minded, empty-headed, four-footed, three-wheeled, glass-roofed, wooded

As some of the examples show, plural inflection does not surface on base noun phrases, in spite of a plural interpretation (see also *four-holed, four-leafed, four-petaled*). The two suffixes *-en* and *-ern* are no longer productive, with *-ern* appearing only on nouns denoting geographic directions (e.g. *northern, western*), and *-en* deriving adjectives from nouns denoting materials or substances (*earthen, silken, wooden*). These unproductive suffixes will not be treated in any more detail.

Note that there are isolated cases of a native extender with *-ly*, when it attaches to nouns denoting geographic directions (*south-er-ly, north-er-ly*). Native adjective-forming affixes as a rule do not attach to bound bases, with the exception of a few archaic or obsolete bases on which we find *-some*, for example *gruesome, handsome, lissome, noisome, winsome*. As is typical of native affixes generally, the adjective-forming suffixes are equally comfortable on native or non-native bases:

(29) a. -ful   *native*: heavenful, deathful

                 non-native: deceitful, beautiful

    b. -ish   *native*: doomish, freeish

                 non-native: caricaturish, modernish

    c. -ly   *native*: deathly, nightly

                 non-native: musicianly, spectatorly

    d. -some *native*: mirthsome, wholesome

                 non-native: adventursome, joysome

    e. -y   *native*: handy, cheesy

                 non-native: actressy, chocolatey

Of the native suffixes, *-ish* and *-y* appear on compound bases, and at least occasionally on phrasal bases.

(30) a. -ish   *compounds*: homeboyish, punk-rockish, show-offish, trailer-parkish

                 phrases: dog-in-the-mangerish, feelgoodish, up-your-buttish

    b. -y   *compounds*: hot-tubby, piss-stinky, woodwork

                 phrases: secret-agenty

As is typical of native affixes, this cohort is associated with neither stress shift nor allomorphy.

The prefix *a-*, which derives what is frequently called an adjective but could often be an adverb, only very occasionally leads to new formations (such as *a-move, a-pant, asmirk* (all from the *OED*), *acrawl*, and, from Barnhart *et al.* (1990), *aclutter, aglaze, asquish, awhir*), all apparently based on verbal bases that are monosyllabic.

14.2.2.2 *Productivity*

Of these suffixes, clearly the most productive are *-ish*, and *-y*, which, as we have seen, attach to virtually any kind of available base, including compounds and phrases; indeed, it seems safe to say that they are among the most productive suffixes of contemporary English. They are most productive, of course, on nominal bases, but there are novel forms on adjectives for *-ish*, and on verbs for *-y*. Apparently novel forms from COCA include: *beginnerish, dungeon-ish, gloomish, bloodyish, familiarish, modernish; kitteny, lummoxy, spoofy, flinchy, moochy, revolvy.* It is not difficult to add examples to these.

The suffix *-ful* is somewhat less productive. It exhibits fewer types overall, and its bases seem to cluster around a specific semantic category that poses natural limitations for potential novel forms. To the extent that new forms can be derived, the suffix *-ful* favours bases that denote psychological states or processes; *verveful, angstful, groundful, importful, learningful,* *driveful, swoonful, despiseful,* and *provokeful* are novel forms attested in COCA. There are only a few other novel *-ful* forms: *fluteful, ghostful, girthful, limbful.* Also only modestly productive is *-some,* for which there are at best a handful of apparently novel forms attested in COCA: *fiercesome, fruitsome, hunksome, problemsome, whoresome, clattersome, droolsome, jinglesome, coosome, rilesome.*

One can very easily find new ornative adjectives with the suffix *-ed,* with new formations having a tendency to have phrases as bases, especially those containing a numeral in the first position of the phrase (*one-horned, two-tailed, three-masted, four-engined, five-sided,* and so on).

Adjectival *-ly* is barely productive, with new forms largely confined to person nouns (*demonly, dudely, speakerly, spectatorly*) and places (*neighborhoodly*). There are relatively few types with this suffix, and most of them are item-familiar. The suffixes *-en* and *-ern* are unproductive, and the prefix *a-* seems to be available for new coinages only to a very limited degree, chiefly in poetic or literary discourse.

14.2.3 Participial adjectives

Both the *-ing* form of verbs and past participle forms are frequently used as premodifiers to nouns, and have sometimes been argued to be categorially adjectival, as evidenced by their frequent ability to accept prefixation with negative *un-,* to form the comparative and superlative, sometimes even the morphological comparative and superlative (see Chapter 6), and to be sub-modified by *very, so,* etc. Formally, the participial adjectives are identical to the present and past participles, and as the formal characteristics of the latter have already been covered in Chapter 5, we will not revisit them here. There is one point that should be highlighted, though, which is the tendency of adjectives formed from past participles to retain archaic strong forms where weak past participles have arisen and are more often used in verbal contexts. Among these are *burnt, cloven, bereft, mown, shorn, shod, smitten, spilt, spoilt,* and perhaps *sewn.*

14.3 SEMANTIC CONSIDERATIONS

The semantic interpretation of adjectival derivation in contemporary English has received far less attention than the semantics of nominalization or verbalization, but it has been touched upon at least by Ljung (1970), Beard (1995), Hamawand (2007), and Kaunisto (2007). In Section 14.3.1 we consider various aspects of the semantics of adjective-forming affixes: what, if any, specific semantic content is carried by various affixes, whether there is a fundamental difference between so called 'relational' and 'qualitative' adjectives, and whether specific affixes can be designated as gradable or non-gradable.

14.3.1 Semantic content

The semantic characteristics of derived adjectives to some extent depend on what sort of base they are attached to. When attached to verbal bases, adjectival affixes typically reference either an argument of the base or the event itself. That is, for a transitive verb VERB whose arguments are X and Y (in other words, X VERBS Y), subject-referencing adjectives can be predicated of X, object-referencing adjectives can be predicated of Y, and event-referencing adjectives can be construed as 'characterized by VERB'. Some deverbal adjectives also have aspectual nuances, as we will see. Except in the case of eventive nouns, adjectives derived from nominal bases do not reference arguments, and generally exhibit more loosely relational meanings. A rather specific non-argumental meaning, however, is associated with ornative -*ed*. We will first discuss deverbal adjectives and then denominal (or de-adjectival) adjectives.

14.3.1.1 *Argument referencing*

As noted above, those adjective-forming affixes that accept verbal bases typically prefer either a subject-referencing or an object-referencing interpretation. The participial -*ing* is somewhat more complex, so we will treat it separately.

Object-referencing

We will begin with the typically object-referencing affixes, as they are less numerous. The most important of these is the suffix -*able* (by which we now mean both the -*able* and the -*ible* allomorphs). As indicated in Section 14.2.1.1, -*able* prefers transitive bases, and adjectives derived with this suffix on transitive bases always reference the object argument. So for a verb like *conceal*, the derived adjective *concealable* refers to the theme, the thing concealed, rather than the agent of the action. Similarly for other typical examples like *adaptable* or *grillable*. In the relatively rare cases where we find -*able* on unaccusative verbs, the -*able* adjective appears to be subject-referencing, for example *perishable*. However, it has been argued in the framework of generative grammar that unaccusative verbs should actually be analysed as having an underlying object, and not an underlying subject argument, in which case we might assume that -*able* is object-referencing here too. Regardless of syntactic analysis, the referent of -*able* in these cases bears the same thematic relation as in the case of the transitives; so forms like *perishable* or *rottable* reference the patient/theme on both transitive and unaccusative bases.

We do find -*able* on the occasional unergative verb, as *stutterable*, attested in COCA. Interestingly, however in this case the -*able* adjective does not reference the subject, the only available argument, but rather a contextually or pragmatically determined referent.

(31) *Psychology Today 1998*: Over that time, he strived for one main goal at local gatherings: "making the atmosphere **stutterable**." He wanted people to have permission to stammer openly; after all, he says, "stuttering isn't something you get over in a week."

In the few other cases where -*able* appears to attach to an unergative verb, the context indicates that those verbs have been coerced into a transitive reading, as for example, in the case of *perspirable* in (32).

(32) *Saturday Evening Post 2003*: To become sensible of this by an experiment, let a person keep his position in the bed, but throw off the bed-clothes, and suffer fresh air to approach the part uncovered of his body; he will then feel that part suddenly refreshed; for the air will immediately relieve the skin, by receiving, licking up, and carrying off, the load of **perspirable** matter that incommoded it.

An -*able* adjective is conceivable for the verb *perspire* as long as it is possible to imagine some output or product of perspiring.

Where we find -*able* on nominal bases, these bases are typically amenable to an eventive or stative interpretation. In such cases, -*able* seems able to reference an implied argument or refer to a participant in the associated event. If the participant is an argument, that argument can be either an implied subject or object. In cases like *knowledgeable* or *pleasurable* we have a subject-referencing interpretation, whereas in *marriageable*, *braillable*, or *impressionable* we have an object-referencing interpretation. A non-argument is focused in *ferryable*, which can refer to the path of the ferrying event, as in *ferryable river*.

The suffix -*able* of course has semantic content beyond its object-referentiality. It is clearly modal in nature, indicating capacity to undergo the action denoted by the verb (*washable*, *heatable*), or occasionally inclination to undergo the action denoted by the verb (*perishable*, *agreeable*) (Bauer and Huddleston 2002: 1707). Bauer and Huddleston point out as well that in particular forms with the 'possibility' reading may shade off into other modalities, as in the 'necessity' reading of *answerable* (as in *to be answerable to someone*) or the 'permissibility' reading of *photocopiable* (as in 'legal to photocopy').

The other typically object-referencing derived adjective is the past participial adjective, which also has an aspectual nuance in keeping with its participial nature. Specifically, the adjectival past participle typically has a completive interpretation. So in phrases like *an eaten apple* or *filtered water*, the premodified noun refers to the object of the verb, and the participial adjective implies a completed action. Transitives predominate (33) and unaccusatives are possible (34), but unergatives are rare. Where we do find apparently unergative verbs, they have been coerced to a transitive reading, as (35) illustrates:

(33) *New York Times 2008*: To better understand their lifestyle and behavior, the Wildlife Conservation Society sent specially **trained** dogs into the piney woods here recently, not in search of actual moose, but their scat, or excrement.

(34) *Health & Social Work 1993*: The findings indicate that a strong sense of personal efficacy was associated with fewer symptoms of depression. However, current refugee resettlement models have not yet developed training programs to enhance and improve personal efficacy among recently **arrived** refugees.

(35) *Harpers Magazine 1998*: The mirrors' remains of sebum and pus and **sneezed** detritus.

The only other affix that bears mention in this section is *-ary*, which only occasionally attaches to verbs. Most of the resulting adjectives are too lexicalized in meaning to merit systematic analysis, but in the few cases of transparent derivations the resulting words are object-referencing. This is the case, for example with words like *documentary* (which applies to the thing documented rather than the documenter); similarly with words like *imaginary*, *salutary*, and perhaps *honorary*.

Subject-referencing

The affixes *-ant*, *-ive*, and *-ory*, all permit a subject-referencing interpretation, as do *-al*, *-ous*, and *-y* when they attach to verbal bases, but these affixes seem more fluid in interpretation than the object-referencing cases discussed above. That is, words derived with these affixes typically do not have fixed interpretations, but can vary between subject-referencing and eventive interpretations depending on context. We will return to the eventive interpretation in the next section.

Examples (36–41) show words derived with these affixes that receive a subject-referencing interpretation.

(36) *Psychology Today 2010*: A woman maybe high functioning as mother to a 4-year-old who remains **compliant** and eager to please, but difficult to a 14-year-old exercising a teen's capacity for criticism and opposition—and yet mellow to a 40-year-old, when her anxieties about a child's independence or difference may have finally been resolved.

(37) *New York Times 2010*: I don't think the American people last year voted for higher taxes, higher deficits and a more **intrusive** government.

(38) *Analog Fiction & Fact 2001*: It's a wasting away, and microscopic **vibratory** forms of life can do that just as well as us big beings.

(39) *Journal of Drug Issues 2010*: Additional research should examine whether the **causal** factors influencing arrest trajectories differ by gender.

(40) *Cosmopolitan 2010*: After weeks of hoping Rob would make a move now that he knew how I felt and his alternating between acting awkward and being **flirtatious** toward me, I finally got fed up and found another job.

(41) *Paul is Undead 2010*: That said, George is nearly as honest as John Lennon, albeit he's less **chatty** and has a significantly lower level of angst.

It is not difficult to find other examples that have this subject-referencing interpretation, especially for the suffix *-ive*.

Participial -ing

Participial *-ing* is strongly subject-referencing, although with an interesting twist. On transitive bases like *annoy*, the adjectival *-ing* participle typically refers to the subject; so an *annoying neighbor* is a neighbour who annoys (as opposed to *an annoyed neighbor*). Similarly with unergative or unaccusative verbs, the *-ing* participle is predicated on the subject, as in for example, a *sneezing parakeet* (unergative *sneeze*) or *the falling leaf* (unaccusative *fall*). What is interesting, however, is that with verbs that vary between transitive/causative uses and unaccusative/inchoative uses—that is, verbs like *open, close, grow, boil, cook*—the *-ing* participle is much likelier to reference the subject of the unaccusative form of the verb, which corresponds to the object of the transitive form of the verb. So we easily find examples like *boiling water* or *growing weeds*, but the sort of example illustrated in (42) is much harder to come by:

(42)   *The Fireman's Fair 1991*: She was not **a cooking woman**, but she liked to be complimented on her shrimp.

The adjectival *-ing* participle has aspectual meaning as well, conveying an ongoing or habitual event.

14.3.1.2 *Event-referencing*

Many of the affixes discussed in Section 14.3.1.1, including participial *-ing*, can also receive an eventive reading, which is to say that adjectives derived with them need not refer to one argument or the other, but can alternatively focus on the nature of the event denoted by the verbal base. Put more simply, such derived adjectives may receive interpretations paraphrasable as 'characterized by VERBing' or 'pertaining to VERBing' or 'involved in VERBing.' (43)–(48) are characteristic examples.

(43)   *Professional School Counseling 2008*: Traumatized children had more intense play, play disruptions, repetitive play, **avoidant** play behavior, and negative affect.

(44)   *Roeper Review 2007*: His teacher embedded a variety of **explorative** activities into her classroom.

(45)   *Antioch Review 2006*: Their machines hum a **vibratory** song like a gather of insects in unison, the monitors clacking and chirring at the bedsides.

(46)   *North American Journal of Psychology 2004*: Given that no decrement in performance is evident, this suggests that the **configural** aspects of the other-race faces are not taken advantage of when the faces are processed.

(47)   *Kenyon Review 1997*: Her eyes, the color of lime slices, always gazed at me with **predaceous** intensity.

(48) *The American Spectator 2009*: And growing up, I would hear in him the breezy, **chatty** style that he must have decided would help him with his customers.

In a sense, the eventive interpretation is very similar to the range of interpretation we find for adjectives derived on nominal bases, to which we turn in Section 14.3.1.3.

14.3.1.3 *Non-argumental*

Adjective-deriving affixes that attach predominantly or exclusively to nominal and adjectival bases are semantically rather different from affixes that take verbal bases, as their meanings obviously cannot depend on the referencing of base arguments. The affixes we have in mind here are *-al, -ary, -ed, -esque, -ful, -an, -ic, -ical, -ine, -ish, -ly, -oid, -ous, -some*, and *-y*. What is critical is to determine to what extent specific meanings are to be associated with particular affixes and to what extent various meanings are dependent on the semantic characteristics of the base rather than the semantics of the affix. We will begin with the adjective-forming suffixes that are more contentful, specifically *-esque, -ful, -ish*, and *-oid*, and then look at the remaining affixes, which are closer to being purely transpositional.

The suffix *-ful* is perhaps the easiest to deal with, as it comes the closest of all these affixes to having a lexical meaning. Often the simple glosses 'full of' or 'having' are appropriate; so *sorrow-ful* is 'full of sorrow' and *insightful* is 'having insight'. Other *-ful* words are also arguably compositional, although their interpretation is slightly different. For example, forms like *dutiful* and *effortful* are more aptly glossed as 'displaying duty' or 'expending effort'. The difference in interpretation is, however, possibly attributable to the difference in bases, the former two being formed on nouns denoting psychological states and the latter on more volitional nouns.

The cohort of formatives *-esque, -ish, -like*, and *-oid* are also relatively contentful, all being what might be termed similative, often paraphrased as 'like X, in the shape of X, in the style of X, resembling X', depending on the kind of base. The affixes *-ly* and *-y* which sometimes have similative meanings are dealt with elsewhere. Comparing triplets and doublets with these forms is instructive. In many cases, there seems to be little or no difference in their semantic content, as illustrated by the doublets and triplets shown in (49), from COCA, and (50), from the BNC.

(49) a. *Washington Post 1991*: Babysitter Courtney and Babysitter Skipper are two **Barbie-ish** dolls that come with infants and Walkmans.

 Fortune 2003: Most branches include a WaMu "store" that sells **Barbieesque** teller dolls for kids and personal[ ]finance books for adults.

 Esquire 1998: The Karen Carpenter Story (which is enacted entirely by **Barbie-like** dolls), Poison, and Safe-Haynes is, like all of his movies, smart and good-looking.

 b. *Men's Health 2004*: And second, it comes with an **iPod-esque** remote, complete with a color LCD screen, that sends your tunes to any "pod" (shown under remote) throughout the house.

USA Today 2005: Receptacle on the dashboard of most versions accommodates **iPod-ish** music machines so you can play your music library through the car stereo.

Time 2005: The Digital Music System is the sleekest solution available— complete with a cool **iPod-like** handheld controller that allows you to play different songs simultaneously in different zones all around your house.

    c. *Town and Country 2009*: Since opening in December, Benjy's has been strictly SRO. The **modernesque** look sets the stage for boisterous fun in the upstairs lounge, where you can enjoy the signature blood-orange margaritas, and downstairs, where the best choices include tuna tartare on a tempura edamame roll, [...]

San Francisco Chronicle 1996: "I always like to do Shakespeare in **modernish** dress because I want to put people into clothes rather than costumes," he explains.

Public Interest 1992: [O]verall, these designs are refreshingly free from formula: no **modernoid** lunar landscapes with lollipop lightbulbs, no "Olmstoid" caricatures of Frederick Law Olmsted's pioneering work of a century ago.

(50)   *Bad dreams*: Its fur was arranged in **punkish** spikes.

New Musical Express: [...] Gary Lee Conner is the band's only obvious showman, a tangle of sweat, hair and **punkoid** Townshend windmill routines [...]

Although, as suggested by these examples, there appears to be no intrinsic semantic difference in these affixes, this is not to say that individual doublets or triplets cannot display different meanings. Such differences often appear with pairs of *-ish* and *-like* words. We find, for example, cases like *amberish* versus *amber-like*, where the *-ish* adjective refers to the color, and the *-like* adjective to the substance in the examples below.

(51)   *Sky and Telescope 2000*: With patience you might see that the yellow looks more specifically **amberish** or apricot orange and that the blue is closest to the ashy blue of the Atlantic Ocean.

Analog Science Fiction & Fact 2005: Then she turned back suddenly, her hand reaching into her jacket pocket and emerging with the **amber-like** keepsake.

Similarly, it would seem that in a pair like *blondish* versus *blonde-like*, the former would refer to a color, and the latter to a type of person, or in the pair *dwarfish* versus *dwarflike* we might suppose that the former is likelier to pick out the quality of small size, and the latter to refer to a kind of person. It might seem then that *-ish* is more likely to denote similarity to individual salient qualities, and *-like* similarity to a whole. The pair *childish* versus *child-like* is another case of two different meanings having developed for the two forms.

    We must reiterate, however, that this is no more than a tendency. There are other *-ish* and *-like* pairs that do not appear to differ at all, as the examples *babyish* and *baby-like* in (52) suggest:

(52) *Callaloo 2005*: In appearance, Marty is **babyish** in his features, a sixteen-year-old chubby-cheeked foul-mouthed infant looking out scornfully at the world from a bonnet of black lustrous hair.

   Literary Review 1994: If he made the effort to turn his head toward her he could see her pudgy hand with its **baby-like** dimples and three silver rings, the kind they used to sell at the Central Bus Station, and which Avner used to buy Rachel by weight.

There seems to be even less difference between *-like* and *-esque* in terms of pure denotation.

(53) *Inc. 2005*: Ostensibly, our destination was Rancho Parsones, as Parsons bemusedly called the **chateauesque** house he was building, but first we had a few errands to run.

   Washington Post 1990: The Trupin house is unmistakably a symbol, sitting vacant on the beach in Southampton, its **chateaulike** turrets still encased in scaffolding, but a symbol of what?

At best we might say that *-like* is the more neutral in connotation than *-esque*, which is somewhat more elevated or academic in style. The suffix *-oid* frequently has a scientific flavour to it, but otherwise seems semantically not clearly distinguishable from the other similative suffixes.

   We should also say a word about these affixes on adjectival bases. We might be tempted to attribute a slightly different semantics to *-esque*, *-ish*, *-like*, and *-oid* when we find them attached to adjectives, as they seem to mean not so much 'similar to X' but 'approximating X'. We would argue, however, that the first meaning is derived by inference from the second. If we say something is similar to *dull*, *baptismal*, *lunar*, or *modern*, the inference is drawn that we cannot mean exactly *dull*, *baptismal*, *lunar*, or *modern* but rather must mean something not exactly the same as those qualities, that is, approximating those qualities. Compare the examples in (54)–(56), and again (49c) above.

(54) *The Southern Review 2004*: Lee Ann remembered watching her parents dance at her and Ted's wedding; they were good, **dullish**, ordinary people, but they were great dancers.

(55) *Houston Chronicle 1995*: Eggs rolled over the body to absorb evil, hands placed over the afflicted area, scented and blessed oils, herbs, and a pool of water for **baptismal-like** cures are a small sampling of the famous folk healer's "remedios."

(56) *Omni 1992*: Devastation Trail is a boardwalk laid out on glistening jet cinders in a setting that looks **lunaresque**—if the moon had burned.

From this inference we derive the approximative sense of the similative affixes.

   The suffix *-ed* has an ornative sense and derives adjectives with the general meaning 'having X, being provided with X'. Examples abound, and we list only a few here: *low-prized*, *large-sized*, *mud-walled*, *propertied*, *short-legged*, *white-robed*.

14.3.1.4 *Transpositional*

The remaining affixes that attach predominantly to nouns or other adjectives are *-al, -an, -ic, -ical, -ine, -ly, -ous, -some*, and *-y*. These are as close as affixes come in English to being purely transpositional, in the sense that they appear to add no specific meaning beyond what would be attributed to their categorial status as adjectives. This is not to say that individual derived adjectives do not exhibit more specific relational meanings, especially in context. As Ljung (1970) points out, specific derived adjectives might mean (given the right context) 'covered in' (*a muddy floor*), 'affected with' (*the furious teacher*), or 'in accordance with' (*a normal temperature*), and the like; indeed, Ljung isolates close to twenty general meanings that can be expressed by denominal adjectives.

It is clear, however, both from his data and from examples gleaned from COCA that specific meanings arise from a combination of the base, the affix, and most importantly the context in which a form appears. The affixes themselves appear to have no fixed meaning beyond the most general meaning of 'characterized by', 'pertaining to', 'relating to'. In this sense their semantic behaviour is very similar to that displayed by non-argumental compounds, where the relationship between first and second elements is constrained only by the sort of reasonable relationships that might be imagined between one lexical base and another (see Chapter 20).

We will illustrate this point in two ways. First we will look at individual forms that may have several interpretations depending on the contexts in which they occur, thus suggesting that specific relationships expressed in the derived adjective are to some extent driven by context. Secondly, we will look at sets of forms that have the same nominal bases, but different adjective-forming affixes, and that nevertheless, in similar contexts appear to mean the same thing.

We concentrate here on the affixes *-al, -an, -ic, -ous*, and *-y*, since the affixes *-ine* and *-some* are only marginally productive. We will return to the suffix *-ical* in Section 14.3.3. The affixes *-al, -an, -ic, -ous*, and *-y* and their variants with extenders are all broadly relational in meaning. As we said above, how we gloss them in individual forms depends heavily on both the nature of the base and the context in which the derived word finds itself.

We will illustrate first with the native affix *-y*. This suffix is unique among the adjective-forming suffixes in preferring mono- or disyllabic bases, often concrete mass or count nouns. In a word like *brothy*, we might be tempted to gloss the suffix as 'containing', for example, but examples from COCA show that a wider range of interpretations is available in context.

(57) a. *San Francisco Chronicle 2005*: Much of it is meant to appeal to a more American palate, but no one would complain over a hot, **brothy** bowl of vegetarian pho with tons of still-crisp vegetables.

   b. *San Francisco Chronicle 2009*: A great version of siu mai $3.20/4 features tender wrappers enclosing a well-seasoned filling with **brothy** undertones.

   c. *The Others 2009*: He pushed the bowl toward her, letting her smell the **brothy** steam.

So in (57a) we get the expected meaning 'containing broth', but in (57b,c) we get something more like 'tasting like broth' or even 'smelling like broth'. It seems more sensible to say that this affix merely transposes the noun to an adjective in which any salient quality of the noun relevant to a particular context can be focused.

Similarly, we can take a word like *rabbinic*, and find it used in a number of distinct senses:

(58)   a.   *Lilith 2005*: The law says count all the days of your menstruation, then check your underwear to make sure there are no more leaks, and then count seven more days till immersion. It's the **rabbinic** way, so we do it, no questions asked.

   b.   *Joy Comes in the Morning 2005*: In **rabbinic** school there had always been students who wrestled with praise and took a[n] attitude toward God, an attitude of human entitlement and anger.

   c.   *Houston Chronicle 2004*: He knew it well, having been born in 1904 into a **rabbinic** family in Leoncin, one of those close-knit villages—shtetls—in which age-old strictures held sway over life even as the Enlightenment, which Singer was to embrace passionately, threatened them.

The word *rabbinic* can be used to describe the practices of rabbis (58a), a school for rabbis (58b), and a family composed of rabbis (58c). Clearly we cannot attribute a specific gloss to *-ic* in this word (much less in others), as the gloss of the derived word is so highly dependent on context. We could provide similar examples for the other adjective-deriving suffixes under consideration in this section.

So on the one hand an individual affix can give rise to many different nuances depending on the base it attaches to and the context in which the derived word is used. On the other hand, different affixes on the same base can give rise to identical meanings; that is to say that with this cohort of affixes we find doublets (and occasionally triplets) that do not seem to differ in meaning.

(59)   *-al* and *-ic*

   a.   *NPR_Fresh Air 2004*: And the more I started to look into it, the more it made absolute sense in a real **epiphanal**, you know, sort of way; I mean, really hitting you like a ton of bricks.

   b.   *Michigan Quarterly Review 2007*: But I don't want this to be one of those **epiphanic** moments when we see ourselves in each other and reconcile.

(60)   *-an* and *-al*

   a.   *NPR_Science 2004*: Case in point: the complete sequences for **microbian** genomes, such as smallpox, anthrax, SARS and Ebola.

   b.   *Science News 2009*: Do-it-yourself DNA Making a complete **microbial** genome from scratch by assembling the individual letters of its genetic code paves the way for making synthetic microbes

(61)   *-ic* and *-an*

    a. *Paris Review 1999*: All except Mrs. Minna, who was at her stove, piling together a **cornucopic** holiday plate for her older son.

    b. *Raritan 1995*: I was looking for olives that afternoon, which, I had not realized until then, come in a panoply of sizes and colors, seasoned with a **cornucopian** array of flavorings and herbs, and preserved through any number of methods.

(62)   *-ous* and *-al*

    a. *Bring Me the Head of Prince Charming 1991*: There, in a shop dedicated to **necrophilious** memorabilia, he was fortunate enough to find a pickpocket's hand for Princess Scarlet.

    b. *Habeas Corpses 2005*: "It's a war story, Bubba, not **necrophilial** porn."

(63)   *-ic* and *-ous*

    a. *Current Psychology 2002*: Despite the employment of **antonymic** relationships in previous work (Brownell, Potter, and Michelow, 1984), it is possible that the use of synonyms might be more appropriate in the present context.

    b. *Atlanta Journal Constitution 1993*: In your letters section of Jan. 6, Mr. Franklin Burke McMahan seeks a well-mannered word that is **antonymous** to misogynist.

(64)   *-ic* and *-y*

    a. *Dark City 1998*: The two men walk cautiously through the **echoic** interior.

    b. *The Answer is Always Yes 2008*: He was a few paces past when his voice returned, borne up from the **echoey** corridor.

(65)   *-an* and *-y*

    a. *PBS_Newshour 1990*: In the center of Leningrad in a red brick dungeon nearly a century old is the **labyrinthy** maze of cells and towers known as "The Crosses", a famous and infamous landmark never before open to foreign television cameras.

    b. *Chicago Review 1992*: My mother told me that convicts and orphans were once sent from the mainland to the island to work, and most times die, in the **labyrinthian** mines.

It is in fact possible to go pairwise through the suffixes we are concerned with here and in nearly every case find doublets in which the individual forms have no discernable difference in meaning, at least in some context, although we will not be exhaustive here.

    Again, this is not to say that pairs cannot differ in meaning. Many of them do: as Hamawand (2007) has shown, there are any number of examples in which the members of pairs have been lexicalized with specific and very different meanings, as for example in *industrious* and *industrial, ceremonial* and *ceremonious,* or *thunderous* and *thundery.* But these differences in meaning cannot reasonably be attributed to any semantic contrast between affixes, and there appears to be nothing systematic about the kinds of differences that get lexicalized or what gets lexicalized with a specific affix.

Our conclusion is not uncontroversial, however. Indeed, Hamawand (2007) contends the opposite, on the basis of an analysis of lexicalized words. We do not find his claims convincing, since we have seen that for unlexicalized, low-frequency forms we frequently do find synonymy, in spite of what happens in lexicalized derivatives.

14.3.2 Relational versus qualitative, gradable versus non-gradable

The distinction is sometimes made in the linguistic literature between relational and qualitative adjectives (Beard 1995; Plag 2003, as well as Huddleston and Pullum 2002, who use the terms associative and ascriptive adjectives rather than relational and qualitative). Relational adjectives are ones which can appear prenominally, but cannot be modified with a degree modifier, and cannot be used predicatively. They are non-gradable, and therefore do not occur in comparative or superlative forms. For example, it is usually said that with relational adjectives we can have a phrase like *a nuclear reactor,* but not **a very nuclear reactor,* or a sentence like **that reactor is nuclear* or **this reactor is more nuclear than that one.* Qualitative adjectives, on the other hand, can occur premodifying nouns, but can also themselves take a degree modifier, can occur predicatively, and can be gradable. It is worth asking, then, whether adjective-forming affixes might be divided into two cohorts—those that form qualitative/gradable adjectives and those that form relational/non-gradable adjectives.

Examination of data available from the corpora, however, suggests that the situation is somewhat more complex. While it seems safe to say that some of the affixes considered in this chapter always derive qualitative affixes, it does not seem to be possible to designate any affix as deriving exclusively relational adjectives. For example, the similative affixes are reliably qualitative, occurring easily in predicative position, or modified by degree adverbs, or in the comparative or superlative:

(66)   a. *Men's Health 2001:* Also, be aware that your fashion-forwardness is indicated by three things: the number of buttons (two is traditional, three is contemporary, one is **hipsterish**).

   b. *Critical Matrix 1994:* Oscar Wilde, whose argument it is, goes on to say with **very un-Dombeyesque** irony that "egotism itself, which is so necessary to a proper sense of human dignity, is entirely the result of indoor life."

   c. *BNC.The Fraxilly fracas:* The spike-skinned exter who had been following me was coming through the door, in company with several other exters, none of them **very humanoid**.

Although it has been suggested that some affixes specifically derive relational adjectives (e.g. Plag 2003: 95–6 for *-al*, *-ary*, and *-ic*), evidence from COCA suggests that this is not invariably the case. Neither specific affixes, nor even particular words derived with those affixes are fixed once and for all as relational. Consider, for example, the adjective *nuclear*, which would seem at first glance to be solidly relational. COCA yields examples like the following:

(67)   a. *Newsweek 1997*: France is second— 75 percent of French electricity **is nuclear**, which has reduced French air pollution fivefold—followed by Russia and Japan.

       b. *USA Today 2005*: The outspoken Texas conservative, who displays the Ten Commandments in his office but admits he has a hard time loving his enemies, declined to run for House speaker in 1998 because he considered himself "**too nuclear**."

These examples suggest that it is possible to coerce just about any relational adjective into a qualitative reading. This is especially true when we focus on specific salient characteristics associated with that adjective, as in (67b) where the sense of *nuclear* that is intended is 'giving off dangerous radiation'. We provide additional examples in (68), with the adjectives *aboriginal* and *dynastic*, which would also seem at least superficially to be solidly relational.

(68)   a. *Washington Post 1996*: Consider shamanism, "probably **the most aboriginal** form of meditation, and most closely associated with nature," said Finbarr Lismore, a Harvard Divinity PhD who spent a summer as the Omega Institute's "answer man," explaining the catalogue to callers.

       b. *NPR_TalkNation 2002*: And there were the Tafts of Ohio, the Browns of California, the Longs of Louisiana, and perhaps **the most dynastic**, the Roosevelts and the Kennedys.

We conclude that while some adjective-forming affixes can be classified as qualitative, and others may tend towards deriving relational adjectives, no relational affix is immune to being coerced to a qualitative reading.

14.3.3 *-ic* and *-ical*

Given the general neglect in the linguistic literature of adjective-forming derivational affixes, there is a surprisingly large literature devoted to determining whether the suffixes *-ic* and *-ical* can be distinguished in any systematic way. Kaunisto (2007) reviews most of this literature, first noting as we have done above, that there are many bases that show forms in both *-ic* and *-ical* (*comic* ~ *comical*, *periodic* ~ *periodical*), as well as many bases that only evidence one or the other (*public, atomic*; *radical, theatrical*) (Kaunisto 2007: 4–5). In his review of the literature, he suggests that much of the discussion of this pair, from Marchand (1969), to more recent studies like Marsden (1985) and Gries (2001, 2003) has taken pains to find systematic distinctions, but has not been terribly successful. Interestingly, all of these studies, including Kaunisto's, have concentrated on a limited number of mostly item-familiar and high frequency pairs (*classic* versus *classical, economic* versus *economical, historic* versus *historical,* and the like); the search has been more to see whether consistent patterns of lexicalization can be found than to see whether there is any intrinsic semantic difference between the two suffixes.

The latter is, of course, the question that more interests us. COCA gives us ample opportunity to consider this issue. It is possible to find many examples in the corpus of *-ic* and *-ical* pairs where neither form is item-familiar. For example, with pairs like *calendric* and *calendrical, cryptologic* and *cryptological, hematologic* and *hematological, herpetologic* and *herpetological, toponymic* and *toponymical,* neither item is particularly frequent, and the contexts in which they are used suggest that there is no semantic distinction between them.

(69) a. *Geographical Review 1991*: Moreover, they are built on complex **calendric** systems analogous to those of neighboring regions.

     b. *Natural History 2000*: You see, poor Dionysius Exiguus (Dennis the Short), the sixth-century monk who devised the B.[C].–A.D. **calendrical** system, made a little error in setting Christ's birth.

(70) a. *Foreign Affairs 1991*: Though the cryptanalysts followed these developments in the newspapers, their inspiration came less from the pressure of events than from fascination with the **cryptologic** problem.

     b. *Mercury 1999*: Astrophysical coding means that a message is designed to yield information through an astrophysical-type analysis of the signal, rather than a **cryptological** analysis.

(71) a. *ENT: Ear, Nose & Throat Journal 2009*: While the diagnosis of this tumor has become more accurate, especially in patients who have a history of **hematologic** abnormalities, it is important to keep this rare entity in mind when faced with poorly differentiated neoplasms of the head and neck in order to provide prompt and appropriate therapy.

     b. *Internet Journal of Rheumatology 2007*: **Hematological** abnormalities included eosinophils of 7.6% (laboratory normal 0 to 5%).

(72) a. *Washington Post 2000*: Deaths from venom are rare even in the **herpetologic** wonderland of Arizona, where about a dozen people have been killed by rattlesnakes in McNally's two decades at the poison center.

     b. *Houston Chronicle 2001*: The sprawl of Greater Houston encompasses much of this **herpetological** Eden.

(73) a. *Geographic Review 2001*: The standard biographical accounts are those of T. L. Venkatarama Aiyar (1968) and R. Raghavan (1975), who also provide **toponymic** information.

b. *Hispanic Review 1996*: Rey understands the **toponymical** misnomers not as lies but as rhetorical ironies precisely because he can see for himself that what they name, describe, or represent is far from their literal meaning.

We might conclude from such examples that whatever their historical source, in contemporary English *-ic* and *-ical* are alternate realizations of the same affix. Some bases will appear exclusively with one or the other of the suffixes. Where either suffix is to be found on a single base, lexicalization may of course take place, although the studies cited above suggest that there is nothing systematic in this process. But it is also possible for pairs to co-exist— especially for low-frequency forms—with no differentiation.

14.3.4 Multiple affixes and semantic interpretation

We return finally to a curious observation that we made in Section 14.2.1.1, namely that it is sometimes possible to find forms which exhibit more than one adjective-forming suffix on a single base; for example, we can find items with the sequences *-or-ial* (*accusatorial, combinatorial, gustatorial, improvisatorial*), *-oid-al* (*arachnoidal, cuboidal, ovoidal, planetoidal*), *-iv-al* (*conjunctival, gerundival*), *-al-esque* (*brutalesque, industrialesque, lunaresque*), *-an-esque* (*africanesque, americanesque, suburbanesque*), *-ar-ian* (*equalitarian, millenarian, sectarian, uniformitarian*). For some of these combinations there seems to be a semantic distinction: the adjective *industrial*, for example, merely means 'related to industry', whereas *industrialesque* seems to mean something like 'industrial in style'.

(74)   *Washington Post 1994*: Actually I, too, sat there, ravenously hungry—on my own unbelievably uncomfortable, spasm-inducing metallic **industrialesque** chair—taking teeny-weeny itsy-bitsy bites and, every now and again, nodding sagely.

A similar contrast can be found with forms like *suburban* versus *suburbanesque*. But there seems to be no discernable difference between, for example, *spheroid* and *spheroidal*, or *gustatory* and *gustatorial* in the following examples.

(75)   *Associated Press 2009*: It has been known through astronomy that spiral disk galaxies are enclosed by a **spheroid** halo of dark matter with a mass about ten times greater than the ordinary mass of the spiral galaxy and also that a weak magnetic field pervades the universe.

Astronomy 2008: Milkomeda's **spheroidal** shape is not unusual, as it characterizes a major class of objects called elliptical galaxies.

(76)   *San Francisco Chronicle 1996*: Prepared by the people who put on the Peninsula's bimonthly Decadent Dinner Parties, EEET!, the so-called Environmental Eating Education Team, this **gustatory** experience will be a veritable vegetarian pig-out, to mix metaphors.

Washington Post 1996: But in **gustatorial** matters, there's really only one bottom line: Maybe they just taste good.

This is not to say that there is never a difference between a form in *-ory* and a corresponding form in *-orial*, or between one in *-oid* and *-oidal*, but merely that there often is not. Why we get this iteration of affixes is an open question, however.

Another frequent combination of affixes that we should point out is *-istic*. Here we appear to have nothing unusual in terms of formal considerations: *-ist* forms nouns, and *-ic* attaches to nouns to form adjectives. Indeed, some forms in *-istic* are also unremarkable in terms of semantics, for example, *atheistic* and *pacifistic*, which could plausibly be interpreted as 'pertaining to atheists', 'pertaining to pacifists'. But there are many forms in *-istic* in which the suffix *-ist* appears to make no semantic contribution to the derived word at all. Consider, for example, forms like *cannibalistic* or *charlatanistic*, which must mean 'pertaining to cannibals' or 'pertaining to charlatans', there being no plausible corresponding forms in *-ist*. Marchand (1969: 295) suggests that such forms are actually derived from forms like *cannibalism* or *charlatanism*, but given other examples of semantically empty derivations like those above, this analysis does not seem completely convincing to us, especially as there are also forms like *analogistic* that lack both the agentive *-ist* form and the corresponding *-ism* form.

....

CHAPTER 15

Derived adverbs

15.1 Prospectus

In this chapter we look at the ways in which adverbs are formed in English. The very fact of this chapter, not to mention its title, implies at least two theoretical assumptions, namely that adverbs are a separate category from adjectives, and then that the affixation involved in creating adverbs is a matter of derivation rather than inflection. Both of these are controversial. We will take up the categorial issue first, and then consider the specifics of adverb-forming processes in English. Although the formation of adverbs is far less central to English word-formation than the other major types we have considered, there are nevertheless interesting questions which are raised in this chapter, especially considering the phonological conditioning of the *-ly* affix, the analysis of forms like *-ways*, and the status and semantics of *-wise*.

15.2 Are adverbs and adjectives the same category?

Scholars have long debated the categorial status of adjectives and adverbs. Payne *et al.* (2010) trace the idea that adverbs and adjectives constitute a single syntactic category to Kuryłowicz (1936), with Lyons (1966) being the first to advocate for a single category for English. Debate has continued in the work of Emonds (1976), Jackendoff (1977), Radford (1988), Bybee (1985), Zwicky (1995), Plag (2003), Baker (2003), and Giegerich (2012) with cogent arguments both for and against a distinction between the two categories. A further, and to some extent orthogonal issue is whether the adverb-forming affix *-ly* is to be classed as inflectional or derivational, an issue to which we will return in Section 15.3.1.

The classic argument for treating adjectives and adverbs as a single category in English is that they appear to occur in complementary distribution: adjectives occur as modifiers to nouns, adverbs as modifiers to other categories. The argument goes that if there is no overlap in distribution, adjectives and adverbs can be treated as positional variants of a single category. Consequently, Payne *et al.* (2010) argue at length for a categorial distinction in English claiming that adjectives and adverbs do overlap in several environments (for example, post-head nominal modifiers, premodifiers to adjectives), and therefore are not strictly in complementary distribution.

Giegerich (2012), however, points out that distributional overlap can sometimes be interpreted as free variation rather than complementary distribution: just as allophones of a phoneme can sometimes be in free variation, adjectives and adverbs might occasionally be found in the same environment, as with the examples in (1) from Payne *et al.* (2010: 52), without requiring us to postulate distinct categories.

(1) a. shortages *both nationally and internationally* of these metals

b. shortages *both national and international* of these metals

Giegerich also argues against overlapping distribution in the preadjectival context on the grounds that items like *blindly drunk, madly keen* are phrasal, whereas *blind drunk* or *mad keen* are compounds. If so, the distributional context is not in fact the same. Giegerich himself offers morphological and phonological reasons for treating adverbs—specifically *-ly* adverbs—as inflectional variants of adjectives, a subject to which we will return shortly.

We will remain agnostic on the subject here, as we do not find the arguments conclusive one way or the other. Our decision to treat adverbial derivation separately from adjectival derivation should therefore be taken as a practical if not a theoretical move.

15.3 SUFFIXATION

15.3.1 The suffix *-ly*

The suffix *-ly* is one of the most productive suffixes in English, added more or less freely to any adjective to create a corresponding adverb. Historically, the suffix *-ly* appears to be the same form as the adjective-forming suffix in words like *neighborly, motherly*, discussed in Chapter 14. In most instances this common origin is no more than accidental homophony in contemporary English.

Adverbial *-ly* has sometimes been argued to be inflectional rather than derivational. Haspelmath (1996) treats *-ly* as category-changing inflection, largely on the grounds of its productivity and regularity. This is not necessarily a strong argument, though, as there are other affixes that are highly productive and semantically transparent (for example *-ness*) that are never claimed to be inflectional.

Giegerich (2012) gives several arguments that *-ly* adverbs are inflected forms of the corresponding adjective. First, he notes that the *-ly* affix in such adverbs cannot be followed by any other affixes, either derivational or inflectional. It is characteristic of inflectional endings that they do not allow further affixation in English. Giegerich draws special attention to the fact that comparative *-er* and *-est* do not occur on *-ly* adverbs, although they can occur on adjectives that end in *-ly* (*likelier, likeliest*) or on other adverbs (*sooner, soonest*). Picking up an argument from Plag (2003: 195), Giegerich also suggests that the absence of any lexical meaning for -*ly* supports its status as inflection.

Giegerich's first argument is the more persuasive of the two; even derivational affixes like -*dom* that do not allow other derivational affixes to attach to them do allow the appropriate inflection at least (*kingdoms*, for example). But we do not find the argument decisive. Note that although -*ly* adverbs cannot take the inflectional suffixes -*er* and -*est*, they do form periphrastic comparatives and superlatives (*more quickly, most swiftly*). The comparative and superlative are among the few inflectional categories in English that alternate with a periphrastic form (the genitive is the other), and as we have seen in Chapter 6, the conditions on the use of the affixal versus periphrastic forms are intricate, so the inability of -*ly* adverbs to take the affixal comparative and superlative might be attributed to other factors. Indeed, Zwicky (1989: 157) points out that there are a number of adjective-forming affixes that together with a monosyllabic base would fit the phonological profile necessary for the affixal comparative and superlative, that nevertheless do not allow -*er* and -*est*: -*ive* (**activer, more active*), -*al* (**brutaler, more brutal*), and for the most part -*ish* (**greenisher, more greenish*; COCA provides one exception *foolisher*). If in contemporary English the adverb-forming -*ly* has become a distinct affix from the adjective forming -*ly* (as implied by the existence of two separate entries for -*ly* in the *OED*), there would be no problem in conjecturing that adjective-forming -*ly* patterns like -*ive*, -*ic*, and -*ish*, whereas adverb-forming -*ly* does not.

Giegerich's second argument is also unconvincing: there are many derivational affixes that are close to purely transpositional and therefore cannot be said to carry lexical meaning (e.g. the -*al* that forms adjectives from nouns, see Chapter 14, or nominalizing suffixes like -*ation* or -*ment*, see Chapter 10).

A final reason to be sceptical of the inflectional analysis of -*ly* is one that we will return to shortly, namely that there are other affixes that derive adverbs and that adverbs are derived from other categories than adjectives, contrary to what Giegerich (2012: 8–9) suggests (see Sections 15.3.2–15.3.5). But there is no reasonable evidence that these might be inflectional as well. In other words, whatever our ultimate decision about the status of -*ly*, we must still acknowledge the existence of derived adverbs in English.

As we have mentioned, -*ly* is highly productive, although there are two major ways in which this productivity is constrained, one apparently phonological, one that looks like blocking. In the first instance, there is a great reluctance to add -*ly* to any base which already ends in <ly>. There are several subcases to be distinguished. The first is where the <ly> is itself a suffix; here we can distinguish between the -*ly* which is added to nouns denoting time periods (*daily, monthly*) and the -*ly* which creates adjectives from person nouns (*friendly, womanly*) or other bases (*courtly, leisurely, comely*). Second is the case where the final <l> of the base is followed by a suffixal -*y* (*oily, steely, woolly*). Third is the case where the base itself ends in the orthographic sequence <ly>, but this has no morphemic value (*holy, silly*).

The time-period -*ly* does not allow a subsequent -*ly*; there is no *hourlily, *dailily, *weeklily, *fortnightlily, *monthlily, *yearlily. The *OED* allows the base forms as adjectives or adverbs:

hourly, daily, weekly, fortnightly, monthly, yearly, and we can find examples of such forms in the corpora.

(2) *Bioscience 2011*: Pattern of carbon dioxide production and retention is similar in adult pigs when fed **hourly**, but not when fed a single meal.

Popular Mechanics 2011: I take the inspection cover off my gas furnace **yearly** and look inside.

The adjectival suffix *-ly*, which attaches to person nouns, does not generally allow a subsequent *-ly*: **gentlemanlily, *motherlily, *neighbourlily, *womanlily*. The OED does list *friendlily*, with citations from the nineteenth century; it appears once in COCA and not at all in the BNC.

(3) *New Yorker 2006*: "It's not an intrusion I hope?" she apologized when she called on them, and was **friendlily** reassured.

Turning to other adjectival formation in *-ly*, we find a variety of bases of sometimes unclear provenance (e.g. *courtly, leisurely, comely, earthly, gainly, kindly, lonely, seemly, worldly*). The OED lists some of these with an adverbial *-ly*: *kindlily, lonelily*, and *worldlily* (this last with a twentieth-century citation) and *seemlily* as obsolete. In many cases, adjectival derivatives in *-ly* are used exclusively as adjectives by some speakers and as adverbs (possibly in addition to their use as adjectives) by others, as illustrated in (4), from COCA.

(4) *Jenny Shank, 1976*: the Police Athletic League was to introduce neighborhood children to what decent and **friendly** guys police officers could be

Literary Review 2004: They talked so **friendly**, he couldn't believe them

Fantasy and Science Fiction 2010: the boys picked up their speed, their water buffalo following them at a more **leisurely** pace.

Brett Battles 2011: Kolya drove the sedan **leisurely** down the street.

Another set of potentially problematic words is adjectival formations in *-y* whose bases end in /l/ (such as *crumbly, curly, freckly, frilly, growly, hilly, oily, smelly, spindly, squally, treacly, wobbly*). Generally there is no adverb form, either with or without the *-ly*.

To items like *holy* and *silly* we can add *early, jolly, (un)ruly, surly, ugly*. These have entries for the adverb in *-ly* in the OED, though *earlily* and *(un)rulily* are marked as obsolete. The others have nineteenth-century citations.

From all such possible words, the BNC has attestations only of the following (and then with few attestations): *beastlily, ghostlily, jollily, oilily, seemlily, surlily, uglily*, and COCA adds only *friendlily, holily, sillily*.

In other words, it appears that users tend to avoid *-lily* endings, whatever their source. The repetition of a *-ly* affix is the least favoured form, the addition of *-ly* to a monomorphemic base seems to be the type which is easiest to use. The fact that we can distinguish the various subcases seems to indicate that speakers have, at some stage or other, made use of the differences in morphological structure, but today the phonological structure seems to be the biggest determinant of the constraint on these forms. The phenomenon could thus be viewed as a case of haplology (see Chapter 9.5).

The second constraint on the productivity of adverbial *-ly* might look, at first glance, like blocking, although closer scrutiny argues against this position. Here we have in mind the simple adjectives which form adverbs by conversion (see Chapter 24). In at least some of these cases the converted adverb has all the functions that a *-ly* adverb would be expected to have. For instance, for many speakers corresponding to *a fast car* we have *he drove fast*, but there is no **fastly*. There is no strict blocking here, however: the *OED*, COCA, and the BNC all illustrate *fastly*, as in the following example from COCA.

(5)   *FIC_Cullum, Paul 1994*: "My point," said Poppy, **fastly** becoming exasperated, "is that he who hesitates is lost."

In the case of several other simple adjectives that can undergo conversion, there is widespread free variation between the adverb with and without *-ly*; among these are *fair, loud, quick, slow, soft*.

We find a few other cases in which there might appear to be blocking. In some, there is an *-ly* adverb but it is not synonymous (*hard* and *hardly*) or does not reflect the central meaning of the base (*bare* and *barely*); potentially transparent forms appear to be avoided in these cases.

Apart from these two constraints, *-ly* is widely productive, occurring on simple bases, native and foreign, suffixed bases, native and foreign, and compound bases. A few examples from the hundreds in COCA are given in (6).

(6)   abdominally, abjectly, accordingly, airily, angelically, anthropologically, artfully, barefootedly, believably, belittlingly, bloodthirstily, bluntly, boisterously, boldly, callously, complexly, compliantly, coquettishly, dearly, drolly, entirely, fluorescently, Freudianly, goodnaturedly, gruesomely, hagiographically, hamhandedly, indicatively, insularly

It is perhaps worth commenting specifically on the combination of *-ic* and *-ly*. Although the preferred orthographic pattern is to use *-ically* rather than *-icly*, the corpora show that this is not always done, and the *OED* provides plenty of historical support for *-icly* forms. The only word in which *-icly* is commonly found in COCA and the BNC is *publicly*. Most others could, from the point of view of the standard, be viewed as errors, but there are sufficient examples to suggest that such a dismissal would oversimplify the actual situation. The pronunciation /ɪkli/ is clearly common, even when the <ically> spelling is used.

In terms of semantics, the suffix *-ly* covers a broad range of meanings. As modifiers of VPs, *-ly* adverbs can express manner, degree, means, duration, frequency, or other temporal relation (using the categories suggested in Pullum and Huddleston 2002: 576), the precise reading of the adverb to a large extent depending on the meaning of the base to which it is attached.

(7) a. *Manner*:

The Cereal Murders 1993: Her golden hair curled **angelically** around her diminutive heart-shaped face.

b. *Means*:

Technology Teacher 2007: PGD is the process by which an embryo is **microscopically** examined for signs of genetic disorders.

c. *Degree*:

Good Housekeeping 2011: Paltrow is the first to admit she doesn't have all the answers on how her **doubly** famous marriage is affecting the children.

d. *Duration*:

Humanist 2011: Retrospectivists see the past as a golden age to be **eternally** reverenced rather than improved upon.

e. *Other temporal*:

Science News 2010: A study of people who **habitually** run barefoot shows that these runners' feet strike the ground in a way that tempers impact forces and smooths the running movement [...]

As clausal modifiers, -ly adverbs can designate a domain or a modality, provide evaluative information, or designate a particular kind of speech act (categories again from Pullum and Huddleston 2002: 576).

(8) a. *Domain*:

To Climb a Flat Mountain 2009: "**Geologically** speaking," she said, "we're on a lava field between two volcanoes."

b. *Modality*:

New York Times 2011: This is **possibly** the next phase of evangelical Christianity's muscle flexing.

c. *Evaluation*:

Academic Questions 2002: Evidently, and **hearteningly**, not everyone feels that the significance of an honorary doctorate has been irredeemably devalued, or that the situation is beyond redemption.

d. *Speech act related*:

Blood: Butchers Tale 2007: **Confidentially**, I think Tony is behind this stealing spree.

15.3.2 The suffix -*s*

The suffix -*s* forms adverbs from a wide variety of bases, including apparently bound bases, as indicated in (9). The lack of any strict pattern here probably reflects a lack of productivity.

(9)   midships, besides, betimes, downstairs, hereabouts, indoors, nowadays, ofttimes, outdoors, overseas, perhaps, sometimes, thereabouts, unawares, upstairs, whereabouts, widdershins

Examples of -*s* in -*wards* and -*ways* have been omitted in (9), and will be considered below. This -*s* suffix appears to be totally unproductive now unless part of -*wards* or -*ways*.

15.3.3 The suffix -*ward(s)*

The suffix -*wards* is used productively to create directional adverbs from prepositions, directional adjectives, and nouns. In (10) standard adverbs of this type are listed.

(10)   a. *prepositional bases*: afterwards, backwards, downwards, inwards, onwards, outwards, upwards

   b. *directional adjective bases*: eastwards, leftwards, north-westwards, northwards, rearwards, etc.

   c. *nominal bases*: homewards, landwards, leewards, sidewards, windwards

The forms *towards* and *forwards* appear to be formed on prepositional bases, although they are semantically opaque. The former is also rather odd, being a preposition more than an adverb. Strikingly, each of these words has a potential synonymous counterpart in -*ward* without the final -*s*. Mostly, the -*ward* form can also be an adjective (*a backward glance, a downward motion, the inward eye, a westward direction*). *Afterward* is unusual in not having this adjectival use.

The suffix is quite productive on nominal bases, as the following less established forms from the BNC suggest.

(11)   bedwards, ceilingwards, choruswards, citywards, deathwards, earthwards, equatorwards, floorwards, goalwards, heavenwards, hubwards, Islingtonwards, officewards, polewards, rimwards, roofwards, seawards, shorewards, skywards, sternwards, Tyne-wards

Interestingly, while -*ward(s)* typically attaches to nouns that express locations, it can turn just about any noun into a directional adverb: in addition to *deathwards* in (11) we find examples like *ankleward* and *bloodward* in COCA.

The difference between the -*ward* form and the -*wards* form is sometimes assumed to be dialectal, aligning with the difference between NAmE and BrE. This is an oversimplification. Not only are the -*wards* forms used in NAmE, but the -*ward* forms are also used in BrE. We can only say that there is variation between the forms.

15.3.4 The suffix -*ways*

In (12) we list adverbs in -*ways* from the BNC.

(12)   always, anyways, arseways, cornerways, edgeways, leastways, lengthways, longways, sideways, widthways

COCA adds the words in (13).

(13)   aways, backways, contrariways, crabways, crossways, elseways, endways, frontways, mostways, noways, slantways, someways

Most of these words are established, but it seems there is some limited possibility of productive usage; *crabways*, *elseways*, and *mostways*, for example, are not recorded in the *OED*.

(14)   *Fantasy & Science Fiction 2010*: His hair has long gone, he must wear sunglasses to protect his bleary eyes, and he shuffles hunched and **crabways**.

Analog Science Fiction & Fact 2004: Of course their god exists, **elseways** the world wouldn't be here, so the fact that the world is here proves that their god exists.

Red River 2008: I was there, watching, like all the women done, up close some of the time but **mostways** from a distance.

The last of these seems to be an attempt to imitate some kind of dialect, but the others are not.

Of these *anyways* is unusual in having a corresponding *anyway*. While there is a *no way*, it is a phrase and not synonymous with *noways*; *away* is not clearly semantically related to *aways*. Some of these words can be used as adjectives (*a sideways glance*), but the adverbial use appears to be primary. This means that the -*ways* affix is probably not analysable, as the -*wards* one is, and the final <s> has no morphemic value of its own.

15.3.5 The suffix -*wise*

The suffix -*wise* is very productive where there is a noun base (15), less so with other types of base (16). The examples here come from COCA.

(15)   accountingwise, actorswise, agewise, appearancewise, babywise, chocolatewise, clockwise, columnwise, computerwise, crabwise, engineeringwise, exercisewise, facultywise, featurewise, flavoringwise, informationwise, lookswise, marketwise, minoritywise, moneywise, perceptionwise, plantwise, presswise, pricewise, profitwise, ratewise, spacewise, specwise, speedwise, trafficwise, weightwise, workwise

(16)   anywise, contrarywise, defensivewise, fitwise, leastwise, likewise, mentallywise, otherwise, palewise, scientificwise, socialwise

Some of the *-wise* forms seem to form direct competitors to forms in *-ways*, including the following from COCA:

(17)   anywise, contrariwise, cornerwise, edgewise, endwise, lengthwise, sidewise, slantwise

In some cases the forms in *-ways* and *-wise* seem to be all but interchangeable.

(18)   *National Review 2002*: **Contrariwise**, suppose you are right. What do we have to lose by failing to reform?

    Cut Quick 1993: **Contrariways**, he's always begging off folks or pestering them to buy his wares.

It is notable that bases may be monomorphemic, as most of the examples above, apparently inflected (*actorswise, numberswise*), derived (*defensivewise, employmentwise*) or neoclassical compounds (*technologywise*). We have no examples with native compounds or phrases, although it is not clear that this is a principled exclusion.

Adverbs in *-wise* can have a number of basic meanings, according to Dalton-Puffer and Plag (2000: 238–9). On the one hand, *-wise* forms what they call manner/dimension adverbs that can roughly be glossed as 'in the manner of X' or 'in an X spatial relation to'. We give examples of the former in (19a) and the latter in (19b).

(19)   a. *American Scholar 2004*: The man clung to a spur of rock near him and moved slowly **frogwise** his green legs in the deep jelly of the water.

    African Arts 2004: And sure enough, when girls are given by their fathers at the Ebuhleni citadel's festival betrothals of affianced couples, bride confers on groom the token of her virginity, the Nazarite version of this ucu, a long twined double-string of pure white new beads, worn wound several times around the neck, then **sashwise** down to a folded handkerchief pendant on the hip or the injobo.

    b. *Art Bulletin 1992*: The artist's conception of the event, spread **beltwise** across the Sistine Ceiling, anticipates by some eighty years a major theme of late Renaissance and Baroque poetry.

Hostage Zero 2010: Rough-finished beige bricks dominated the walls, arranged **edgewise** in horizontal courses that rose from the brown tiled floor to the acoustic tiled ceiling.

A more common reading is what they call the 'viewpoint' reading, which can be glossed roughly as 'from the point of view of X'.

(20) *Bazaar 2005*: **Fashionwise**, that decade was heralded by the explosion of such designers as Helmut Lang and Martin Margiela and Jil Sander.

San Francisco Chronicle 2009: "I may be the one with the offbeat career, but **personalitywise**, it was the eldest of our five siblings who were the most rebellious," he says.

Dalton-Puffer and Plag (2000) suggest that the viewpoint *-wise* adverbs, although displaying a smaller number of tokens in the BNC than the manner/dimension ones, appear to provide the larger number of hapaxes, which suggests that this type of formation is actually the more productive of the two. Our scrutiny of the COCA data corroborates this suggestion.

The morpheme *wise* can also be used in forming adjectival compounds, where it has roughly its expected lexical meaning; examples like *streetwise* in the sense 'being aware of how to behave in a city' are not hard to find. Businesses frequently capitalize on the ambiguity between the adjectival compound form and the viewpoint *-wise* adverb in creating names for services or products. For example, *pricewise* is most likely to mean 'in relation to price' but could mean 'wise about prices'. COCA gives us examples of this type like *Travelwise* (presumably a travel agent), *Medwise* (a chain of medical clinics), *Moneywise* (the name of a television programme), and *Worldwise* (a company that makes recycled products).

15.4 THE PREFIX A-

The prefix *a-* is used to form some adverbs. Historically this is often a reduced form of the prefix *on-*, although *on-* is no longer used in this sense. Given its origins, it is not surprising that this prefix is most often locational in sense, although it sometimes adds an aspectual flavour of ongoing action, as is illustrated in the COCA example in (21).

(21) *Washington Post 1996*: On one court, Marla O'Hara, 35, kicks the sand and stalks the court in a leonine fashion, a long mane of brunette hair **afly**.

Many of the forms in *a-*, however, are highly lexicalized in meaning, as exemplified in (22).

(22) aback, abeam, abed, aboard, about(s), abreast, abroad, abuzz, adrift, afar, afield, afire, afloat, afly, afresh, agape, aglow, agog, aground, ahead, ahold, ajar, akin, alike, alive,

aloft, alone, along, aloof, aloud, amid, amidships, amiss, anew, apace, apart, apiece, aquiver, aright, around, ashore, aside, askance, askew, aslant, asleep, asprawl, astern, astir, astray, atop, away, aweigh, awhile (*often written as two words*), awry

As a prefix, *a-* may have some residual productivity on nouns and verbs, but only in poetic styles. The *OED* cites *amove, apant, asmirk*; COCA gives us *afly*, exemplified above, which is not also attested in the *OED*.

In some instances the same form may be an adjective and an adverb: *abroad, acrawl, afloat, away*, etc. In some instances it may be difficult to tell whether the word is an adverb or an adjective, even in context.

15.5 CONVERSION

As discussed in Chapter 24 and repeated above, there are instances of conversion between adjective and adverb.

In cases like *fast, hard, loud, quick, soft* it seems that the adjective is the base and the adverb is the converted form. One argument for assuming that conversion goes from adjective to adverb, rather than the other way around, is that all adverbial forms of this sort have corresponding adjectives, but it is not the case for every adjective that there is a corresponding adverb formed by conversion. See Chapter 24 for further discussion.

In instances with *-ward* it is less clear which form is the base and which is the derivative. However, we can build up a case that the adverb is primary. In etymological terms, the adverb comes first. At least *afterward* is an adverb but not an adjective; it is not clear that there are any the other way round. The adverbs appear to be more common than their corresponding adjectives in the BNC. The *OED* does not list the *-wards* forms as adjectives, but they seem to have such uses, as, for instance, in (23) from the BNC. This implies that such extensions are recent.

(23)   *W_fict_prose 1991/2*: you go faster and faster in an **upwards** direction

The instances with the prefix *a-* and the suffix *-ways* seem to be primarily adverbs with the adjective as the converted form.

There are also instances where there is conversion involving prepositions. This is perhaps not surprising, since there is a class of adverbs which is sometimes treated as intransitive prepositions (Huddleston 2002a: 272). Examples include *abreast, amid, around, besides, toward(s)* and the *OED* lists several other *-ward* forms (*downward, inward, upward*, etc.) which used to be prepositions. There does not appear to be any productive process involved here.

CHAPTER 16

....

Locatives of time and space

16.1 PROSPECTUS

In this chapter we survey the affixes used in English to express spatial and temporal concepts. All such affixes are prefixal, and many of them do double duty with spatial or temporal readings depending on context. English has two cohorts of such prefixes, non-native ones and native ones, and there are generally pairs (or sets) that overlap in meaning, with only subtle differences apparent. Several of the prefixes (*super-, sur-, extra-, over-, under-*) mix spatial readings with quantitative (or at least scalar) readings, a connection we will explore in Section 16.3 (see also Chapter 18). With few exceptions (Williams 1992; Southerland 1994; Lehrer 1995; Bauer 2003a; Börger 2007), these prefixes have largely been ignored in the literature on English word-formation. We begin in Section 16.2 with their formal characteristics and go on to semantic considerations in Section 16.3.

16.2 FORMAL CONSIDERATIONS

The non-native prefixes that convey spatial and temporal meanings in English are *ante-, arch-, circum-, cis-, co-, contra-, counter-, epi-, ex-, extra-, inter-, intra-, meta-, neo-, para-, peri-, post-, pre-, proto-, retro-, sub-, super-, supra-, sur-,* and *trans-*. The native locatives are largely coextensive with prepositions, and we will discuss our reasons for treating them as prefixes rather than as the first elements in compounds in Section 16.2.2. These include *after-, back-, by-, down-, fore-, in-, mid-, off-, on-, out-, over-,* and *under-*. Table 16.1 summarizes pertinent formal information including the syntactic categories of base the prefix attaches to (N = noun, V = verb, A = adjective, ✓ indicates attachment to the relevant category), whether the affix attaches to bound bases, to native or non-native bases, and to compounds or phrases. In the following sections we will discuss each prefix in more detail.

Table 16.1 Formal characteristics of locative prefixes

	N	A	V	Bound base	Native	Non-native	Compound	Phrase
after-	✓	✓			✓	✓		
ante-	✓	✓	✓	✓	✓	✓		
arch-	✓				✓	✓	✓	✓
back-	✓		✓		✓	✓		
by-	✓	✓	✓		✓	✓		
circum-	✓	✓	✓	✓		✓		
cis-	✓	✓				✓		
co-	✓	✓	✓		✓	✓	✓	✓
contra-	✓	✓	✓	✓	✓	✓		
counter-	✓	✓	✓	✓	✓	✓		
down-	✓	✓	✓		✓	✓		
epi-	✓	✓		✓		✓		
ex-	✓		✓		✓	✓	✓	✓
extra-	✓	✓			✓	✓	✓	
fore-	✓		✓		✓	✓		
in-	✓	✓	✓		✓	✓		
inter-	✓	✓	✓	✓	✓	✓		
intra-	✓	✓			✓	✓		
meta-	✓	✓	✓	✓	✓	✓		
mid-	✓	✓			✓	✓	✓	✓
neo-	✓	✓		✓	✓	✓	✓	
off-	✓	✓	✓		✓	✓		
on-	✓	✓	✓	✓	✓	✓		
out-	✓		✓		✓	✓	✓	✓
over-	✓	✓	✓		✓	✓		
para-	✓	✓	✓	✓	✓	✓		
peri-	✓	✓		✓	✓	✓		
post-	✓	✓	✓	✓	✓	✓	✓	✓
pre-	✓	✓	✓	✓	✓	✓	✓	✓
proto-	✓	✓			✓	✓	✓	✓
retro-	✓	✓	✓	✓	✓	✓	✓	
sub-	✓	✓	✓	✓	✓	✓	✓	✓
super-	✓	✓	✓	✓	✓	✓		
supra-	✓	✓			✓	✓		
sur-	✓	✓	✓	✓	✓	✓		
trans-	✓	✓	✓	✓	✓	✓	✓	
under-	✓	✓	✓		✓	✓		
up-	✓	✓	✓		✓	✓	✓	

16.2.1 Non-native prefixes

All of the non-native prefixes can be found attached to nouns, almost all to adjectives, and many to verbs. In (1) we find examples from COCA in which the prefix does not change the category of the base. Derivations on native bases are marked in italics in these examples.

(1) a. ante-   *On N*: ante-building, antechamber, antechoir, anteroom

                   On A: antenatal, antenuptial, antetypal

                   On V: antedate

     b. arch-   *On N*: archabbey, archangel, archbetrayer, archlute

     c. circum-   *On N*: circumstance

                   On A: circumambient, circum-Atlantic, circumpolar

                   On *V*: circumambulate, circumlocute, circumnavigate

     d. cis-   *On N*: cisplatinum

                   On A: cisalpine, cislunar, cismoral

     e. co-   *On N*: co-agent, co-biographer, co-compost, co-denizens

                   On A: co-conscious, co-ethnic

                   On V: co-adjust, co-adopt, co-construct, co-sleep

     f. contra-   *On N*: contra-bass, contra-dance, *contraflow*, contra-perfume

                   On A: contra-causal, contra-factual, contra-lateral

                   On V: contra-distinguish, contra-indicate

     g. counter- *On N*: counteragent, counterbeliefs, counterchagrin, counter-odor

                   On A: counter-incentive, counter-pastoral

                   On V: counteract, counterbalance, counterrotate

     h. epi-   *On N*: epi-cells, epi-bacteria, epicenter, epiphenomena

                   On A: epicritical, epideictic, epinucleic

     i. ex-   *On N*: ex-addict, ex-billionaire, ex-cat

     j. extra-   *On N*: extra-mission, extranet

                   On A: extrabiblical, extracorporeal

     k. inter-   *On N*: intercolitis, intercooler, internet, intersex

                   On A: interabdominal, interaural, intercanine, interracial

                   On V: interact, *interbreed*, interchange, intermarry

     l. intra-   *On N*: intramarriage, intrameasure, intranet, intraspace

                   On A: intraabdominal, intracoastal, intracutaneous, intraracial

     m. meta-   *On N*: meta-account, meta-computer, meta-drama, meta-glass

                   On A: metacarpal, meta-ironic, metaliterary, metaweird

                   On V: meta-analyze, meta-reflect

n. neo-   *On N*: neo-allergens, neo-beatnik, neoether, neo-folkies

On A: neo-abstract, neo-cool, neo-feudal, *neo-Norse*

o. para-   *On N*: para-athletes, paracone, paraeducator

On A: paraclinical, para-formal, para-Islamic, para-limbic

On V: paraglide, parasail

p. peri-   *On N*: periapse, periclaw, perilymph, perimenopause

On A: perianal, periglacial, perinatal, periurban

q. post-   *On N*: postadolescents, postblackness, postdoc, postfeminist, posttest

On A: postapostolic, postblack, post-conservative, post-digestive, post-glam

On V: postdate

r. pre-   *On N*: preadult, precalculus, predead, preembryo

On A: preacademic, precanonical, predark, pre-egoic

On V: preacquire, preapprove, prebake, preclear

s. proto-   *On N*: proto-adult, proto-chordate, proto-elephant, protoheart

On A: proto-bourgeois, proto-classic, proto-feminine, protoglyphous

t. retro-   *On N*: retro-chiffon, retro-comedy, retrohead, retro-logic

On A: retroactive, retrobulbar, retro-campy, retro-chic

On V: retrofit

u. sub-   *On N*: subaccount, subarea, subcamp, subclause

On A: subabusive, subalpine, sub-brown, sub-cheap

On V: subcategorize, subcontract, subdivide, subgroup

v. super-   *On N*: superaddressee, superblock, supercabinet, supercavity, superego

On A: superconscious, superfamilial, supergalactic, superlunary

On V: superintend

w. supra-   *On N*: supracommunities, supraconductivity, supra-identity, supra-molecule, supraspan

On A: supraannual, supra-basal, supraethnic, suprahuman

x. sur-   *On N*: surcharge, surcoat, surfiction, surname

On A: surreal

On V: surcharge, surmount, surpass

y. trans-   *On N*: transaxle, trans-children, transfat, transgenes

On A: trans-Baltic, trans-cervical, trans-ethnic, transglobal

On V: transact, transfigure, transform, transload

Items derived with these prefixes can be spelled with or without hyphen. Here we have preserved the spelling found in COCA.

In (2) we give examples of the prefixes that can be found on bound bases. Many of the examples we give here might not be considered complex words by contemporary speakers, but based on our considerations in Chapter 3 we include them here.

(2) a. ante-   antecede, antediluvian

     b. circum-   circumcise, circumference, circumspect

     c. contra-   contraceptive, contradict, contravene

     d. counter-   counterfeit, countermand, countervail

     e. epi-   epicanthic, epidemic, epigram

     f. ex-   exceed, expect, expose, extend

     g. inter-   intercept, intercede, interdict, interpellate

     h. meta-   metamorphosis

     i. neo-   neophyte, neoteny, neoteric

     j. para-   parabellum, parabrachial, paraphilic

     k. peri-   perianth, pericardium, periphery

     l. post-   postdict, postlude, postpone

     m. pre-   precede, preclude, predict, preempt

     n. retro-   retrocede, retrodict, retroflex, retrogress

     o. sub-   subduct, subjugate, subject, submit

     p. super-   supercede, supercilious, superficial, superlative

     q. sur-   surface, surfeit, surmise, survive

     r. trans-   transceiver, transcend, transduce, transfer

Several of the locative prefixes can be found attached to compounds or phrases.

(3) a. arch-   arch-Clinton loyalists, arch-comical designs, arch-dipshit, arch-liberal columnist

     b. co-   co-artistic director, co-boat-owner, co-cave-dweller, co-medical director, co-topdog

c. ex-   ex-aerial gunner, ex-ballplayer, ex-battleship, ex-big band, ex-boomtown, ex-French colony

d. extra-   extra-Chinatown

e. neo-   neo-baby boom, neo-bullshit, neo-deathwish, neo-hunter-gatherer

f. post-   post-affirmative-action, post-babyboom, post-baby-on-board, post-baseball, post-budget-cut, post-communist-era, post-Connery-as-Bond, post-death-of-God

g. pre-   pre-air-conditioned, pre-baseball, pre-complaint-filing, pre-Cold War, pre-first-grade, pre-leveraged-buyout, pre-main-sequence, pre-Redford-and-Hoffman

h. proto-   proto-daily-paper, protohighlands

i. sub-   sub-cabinet-level, sub-five-second, sub-freshman, sub-headline, sub-lightspeed

j. trans-   trans-lightspeed, trans-windshield

Interestingly, quite a few of the locative prefixes appear to be category-changing. While the examples in (1) and (2) are category-preserving, the examples we present in (4) raise the issue of whether locative prefixes can effect category change. We find abundant examples in which nouns with locative prefixes appear as pre-modifiers to other nouns.

(4) a. *nominal bases*

Anthropological Quarterly 2007: But though these **extra-household** activities may extract energy and time from women's focus on immediate domestic duties, they are seldom demonized in the same way that the career women's working is.

Atlanta Journal Constitution 2000: United Airlines and Air Canada began offering an **inter-airline** electronic-ticketing service, which links the computer reservation systems of both carriers.

Current Psychology 1996: Because the study was designed to explore how males and females would evaluate the trait-pairs with and without a biologically relevant "starting point," **intragender** comparisons among Conditions 1 and 2 were performed.

Inc. 1999: we should expect only that these complaints will get to be higher and higher complaints; that they will move from lower-grumble levels to higher-grumble levels and finally to **metagrumble** levels…

Washington Post 1992: And who could have imagined a poetry reading inside the 15 Min. nightclub on 15th Street between K and L, a sullen little nook with creepy button-tufted couches and a high-grunge, proto-funk, black-light decor with **neo-brothel** red walls and ridiculous cupids.

Denver Post 2003: "That's the reality of the world we now live in, post-Sept. 11 and **post-anthrax** letters," said Harris, a staffer with the National Security Council from 1993 to 2001.

Night Embrace 2003: But the **retro-beatnik** Coffee Stain had nice artwork on the walls and her friends seemed partial to drinking gallons of the tar-liquid.

PSA Journal 2003: Other than a very old female, and a **sub-adult** male, the adults were gone.

CNN_On Story 2004: The only recommendation that I've heard that has sort of gotten out there is, OK, we need a superagency, a **supercabinet** position, to overlook intelligence, to bring it all together.

America 1994: In many ways, the liberal or mainline churches and their **suprachurch** organizations are intolerant of religious plurality and particularity, even if their vocabulary is more open.

Geographical Review 2008: It was close to the bus and train station--an ideal location for serving **transborder** shoppers.

b. *verbal bases*

Houston Chronicle 1996: A **post-emerge** herbicide is needed to treat a perennial broad-leaved weed such as dichondra.

Some theorists might want to take examples such as these as evidence that the locative prefixes can change nouns to adjectives, but given the existence of monomorphemic nouns occurring as premodifiers of other nouns (for example, *stone wall*), we are somewhat reluctant to do so (for further discussion see Chapter 19). The example in (4b) is, however, different as monomorphemic verbs typically do not occur as premodifiers to nouns; although examples like this appear to be quite rare, they suggest that further study would be useful here.

For the most part, non-native locative prefixes neither undergo allomorphy themselves nor induce allomorphy on their bases. Placement of stress seems not to be systematic. While there is a tendency for stress to be on the prefix in nouns and on the base in verbs, Wells (2008) shows both patterns for the verb *antedate*, for example, stress on the prefix for the verb *countersign*, and stress on the base for the noun *counterirritant*. We also find stress on the second syllable of the prefix, for example in forms like *extrapolate, interpret, interpolate, periphery, superfluous, superlative*. Most of these can be accounted for by the general prosodic constraints imposed on these derivatives by the suffixes in these words. For example, verbs in *-ate* as well as *-y* formations on the basis of neoclassical formations are characterized by antepenultimate main stress (see Chapter 13.2.2.2 and Chapter 12.2.5, respectively).

The non-native prefixes vary in productivity. The prefix *cis-* is the least productive, with very few types occurring in COCA. The prefixes *ante-, circum-, contra-, epi-, para-, peri-, supra-,* and *sur-* show moderate productivity, as do *extra-* and *super-* with their spatial readings; these last two are wildly productive, however, in their quantitative readings. The remaining prefixes (*arch-, co-, counter-, ex-, inter-, intra-, meta-, neo-, post-, pre-, proto-, retro-, sub-,* and *trans-*) all show a high level of productivity.

16.2.2 Native prefixes

The first formal issue we must raise here is why we choose to treat the native morphemes *after-*, *back-*, *by-*, *down-*, *fore-*, *in-*, *mid-*, *off-*, *on-*, *out-*, *over-*, *under-*, and *up-* as prefixes rather than as the first elements of compounds, as some scholars do. Marchand (1969) treats *fore-* and *mid-* as prefixes, but the others are covered in his section on compounds as what he calls 'combinations with locative particles as first elements', on the grounds that the former are no longer free morphemes whereas the latter are. Although neither treats the whole range of locatives we consider here, Bauer (1983) and Adams (2001) both consider the non-native elements as prefixes, and the native ones as the first elements in compounds. Lehrer (1995), however, claims that distributional evidence justifies treating both native and non-native elements as prefixes, although again she does not discuss the entire range of locatives.

We have several reasons to adopt Lehrer's position, one practical and two theoretical. Our practical reason is that both formally and semantically the native forms show parallels to the non-native ones; treating them in the same chapter allows us to make comparisons. Our theoretical reasons are perhaps more convincing. First, a few of the native morphemes have effects on the argument structure of verbal bases, something that we would not expect to see if they were the first elements of compounds. We return to this point in Section 16.3.3.

We take our second theoretical argument from Dalton-Puffer and Plag (2000), who argue that a formative can be considered to be an affix (as opposed to an element of a compound) to the extent that it shows a coherent semantics that is at least partially distinct from a homophonous free form. The native prefixes *after-*, *by-*, *down-*, *in-*, *off-*, *on-*, *out-*, *over-*, *under-*, and *up-* are obviously homophonous with prepositions in English and we find when we compare their semantics that their meanings are not always perfectly coextensive. On the one hand, the prepositions often show a wider range of meanings than the prefixes, but we also find meanings for the prefixes that do not occur in the free forms.

For example, the prefix and preposition *after* both express core meanings like 'subsequent in time' (*aftershock*, *after the earthquake*), 'posterior to' (*afterdeck*, *to follow after*), but the preposition also has specialized uses like 'in imitation of' (*a painting after Michelangelo*) or 'in accordance with' (*after my own heart*). Similarly, the prefix and preposition *by* share the core meaning 'alongside' (*bystander*, *by the river*), but the preposition also indicates means or instrument (*by foot*) or, in a construction with a reflexive, 'alone' (e.g. *by myself*).

There are also senses that can be found in the prefixes but not in the prepositions. With *by-*, for example, the prefix sometimes conveys the sense of 'not major' (*byroad*, *bylaw*, *byproduct*), which in turn leads to more specialized meanings like 'accidence' (*by-catch*, *by-kill*), or meanings that are not typically found with the preposition. Sometimes a meaning can be found with both, but is much more prominent in the prefix than with the preposition, as with the 'excess' meaning of *over-*. This sort of non-overlap in meaning provides another piece of evidence for treating the native formatives as prefixes.

Like the non-native prefixes surveyed in Section 16.2.1, the native locatives typically attach to nominal bases, and sometimes to adjectival and verbal bases as well. Either native or non-native bases seem to be possible, although native bases are more frequent with this cohort than with the non-native prefixes. Because of the extent of conversion in English, it is not always possible to identify the category of the base uniquely, and some of these forms may have more than one analysis.

(5) a. after- *On N*: afterbirth, afterdeck, afterglow, afterscent

                     On A: after-shocking, after-sweet

      b. back- *On N*: back-action, back-country, backhoe, backporch

                     On V: back-annotate, back-announce, back-comb, backfire

      c. by-   *On N*: by-blow, byhikers, bykill, byproduct

                     On V: bygone, bypass

      d. down- *On N*: downbeat, downblast, down-gusts

                     On A: down-deep, downlow, downright

                     On V: download, downsell, downshift

      e. fore- *On N*: forearm, forebrain, forefin, forenoon

                     On V: forebear, forebode, foreclose, forejudge

      f. in-   *On N*: in-basket, in-break, in-crowd, infield

                     On A: inborn, inbuilt, ingrown, in-marrying

                     On V: indwell, ingather, inmix

      g. mid- *On N*: midabdomen, midbite, midchannel, midengine

                     On A: midaxillary, mid-Cambrian, mid-distal, mid-gibbous

      h. off-   *On N*: off-flavor, off-months, off-ramp, off-taste

                     On A: off-blond, off-diagonal, off-gray, off-width

                     On V: off-load

      i. on-   *On N*: on-passing, onrush, onset

                     On A: onmoving, onsweeping

                     On V: on-load, onlook

      j. out- *On N*: out-agent, outcamp, outfield, outhouse

                     On V: outdate, outgrow, outlay, outsource

      k. over- *On N*: overbag, over-bite, overboot, overdog

                     On A: (quantitative/scalar reading only): over-academic, over-arty, overbold, overdark

                     On V: overarch, overfly, overhang, oversee

l. under-   *On N*: underarm, underbark, underbody, underbrush

On A: under-diagonal, underlit, underslung, underthrown

On A: under-diagonal, underlit, underslung, underthrown

On V: undercut, undergo, underlie, underline

m. up-   *On N*: up-angle, up-chute, up-cropping, updraft

On A: upclose, upcoming, updrawn, upright

On V: upbring, upconvert, update, upgrade

As with the non-native locative prefixes, forms may be spelled either with or without hyphen.

Not surprisingly, the native prefixes do not appear on bound bases (the form *onslaught* is perhaps an exception, if the obsolete *slaught* is to be treated as bound at this point). Most of them do not appear on either compounds or phrases, the exception being *mid-*.

(6)   mid-   *On compounds*: mid-dogfight, mid-freefall, mid-grain-filling, mid-photo-spread

On phrases: mid-five-figure, mid-single-digit, mid-wanna-escape

The prefixes *over-* and *out-* can be found on compounds and phrases, but only with a quantitative/scalar (as opposed to purely locative) meaning (*over-aircondition, out-fund-raising, out-redneck*); see Section 16.3.1 for a full treatment of the semantic distinction.

As with the non-native locatives, we find many cases in which the prefixed items occur as premodifiers to nouns and raise the same theoretical issue with regard to syntactic category specification that we discussed with regard to the examples in (4).

(7)   a. *nominal base*

Todays Parent 2004: Take that sensation a step further by smoothing on an **after-bath** gel after you dry off.

Backpacker 2011: The best **backcountry** meals don't come from chichi cookbooks that use words like "nap" to refer to a sauce coating instead of a siesta.

Atlantic Monthly 2007: These ranged from those that confront all senators—how should they tend to the interests of **downstate** constituents?—to those that confront only a few.

College Student Journal 2011: This can take the form of group projects, before or after class interactions, office hour visits, and **in-class** discussions that require students to interact with each other.

Ethnology 1993: Vetale vaLLi and nuulam paTai are found from altitudes of about 1,250 meters down to 300 meters; that is, from the forested flanks and **midaltitude** plateaus of the mountains down to the very edge of the agricultural plain.

PC World 2000: The machine you get is an **offbrand** computer, and you have to purchase the monitor separately.

CSM 2009: One was the development of the American crawl, an **overarm** thrashing stroke known today as freestyle.

PBS Newshour 2011: The prime minister of a major European economy, not just accused, but now formally charged with **underage** prostitution and abuse of power.

NPR Science 2011: Tennessee has a lot more of **upland** limestone, and it's pretty riddled.

b. *verbal base*

Environment 1991: Groins and jetties built perpendicular to the shore intercept shifting sand on the **updrift** side, but deny sand to the opposite, or **downdrift**, shoreline.

Again, it is not clear whether this is to be counted as a category-changing phenomenon, but we do not rule this analysis out.

There is one case, however, where *out-* really does seem to be category-changing. Consider the examples in (8).

(8)   a. *adjective to verb*

USA Today 2000: He would do one pose, and I would try to **out-absurd** him.

Chicago Sun Times 2008: A critical part of McCall's spring charge will be to merge smash-mouth, forward football into an offense that far too frequently tried to '**outcute**' brute opponents.

Houston Chronicle 2003: He didn't fight it. He didn't **outsmart** himself, didn't **outdumb** himself, didn't get too greedy or too cautious.

b. *noun to verb*

Journal of International Affairs 2002: Serbia: If You Can't **Out-Birth** Them, Make Them Run Away

Houston Chronicle 2002: Both candidates are already using television advertisements, and are trying to "**out-Bubba**" one another for the rural audience.

CBS_Sixty Minutes 2004: Fuller first gained notoriety in 1997 when she was named editor-in-chief of the racy "Cosmopolitan" magazine, where she soon **out-Cosmoed** even "Cosmo."

San Francisco Chronicle 1991: And when money buys the senator's vote…we're outnumbered and **outdollared**.

Here we have *out-* occurring on either adjectival (8a) or nominal (8b) bases. This pattern is highly productive in contemporary English and raises an interesting theoretical issue. For the most part, the examples with the nominal forms in *out-* are purely locative (*outhouse*, *outfield*), and the verbal forms on verbal bases are sometimes locative (*outsource, outbreed* 'breed out-side of a particular population'), whereas the verbs formed on nouns and adjectives always seem to have a comparative meaning. This raises the question of whether we have here one polysemous prefix or two homophonous prefixes. We will return to this issue in Section 16.3.1.

One way in which the native prefixes differ from the non-native ones is that the former occasionally appear to function as heads of their words. That is, at least the prefixes *down-*, *up-*, *in-*, and *out-* can derive words that are distributionally identical to prepositions or prepo-sitional phrases (or adverbs, in traditional terms), for example, forms like *up-river, down-stream, in-house,* and *outside.* The prefixes *down-* and *up-* appear to be productive in this function, at least with topographical nouns (*up-canyon, downbeach*), but *in-* and *out-* are not, being confined, as far as we can see, to a number of item-familiar and high frequency bases.

The native locative prefixes neither induce allomorphy in their bases nor undergo allo-morphy themselves. As was the case with the non-native prefixes, nouns derived with the native prefixes are typically stressed on the prefix. Derived verbs and adjectives seem to be somewhat variable in stress pattern. With respect to verbs, Wells (2008), for example, gives both pronunciations to *download* and *offload,* stress on the prefix for *backcomb* and *bypass,* and stress on the base for *indwell.* The verb *outgrow* is stressed on the base, but *outsource* on the prefix. Verbs in *fore-* are typically stressed on the base.

As with the non-native prefixes, the native locatives vary widely in productivity. The pre-fixes *fore-, by-,* and *on-* are perhaps the least productive. Somewhat more productive are *after-, back-, down-, in-, off-,* and *up-,* and most productive are *mid-, out-, over-,* and *under-.* It should be kept in mind, however, that the prefixes *out-, over-,* and *under-* are a great deal more pro-ductive with their scalar/quantitative readings than with their locative readings.

16.3 SEMANTIC CONSIDERATIONS

Locative prefixes are those that denote position with respect to either a spatial or a temporal referent, or both; we include in this cohort the prefixes *arch-* and *meta-* which are metaphori-cally but not literally locative. In this section we will first consider basic meanings of the loca-tive prefixes (Section 16.3.1), then compare denotationally similar native and non-native pairs (or triples) (Section 16.3.2). Finally, we will turn to the native prefixes which have valency-changing effects when they occur on verbal bases (Section 16.3.3).

16.3.1 Core meanings

We can distinguish the semantic features of locative prefixes along several dimensions. We will first look at the general semantic characteristics of the locative prefixes, distinguishing those prefixes that are primarily spatial, those that are primarily (or exclusively) temporal, those that do double duty as both temporal and spatial locatives, those that have both spatial and quantitative meanings, and finally those that are primarily metaphorical in nature.

Like locative prepositions, locative prefixes can be characterized semantically according to the implied geometric characteristics of their referents. By 'referents' we mean the objects of those prepositions, or the bases of the prefixes. Some prefixes make reference to a one-dimensional object, that is, to a line, and more specifically to a line with either a horizontal or a vertical orientation. The prefixes *up-, over-, super-, supra-, sur-, sub-, down-,* and *under-,* for example, make reference to a vertical axis of orientation, whereas *ante-, fore-, pre-, after-,* and *post-* make reference to a horizontal axis. We can further divide these into those prefixes that refer to the positive end of the axis (*up-, over-, super-, sur-, meta-, arch-; after-, post-*) and those that make reference to the negative pole (*sub-, down-; ante-, fore-, pre-*). The prefix *mid-* can refer to either axis but to an area between the two poles.

(9)

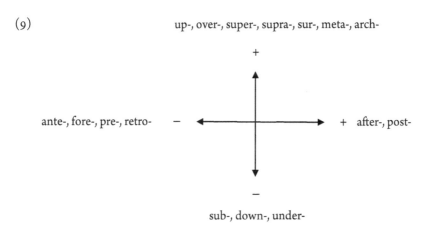

Other prefixes are best described with reference to a two- or three-dimensional space (*back-, circum-, para-, peri-, by-, off-, on-, out-, in-, epi-, extra-*):

(10)

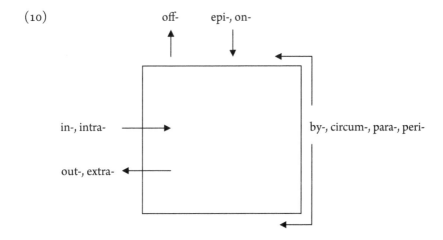

For the latter group, *in-* and *intra-* make reference to the interior of the referent, *on-*, and *epi-* to a surface, *extra-*, *off-*, and *out-* to the area exterior to the referent, and *circum-*, *peri-*, *by-*, and *para-* to the edge or border. The latter four are distinguished in that *circum-* makes reference to the whole of the periphery, whereas *by-*, *peri-*, and *para-* merely reference the vicinity of the referent. The prefix *back-* refers to the rear surface of a three-dimensional referent, or the area behind that surface.

Finally, several prefixes can be described as relating one point of reference to another (*cis-*, *trans-*, *inter-*, *co-*, *counter-*, *contra-*).

(11)   a. • ——————▶ •
        cis-, trans-

       b. • ◀——————▶ •
            inter-

       c.   • •
                  co-

       d. • ——▶ ◀—— •
          counter-, contra-

The prefix *trans-* may focus on the path (going through or across something), or on the final destination, as being beyond something from the speaker's perspective (*trans-Alpine Gaul*).

In (12) we group the locative prefixes according to their main semantic functions:

(12)   a. *Primarily spatial*: by-, circum-, cis-, contra-, counter-, down-, epi-, in-, off-, on-, para-, sub-, supra-, trans-, up-

       b. *Exclusively temporal*: ex-, neo-, proto-

       c. *Both spatial and temporal*: after-, ante-, back-, co-, fore-, inter-, intra-, mid-, peri-, post-, pre-, retro-

       d. *Both spatial and quantitative*: extra-, out-, over-, super-, sur-, under-

       e. *Metaphorical*: arch-, meta-

Simple temporal reference to a point on a timeline is generally accomplished by a prefix that does double duty as a spatial prefix. So we have spatial/temporal pairs such as the following.

(13) | *Spatial* | *Temporal* |
       |---|---|
       | afterdeck | aftercare |
       | antechamber | antedate |
       | backcountry | backdate |
       | co-author | co-consider |

forearm	foresight
intercampus	intermenstrual
intragroup	intrasemester
midbrain	midargument
perianal	perimenopause
postauricle	post-acne
preschool	preadolescent
retrocurved	retro-date

We find spatial readings more frequently than temporal for *back-* and *intra-*, and temporal readings more frequently for *post-*, *pre-*, and *retro-*, but the majority allow both readings with relatively equal frequency. Where the spatial readings are dominant, it is often necessary for the base to be explicitly temporal in reference (*intra-annual*) or to be readily interpreted as eventive (*intra-semester*) to get the temporal reading from the prefix. Where the temporal reading is dominant, even completely non-eventive bases can be interpreted temporally, as we find when *post-* is attached to any proper noun (for example, *post-Clinton*).

Several of the locative prefixes have come to combine both locative and quantitative meanings. These are typically prefixes that express endpoints on an axis, usually the vertical axis (*over-*, *super-*, *sur-*, *under-*; *extra-* and *out-* are the exceptions here). The semantic extension takes us from the spatial endpoint of a scale to beyond that endpoint, thus inviting the inference of excess (for *extra-*, *out-*, *over-*, *super-*, *sur-*) or dearth (*under-*) depending on whether reference is to the positive or negative pole. The prefix *out-* is somewhat different in that its quantitative/scalar reading on derived verbs is comparative in nature.

The prefix *out-* raises an interesting theoretical issue: as mentioned in Section 16.2.2, it is typically locative in meaning when it derives nouns (*outfield*, *outhouse*), and when it derives verbs on verbal bases it can bear either a locative meaning (*outsource*, *outbreed* 'breed outside of a particular population') or a comparative meaning (*outdance*, *outcompete*), but in its category-changing guise (*out-absurd*, *out-Bubba*) it is exclusively comparative in meaning. On the one hand, the semantic uniformity and robust productivity of the category-changing version of the prefix might be taken as evidence that *out-* has evolved into two distinct homophonous affixes. On the other hand, the existence of an overlap between the two meanings in forms derived from verbs might argue for a polysemy analysis. We will not decide between these two possibilities here.

English has three prefixes that seem to be exclusively temporal: *ex-*, *neo-*, and *proto-*. *Neo-* and *proto-* are fairly straightforward, the former denoting 'new' (*neo-family*) or 'revived from an older form' (*neo-conservative*), and the latter 'earlier' or 'original' (*proto-Indo-European*). The prefix *ex-* is somewhat more complex. Meaning 'former', it occurs more comfortably on stage-level nouns, that is, nouns like *pedestrian* or *musician* that denote temporary states, than on individual level nouns like *car* or *horse* that denote permanent states of being (we take Monty Python's *ex-parrot* to be an instance of coercion). The prefix *ex-* can occur on individual level nouns if they are preceded by a possessive, in which case the prefix actually takes scope over the possessive rather than the noun to which it is attached; in other words, *my ex-car* normally refers to a car that no longer belongs to me, as opposed to something which is no longer a car. With more complex noun phrases, the prefix *ex-* can take wide scope over an entire phrase as well as narrow scope over the base to which it is phonologically attached. So if we have a phrase like an *ex-ballplayer for the Red Sox*, the person in question might no longer be a ballplayer (narrow scope), but might equally well still be a ballplayer, but for another team (wide scope).

The final two prefixes we consider here are *arch-* and *meta-*. These differ from the rest of the locatives in that their spatial sense is purely metaphorical. The prefix *arch-* is typically used on personal nouns (*arch-critic*, *arch-dipshit*, *archsorcerer*) to indicate higher status. The prefix *meta-* favours abstract nouns (*belief*, *pathology*, *theory*) and relational adjectives (*aesthetic*, *cognitive*) as bases and denotes an over-arching or a higher-level form of the base. They may both be considered figurative analogues of prefixes like *over-* or *super-* in their spatial (as opposed to quantitative) senses.

16.3.2 Native and non-native cohorts: a comparison

As the diagrams in examples (9), (10), and (11) suggest, some of the spatial relationships we have looked at are associated with both a native prefix and a non-native one (and sometimes with more than one non-native one). The question therefore naturally arises whether the cohorts of prefixes can be distinguished semantically in any way. This is the question we turn to here.

16.3.2.1 over- *versus* super-, supra-, sur-

Despite the similarity in core denotation, these prefixes are not identical either in productivity or in semantic nuance. The prefix *sur-* is at best minimally productive, although the term *surfiction* (found in COCA) does seem to be a neologism—albeit an extremely self-conscious one. The other non-native prefixes are more productive, but only on nouns and adjectives. The native *over-* is the only one of this cohort that can be freely used to coin verbs.

While both *over-* and *super-* frequently have a nuance of 'excess', with *over-* this nuance is typically intended in a negative sense and with *super-* often (but not always) in a positive sense, as the examples in (14) illustrate.

(14) a. *Field and Stream 2005*: Audubon Pennsylvania agrees with the overwhelming scientific evidence that **overabundant** whitetail deer have seriously degraded habitats throughout the commonwealth.

b. *Skiing 1995*: Targhee was a super place to test fat skis, with its abundant terrain and **super-abundant** snow (the area's slogan is "Snow from heaven, not hoses").

The prefix *supra-*, in contrast to *super-*, does not have the nuance of 'excess' and is sometimes used in distinction to *super-* to convey a spatial sense.

(15)   a. *America 1994*: In many ways, the liberal or mainline churches and their **suprachurch** organizations are intolerant of religious plurality and particularity […]

   b. *New York Times 1995*: "[…] I do think that's a danger you face in the **superchurch**," said Dr. Gregory, who described his experience in a book, "Too Great a Temptation" "[…] A megachurch minister can," he said, "get promoted right out of reality."

16.3.2.2 under- *versus* sub-

These prefixes sometimes overlap in sense. Both can be straightforwardly spatial, as we find in the examples in (16) and (17).

(16)   a. *Esquire 2004*: Everybody at Sony Pictures says they're happy—the top boss, the various **sub-bosses**, the would-be bosses.

   b. *Nightline 2010*: FBI wiretaps have captured this **underboss** of the Colombos bragging about the dozens of men he's killed and describing his favorite way to dispose of bodies, using knives, a kiddy pool and a trash compactor.

(17)   a. *Airforce One 1997*: Korshunov pushes Alice down the stairs to the **underdeck**.

   b. *Skiing 1994*: The wooden deck, which is shaped like a skateboard, is attached to a **subdeck** with a plastic rail along the length of the bottom.

While *under-* frequently has a quantitative nuance, the prefix *sub-* only occasionally does. Where *sub-* does carry a quantitative nuance, it seems generally more neutral in tone than *under-*.

(18)   a. *Mechanical Engineering 2007*: Boeing has the new **subjumbo** 787, designed to serve what the company sees as the future demand of air travel, as well as a "new" superjumbo 747-8 family.

   b. *Education 2000*: Swart (1987:163) maintains that too little stress may even lead to **underaverage** achievement.

The pejorative reading is particularly prominent when *under-* is attached to verbal bases (*underachieve, underbake, underproduce*). The prefix *sub-* has one nuance that *under-* lacks. Forms with *sub-* on nominal or verbal bases frequently carry a meaning of partition or hierarchy, rather than a purely spatial meaning, as we find in *subclause* or *subdivide*, for example.

16.3.2.3 fore- *versus* ante-, pre-

These three prefixes appear to be denotatively similar, although of the three, only *pre-* shows any substantial degree of productivity. We only rarely find doublets. In (19) the forms are denotatively identical, although the form in *fore-* is meant to convey a self-consciously archaic flavour.

(19)   a. *Fantasy & Science Fiction 2007*: When I set out in the **fore-dawn**, methought I wore a shadow of subtle tints and colorations invisible in dawnlight.

   b. *Fantasy & Science Fiction 2010*: Now, in the **predawn**, I arrived at an almost empty skyscraper, signed in with security in a silent lobby, went up to the shabby station where an engineer and a couple of other guys sat around gossiping.

In (20) we have an apparent neologism *forecheck*, but on a sense of *check* that is peculiar to certain team sports (ice hockey, field hockey, etc.).

(20)   a. *USA 2009*: "It's just key to have people who can **forecheck** and possess the puck and still maintain that scoring ability and poise once they get it," Cahow said.

   b. *PSA Journal 1996*: But many times, the presenter did not **precheck** the equipment or was not familiar with the local setup.

16.3.2.4 after- *versus* post-

This pair is not only similar in denotation, but also in connotation, neither having a particularly evaluative flavour. The prefix *after-* occurs productively only on nouns, although the prefixed forms, as mentioned in Section 16.2.2, frequently occur as premodifiers of other nouns. The prefix *post-* is productive on both nouns and adjectives, and on nouns can also form premodifiers. As the doublet in example (21) illustrates, the two prefixes appear to be semantic equivalents.

(21)   a. *Ebony 2004*: The typical teen, experts say, could spend in excess of $1,000 for the prom ticket, limo rental, photos, corsage, spectacular one-of-a-kind dress and matching garter belt, tuxedo rental (or purchase) personal grooming and, of course, the **after-prom** celebration which typically caps off the evening.

   b. *Atlanta Journal Constitution 2002*: As the PTA president at Harrison High School in Kennesaw, she has hosted a **post-prom** party for several years at U.S. Play near Town Center mall and planned to carry it on this spring.

Neither prefix attaches freely to verbs, although we do find the occasional exception such as *post-date*.

16.3.2.5 by- *versus* peri-

These two are perhaps not really parallel in the way that the previously discussed pairs are: the prefix *by-* can be glossed as 'beside', *peri-* as 'round about', but pragmatically this often amounts to the same thing. The prefix *by-* is at best minimally productive. We find the form *by-kill* attested in COCA but not in the *OED*; most forms with this prefix are high-frequency and well-established. The prefix *peri-* is somewhat more productive, but is most frequently used in learned and especially medical contexts (*pericranial, peri-tumoral*).

16.3.2.6 out- *versus* extra-

Although these prefixes share a core meaning 'external to', they in fact do not overlap. The prefix *extra-* is primarily productive on adjectives, and where it occurs on nominal bases the derived forms typically function as premodifiers of other nouns. The prefix *out-* does not attach to adjectives or form premodifiers, and in fact is most productive on verbal bases, where it has a clearly comparative sense.

16.3.2.7 in- *versus* intra-

Denotatively, these two prefixes are quite close, although in terms of potential bases there is relatively little overlap. Of the two, only *in-* can attach to verbs, and on nominal and adjectival bases *intra-* tends to favour non-native and especially learned bases, whereas *in-* favours native bases. There are small areas of overlap, however, which illustrate the denotative similarity.

(22) a. *Denver Post 1996*: "I think the rivalry is more **intra-division**, rather than cross-division," Neuheisel said.

   b. *San Francisco Chronicle 1990*: If you're a Giants fan, you can say good-by to the West for a while, catch your breath and hope things are still as interesting when the traditional round of **in-division** games start in September.

Neither of these prefixes has a particularly evaluative force.

16.3.3 Argument structure effects

Non-native prefixes do not affect argument structure when they attach to verbal bases. With native prefixes, however, we sometimes do find changes to verbal diathesis that seem to be induced by the prefix. This is especially true of the native prefixes *over-* and *out-*, occasionally true of *under-*, and only sporadically true of the other native prefixes that can be found attached to verbs. This phenomenon has occasionally been noted in the literature (Fraser 1974; Bresnan 1982; Williams 1992; Lieber 2004) at least for the first two prefixes, although it has not to our knowledge been studied systematically for all locative prefixes.

   With *over-*, two sorts of argument structure effect can be found. On verbs of change of state or directed motion like *flow, fly, grow,* or *leap,* the affixation of *over-* allows the addition of a locative NP argument, as the examples in (23) illustrate.

(23) a. *Christian Science Monitor 2006*: Without the grazing species, the seaweeds these small organisms ate soon **overgrew** the seafloor, crowding out other species and making it much harder for already stressed coral reefs to regenerate.

b. *Futurist 2003*: Recycling has delayed the "garbage glut" that threatened to **overflow** the world's landfills, but the threat has not passed simply because it has not yet arrived.

c. *Natural History 2003*: Wallace's Line is now understood to **overlie** a region incorporating three major tectonic plates and several smaller ones.

In these cases, *over-* often has its locative rather than qualitative reading. On other verbs (often, but not always activity verbs) the prefixation of *over-* allows for the deletion of an argument, so that a normally transitive verb can be used intransitively.

(24) a. *ABA Journal 1994*: Solving problems others created or succeeding for someone else's benefit develops stress or a compulsion to **overachieve**.

b. *Atlanta Journal Constitution 2008*: Pros are strategic in what storage containers they have clients purchase, whereas someone desperate to declutter in a single weekend will tend to **overbuy**.

c. *Christian Science Monitor 2009*: Lithium-ion batteries using cobalt chemistry, popularly used in laptop computers and cellphones, have in the past shown a propensity to **overheat**, resulting in a few laptops going up in flames.

In these cases, *over-* tends to display its quantitative/scalar reading.

The prefix *under-* is much less productive in forming verbs than *over-* is, but where it does occur on verbal bases, it shows some of the same argument structure effects. We find verbs like *underachieve* and *underearn* that are predominantly used intransitively, as in (25a) and (25b); there is at least one verb, *bid*, that normally selects a prepositional object when unprefixed, but which, with the prefix *under-*, can appear with an NP object (25c).

(25) a. *Community College Review 2009*: These results suggest that there might be an interaction with income to explain why White students with Pell grants and Stafford loans **underachieve** compared to African American and Native American students without these forms of aid.

b. *PBS_Tavis 2006*: Cause I ain't never met nobody, including Bill Gates, who thinks he **underearns**.

c. *USA Today 2006*: The Revolutionary Guards' preferential access to state financing allows them to **underbid** private firms, says Bijan Khajehpour, chairman of Tehran-based Atieh Group, which advises foreign firms on the Iranian market.

The prefix *out-* quite regularly derives transitive verbs, something which makes sense, given its comparative semantics. If the verbal base is transitive to begin with, there is of course no change in verbal diathesis, although the semantic category of the NP object may be different. That is, whereas a verb like *eat* normally takes food items as its object (*Fenster ate a pickle/*Raoul*), when prefixed with *out-*, the object must be another animate NP (*Fenster outate *pickles/Raoul*).

If the verb is intransitive to begin with (for example, *fart, guffaw, linger, sleep*), or takes a prepositional (*stare, yell*) or clausal object (*think*), the prefixation of *out-* triggers the addition of an NP argument, as the examples in (26) illustrate.

(26) a. *Cosmopolitan 2003*: On and off camera, more girls are dishing about discharge, **outfarting** their friends, and taking part in other beyond-ribald behavior.

   b. *Christian Science Monitor 1993*: Jim Mezon inhabits the role of Simon with an uncanny feeling for the speech and habits of a man who hasn't forgotten the folks from the old neighborhood, but who can outwit and **out-guffaw** the sleaziest politician.

   c. *Radiance 1999*: In spite of her tenderness, Aunt Jenny could outshout, outgesture, and **outstare** the loudest of my Italian relatives.

   d. *Boys Life 2007*: As an Eagle Scout in Mesa, Beck learned the importance of being prepared. His favorite activity was fly-fishing, a sport in which you have to study the behavior of fish, then try to **outthink** them.

Where *out-* derives verbs from adjectives or nouns, the result is typically transitive as well.

(27) a. *USA Today 2000*: He would do one pose, and I would try to **out-absurd** him.

   b. *Atlanta Journal Consitution 1996*: Hammerin' Hank did not **out-Babe** the Babe!

In all of these cases, *out-* has its scalar or quantitative reading, rather than a purely locative one.

The only other native locative prefixes that can be found on verbs are *back-, down-,* and *up-,* although none of these is particularly productive. Generally *back-* has no effect on the argument structure of the base verb, although we do find the form *backtalk* in COCA used with an NP object rather than a prepositional object. Similarly, where *down-* occurs on verbal bases, it generally leaves verbal diathesis untouched, exceptions being *downcut* and *downtalk*, both attested in COCA.

(28) a. *Killing Mister Watson 1990*: And she said, Don't you **backtalk** me, you are my child!

   b. *Bioscience 1993*: In addition, channels may erode, or **downcut**, triggering rejuvenation of tributaries, which themselves begin eroding and migrating headward.

   c. *Analogue Science Fiction & Fact 2010*: I suspected the boy had the right of it, but it does no good to **downtalk** leaders.

It is difficult to say whether there is anything systematic about the effects illustrated in (28), as they are limited to these isolated examples.

....

CHAPTER 17

Negatives

17.1 PROSPECTUS

In this chapter we will examine affixal negation in English. We use a broad definition of negation here, including along with standard negatives ('not X') also privatives ('without X' or 'remove X from'), reversatives ('reverse action of VERBing'), and verbal pejoratives ('do X wrongly, badly'). The affixes we will examine are *in-, un-, non-, a-, dis-, de-, -less, mis-,* and *mal-*. The semantically related formations involving *-free* and *ill-* are sometimes treated as affixes or affixoids, but we consider formations with these elements as compounds, on the grounds that there are no compelling arguments for their status as affixes or affixoids (see Chapter 16 and Dalton-Puffer and Plag (2000) for pertinent tests). At least the first four of these affixes have received extensive discussion in the literature, including Jespersen (1917), Zimmer (1964), Marchand (1969), Bauer (1983), Horn (1989, 2002), Bauer and Huddleston (2002), Plag (2003, 2004), Lieber (2004), and Hamawand (2009).

The corpus data indicate that these affixes are frequently polysemous, displaying more than one of the meanings/functions mentioned above and suggesting that to some extent the semantic interpretation of the derived words is not solely a function of the meaning of the affix, but is the consequence of combining the broadly negative content of the affix with the meaning of the base; that is, straightforward negatives tend to occur with certain kinds of bases, privatives with others, and so on. In this conclusion, we depart from much of the above-mentioned research. From a different, base-driven, perspective, we note that one base can take more than one of these affixes, sometimes with the formally different derivatives having the same meaning, sometimes having different meanings.

We begin with formal considerations in Section 17.2 and continue with semantic considerations in Section 17.3. Examples are taken from COCA, unless otherwise specified.

17.2 FORMAL CONSIDERATIONS

17.2.1 Basic characteristics

Table 17.1 sets out the basic formal characteristics of this cohort of affixes and affixoids, examples of which are then given in (1). Clearly, there is a great deal of overlap in formal properties among the negative and privative affixes of English.

Table 17.1 Formal properties of negative and privative affixes (native affixes are italicized). Parenthesized items are rare

	Input category			Output category				Category changing	Native bases	Non-native bases
	A	V	N	bound bases	A	V	N			
in-	✓	✓	(✓)	(✓)	✓	✓	(✓)	sometimes N→A, occasionally N→V	✓	✓
un-	✓	✓	(✓)		✓		✓	sometimes N→A	✓	✓
non-	✓		✓		✓	✓	✓	sometimes N→V	✓	✓
dis-	(✓)	✓	✓	(✓)	(✓)	✓	✓	very occasionally N→A	(✓)	✓
de-	✓	✓	✓	(✓),✓		✓	(✓)	N→V	✓	✓
a(n)-			(✓)	(✓),✓			✓			✓
mis-		✓	✓	(✓),✓		✓	✓		✓	✓
mal-		(✓)	✓	?	✓	✓			✓	✓
-less	✓		✓		✓			N→A	✓	✓

The following examples list pertinent derivatives for illustration. Note that since *dis-* can safely be considered non-category-changing, potentially ambiguous examples (e.g. *discomfort*) have been analysed with this assumption in mind.

(1)   a. in-

on *adjectives*: inaccurate, inappropriate, inartistic, incoherent, incorrect, indifferent, ineffective, infertile, inhumane, inorganic, insane, intemperate, invariable, involuntary

on *nouns*: indecorum, indigestion, inefficacy, inexperience, inutility

on *bound bases*: inane, incognito, incommunicado, inept, inert, innocent, inoxia

b. un-

on *adjectives*: unable, unactorish, unbandaged, unbegrudging, uncatlike, un-devout, unemotionless, unfair, unfishy, unghosted, ungreen, unimpressive, unlevel, unmanifest, unorthodox, unpoisonable, un-rebuilt

on *nouns*: unbelief, unburger, unconcern, undeath, unhero, un-tundra, un-chicken, unchurch, uncircumcision, un-commercial, uncorrection

on *verbs*: unbelt, unbraid, uncheck, undecorate, unenter, unfold, unglue, unharness, unimagine, unlearn, unleash, unpeel, unpry, un-relax

c. non-

on *adjectives*: non-anxious, nonartsy, nonbasic, noncelibate, non-deceptive, non-editorial, non-fearful, non-geeky, nonimpaired, non-kosher, non-manual, non-palatal, nonrandomized, nonsanitary, non-soulful

on *nouns*: non-astronaut, non-baseball, noncatch, nonconformity, non-dancer, nonfeminists, nonguest, nonhighway, non-latino, non-marriage, nonnun, non-peanut, non-question, nonresident, non-speech

d. dis-

on *adjectives*: disconjugate, dishistorical, dishonest, disloyal, disordinal, displastic, dissimilar, distemperate

on *nouns*: disanalogy, disarray, disbenefit, disbelief, discomfort, discontinuum, disequilibrium, disharmony, disidentity, disorder, disquiet, disrespect, distaste, distolerance, disunion

on *verbs*: disavow, disband, disengage, disinherit, dislocate, dislodge, dislove, dismount, disoblige, dispossess, dispraise, disqualify, disreport, dissave, disthrone, disunite, disvalue

on *bound bases*: discarnate, discrepancy, dispel, dissent, disphonia, distort, distract

e. de-

on *verbs*: deacidify, decaffeinate, decarbonize, decommit, de-erotify, de-fry, deglamorize, de-merge, demodulate, demythify, depenalize, deracinate, dereify, desaturate

on *nouns*: debarb, de-bling, debulk, decrud, defat, defrock, degender, delead, demoss, depretzel, desilk, dethrone, detoad *on bound bases*: deflect, deflate, deplenish, deplete, deport, depose, deprive, detract, devolve

f. a- (*with its allomorph* an-)

on adjectives: acaucasian, acultural, adeictic, anestrous, arhetorical, asemantic, apolar, aseismic, asexual, athematic, acephalous

on bound bases: agenic, aphelic, acephal, amorphous, anaemia, anarchic, anomic

g. mis-

on verbs: misact, misallocate, misbehave, misbutton, miscall, misclassify, misdefine, misestimate, misfuel, mishandle, mishit, misinvest, mislead, misname, mispredict, misreport, misscore, mis-tally, mistype, misu[z]e, misvote

on nouns: misadventure, misanalogy, misbelief, misbirth, mischance, misconceit, misconduct, misdeed, misfortune, misjustice, mistruth, misu[s]e

on bound bases: misanthrope, miscreance, misfeasance, misnomer, misogyny

h. mal-

on adjectives: maladjusted, malaligned, malcontent, maleducated, malgoverned, mal-hygienic, malplaced

on verbs: malabsorb, malform, malnourish, maltreat

on nouns: malfunction, mal-intent, malnutrition, malodor, malunion

on bound bases: malediction, malevolence, malversation

i. -less

on nouns: ageless, airless, antless, batteryless, bosomless, captionless, dairyless, flangeless, hasteless, ladderless, mooseless, pastorless, roseless, secretless, tableless, visionless

on verbs: doteless, resistless, quenchless

on bound bases: feckless, gormless, reckless

There is an orthographic variant of *dis-*, *dys-*, which is strictly a neoclassical element and which is used mainly on Greek bases, mostly in the area of medicine. Examples include *dysarthia, dysfunction, dysgraphic, dyslexia, dyspeptic, dysplasia, dysrhythmia, dystrophy.*

Of the affixes that we consider in this chapter, only *un-*, *mis-*, and *-less* are native in origin. The prefix *mis-* is a difficult case, however, as it is both native and non-native in origin. Old English had many forms with this element, to which later some French loans with the corresponding French prefix were added. How these French forms influenced the later development of the prefix is unclear.

Apart from *un-*, *mis-*, and *-less* all other negative affixes are non-native. The prefixal negatives almost always attach to more than one category of base. Only *a-* is restricted to a single category, adjective. The prefixes *un-*, *dis-*, and *mal-* all attach to all three lexical categories, *in-* and *non-* to adjectives and nouns, *de-*, *mis-*, and *-less* to verbs and nouns. With the exception of *de-*, the other prefixes usually do not change category, but occasional category changes with *dis-* (*disrobe*) and *un-* (*unbosom, unearth*) can be found. Nouns negated with *un-* are sometimes used, adverbially modified as in (2a–c), as premodifiers, occasionally even predicatively as in (2d), and could thus be argued to have become adjectives.

(2) a. *Backpacker 1994*: the most **unbackcountry** part of the Florida trail

  b. *San Francisco Chronicle 1993*: Admittedly the goal is a notoriously **un-Berkeley** one: profit.

  c. *Esquire 2000*: A most **un-Boomer** sentiment, indeed.

  d. *The Big Lebowski 1998*: Come on. You're being very **unDude**.

Like *un-*, *non-* also sometimes appears to form adjectives, or at least nominal-premodifiers, from nouns:

(3) *CNN_SunMorn 2006:* So you might have a candy, for example, that is processed on a machinery that had peanuts on it right before they manufactured your **non-peanut** candy, or vice versa.

  San Francisco Chronicle 2002: From Hollywood, visitors can easily take a 20-minute train ride to Universal Studios or get in the car and visit Beverly Hills, about 25 painless, **non-highway** minutes away.

The negative prefixes *in-*, *mis-*, and *mal-* appear to be uniformly non-category-changing.

Of the negative prefixes, only *a-* is found with some frequency on bound bases. This is not surprising, as many of the words found with this affix were borrowed directly from the classical languages. The suffixes *in-*, *de-*, *dis-*, *mis-*, and *mal-* are sometimes found on bound bases, although it seems safe to say that these have come into English as borrowings and are not productively derived in contemporary English. It is thus doubtful that native speakers perceive the *in-* in *innocent*, the *de-* in *detract*, the *dis-* in *distort*, or the *mal-* in *malediction* as being prefixes at all, or as being the same prefixes as found in *intolerable, destabilize, disable,* or *maltreat*. One obvious difference is the fact that the former forms are not so easily segmented, since they involve bound bases, whose meaning is not easily recoverable (*-nocent, -tract, -tort*), or show a phonology different from that of the productive prefix (e.g. unstressed versus secondarily stressed: *detráct* versus *dèstábilize*).

All of these prefixes can be found on non-native bases, *in-*, *a-*, and *mal-* exclusively so. Only a small minority of bases found with *dis-* are native (*disbelief, disbelieve, disband, disbond, dishear, dishearten, dislike, dislove, disown, disfathered*). Note that the last of these is to be found in COCA but not in the *OED*, suggesting that it is still marginally possible to coin new *dis-* words on native bases. The remaining negative prefixes are indifferent to the origin of their bases, being formed with equal ease on native or non-native bases.

Of all negative affixes, only *-less* is suffixal. It is category-changing, forming adjectives largely from nouns. We do, however, occasionally find both morphemes on bases of other categories. The suffix *-less*, for example, is found on several bases that seem unequivocally to be verb stems:

(4) *Psychology Today 1996*: We need a clearinghouse for grown-ups who want to put themselves up for adoption—there are many of them but I've seen only grief for everyone when men kick their own children out of the nest and replace them with some **doteless** damsel.

Field and Stream 1995: Men may never have been killed by these flies as they have been by the fever-carrying mosquitoes of Southern latitudes, but the poisonous afteraffects [sic] of the gnat's sting produce a **resistless** drowsiness amounting to stupor, or coma, and is very slow to work off.

National Review 2001: The great advertising industry has helped by producing a **quenchless** flow of effective, if sometimes crude, propaganda.

In the words *feckless*, *gormless*, and *reckless*, the suffix is found with three native bases that might conceivably be analysed as bound, although their status is unclear. The bases *gorm* and *reck* were historically or dialectally free morphemes, but arguably are no longer so in contemporary English, and *feck* is conjectured by the *OED* to be either a clipping of *effeck*, an aphetic pronunciation of *effect*, or a backformation from *feckless*.

17.2.2 Phonological and orthographic properties

Of the negative affixes, *in-*, *a-*, and arguably *un-* exhibit allomorphy. The prefix *in-* undergoes assimilation to the point of articulation of a following stop or nasal, and is deleted before liquid-initial bases, without gemination (see Chapter 9). Example (5) illustrates these effects.

(5) inalienable   /ɪnˈeɪliənəbl/

  implausible   /ɪmˈplɔːzəbl ‖ ɪmˈplɑːzəbl/

  immortal   /ɪˈmɔːtl ‖ ɪˈmɔːrtl/

  intolerable   /ɪnˈtɒlərəbl ‖ ɪnˈtɑːlərəbl/

  innumerable   /ɪˈnjuːmərəbl ‖ ɪˈnuːmərəbl/

  incongruous   /ɪŋˈkɒŋgruəs ‖ ɪŋˈkɑːŋgruəs/

  irrational   /ɪˈræʃnəl/

  illegal   /ɪˈliːgl/

The assimilation is orthographically sanctioned—except for <n> pronounced /ŋ/ before velars—and is largely automatic (see Chapter 9). However, we find a few instances in COCA such as *inbalance, inbearable, inbelievable, inperfections, inpracticable* which suggest that the process may not be fully automatic. In these instances, there is an alternative explanation in an <n> for <m> typographical error.

The prefix *in-* occasionally attracts stress, but this does not seem to be a systematic process. We find stress on the prefix in such words as *ínfidel, íngrate, ínnocent, ínclement* (although Wells (2008) considers this pronunciation incorrect), *ínfinite, ímpotent*, and *ínvalid* (when it means 'ill', but not when it means 'not valid'). Jespersen (1917: 139) mentions *impious* as another word in which the prefix has attracted stress, but this pronunciation is becoming less common in BrE according to Wells (2008), and is not found in NAmE. Notably, stress on the prefix is often accompanied by semantic opacity, as in *impotent, infamous*, and *invalid*, or happens with bound bases (e.g. *infidel*).

The prefix *a-* has an allomorph *an-* which appears before bases that are vowel-initial or that begin with /h/. The selection of the allomorph is somewhat variable (across and within types) preceding /h/.

(6)   a. *before vowel initial bases*: anemia, anerobic, anesthesia, analphabetic, anastigmatic, anechoic, anencephalic, anorexia, anorgasmia, anovulant, anoxia, anuria

　　　b. *before bases beginning with* /h/: anharmonic, anhedral, anhedonia, anhydride, anhydrous (*but cf.* ahistorical ~ anhistorical)

　　　c. *before consonant initial bases*: abiotic, acalculia, achromatic, agraphia, akinesia, alogical, amitotic, amoral, aperiodic, apolitical, asexual, asocial, asymmetry, asymptomatic, atheism, azoic

The *a-* allomorph is usually pronounced /eɪ/ (*abiotic, achromatic, asexual*), but is occasionally pronounced /æ/ (*apathy, asymptote*, *asphyxiate) or reduced to /ə/ (*anomaly, amorphous, aphasia*, *asphyxiate). The distinction in pronunciation is not entirely predictable, but it does seem to depend to some extent on the degree to which the form has been lexicalized, with a higher degree of lexicalization correlating with reduction of the vowel. The form *an-* is always /æn/.

The prefix *un-* is orthographically invariant, but at least in rapid, informal speech can undergo assimilation of /n/ to the point of articulation of a following stop. See Chapter 9 for details.

The remaining negative and privative affixes are largely invariant, apart from two phenomena. There are a number of forms like *deport, depose, deprive, detract, devolve* that have no secondary stress on <de>. In fact, it is not even clear whether these forms are morphologically complex as their meaning cannot be derived on the basis of the would-be prefix and the base. Second, there is a small handful of forms with *dis-* that take stress on the prefix, rather than on the base: *disparate, dissonant, discord, discount, disjunct, dissolute, dissident, dissipate*. It is not clear, however, that there is anything systematic about this stress shift, especially since we, again, have to deal with bound bases and semantic opacity in most cases. In a few cases (e.g. *discord*) it may be a matter of the sort of stress shift we find with other Latinate noun–verb pairs (e.g. ʹpermit_N versus perʹmit_V), but this does not account for all of the cases.

17.2.3 Productivity

It is usually said that of the negative prefixes *in-*, *un-*, *a-*, *dis-*, and *non-* only *un-* and *non-* are robustly productive in contemporary English. Bauer and Huddleston (2002: 1688), for example, echo earlier literature (e.g. Jespersen 1917; Zimmer 1964) in saying that 'Negative *in-* is no longer productive, while *a-* and *dis-* are now rarely used to create new words.' The corpora suggest that this is not quite right, however. While it is certainly true that *un-* and *non-* are the most productive of this cohort of affixes, it is not entirely clear that *in-*, *a-*, and *dis-* are completely unproductive. This productivity is shown in new words illustrating the use of *in-* (7a), words where we find *in-* where some other allomorph might be expected (7b), and words where we find *in-* even though a different negative prefix is established (7c).

(7) a. *new words*

    immedical, inactual, inadult, inattentional, incompoundable, inconservative, indescriptible, indominable, inexorcizable, inexplicatable, inextractable, injuvenile, intesticular

  b. *words with an unexpected allomorph*

    inbalance, inbearable, inbelievable, inperfections, inpracticable, inprecision, inprescribable

  c. *words where another prefix is established*

    inbalance, inbearable, inbelievable, inconservative, incordial, indisciplined, induplicable, inerect, inesthetisable, infungibility (*no infungible in* OED), ingovernability (*no ingovernable in* OED), inintelligent, inobjective, inspecific, insupportive, immorbid, impleasant, irreal, irrelational, irrhythmic, incertainty (*last* OED *attestation 1792*), imprompt (*last* OED *attestation 1759*)

Although Zimmer (1964) claims that *a-* is unproductive in contemporary English, and Bauer (1983: 218) that the affix is only 'marginally productive', we find to the contrary that this prefix is still surprisingly productive in specific registers like medical or academic writing. Indeed we find quite a few forms in *a-* or *an-* in COCA that either do not occur in the *OED* or were last attested in the seventeenth or eighteenth centuries, suggesting them to be novel coinages in their recent appearances:

(8) a. abiotrophic, acaucasian, achronic, acontextual, acultural, adeictic, adimensional, agametic, agenic, ageotropic, aglycal, alanate, amelanotic, ameloblastic, amenorrheic, amillennial, amodal, amotivational, anarchival, anestrous, anhedonistic, anhepatic, anhydrobiotic, anhypothetical, anisogamic, anisogamous, anparasitaemic, apoetic,

areligious, arhetorical, arrhythmogenic, asectic, asemantic, astereotypical, astrategic, ateleological, athermal, avenal, averbal

b. *Style 1990*: The male's "castration anxiety" is just as "**anhypothetical**" […] a hypothesis as the woman's "penis envy."

Houston Chronicle 1999: The pope and his lieutenants emphasize that their millennium program is not done with an eye toward the apocalypse or Jesus' second coming. Catholic "**amillennial**" teaching, they say, is that the end of time is a historical process that has already begun.

Good Housekeeping 2008: But not all melanomas conform. One type, **amelanotic** melanoma, for example, has no brown or black.

The prefix *dis-* is at least marginally productive on bases of all kinds (contrary to, e.g., Zimmer 1964). We find apparent new formations with *dis-* such as those in (9) from COCA:

(9) a. *on adjectives*: disconjugate, dishistorical, disordinal, displastic, discheerful, dis-aggrieved, disalienated, disfathered, disglobalized, disnarrated, disorbited, disshelved, distopic

on nouns: discensus, disidentity, distolerance, disbond, disgodding, disrealness

on verbs: dis-align, disattend, discomplicate, disconstrue, dis-elect, disenroll, disenthrall, disimpact, dispray, dissanction, disadjectivize

b. *Art Bulletin 1994*: In terms of its qualities of displacedness, dispersal, and distribution, however, networked history might more appropriately be called **dishistorical**.

American Studies International 1993: Only by the play of **discensus**—not consensus—can we anticipate change and live together heterogeneously?

Atlantic Monthly 1997: a taxi took him … to Posse Motors, where lax salesmen drifted like **disorbited** satellites and where he bought a second hand Cadillac.

PBS Newshour 1996: It unelected Bill Clinton's Democrats in 1994, it elected a Republican Congress. It's about to **dis-elect** a Republican Congress in '96.

Although the three prefixes already discussed are generally more productive than might have been thought, it is nevertheless quite clear that the most productive of the negative prefixes are *un-* and *non-*. *Un-* is the default negative prefix for adjectives and for verbs that have the requisite semantic characteristics to give rise to a reversative reading (see Section 17.3.2). We find *un-* used on a wide range of monomorphemic adjectives, including ones which are themselves negative in tone (*unsordid, unpoor, unugly*) and ones that have obvious monomorphemic antonyms (*unrich, unlarge, unheavy*); see Section 17.3.5 for further discussion. It is especially productive on adjectival participles of various sorts and on adjectives derived with such suffixes as *-able, -ous, -ic, -al*, and *-ive*. *Non-* is also fully productive on adjectives, and is the preferred negative prefix on nouns.

What is perhaps surprising, however, is the degree to which *un-* has become productive on nominal bases. This is pointed out by Horn (2002), and is corroborated by the data we find in COCA. A few of these are item-familiar (*unbirthday*, *unperson*), but quite a few are novel forms.

(10) un-advice, un-ass, unbachelor, un-baguettes, unbirthday, unblessings, un-boomer, un-brat, un-car, un-chicken, unchurch, uncircumcision, un-commercials, uncorrection, undeath, undiet, undinner, un-difference, un-diva, undude, unevent, unexistencehood, un-fact, unfaith, unfreedom, ungame, unhealth, unhero, un-hollywood, unlife, unlogic, un-music, unperson, unquality, unrock'n'roll, unsleepover, unsuccess, unsun, unsystem, un-tundra, un-turkeys, unveracity, un-war

As pointed out in Section 17.2.1, some of these appear in the corpus functioning as premodifiers, allowing for the interpretation that *un-* can be category-changing when attached to a noun.

Un- also exhibits a small degree of productivity with compound and phrasal bases. We find several examples like those in (11).

(11) unblockbusterish, un-boondocksy, uncomputer-savvy, undoublespace, un-bad-guy-like, un-deep-friable, undinosaur-looking, un-fall-in-love, un-hello-kitty-like

The privatives *de-* and *-less* are all highly productive in contemporary English. *De-* regularly forms new verbs both from nominal bases and verbal bases, especially those derived with the suffixes *-ize* (*dehazardize*, *depenalize*) and *-ify* (*de-erotify*, *denitrify*), but also with verbs in *-ate* (*deaerate*, *degranulate*), and less frequently with underived verbs (*deblur*, *declutch*). The suffix *-less* attaches to nouns with great freedom; only rare examples can be found formed on verbs.

Both of the pejorative prefixes exhibit some degree of productivity. The prefix *mis-* is probably the more productive of the two, with the following examples appearing in COCA that are not recorded in the *OED*.

(12) a. mis-activate, misarticulate, misassemble, misbalance, misbase, mis-beginnings, miscarved, miscognition, misconfusion, miscover, miscrawl, misdropped, misflying, misforgotten, misfuel, misgrab, misgruntlement, misgust, misintuit, misjustice, mismix, misnavigate, misnomial, mis-overheard, misplot, mispreread, mis-raise, misreputation, misshipment, mis-species, mis-spin, mis-story, mis-sync, misunderattribute, misunderestimate, miswant

  b. *CNN_Sonya 1993*: But then we get to the justice system, and you and I first met many years ago dealing with the **misjustice** of the justice system with your own daughter, Dominick.

  Psychology Today 2002: In reality, note Gilbert and his colleague Timothy Wilson, Ph.D., of the University of Virginia, we often "**miswant**." People who dream of a holiday on a deserted tropical island may in fact be disappointed when they see "how much they require daily structure, intellectual stimulation or regular infusions of Pop Tarts."

We find apparently novel formations on nouns (*misjustice, mis-story*), and verbs (*miswant, miscarved, miscovered*). The existence of complex formations like *mispreread* and *misunderat-tribute* shows that *mis-* is also productive before other prefixes.

There are also a few apparently novel forms with the prefix *mal-*, although not nearly as many as we find with *mis-*, but perhaps because this prefix in general exhibits fewer types in COCA than the others.

(13)   a.   malaligned, malapportion, malgoverned, mal-hygienic, malknotted, malplaced, mal-socialized, malunited, maldigestion, mal-intent, malplacement, malunion

   b.   *Internet Journal of Gastroenterology 2007*: Infection in humans arouse from ingesting water plants (eg. wild watercress) with metacercaria in **mal-hygienic** conditions.

   Kenyon Review 1998: It limps when it walks, one leg bent out at an angle, like a **malplaced** cane.

   Orthopoedic Nursing 2006: Acute compartment syndrome, infection, and **malunion** or nonunion of a fracture can lead to loss of a limb or impaired limb functioning.

17.3   SEMANTIC CONSIDERATIONS

17.3.1   Types of negativity

In order to understand the semantic range of this cohort of affixes, we must first clarify some terms. At various points in this chapter we have used terms like 'negative', 'reversative', 'priva-tive', and 'pejorative' in an intuitive way. Here we first try to make these terms precise and add some other necessary terminology, and then examine the meanings of complex formations in light of them.

We can use the general term 'negative' as a default for readings that are neither reversative nor privative nor pejorative, but in some cases it will be useful to further distinguish among several sorts of negativity. Before turning to these distinctions we need to mention a negative interpretation that is very similar to clausal negation. This type of negation can only be expressed by a subset of verbs prefixed with *dis-*, namely those expressing psychological states (e.g. *disagree, dislike, disobey*).

Of the other types of negation, the contrast between so-called 'contrary' and 'contradic-tory' negatives is well-described in the literature (Jespersen 1917; Zimmer 1964; Horn 1989). The distinction is predicated on the relation obtaining between the negative 'not-X' and its corresponding positive 'X'. In contrary negatives 'X' and 'not-X' are terminal points on a gradable scale, such that there are conceivable points between them. For example, between *happy* and *unhappy* there are intermediate states such that someone can be neither *happy* nor *unhappy*. With contradictory negation, something is either 'X' or 'not-X'; there is, for example, no intermediate state between *animate* and *inanimate* or between *attached* and *unattached*. Contrary and contradictory negative readings correlate with the gradability of their bases; to the extent that we can conceive of a given base as denoting a scale, a contrary reading will be possible. If the two polar opposites exhaust all possibilities, the negation will be contradictory.

It may be worth digressing for a moment to note the difficulty in determining unequivocally whether a given adjective is gradable or not (see Chapters 6 and 14 for further discussion). Judgements on gradability are notoriously labile, differing from speaker to speaker, and from one context to another. Another problem is that even adjectives that would seem to be clearly ungradable frequently have possible interpretations that are gradable. This phenomenon is also known under the label of coercion (see Chapter 6.2, Chapter 25), that is the contextual interpretation of an expression that would otherwise not show this type of polysemy (Swart 2011). This said, it is possible that readers will sometimes disagree with our judgements on whether a given word has a contrary or contradictory reading.

To the relatively well-known distinction between contrary and contradictory negation, we might add two further distinctions. One of them will be useful in describing the semantics of the negative affix *a-*. That is, there is a mode of negation which presupposes a scale or a pair of polar opposites, but in which what is denoted is not one pole in the opposition or one part of the scale, but the complete irrelevance of the scale or polar opposition in question. In this kind of negation what is highlighted is a semantic space entirely external to the scale. So something which is *amelodic* is neither *melodic* nor *unmelodic* (or anything in between), but is outside the realm of melody. For lack of an established term we will call this sort of negation SCALE-EXTERNAL NEGATION.

The other term that we will need to add is 'stereotype negation'. In cases of STEREOTYPE NEGATION, a noun is taken to denote a bundle of characteristics or qualities {x, y, z, ... }. When certain affixes are attached, what is negated is not the meaning of the noun as a whole, but a number of its semantic characteristics or qualities. The resulting derivative still generally denotes the same entity or something close to it, but one that is missing several key characteristics. In effect, the noun denotes a non-stereotypical exemplar of its category. We will return to this kind of negation below when we discuss *non-* and *un-* on nominal bases.

We will use the term REVERSATIVE for verbs like *untie* which can be roughly paraphrased as 'reverse the action of *tying*'. 'Reversative' is not a primitive notion, however. Rather, for verbs whose meaning implies some sort of result, reversatives occur when an affix negates the result, as has been pointed out by Marchand (1969) and Horn (1989, 2002). So with a verb like *zip* whose result is that the object is 'zipped', a negative prefix will denote an action such that the endpoint is an object which is 'not-zipped'. The derived verb is thus interpreted as a reversal of the action.

The term PRIVATIVE is used for verbs like *debug* or *demilitarize*, or adjectives like *shoeless*. So at the core of a privative based on 'X', we have 'no X'. With an affix whose output category is verb, the output normally has both a causative and a negative meaning, even though the base of the verb does not have that causative meaning. The causative sense typically accompanies the negative meaning 'no X', giving 'cause to be no X'. So to *debug* is to cause there to be no bugs, to *demilitarize* is to cause there to be no military. The result is a reading which implies removal. Clearly, with verbal bases derived with *-ize, -ify*, or *-ate*, the causative sense may already be supplied by the suffix. With *-less*, a sense of absence or loss is implied; so *shoeless* denotes the absence or lack of shoes.

We turn finally to pejoratives, which arguably lie somewhere between the morphology of negation and evaluative morphology (see Chapter 18). The pejoratives we are considering here are morphemes like *mal-* or *mis-*, in which a negative evaluation is associated with the base. For a base X, such forms can be paraphrased as 'X wrongly or badly'. What is targeted by the negative in such cases is the manner in which an action is done.

Let us summarize the above theoretical considerations by listing the different semantic categories and their semantic interpretation. The brackets contain the argument on which negation operates, 'X' stands for the denotation of the base and 'x, y, z' for specific properties of X.

- Reversative: NEG [result]
- Privative: NEG [existence of X]
- Negative: NEG [X]

  Contrary: intermediate states possible between X and not X
  Contradictory: no intermediate states between X and not X
  Scale external: NEG [scale defined by X]
  Stereotype negation: X [x, NEG-y, NEG-z, ...]

- Pejorative: NEG [manner]

17.3.2   Ranges of meaning

What is most interesting to note with the cohort of negative affixes is that they do not carve up the semantic nuances of negation in any neat one-to-one fashion. While a few of the affixes appear to have more or less fixed semantic content, and a few have a tendency towards one reading or another, the majority of them are polysemous, with specific readings depending on the nature of the base, the degree of lexicalization, and in novel forms often on the context in which a given form is used. In other words, for some affixes, multiple readings are available and result from the interaction of a general affixal negative meaning 'not' with the semantic composition of a base. We summarize the correlations of possible readings with affixes in Table 17.2.

Table 17.2 Distribution of readings

Base Category	Category change	Negative		stereotype negation	scale extension	Reversative	Privative	Pejorative
		contrary	contradictory					
Adjective								
in-		✓	✓					
un-		✓	✓					
non-		✓	✓					
dis-		✓	✓					
a(n)-		✓	✓		✓		✓	
mal-								✓
Noun								
in-	sometimes A or V	(✓)						
un-	sometimes A	✓		✓			✓	
non-				✓			✓	
dis-							✓	
de-	V						✓	
mis-								✓
mal-								✓
-less	A						✓	
-free	A						✓	
Verb								
un-						✓	✓	
dis-		(✓)				✓	✓	
de-						✓	✓	
mis-								✓
mal-								✓

We begin with the affixes that appear to be relatively fixed in meaning. Among these are the pejoratives *mis-*, and *mal-*, which seem to be used almost exclusively in this reading. With the exception of a couple of forms to be found in COCA (*mislike*, used in context to mean 'dislike'; *misfortunate*, used in context to mean 'unfortunate'), *mis-*, and *mal-* consistently give a negative evaluation of manner, that is, they add meanings like 'wrongly, mistakenly, badly' to the bases they attach to.

Also quite fixed in meaning is the suffix *-less*. It is consistently privative in interpretation, but often with an evaluative component, especially if compared with corresponding compounds with *free* as the head (Górska 1994; Slotkin 1990). For example, although both *salt-less* and *salt-free* denote the absence of salt, the former marks that the absence of salt is a negative or at best neutral quality, whereas the latter generally suggests that the absence of salt is something desirable. There are some instances, however, where the two rival forms seem all but identical in force, as the examples in (14) suggest:

(14) *New York Times 2007*: Kathleen Marshall directs and choreographs a **charisma-free** ensemble, whose leads (Max Crumm and Laura Osnes) were cast via reality television (2:15).

Wolf at the Door 2006: "Drank three pints straight from the bags before I was fit company again," the **charismaless** wonder said, peppering his delivery with a few smug chuckles. [...]

At best *charisma-free* conveys a slightly ironic edge that *charismaless* lacks, but the difference is very small.

For the remaining affixes, it is usually the case that the wider the range of bases to which an affix can attach, the wider the range of readings that it is compatible with. For example, *in-* occurs almost exclusively with adjectival bases, there being only a few examples of *in-* on nouns. We find that *in-* is consistently negative in force, either contrary or contradictory depending on the gradability of its base. For example, *inappropriate* or *incompatible* are contraries, it being possible for things to be more or less *inappropriate* or *incompatible*. But *inanimate* and *inexact* are contradictory (for us, with the usual caveats). A very large proportion of *in-* words are high-frequency and item-familiar, and with these characteristics, as might be expected, we often find lexicalization. For example, *indifferent* does not mean 'not different' but rather 'neutral', and *inhuman* does not mean 'not human', but 'cruel'.

The prefix *a-* is also confined to adjectives and bound bases, covering most of the range of negative readings (contrary, contradictory, and scale external), with a few examples of privatives also attested:

(15) a. *contrary*

Journal of Sports Behavior 2009: First, it may be that the same behavior is seen as equally aggressive when exhibited by women or men but that the women are punished more because, for women, the act is **astereotypical**.

b. *contradictory*

Symposium 1999: However, Todorov also demands a non-allegorical, **apoetic** reading of the text, which means that fairy tales are necessarily and unfortunately excluded from the genre, instead classified as the "merveilleux" (59).

c. *scale external*

Raritan 1990: Viewed this way, the inversions of carnival where kings and paupers exchange clothes, the subversions of jokes where, say, the well-dressed lady slips on a banana peel, and the reversions from self-conscious and constrained adulthood to playful or spontaneous childhood that are prominent in texts like Alice in Wonderland let us abandon, imaginatively at any rate, conventional social differences for participation in delightfully "real" human unions or communions that are **acultural** and **ahistorical** in nature.

d. *privative*

Fantasy & Science Fiction 2005: The Blemmye had no head; he was **acephalous**.

It would appear that the default affix for forming scale-external negatives from adjectives is *a-*, but *a-* is not restricted to this sense.

Also relatively limited in scope is *de-*. Much of the semantic range of this prefix can be attributed to its formal characteristics—namely that it attaches to nouns or verbs and uniformly derives verbs. The vast majority of words derived with *de-* are either privative or reversative in force. On nouns, we find almost exclusively privative forms, as these COCA examples illustrate:

(16) *Prevention 2007*: It significantly helps to **degunk** her pores, which, she says, "started looking bigger with age."

US News and World Report 1993: It costs between $350 and $1,800—depending on helicopter flight time—to **dehorn** a single rhino, and the procedure has to be repeated every three years as the horn regrows.

This is especially consistent where the nouns are concrete, count nouns. Interestingly, different arguments can be referenced. While with most formations the entity denoted by the base is the entity that is removed, there are cases where the source can be referenced, instead of the object. Thus, *dethrone* means 'remove from the throne', not 'remove the throne' (cf. also *decart, debus*).

On verbal bases, either reversatives or privatives may be found, although the distinction between the two is sometimes hard to make. If the verbal base is itself derived from a noun (as in *decarbonize, dechlorinate*), we often find the same sort of privative reading that we find on purely nominal bases. Where the verbal base is derived from an adjective, the reversative meaning is dominant:

(17)   a. *privative*

      ABC_Special 1994: On the other hand, if you take decaffeinated coffee, sometimes the process to **decaffeinate** it has exposed the coffee to a chemical that isn't good for you.

      Popular Mechanics 2009: Mechanical, chemical and thermal energy act together in your central air-conditioning system to cool and **dehumidify** indoor air.

    b. *reversative*

      Washington Post 2008: Following the adoption of a new constitution in 2005 and the first multiparty elections in decades, Congo is aiming to **decentralize** government from the capital of Kinshasa to newly elected legislatures in 11 provinces.

      Review of Contemporary Fiction 2006: If the great sorcerer showed them under the title, "How to **de-erotify** the erotic object," they would be the epitome of what not to do.

For some verbs, either interpretation is plausible: for example, to *dechlorinate* can equally well be construed as meaning 'remove the chlorine from' or 'reverse the process of chlorinating'.

The prefix *non-* attaches productively to both adjectives and nouns. On adjectives it shows both contrary and contradictory negative readings:

(18)   a. *contrary*

      Children's Digest 2002: There are different types of fish that will be best suited for the type of tank you choose. Choose from the four main categories of freshwater fish: goldfish, **non-aggressive**, semi-aggressive, or aggressive.

      CNN_LiveSun 2003: I considered it but because my parents are divorced I took it very, very, very seriously and I've always said that if I was to be engaged that it would be a very **non-traditional** engagement and I would take a very long time.

    b. *contradictory*

      African Arts 1996: The same associations underlie the geometric designs and pictorial ideographs on both mnemonic devices like the lukasa and royal emblems in **non-beaded** media such as wood, metal, painting, pottery, and weaving.

Where *non-* occurs on nouns, we most frequently get a general negative reading, the distinction between contrary and contradictory being neutralized, as nouns are not gradable or scalar:

(19)   *Denver Post 2005*: Myers wears a green Pirates cap and is the only **non-coach** allowed on the St. Mary's sideline during games.

    Houston Chronicle 1995: Composed of six dentists and six **non-dentists**, the committee figures to play an important role as the Health Department tries to improve its much-criticized system of detecting fraud and abuse in the state's Medicaid dental program.

A *non-coach* is someone who is not a coach, a *non-dentist* someone who is not a dentist.

Contrasting with examples like these, we also sometimes find *non-* used as a stereotype negator. A lexicalized example is the word *non-person*, which denotes someone who is indeed a person but is not acknowledged as a person, or is not treated fully as a person. Algeo (1971: 92) offers the example of *nonbook*, which is intended to denote the sort of coffee-table book that has lots of pictures, not much text, and is meant to be flipped through, rather than read cover-to-cover. Non-lexicalized examples of stereotype negating *non-* are not too difficult to find, as the examples from COCA in (20) suggest:

(20)   *The Paris Review 1997*: The man in the tweed suit wore his hair clipped short, in a crew cut. It was a flat metallic color, a **non-color**, like his eyes.

   NPR_Weekend 1992: Well, he's not saying he has the answers. That's—that's what's so novel about this campaign. It's almost like a **non-campaign**. It—it's like we're running to get him on the ballot.

In the given context, a *non-color* is a colour, but one that lacks the vibrancy of a true colour. A *non-campaign* is a campaign, but one that is not characteristic in certain ways. As Algeo (1971) points out, *non-* words of this sort are frequently used with a disparaging tone.

As mentioned in Section 17.2, nominal *non-* words often occur in prenominal position, and in such cases we might argue that *non-* has had a category-changing function; where this occurs, the *non-* word can have a privative reading. We have in mind here forms like *non-fat*, as in *non-fat milk*, or *non-fish*, as in the example in (21):

(21)   *San Francisco Chronicle 2000*: My only regret with these **non-fish** sushi was the absence of two wonderful flavor elements: shiso, a fragrant relative of mint; and ume or Japanese plum, a tangy, pickled fruit paste that's delicious in sushi.

In cases such as these, the interpretation of the *non-* words is close to that of adjectives derived with *-less*, the difference being that whereas *-less* can evaluate the absence of the base negatively, *non-* is neutral in evaluation.

The affixes with the widest range of potential readings are *un-* and *dis-*, both of which attach to adjectival, nominal, and verbal bases. On adjectival bases, *un-* productively derives both contrary and contradictory negatives, but apparently not scale external readings. Although there are clearly many high frequency item-familiar forms among the *un-* words, we in general find less lexicalization than we find with *in-*, and the vast majority of forms are completely transparent in meaning. Examples like *unactorish, unbacked-up, unbeany, un-chain-store-afflicted, uncherrylike, unduckable, uneventual*, and so on, are easily found in the corpora (these from COCA). They are, not surprisingly, not recorded in the *OED*, and surely have no need to be, their meanings being so clearly compositional. Indeed it is hard to conceive of any derived adjective that could not potentially be negated with *un-*, even when lexicalized alternatives with *in-* are available; in COCA we find cases like *unaccessible, uncomplete, uncorrect, uneffective*, among many others for which there are well-established *in-* forms (see Section 17.3.4 for further discussion). Similarly, there are few underived adjectives to which *un-* cannot be attached, even those adjectives that have clear mono-morphemic antonyms (*ungood* as opposed to *bad*), and those that have evaluatively nega-tive semantics (*unugly* as opposed to *unattractive*). Since the existence of forms like these has been a matter of controversy in the literature, we will explore this issue in detail in Section 17.3.5.

In contrast to *un-*, the prefix *dis-* occurs only infrequently on adjectival bases, producing either contrary or contradictory negatives, and as mentioned above, seems to be only slightly productive with this category of bases. We find examples in COCA like *displastic, dishistori-cal, disordinal, disconsonant, discontiguous, dishonest, disingenuous, disloyal, dissimilar, dissocial*, and *distemperate*. The first four of these are not recorded in the *OED*, and occur in medical or scholarly contexts.

It has been pointed out several times in the literature (Jespersen 1917; Zimmer 1964; Marchand 1969; Algeo 1971; Horn 2002), that *un-* and *dis-* adjectives frequently carry a depre-ciatory nuance that is absent with *non-*. Examples that are often given to support this claim are pairs like *unAmerican* as opposed to *non-American*, or *unprofessional* as opposed to *non-professional* (Horn 2002: 9). This appears to be the case from pairs like those above, but we have pointed out that *non-* can be quite depreciatory, when used as a stereotype negator (Algeo 1971). We will return to this topic in Section 17.3.5 and evaluate it in further depth there.

Dis- and *un-* also both occur on nominal bases. The prefix *dis-* generally expresses priva-tion. For example, *disanalogy* is privative, according to the *OED*, which defines it as 'want of analogy':

(22)   *Monist 1998*: Surprisingly perhaps, it does not follow from this concession that there is a radical **disanalogy** between divine creation and intrasubstantial causality.

We find a similar force in examples like *disfunction, disbelief, disaccord*, and *distrust*, all of which express the lack of what is denoted by their base.

The prefix *un-* can form privatives, but unlike *dis-*, it can also act as a stereotype nega-tor. Examples like *unfaith, unfreedom, unhealth*, and *unsuccess* seem to have the privative reading:

(23)   *Christian Century 1995*: I have sought for some years to find a theological dialogue where a serious methodological discussion is taking place about how to draw some line between faith and **unfaith**, between orthodoxy and heresy.

Anthropological Quarterly 2004: In a way, while the socalled real kin are re-assigning the kinship a new morality of humanitarianism beyond consanguinity, as in the case of Mr. Yu's daughters, the invocation of kinship relations is multiplying, reflecting the strained conditions of **unfreedom** under the paternalistic totalitarian regime of North Korea.

Southern Review 1999: The life had gone out of her red hair, and what should have been pale Irish skin was pasty, the picture of **unhealth**.

Lens of the World 1990: I disapproved heartily and wished them every sort of **unsuccess** if only they didn't drag me down with them.

In examples like *unchurch, undiet*, and *unsleepover party* on the other hand, *un-* has the force of a stereotype negator:

(24) *CNN_SunMorn 2006*: It's not the traditional place of worship [...] Deron Cloud, founder and pastor of the Soul Factory, called it the "**unchurch**".

   Shape 2000: She calls her new way of eating the "**undiet**" because it has no restrictions—and it and her weight loss have been lasting.

Clearly in some ways *unchurches* and *undiets* really are churches and diets, but they lack certain key characteristics of stereotypical ones.

Horn (2002: 30) rightly observes that in some cases, the *un-X* noun actually denotes something that is in fact not an X, but which nevertheless can be compared to X or considered in relation to X by virtue of sharing certain characteristics of X. Consider the example in (25):

(25) *Parenting 1999*: Host an "**unsleepover**" party: The guest comes dressed in pajamas and brings a sleeping bag to lounge around on, and the kids eat, play games, and watch a video while they munch popcorn. At around 9 P.M., the parents pick up their child, and everyone gets some sleep that night.

In the case of an *unsleepover*, we do not in fact have a sleepover party, as the children go home to sleep. But we do have many of the qualities that can be found in a stereotypical sleepover: wearing pajamas, bringing a sleeping bag, watching movies, and so on. *Un-cola* and *un-turkey* are other examples of this sort. As Horn points out, not just anything can be an *un-cola*; in order to be one, a product has to be at least functionally similar to a cola (e.g. something to drink, preferably sweet and fizzy).

We turn now to *un-* and *dis-* on verbal bases. It appears that *un-* and *dis-* produce similar readings where they attach to verbs that belong to the same semantic class; however, to some extent the two prefixes select different kinds of verbal bases. *Un-* is quite consistent in selecting for verbs that imply non-permanent results. The vast majority of these are straightforwardly causative in nature (26a), although a few can be found with both causative and inchoative senses as well (26b):

(26) a. unclip, uncompress, undelete, unentwine, unfix, ungarble, unhitch, unkennel, unmold, unname, unpersuade, unrelease, unsell

   b. untense, untwist, uncoil, uncurl, unfold

Whether the verbal base is purely causative or alternates between causative and inchoative depends largely on whether the action denoted is one in which external causation is necessary. Pure causatives presuppose external causation; verbs that alternate between the senses allow either internal or external causation. On bases such as those in (26), the *un-* verb is reversative in force, that is, denotes the negation of the result.

There are, however, at least some instances where the verbal base lends itself to a privative interpretation, or to an interpretation which could be either privative or reversative. Among these, Marchand (1969) cites *unsex* and *unvoice*, and to these we can add *unbridle, unblock, uncap, unchain, unclog, uncover, undress, unkink*, and a variety of others in which the base is denominal.

Interestingly, although *un-* typically does not attach either to verbal bases that are non-causative or to bases that denote results that are permanent, the prefixation of *un-* to such bases is not impossible; where it occurs it has the effect of coercing the verbal base to be semantically like the verbal bases that *un-* normally selects. That is, *un-* can take a stative, activity, or other kind of verb and force it into a causative/inchoative verb that implies a reversible result. Consider the examples in (27), where *un-* occurs on a stative verb (27a), a verb of perception (27b), and a verb whose result is normally taken to be non-reversible (27c):

(27) a. *stative verb*

   Iris 1997: From the broad window of the caf, the office buildings erupt. Bodies spill out in their gray and black suits. In one of her classes, she shows an avant-garde film. A hand is opened. Insects swarm out. She thinks of this now as the buildings **uninhabit**.

   b. *verb of perception*

   Cross Currents 2001: When hunger is understood as an acceptable reality in the politics of competing states, the conviction that hunger is intolerable is itself revolutionary. The attempt to **unimagine** its necessity in our present actions transcends and relativizes national commitments.

   c. *verb with non-reversible result*

   Bioscience 2005: This result was most surprising and unexpected, yet consistent with the hypothesis that ancestrally both sexes may have expressed thoracic horns in this species, and that females lost their horns by evolving mechanisms to **un-grow** them, rather than not growing them in the first place.

In the context above, to *uninhabit* is 'to become uninhabited', to *unimagine* is 'to remove from the imagination', and to *un-grow* is to reverse the process of growing. Horn (2002: 15) observes that such *un-* verbs always denote 'telic achievements', using the terminology of Vendlerian verbal classes, regardless of the class to which the base would normally belong.

It is also relatively common to find verbs like those in (28) in what Horn (2002: 16) calls counterfactual contexts, that is, contexts that cancel the seemingly anomalous interpretation of the verb:

(28)   *Fantasy & Science Fiction 2003*: And once you've seen it, you can never **unsee** it.

     CNN_Sonya 1993: The other big difference is once you have AIDS, you can't **unhave** it.

     Southwest Review 2007: She saw that she had hit a nerve and that there would be no way to **unhit** it.

The negative contexts in effect highlight the unreversibility of the implied result.

The prefix *dis-* frequently attaches to the same sort of verbs that *un-* favours: causative or causative/inchoative verbs that imply reversible results. The resulting derived verbs are reversative or sometimes indeterminate between reversative and privative readings. We find examples like the following:

(29)   disarm, disband, disbud, disconnect, discredit, disembed, disinfest, disinvite, disrobe, disthrone

Many of these are transparent in meaning, but quite a few are lexicalized, among them *discharge, disclose, discover, discredit, disgorge, disintegrate, dismantle*, and so on. Indeed, lexicalization seems more common with *dis-* verbs than with *un-* verbs.

Where *dis-* differs significantly from *un-* is that when it attaches to non-causative verbs, it generally results in either negative or pejorative verbs:

(30)   a. *negative*
      disaffirm, disagree, disallow, disapprove, disbelieve, disconfirm, discontinue, discount, disimprove, disincline, dislike, dislove, disobey, displease, dissatisfy, disuse

      b. *pejorative*
      discolor, disidentify, disinform, disremember, disvalue, disconstrue, dishear, dispray

In other words, although *dis-* sometimes attaches to verbal types other than causative/inchoative, affixation of this prefix does not have the effect of coercing these other verbal types to a causative/inchoative interpretation. Rather, it delivers either a simple negative or a pejorative reading, depending on the nature of the base verb.

17.3.3 Redundancy

It has been noted in the literature that the negative verb-forming affixes are sometimes used redundantly such that the sense of the bare base and the sense of the base with the negative affix are identical. Both Thomas (1983) and Horn (2002: 19) observe that this is the case for verbs like *unravel, unloose, unrip,* and *unthaw*. In addition to these examples, we find in COCA examples like *unpeel* and *unpry* which in context mean precisely the same thing as their bases:

(31)   *American Studies International 1997*: On a slanting stone lay a drowned man, naked, swollen, purple; clasping the fragment of a broken bush with a grip which death had so petrified that human strength could not **unloose** it...

   The Mercury Visions of Louis Daguerre 2006: Louis cracked an egg on the side of the plate and began to **unpeel** it.

   Sewanee Review 1998: It would take near an hour to **unthaw** the sand, which meant a shorter day for the brick crew, which meant they'd be grumpy at Ray and old Henry, the other hodcarrier.

Echoing Covington (1981: 34), Horn attributes this seemingly redundant interpretation to the propensity of reversative *un-* to return the base verb to what he characterizes as a state of entropy, that is, movement from a more marked state to a less marked one, for example, from closed to open, from frozen to thawed, and so on. If the verbal stem intrinsically denotes movement towards the state of entropy, the *un-* does not reverse the direction of movement, but reinforces it.

   As with *un-*, the affixes *de-* and *dis-* are sometimes found in redundant forms. For *de-*, Horn (2002: 20) gives such examples as *debone, dehusk, deworm,* and for *dis-, disannul,* and *dissever*. To these we can add *debar, degut, dehull, delimit, dedust, de-joint, dejuice, depulp, de-shell, de-skin,* and *de-stem,* all attested in COCA with the redundant meaning. It is worth noting that the bases to which *de-* attaches are sometimes ambiguous, having the capacity to mean both the action of putting in (what Horn calls goal-orientation) and the action of removing (source-orientation). It is likely in these cases that the affixation of *de-* is felt to disambiguate the base. As Horn (2002: 22) says, 'But when goal- and source-oriented readings are both plausible for a given base verb in combination with a given patient, the *un-* or *de-* verb will serve usefully and unambiguously to signal the source or entropic interpretation.'

   An alternative analysis in all of these cases is that *de-* is a class-changing prefix and that the bases are nouns. In some instances, conversion (*to skin*) and *de*-prefixation (*to deskin*) can operate on the same bases and give rise to synonymous forms, without there being any real redundancy.

   While Horn generally seems correct about the propensity of negative verbal affixes to signal a change of state moving towards entropy, we should probably see this as a tendency, and not a strict rule. Given the right context, it is quite possible for an *un-* verb to signal a change of state away from entropy, as we see in this example from COCA:

(32) *Deep Rising 1998*: FI[R]ST MATE We have a main frame meltdown!! CANTON Well **unmelt** it!!

Examples of either sort are relatively rare, however, and it does not seem possible to make a conclusive determination on this point.

17.3.4 Rivals

As Section 17.3.2 has shown, there is significant overlap in the functions of several of the negative prefixes. The prefixes *in-*, *un-*, *non-*, and *a-* all attach to adjectives, and *de-*, *un-*, and *dis-* all attach to verbs. Such clusters can be seen as cohorts of rival affixes, and the question therefore arises whether the existence of a form with one affix blocks the derivation of forms with the other affixes. Similarly, if we find doublets (or triplets or even multiples) with these affixes, we can ask whether consistent semantic contrasts can be found, such that each affix can be seen as specializing in a particular sort of negative semantics.

We can begin with blocking. It seems quite clear that there is little or no blocking to be found in these cohorts of affixes. While there certainly are established forms in which a particular prefix is associated with a particular base, and while native speakers often have a sense of which forms are prescriptively 'correct', we nevertheless frequently find novel or low-frequency formations with two or more rival prefixes. Kjellmer (2005: 158), for example, estimates that 17 per cent of the adjectives in the 57 million word Cobuild corpus he uses occur with more than one negative prefix. Looking at the negative prefixes on adjectival bases, we find sets like the following in COCA (not an exhaustive list):

(33)

	a-	*in-*	*non-*	*un-*
accessible		inaccessible	non-accessible	unaccessible
attentive		inattentive	non-attentive	unattentive
credible		incredible	non-credible	uncredible
obvious		inobvious	non-obvious	unobvious
plastic	aplastic		non-plastic	unplastic
poetic	apoetic		non-poetic	unpoetic
rational		irrational	non-rational	unrational
religious	areligious	irreligious	non-religious	unreligious

As for our second issue, whether there is a consistent semantic value that can be associated with each affix in sets like those above, we find ourselves at odds with the literature. Horn

(1989: 282–3) argues, for example, that *in-* is 'generally depreciatory', evaluative, and lexicalized, that *non-* tends not to be evaluative or depreciatory, and that *un-* stands somewhere in between the two. Similarly, Bauer and Huddleston (2002: 1689), while acknowedging that there is sometimes little difference between the affixes, nevertheless suggest that where pairs of *un-* and *non-* words exist, 'The forms with *non-* are emotively neutral and non-gradable, while those with *un-* have a wider range of meaning, so that they may convey criticism and gradability (allowing them to take such degree modifiers as *very, extremely,* etc.).' Hamawand (2009: 128) claims that synonymy of negatively prefixed forms is in fact impossible.

We, however, find the corpus data to be somewhat at odds with these characterizations. First, it is clear, as we have suggested above, that *non-* words can be either gradable or not, and either depreciatory or not, depending upon the base to which they are attached (see (18)).

Further, while it is true that there are sometimes clear distinctions among the words in each set, often this is not the case. For example, it appears that *inobvious, unobvious,* and *non-obvious* all mean more or less the same thing, namely 'not obvious'.

(34)   *Ploughshares 2002*: Basha folded herself into me. Everything about her seemed perfect just then: her cheeks, the way her mouth smooshed vowels, her new decadence, her pale body. She was emotionally **inobvious**.

Monist 1993: What these senses will tell us…is on occasion accurate enough as far as it goes, but will never get us beyond descriptions of a world of variety and change and obvious connections (ft. 54) to a description of that more significant, unified world of **unobvious** connections that tends to lie concealed (ft. 123).

Harvard Journal of Law and Public Policy 2002: Thus, sexually explicit websites get traffic through obvious and **non-obvious** ways, enhancing their vast reach.

We find a similar triplet of apparently synonymous negative forms in COCA with the words *inattentive, unattentive,* and *non-attentive.*

Where there are distinctions, these distinctions are not always to be attributed to the contribution of the affixes. For example, *unplastic, non-plastic,* and *aplastic* are all attested in COCA and have different meanings, but their differences appear to have more to do with the polysemy of the base *plastic* than with nuances of the prefixes:

(35)   *People 1992*: More important, Ross captivated a whole generation with her lush-lipped and decidedly **unplastic** beauty—here was someone worth snatching from the altar (or spiriting down to Bolivia, as in the 1969 megahit Butch Cassidy and the Sundance Kid).

USA Today 2005: He's also added some products made from **non-plastic** materials, including wooden furniture and fabric inflatables.

Ear, Nose and Throat Journal 1996: The external canal is hypoplastic, **aplastic**, or ends in a blind pouch with fistulous tracts leading to a rudimentary TM.

The *un-* and *non-* words both refer to the material 'plastic', although the *un-* word in (35) does so in a metaphorical sense and the *non-* word in the literal sense. The *un-* form is clearly more evaluative than the *non-* form, but we would observe that the metaphorical use of *plastic* is itself evaluative; *plastic* is intended to mean 'fake' in this context. The *a-* form selects the learned or medical sense of the base (something like 'shapeable' or 'moldable'). The prefixes, however, in each case add a simple negative force.

There are, of course, cases in which the base maintains more or less the same meaning, and the affixes provide clearly different nuances. Consider, for example, the quadruplet *irreligious, unreligious, non-religious, areligious*:

(36)   *Ms 2003*: "I also wanted to write about what a spiritual quest might look like at the end of the twentieth century—a spiritual quest by someone who, like so many of my friends, was basically **irreligious** and resistant to spiritual thought."

   NBC_Matthews 2007: Can he be the **unreligious** candidate, the secular candidate who wins the East Coast states of New York, Connecticut, New Jersey, Florida?

   Anthropological Quarterly 2008: That is, the Turkish state promotes the notion that Islam can be separated out from other types of social activities, including politics, to create a neutral, **non-religious** public space and institutions.

   Church History 2002: Religious symbols and acts may have saturated life, but Guibert had encountered someone who was (in our language) "**areligious**," indifferent to such tugs or claims.

What we find here is that the *in-* form does have a clear depreciatory flavour; *irreligious* in this context implies hostility to religion. The *un-* form is more evaluatively neutral, though, being more or less equivalent to 'secular'. The *non-* and the *a-* forms are also evaluatively neutral, but express scale-external negation, rather than contrary or contradictory negation. Given the previous examples, the important observation is that the differences that we find appear to depend more on context of use than on some inherent and consistent semantic property of the affixes.

We do, of course, find lexicalized meanings more frequently with *in-* forms than with any of the other prefixes. For example, *irrational* means 'unreasonable', *incredible* can mean 'excellent', and *inaccessible* can mean 'difficult to understand'. And such lexicalized forms are often but not always depreciatory in sense (for example, *incredible* clearly is not). But there are also many *in-* words that are quite transparent.

What we find, then, is that the data in the corpora do not clearly corroborate the claims made by Horn, or by Bauer and Huddleston. At best we might say that *in-* is more likely to have a depreciatory sense than *un-*, and *un-* is more likely to have one than *non-*, but that this is no more than a tendency having to do with the degree of lexicalization found with each prefix. All four rival affixes can be negative without being depreciatory. We must conclude that lexicalization and depreciatory nuance are a matter of individual lexical items, and not of the affixes themselves.

A similar story can be told about the negative affixes that take verbal bases. With the rival cohort *un-*, *de-*, and *dis-* on verbal bases, we only occasionally find triplets, but doublets are not difficult to find, again suggesting that blocking is not a real phenomenon.

(37)   a. *triplets*: unbar, disbar, debar; uninvest, disinvest, de-invest

   b. *doublets* (un-, dis-): unarm, disarm; uncharge, discharge; uncover, discover; uninvite, disinvite; unmount, dismount; unelect, dis-elect

   c. *doublets* (un-, de-): uncenter, decenter; uncertify, decertify; uncode, decode; uncompress, decompress; unconstruct, deconstruct; unlink, delink; unpretzel, depretzel; unselect, deselect; untrain, detrain

   d. *doublets* (de-, dis-): decolor, discolor; decompose, discompose; de-identify, disidentify

As with the adjectival cohort, with this set of affixes we find some pairs that appear to mean precisely the same thing, and others in which one or more members are lexicalized or have different meanings:

(38)   *Military History 2006*: British soldiers crossed the parade field to **unbar** the main gate, admitting more Redcoats.

   ABC_GMA 2007: The question is, will this panel **disbar** him, take away his law license, prevent him from practicing law at all, as a civil lawyer, as a corporate lawyer, as a transactional lawyer?

   Washington Post 1999: But some corruption experts said that if the accusations pan out, the firms should be "**debarred**" by the World Bank—that is, prohibited from bidding on projects funded by the bank, a major source of financing for dams in developing countries.

(39)   *Sewanee Review 1997*: "People can invest other things besides money," Ginger said, taking their dishes to the sink. "Maybe I already have." # "Well, then you'd better **uninvest** it," Lucky said.

   Journal of International Affairs 1992: Companies wishing to **disinvest** were forced to do so in a buyers' market; South Africans could therefore acquire former subsidiaries, whose profits would no longer be taken out of South Africa in the form of dividends, at cut-rate prices.

   Boston College Environmental Affairs Law Review 1999: EPA has **de-invested** in Part 503, while diverting fiscal resources to other programs under the CWA.

So *unbar* appears to have a literal privative meaning 'remove the bar', *disbar* a lexicalized meaning 'to remove from the bar, i.e., to be disqualified from practicing law', and to *debar* an apparently redundant sense identical to 'bar, i.e., to prevent from doing something' (see Section 17.3.3). On the other hand, there does not seem to be any difference in sense between *uninvest*, *disinvest*, and *de-invest*; all three seem in context to mean 'cease to invest' or 'remove investment'.

Nor is there any clear trend towards differentiation of meaning overall in sets of rivals. Of the doublets listed above, nine appear from the contexts in which they are used in COCA to have the same meaning (mostly reversative or privative), five pairs have different meanings, with either one or both of the meanings being lexicalized, and two pairs display a complex pattern of overlapping senses. What this suggests again is that blocking does not seem to occur, and that to the extent that items with these prefixes differ in sense, the difference can only be attributed to the effects of lexicalization on an item-to-item basis, and not to any systematic difference in the meanings of the affixes.

17.3.5 Semantic restrictions on bases

The last issue we will examine in this section is one that has a venerable history in the study of English morphology, namely whether negative affixes are prohibited from attaching to certain semantic categories of base: bases which themselves are negative, bases that have monomorphemic antonyms, or classes of bases like colours; the issue is discussed at least by Jespersen (1917), Zimmer (1964), Marchand (1969), Funk (1986), Horn (2002), Kjellmer (2005), and Dixon (2010).

We begin with the issue of negative bases. Jespersen (1917) frames the claim as follows:

> Not all adjectives admit of having the negative prefix *un-* or *in-*, and it is not always easy to assign a reason why one adjective can take the prefix and another cannot. Still, the same general rule obtains in English as in other languages, that most adjectives with *un-* or *in-* have a depreciatory sense: we have *unworthy*, *undue*, *imperfect*, etc., but it is not possible to form similar adjectives from *wicked*, *foolish*, or *terrible*. (Jespersen 1917: 144)

Zimmer's (1964) monograph is entirely devoted to the issue of whether negative prefixes are restricted to non-negative (that is, evaluatively positive or neutral) bases. He states (1964: 15) the hypothesis as follows:

> Negative affixes are not used with adjectival stems that have a 'negative' value on evaluative scales such as 'good - bad,' 'desirable - undesirable.' (Zimmer 1964: 15)

After a careful study of data from then-contemporary English dictionaries, Zimmer's results are equivocal (1964):

> We can thus say that for the group of forms in question, and especially for the monomorphemic-base component of it, our hypothesis that *un-* prefixation is not applied to 'negative'

bases seems to be substantially correct, although some exceptions do occur. An extension of the corpus leads, however, to the addition of further rather surprising exceptions; thus *uncruel, unevil, unignorant, unignominious, unsick, unsilly, unstupid* (and possibly other exceptions that we have missed) are all listed in [*Webster's* 1957]. (Zimmer 1964: 36)

He acknowledges that there are many complex bases that are negative in connotation to which negative affixes can nevertheless attach (for example, *unbigoted, undegenerate, unfaulty, unguilty, uninjurious, unmalicious, unobnoxious, unselfish, untroublesome*), but very few that are simplex (*unbitter, unhostile, unsordid, unvulgar*, and possibly a few more, as the quote above suggests).

What corpus data from COCA suggest, however, is that what Zimmer calls 'surprising exceptions' are neither particularly exceptional, nor particularly surprising. For example, we find the negative forms on negative bases in (40) in COCA.

(40)   unafraid, unangry, unanxious, un-bald, unbare, unbitter, unbogus, uncoy, uncrazy, uncruel, undead, unevil, unfake, unfraught, unhostile, unhumid, unjealous, unlame, unlazy, unmad, unsordid, unsurly, unvulgar, unweary, unpoor, unsick, untimid, unugly

While individuals might quibble about whether all of the bases above are indeed negatively evaluative (maybe *bald* is beautiful?), it is clear that the vast majority of these are counterexamples to Zimmer's hypothesis.

Furthermore, there is a clear pragmatic reason why they occur: there is a need for both the positive term and for the negative-prefixed term. What, for example, is the antonym of *angry*, or of *sordid*? There are surely several possibilities for each, but the most straightforward is the *un-* word. And even where there is an institutionalized antonym, it may be too strong for the context in which the word is needed. Someone who is *untimid* is not necessarily *bold*. Horn (2002: 9) says with regard to forms like *unhappy* or *unintelligent*, that 'their meanings are palpably different from (and in particular, weaker than) those of the corresponding underived *sad* and *stupid*', and we might say precisely the same thing about what Zimmer calls *un-* adjectives on negative bases.

Kjellmer (2005: 160) goes a step further than Zimmer, in suggesting that any word which has a morphologically simple antonym is excluded as a base in negative-formation. We also disagree with this claim. COCA yields the following examples that Kjellmer would predict to be unacceptable, with the obvious non-prefixal antonym in parentheses.

(41)   unadult (child), un-big (small), unclear (opaque), unclever (stupid), uncomplex (simple), uncrazy (sane), undead (live), unfake (real, genuine), unfancy (simple), unfresh (stale), ungentle (rough), ungenuine (fake), ungood (bad), ungreat (small), unhappy (sad), unheavy (light), un-hot (cold), unhumid (dry), unkosher (trayf), unlarge (small), unlight (heavy, dark), unlive (dead), un-meek (bold), unopaque

(clear), unplain (fancy), unpoor (rich), unpresent (absent), unpretty (ugly), unprofane (sacred), unpublic (private), unrare (common), unrich (poor), unsick (well), unsmart (stupid), unstraight (crooked), unstrong (weak), untame (wild), untidy (messy), untiny (large), untrue (false), unugly (pretty), unwarm (cool), unwell (ill, sick), unwet (dry), unwide (narrow), unwild (tame)

As with the examples of negative prefixes on negative bases, these examples may be far less frequent than the morphologically simple antonym in parentheses, but they clearly provide an alternative, and sometimes serve a distinct purpose in identifying a region on a scale that is more central, less close to the opposing pole than the direct antonym. So, *ungood* is not exactly the same thing as *bad*:

(42)   *Houston Chronicle 1992*: Templeton, who isn't very talkative these days, even with his wife and children, says he feels good. He's seen numerous 10th-floor neighbors emerge from the transplants feeling distinctly **ungood**.

Examples like those in (40) are also common in contrastive contexts, paired either explicitly or implicitly with the corresponding positive:

(43)   *Fantasy & Science Fiction 1995*: And when I win, the Net tells me, "Congratulations," with its changeless voice, nothing warm or **unwarm** about it, no trace of involvement, and nothing behind the words but an unshakable politeness.

        Esquire 2005: The island is a leveler. It takes the greatest players on earth and makes them...**ungreat**.

In the first example in (43), the contrast is overt, in the second implied. In all three cases it is clear that the *un-* form provides a nuance of meaning that the simple antonym would not supply.

A final claim concerning potential semantic restrictions on the derivation of negatives that we might evaluate is that of Dixon (2010: 53). He states that, 'the prefix *un-* may be used with many adjectives from the HUMAN PROPENSITY type, with some from the VALUE and with a few from PHYSICAL PROPERTY, but with none from DIMENSION, COLOR, or AGE.' The list in (41) provides a number of counterexamples (*un-big, ungreat, unlarge, untiny, unwide, unadult*), to which we can add colour adjectives like *unblue* and *ungrey* from COCA, and *unred* and *unyellow* from internet discussions of haircolouring products.

The conclusions that we must draw from the corpus data are that there is no real prohibition against affixing negative prefixes to negative bases, that the existence of simple antonyms does not block the attachment of negative prefixes to either the positive or the negative antonym, and that even adjectives denoting size, age, and colour may occur with a negative prefix in appropriate contexts. Indeed, there are contexts in which such words are indispensible, and native speakers do not hesitate to produce them. Further, it seems important to observe, given the extensive discussion that these issues have received, that derived forms that might seem odd or marginal when encountered out of context, or when judged against our intuitions, are both possible and natural when encountered in context.

....

CHAPTER 18

Size, quantity, and attitude

18.1 PROSPECTUS

In this chapter we consider morphological ways of marking size, frequency, and quantity. The pertinent expressions are also often used to show attitude or evaluation and this is the reason why we treat all of them in one chapter. The categories in question often involve prefixes, though some suffixes and also other types of process are considered. Finally we consider the morphology of numbers in English.

In terms of the semantics of the processes considered here, there is also a certain amount of leakage. Many of the processes that are used to mark quantity are also used to show location (presumably via semantic extension of the notion of location to location on a scale of quantity, as, for example, with the prefix *super-*). We have divided the treatment of potentially relevant morphological categories between this chapter and Chapter 16 according to what seems to be the major focus of the respective category, but the reader may need to consult both chapters for a full report on all potentially relevant categories.

We will begin with categories that primarily mark evaluation and size, then turn to those expressing non-evaluative attitude, and then turn to quantification and numbers.

18.2 EVALUATION AND SIZE

18.2.1 Preliminaries

In this section we will deal with those word-formation processes that are used to denote the size of the referent associated with the base. The main products of such processes that come to mind are diminutives and augmentatives. The notion of diminutive in particular is not easy to define clearly. One problem with this notion is the semantics, the other the kind of formal means employed to express diminutive meaning. Hence, before entering the discussion of the pertinent morphological processes we will first lay out our understanding of this domain at large.

Traditionally, the term DIMINUTIVE refers to morphological categories that express smallness. However, as noted by many authors, diminutives also express familiarity with the referent, and positive or negative attitude (i.e. appreciation or depreciation, e.g. Jurafsky 1996;

Schneider 2003). In order to explain that the same form can have apparently opposite readings, we must consider the specific context in which a certain diminutive form is used. Which
reading a given diminutive form receives in that context may depend on the nature of this
linguistic and situational context as well as on the meaning of the respective base. As nicely
pointed out by Schneider (2003), *wifelet* is probably always negative in evaluation, while
cubelet perhaps never is. Referring to a child acting as a king in a play, with the diminutive
kinglet may convey a positive attitude, while referring with the same word to an adult sover-
eign probably never does. The meaning 'small' is often extended to 'young' or to 'dear', but
these meanings are relevant only with nominal bases.

We will refer to the meaning complex of small size, familiarity, appreciation, or depreciation as the notion of 'diminution', and the forms conveying these meanings as diminutives.
English has a rich inventory of forms expressing diminution, most of them morphological in
nature. Schneider (2003) arrives at 15 suffixes (*-a*, *-een*, *-er*, *-ette*, *-ie*, *-ing*, *-kin*, *-le*, *-let*, *-ling*, *-o*,
-pegs, *-poo(h)*, *-pops*, *-s*) plus truncation (referred to here as clipping), and reduplication. In
addition, there is also the possibility of expressing diminution analytically, with the adjective
little (see Schneider 2003 for details). We will only be concerned here with the morphological
expressions of diminution.

Precisely which word-formation processes should go under the label of diminutive seems
to vary a great deal in the literature, mostly depending on how much emphasis is laid on the
attitudinal component versus the size component of the meaning of the process. Thus one
could distinguish between terms of endearment, which lack the meaning component 'smallness' and other diminutives, which have both meaning components. In practice, however, it
is often very hard to distinguish properly between the two, as most diminutive morphological categories can express both concepts, even if not always simultaneously in each of the
pertinent formations. Furthermore, clippings or reduplications often express attitudinal
meaning and are therefore also subsumed under the rubric diminutive by many authors (e.g.
Schneider 2003). We remain largely agnostic as to these taxonomic questions and have
grouped processes expressing evaluation and size using a mixture of formal and semantic
criteria. As in the other chapters, we focus on productive processes.

18.2.2 Diminution by affixation

18.2.2.1 *Native affixes:* -let, -ling, -ie, *and the minor suffixes* -o, -s, -er *and* -kin

The suffix *-let* is still slightly productive in a number of uses. In (1) we find examples from the
BNC illustrating *-let* with the meaning 'small of a species', occasionally 'young of a species'.

> (1)   auklet, basslet, catlet, froglet, gooselet, murrelet, piglet, swiftlet, toadlet

The examples in (2) show *-let* with a simple meaning of small size used on inanimate
entities.

(2)   applet, bomblet, booklet, brooklet, budlet, cloudlet, droplet, eyelet, firmlet, flatlet, leaflet, manorlet, moonlet, platelet, rootlet, spinelet, spirelet, statelet, streamlet, tartlet, twiglet, wavelet

The examples in (3) show *-let* with a slightly disparaging meaning.

(3)   godlet, playlet, starlet

The examples in (4) show *-let* with the meaning of 'piece of jewellery or adornment', where the base denotes the place where it is worn (*corse* is an old form meaning 'body', from the French).

(4)   armlet, bracelet, corselet, necklet, wristlet

The examples in (5) illustrate the suffix with an obligatorily bound base, in the relevant meaning.

(5)   chaplet, gauntlet, hamlet, pamphlet, rivulet

For bases ending in <l> it may be sometimes difficult to determine whether we are dealing with the suffix *-let* or *-et*. For instance, it is not clear whether forms like *tablet* are best analysed as containing the more common *-let* and some simplification of the resulting double <ll>, or whether they contain the rarer suffix *-et*. Another problematic case would be *hamlet*, which, according to the *OED*, has a historical root *hamle*, but neither *ham* nor *hamle* is available with a suitable meaning in current English.

The suffix *-ling* is of extremely restricted productivity; even where a word containing this suffix is used with a meaning not listed in the *OED*, which might indicate productive coinage, the form itself is usually listed. The examples below are mainly from COCA. We can distinguish between words with adjectival, nominal, and verbal bases and there are very few examples, like *underling, overling (OED)* which have none of these. Within the denominal formations, there seem to be various semantic classes (see below).

De-adjectival formations are given in (6). The base in *darling* is etymologically from the root that gives *dear*, though this is no longer transparent.

(6)   darling, firstling, foundling, grayling, greenling, lostling, scantling, weakling, wildling, youngling

In the denominal series, we first have those which denote the young or a small exemplar or type, as in (7). *Codling* has several meanings, here it means 'small species of cod'.

(7)   codling, duckling, gosling, kidling, mouseling, pigling, ratling, spiderling

In the next series, in (8a), the diminution may be read as implying insignificance, illustrated with an example from COCA in (8b).

> (8)   a. godling, lordling, priestling, princeling
>
>   b. *The Helper and His Hero 2007*: Now it was Bandar's turn to be surprised: even a provincial **lordling** ought to have heard of Rovers.

In the series in (9), the words all seem to denote young creatures (people, animals, even plants), but the relationship to the base is much less transparent. A *fingerling* (when it denotes a fish or a potato) resembles a finger, a *nestling* is found in a nest, and a *yearling* is a year old, for example.

> (9)   fingerling, fosterling, nestling, nursling, seedling, stripling, yearling

In the examples in (10) the semantics is obscure, and the *-ling* appears to denote little more than 'thing or creature in connection with X'. *Starling* is included here following the etymology suggested by the *OED*, from the noun *stare*.

> (10)   bratling, earthling, fleshling, groundling, halfling, heartling, potling, sideling, starling, witling

The deverbal formations in (11) are object-referencing, and the suffix is similar to *-ee* in this regard (see Chapter 11). The semantics fits with *fatling* 'an animal which has been fatted' (see the *OED*). Note that *weanling* has a synonymous form *weaner*.

> (11)   changeling, fatling, hatchling, hireling, starveling, weanling

Finally, there is a small set of words from COCA in (12) which all denote some kind of creature. They are not listed in the *OED*, and all of them arise in the context of science fiction or fantasy fiction. Such sources also account for the attestation of a number of other rare forms in COCA (*fleshling, halfling, kidling*). This type of prose seems to provide the only reliable domain of productivity for this suffix in contemporary English and can be seen as evidence for the extended meaning '(small) creature'.

> (12)   sisterling, stepling, witchling, wyrmling

In spelling terms, note the lack of <e> in *nursling* and *starling*, but not in *hireling, mouseling, sideling* (although this last has an alternative spelling with no <e>).

The suffix *-ie* (also frequently spelt as <y> as in <Tommy>, and much more rarely as <ey>, as in <Barney>) has an obscure history. It is related to the Germanic suffix that gives us Dutch

-tje and German *-chen*. Zandvoort (1962: 302) claims that English is more restricted than those languages in its use of diminutives (see also Strang 1968: 138), but we know of no empirical study to show this with solid quantitative data. Quite to the contrary, Cannon (1987: 185) presents evidence that *-ie* is among the most productive suffixes of English. Claims that pertinent forms are largely restricted to the language addressed to or coming from children (*doggy, hankie, girlie, grannie, mousie, nighty, piggy, sweetie, tummy*) also seem empirically weak, as such forms are also common outside this domain (e.g. *bookie* ◆ *bookmaker, darkey* ◆ *dark* (now taboo sl.), *goalie* ◆ *goalkeeper, roadie* ◆ *road manager*, and the examples in (13)). Hypocoristic names with this suffix are also very common (*Annie, Betty, Bobby/Bobbie, Charlie, Davy, Freddy, Georgie, Jackie, Kitty, Laurie, Lizzie, Mandy, Teddy, Tommy*). These are dealt with in more detail in Section 18.2.3, as they are subject to slightly different restrictions.

The use of *-ie* seems especially strong in ScE, providing forms like *laddie, lassie*, and exporting the suffix to Australia and New Zealand, where it thrives. In South Africa it met a homophonous Dutch diminutive, which must have supported this form although the Dutch allomorphy is often retained (Silva 1996). The suffix is, however, also widely used in other varieties of English. It is not entirely clear whether the rules for *-ie* suffixation are the same in all these varieties, but in this chapter words from different varieties will not be treated separately. Hypocoristics of place names will also be treated on a par with diminutives from ordinary words, though personal names will be left to one side here, since they are often formally more complex than other *-ie/-y* forms (see Section 18.2.3 for more discussion).

In the examples of *-ie* formations that follow, many words are taken from the literature, which has often concentrated on *-ie* formations in particular varieties. The words are marked as being AusE, NZE, SAfrE, or ScE as appropriate, although there is no expectation that they are different in kind, or that they might not at all occur anywhere else. The ScE forms are from Bulloch (1924) unless otherwise stated. Many of the AusE and NZE forms are from Ramson (1988), Sussex (2004), and Bardsley and Simpson (2009). South African forms are from Silva (1996), other forms from Schneider (2003) or Lappe (2007).

Examples are given in (13). All or nearly all of these are established, although some forms appear to be restricted in usage to certain groups of speakers and therefore will not necessarily be known to every reader. The suffix is, however, highly productive. In (13), we use regional designations if pertinent or if given as such in the sources. Such designations do not preclude that the item in question may not also be found in other varieties.

(13) baddy ◆ bad
      bankie ◆ bank 'bench' (SAfrE)
      barbie ◆ barbecue (AusE/NZE)
      boatie ◆ boat (ScE)
      bootie ◆ boot
      cardie ◆ cardigan (NZE)

ciggie ◆ cigarette

cocky 'farmer' ◆ cockatoo (AusE/NZE)

coldie ◆ cold beer (AusE)

combie ◆ combination

curlie ◆ curl (ScE)

drillie ◆ drill sergeant (AusE)

eggs benny ◆ eggs Benedict (NZE)

footie ◆ football

girlie ◆ girl

gummy ◆ gumdigger (NZE)

hammy ◆ hamster

hanky ◆ handkerchief

homie ◆ home boy 'friend' (NAmE)

indie ◆ independent

kindy ◆ kindergarten (AusE/NZE)

lairdie ◆ laird (ScE)

lassie ◆ lass (ScE)

Palmie ◆ Palmerston North (NZE) / Palm Bay (AusE)

Phillie ◆ Philadelphia (NAmE)

pollie ◆ politician (AusE)

pokey ◆ poker

pommy ◆ pomegranate 'Englishman' (AusE/NZE)

pozzy ◆ position (AusE)

pressy ~ prezzie ◆ present 'gift' (AusE/NZE)

prossie ◆ prostitute (BrE)

Rangy ◆ Range Rover (AusE)

rhodie ◆ rhododendron

roey ◆ Rohypnol (AusE)

scotchie ◆ scotch thistle (NZE)

steppie ◆ stepmother (AusE)

swaggie ◆ swagman (AusE)

Tassy /tæzi/ ◆ Tasmania (AusE)

titty ◆ tit

As expected from our discussion of the semantics of diminutives, derivatives with the suffix *-ie* do not necessarily imply a particularly small size, but are often about attitude, as, for instance, illustrated by the examples *steppie* ◆ *stepmother* or *homie* ◆ *homeboy* listed in (13). The connotations are perhaps mostly positive or mark familiarity, but may also be negative, as evidenced by the established forms *blowie* • *blowfly* (AusE) and even with *rellie* • *relative, relation* (AusE/NZE).

The suffix attaches most frequently to nouns and forms count nouns, except in the case of *Aussie*, which, like its base *Australian*, may be either an adjective or a noun. We also find formations based on adjectives (e.g. *baddie, blackie, goodie, greeny, softy, stiffy*), in which case the derivatives are nouns. Very occasionally it attaches to other parts of speech, such as prepositions (again forming nouns, e.g. *innie, outie* 'types of navel'). One might even be tempted to analyse forms such as *howdy, all righty, thanky* as being derived from phrases, that is from *how do you do, all right*, and *thank you*, respectively. At least with *howdy* and *thanky* such an analysis is problematic, as these forms probably result from univerbation and phonological erosion. Furthermore, there is the problem that all three forms are not nouns, as all other *-ie* diminutives seem to be.

Our analysis implies that the adjective-forming *-y* suffix which gives *cheery, crazy, dotty, shotty* ('excellent', NZE children's sl) is a different suffix, despite its homophony with the diminutive suffix *-ie* and—at least in the instances cited—similar connotations (see Chapter 14).

Let us now turn to the phonological aspects. Derivatives in *-ie* are almost all disyllabic trochees, which necessarily leads to the loss of phonological material of the base with multisyllabic base words. A further peculiarity that arises through this prosodic requirement is the fact that with many derivatives it is actually unclear whether they are suffixed. Derivatives like *indie* on the basis of *independent*, or *combie* on the basis of *combination*, might be analysed as not having a suffix at all and being simply truncated. However, from an output perspective, such an analysis is unwarranted and cannot explain why the putatively unsuffixed forms behave exactly like the clearly suffixed forms, both in terms of phonology and semantics. We adopt an output-oriented view here and define *-ie* diminutives as diminutive forms that are disyllabic trochees ending in /i/. For the sake of convenience we will nevertheless keep using the traditional 'suffix'-based terminology.

Monosyllabic bases take *-ie* and integrate the suffix phonologically (e.g. *po.key* • *poker*). The truncation patterns found with polysyllabic bases are quite intricate and are closely linked, but not fully identical, to the ones found with clippings, which we discuss in Section 18.2.4. There are three main problems associated with base truncation in this morphological category. The first is what material from the base survives. We will refer to this problem as 'anchoring'. The second is the phonotactics and syllable structure of the derivatives, and the third is the segmental stability, that is whether segments from the base have the same quality as their corresponding segments in the derivative. Our treatment is largely based on the findings in Lappe (2007).

The vast majority of *-ie* forms anchor to the first syllable of the base (e.g. *hammie* • *hamster, pokey* • *poker*), irrespective of where the base is stressed. Thus we find forms anchoring to the initial base syllable in spite of non-initial base stress (*combie* • *combinátion, indie* • *indepéndent*). How much of the base is preserved is quite variable, but also clearly constrained. Diminutives of this category preserve contiguous strings starting from the left edge of the first syllable.

There are no extra restrictions on the syllable structure of the derivative apart from the fact that the second syllable needs to have an onset. As a consequence, deletion patterns vary within the regular confines of English syllables and the prosodic requirement imposed by the morphological category. Thus we find some variation in the preservation of consonant clusters. Sonorant–obstruent clusters favour preservation (e.g. *barbie* • *barbecue, alkie* • *alcohol*), while obstruent–obstruent clusters are more variable. For example, the diminutive of *prostitute* is attested as *prossy*, while *hostess* has the diminutive *hosty*. The only clusters that seem to be always subject to deletion are those in which the second consonant is more sonorous than the first consonant (*seggy, *segry* • *segregation; Chevvy, *Chevry* • *Chevrolet*)

The overwhelming majority of derivatives faithfully preserve the quality of the segments of the base, but changes from schwa to full vowel can be observed with those forms where the derivative anchors to a base-initial schwa syllable, as in *s*[ʌ]*ssy* • *s*[ə]*spicious*. Consonantal changes are even rarer and show only one recurrent, but not consistent, pattern, the voicing of /s/ in intervocalic position, as in *Au*[z]*ie* <Aussie> • *Australian*, or *co*[z]*ie* <cossie> • *costume*.

Exceptions to the general patterns just described are occasionally found. They may retain more than one syllable, may anchor to a non-initial syllable, or other phonological changes to the root are made. It is unclear how much the pertinent forms may in fact reflect regular patterns in regional dialects. Some such forms are listed in (14), with a few of them apparently being neologisms.

(14)　breakfastie (ScE)

　　　bullocky 'beef', 'bullock driver' (AusE)

　　　cradlie (ScE)

　　　gyppie • Egyptian (AusE)

　　　littlie 'small child' (NZE)

　　　messagie 'errand' (ScE)

　　　second handy (NZE)

　　　Shorty/Landy/Streety • Shortland Street (NZ TV soap)

　　　smooy /smuːi/ • smoodge 'display of amorous affection' (AusE)

　　　steenbokkie (SAfE)

　　　tammie • Temazepam tablet (AusE)

Diminutive formation in *-ie* is certainly the most productive diminutive category in English, but a couple of minor classes of words, those ending in *-o, -a,-er, -s,* and *-kin*, should not go unmentioned. Formations in *-o* (*journo* • *journalist*) are the next most common, while formations in *-er* (also very rarely spelled <a>) are very rare (e.g. in *Maccas* • *Macdonalds*). Diminutives ending in *-o* seem more frequent in, but are certainly not restricted to, Australasian varieties of English, and then in AusE rather than in NZE. Attested words across varieties are a*ggro* ✦ *aggravation, ammo* ✦ *ammunition, arvo* ✦ *afternoon, combo* ✦ *combination, doggo* ✦ *dog* (in the expression *to lie doggo* 'keep a low profile'), *journo* ✦ *journalist, kiddo* ✦ *kid, muso* ✦ *musician, weirdo* ✦ *weird*.

Some examples from Sussex (2004) and Bardsley and Simpson (2009) are listed in (15); see Lappe (2007) for many more forms.

(15)
ambo	'ambulance officer'
Catho	'Catholic'
hospo	'worker in the hospitality industry'
lezzo	'lesbian'
maco	'immaculate'
metho	'methylated spirits'
Missos	'The Miscellaneous Workers' Union'
obno	'obnoxious'
Proddo	'Protestant'
reffo	'refugee'
rego	'(car) registration'
Rotto	'Rottnest Island'
Salvo	'member of the Salvation Army'

As was the case with *-ie*, we find forms, such as *demo* ✦ *demonstration*, or *condo* ✦ *condominium*, that appear to be simply truncated, and not necessarily to be analysed as suffixed with *-o*. Following the same arguments as with *-ie* diminutives, *-o* diminutives are thus best defined in an output-oriented fashion as disyllabic trochees ending in *-o*.

Derivatives in *-o* are mostly nouns that are based on nouns, but, as shown by some of the above data, we also find de-adjectival and de-phrasal nouns (*weirdo* ✦ *weird, metho* ✦ *methylated spirit drinker*, respectively). Monosyllabic bases take *-o* and integrate the suffix phonologically. The derivatives anchor to the initial base syllable and preserve contiguous strings starting from the left edge of the first syllable, and, unlike *-ie* derivatives, they almost categorically preserve all clusters, even those in which the second consonant is more sonorous (*obno* ✦ *obnoxious*). Segmental alternations are very rare, one example is *l*[aɪ]*no* <lino> ✦ *l*[ɪ]*noleum*.

Diminutive formations in *-o* and *-ie* are in obvious competition and we find a number of bases that are attested with both suffixes: *prossie* ✦ *prosso* ✦ *prostitute, Proddie* ✦ *Proddo* ✦ *Protestant*. Diminutives in *-ie* are however, much more common.

Another type of diminutive comprises disyllables ending in schwa, normally spelled <er> in the non-rhotic varieties where this suffix seems to be mostly found. It has been noted to be in-group marking, particularly in academic institutions and many words refer to concepts pertinent in such environments (*nipper* ✦ *nip, rugger* ✦ *rugby*, and *topper* ✦ *tophat, footer* ✦ *football, prepper* ✦ *prep(aratory) school, fresher* ✦ *freshman*). The form triggers truncation in a similar fashion to *-ie* and *-o* but there seem to be too few forms to establish more detailed generalizations. Diminutives in *-er* derive nouns, mostly on nouns. Often, it co-occurs with an additional *-s* as in *champers* ♦ *champagne, starkers* ♦ *stark naked, butters* ♦ *butt ugly* and *preggers* ♦ *pregnant*. Some forms are actually ambiguous between a person noun *-er* and a diminutive *-er* interpretation, as in *fresher* ♦ *freshman, tucker* ('food') ♦ *tuck in* 'eat heartily' (see Schneider 2003 for more discussion and further references).

The suffix *-s* frequently arises in instances where there is multiple marking of diminutiveness. Its function is often one of marking a hypocoristic (see Section 18.2.3). Various uses can be distinguished. It is found by itself or with a clipped base on nouns which are either hypocoristics or terms of address (the two may intersect, of course). Examples include *Babs* ♦ *Barbara, Debs* ♦ *Deborah, ducks* (BrE), *Jules* ♦ *Julia/Julian, Mags* ♦ *Margaret, moms, pops.*

As already mentioned above, it occurs after the diminutive *-er* in BrEsl, as in *Honkers* ♦ *Hong Kong, Wimblers* ♦ *Wimbledon*. This combination of forms is usually attributed specifically to British public schools (mainly Rugby) and the University of Oxford, though some of the forms have become item-familiar for a wider portion of the British English community and even the Australian community. *Rudders* ♦ *Rudiments of Divinity* (see the *OED* sv. *-ers*) would not be easily interpreted outside of Oxford (possibly Oxford of the relevant period). *Bonkers* and *crackers* (both meaning 'mad') may illustrate the same process, though the relationship with the base is less clear. Quirk *et al.* (1985: 1584) also put *bananas* in the same category, but it is questionable whether this form expresses diminution.

The suffix *-s* also occurs along with the *-ie* suffix, for example in the language of the playground. Bauer and Bauer (1996) cite examples such as *ankles, kneesies*, and *under-bums* as variants of a playground jumping game from New Zealand. Note the triple diminutive marking in *kneesies*. The item-familiar child-language word *tootsie* ('foot') (and the more adult formation *play footsie*) seem to illustrate the same combination of affixes. It is less clear whether it is found (or may be analysed) in words like *the heebie jeebies, the (blue) meanies, walkies*, and *the willies*.

Let us turn to the suffix *-kin*. Most of the words where *-kin* can be analysed as a genuine suffix are names, often surnames, where the *-kin* seems to function just like *-son*, so that *Dickson* (or *Dixon*) and *Dicken* (or *Dickens*) are parallel forms. There are only a few examples of ordinary words with the suffix *-kin*, and in most of these the base is no longer recuperable from the word. Examples from the BNC include those in (16). All of these are established, often old-fashioned. Many of them represent loans from Dutch rather than genuine English derivations. Even where the elements are clear, the meaning relationship between the elements is often obscure, with only *bunnikin, catkin, lambkin*, and *manikin* being at all transparent.

(16)   bodkin ('dagger, needle'), bumpkin, bunnikin (*defined as a flower in the* OED), catkin, firkin ('quarter barrel'), gherkin, lambkin, lumpkin, manikin, munchkin (*Baum 1900*), napkin, pipkin ('drinking vessel'), ramekin, siskin ('small bird')

Mannequin is probably a parallel development of the same source as *manikin*, but one which has come through French.

18.2.2.2 *Non-native affixes:* -ette, hypo-, mini-, micro-, nano-

The suffix *-ette* is French in origin, and there are still a large number of recognizably French words which end in this sequence. The suffix occurs on bound bases, as well as on simple and compound nouns, as the examples in (17) and (18) illustrate. It is no longer productive on bound bases.

> (17)   baguette, banquette, briquette, brunette, camionette, coquette, couchette, croquette, florette, lazarette, lorgnette, marionette, marquisette, vinaigrette

The suffix *-ette* is one of the auto-stressed suffixes of English and as such carries the main stress of the derivative (with the exception of the single example *cigarette*). It is remarkably productive in a number of distinguishable meanings. While there are many established items in the lists from the BNC and COCA, there are many neologistic items which occur in only one of the corpora.

A list of examples which appear simply to denote smallness is presented in (18). In some of these cases there may be overtones of disparagement, but those do not appear to be dominant.

> (18)   cigarette, clubette, coffinette, crashette, crisisette, diskette, featurette, festival-ette, filmette, flingette, ghetto-blasterette, iconette, jaunt-ette, jobette, mealette, partyette, recessionette, seatette, sermonette, snackette, spinnerette, statuette, suburbette, novelette

There are rather more specific series of words where size appears to be more important than attitude, distinguished here as businesses (19) and rooms/buildings (20), although that distinction may be slightly artificial at times. These seem to be semantic domains where *-ette* is particularly favoured.

> (19)   laund(e)rette, luncheonette, ranchette, shoppette, washerette

> (20)   dinette, hangarette, hotelette, kitchenette, loungette, maisonette, pullmanette, roomette, sleeperette

Note the example in (21), which specifically mocks the use of the suffix on the names of rooms.

> (21)   I've been allocated a little house or 'maisonette', as it's called (a twee fake-French word I've always disliked) on the campus, at the end of a terrace of five....An open-plan living room with 'kitchenette' downstairs and a bedroomette and bathroomette upstairs. (*Lodge 2001: 10*)

Another well-known meaning for this suffix is 'fake, imitation' when applied to fabrics. There are few of these words in the corpora, and those that occur are all established, sometimes having a non-transparent, lexicalized meaning (e.g. *towelette* 'pre-moistened small towel sealed in a foil packet').

(22)   flannelette, leatherette, towelette

The largest group of *-ette* words with an identifiable meaning are those where the suffix means 'female'. Many of these are clearly disparaging, but not all are, though they are rarely completely serious words. Very few of these are item-familiar, which implies considerable productivity in this meaning. The suffix *-ette* may, in fact, be the main gender-marking suffix available in English, more used than *-ess* (see Chapter 11), but with far more strongly marked connotations.

(23)   bachelorette, baronette, bimbette, bumette, chaufferette, chefette, choir-
        ette, columnistette, conductorette, daemonette, deanette, demonette, disciplette,
        drumette, dudette, goblinette, gothette, grocerette, hustlerette, idolette, jockette, major-
        ette, nerdette, nymphette, professorette, punkette, rabbinette, raiderette, redskin-
        ette, reporterette, rock-ette, santa-ette, scionette, shrinkette, smurfette, suffragette,
        trooperette, usherette, wenchette, wifette, yeomanette

The suffix *-ette* strongly disprefers bases ending in /t/, which can be interpreted as a haplology effect, in this case the avoidance of identical onset and coda in the final syllable of the derivative (see Chapter 9 for discussion). Among the hundreds of derivatives in the BNC and COCA we found only three forms of this kind, *columnistette, Dustette* (the name of a vaccum cleaner model), and *seatette*.

The prefix *mini-* is extremely productive in modern English, a point which we illustrate with just a handful of the examples we find in COCA which are not listed in the *OED*.

(24)   mini-DVD, mini-illustration, mini-mask, mini-minivan, mini-moon, mini-novel,
        mini-researcher, mini-supermarket, mini-Supreme court, mini-vineyard, minibottle,
        minihomily, minipizza, minireferendum, minisat, miniski, minisnowbank, minispace,
        minitelescope, minitremor, minizoo.

The examples in (24) show that hyphenation is inconsistent, that *mini-* can be prefixed to clippings, initialisms, derivatives (including prefixed words), to native and neoclassical compounds, and to phrases and that *mini-* can be recursive. Stress is variably placed on the prefix or on its host, with longer base words tending to carry the main stress of the derivative.

Mini- appears to refer purely to size and not to be biased towards positive evaluation. While nearly all of the bases are nouns, we occasionally find an adjective or a name used as a base.

(25)   a. *Popular Mechanics 1997*: The undermounted handles and spout on this Monticello **mini-wide** faucet will fit any standard 4-In. centerset basin

    b. *San Francisco Chronicle 2008*: It was a **mini-Woodstock** for the public transit set.

The explosion in the use of forms with *mini-* appears to have begun in the 1960s (despite a few earlier examples—see the *OED* sv. *Mini-*) and to continue to the present time. The prefix *mini-* is probably now the preferred affix for marking small size (with no other implications) in contemporary English.

The prefix *micro-* derives from the Greek word meaning 'small', but gains a number of distinguishable meanings in English, though these should almost certainly be attributed to polysemy of the prefix rather than to a series of homophonous affixes. The meanings include 'small', sometimes 'abnormally small' (26), 'microscopically small', 'concerned with microscopically small entities', or perhaps 'involving the use of a microscope' (27), 'smaller-scale than with the contrasting *macro-*' or 'smaller than something denoted with the prefix *mini-*' (28), 'a one millionth part' (29), 'created by microphotography' (30), and so on. While derivatives in *micro-* are largely derived from nouns, there are occasional exceptions where *micro-* is found in verbs, adjectives, and adverbs (e.g. *microetch, micro-fresh, microneural, microsocial, microthin, microurban*). The examples below are all taken from COCA.

(26)   micro-adjustable, microbrewery, microcassette, microcellular, microclimate, microexpression, microhabitat, microhouse, microlivestock, micromastia, micropenis, microthin

(27)   microbiology, microfauna, microfossil, micrometeoroid, micrometer, Micronesia, microspectrography

(28)   micro-economic, microbus, microcredit, micromanagement, microskirt

(29)   micro-henry, micro-kelvin, microliter, microsecond, microwatt

(30)   microdot, microfiche, microfilm, microprint

The prefix *micro-* can carry primary or secondary stress on its first syllable (e.g. *microbiólogy, mícrobrewery*), with the distribution of the two patterns being essentially unclear. Primary stress may also occur on the second syllable of *micro-* if the prefix is part of a form with a stress-shifting element, as in *micróscopy* (see Chapter 10, *-y*).

The prefix *nano-* originated as a number prefix in the metric system, denoting $1/10^9$ (see Section 18.5.4). It has made its way into the general language with the meaning 'extremely small', or 'with regard to very small entities'. COCA lists hundreds of derivatives, most of them nouns (e.g. *nanoaccelerator, nanobacteria, nanobacterium, nanobattery, nanobiology, nanoboat, nano-brain, nanobug*). Many adjectives can also be found, however (*nanobased, nanobiological, nano-biomedical, nanocrystalline, nano-enhanced, nano-generated, nano-inspired, nanoimpregnated, nanostructured*). Some of them appear to be back-formations from related nouns, others do not. Derived verbs are hard to find and seem to be back-formations (e.g. *nano-optimize* • *nano-optimized, nano-process*$_N$ • *nano-process*$_V$, *nano-fabricate* • *nano-fabrication*). Stress-wise, *nano-* behaves like *micro-*, as shown by the examples *nánomachine* versus *nànotéchnology* versus *nanógraphy*.

The three prefixes *micro-*, *mini-*, and *nano-* appear to be interchangeable in some contexts, with no precise difference in meaning in a non-contrasting environment.

(31)   *Analog Science Fiction & Fact 2001*: A stray reflection from the overhead lights, Pancho thought, an unavoidable momentary glitter off the array of **nanocameras** and projectors.

Analog Science Fiction & Fact 2001: Arrays of the church's **microcameras** scanned the preacher, the audience, and the lifelike images of the elderly couple, transmitting the memorial services around the world to other family members and friends who were attending electronically, plus a few million interested or at least voyeuristic webbies.

USA Today 1997: Baseball has PC-toting managers and **minicameras** attached to catchers' face-masks for TV viewers, basketball coaches churn statistics on laptops and golfers boom big drives with titanium clubs.

Of the three, *mini-* seems most colloquial, *micro-* has a somewhat scientific nuance, and *nano-* is used in scientific or pseudo-scientific contexts. The quote from *Tech Review* illustrates this excellently.

(32)   *Technology Review 1999*: It's somewhere around here that the science starts getting mixed up with science fiction. If you can make a **nanowheel**, why not a **nanogear**? A self-powered **nanoboat**? Why not build a **nanorobot** to move around the atoms for you? # And while you're at it, why not make **nanorobots** that can replicate themselves, making it possible to staff **nanofactories** capable of piecing together almost anything out of the basic building blocks of atoms? # Welcome to molecular manufacturing, as preached by **nanoevangelist** Drexler.

Nano is frequently used in brand names to make the product sound more scientific, even when it's not clear that the product involves anything small.

(33)   *Sunset 2007*: Sandwiched inside the glass panels is **Nanogel** aerogel (nanogel.com), a Cabot Corporation product that improves the insulating properties of glass.

Nano- is also the one that seems to be used disparagingly:

(34)   *Southwest Review 2000:* "He said, 'Tell **nano-brain** to write me when he learns how.'" Rufus gives his younger son a sort of shoulder punch of affection, in the oblique male manner.

> *The Albino Knife 1990*: Finally, the little gadget's **microbrain** could recognize a couple
> dozen explosives by using no more than a few stray molecules.

18.2.2.3 *Miscellaneous diminutive affixes and multiple affixation*

There are a number of historical diminutives whose force has now vanished, minor diminutive markers, and some isolated diminutive forms in English.

The *OED* recognizes a historical *-en* diminutive in words like *chicken, kitten,* and *maiden*. This is not recognizable as such today, and is not productive. Marchand (1969: 281-2) recognizes a suffix *-rel* or *-erel* in words such as *cockerel, gomerel* (ScE 'fool'), *kestrel, mackerel, mongrel, scoundrel, wastrel,* but comments that this has not been productive since the seventeenth century. The suffix *-et* may be difficult to separate from the suffix *-let* when the base ends in <l>, and from the suffix *-ette*, with which it is segmentally homophonous. Nevertheless it may be recognized in items like those in (35).

(35)   bullet, freshet, hogget, midget, owlet, rivulet, snippet, spinneret

Marchand (1969: 288-9) discusses this affix at greater length, but many of the words he discusses are no longer current. This affix is not productive.

The *OED* lists a diminutive suffix *-ot*, but the only current word it lists as an example is *eyot* ('small island') perhaps from the base *ait* 'small island'. *Ballot, spigot* might be seen as carrying the same suffix. This affix has not been productive for many centuries.

The *OED* also recognizes a diminutive in *-ola*, though it is mostly present in borrowings and not easily analysable in English. Some of the relevant words are in (36). This *-ola* should probably be distinguished from the homophonous suffix which the *OED* describes as being used for humorous effect, which occurs in *payola* (see also below Section 18.2.5.8).

(36)   aureola, cupola, fasciola, foveola, pergola, roseola, rubeola

There are a few isolated forms which seem to function as diminutives, but these forms do not seem to give rise to larger extendable series. A few pertinent forms are illustrated in (37a). In (37b) we list all pertinent forms from COCA involving the suffix *-poo*. Such forms are typically based on diminutives in *-ie*, which in turn are mostly, but not exclusively, based on nouns.

(37)   a. beddy-byes, daddypegs, girleen (*IrE*)

      b. bonkers-poo, bunny-poo, chickie-poo, cutesy-poo, drinky-poo, Evey-poo, hankypoo, giggledypoo, grumpy-poo, icky-poo, kissy-poo, matchy-poo, Neddy-poo, Putie-poo, sneaky-poo, stinky-poo

Markers of diminution are known cross-linguistically for being recursive, either in the sense that the same affix may be repeated, or in the sense that multiple markers of the same category may accrue. Although this is not automatically the case in English, there are many such examples, some of which we have already mentioned. Consider (38).

(38)   Debs/Debsie/Debso, goofies (♦ goef 'swim' = 'swimming baths' SAfE), Honkers, kneesies, micro-miniskirt (COCA), micro-minivan (COCA), microdroplet, mini-microwave (COCA), mini-minivan (COCA), mumsy ‖ momsy, preggers, tootsie.

18.2.3 Proper noun diminution: Hypocoristics

Hypocoristics are pet names, usually for people but also occasionally for places. These are marked in the same way as diminutives for the most part, but they are also marked in other ways.

Various examples have been given in Section 18.2.2 of diminutive suffixes being used for hypocoristics. Some of these are repeated below, according to the suffix used. Many of these are based on a clipping.

(39)   Babs, Debs, pops

(40)   Honkers (♦ Hong Kong), Wimblers (♦ Wimbledon)

(41)   Annie, Bobby, Charlie, daddy, Freddy, Georgie, Jamie, Jeannie, Lizzie, mummy ‖ mommy, Sally (♦ Salvation Army) (*NZE*); Brizzie (♦ Brisbane), Gissy (♦ Gisborne), Palmie (♦ Palm Bay *or* Palmerston)

(42)   Maccas (♦ Macdonald's) (*AusE*)

(43)   Salvo (♦ Salvation Army) (*AusE*); Rotto (♦ Rottnest Island) (*AusE*)

Hypocoristics can also be formed by clipping, that is by deleting phonological material of the base word. Some clippings that show no modification beyond the shortening are exemplified in (44). Many of these names have become names in their own right, but began as clippings of a longer name.

(44)   Alex, Chris, Dan, Dave, Deb, Di, Don, Ed, Geoff, Greg, Jake, Jan, Jess, Joe, Ken, Lena, Liz, Lou, Manda, Mike, Nick, Pete, Ray, Reg, Rob, Sam, Steve, Sue, Tim, Tom, Trina, Val, Vic, Will, Zach

The highly productive morphological categories of monosyllabic name clippings and suffixed hypocoristics impose severe prosodic restrictions on their members. The restrictions are similar to those we find in the *-ie* diminutives discussed above and in the clippings discussed in Section 18.2.4 below, but are not fully identical to them. The following treatment of the phonological characteristics of clipped names is largely based on Lappe's (2007) analysis of a large number of such forms. As will become clear, clipped names and suffixed hypocoristics are highly regular, in spite of the existence of a significant amount of variation. As shown in Lappe (2007), the regularity of the patterns is most insightfully recognized if one takes an output-oriented approach that focuses on the relationship between what is preserved from the base word and not on what is deleted (see, for example, Berg 2011 for the latter kind of approach). It is useful to treat the different categories separately, as their restrictions differ slightly.

18.2.3.1. *Clipped names*

Clipped names are monosyllables that need to have a heavy rhyme and at least one consonant, so that forms like **D[e] ◆ Dexter*, or **A ◆ Abraham* are ruled out. Clipped names anchor either to the first syllable or to the main-stressed syllable (*Pat ◆ Trish ◆ Patrícia*). Very occasionally, the secondarily stressed syllable is chosen as anchor (as in *Gail ◆ Ábigàil*). Anchoring to an onsetless first syllable is largely avoided if that first syllable is not stressed. In such cases the main stressed syllable is the anchor (e.g. *Tave ◆ 🖐Oc ◆ Octavia*). Exceptions to these anchoring patterns are extremely rare (e.g. *Al ◆ Alónzo, Ron ◆ Áaron*), but where found, the derivatives often have homophone clippings derived in a regular fashion from other bases (cf. *Al ◆ Álfred, Ron ◆ Rónald*).

As was the case with *-ie* diminutives, the derived form preserves contiguous segments starting from the left edge of the anchor syllable. To fulfil the constraint on heavy rhymes, the first consonant of the following syllable often makes it into the clipping (as in *Cliff ◆ Clifford*). Some forms show exceptional violation of the contiguity requirement *Ike ◆ Isaac* or *Floss ◆ Florence*. Such violations are systematic with derivatives that would otherwise end in /r/ (**Flor*). Preservation of consonant clusters is generally variable (e.g. *Clif ◆ Clift ◆ Clifton, Jasp ◆ Jas ◆ Jasper, Bren ◆ Brend ◆ Brendan, Mel ◆ Melv ◆ Melvin*), but there are specific clusters that are never preserved (e.g. stop-stop clusters, as in *Hec ◆ *Hect ◆ Hector*), while other cluster types never seem to undergo deletion (e.g. /ŋk/, as in *Frank ◆ *Fra[ŋ] ◆ Franklin*).

The segments that make it into the name clipping are mostly unaltered, but some exceptions occur. A large group of rather systematic segmental alternations concern schwas in base-initial syllables. In such cases the schwa is replaced by a full vowel. Which vowel is chosen is mostly dependent on the spelling. For example, schwas spelled as <a> in the base may become /æ/ in the clipping (*Al ◆ Alyssa, Pat ◆ Patricia*), schwas spelled as <e> typically becomes /e/ (*Del ◆ Delila*). Apparently more random vowel changes also occur, examples include *Bab ◆ Barbara, Kate ◆ Kay ◆ Catherine, Meg ◆ Margaret, Ray ◆ Regina*. Again it is noteworthy that these exceptional forms may be homophonous to the completely regular derivatives of other bases. The vast majority of name clippings do not alter the consonants taken from the base. If they do, the change is systematic with regard to two phenomena. The dental fricative /θ/ is often replaced by a /t/ (e.g. *Bart ◆ Bartholomew, Ted ◆ Theodore*), and post-vocalic /r/ is avoided as a final segment and in that position is often replaced by a consonant occurring later in the base (*Chat ◆ Charity, Floss ◆ Florence, Jem ◆ Jeremy, Lon ◆ Lawrence*), or it is replaced by /l/ (*Hal ◆ Harold, Sal ◆ Sarah*, but note the exception *Lor ◆ Lorraine* NAmE).

18.2.3.2. *Suffixed hypocoristics:* -ie, -o, -s, -zza

Of all suffixed hypocoristics, those in *-ie* are by far the most common. Suffixed hypocoristics *-ie* and *-o* are phonologically restricted in much the same way as the *-ie* diminutives described in Section 18.2.2.1, with two differences. The hypocoristics can freely anchor to the first and to the stressed syllables, while the other diminutives have a tendency to be restricted to the first syllable of the base. With regard to consonant clusters, hypocoristics are less tolerant of certain clusters. Thus, suffixed hypocoristics do not allow non-homorganic second consonants in nasal-initial clusters, while clippings do. Derivatives exhibiting these two regular patterns are, for example, *Winny* ◆ **Winfy* ◆ *Winfred* versus *confy* ◆ *confidential*.

Hypocoristics in *-s* (e.g. *Babs, Debs, Fats, Lyds*) are monosyllabic and are perhaps best described as being based on clippings, as all attested forms that we have come across have bases that are also attested as clipped names. There seems to be a preference for bases ending in a plosive, but the data sets are too small to make more reliable generalizations.

Another type of hypocoristic formation is comprised of trochaic disyllables ending in *-zza*, which are of relatively recent use, and especially prevalent in BrE and AusE. Some examples are given in (45) from various sources including the BNC and COCA.

(45)   Bazza ◆ Barry, Dazza ◆ Darren, Gazza ◆ Gary / Gascoigne, Hezza ◆ Heseltine, Lazza ◆ Larry, Mazza ◆ Amanda, Mozza ◆ Morrissey, Ozza ◆ Owen, Shazza / Shazzer / Shaz ◆ Sharon, Tezza ◆ Terry

The truncation patterns are very similar to the other suffixed hypocoristics (anchoring to first or stressed syllable, contiguity, and relative stability of the segments taken from the base). Base words with intervocalic /r/ or /s/ seem very much overrepresented, and in these derivatives /r/ does not survive, which is reminiscent of clipped hypocoristics.

18.2.4 Clipping

Non-hypocoristic clippings express primarily the attitudinal component of diminution, marking familiarity with the denoted object or concept. Like abbreviations, they often convey the in-group status of the speaker and are often restricted in usage to sub-groups of the speech community at large. Like other diminutives, they may express equal status or reduced social distance. Eventually, through the process of lexicalization, clippings may become the standard words for the relevant denotatum. Clippings may be formed from nouns, adjectives, verbs, and phrases. They do not change the syntactic category of their bases and in the case of phrasal bases they have the category of the head of that phrase, even though the clipped word may not be the head and have a different syntactic category (e.g. pub_N ◆ $[public_{ADJ} house_N]_{NP}$).

Clippings based on polysyllabic bases involve loss of phonological material in rather complex ways. In order to explore potential patterns, clippings have been classified according to which part of the original base is removed, as reflected in the terminology 'back-clipping' and 'fore-clipping' (e.g. Marchand 1960; Bauer 1983; Berg 2011). However, it is more insightful to focus on what is preserved in the output and how the material preserved in the derivative relates to the base (see Lappe 2007; see also Nelson 1998 for French, or Piñeros 1998 for Spanish).

The overwhelming tendency in clipping formation is to form monosyllables. The majority of clippings anchor to the first syllable (e.g. 93 per cent in Lappe's database, Lappe 2007:174). This pattern is exemplified in (46).

(46)   ad • advertisement, app • application, caff (BrE) • café, dem • democrat, doc • doctor, fax • facsimile, gas (NAmE) • gasoline, lab • laboratory, mike • microphone, pram (BrE) • perambulator, pub • public house, sub • submarine sandwich, submarine vehicle, substitution, ute (AusE/NZE) • utility truck

If the base starts in an unstressed syllable followed by a stressed syllable, we also find disyllabic clippings, as in (47). Example (47a) shows forms based on a main-stressed syllable, (47b) forms based on a secondarily stressed syllable.

(47)   a. artíc (BrE) • artículated lorry, binócs • binóculars, celéb • celébrity, exéc • exécutive, idént • idéntity, posísh • posítion, *postóp • post-óperative, *prelím(s) • prelíminaries

        b. co-éd • coèducátion, congráts • congràtulátions, colláb • collàborátion, exám • exàminátion

Other clippings that are longer than one syllable involve truncation that is not purely phonological, but targets sublexical morphemes. This can be found frequently with prefixed or compound bases. In such cases the surviving material may anchor to and comprise initial, medial or final (pseudo-)morphemic constituents. We can thus distinguish terminologically between purely phonological clippings and morphemic clippings. Examples of morphemic clipping are given in (48).

(48)   blog • weblog (*with shifted morpheme boundary*), bus • omnibus, fiche • microfiche, fridge • refrigerator, mini • minicar / miniskirt, pike (NAmE) • turnpike, phone • telephone, plane • aeroplane ‖ airplane, shrink • head-shrinker 'therapist', stereo • stereophonic record-player, uni • university, video • videorecorder / videotape

A closely related phenomenon that is usually not treated as a case of word-formation is ellipsis in lexicalized phrases, as in *fries* for *French fries*, *the House* for either *the House of Representatives* or *the State House*, and *the States* for *the United States of America*.

Exceptions to the three major patterns of monosyllabic, disyllabic, and morphemic clippings exist, but are rare. Some are collected in (49).

(49)   flu • influenza, gator (NAmE) • alligator, jams • pyjamas, tache (BrE) • moustache, tec (BrE *now arch.*) • detective

Clippings are frequently used in compounds, either being compounded with a full word (50) or with another clipping (51).

(50)   behavior mod, con-man, interrobang, petrodollar, teletext

(51)   biopic, edbiz, hi-fi, kidvid, sci-fi

As we have seen, morphemic clippings faithfully preserve the phonological structure of their base morpheme. Phonological clippings are more intricate. In the following passages we return to phonological clippings and their properties.

Phonological clippings preserve contiguous segments starting from the left edge of the first syllable. In addition, they need to have a heavy rhyme. In order to satisfy both requirements, they preserve as many segments as needed, sometimes even more (cf. *cue* ~ *cuke* ◆ *cucumber*). Consonant clusters are variably preserved, as in *amp* ◆ *amplifier* versus *sis* ◆ *sister*, but there is a preference for preservation. Clusters that begin with /l/- seem to be categorically preserved (*Alb* ◆ *Albania, alt* ◆ *alternative*). Very rarely, contiguity is violated (e.g. *crab* ◆ *karabiner*). Such violations are predictable, however, if the clipping is based on a form that has an -*s* suffix. In such cases the suffix is often preserved (e.g. *avs* ◆ *average results, binocs* ◆ *binoculars, comps* ◆ *comprehensive exams, maths* (BrE) ◆ *mathematics, stats* ◆ *statistics, specs* ◆ *spectacles*).

The segments surviving in the clipped form are normally faithfully preserved except that schwas in base-initial syllables are regularly turned into full vowels, as in *pro* ◆ *professional, fan* ◆ *fanatic* (with specialized meaning), based on the possible sound–spelling correspondences. Other vowel changes occur very rarely, and seem to be triggered by the prosodic constraints discussed above, for example the change from short vowel to long vowel (in an open syllable) to fulfil the requirement of having a heavy rhyme, as in *bro* ◆ *brother*. Consonantal alternations are rare (e.g. *prink* ◆ *principle, spaz* ◆ *spastic*), and do not seem to affect the consonants that are prone to alternation in clipped names, that is /r/ and /θ/ (cf. *cath* ◆ *cat* ◆ *catheter*, or *ter* ◆ *tel* ◆ *tess* ◆ *terrorist*, as against *Nat* ◆ *Nathaniel, Sal* ◆ *Sarah, Floss* ◆ *Florence*).

Overall, it is clear that, in spite of the variation this morphological category exhibits, the formation of clippings is heavily constrained and to a large extent regular and predictable. Notably, the patterns displayed by hypocoristic clippings (as discussed in Section 18.2.3) are similar, but not quite identical to the patterns observed by the clippings described in this section, which substantiates the claim that we are faced with distinct morphological categories.

18.2.5 Augmentatives

18.2.5.1 *The prefix* hyper-

The prefix *hyper-* is extremely productive in both technical and non-technical domains, attached commonly to both nouns and adjectives and less commonly to verbs. Where it is relevant, the use of the prefix *hyper-* often seems to imply some pathological case or, the non-technical equivalent, something which is excessive. In most ways the semantics of *hyper-* is comparable to that of *super-* (with which it is cognate). While *super-* came into English as a prefix, *hyper-* was originally a combining form (Bauer 1983: 215). The prefix *hyper-* continues to be able to attach to other combining forms, but both prefixes now attach freely to words. A few of the many examples from COCA are given in the following examples, divided according to the bases, with nominal (52), adjectival (53), verbal (54), and neoclassical elements (55) treated separately.

(52)   *nominal bases*: hyperachiever, hyperagency, hyperarousal, hyper-deflation, hyper-elite, hyper-investment, hyper-pension, hyper-steel, hypercar, hypercello, hyperclarity, hypercoffee, hypercognition, hypercompetition, hypercomputer, hypercube, hyperdrive, hypergravity, hyperhonesty, hyperindividualism, hyperinsecurity, hyperirritability, hyperlaw, hypermarket, hypermedia, hypermiler, hypernova, hyperparasite, hyperplane, hyperreggae, hyperspeed, hypersuccess, hypersurface

(53)   *adjectival bases*: hyper-abrupt, hyper-awake, hyper-fertile, hyper-grossing, hyper-health-conscious, hyper-miniature, hyper-optimistic, hyper-rapid-fire, hyper-svelte, hyperacerbic, hyperactive, hyperalert, hyperambitious, hyperarid, hyperaware, hyperblue, hypercarnivorous, hyperchic, hyperchronic, hypercool, hyperdense, hyperelegant, hypermacho, hypermeticulous, hyperobsessed, hyperpermissive

(54)   *verbal bases*: hyperaccumulate, hyperanalyze, hyperbrowse, hypercharge, hypercorrect, hyperextend, hyperovulate, hypersoar

(55)   *bound bases*: hyperaemia, hyperalgesia, hyperaspis, hyperbole, hyperborea, hyperdermic, hyperemia, hypergammaglobulinemia, hypergamy, hypergolic, hyper-graph, hyperhomocysteinemia, hyperlect, hypermnesis, hyperonymy, hyperostosis, hypertrophia

In many of these cases the order of affixation is underdetermined. For example, *hypervegitarianism* may be seen as a case of *hyper-* prefixation to a base *vegetarianism*, or as a case of *-ism* suffixation to a base *hypervegetarian*. Some examples like this have been included to show that potentially the bases are complex, but many more have been omitted for this reason.

The prefix is generally secondarily stressed (on the first syllable), but if the prefix combines with a neoclassical form that attracts stress to the syllable immediately preceding it (see Chapter 9.4.5 for discussion), the second syllable of the prefix receives the main stress of the derivative, e.g. *hypérgamy, hypérbola, hypértrophy.*

18.2.5.2 *The prefixes* maxi- *and* midi-

The prefix *maxi-* is attached mainly to nouns to show great size. It often contrasts implicitly or explicitly with the prefix *mini-* (see Section 18.2.2.2). Some examples from COCA are given in (56).

(56)   maxiboat, maxicab, maxi(-)coat, maxi-manor, maxi(-)pad, maxi(-)skirt

The prefix is considerably less profitable than *mini-*, but is nevertheless productive, as indicated by the fact that most of the relevant words in COCA are hapaxes. The prefix is mostly main-stressed (e.g. *máxicircle*, *máxi-skirt*), sometimes secondarily stressed (*màxi per-fórmance*). As with *mini-*, the question can be raised as to whether this is a prefix or a compound element, especially since *maxi* is frequently spelled as a separate word, which probably reflects the writers' intuition about the lexical tightness of the derivatives. Where *maxi* occurs as an independently spelled word, it is frequently being used as an adjective, and it is not clear that this usage is, in reality, anything other than a different representation of the prefix. Some examples are given in (57).

(57)   *Bicycling 1998*: Here's a mini bike capable of **maxi** performance

   Mechanical Engineering 2002: Select **maxi** systems can allow pump-down of a supply cylinder as low as 150 psi

Just occasionally, *maxi-* is prefixed to an adjective, yielding an adjective that is intensified in its meaning (paraphrasable as 'extremely X'). Two examples from COCA are presented in (58).

(58)   *Gregory Macdonald 1994*: You're marrying into a **maxi-wealthy** family

   Town and Country 2007: The country may be minisized (999 square miles, slightly smaller than Rhode Island), but it's **maxirich**.

Closely related to *maxi-* is the prefix *midi-*, which denotes medium size. Strictly speaking, it should perhaps not be classified as an augmentative, but we treat it here nevertheless, as it stands at least in a paradigmatic contrast with *mini-*. It is not very productive and occurs chiefly with reference to garments or audio equipment, as in *midi(-)coat, midi-dress, midi-length, midi-skirt, midi(-)cd-player, midi-hi-fi-system*. Orthographically, it seems to behave like *maxi-*, with two-word spellings being preferred for most formations. Stress-wise it also shows the kind of variability found for *maxi-*.

18.2.5.3 *The prefix* mega-

The prefix *mega-* has a number of distinguishable uses. First it can be used as a combining form, that is, in combination with another neoclassical element, as in (59) (see Chapter 19). Here it is sometimes in competition with *megalo-*, which is used exclusively as a combining form. A second use of *mega-* is in the names of units to multiply the unit by one million, as in (60). In its third use it can be used as an ordinary English prefix to mean 'extremely large'. In this last kind, it is usually attached to nouns (61), but is also found on adjectival bases, meaning 'extremely' (62). The examples below are all from COCA.

(59)   megakaryocytes, megalith, megaphone, megapod, megapode, megapolis, megaptera, megatherium

(60)   mega-decibel, mega-dollar, megaflop, mega-joule, mega-kilowatt, mega-pixel, megabar, megabit, megabits/sec, megabyte, megacalorie, megadecibel, megahertz,

megahorsepower, megajoule, megajoules/kg, megakilometer, megamile, meganewton, megaparsec, megapascal, megapixel, megaton, megavolt, megawatt, megawatt-hour

(61) mega-acquisition, mega-amount, mega-artist, mega-attraction, mega-book, mega-box, mega-budget, mega-chain, mega-crayfish, mega-ego, mega-events, mega-market, mega-selling, megabrain, megabrand, megacorridor, megadealership, megafarm, megamachine, megamansion, megamedia, megamind, megamouth, megamusical, megaproject, megastore, megastructure, megatap, megatask, megateam, megatech, megathrust, megatonnage, megazillionaire, megazit

(62) mega-bad, mega-best-selling, mega-funky, mega-personal, mega-quick, mega-scaled, mega(-)rich, mega(-)sized, mega(-)successful, megacool, megafamous, megapopular, megawide

In the first two types of formation *mega-* always carries main stress, while in the third type, meaning 'extremely (large)', it seems variably main-stressed, or secondarily stressed. The spelling is variable between one-word, hyphenated and two-word spellings, with established formations having a tendency toward one-word spellings, and new formations occurring hyphenated or even as two words (e.g. *mega churches, mega famous, mega drool-inducing, mega success*, all from COCA).

18.2.5.4 *The prefix* super-

The semantics of *super-* is particularly difficult to specify. There are a number of sub-meanings which can be distinguished, but they are often interchangeable for the same lexeme, and one meaning often shades into another. Given that the original meaning of *super-* is 'above', there are cases where *super-* means 'in a class above', and, indeed, this might be an over-arching meaning for the prefix. The locative uses of the prefix are discussed in Chapter 16. Many of the derivatives also carry an attitudinal shade of meaning, expressing either excessiveness or appreciated large size in the eyes of the speaker. This attitudinal meaning can be found alongside the other meanings in one and the same derivative, or may occur on its own.

The augmentative meaning can have various more specific readings that emerge in the interaction of the prefix with its particular base. We find readings where the augmentative denotes qualitative superiority either with an adjectival base, as in (63) or with a nominal base, as in (64).

(63) super-easy, super-powerful, super-quick, super-sharp, super-simple, super-skinny, super-smart, super-sophisticated, super-thin, superabsorbent, superabundant, superbright, supercheap, supercold, superfit, superpowerful, superskinny, superslim, supersmooth, superthin

(64) supercar, superhero, superinsulation, superlawyer, supermodel, supermom, supernanny, superstar, superwoman

The derived word can also denote something which is of a similar type to the thing denoted by the unprefixed lexeme, but one step up some notional scale; again this can be with a nominal (65) or adjectival base (66).

(65)   super-ego, super-glue, super-heavyweight, super-organism, superalloy, superbike, supercollider, supercow, superdrive, superhumans, superintelligence, superspy, supersymmetry, superweed

(66)   supernormal, supersensory

The augmentative may also be interpreted as denoting something which is simply bigger than the thing denoted by the unprefixed lexeme, as in (67).

(67)   superbomb, supercluster, supercomputer, supercontinent, supercroc, supergiant, supergun, superhighway, superjumbo, superliner, superspeedway, superstore, supertanker

As already mentioned, the derived lexeme can, in the appropriate context, also carry the meaning of 'excessive(ly)', based on a nominal, adjectival, or verbal base (68a). Example (68b), from COCA, illustrates this reading.

(68)   a. super-expensive, superabundance, supercool, supercritical, superovulate, supersensitive

   b. *Redbook 2003:* And I came to understand some of the theories experts had as to the cause of IC-from the leaky-bladder hypothesis, in which microscopic tears allow urine to irritate the bladder wall, to a theory that suggested **supersensitive** nerve endings were to blame

Despite the classifications of the various shades of meanings provided in (63) to (68), the readings mentioned so far are often not clearly distinguishable, as the examples in (69) illustrate. For example, a *superministry* may be one that is simply larger than a usual ministry, or it may be one that is perceived as excessively large, or a step up on a scale of significance.

(69)   super-agent, superagency, superministry, superpredator, superregion, superscience, supervillain

The prefix is either main-stressed or carries secondary stress. The distribution of the two stress patterns is not quite clear, but more lexicalized words tend to have main stress on the prefix (e.g. *Súperbowl*). Following the same patterns as the previously discussed prefixes, *super-* is normally left-prominent, but may also be main-stressed on its second syllable with some lexicalized forms, or if the following element attracts stress to that syllable (e.g. *supérfluous, supérlative, supérnal*).

The potentially problematic form *superette* ('small supermarket') is not current in all parts of the English-speaking world, but provides a superficial instance of a prefix and a suffix without a base. However, it is probably best analysed as a morphemic clipping of *supermarket-ette*. This analysis is supported by the fact that *-ette* avoids attachment to /t/-final bases.

18.2.5.5 *The prefix* ultra-

Ultra-, coming from the Latin word meaning 'beyond', has a scientific or social-scientific usage (70) where it retains that Latin meaning and a more colloquial usage where it is prefixed to adjectives in particular with a meaning of 'extremely' (71). There are instances where it can be difficult to determine which use is which. The examples here are from COCA. They show that *ultra-* attaches to a wide variety of bases, including adjectives, compounds, and phrases. The prefix usually carries secondary stress, but a small minority of forms have initial main stress (e.g. *últrasound*).

(70)   ultra-heat-resistant, ultra-high-density, ultra-high-efficiency, ultra-Keynesian, ultra-left-wing, ultra-low-dose, ultra-loyalist, ultra-maoist, ultra-uv, ultrabroadband, ultracentrifuge, ultradense, ultralow-frequency, ultramarathon, ultramicrobacteria, ultranationalism, ultraorthodox, ultrapacifist, ultrasaurus

(71)   ultra-absorbent, ultra-accurate, ultra-ambitious, ultra-American, ultra-aware, ultra-exaggerated, ultra-svelte, ultra-swanky, ultraclassy, ultraclean, ultraexclusive, ultraexpensive, ultralurid, ultralush, ultralusty, ultraminiature, ultramobile, ultrarapid, ultrarare, ultrarational, ultrasexy, ultrasweet

The prefix *ultra-* is also found prefixed to nouns, as in (72). Here the meaning may not be clear out of context and may vary from the scientific to the rather colloquial.

(72)   ultra-coach, ultra-elf, ultra-kiosk, ultra-nerd, ultra-poppy, ultra-underdog, ultrabike, ultracop, ultradog, ultrafluid, ultrahero, ultrahit, ultraluxury, ultramarina, ultrasun, ultratorque, ultrawife

18.2.5.6 *The prefix* turbo-

The element *turbo-* originally meant 'driven by a turbine' as in *turbo-charge, turbo-fan, turbo-jet, turbo-prop*. In modern usage this has become a quantitative and attitudinal prefix indicating desirable high speed and power. COCA provides *Turbolinux, Turbotax, TurboChip, TurboChef* (all brand names) and *turbochat, turbonews, turbosled, turbospeed*, and *turbowash*. It carries the main stress of the derivative on the first syllable.

18.2.5.7 *Prefix rivalry:* hyper-, maxi-, mega-, super-, ultra-

Given that the meanings of these prefixes are very similar to each other, and that they often attach to the same kinds of bases, it is not surprising to find examples where these suffixes seem interchangeable, with no, or only very little, difference in meaning. *Hyper-* can be used neutrally, but when it occurs in medical, technical, and science fiction contexts it is the one used to convey 'large in a negative, pathological sense'. The prefixes *maxi-, mega-, ultra-*, and *super-* seem most often to be used in a positive sense. It is possible to find doublets for any pair of these prefixes. The examples in (73) to (79) illustrate this, with (77d) being from the BNC, all others from COCA.

(73)   a. *Rolling Stone 1990*: The Police were the first video-era rock & roll band of any magnitude. They grew into that era, and it was sort of **hyper-accelerated** through video, through MTV.

   b. *Analog Science Fiction & Fact 2001*: The engines don't hum—no devices move within them but the **super-accelerated** particles pushing the Resurrection slowly to greater and greater speed, and even when you stand next to the reactors, there's no sound.

(74)   a. *Ear, Nose, & Throat Journal 2004*: **Hyperacute** forms progress in only a few hours, but most cases progress over a period of days, probably because patients undergo antibiotic treatment at the onset of symptoms.

   b. *USA Today 2003*: Early in the film, blind attorney by day, vigilante by night Matt Murdock uses his other **ultra-acute** senses to trail the hard-to-impress Elektra, a dazzling practitioner of martial arts.

(75)   a. *Total Health 2006*: Yet if the immune system is continually on **hyperalert**, inflammation can become chronic.

   b. *Outdoor Life 2007*: If you really want to challenge an antelope with all your skills, try the animal with a bow or muzzleloader. You'll know you've been on a hunt once you do. The need to get very close to this **ultra-alert** speedster will test all your abilities as a hunter.

   c. *Patchwork Planet 1998*: It wasn't even ten o'clock, but she must have been in bed, because she answered so immediately, in that **superalert** tone people use when they don't want to let on you've wakened them.

(76)   a. *Skiing 1998*: I suggest that you spend at least a few hours on this **hyperfriendly** terrain making very big, round long-radius turns.

   b. *Redbook 2010*: Everyone was **superfriendly**—and very concerned about my hydrating needs: Every single person who spoke to me asked if I wanted water.

   c. *Newsweek 1998*: Acer preloads two especially useful programs on its machines: the My Aspire Guide, an **ultrafriendly** software that will hold your hand should you run into problems, and a !just for kids! browser for tapping into kid-safe Web sites.

(77)   a. *Smithsonian 1994*: He is explaining why ostensibly mature men and the occasional woman buy his hyperpowered, handmade **ultracars** like CheZoom.

   b. *Journal of International Affairs 1999*: Ultimately, plug-in **Hypercars** could provide five to 10 times as much generating capacity as all utilities now own—enough in principle to displace essentially all central thermal power stations at a profit.

   c. *Popular Science 2008*: Now that Nissan has proven that it can be done, expect more accessible, technology-rich **supercars** in the years ahead.

d. *w_fict_prose 1991*: And he had a status-symbol **mega car** which he drove very slowly in the middle lane

(78) a. *Consumers Research Magazine 2004*: Independent Rear Suspension will, however, be fitted to the more expensive, **ultra-performance** SVT Cobra.

b. *Bicycling 1998*: Here's a mini bike capable of **maxi performance** thanks to a welded-aluminum frame

(79) a. *USA Today 1990*: Reggie Fountain, in Fountain, averaged 107.94 mph to win the **Super Boat** class at the Popeye's Racefest in New Orleans

b. *USA Today 1991*: Goetz, who rolls up his sleeves and works alongside his employees, has worked with Conner since 1979 and built Koch's prize-winning **maxiboat** Matador in 1990.

18.2.5.8 *Non-prefixal augmentatives*

The overall rule is that English does not have augmentative suffixes. However, there are pertinent forms that use *-rama*, what appears to be what we call a 'splinter' (see Chapters 2 and 23), and some with the putative suffix *-ola*. Examples are listed in (80).

(80) a. Hardboiled homicide cops dancing the **fawnorama**. (*McClister 1999: 75*)

b. Leaves us with a gigantic **hole-o-rama** in our December release schedule. (*Cannell 2003: 252*)

c. *Christian_Science_Monitor 2007*: I wrote about the sport in the 1960s and 1970s, which was the medieval age compared with today's big-bucks **cashorama**.

c. there's a huge **problemola** with fetchmail (*Newbie 2001*)

d. the screen debut of Jimmy Durante, he of the large **sch[n]ozzola** (*OED* cit. 1930)

The suffix *-ola* shown here is presumably the non-diminutive suffix which is usually assumed not to have a specific meaning in English. It is often assumed that the same suffix appears in *payola* and *granola* (despite the different meanings in the two words, see Randle 1961; Glowka 1985).

18.2.6 Reduplication

There are a number of patterns of reduplication in English whose main function, apart from the creation of new words, appears to be attitudinal. The examples can be classified in a number of different ways which interact. One classification is in terms of two words with some phonological constituent in common that are both words, while in other instances one or both of the elements may be items without independent occurrence. A formal classification is in terms of the process of reduplication involved. The examples below are all established, and are mainly taken from Matthewson (1991). All examples have elements of matching length, and each element is maximally disyllabic in itself.

First we find examples where there is real reduplication, the two elements are homophonous. The examples in (81) all illustrate nursery language.

(81)   chuff-chuff, choo-choo, doo-doo, quack-quack, woof-woof

Second we find instances where the two elements retain the consonantism from the stressed syllable of the foot, but show ablaut between the two elements. There are two common patterns of ablaut: items with /ɪ/ in the stressed syllable of the first element and /æ/ in the stressed syllable of the second, see (82), and items with /ɪ/ in the first element and /ɒ/ ‖ /ɑː/ in the second, see (83).

(82)   chitchat, dilly-dally , fiddle-faddle , flimflam, jimjam(s), kitcat, knick-knack, mishmash, pitter-patter, rickety-rackety, shilly-shally, tittle-tattle, whim-wham

(83)   clip-clop, criss-cross, dingdong, flipflop, pingpong, singsong, ticktock, tip-top, wishy-washy

In a third case, the rhyme of the stressed syllable and any remaining material in the foot remains the same, but the onset is changed. Examples are in (84).

(84)   argy-bargy, boogie-woogie, easy peasy, fuddy-duddy, fuzzy-wuzzy, hab-dabs, hanky-panky, heebie-jeebies, helter-skelter, higgledy-piggledy, hocus-pocus, hoity-toity, hokey-pokey, holus-bolus, humdrum, hurdy-gurdy, hurly-burly, incy-wincy, killer-diller, lovey-dovey, mumbo-jumbo, pow-wow, raggle-taggle, roly-poly, silly-billy, super-duper, teensy-weensy, teeny-weeny, walkie-talkie, wham-bam, willy-nilly

There is a slight preference for a bilabial consonant in the onset of the first syllable of the second element where this is not predetermined by the original, and there is also a slight preference for plosives in the same position. The examples illustrate, though, that neither of these preferences is categorical.

There are also words which can be viewed as genuine compounds whose elements happen to rhyme. The rhyme is certainly part of the motivation for the coining of the compound, and the rhyme certainly makes the compound more striking. Examples are in (85). In these cases, though, it is not clear that the alliteration is any different in principle from that which affects expressions like those in (86).

(85)   backpack, cop-shop (BrEsl 'police station'), culture vulture, hotpot, hot shot, hurry-scurry, peg leg, ragbag, sin bin

(86)   come hell or high water, cool as a cucumber, fit as a fiddle, kith and kin, might and
main, now or never, Peter Pan, ring-a-ring-o'-roses, vim and vigor

Bauer and Huddleston (2002) suggest compounds like those in (85) are trivializing, and that
is certainly true in cases like *gang-bang* and *culture vulture*, but not necessarily in the case of
hotpot. Perhaps the best we can say is that these words involve a ludic element.

A specific type of the rhyme-motivated construction arises in NAmE (based on Yiddish)
use of /ʃm/ to replace the onset. This is generally treated as syntax rather than word-formation, in the sense that the /ʃm/word is usually separated from its base by a comma (and
occasionally by more). Examples from COCA are given in (87). They are clearly dismissive
and disparaging.

(87)   a. acting, shmacting; chemistry shmemistry; children, shmildren; cover, shmover;
eloquent, shmeloquent; fantasy shmantasy; innovative, shminnovative; millennium,
shmillennium; organic, shmorganic; parked, shmarked; peace, shmeace

b. *Cobb 1994*: I don't know baseball from shmaseball

It is perhaps worth noting that many discussions of English word-formation include these
reduplicative constructions as compounds, seeing them as parallel to the examples in (85).
For reasons discussed in Chapter 19 we prefer not to count these as compounds at all.

18.2.7 Expletive insertion

Expletive insertion is a phenomenon in contemporary English whereby words like *fucking*,
bloody, and *frigging* can be inserted into the middle of a word, giving words like *kanga-bloody-
roo*, *guaran-frigging-tee*, *Tala-fucking-hassee*, *abso-bloody-lutely*. This process appears to be marginal in the sense that some speakers do not control it, though most speakers do. Some sources
(e.g. Aronoff 1976; Plag 2003) term this infixation, but it is not strictly affixation, since the elements that are inserted are words rather than affixes. Part of the puzzle of these formations is,
therefore, their precise nature. If it is a relevant process, it is one whose main function appears
to involve the attitude of the speaker: the formations created in this way are emphasized but in
a pejorative way, as well as having their style-level changed by the presence of the expletive.
Although we talk of expletive insertion here, in some instances, as is pointed out by McMillan
(1980: 163) non-expletives can be inserted: *Jesus H. Christ, terra-extremely-firma, theo-jolly-logical*.
Typically, such alternative inserts are perceived as euphemisms for an expletive.

The phonology of this process has been dealt with as an instance of prosodic phonology
(Chapter 9.6.3). The implication of the required prosodic structure of words into which
expletives can be inserted is that there are words which cannot be used as bases. In such cases
the expletive can still be used, but it is preposed to the noun, as in (88).

(88)   *bk:Senseless 2011*: Nobody here ordered any **fucking** flowers.

HarpersBazaar 2011: We've spent the **fucking** lot.

ACAD_Commentary 2010: Finkler's wife asks the increasingly obsessive Treslove if he doesn't wish that Jews would just "shut up about themselves…whether the world hates them or it doesn't, the **fucking** Holocaust, **fucking** Palestine?"

The implication of this might be that this is a case of prosodic syntax. The expletive is placed in such a position as to strengthen a strong syllable in the original; where necessary, it migrates across the word-boundary into the word in order to do this. The last example in (88) suggests that this is not the whole story. Given that *holofuckingcaust* would fit the prosodic pattern of typical outputs of this process, the writer must have chosen to use the preposed expletive, which means that the two structures are alternatives, not variants of the same underlying pattern.

There are other indications that the expletive insertion is a morphological process. The first is that while the preferred structure is for the expletive to be placed relative to a stressed syllable, in some instances it can be placed between morphs. Thus alongside prosodically expected *unbefuckinglievable*, we find (89a), and there are even rare examples like (89b, c), where morphology seems more important than prosodic structure.

(89)   a. *MAG_Esquire 2000*: well…it was amazing, incredible, unfuckingbelievable.

b. *Triquarterly 2005*: He wanted a huge dog, a humongous dog, the world's most enor-fucking-mous dog in the universal pound.

c. In-goddamn-consistent (*McMillan 1980*)

Whatever the precise nature of this phenomenon, therefore, it has morphological implications, and in some cases the insertion point is determined by morphological structure. It might be possible to view this phenomenon as a prosodically-driven version of compounding with an expletive.

18.2.8 The prefixes *pseudo-* and *quasi-*

Another affix which, at least in colloquial usage, denotes an attitude is *pseudo-*, where it indicates something sham or less than genuine. In scientific usage the negative implications are absent. The colloquial usage is illustrated in (88), where the bases are nouns or adjectives. The examples are from COCA.

(90)   pseudo-Arabic, pseudo-celebrity, pseudo-classical, pseudo-conservative, pseudo-diary, pseudo-environment, pseudo-independent, pseudo-issue, pseudo-linguistics, pseudo-news,

pseudo-philosopher, pseudo-reality, pseudo-religious, pseudo-science, pseudo-superhero, pseudo-Victorian, pseudocapitalism, pseudocoffeehouses, pseudofeminists, pseudoscience

The scientific usage is exemplified in (91a). There are also neoclassical formations with *pseudo-* in the first position. A few examples are provided in (91b).

(91)   a.   pseudo-cells, pseudoacacia, pseudoaneurysms, pseudoarthrosis, pseudobinary, pseudocysts, pseudoephedrine, pseudopod, pseudorandom, pseudosarcoma, pseudoscorpion, pseudotumor, pseudoxanthoma

        b.   pseudoceros, pseudodoxia, pseudomorphic, pseudonym

The prefix is either main-stressed or secondarily stressed. If main-stressed, it has three allomorphs. One with initial stress and a final schwa, as in *pséudonym*, one with initial stress and a final diphthong, as in *pséudopod*, and one with final stress, which occurs if a stress-shifting form follows it, as in *pseudónymous*. In scientific usage, the prefix may (sometimes variably) lose its final vowel if followed by a vowel-initial base, as in *pseudepisematic, pseudaposematic, pseudarthrosis ~ pseudo-arthrosis* (all from *OED*).

There is another prefix that expresses the speaker's doubtfulness about the presence of all the necessary properties in the referent denoted by the base, the prefix *quasi-*. It is glossed by the *OED* as 'resembling or simulating, but not really the same as, that properly so termed; having some but not all of the properties of a thing or substance'. The prefix is quite productive and attaches to nouns, adjectives, adverbs, compounds, and phrases as shown in (92), with derivatives found in COCA. The prefix is either main-stressed or secondarily stressed.

(92)   a.   quasi-editor, quasi-homophony, quasi-intuition, quasi-radio, quasi-shoe, quasi-sleep, quasi-slavery, quasi-zombie

        b.   quasi-experimental,   quasi-hip,   quasi-hypnotic,   quasi-public,   quasi-stable, quasi-stellar, quasi-utopian, quasi-violent

        c.   quasi-accidentally, quasi-anonymously, quasi-clockwise, quasi-elastically, quasi-facetiously, quasi-simultaneously,

        d.   quasi-backcountry, quasi-flat-rate, quasi-newsgroup, quasi-market-based

        e.   quasi-American-style, quasi-free-market, quasi-global-scale, quasi-working-class

A comparison of *quasi-* and *pseudo-* reveals that the two prefixes share the meaning component that the derivative does not refer to a genuine exemplar of its head's category. However, *quasi-* lacks the element of falseness that *pseudo-* generally carries. This can be illustrated with the examples in (93) and (94), from COCA:

(93)   a.   *Consumers Research Magazine 1999*: One of the first countries to reform ATC in this way was Britain, which created the National Air Traffic Services as a

quasi-independent corporation in 1972. While still nominally part of the U.K. Civil Aviation Authority (their equivalent of our FAA), NATS is funded mostly by user fees and is regulated for safety by the safety branch of the CAA.

b. *Africa Today 1998*: Second, the plurality system provides greater opportunity to manipulate the size of single-member constituencies through malapportionment. An incumbent government (represented by a **pseudo-independent** Electoral Commission) can adjust the size and boundaries of constituencies according to its needs.

The 'not genuine' meaning component leads to the negative evaluative meaning component that can be found with many *pseudo-* derivatives as the falseness is often seen as an intentional act of deception or obfuscation. Notably, and as already mentioned above, the scientific usage of *pseudo-* lacks the evaluative attitude, which makes both prefixes eligible for the coinage of a new scientific term, and we do find both, perhaps with a preference for *pseudo-* (for example, astronomical *quasi-stellar* for *quasi-*, and the examples in (91a) for *pseudo-*).

Other potential rivals of *pseudo-* and *quasi-* are the suffixes *-ish*, *-esque*, and *-oid* whose derivatives also denote something that is similar, but not identical, in shape or quality to what the base denotes (see Chapter 14). Like the prefix *quasi-*, the suffixes lack the element of falseness. The exact difference in meaning, if any, between *quasi-*, *-ish*, *-esque*, and *-oid* is not entirely clear and the distribution perhaps a matter of register or domain. The examples in (94) illustrate the use of the five affixes with the same base, *modern* (examples from COCA).

(94)   *Geographical Review 1998*: One need not admire flimsy construction, the short-sighted planning, the overdramatized, over-colored, **pseudo-modern** ranch houses which are rising all over the country;

Foreign Affairs 2009: This is both more modest and more realistic than earlier notions of building a modern democracy in a society in which only the urban sectors are more or less **quasi-modern** and the rural areas are in many respects still quite medieval.

Town and Country 2009: Since opening in December, Benjy's has been strictly SRO. The **modernesque** look sets the stage for boisterous fun in the upstairs lounge, where you can enjoy the signature blood-orange margaritas, and downstairs, where the best choices include tuna tartare on a tempura edamame roll, […]

San Francisco Chronicle 1996: "I always like to do Shakespeare in **modernish** dress because I want to put people into clothes rather than costumes," he explains.

Public Interest 1992: [O]verall, these designs are refreshingly free from formula: no **modernoid** lunar landscapes with lollipop lightbulbs, no 'Olmstoid' caricatures of Frederick Law Olmsted's pioneering work of a century ago.

18.3 NON-EVALUATIVE ATTITUDE: *ANTI-* AND *PRO-*

Two affixes which show attitude in a rather more specific way are *anti-* and *pro-*. These do not show attitude in the sense that they have connotations attached to them, but in the sense that they specify an attitude.

Anti- has at least three distinct uses. The first is the attitudinal meaning, where it attaches to a noun, a name, or an adjective to show opposition to whatever is denoted by the base. Examples are provided in (95a). The second is the medical or scientific usage, where the prefix is usually attached to an adjective, though may also be attached to a noun, to show the effect of something in attacking or counteracting something else. Some of the examples in this set are less scientific, but retain that meaning. Examples are in (95b). In the third usage, illustrated in (95c), the prefix seems to express a negative meaning with readings like 'reversed', 'non-', or 'opposite to'. Examples are from COCA.

(95)   a. *attitudinal*

antiabolitionist, antiabortionist, antiacademic, anti-additive, anti-appeasement, anti-Aquino, anti-aristocratic, anti-Aristotelian, anti-Bergsonism, anti-Blair, anti-British, anticensorship, antichoice, anti-environmentalist, anti-free-speech, anti-hate-speech, anti-Kissinger

b. *medical or scientific*

antiacid, antiacne, antiaddiction, antiaircraft, antiamoebin, anti-amyloid, antibody, anticholera, anticholesterol, anticonvulsant, antidiuretic, antiflatulence, antifreeze (*note the verbal base*), antifungal, antigenic, antineutrino, antioxidant, antitussive,

c. *negative*

anti-alphabetical, anti-biography, antichrist, anti-election, antihero

In a few instances, *anti-* combines with final combining forms (and thus behaves like a combining form itself), creating neoclassical compounds, as in (96).

(96)   antidote, antiphony, antipodes, antiptosis, antisoma

Anti- has the allomorph *ant-* before <h> or before a vowel in neoclassical formations as in *antagonist, anthelion, antonym*. Occasionally this occurs where the element is added to a word rather than to a bound morph, as in *antacid*. More often, though, as illustrated in (95) and (96), the <i> is retained. The prefix can be recursive, as in *anti-anti-muslims, anti-anti-porn, antiantiquarks, antiantirelativism, anti-anti-semitism*.

The prefix *anti-* is most often secondarily stressed (*ànti-abórtion, ànti-magnétic*), but can also occur with main stress on the first syllable (*ántibòdy, ántimàtter*) and with main stress on its second syllable, when stress-shifted (*antónymy, antípathy*).

We now turn to the prefix *pro-*. There are two types of instance of the string <pro> that should not be confused with the prefix under discussion here. First there is the Latin prefix *pro-*, whose reflex can still be seen in words like *produce, prosecute, provide, provoke*, but which is no longer analysable as a prefix in English. Second there is the clipped form of *professional*, which can occur as a compound constituent (e.g. in *pro-am, pro-football, pro-level*). There are two meanings of the actual prefix *pro-*, only one of which is clearly productive. The productive meaning is the attitudinal one ('in favour of'), illustrated by the words from COCA in (97).

(97)   pro-abortion, pro-apartheid, pro-Arab, pro-Aristide, pro-British, pro-business, pro-Clinton, pro-communist, pro-consumer, pro-death, pro-democracy, pro-environment, pro-European, pro-gay, pro-German, pro-industry, pro-inflammatory, pro-Iranian, pro-Islamic, pro-Israel, pro-life, pro-NAFTA, pro-Nazi, pro-prosecution, pro-war, pro-western, pro-woman, pro-Yeltsin, proactive, proslavery

The probably non-productive meaning is 'in place of', which is found in established words like those in (98).

(98)   proconsul, pro-form, pronominal, pronoun, pro-Vice-Chancellor

Established uses of *pro-* in words like *prolapse, prolong* ('movement forwards') and *prodrug* ('before') are typically hard to analyse in English words.

18.4   QUANTIFICATION AND MEASURE

18.4.1 Nominal *-ful*

The suffix *-ful* to be considered here is the one which creates nouns (or, more specifically, noun classifiers, see Dalton-Puffer and Plag 2000) from nominal bases which denote objects viewed as containers. The derivative denotes a measure. This suffix is very productive in its domain, as is illustrated by the sample of words from the BNC in (99). The words in (99) show a preference for monomorphemic bases, but include derivatives and compounds.

(99)   armful, barnful, barrelful, barrowful, basketful, bathful, beakful, bellyful, bottleful, bowlful, boxful, caveful, cellarful, cupboardful, cupful, diskful, drawerful, earful, eggcupful, eyeful, fistful, gutful, hatful, headful, houseful, jugful, kettleful, lungful, mouthful, mugful, neckful, nestful, noseful, officeful, pipeful, planetful, pondful, potful, pramful, purseful, quiverful, sackful, screenful, sinkful, skyful, sporranful, syringeful, tankful, teaspoonful, thimbleful, townful, trainful, truckful, trunkful, tubful, tumblerful, wineglassful

There is a prescriptive position that these nouns pluralize by marking the plural on the base (*spoonsful*, etc.), but it is more common to find the plural marked on the right-hand edge of the word (*spoonfuls*, etc.). The BNC has only one form with the internal *-s*, and many with the final *-s*. While COCA has rather more forms with internal inflection, those with final inflection still predominate.

18.4.2 Verbal *re-*

The prefix *re-* is relevant to a chapter on quantification because it quantifies over events by indicating iteration. It is primarily added to verbs (according to *OED* particularly transitive verbs), though nouns and adjectives may subsequently be derived from these verbs. Examples of relevant verbs from COCA are presented in (100). The examples illustrate the use of transitive and intransitive bases, simple, derived and compound bases, established (sometimes idiomatized) and novel uses, and varying hyphenation.

> (100) reabsorb, reaccess, reaccumulate, readapt, readdress, readjust, readmit, reaffirm, re-alphabetize, reapproach, reargue, rearm, re-ask, reassemble, re-attack, rebabyproof, re-bid, rebloom, reboot, rebottle, re-button, recalculate, recapture, recategorize, recertify, re-choose, reclaim, recode, recolonize, reconfigure, recycle, redeciphering, redevelop, redig, rediscover, redo, re-download, re-endear, re-enlist, re-erupt, re-evolve, re-exit, re-fall, refilm, refloat, refocus, reformulate, refuel, regraft, re-grout, rehaunt, rehistoricize, reimplant, reimprisoning, reinforce, re-kill, relandscape, re-listen, relook, remortgage, repopulate, rerefine

As shown in Lieber (2004), arguing against Smith (1997), the suffix generally attaches to those verbs that imply some sort of non-permanent result. Verbs denoting events with no inherent result are impossible bases (e.g. **resleep*, **repush*), and so are verbs which imply a result which cannot be reversed. For example, it would be impossible to **reeat the apple* or **reexplode the bomb*, unless we imagine a world where such things can actually happen (cf. the science fiction horror movie title *Re-Kill*).

Note the examples *recork, refit, refresh, reinstate, renew*, where the *re-* may indicate the return to an original state rather than a repetition and where the bases are not all verbs. Another example of this reading is intransitive *re-eat* as attested in COCA, shown in (101), signifying the return to a state in which the speaker ate, and not the reversal of an eating event.

> (101) *ABC_GMA 2009*: No kidding, eat your breakfast. That's what I didn't do is I stopped eating, and I learned to **re-eat**. So, that's a very important thing.

What we might see here at work is the same kind of ambiguity we find with the free form *again*, which can indicate repetition as well as 'back', that is the return to a former position or state (*OED*, sv. *again*). It is not clear, however, that we have to recognize the latter reading as a meaning of the prefix *re-* in contemporary English, where iteration seems the appropriate interpretation in productive uses.

The prefix has a tense /iː/ and is secondarily stressed, but some lexicalized formations may deviate from this pattern (e.g. *recreation* 'refreshment' versus *re-creation* 'action of creating again'). Hyphenation is usually used to distinguish between pairs which would otherwise be homographs where one has and the other does not have the prefix (note also the respective presence or absence of secondary stress on the first syllable). Examples include *react* versus *re-act, recover* versus *re-cover, reform* versus *re-form, represent* versus *re-present, review* versus *re-view*.

18.4.3   The suffix *-fold*

The suffix *-fold* is added to numbers and other semantically suitable quantifiers to create adverbs meaning 'times the value of the base', so *five-fold* means 'five times'. It is surprisingly productive, as the short list of examples from the many in COCA provided in (102) indicates. Note the variable hyphenation and variable writing of the number in the base.

(102)   1,700-fold, 14-fold, 162-fold, 2.5-fold, 37-fold, 5-fold, 800-fold, billionfold, five-and-a-half-fold, manifold, many-fold, one-fold, sixty-sevenfold, trillionfold, twelvefold, zillion-fold

18.4.4   The suffixes *-some*

There are two distinct suffixes of the form *-some* used with bases which are numbers, and in usage they appear to be in complementary distribution.

The first of these is the nominalizing suffix used in *twosome, threesome* or with any other number under ten, and also found in *ownsome*. It denotes a group (usually of people, but occasionally of other entities) of a size denoted by the number in the base. Some textual examples from COCA are provided in (103).

(103)   *Harpers_Bazaar* 2007: Going away can be an inflammatory enterprise for any **twosome** or **moresome**.

   Golf_Magazine 2004: Balls must be at least 1.62 inches around and no heavier than 1.62 ounces. The reason for the 1.62 **twosome**, if any, is lost to history.

   Parenting 2008: a toddler **twosome** eating ice cream.

The other suffix of form *-some* to be dealt with here is the one found, for example, in *20-some*, which means the same as in the syntactic construction *some twenty*, that is 'approximately' (cf. *-ish*, Section 18.4.7). The majority of the bases are round numbers—numbers of twenty or greater which end in zero. COCA does provide occasional exceptions, though, as shown in (104).

(104)   *Bicycling 1994*: You're talking **12-some** hours in the saddle.

       NBC_Dateline 2008: the one act in combat that has been a burden for me for **33-some** years.

The suffix *-some* is in obvious competition with its syntactic equivalent *or so*, which has a wider distribution. For the *-some* which creates adjectives, see Chapter 14.

18.4.6 The suffix *-ton*

The nominalizing suffix *-ton* is established only in the word *singleton* 'one that is isolated, unique or alone', but is occasionally found in some analogical forms, as illustrated in (105). The *OED* suggests that this is the same suffix as in *simpleton*, but the meaning is so different as to raise queries about this in the current state of the language. There is no evidence of productivity for this suffix beyond what is listed in (105).

(105)   *Journal_of_Sports_Behavior 2010*: Beginning with a five-factor solution, a process of eliminating singleton and **doubleton** items was conducted.

      New York Times 2007, cited in *Wiktionary*: It means that you lead low from a doubleton and the middle card from a **tripleton**.

18.4.7 The suffix *-ish*

The suffix *-ish* creates adjectives of similarity or approximation, and occasionally adjectives of nationality, as shown in Chapter 14, but is listed here because of its approximative use with number bases, as in the examples in (106), all attested in COCA or the BNC.

(106)   10-ish, 25-ish, 500-ish, fortyish, twelve-ish, twentyish, two-ish

18.4.8 The prefix *hypo-*

The prefix *hypo-* is the counterpart for *hyper-* (see Section 18.3.4) in some of its uses. When used in a locative sense, it can mean 'under' (sometimes a metaphorical locative, as with 'lower' orders of animals), in which case it may be in competition with *sub-* (see Chapter 16). But it also has a quantitative sense in which it means 'less than is normal or desirable'. It is usually used with this quantitative sense in medical and scientific contexts, attached to a noun or an adjective (107), or in a neoclassical formation (108).

(107)   hypo-allergenic, hypo-production, hypo-reactivity, hypo-sensitization, hypo-skeptical, hypo-ventilation, hypoactivity, hypocretin, hypocritical, hypodense, hypoechoic,

hypoelastic, hypofunction, hypoglycaemic, hypogonadism, hypointensity, hypopharynx, hypophthalmus, hypopituitarism, hyporesponsive, hyposensitivity, hypotension, hypotext, hypothermia, hypotragedy, hypotympanic, hypoventilation

(108)   hypobaric, hypochloric, hypochondria, hypocrisy, hypoderm, hypodermic, hypogamous, hypogram, hypokinesis, hypokinetic, hyponymy, hypoplasia, hypopnea, hyporheic, hyposmia, hypostasis, hypotaxis, hypothalamus, hypothalmus, hypothesis, hypotrophy, hypoxaemia, hypoxia

Unlike its congener, *hyper-*, *hypo-* is rarely used in a colloquial context. Even *hypo-skepticism* and *hypotext*, cited in (107), are technical terms of psychology and literary criticism respectively.

The prefix *hypo-* carries secondary stress, unless it is followed by a neoclassical form that attracts stress to the immediately preceding syllable (see Chapter 9.4.5 for discussion). In this case, the second syllable of the prefix is main-stressed (*hypónymy, hypóstatis, hypótenuse, hypóthecate, hypóthesis*). In one set of forms the first syllable of the prefix is reduced to a short vowel, [ˈhɪ]*pocrite*, h[ɪ]*pócrisy* and h[ɪ]*pocrítical*.

18.5   CARDINAL AND ORDINAL NUMBERS

The basic numbers of English are *one, two, three, four, five, six, seven, eight, nine, ten, eleven, twelve, hundred, thousand, million* and, since the 1940s, *googol*, and *googolplex*. *Twelve* can be considered a suppletive form for an unattested **twoteen*, and the *tw-* initial cluster is also found in *two* (in the orthography only), *twin, twain*, and *between*, and possibly in *twine*. The orthographic <tw> no longer has morphemic value in these words. It is not clear that there is a number word corresponding to the notation 'o', since *nil, null, nought/naught, oh* /əʊ ‖ oʊ/, *zero*, and, for some speakers, *nothing*, divide this area between them in a not entirely regular way.

18.5.1   The suffixes *-teen* and *-ty*

The suffix *-teen*, meaning 'plus ten' can be added to the numbers from *three* to *nine*, and the suffix *-ty*, meaning 'times ten' can be added to the numbers from *two* to *nine* as shown in (109). The suffix *-teen* is auto-stressed, *-ty* is unstressed and base stress is preserved.

(109) | *base* | 'plus ten' | 'times ten' |
|---|---|---|
| two | twelve | twenty |
| three | thirteen | thirty |
| four | fourteen | forty |
| five | fifteen | fifty |
| six | sixteen | sixty |

seven	seventeen	seventy
eight	eighteen	eighty
nine	nineteen	ninety

Phonological alternations can be observed in four of the nine series, that is with derivatives based on *two, three, five,* and *eight.* We find suppletion (*two • twelve • twenty, three • thirteen • thirty*), vowel alternation and consonant devoicing (*five • fifteen • fifty*), and degemination, or loss of final /t/, depending on the analysis (*eight • eighteen • eighty*). The orthography reflects these alternations but also introduces a further irregularity, namely a different spelling of the base *four* in *forty.* The orthographic distinction between <our> and <or> in *four* and *forty* is not reflected in the pronunciation in most varieties of English, but a phonological distinction is made in ScE. Some Americans have a different vowel in *fourteen* from that in *four* and *forty* (Wells 2008).

Because of the phonological similarity of *-teen* and *-ty,* the pronunciations are often exaggerated, and in speech the figures are often given alongside the figure: *It cost $40, four oh.*

There also seems to be an unspecified one-digit number *ump-,* to which *-ty* can attach, as in *She's just had her umpty umpth birthday,* expressing the meaning 'an unspecified number'. The unspecified number *ump-* may also combine with *-teen* to form *umpteen* 'many', and an ordinal number can be formed on the basis of *umpty-ump* and *umpteen,* as in *umpty-umpth* and *umpteenth.*

There is also a free form *teen,* which can occur as a plural form in expressions like *somewhere in their teens* 'aged between 13 and 19' and as a metonymic singular form *teen* 'a teenager, a person in their teens'. The formative *-ty* is also occasionally (and usually jocularly) added to *eleven* (see, for example, Tolkien 1954: 43), is used on *naught* to give the punning *naughties* ('the years between 2000 and 2009').

18.5.2 More complex numbers: beyond 20

More complex numbers are derived by the combination of the simplex and complex numbers described in the preceding section. The numbers between 20 and 99 are created by taking the number in *-ty* and then adding the relevant unit number: *twenty-seven, thirty-two, ninety-one,* and so on. The hyphen is generally used, and the stress is on the second element. These numbers might be argued to behave semantically like additive coordinative compounds such as *Alsace-Lorraine* in that their meaning is the sum of the parts, and they are exocentric, not being a hyponym of either of the parts.

Three digit numbers consist of one of the numbers from 1 to 9 followed variably by *hundred* or *hundred and* (with *and* being often phonetically reduced to /ən/ or /n/), followed by one of the numbers from 1 to 99: *one hundred (and) thirty-nine* (i.e. 139), *six hundred (and) two* (i.e. 602). *One* before *hundred* may be replaced by *a,* as in *a hundred (and) sixty-three* (i.e. 163).

An alternative way of reading or saying three-digit numbers is by having one of the numbers from 1 to 9 followed by one of the numbers from 10 to 99: *two fifty-three* (i.e. 253), *eight ninety-eight* (i.e. 898). If the number following the first digit is below ten, the second digit is pronounced as /əʊ ‖ oʊ/, as in *two oh seven* (i.e. 207).

Numbers for thousands and millions are added recursively before the numbers as explained so far, except that the alternative variant just discussed is no longer possible (10,898: **ten thousand eight ninety-eight* versus *ten thousand eight hundred (and) ninety-eight*). Typically there are intonational breaks possible after the word *million* and after *thousand* when a number of hundreds follows. This is reflected by commas in the mathematical notation of the numbers. Thus we get numbers like *two thousand nine hundred (and) thirty-three* (i.e. 2,933), *six hundred (and) twenty-nine million, nine thousand and five* (i.e. 629,009,005), *seven million, nine hundred (and) twenty-one thousand, three hundred and seventy-nine* (i.e. 7,921,379). Notably, *million* and *thousand* must be followed by *and* (full form or reduced form) if the overall number has more than four digits and there are only zeros between the *thousand*, or *million*, and the last digit, see (110a). If the overall number has only four digits and there are only zeros between the first and the last digit, the use of *and* is variable (110b).

(110)   a.   235,000,002:

two hundred (and) thirty-five million and two
*two hundred (and) thirty-five million two

345,006:
three hundred (and) forty-five thousand and six
*three hundred (and) forty-five thousand six

b.   8005:
eight thousand and five
eight thousand five

Although numbers like *sixty-five* may look like compounds, larger numbers look far more syntactic in structure. Not only may they have the syntactic coordinator *and* in them, but with numbers with millions and thousands, the intonation also suggests that they are phrasal rather than lexical, especially if the number is said more slowly. Phonologically and semantically, therefore, a number like 7,302 may be parallel to a syntactic phrase like *Peter, Paul (and) Mary*. The rather strong co-occurrence restrictions show, however, that we are dealing with a tight-knit lexical system.

Although we have outlined a system for number names above, there is an alternative system in operation for numbers between 1,100 and 9,999. This alternative system is not based on a segmentation with three digits, but uses two digits as a boundary. This alternative system is more usual with the lower numbers in this scale. According to this system, the first two digits are pronounced as numbers between 11 and 99 followed by *hundred*, followed by the number given by the last two digits. Thus, instead of *one thousand one hundred (and) twelve* the number 1,112 may be spoken as *eleven hundred (and) twelve*. This option is available even when there are numbers in the tens and units: *fifteen hundred (and) forty-nine*. While *ninety-nine hundred (and) ninety-nine* would be odd, such figures occur with lower numbers, such as *twenty-five hundred (and) six*. This alternative system also has a variant without the word *hundred*, used from 1,000 onwards, so that 1,549 could be *fifteen forty-nine*; this formulation is frequently used for dates. Without the word *hundred*, 9,999 could well be *ninety-nine ninety-nine*, and would then be homophonous with a price of $99.99 or £99.99.

In principle words containing *billion, trillion, quadrillion*, etc. are built up in the same way as the numbers including millions; in practice, such numbers are rarely spelled out in full: they are used in whole numbers (*five trillion*) or with decimal points (*five point seven trillion*).

Morphologically, however, these higher numbers are hard to deal with, since there are two distinct systems in use. These are sometimes referred to as 'British' and 'American' systems, but there is no such simple division. One system includes forms in *-lliard*, the other does not, as shown in (110). Note that the use of these numbers is common only in specialist circles.

(111)	10^{24}	septillion	quadrillion
	10^{21}	sextillion	trilliard
	10^{18}	quintillion	trillion
	10^{15}	quadrillion	billiard
	10^{12}	trillion	billion
	10^{9}	billion	milliard

The system in the righthand column appears to be yielding to that in the lefthand column. The formative *-illion* is also added to nonsense onsets or syllables to give *bazillion, bajillion, frillion, jillion, gajillion, gazillion, kajillion, kazillion, squillion, zillion*, each of which simply means 'an indeterminately large number'.

18.5.3 Ordinals and fractions

The ordinal numbers are created from the cardinal numbers with the addition of the suffix *-th*, except that **one + th* has the suppletive form *first*, **two + th* has the suppletive form *second*, and **three + th* has the suppletive form *third*. Following numerals in *-ty*, there is an extender /ə/ <e> before the *-th*: *thirtieth, ninetieth* and a spelling alternation of <y> ~ . *Five* and *eight* show the same allomorphy before *-th* as they do before *-teen* and *-ty*: *fifth, eighth*.

Fractions are formed using the same process, except that the word *half* is used instead of the expected *second*: ½ is *a half* (or *one half*) and not **a second*, and *quarter* is often used in place of *fourth*. When fractions are made plural, the sequence of /θs/ is often simplified to [sː] or [s], so that 5/6 may be pronounced [faɪv sɪksː], scarcely distinct from *five six*. On the other hand, for some speakers, an epenthetic /t/ may be inserted before the /θ/ in particularly clear speech, to give, for instance, /fɪftθs/, /sɪkstθs/, /naɪntθs/.

18.5.4 Number prefixes

A series of prefixes is used for fractions; these are presented in (112). The earliest such prefixes come from French, Latin, and Greek, but invented elements based on other languages have been added as smaller fractions have become required for scientific study.

(112)	number	prefix	example
	1/2	demi-	demi-cup
		hemi	hemisphere
		semi-	semicircle
	1/10	deci-	deciliter
	1/100	centi-	centigram
	1/1000	milli-	milliliter
	$1/10^6$	micro-	microsecond
	$1/10^9$	nano-	nanotube
	$1/10^{12}$	pico-	piconewton
	$1/10^{15}$	femto-	femtometer
	$1/10^{18}$	atto-	attosecond

Demi-, from French, can be used literally to mean 'a half', but usually means 'of lower quality' as in *demigod*. *Semi-* and *hemi-* are etymologically Latin and Greek respectively, and this sometimes affects their distribution, though note the BrE *hemidemisemiquaver* ('1/32nd note'), where the ordering seems random, and there is nothing in the environment to help predict the distribution.

   It is always possible to use the English numbers in combination with other elements to create forms like *six-ball*, *six-bedroom*, *six-sided*, *six-strong*, *six-wheeler*. However, English has specific prefixes from Latin and Greek to make single words that involve specific numbers and quantifiers. Many of these are borrowed but analysable, and they tend to be stylistically more formal than the English constructions.

(113)	number/ quantifier	Latin	Greek
	1	unicycle	monologue
	2	bicycle	diphthong
	3	tricycle	tripod

4	quadrangle, quadraphony, quadrimanual, quadruped	tetrahedron
5	quincentenary, quinquereme	pentagram
6	sexfoil	hexagon
7	septennial, septivalent	heptathlon
8	octosyllable	octahedron
9	nonagon	ennead
10	decennial	decalogue
20	vigesimal	
100	centipede	hectogram
1000	millipede	kilogram
Many	multi-national	polyvalent
All	omnivore	pan-American
Both	ambisyllabic	

Some of these forms are subject to allomorphy whose analysis is unclear, possibly involving extenders in the contemporary language.

For some larger multiples of 10 there are prefixes, as illustrated in (114), all carrying main stress. These are used largely in scientific discourse, often within the fields of astronomy, computer science, and economics.

(114) 10^6 megabyte

10^9 gigaflop

10^{12} terawatt

10^{15} petabyte

10^{18} exajoule

10^{21} zettabyte

10^{24} yottabyte

PART IV

Compounding

....

CHAPTER 19

Compounds: formal considerations

19.1 PROSPECTUS

This chapter and the following one are concerned with compounds. The present chapter will deal with the formal properties of these formations while Chapter 20 discusses their semantics. We will start out in Section 19.2 by clarifying one of the most controversial issues in the study of compounds and their formation, that is the question of which kinds of constructs should be classified as compounds and which ones should not. This is followed by a discussion of the internal structure of compounds in Section 19.3, followed by an overview of the formal properties of different types of compound (Section 19.4).

19.2 BOUNDARY ISSUES: WHAT IS A COMPOUND?

Derivation is conceived of in this book as the formation of words by combining affixes with bases, and also the operation of some non-combinatorial processes on a base, as in conversion or clipping. In contrast to this, compounding can be regarded as the formation of words through the combination of bases (see also Bauer and Huddleston 2002: 1626). Since bases are also concatenated to form syntactic phrases, the issue arises of how compounds can be distinguished from syntactic phrases, and indeed the literature is full of discussions of this question. Another issue is to determine whether a given base is really a base or perhaps better analysed as an affix. A third issue concerns the problem that not every word that contains two (or more) bases, and thus would fall under this rough definition of compound, arises as the result of the same process of base-combination by which compounds are normally formed. These three issues will be discussed in Sections 19.2.1 to 19.2.3.

19.2.1 Compounds: morphological or syntactic?

Discussions of the boundary between compounds and syntactic phrases have focused mainly on noun–noun (NN) combinations, and especially on those NN combinations that are spelled as two separate orthographic words. In contrast, NN combinations spelled as one word or hyphenated are generally taken to be words, that is, compounds, not phrases. Examples of all three kinds are given in (1). Following the terminology introduced in Chapter 4.5.2, we will refer to words like those in (1b) as being written solid, those in (1c) as being hyphenated, and we will say that those in (1a) are spaced. Compounds written solid or hyphenated may be grouped as being 'concatenated'. The examples are taken from the Boston University Radio Speech Corpus (BURSC, Ostendorf *et al.* 1996), the transcriptions of which were provided by native-speaking research assistants, and did not undergo a centralized editorial process.

(1)　a.　birth control, hospital staff, housing subsidies, state official, wind erosion

　　　b.　cornerstone, jailbird, lawmaker, workday, wristband

　　　c.　hoop-junkie, life-span, tissue-type

Instead of restricting our discussion to constructs spelled in a certain way, we will focus here on general criteria that have been used to distinguish compounds from phrases. Furthermore, we will look not just at NN combinations, but at combinations including verbs and adjectives as well.

19.2.1.1 *Criteria for NN compounds*

There are a number of general criteria that are standardly adduced to test the status of NN constructs as phrases or words. One problem with these criteria is that they sometimes rest on questionable assumptions, which makes them potentially unreliable. Furthermore, as shown, for example, by Bauer (1998a), it is frequently the case that the outcomes of the various tests contradict each other, which further undermines the value of these diagnostics. Huddleston and Payne (2002: 449) claim that it is enough to fulfil only one criterion of phrasehood to decide the issue, but do not give reasons why such an approach would be justified.

The first test criterion to mention is an aspect of syntactic atomicity, which says that words are uninterruptable units, hence it should not be possible to insert an affix or another word into a compound. The examples in (2) illustrate this. Examples like those in (3) are not counterexamples, because they arise from the recursiveness of the compounding process, that is, from the attachment of *council* to the left of *health program* and not from the insertion of *health* into *council program*.

(2)　council program *versus* *council recent program
　　　state deficit *versus* *state big deficit

(3)　council health program, state budget deficit

The second criterion holds that compounds be listed in the lexicon, while phrases are not. This criterion is unclear and thus questionable. It is unclear since the notion of listedness is not well defined. Psycholinguistic studies (e.g. de Vaan *et al.* 2007) have shown that even a single mention of a word leaves a trace in memory and that words may be present in the lexicon in varying degrees of strength. A way out of this problem may be to define 'listed' as 'listed with some idiosyncratic property'. Such a move would, however, make listedness a questionable, if not utterly useless, criterion, because it would lead us to classify all non-idiosyncratic compounds as syntactic and therefore unlisted (apparently the view of Lyons 1977: 535). This is an undesired result, for at least two reasons. First, there is good psycholinguistic evidence that non-idiosyncratic complex words are also stored in the mental lexicon (de Vaan *et al.* 2007). Second, under this approach any regular complex word would have to be regarded as a syntactic entity instead of a word.

A third criterion tests whether the second element can be replaced by anaphoric *one*, which is taken as an indication that the construction is a phrase. The criterion itself is not reliable, however, since it rests on the assumption that sub-lexemic elements are not accessible to pronominalization, which has been shown to be false (e.g. by Ward *et al.* 1991; Lieber 1992: 122–4). Instead, the possibility of anaphoric reference is restricted by pragmatic rather than structural principles. The problem with this criterion is illustrated in (4), where all the examples show that words are not anaphoric islands (all the extracts in (4) are attested, the first from COCA, the second from a web-site, the others in conversation).

(4) a. *ABC_Nightline 1991*: as both a North supporter and a Reagan supporter, I still support both without reaching the conclusions that Ollie reaches in his book […]

   b. …cash withdrawal fees generally average two per cent for credit cards and 1.5 per cent for debit ones. (http://www.newsletter.co.uk/news/business/pack_the_right_plastic_1_1839384 9 June 2011 cited by Bell 2011)

   c. I'm trying to give myself a headache by banging it on the floor.

   d. He opened the garage door and drove straight into it [viz. the garage]

A fourth criterion is modification. Payne and Huddleston (2002: 449) argue that the possibility of expanding NN constructs into [N[A N]] or [[A N]N] constructions can be taken as evidence for their being phrases. According to Bell (2011) this argument is not compelling. Based on the idea that a nominal head in syntax should be able to project full phrases, the potential phrase headed by the left noun in the structure [[A N]N] would be expected to allow complements, specifiers, and modifiers as dependents. Bell shows, however, that the noun is unusually restricted in its capacity to carry these, as is the adjective. This would make this premodifying noun phrase very atypical, and the force of the criterion dubious. She cites examples such as *red tulip collection*, which does not allow **very bright red tulip collection*.

The fifth test to mention here is coordination, which assumes that sub-lexemic units may not be syntactically coordinated, for example with *and*. This test is not very useful either, because sub-lexemic units can easily be coordinated syntactically, provided that certain prosodic (and semantic) requirements are met (see Plag 2003: 84; Bell 2011; unless otherwise noted the examples in (5a, b) are from COCA).

(5)   a.   *Education 2010*: **pre- and post-test** methodology

Ms. 2008: No alumnus, whether **pro- or anti-feminist**, should be able to determine a college curriculum

Mechanical Engineering 2001: the two or three large engines are replaced by many **mini or micro engines**

   b.   **child- and home-less** (*Plag 2003*)
         business and family-wise

   c.   speech-perception and production
         word and sentence structure
         sugar- and fat-free

The sixth criterion is stress, with the traditional distinction of right stress for phrases and left stress for compounds. As will be discussed in detail in Section 19.3.3, this criterion only works in one direction: left-stressed NNs are uncontroversially considered to be compounds, but right-stressed ones are not necessarily phrases.

Spelling is the final criterion mentioned in the literature, but the observable variability in spelling makes this criterion difficult to apply. If anything, compounds that frequently occur with concatenative spellings are uncontroversially regarded as compounds.

In sum, there seems to be no established set of trustworthy procedures that could tell us reliably and theory-neutrally for a given NN construction whether it is a noun or a phrase (see also the survey in Lieber and Štekauer 2009). We will therefore be inclusive rather than exclusive and consider NN constructs as compounds, unless there is clear evidence to the contrary.

However, even if we are as inclusive as possible, the question of determining what are compounds and what other types of complex nominal remain, and we now turn to look at a number of potential candidates for compound status.

For example, we do not consider names consisting of two proper nouns (e.g. *Alice Miller*) or appositive NNs (such as *Governor Dukakis*) as compounds. We include in this set NN constructions which are left-headed; *the letter A, the number nine, a Model T, the year 2000, the play 'Macbeth'.*

19.2.1.2   *AN combinations*

We now consider a number of types of AN construction. The first is made up of basic, usually etymologically Germanic, adjectives which are usually written solid with the noun and stressed on the leftmost element. Examples are *blackboard, greyhound, highlight, hotplate, longboat, lowland, madman, shorthand, short wave, sweetcorn, whitehead*. Typically the adjectives are monosyllabic, but there is the occasional disyllabic adjective in this class, as in *narrow-boat*. Some of these words may be exocentric like *redcap, redskin, whitehead*, others are endocentric. There is virtually no dispute in the literature that these are compounds (but see Spencer 2003). Typically the adjective creates classes of objects denoted by the noun, and cannot be sub-modified by *very, rather, so*, etc.: *a very hot plate* is not a hotplate, but a plate that is very hot.

Next we have two classes made up of AN where the adjective is a relational adjective. Relational adjectives are usually derived from nouns, cannot be graded or intensified, cannot occur in predicative position and express the meaning 'in relation to X' with 'X' being the denotation of the base: *dental surgery, electrical engineer, financial advisor, polar climate, postal service, vernal equinox*. The first group of constructions with these adjectives are rather like the AN compounds discussed above, except that they are not written solid with the noun. Importantly, like the compounds discussed above, they take left stress. Examples in this group include *cúltural club, dramátic society, %flóral arrangement, prímary school, romántic period, sócial worker, sólar system*. The reason for the occurrence of left stress in these constructions is not entirely clear: to some extent, it is probably a function of the frequency of the combinations, but the fact that we find sets like *archeológical society, chóral society, dramátic society, horticúltural society, operátic society, zoológical society* all with left stress suggest that there is some influence of the paradigm, despite *royal socíety* and *national socíety* with right stress (see Section 19.3.3 for a detailed discussion of stress). These constructions are not much discussed in the literature, but would probably be generally accepted as compounds.

The second type with relational adjectives looks similar, but does not have left stress. These are expressions such as *atomic bomb, Chomskyan analyses, fungal spore, human genome, linguistic behavior, moral philosophy, phocine distemper, prosodic analysis*, and so on. Levi (1978) classifies these constructions as 'complex nominals', along with constructions that would generally be regarded as compounds. Some subsequent scholars (see Giegerich 2006; Bell 2011 for discussion) have classified them as compounds. The question remains controversial, and may amount to no more than a matter of definition; because these constructions are not clearly morphological, we do not treat them in any more detail here.

Next we have a set of constructions with usually monosyllabic and usually Germanic adjectives that behave just like the first set except that they do not take left stress. Examples are *black íce, brown ále, green téa, high córt, light ráilway, red gíant, red squírrel, thin áir, white wítch*. The difference between these and the compound set is largely one of frequency (Bauer 2004a). Nevertheless, we know of no authorities who include these as compounds, and we will treat them as lexicalized noun phrases. We note, however, that their semantics seems indistinguishable from that of compound AN constructions, and that the adjective seems similarly isolated, in that we cannot have *a very red squirrel* without losing the lexical meaning of *red squirrel*, and that *brown red squirrel* is not necessarily a contradiction.

Finally, there are free combinations of adjective and noun, typically adjectives not derived from nouns, which can frequently be sub-modified, in which the adjective is descriptive of the head (rather than relational), and which typically are not lexicalized, although there are lexicalized examples: *red light* is lexicalized to some extent (especially when it occurs in a larger collocation such as *red-light district*, but even in the sense of 'traffic light'), but *brown trousers, green leaf, inveterate liar, short walk, sloppy kiss, tall tower, wet grass* are all simple noun phrases, and not part of word-formation at all.

19.2.1.3 *Other cases*

The first of the special constructions we need to consider involves the combination of two words of the same category being used as modifiers of a nominal head, such as *father–daughter (dance), mind–brain (connection), true–false (question),* or *push–pull (gizmo).* Plag (2003: 221–2) advances three arguments for treating them as compounds, none of them being particularly forceful, however. First, insertion of adjectives seems to lead to odd results. Second, the relation between the two constituents is normally expressed overtly by a conjunction, if clearly syntactic means are chosen (e.g. *the connection between mind and brain*). Furthermore, inflections seem to be obligatorily missing (*fathers-daughters-dance*). We will also treat such structures as compounds; see Chapter 20.3.2 on coordinative compounds.

A second potentially problematic case is what has been labelled 'descriptive genitives', by which we mean (following Rosenbach 2006) the whole N'sN construction. Some examples are given in (6).

(6)   Broca's aphasia, driver's license, fool's errand, men's room, men's suit, mother's milk, smoker's cough, writer's block

Some descriptive genitives sometimes have rival NN constructions without *'s*, some do not, as the examples in (7) show. The existence of doublets is presumably partly dependent on the degree of lexicalization.

(7)   lawyer fees *versus* lawyer's fees (*both in* COCA)
       people power *versus* people's power (*both in* COCA)
       *mother milk *versus* mother's milk
       frog spawn *versus* ?frog's spawn

Although descriptive genitives may look like straightforward phrases, their status as phrases is arguable. Descriptive genitives differ systematically from more prototypical, so-called 'determiner genitives' in that their pre-head structure is clearly a noun and not a noun phrase, as is possible with determiner genitives (Huddleston and Pullum 2002: 354–5). In addition, the pre-head structure in determiner genitives makes the whole possessive NP definite, even if the possessor itself is indefinite, as in *a smoker's car*, which corresponds to *the car of a smoker* (note also that *a car of a smoker* does not have a corresponding *'s* genitive construction).

Conversely, descriptive genitives are very similar to NN compounds in that their first element has word status rather than phrasal status, has a classifying semantic function, and tends to be non-referential. Furthermore, many descriptive genitives have left stress and have lexicalized meanings. Applying the usual tests (such as coordination, modification, etc.) leads, as with so many NN constructions, to contradictory results (see Rosenbach 2006 for detailed discussion), and Rosenbach uses the mixed behaviour of genitives as an argument for the view that categories are gradient.

We see here a number of constructions which are formally more or less syntactic and semantically more or less compound-like, with some gradience even within the individual subtypes. Arguments as to whether some of these 'are' or 'are not' compounds are likely to become matters of definition rather than questions that can be answered by the production of evidence. We will not treat descriptive genitives here, even though we acknowledge the semantic similarities between the various constructions.

The next potentially problematic kinds of structure are so-called 'phrasal compounds'. This class is characterized by a phrase as first element of a compound. Examples are numerous, some of them, as taken from COCA, are listed in (8a). They are often highly specific in meaning and unlikely to become institutionalized, as shown in example (8b), which illustrates one in its original context.

(8) a. circle-a-word puzzle, soon-to-be-divorced wife, strawberries-in-July talk

     b. Watchful parents need to know: Where will my precious child be safe from the scourge of drugs? At the service academies, of course, which score four of the five places in the **"Don't Inhale" rankings**. (*Boston Globe,* 24 August 2010)

These structures have featured prominently in discussions of the syntax–morphology interface, but it seems that they are less spectacular than assumed by many theorists. As shown in the previous chapters and later in Chapter 22), phrases can function as bases for many derivational processes, in other words phrases must be included anyway in the set of possible bases in English word-formation. From this, and from our definition of compounding as the combination of bases, it follows naturally that phrases can occur as compound elements, and that phrasal compounds are compounds. It is less clear, however, why phrases may not occupy the right position in compounds, unless it is axiomatically (and perhaps sensibly) assumed that heads are lexical (see, for example, Zwicky 1985: 5).

Similar to phrasal compounds are those structures that contain phrase-like first elements, given in bold in (9). The unproblematic insertion of an adjective between the hyphenated modifier and the head noun (shown in (9a)) suggests that the structure as a whole is not a compound. Yet these first elements are not clearly phrases since they lack certain properties, for example agreement marking (consider *a three-syllable word*). This lack of agreement marker in (9a) and the wider set of examples in (9b) suggest that these may all be compounds (some of them exocentric ones) albeit non-canonical ones in some cases (see Section 19.2.3).

> (9)   a. a **three-syllable** English word, the **two-year** formative period, a **four-term** congressman
>
> b. a **go-go** dancer, a **no-go** area, a **pass–fail** test, a **tow-away** zone, **before-tax** profits

Rarely featuring in discussions of compounding, numerals (such as *twenty-four, three hundred (and) fifty-five*) seem also to be borderline cases. They are discussed in detail in Chapter 18.

Perhaps less controversial are combinations of adverbs with adjectives, whose spelling in premodifying position with a hyphen may suggest compound status (e.g. *ill-advised decision, well-chosen example*), but following the arguments developed in Chapter 4.5.3, we do not consider these compounds.

Similarly, lexicalized phrases such as *forget-me-not, jack-in-the-box, lady-in-waiting, matron-of-honor, son-in-law* or structures such as *book-turned-movie, coach-turned-commentator* (all from COCA) are excluded from the set of compounds, though some authorities (e.g. Quirk *et al.* 1985) list them as such.

Consider specifically constructions which consist of two or more words combined under inclusion of a linking element *cum* or *-cum-*, as shown in (10), with examples taken from COCA. The construction is productive and works with nouns (10a) and (much less frequently) with adjectives (10b).

> (10)   a. bookstore cum restaurant, café-cum-bookstore, cricketer-cum-politician, deli cum takeout fish market, earth rock cum paperweight, intentionality cum responsibility, soap opera cum sex farce, soccer player cum musician
>
> b. cognitive-cum-affective, civic-cum-cultural, cosy-cum-corny

The element *cum* is listed as a preposition in the *OED*, but outside genuine Latin expressions such as *summa cum laude* it occurs only as a conjunction-like coordinating formative between words of the same syntactic category. The expressions are spelled either with or without hyphens and may contain more than just two elements (e.g. *wagon-cum-car-cum-truck*, from COCA). The resulting expressions refer to a single entity that combines characteristics of the denotations of its constituents, which makes the constructions similar to coordinate, more specifically appositional, compounds (see Chapter 20 for discussion). The constructions have rightward stress, which is typical of both coordinate compounds and phrases.

The phrasal analysis is, however, strongly supported by the placement of plural marking. In the few attested constructions in COCA that have plural marking, the inflectional suffix always occurs on both constituents. In (11) we provide an exhaustive list of attestations of pluralized constructions in COCA.

(11) a. boarding schools cum penal institutions, doctors-cum-soldiers, embassies-cum-fortresses, guides-cum-chefs

This kind of plural marking is the same as we find with syntactically coordinated noun phrases (e.g. *boarding schools and penal institutions*), and it is very rarely attested for coordinative compounds (as in *producers-directors*, COCA). For example, COCA has 59 plural forms of the rather high-frequency compound *singer-songwriter* with plural marking only on the second noun, and no attestation of this compound with plural marking also on the first noun (🖐*singers-songwriters*). Renner (to appear) also finds for his collection of *cum*-constructions that double plural-marking is the norm, with 19 out of 20 pluralized forms showing this pattern (across different types).

The fact that *cum*-coordination is restricted to nouns and adjectives is interpreted by Renner (to appear) as evidence against the syntactic status of the construction. This interpretation is not compelling, however, as we know from other languages that coordinators may be restricted to the coordination of certain types of constituent. For example, many languages have different coordinating conjunctions for NPs as against clauses or verb phrases (see Haspelmath 2007: 20–2).

Due to its rather controversial status as a morphological construction we do not treat *cum*-constructions in any more detail in this volume. The reader is referred to Renner (to appear) for a recent and more detailed study of the properties of these expressions.

Some authors (Bauer 1983; Katamba and Stonham 2006: 305) take reduplicative compounds such as *easy-peasy, killer-diller, lovey-dovey* to be compounds. Since they do not fit thedefinition of being constructed of two bases, we reject this classification. We then extend this to the few examples where the two elements do exist independently, such as *silly-billy, wham-bam*. These constructions are dealt with in Chapter 18.2.6.

Finally, there are several lexical items with the head on the left that are originally borrowed from French. These include items such as *attorney general, court martial, governor general, notary public*, and so on (for further examples see Chapter 7). Some authorities (e.g. Quirk *et al.* 1985: 313; Plag *et al.* 2008) treat these as compounds. We consider these to be pieces of lexicalized syntax, just like the phrases such as *forget-me-not* discussed above, the only difference being that the original syntax here is French. The same may be true of expressions like *Chicken Kiev, Steak Diane*. The only example of which we are aware that seems exceptional in this regard is *girl Friday* (an analogy on *man Friday*, which is more clearly an instance of apposition), which appears left-headed without any French syntax (although in COCA its plural is always *girl Fridays*).

Having clarified the boundary between compounds and syntactic constructions, we will now turn to the boundary between compounding and derivation.

19.2.2 Compounding versus prefixation and suffixation

While for most compounds this boundary is not an issue, there is a set of complex words where it is not so clear whether the constituent elements should be regarded as bases or affixes. This set can be subdivided into one that is traditionally described as having affixoidal elements and one that consists of neoclassical compounds. We will discuss each in turn.

19.2.2.1 *Affixoids*

The category of 'affixoid' or 'semi-suffix' has been invoked for those complex words where the status of one of the elements as a base is felt to be ambiguous between an affix and a base (e.g. Marchand 1969: 357). A standard example is *-man* in words like *postman, chairman, milkman*.

Instances of this phenomenon are often brought about by historical processes of grammaticalization, accompanied by semantic bleaching, and it is uncontroversial that the development of an affix out of a free morpheme is a gradual process. The question for the synchronic linguist is, however, whether a better understanding of these phenomena can be achieved by positing an intermediate category. It seems that this is questionable.

Again, we would need sensible criteria to classify formatives as either base or affix. Two kinds of properties come to mind: morpho-phonological and semantic. The more integrated morpho-phonologically a formative is, the more affix-like it is. We have to be careful, however, with this criterion. While it is true that phonologically highly fused elements tend to be affixes, the reverse is not necessarily the case. Even among affixes, phonological integration can vary a great deal (see Chapter 9 for discussion). To mention only one complication, most vowel-initial suffixes in English are integrated into the host's prosodic structure, most consonant-initial suffixes are not, and many prefixes (e.g. *pre-, post-, anti-, de-, dis-, mis-*) behave prosodically like independent words. The degree of phonological integration and morphological status thus do not always match and the criterion of morpho-phonological integration does not tell us whether we are dealing with a compound element or an affix.

Another issue is the phonological weakening of formatives, as in *postman*, with a schwa realization in *-man*. This indeed questions the degree of morphological complexity of this particular form to some extent. But given that the reduction of the vowel seems to be an epiphenomenon of lexicalization (appearing on very frequent forms like *postman* but not on *stunt man*) linked with phonological effects (two unstressed syllables are not permitted before an unstressed vowel in *man*, so that *cameraman* has /æ/), it is unlikely that we need to posit two lexical entries, with one of them being an affix. This brings us to other criteria.

Semantic opacity and a high degree of lexicalization have been adduced in the literature as typical properties distinguishing derivational morphology from inflectional morphology (Plag 2003: 15–16, for example), with compounding being allegedly more transparent. However, compounds can be non-transparent and productive derivation is by definition transparent.

The most important criterion in distinguishing a compound element from a suffix seems, therefore, its relatedness to a free form. If the constituent in question occurs with the same meaning as a free form, no additional affix should be assumed. If, however, the bound form consistently differs in meaning from the free form, one should assume the existence of an affix. If we apply this reasoning to formations with *-man*, there is clear evidence that *-man* and *man* are semantically identical, as is clear from low-frequency formations such as *balloonman*, *barnman, gloveman, holyman, taxi-man* (all from COCA or BNC). A second relevant case is that of *over-* or *under-* which we have in earlier work individually analysed as compound elements (Plag 2003: 222–3) or as prefixes (Lieber 2004: 126–33) (see also Chapter 16), but which by these criteria are prefixes. Finally, we mention *-like* which Marchand (1969: 356) analyses as a 'semi-suffix' and Adams (2001: 36) as a suffix, but which we take to be a compound element (see Chapter 14).

In any case, there seems no need for an in-between category of affixoid and we will not make use of this term.

19.2.2.3 *Neoclassical compounds*

Another group of complex words that are made of formatives of potentially unclear status as base or affix are so-called 'neoclassical' formations. These are generally characterized as forms in which lexemes of Latin or Greek origin are combined to form new combinations that may or may not be attested in the original languages; the classical elements may sometimes also be used in English as free forms. Example (12) lists a selection of forms featuring the neoclassical elements *bio-*, *photo-*, and *-logy*.

(12) | | | |
|---|---|---|
| biodegradable | photometric | geology |
| biorhythm | photolyse | narratology |
| biofuel | photolabile | eurology |
| bionomic | photovoltaic | analogy |

It is not obvious whether these neoclassical elements should be regarded as affixes or as bound roots. If such data are interpreted as evidence for the prefix status of *bio-* and for the suffix status of *-logy*, we are forced to assume that *biology* would consist of a prefix and a suffix, which in turn would go against our basic assumptions that complex words need to have at least one base. The obvious alternative is that we are not dealing with affixes, but with bound bases, hence with compounds. This would also nicely account for the interpretation of these forms. As in other kinds of non-coordinative compounds, the first element modifies the meaning of the head by specifying its type. Thus, *biofuel* refers to a kind of fuel, *biorhythm* is a kind of rhythm, etc. The same argument would hold for *photo-* 'light' or *geo-* 'earth'. The only difference between the neoclassical forms and native compounds is that many of these non-native elements are obligatorily bound. This is also the reason why the neoclassical elements are often called 'combining forms'. We can thus state that neoclassical formations are best treated as compounds, and not as cases of affixation. For a detailed treatment of the formal properties of neoclassical compounds, see Section 19.4.5.

19.2.3 Compounding and compounds: Process versus product

There are two ways of determining what should be considered a 'compound'. We can view a compound as a synchronic product, anything that fits the definition of consisting of two bases. If we take this view, we ignore the fact that such forms may have arisen historically by any number of morphological processes (including, among others, back-formation and conversion). The second way is to view compounds as entities which are formed by a process of compounding (i.e. a process of putting two bases together to form a larger word, with certain predictable qualities). In this section we will have a closer look at the consequences of these two competing views on compounds. It is clear from the two definitions that the process-oriented approach is more restrictive. In this section we will examine those cases where the resulting structures were apparently not formed by a speaker combining two bases. We will use the term CANONICAL COMPOUND for compounds formed by productively combining two or more bases, and NON-CANONICAL COMPOUND for forms that came about through other processes. As will become clear, non-canonical compounds may differ from canonical compounds not only in terms of their derivational history, but also in terms of some of their properties, for example headedness, or internal structure (as discussed in the next subsection).

One mechanism that can result in a non-canonical compound is univerbation, that is the merging of two (or more) words due to their frequent adjacent co-occurrence in discourse. Prepositions and other closed class items such as *into, onto, throughout, whereafter, therefore, notwithstanding, hereby* are a case in point.

Another group of non-canonical compounds is best analysed as being historically derived through a process of inversion (see Berg 1998 for details). This group involves forms with a preposition in first position and a verb or adjective in second position, as in *download, outsource, input* and *inbuilt, upcoming, outgoing*.

Third, there are forms derived by conversion into nouns from phrasal verbs, accompanied by a stress shift (as in, for example, *break dówn ◆ bréakdown, push úp ◆ púsh-up, rip óff ◆ ríp-off*). Sometimes, the suffixation of *-er* to phrasal verbs may also lead to non-canonical compounds, as in *hanger-on, passer-by* (see Chapter 11 for details).

Fourth, there is a large group of non-canonical compounds that are created through back-formation (see Chapter 23 for detailed discussion). This process is especially prevalent with compound verbs that are back-derived from synthetic compounds, as evidenced in *babysit ◆ babysitter, chainsmoke ◆ chain-smoker, brainwash ◆ brainwashing*.

Finally, consider the rather transient formation pattern of the form verb plus *-in*, as in *sit-in, love-in, sleep-in, teach-in*. These non-canonical compounds systematically violate the right-headedness that is characteristic of canonical compounds, as discussed in the next section.

19.3 INTERNAL STRUCTURE

In this section we will look in more detail into certain properties of canonical compounds, that is headedness, constituency, stress, and spelling.

19.3.1 Headedness

It can be observed that canonical compounds have the peculiar property that, in general, the righthand member determines the grammatical properties of the whole compound, and is therefore called the head of the compound. For example, if the righthand member is a count noun, the compound will also be a count noun, irrespective of the grammatical properties of the left member (consider *blackboard, rice cooker, milk bottle*). This generalization is known as the righthand head rule (Williams 1981). The head also carries the inflection, as in pluralized compounds (*blackboards, milk bottles*). Despite some claims in the literature (see, for example, Pinker 1999: 178–87) that NN constructions with a plural in the lefthand element are not canonical compounds, we treat such forms as canonical. Crucially, and in accordance with the righthand head rule, these compounds do not receive a plural interpretation, unless the head is also plural, as can be seen in examples like *clothes basket, admissions officer, parks commissioner, assists record, mammals CD-ROM, spoons player* versus *whales deaths* (COCA).

The concept of headedness is quite problematic in its application to coordinative compounds. Knowing the head of a non-coordinative compound allows us to predict certain properties of that compound. For example, if the head is a count noun, the compound will be a count noun, if the head is a gradable adjective, the compound will be a gradable adjective. With coordinatives, matters are different. As the constituents of a coordinative compound are always very similar in terms of their morphosyntactic (and semantic) properties, either constituent might be considered the source of the compound's properties. The fact that the inflection is attached to the rightmost constituent might be taken as an argument for this constituent being the head, but this argument is theory-dependent. Under a theory in which the phonological host (in this case the rightmost constituent) need not be identical to the morphosyntactic host (in this case the compound), it loses much of its force. In view of this situation headedness seems not to be a useful concept in the analysis of coordinative compounds.

19.3.2 Constituency

In the above definition we used the formulation 'two or more bases'. In fact, we find many compounds that consist of more than two constituents. However, all canonical compounds (except coordinatives, to be dealt with shortly) can be analysed as having an essentially binary structure. In the case of more than two bases involved, one can find binary structures embedded in binary structures, as shown in the examples in (13).

(13)   [Alabama [[health department] official]]

       [[Magnolia Terrace] [Guest House]]

The interpretation of these compounds follows straightforwardly from the assumption of binarity and the righthand head rule. An [*Alabama* [[*health department*] *official*]] is an official of a health department and is located in, or employed by, the state of Alabama. Note that the meaning of such long compounds may be ambiguous as a result of different possible bracketings. Hence, *Alabama health department official* could also be analysed as denoting an official employed by the Alabama health department, in which case the constituency would differ slightly from that shown in (13).

Coordinative compounds are not restricted to binary structures (see further Chapter 20). Examples like those in (14) (from COCA, see also Olsen 2001) illustrate structures with more than two linguistically equal elements (in terms of history, it may be possible to determine what the internal structure of a name like *AOL-Time-Warner-EMI* is, but that is not reflected in the linguistic structure).

(14)   *Bk:LiarsGame 2001*: She took my digits, gave me her **red-white-blue** business card.

       News_CSMonitor 2000: Chuck D has a message for the **AOL-Time-Warner-EMI** conglomerate.

       Mag_Time 2007: Knocked Up certified leading-man status for this **writer-producer-actor.**

       Acad_Education 1992: The study attempted to identify the **personal-social-career** development needs of the school.

19.3.3 Stress

Compound stress is an extremely intricate phenomenon. First, we have to distinguish between compounds that have only two bases and those that have more than two bases. The standard view of compound stress with two-member compounds is that they are stressed on the left constituent (e.g. Bloomfield 1935: 180, 228; Chomsky and Halle 1968: 1–4). However, it has also been observed that many compounds do not seem to observe that rule. In order to solve this problem some researchers, like Bloomfield, claim that right-stressed compounds cannot be compounds, but this kind of reasoning has been proven to be circular and unconvincing.

Another complication arises from the acoustic manifestation of the two stress patterns. As shown in Farnetani *et al.* (1988), Kunter and Plag (2007), Nguyên *et al.* (2008), and Kunter (2011), right-stressed compounds are characterized by more or less level pitch, while left-stressed compounds have a clear drop in pitch from the first member to the second. It is these acoustic properties that have apparently led some researchers to posit three stress levels: left stress, right stress, and an additional type labelled 'level stress' or 'double stress' (e.g. Marchand, 1969: 22; Faiss, 1981: 132). However, the phonetic studies mentioned above suggest that so-called level stress is simply a variant of right stress, not a separate category at all.

There is also some debate on the phonological status of compound prominence as either a kind of lexical stress or a kind of accentuation. Thus an accent-based account of English compound stress would hold that left-prominent compounds have only one pitch accent, namely on the left member, while right-prominent compounds have two pitch accents, one on each of the two members (e.g. Gussenhoven 2004: 19, 276–7; Kunter 2011). We remain agnostic here and use the terms 'prominent' and 'stressed' interchangeably, without any theoretical implication.

The important question remains: what determines the distribution of leftward and rightward stresses? One factor that plays a role is the type of compound in question. Thus, noun–noun compounds seem to behave slightly differently from adjective–noun compounds, and other combinations of word classes may show yet other characteristics. In the following we will mainly deal with stress assignment to noun–noun compounds for the simple reason that all empirical studies available deal exclusively with this type of compound. We will complement our discussion of noun–noun compounds only with a few tentative remarks on other compound types.

In the literature on noun–noun stress, a number of influential factors for the distribution of the two stress patterns have been proposed, such as argument structure, semantics, lexicalization, spelling, analogy, and informativity. Recently, some empirical studies have become available that have tested various hypotheses using large amounts of experimental and corpus data, and we will summarize their results. The theoretically most important result is perhaps that none of the determining factors works in a categorical fashion. Rather, different studies find different effects at work, all of them having a probabilistic effect. We will discuss each factor in turn.

Before discussing the above-mentioned individual factors that determine the distribution of left and right stress, it should be pointed out that compound stress may also vary along other dimensions. First of all, contrastive stress may generally override the stress pattern normally assigned to a compound (as in *She meant Park Stréet, not Park Róad*). In the following, we will ignore this source of variation and only deal with compound stress in non-contrastive environments. Second, we find regional differences, that is dialects may differ in the stressing of particular forms, or even whole sets of forms (e.g. NAmE *drý-clean* versus BrE *dry-cléan*). Third, a given compound may show variation even within and across speakers of the same dialect. Kunter's (2011) corpus study indicates that this type of variation seems to be restricted to certain compounds and is absent from other compounds. It remains unclear, however, what makes a given compound variable (e.g. *ice-cream*) and another one non-variable (e.g. *ice-cap*). Speaker-variation will inevitably lead to disagreement about the stress of some forms exemplified below. All forms we cite with a particular stress pattern have been taken from speech corpora, from the literature on compound stress (including dictionaries) or have been elicited from or judged by phonetically aware native speakers.

Let us now turn to factors that have been more thoroughly investigated. Giegerich (2004) claims that what he calls argument-head compounds such as *ópera singer* (a subset of our argumental compounds, see Chapter 20) have left stress, while modifier-head structures like *steel brídge* (our attributive compounds) are right-stressed. He concedes that there are many left-stressed modifier-head compounds (such as *ópera glass*) and explains this phenomenon as a lexicalization effect. There is also potentially an important distinction to make between subject and object arguments. Liberman and Sproat (1992) claim that subject-referencing compounds (such as *government cláim*) are right-stressed, while object-referencing compounds (such as *bookseller, squadron leader*) are left-stressed, and Kunter (2011: 134–5) finds empirical evidence for a tendency in that direction. In view of the many counterexamples (e.g. Chapter 20, example (5)) further study is called for.

Empirical evidence for the general argument structure effect as proposed by Giegerich was found, for example, by Plag (2006) and Plag *et al.* (2007, 2008), but the latter two studies (using different corpora) both found that the effect was restricted to compounds whose head ended in agentive -*er* (as in *opera singer*), which corresponds largely to the group of object-referencing compounds mentioned above. Furthermore, the lexicalization effect as gauged by frequency (with higher frequency indicating a higher degree of lexicalization) was found to hold equally for argumental compounds and attributive compounds. Overall, the structural distinction does not turn out to be a good predictor of compound stress.

On the other hand, a very robust general effect of lexicalization has been empirically substantiated in a number of studies. While Plag (2006) finds no correlation between frequency and stress for his small set of experimental items, studies using larger numbers of compounds (e.g. Plag *et al.* 2007, 2008; Bell and Plag 2012) have supported the claim that with rising frequency the chances of left stress increase. Another way to assess lexicalization is spelling. Sepp (2006) and Plag *et al.* (2008) showed that spelling and frequency are related. The higher the frequency of a compound, the more likely a concatenated spelling becomes. Since concatenated spellings are most prevalent among lexicalized compounds, it can be predicted that the proportion of left stresses is highest with compounds that occur with a concatenated spelling. The studies by Plag and colleagues (2007, 2008; Bell and Plag 2012) show that this prediction is correct.

Semantics has also played a role in discussions of compound stress. For example, it has been claimed that certain semantic relations between the two members go together with particular stress patterns (see e.g. Kingdon 1958; Fudge 1984; Olsen 2001; Plag *et al.* 2008; and Lieber and Štekauer 2009: 8–11 for a review). A very robust generalization in this domain is that coordinative compounds (such as *singer-sóngwriter, nerd-génius*) are stressed on the right constituent. Other relations taken to trigger rightward stress are, for example, 'N2 is temporally or spatially located at N1' (*summer dréss, Boston hárbor*), 'N2 is made of N1' (*aluminum lég*), 'N2 is created by N1' (*Mahler sýmphony*). However, although they have been shown to be influential, the effects of these semantic classes do not turn out to be categorical in any of the empirical investigations that tested them (e.g. Plag *et al.* 2007, 2008; Bell and Plag 2012). In other words, the semantic approach works for many, but by no means all compounds for which it makes predictions. Other semantic approaches have taken recourse to the properties of individual constituents or of the compound as a whole. Often, the respective claims coincide with claims based on semantic relations and have the same drawbacks. More exotic categories held to trigger rightward stress are also mentioned in the literature, for example, first nouns denoting food items (e.g. Gussenhoven and Broeders 1981), but empirical investigation has not found any independent effect (Bell and Plag 2012).

From a theoretical perspective the question arises as to what unites the mixed bag of semantic categories and relations that are held responsible for rightward stress assignment. In other words, why would a compound showing a locative relation behave stress-wise in the same way as a coordinative compound? Giegerich (2009b) suggests that the semantic factors can be subsumed under the notions of semantic transparency and ascriptive versus associative semantics. According to Giegerich, in ascriptive attribution, the modifier denotes a property of the head, as in *metal bridge* which can be paraphrased as 'the bridge is metal'. In contrast, in associative attribution, the modifier denotes an entity associated with the head (e.g. *metal fatigue*), where a paraphrase 'the fatigue is metal' is nonsensical, but the fatigue 'is associated with metal'. Giegerich (2009b: 5–6) claims that only modifier-head compounds ('attribute-head' in his terminology) can be right-stressed, and that right stress typically occurs with semantically transparent compounds and with compounds that express an ascriptive relationship.

There are at least two problems with this attempt to unify the semantic effects. First, as shown in the empirical studies mentioned above, the assumption that only modifier-head compounds can carry rightward stress is empirically wrong (examples like *party léader* prove the hypothesis wrong). Second, the distinction between an ascriptive and an associative relationship is often very hard to apply. For example, it seems that linguists may disagree as to whether *door* in *doorknob* is associative (the knob is associated with a door) or ascriptive (the knob has the property of being on a door) in nature.

The most successful approaches to the compound stress problem to date are those that do not relate to categorical rule application but to effects of lexical relatedness and lexical representation. One set of these approaches focuses on analogical effects, another on informativity. We will discuss each in turn.

It has long been observed that compounds with the same rightward or leftward constituent behave rather uniformly in terms of stress assignment. The sets of compounds that share a constituent are called 'constituent families', and a prime example of such constituent family effects are compounds with the right constituent *street* as against compounds with the right constituent *road*, the former of which are all left-stressed (e.g. *Óxford Street*), the latter of which are all right-stressed (*Oxford Róad*). Corpus-based studies (e.g. Plag 2010; Arndt-Lappe 2011) have shown that the constituent family effect is an extremely powerful mechanism across the board in predicting the stress pattern.

Another promising take on compound stress is inspired by the idea that generally, those expressions tend to receive prosodic prominence that are most interesting or informative for the speakers and hearers. What does it mean for an expression, or a linguistic sign, to be informative? Shannon (1948) operationalized the informativity of a sign as the inverse of the probability of occurrence (i.e. the frequency) of that sign. Applying the idea of the connection between informativity and stress placement we arrive at the prediction that the right member of a compound receives stress if it is especially informative. This idea has been around for a long time (see, for example, Sweet 1892: 288), but has been tested only recently. Sweet himself suggests using frequency and semantic specificity as correlates of informativity, with high frequency and semantic non-specificity being indicators of low informativity, and Bell and Plag (2012) find the predicted effects in a large corpus.

To summarize, stress assignment to noun–noun constructs is an intricate phenomenon where many different, sometimes even conflicting, influences play a role. It is presently unclear how the different factors can be unified or related to each other. What is clear is that deterministic rules do not lead to adequate results.

Let us turn to other kinds of compound, for which, however, no systematic research has been carried out. Adjective–noun compounds (such as *blúeprint*, *hóthouse*) normally have initial stress. This is scarcely surprising, since stress was taken as one of the crucial factors in identifying adjective–noun compounds (see Section 19.2.1.2). However, adjective–noun constructions without left stress are generally accepted as being normal syntactic structures, so the weight of having left stress is greater here than in the noun–noun cases where the stress is not necessarily decisive. Note that as well as the stress pattern, which distinguishes these adjective–noun compounds from the corresponding phrases, there is often reduced transparency. Right stress can also be found with adjective–noun compounds which act as adjectives (e.g. *small-scále*). The leftward-stress pattern can also be commonly found with verb–noun compounds (*crýbaby*, *spóilsport*).

Adjectival compounds show the additional complication that with many compounds stress may vary according to sentential position. In premodifying position, there is a tendency towards left stress (e.g. *a ský-blue dress*), while in predicative position we tend to find right stress (e.g. *it is sky-blúe*). Spoken in isolation, coordinative adjectival compounds (e.g. *sweet-sóur*, *grey-gréen*) as well as most modifier-head adjectival compounds (e.g. *knee-déep*, *bone-drý*, *dog-tíred*, *London-básed*) are right-stressed. Argument-head adjectival compounds may take either pattern. While some are more prone to right stress (*university-contrólled*), others are left stressed (*áwe-inspiring*, *háir-raising*).

Verbal compounds seem to generally prefer left-stress in NAmE, although right-stressed items are also found (cf. *swéet-talk* versus *soft-sóap*). In BrE, coordinative verbal compounds show a certain amount of variation (e.g. *dry-cléan*, *freeze-drý* ~ *fréeze-dry*, *stir-frý* ~ *stír-fry*), while all other verbal compounds have a tendency towards left stress (*déep-fry*, *shórtcut*, *blíndfold*, *próof-read*, *tálent-spot*, *cháin-smoke*, but see also *spring-cléan*).

Let us turn to stress assignment on compounds with more than two members. Again we concentrate on compounds with only nouns as constituents, since there are no other combinations of bases that have been systematically investigated. The standard assumption for triconstituent nominal compounds is that the branching-direction determines stress assignment. In left-branching compounds, that is those of the structure [[NN] N], the leftmost noun receives main stress, whereas in right-branching compounds, that is [N [NN]], the second noun is the most prominent one (so-called 'Lexical Category Prominence Rule', e.g. Liberman and Prince 1977). This assumption is built in turn on the ill-conceived idea that all compounds are left-stressed. And indeed it has been shown that branching direction does not work properly as a predictor of triconstituent compound stress (e.g. Giegerich 2009a; Kösling and Plag 2009; Kösling 2011). Giegerich (2009a: 10) gives the following examples, which show that all constituents may in principle be stressed, no matter what the bracketing is.

(15) a. *right branching*
          steel [wáre-house]
          university [spring térm]
          ówl [nest-box]

      b. *left-branching*
          [sand-stone] wáll
          [óil-tanker] driver
          [garden shéd] exhibition

The crucial point is that the stress of triconstituent compounds seems to be subject to the same mechanisms as the stress of two-member compounds (Kösling 2011). The only difference between the two kinds of compound is that with triconstituent compounds these mechanisms work at two levels, namely at the level of the immediate constituents and at the level of the embedded compound. Still, the Lexical Category Prominence Rule makes correct predictions for the majority of compounds. As shown by Kösling and Plag (2009), the many cases of correctly predicted stress patterns result from the fact that there is a skewed distribution of different kinds of bracketings and stress patterns. Thus most triconstituent compounds are left-branching, and most two-member compounds are left-stressed, which gives the Lexical Category Prominence Rule a quantitative advantage which belies the rule's theoretical and empirical inadequacy.

19.3.4 Orthography

As already mentioned, the spelling of compounds is variable, with three possibilities: solid (*butterfly, wristband*), hyphenated (*child-care, loop-hole*) and spaced (*state official, seat belt*). Some types have three variants (e.g. *cell phone, cell-phone, cellphone*), but most compounds prefer one spelling. Thus, in the corpus of noun–noun compounds used in Sepp (2006), there are 91,868 compound types, but including all spelling variants increases the numbers by only an additional 3 per cent ($N = 3{,}009$). Depending on the corpus one chooses the different spellings occur in variable proportions. Table 19.1 summarizes the results for noun–noun compounds from three corpora. Sepp (2006) is a balanced corpus with texts from different domains, Plag *et al.* (2008) extracted their compounds from the Boston University Speech Corpus (BURSC, Ostendorf *et al.* 1996), which contains news speech, and CELEX (Baayen *et al.* 1995) is a lexical database with compounds taken from two dictionaries.

From such results we can conclude that in normal usage there is a strong tendency for noun–noun compounds to be spelled as two words. The discrepancy between the text corpus-based figures and the dictionary-based figures indicates one important factor determining the choice of the spelling, that is lexicalization. The more lexicalized the compound the more likely it becomes that we find a solid spelling. Thus, as already mentioned, Sepp (2006), Plag *et al.* (2007, 2008) and Bell and Plag (2012) find a correlation of frequency and spelling (and stress), with solid spellings being more probable among more frequent compounds. Other factors influencing the spelling choice (empirically verified in Sepp 2006: 88–116) are length (longer compounds tend to avoid solid spellings) and the segmental make-up across the internal boundary. Identical consonants across the word-boundary and vowel hiatus disfavour a solid spelling. Finally, we find analogical effects based on constituent families. For example, a solid spelling for a given compound is more likely if its constituents also occur in many other solid compounds. It also seems that there may be in-house spelling rules for compound orthography; for example, *The Chambers Dictionary* (Marr 2008) is more conservative in using large numbers of hyphens than *Collins English Dictionary* (2006).

The above findings all refer to noun–noun compounds, and it is not clear whether they easily transfer to other types of compound. On the contrary, it seems that the spelling of compounds with an adjectival or verbal head show a different kind of variability. Unfortunately, there are no systematic empirical studies available on the spelling of adjectival and verbal compounds, but adjectival compounds seem to generally prefer hyphenation (e.g. *dog-lean, girl-crazy, sugar-free, university-controlled, Cambridge-based*), with solid or spaced spellings being much rarer (e.g. *footloose, threadbare, toll free*). For illustration, consider the

Table 19.1 Proportion of spellings in three corpora in percent

Spelling	Sepp (2006) types (N = 94,877)	Sepp (2006) tokens (N = 265,991)	BURSC tokens Plag *et al.* (2008) (N = 4,353)	CELEX
Solid	5.4	27.5	8.4	42.1
Hyphenated	10.3	7.5	0.1	29.6
Spaced	84.2	65.1	90.9	28.2
	100	100	100	100

distribution of spelling variants for the noun–adjective combination N-*prone* (as in *accident-prone*). In COCA the vast majority of relevant forms are hyphenated. Solid spellings (e.g. *repairprone, floodprone*) are extremely restricted and can be found for only 12 types (as against 227 hyphenated types), with only 18 tokens (as against 935 hyphenated tokens).

A similar picture holds for the verbal compounds, which also show a clear preponderance of hyphenated spellings (*stir-fry, finger-catch*), with only the occasional solid spelling or spaced spelling (e.g. *smellsip, flash photograph*, from Erdmann 1999).

The above discussion tacitly related to contexts in which the different spelling variants are functionally equivalent. This is, however, not always the case. Hyphenation, for example, is frequently used to indicate correct parsing with premodificational adjectival compounds (*a disease causing headache* versus *a disease-causing headache*) or with triconstituent compounds (e.g. *company whistle-blowers*, Kösling and Plag 2009: 210). In larger compounds, especially phrasal compounds, the use of hyphenation also reflects structural relations as represented by syntactic bracketing (cf. [*noun-plus-adjective*] *compounds*, or [*late-twentieth-century*] *Britain*. In such cases, the hyphenated portions represent the first immediate constituent of the compound. Especially with adjective–noun compounds, solid or hyphenated spellings may be used to indicate the status of the construct as a (lexicalized) word instead of a phrase (*whiteboard* versus *white board*). However, this is also linked with frequency so that relatively less frequent *red squirrel* is lexicalized but spelled spaced.

19.4 TYPES OF COMPOUND

In this section we will look in more detail at the formal properties of specific types of compound. These types are grouped according to the formal (syntactic, morphological, phonological) properties of the kinds of elements that they consist of. Table 19.2 gives an overview of the compound types by syntactic category, using a product-oriented definition of compounding, including canonical and non-canonical compounds. The examples in Table 19.2 simply illustrate in a pretheoretical manner forms with words of the stated category in the stated position.

Quite strikingly, all combinations are attested. As we will see, however, the different combinations differ widely in their derivational history and productivity. In the next four subsections we will discuss each of the cells in Table 19.2. We will do so column-wise, that is according to heads. The semantic properties of these compounds will be discussed in detail in the next chapter, for questions of spelling and stress assignment see the preceding subsections.

19.4.1 Nominal compounds

Noun–noun compounds are the most productive kind of compound in English, and they are semantically extremely diverse (as will be illustrated in Chapter 20). The productivity of

Table 19.2 Compound types by syntactic category

	Noun	Verb	Adjective	Preposition
Noun	film society	brainwash	knee-deep	year-in
Verb	pickpocket	stir-fry	go-slow	breakdown
Adjective	hothouse	hot glue	light-green	tuned-in
Preposition	afterbirth	downgrade	inbuilt	into

adjective–noun compounds is hard to determine, since there may be some variation in stress in individual collocations and since the compounds seem to arise from stress shift in phrases (Bauer 1983: 205–6). An example like *slow food* may be indeterminate, even though its congener *fast-food* has left-stress in attributive positions as in *fast-food outlets*. Spelling is not necessarily helpful, since the majority of adjective–noun constructions linked by a hyphen are in attributive position, and the hyphen is used according to standard orthographic norms. It is sometimes implied that exocentric adjective–noun compounds cannot be productive (Jackendoff 1975), although this seems unlikely since various meanings for a form like *redskin* (North American native, potato, apple, tomato) can readily be found.

Next, there is a class of compounds in which the first element is ambiguously analysed as a noun or a verb, for example, *boarding pass, livingroom, surfing lesson, killing field*. These sometimes alternate with forms that lack the *-ing*, as in *board pass, surf lesson*, in which case they are unambiguously verb–noun compounds. New endocentric verb–noun compounds in which the noun plays various roles in relation to the verb are regularly found; examples include *dive suit, drown-proofing, dump truck, write-performance, think-tank, wait-time*, as well as those immediately above (see Chapter 20.3.1.1 for discussion). The *pickpocket* type illustrated in Table 19.2 is exocentric, and not really productive in current English.

Finally, we find numerous constructions with prepositions as first elements, as in *afterbirth, afterthought, backseat, back-office, downtown, downside, upland, uplight*. However, there are good reasons to analyse these as derived words rather than compounds (see Chapter 16).

19.4.2 Verbal compounds

Most compounds with verbal right elements seem to be non-canonical, that is derived by processes other than the combination of two bases. The effect is so strong that Marchand (1969) claims that there are no verbal compounds in English. Erdmann (1999) finds the following sources for compound verbs.

They can be converted from nominal or adjectival compounds or even phrases (*bear-proof, breath test, carbon-copy, cold shoulder, head-shake, white-lie*), derived by inversion from phrasal constructions (e.g. *upgrade* ◆ *grade up* 'to improve the breed of (stock) by grading' *OED*), back-derived from nominal or adjectival compounds (de-nominal: *ghetto-blast*

♦ *ghetto-blaster, crash-land* ♦ *crash-landing*, de-adjectival:*horror-strike* ♦ *horror-struck, tailor-make* ♦ *tailor-made*). In many cases, however, the evidence (e.g. from earliest attestations) is not very clear concerning the question of whether the compound verb was first or some nominal or adjectival compound from which it was potentially derived. Erdmann (1999) gives many examples of compound pairs where the dates of the earliest attestations are very close to each other, or where there is even an earlier attestation for the verbal compound. Especially among the latter group, one often finds whole sets of verbal compounds with the same right element, which suggests that analogy is also a very important factor at work. For example, the twentieth-century neologisms *drip-dry, spin-dry, blow-dry* are all attested before their adjectival counterparts came into existence (*drip-dried, spin-dried, blow-dried*). Crucially, at the time there was already a large right constituent family of verbal compounds in *-dry* that served as an analogical model for these new canonical formations (*kiln-dry, smoke-dry, sun-dry*).

There are, however, also verbal compounds that apparently have been coined without recourse to any of the above mechanisms and should be considered canonical compounds. Such compounds can be either attributive, as in *tip-touch, window-shop, sugarcoat*, or possibly coordinative, as in *blow-dry, stir-fry, trickle-irrigate*.

Given the diverse derivational histories of compound verbs, it comes as no surprise that we find nouns, adjectives, verbs, and prepositions as first elements.

19.4.3 Adjectival compounds

Canonical adjectival compounds can be productively formed with nouns or adjectives as first elements. With nouns in initial position the compound is generally argumental (e.g. *ankle-deep, butter-yellow, crime-prone, resource-expensive, word-final*) with adjectival non-head it is coordinative (*blue-green, spicy-mild, icy-hot*). Non-canonical adjectival compounds arise through the use of phrases in premodifying position (as in *they want a go-slow approach*, COCA). Whether the *slow* in *go-slow* should be analysed as an adjective or as an adverb may be controversial, and it is a problem which faces many such forms. Adjectival compounds with prepositions in non-head position seem to be restricted to participles as heads (*down-sized, in-turned, out-sourced, up-graded*), and are derived by inversion from phrasal verbs, or are participles of compound verbs.

19.4.4 Prepositional compounds

None of the four types of prepositional compounds are canonical. The combination of two prepositions as in *into, upon* has arisen via univerbation. Noun–preposition combinations are not restricted to fixed expressions such as *year-in, year-out*, but appear to be moderately productive, as shown in (16).

(16)   *2010 FIC Bk:AmorFugit*: I hold the book **face-out** so he can read the lettering

2004 MAG TodaysParent: Can be worn in five positions (front face-in and face-out, back **face-out** and face-in and a fifth "nursing" position)

1999 MAG PopScience: Each has 16MB of memory, a color LCD, and a **video-out** port.

2005 FIC SCarolinaRev: they drank until **sun-up**

The syntactic category of these formations is not always clear, but it seems that they cannot be straightforwardly analysed as prepositions (*sun-up* is a noun, *face-out* an adverb, *video-out* is even less clear), in other words, these forms are syntactically exocentric. Yet another case of noun–preposition compounds are forms arising from the suffixation of *-er* to phrasal verbs (e.g. *runner-up, passer-by, picker-up*).

Verb–preposition compounds are either nouns converted from phrasal verbal constructions (e.g. *breakdown, hold-up, sleep-over*), or analogical formations on the basis of converted phrasal constructions (e.g. *sleep-in* on the basis of *sit-in*—there are also other meanings of *sleep-in*). Adjective–preposition compounds are adjectives and seem to be restricted to verbal participles as heads (e.g. *tuned-in, tied-up*).

19.4.5 Neo-classical compounds

Neoclassical compounds have a number of peculiarities that deserve special attention. First, the position and combinatorial properties of the elements involved; second, the phonological properties of the resulting compounds; third, the status and behaviour of the vowel that often appears in the middle of such forms; and finally the syntactic category of the elements in question.

The list of forms that can be argued to belong to the class of neoclassical forms is long, and it is not entirely clear which elements should belong to this class (see, for example, Bauer 1998b; Baeskow 2004 for discussion). (17) shows some of them.

(17)		*form*	*meaning*	*example*
	a.	astro-	'space'	astro-physics, astrology
		bio-	'life'	biodegradable, biocracy
		biblio-	'book'	bibliography, bibliotherapy
		electro-	'electricity'	electro-cardiograph, electrography
		geo-	'earth'	geographic, geology
		hydro-	'water'	hydro-electric, hydrology
		morpho-	'figure'	morphology, morpho-genesis
		philo-	'love'	philotheist, philo-gastric
		retro-	'backwards'	retroflex, retro-design

	tele-	'distant'	television, telepathy
	theo-	'god'	theocratic, theology
b.	-cide	'murder'	genocide, insecticide
	-cracy	'rule'	bureaucracy, democracy
	-graphy	'write'	iconography, bibliography
	-itis	'disease'	laryngitis, lazyitis
	-logy	'science of'	astrology, lichenology
	-morph	'figure'	anthropomorph, pythonomorph
	-phile	'love'	bibliophile, jazzophile
	-phobe	'fear'	bibliophobe, commitmentphobe
	-scope	'look at'	iconoscope, telescope

Most of the forms in (17) do not occur as free forms. There are elements like *morph-/-morph* and *phil-/-phile*, which can occur in both initial and final position, while most forms occur in only one position. Hence a distinction is often made between initial combining forms and final combining forms. Combining forms can either combine with bound roots (e.g. *glaciology, scientology*), with words (*lazyitis, hydro-electric, morpho-syntax*), or with another combining form (*hydrology, morphology*).

With regard to the phonological properties of neoclassical elements, we see that they vary in their segmental structure and in their stress contour, depending on whether initial combining forms combine with free forms or with certain other combining forms.

(18)   a.   astro-phýsics   b.   astrólogy
            biodegrádable   bíocracy
            biblio-thérapy   bibliógraphy

Initial combining forms that take a word as second element, as in (18a), regularly have their main stress on the righthand member of the compound. Many final combining forms, such as *-graphy*, *-cracy*, and *-logy*, as in (18b) impose antepenultimate stress on the compound, accompanied by a different vowel quality (/əʊ/‖/oʊ/ versus /ɒ/‖/ɑ/). Combining forms such as *-graphy*, *-cracy*, and *-logy* thus behave phonologically like certain stress-influencing suffixes (such as *-ity*).

Note that we have accepted here a general analysis whereby words such as *geology* are usually seen as being made up of *geo-* and *-logy* (see below for the status of the *-o-*). In many instances we might consider the final *-y* here an affix (as in *allomorphy*, for example), parallel to *-ist* in *geologist* (see Chapter 12.2.5 on *-y* in particular). If we accept items like *-logy* as units, rather than as sequences of *-log-y*, it is because they are treated as independent items by speakers (e.g. Urdang *et al.* 1986: 7, where several such items are treated as unanalysable).

The next characteristic of neoclassical compounds that needs discussion is the status of the vowel that appears at the boundary of the two elements. This vowel, orthographically represented mostly as either <o> (mainly with Greek-derived bases) or <i> (mainly with Latin-derived bases), could be analysed as the base-final vowel of the initial element (e.g. Bauer 1998b) or as an independent element intervening between the two bases, similar to linking elements in native compounds in other Germanic languages (e.g. Baeskow 2004). In English, combining forms are used with the attached vowel when added to lexemic bases: *insect-icide, morpho-syntax, geo-thermal, lichen-ology*. This might lead to an analysis whereby the vowel belongs with each combining form and is part of the lexical specification of the element. This would account for the differing vowels in *tele-printer, insect-icide* and *socio-linguistic*. It would also imply some kind of haplology to simplify a sequence of vowels in cases like **geo-ology*.

There is an alternative analysis of what is going on here. We could see the vowel as an element placed between the two roots to ameliorate the phonotactics so that *morphology* comes from **morph-logy* with an inserted *-o-* (this is historically the case in Greek, but, of course, it does not follow that this is the best analysis for modern English). This fails to account for the variation in the vowel, but does account for the fact that the vowel may be omitted where the morphology does not bring two consonants into contact across the boundary: *homo-taxis, laryng-itis, mono-semy, poly-gon*, It also accounts for the vowel in formations such as *steroid-o-genesis* (COCA) which appear to be made up on the basis of two English lexemes.

Ancient Greek formations and modern English formations differ slightly in their patterns of constructions where there is an initial <h> in the second combining form. Such differences are also seen with Greek prefixes. For instance, consider the difference between *anthelion* and *anti-hydrophobic*, both of which contain the prefix *anti-*. In *anthelion*, the final <i> of *anti-* is deleted to avoid the vowel–vowel sequence because the <h> is treated as a vowel. In *anti-hydrophobic*, the <h> is treated as a consonant, and there is no deletion. Similar instances are found with neoclassical formations. *Glycemia* and *glycohemia* are synonymous words made from the same elements, the first with vowel (and <h>) deletion, the latter with no deletion, in the modern manner.

Finally, we turn to the problem of syntactic category. In general, we find that neoclassical formations are nouns. This may be surprising since bound roots are normally assumed to have no syntactic category specification (e.g. Giegerich 1999: 72–6). Neoclassical compounds may undergo further morphological processes, in which case the new formation largely inherits the formal properties of its base. For this reason such derivations are sometimes called 'neoclassical derivations' (Baeskow 2004).

19.4.6 Phrasal compounds

Phrasal compounds are right-headed structures and seem to be largely restricted to nominal heads, although, for example, adjectival heads do allow phrases as left sisters. This class of compounds is very productive, some examples from COCA are given in (19).

(19) burned-rope-and-sugar taste, soon-to-be-divorced wife, less-than-successful husband,
      empty-nest syndrome, one-on-one conversation, work-at-home husband, on-air
      puzzle, this-person-is-a-jerk attitude

There seem to be very few restrictions on the phrases that can be used in first position: we
find noun phrases, adjective phrases, verb phrases, prepositional phrases, and clauses. It is
even possible to use strings that are not syntactic constituents as initial elements (e.g. *thumbs-up sign*). There is, however, a restriction on the kinds of noun phrases that may occur in
phrasal compounds. Thus, it has been pointed out in the literature (e.g. Lieber 1992: 12) that
determiner phrases seem not to be allowed (**a the-burned-rope-and-sugar taste*). Why it is
exactly that these phrases are excluded is still under debate.

Although many phrasal compounds feature phrases that seem lexicalized or rather fre-
quent, it is by no means impossible to use completely new phrases (e.g. *this-person-is-a-jerk-attitude*, COCA).

19.4.7 Reduplicative compounds

There are various types of reduplication whose main function appears to be to indicate attitude, and these are dealt with in Chapter 18.2.6. Here we deal with a pattern of full reduplication also known as contrastive reduplication (Ghomeshi *et al.* 2004) or identical constituent
compounds (Hohenhaus 2004) which involves the full phonological copying of bases, that is
of words or phrases. Ghomeshi *et al.'s* (2004) examples reproduced in (20) illustrate the
phenomenon.

(20) a. Are you LEAVING-leaving? *[i.e., are you "really" leaving (for good), or are you just
         stepping out for a minute?]*

      b. **A:** Are you nervous?

         B: Yeah, but, you know, not NERVOUS-nervous. *[i.e. not "really" nervous]*

      c. Lily: You have to get up.

         Rick: I am up.

         Lily: I mean UP-up.

Semantically, contrastive reduplication restricts the meaning of the head to some type of
prototypical meaning. As a consequence, Ghomeshi *et al.* (2004) suggest that function words
lacking the necessary semantic variation cannot be contrastively reduplicated.

(21) **A:** I will visit my mother next week.

      B: *You will, or you WILL-will?

Note, however, the title *The Foods you Must Must Eat Before You Die* (Men's Health 2011) which suggests that such constraints may be overstated.

Contrastive reduplicative compounds are categorically stressed on the first immediate constituent, which is, however, a fact that automatically follows from the contrastive pragmatics and semantics.

19.4.8 Blends

Blends are compounds where at least one constituent lacks some of its phonological material. Semantically, they behave like other compounds, as shown in more detail in Chapter 20, but stress-wise they behave like a single word, normally adopting the stress pattern of one of the two source words.

There is no agreed definition of the phenomenon and the boundaries of what is called 'blend' in the literature are fuzzy. For example, a distinction has been proposed (e.g. Bauer 2006b) between 'blends' (which involve the loss of medial segmental material, as in *brunch*) and 'clipped compounds' or 'complex clippings' (which involve the loss of final material of both bases, as in *mod*em < **mod**ulator-**dem**odulator). The two patterns can be formalized as in (22), where AB stands for the left base (with its two parts A and B) and CD stands for the right base, with its two parts C and D.

(22)   a. AB + CD → AD

        b. AB + CD → AC

In many blends, the surviving material may be shared by the two bases, as in *boatel* or *scrapnel*, where the rhyme of the first syllable of the blend corresponds to the same sequence of sounds in both bases (*boat* and *hotel*, *scrap* and *shrapnel*, respectively). It is also possible to find blends in which the whole left base word is preserved (e.g. *painstation* ◆ *pain* + *playstation*). Either of these patterns may be analysed as an AD blend, in accordance with (22a).

It is not immediately obvious whether the distinction between blends and clipped compounds is theoretically or empirically informative. Gries (2006) shows, however, that the two kinds of formation do indeed differ in important respects, so that it may be justified to posit two distinct processes with their own properties. Thus, in Gries's data set, clipped compounds systematically preserve much less material than blends normally do. Furthermore, overlaps of segmental material are underrepresented in clipped compounds. Finally, blends and clipped compounds differ with regard to their base words. While bases of blends tend to be orthographically and phonologically highly similar to each other, clipped compound bases are significantly less similar to each other (only half-way in similarity between blend bases and arbitrarily chosen words in the lexicon).

There is also a clear difference in productivity, with clipped compounds being in the clear minority, with a proportion ranging from 3 to 6 per cent in different empirical studies (cf. Kubozono 1990; Gries 2006; Arndt-Lappe and Plag 2012).

Given that the literature on clipped compounds is scarce, we will say very little about this category and concentrate on blends of the type given in (22a). The reader should note, however, that some of the empirical results we summarize here are taken from studies that may not have neatly distinguished between the two types of blend.

Another problem in delimiting the category of blend is the occurrence of splinters. We defined splinters as originally (mostly) non-morphemic portions of a word that have been split off and used in the formation of new words with a specific new meaning. The line between a derivative with a splinter and a blend may sometimes be hard to draw (see also Chapter 23 for discussion). For example, *freeware* might be treated as a blend of *free* and *software*, or as a case of suffixation of the splinter *-ware* to the base *free* (as in *crimeware, eduware, malware, netware, spyware, trialware*).

In a large collection of more than 1,018 formations, Reischer (2008) finds that nouns are the most frequent output category of blends in English (almost 80 per cent, e.g. *brunch, buffeteria, diagnonsense*), followed by adjectives (11 per cent, e.g. *bleen ◆ blue + green, dramastic ◆ dramatic + drastic*, and verbs (4 per cent, *guesstimate*). Reischer's figures, however, include instances of syntactic wordplay that we do not consider to be part of word-formation such as *I drink, therefore I am* or *A car is born*. Such examples amount to only 1 per cent of all forms in Reischer's collection.

The four most frequent input combinations (in descending order) are noun + noun, adjective + noun, adjective + adjective, and verb + verb. Example (23) illustrates the different patterns.

(23) *noun + noun*
      brainiac, infotainment, netizen, painstation (◆ pain + playstation), sitcom (◆ situation + comedy), smog, spork (◆ spoon + fork), suicycle, skort (◆ skirt + shorts), textpert, wreader (◆ writer-reader)

      adjective + noun
      britcom (◆ British + sitcom), prosumer (◆ professional + consumer), quicktionary

      adjective + adjective
      abnormous, delishful, fabtastic, obsolute, prezactly, rurban, solunar

      verb + verb
      correctify (◆ correct + rectify), gesplain (◆ gesture + explain), scarify (◆ scare + terrify), suspose (◆ suspect + suppose)

Such examples raise a number of questions, the most important of which is, given two input forms, how one can determine the phonological or orthographic structure of the output?

Which parts survive, which parts are deleted? Where does the stress pattern come from? What kinds of entities play a role in the process (e.g. graphemes, segments, onsets, codas, rhymes, syllables, or feet)?

As will become clear, the diversity of the observable patterns is considerable and the apparent variability in the outcomes has led researchers to claim that the phonological-orthographic output properties of blends are largely unpredictable (e.g. Marchand 1969; Bauer 1983: 225; Cannon 1986: 744). Notably, such pessimistic statements stem from an era in which deterministic rules predominated the conceptualization of structural linguistic phenomena. More recent developments in probabilistic grammar, prosodic morphology, and statistical linguistic modelling have contributed to the emergence of many studies that have shown that blends are not to be conceived of as 'extragrammatical' (Dressler 2000). Instead, the formation of blends is prosodically highly constrained and essentially predictable within a well-defined space of variation.

Constraint-based approaches in the theoretical framework of Prosodic Morphology such as Lappe (2007) have shown that subtractive morphological processes such as the formation of clippings are largely regular, despite the conclusions in much of the earlier literature (see Chapter 18). These processes rely heavily on the manipulation of prosodic constituents instead of on the agglutination of morphemes. Blending is another such process in which prosodic categories play a prominent role in shaping the phonological form of the output. Approaches using this perspective have achieved considerable success in describing the phonological properties of blends and in suggesting mechanisms through which these properties emerge (e.g. Kubozono 1990; Bat-El 2006; Bat-El and Cohen 2012; Arndt-Lappe and Plag 2012). Complementing constraint-based approaches, statistical, and computational investigations such as Gries (2004a, 2004b, 2004c, 2006, 2011), Reischer (2005, 2008), or Cook and Stevenson (2010) have revealed that many aspects of blends lend themselves to successful quantitative and computational modelling. In the following we summarize some of the most important findings with regard to the above-mentioned questions.

In general, there are two competing forces at work that generally constrain the form of phonologically reduced compounds (and other prosodic-morphological formations). One is the shortening of the combination into a single word, the other the need to preserve as much material as possible in order to establish a formal relationship between the output and the input forms.

The two counteracting principles just mentioned conspire to influence not only the size, but also the order of the two elements, such that in coordinative blends, where order is not determined by semantic considerations, there is a strong tendency to prefer an order that preserves as many segments as possible. Thus, we get, for example, *spork* instead of **foon* from the combination of *spoon* and *fork*. However, this tendency does not seem to hold for formations that involve source words with more than one syllable, a point which illustrates the complexity and interaction of the restrictions involved.

One general restriction on blends is that the output must obey the normal constraints on the phonological structure of words in English. For example, Davis (1988) suggests a form like **smang ◆ smash + bang*) preserves more material than the competitor *bash* but is ruled out for phonotactic reasons, since English words of the structure *sCVC* may not contain two nasals in the two C positions (Davis 1988).

Another combinatorial mechanism that reconciles the two basic competing principles with regard to the size of the output form is the tendency of blends to have as many syllables as one of the bases, usually the second base (as in *boatel, brunch, guesstimate*). Counterexamples preserving more syllables can be found (e.g. *correctify*), but they often involve a considerable overlap of phonological (or sometimes purely orthographic) material, which facilitates the recoverability of the relationship between base words and blend. Example (24) provides an illustration of overlaps, with the overlapping part in bold print. The form *brainiac* shows a phonological overlap, *netizen* an overlap at the phonological and orthographic level, *smog* an orthographic overlap, and *suicycle* an intricate mixture of both, with the first <i> overlapping orthographically, but not phonologically, and the onset and nuclei of the respective second syllables (<ci> and <cy>) overlapping phonologically but not orthographically. Finally, especially with longer words, there can be no overlap (as in *infotainment*).

(24) br**ain** + m**an**iac ◆ brainiac

net + ci**t**izen ◆ netizen

sm**oke** + **fog** ◆ smog

su**ici**de + **bicy**cle ◆ suicycle

info/information + entertainment ◆ infotainment

The examples in (24) may suggest that overlaps are always and only medial. This is, however, not true. Overlaps may also occur in other positions, and given the fact that the two bases are often phonologically very similar to each other, this is even to be expected, consider *Chunnel ◆ Channel + tunnel, hesiflation ◆ hesitation + inflation, Turlish ◆ Turkish+ Polish.* There is no empirical study available that specifically addresses the question of where the cut-off points are located in blends that have a medial overlap as against blends that do not have a medial overlap. It seems, however, that blends with medial overlaps also conform to the restrictions that hold for blends with a different kind of overlap or without any overlap. In general, in an output-oriented analysis, forms that show overlaps can be more easily accommodated to structural restrictions than blends with no overlap, as correspondence relations between bases and blend can be established more flexibly.

Some of the prosodic restrictions on blend formation concern syllable structure and stress. For the description of the pertinent phenomena it is useful to distinguish between monosyllabic and polysyllabic blends. With monosyllabic blends there is a strong tendency to combine the onset of the first word with rhyme of the second, as we see it in *br#unch, sp#ork,*

Sw#atch. However, certain initial clusters of the left base may be broken up if the initial part of the left word onset can form a new onset with the right word onset (irrespective of the number of syllables). For instance, Arndt-Lappe and Plag (2012) find systematic variation in their experimental data with forms such as *bleen ~ breen* (• *blue + green*) and *scinter ~ scrinter ~ sprinter* (• *scanner + printer*). They also show that base stress has an influence of the cut-off-points. Thus, the cut-off point of the second word has a tendency to be chosen in such a way that (parts of) the stressed syllable makes it into the blend (e.g. *ginórmous* • *gigántic + enórmous*), a tendency that we do not find for the left base.

How much of the base survives is also dependent on the overall length constraint mentioned above, namely that blends are usually as long as the longer base word, which, if the two words differ in length, is mostly the second word. In general, we find that the second word also provides more material than the first and that the stress pattern of the blend tends to be the same as the stress pattern of the second word.

Interestingly, these structural restrictions or tendencies have psycholinguistic correlates. Gries (2006) shows that the cut-off points are correlated with what he calls 'selection point', that is the position in the word where the selection of the base word among its lexical competitors becomes highly likely (according to the particular metric he develops).

To summarize, blends are a productive word-formation process in English which, in spite of the considerable variability, conforms to a number of general principles and tendencies that highly restrict the structure of possible formations. Given the intricacies involved and the comparative scarcity of pertinent studies, blends certainly merit much further study.

....

CHAPTER 20

Compounds: semantic considerations

20.1 PROSPECTUS

In this chapter we move from a formal consideration of compounds in English to a consideration of semantics, a subject that has drawn an enormous amount of attention in the linguistic literature. Previous accounts of the semantics of English compounding can be found in Jespersen (1942), Lees (1960), Hatcher (1960), Marchand (1969), Brekle (1970), Adams (1973, 2001), Levi (1978), Bauer (1978, 2008, 2010c), Lieber (1983, 2004, 2009, 2010), Ryder (1994), Plag (2003), Jackendoff (2009), among others. Blends and neoclassical compounds have received less attention, but we will see that their semantic properties are similar to other compounds.

We begin in this section with a consideration of some general semantic characteristics of English compounds and with a justification of the basic terminology we will need in order to organize further discussion, especially the distinction between ARGUMENTAL and NON-ARGUMENTAL compounds that will be the basis for our classification. We will treat argumental compounds in Section 20.2, and move on to non-argumental compounds in Section 20.3. Section 20.4 will discuss cases in which the boundary between argumental and non-argumental compounds is blurred. In Section 20.5 we will look at the semantics of both blends and neoclassical compounds and assess the extent to which their semantics is similar to that of other compounds. Finally, in Section 20.6 we will look at several marginal or disputed compounding patterns including compounds with verbs as their second elements (*henpeck*), phrasal compounds (*over-the-fence gossip*), and reduplicative compounds (*friend friend*).

20.1.1 General remarks

We intend here to explore the semantics of those compounds whose meanings are compositional in nature, but we should make clear at the outset what we mean by compositionality. Compounds, like any other complex words, can be semantically opaque and be lexicalized with non-transparent meaning. Lexicalization is not a homogeneous phenomenon, however.

Here we will not be concerned with the semantics of item-familiar compounds whose meanings are in no way predictable from their parts—for example, compounds like *butterfly* or *honeymoon*. Unlike derived forms, however, newly coined compounds frequently have the potential to be multiply polysemous, at least when considered out of context. In context and especially if they become established and item familiar, many of the potential meanings of course fall by the wayside; at this point, the meaning of the compound becomes lexicalized, although still compositional.

We will be concerned here with the semantics of newly coined compounds and those lexicalized/institutionalized compounds whose meanings continue to be transparent, and we will leave aside the semantics of compounds that have ceased to be compositional in nature.

There are two general characteristics that form the basis of most accounts of the semantics of English compounds: first, that the compound as a whole is a hyponym of the second element of the compound (or put otherwise, that English compounds are right-headed semantically as well as syntactically); and second, that the first element of the compound is non-referential in nature. While both of these generalizations are true of the majority of compounds in English, they are of course not exceptionless. We will have occasion in the sections below to explore in depth the extent to which hyponymy obtains in English compounds, but we should first say a few words about the issue of non-referentiality.

The problem of referentiality in compounds is necessarily restricted to compounds in which the first element is a common noun. It is certainly the case that in the vast majority of such cases, that noun is intended non-referentially; clearly, *cat* in *cat litter* does not and cannot refer to any specific cat, nor can *truck* in *truck driver* refer to any specific truck. It should be kept in mind, however, that compounds can be formed in English with proper nouns as the first element, as we find in examples like *Amadinejad supporter* or *Beatles fan*. In these, the first element is clearly meant to refer specifically to the President of Iran or the musical group comprised of Lennon, McCartney, Harrison, and Starr. Similarly, in compounded names of businesses, countries, or individuals (e.g. *Hewlett-Packard*, *Bosnia-Herzegovina*, etc.), both elements of the compound are clearly referential. Similarly, compounds with common noun modifiers that have unique reference, such as *moonlight*, *earth sciences*, *sunset* have referential first elements. Furthermore, it seems that the discourse context may make the first element of a given compound referential. Thus, in a parliamentary debate about the budget for the nation's army, the word *army* in *army budget* will receive a referential interpretation, namely as referring to the army of that country. These complications aside, it seems safe to say that the first element of English compounds is usually non-referential.

20.1.2 Classification

Any discussion of the semantics of compounding must inevitably be organized on the basis of some underlying scheme of classification. The classification of compounds, however, has been a matter of much controversy among morphologists; see for example Scalise and Bisetto (2009), and references cited therein. One significant problem has been the failure of many researchers to look at the full scope of compounding in English or to look at English in the context of types of compounds found in other languages. Another has been the welter of overlapping and conflicting terminology. It behooves us, therefore, to begin by setting out clearly the terminology we will use and briefly justifying the way we propose to divide up the landscape of compounding.

In Chapter 19, we looked at formal properties of compounds, including their categorial composition, (morphosyntactic) headedness, and phonological properties. Here, we concentrate on surveying the semantic types of compounds that can be found in English and the extent to which particular semantic types and subtypes can be deemed productive. We will therefore not divide compounds on the basis of their syntactic categories; for example, where nominal and adjectival compounds share semantic characteristics, they will be treated together. There have been a number of recent surveys of the semantics of English compounds that will be useful to us, including Adams (2001), Plag (2003), Bisetto and Scalise (2005), Bauer (2008, 2010c), Scalise and Bisetto (2009), and Lieber (2009, 2010). The system that we will introduce here is a synthesis of various proposals introduced in those works. We will begin with an overview of the basic terminological distinctions of which we will make use.

A distinction is commonly made between ENDOCENTRIC and EXOCENTRIC compounds. The most comprehensive discussion of exocentricity can be found in Bauer (2010c), which we will largely follow here. Briefly, endocentric compounds are ones in which the compound as a whole denotes a subset of the head element of the compound. In semantic terms, in endocentric compounds the compound as a whole is a hyponym of the head. Exocentric compounds are ones in which the compound as a whole does not denote a kind or subset of the head.

However, as Bauer (2010c) points out, exocentricity is not a homogeneous phenomenon; there are a number of ways in which compounds can count as exocentric. One type of exocentricity might be seen as purely semantic, that is, cases in which the compound as a whole is not (literally or figuratively) a hyponym of its head. Items like *pickpocket* or *cutpurse* are exocentric in the sense that they denote types of people, and not objects like pockets or purses; these are frequently literal in nature: a *pickpocket* literally is 'someone who picks pockets'. Items like *blockhead* or *air head* are also exocentric, and might be termed POSSESSIVE compounds (similar to the Sanskrit designation BAHUVRIHI). These compounds frequently denote types of people, and are often meant metaphorically or metonymically: a *blockhead*, for example, is a person whose head is like a block, hence a stupid person, a *redshank* a bird with red shanks.

The next basic division we make is between ARGUMENTAL and NON-ARGUMENTAL compounds. The former are compounds, one element of which is interpreted as an argument of the other element. Argument-taking elements can be relational nouns (e.g *member*, as in *club member*), or verbs, or nouns derived from verbs via affixation or conversion (e.g. *soccer player*). In the case of an argumental compound with a verbal or deverbal head the non-head constituent is interpreted as a subject, object, or prepositional object. The argumental compounds that have overt affixes (for example, *truck driver, cost containment*) have frequently been referred to as SYNTHETIC compounds in the English tradition. Those that involve underived verbs or nouns formed from verbs by conversion (e.g. *attack dog, dog attack*) have frequently not been identified as a coherent type, and indeed have sometimes only been discussed in passing (but see Bauer and Huddleston 2002, and especially Lieber 2010, who calls them 'non-affixal (de)verbal compounds').

Non-argumental compounds are those in which neither member bears an argumental relation to the other. Among these, we can distinguish two major types, ATTRIBUTIVE and COORDINATIVE compounds. In attributive compounds the relation between the first element and the second is one of loose modification. Such compounds have often been called ROOT or PRIMARY compounds. In coordinative compounds we find a variety of relationships, but always ones in which both elements of the compound have equal semantic weight; in other words, where neither element can be said to modify the other. Note that the distinction between attributive and coordinative compounds is not always clear. For example, it seems that the putative coordinative compound *zebra-dog* could also be analysed as an attributive one, as can be seen by the potential semantic difference between *zebra-dog* 'a dog with black stripes' and *dog-zebra* 'a zebra with the appearance of a dog'.

We should note here that the endocentric/exocentric distinction and the argumental/non-argumental distinction are orthogonal; argumental compounds can be endocentric or exocentric, as can non-argumental compounds. It is also worth pointing out that the dividing line between argumental and non-argumental compounds is not always crystal clear as deverbal nouns and adjectives can serve as the second element in non-argumental as well as in argumental compounds. We will return to this subject in Section 20.4.

20.2 ARGUMENTAL COMPOUNDS

We will first discuss argumental compounds whose head is argument-taking and deverbal (Section 20.2.1), then turn to argumental verbal compounds (Section 20.2.2), and to those with relational nouns and non-deverbal adjectives as heads (Section 20.2.3) and then treat argumental compounds whose non-head is argument-taking (Section 20.2.4). In Section 20.2.5 we will briefly discuss the extent to which we find exocentric examples among argumental compounds in English.

20.2.1 Argumental compounds with deverbal heads

This group of compounds comprises those with a deverbal element derived by suffixation with, for example, *-er, -ation, -ment, -ure, -al, -ing, -ent, -ive*, or a past participle form (henceforth AFFIXAL ARGUMENTAL COMPOUNDS), and those in which there is a noun formed from a verb via conversion. The semantics of argumental compounds with deverbal heads, otherwise known as SYNTHETIC, VERBAL, or DEVERBAL COMPOUNDS, has been well-explored in the literature on English word-formation, both descriptively (Jespersen 1942; Marchand 1969; Adams 2001; Bauer and Huddleston 2002) and theoretically (Lees 1960; Levi 1978; Roeper and Siegel 1978; Selkirk 1982; Lieber 1983, 1992, 2004; Roeper 1988; Ryder 1994, among many others). Nevertheless, we find that scrutiny of the corpus data adds depth and nuance to our understanding of compound use and interpretation in contemporary English.

Most commonly discussed in the literature on affixal argumental compounds are compounds whose second elements are nominalizations in *-er* (*truckdriver*), *-ation* (*air circulation*), and *-ing* (*ball-playing*), but such compounds can in fact occur with any deverbal nominalization as head; we find compounds with *-ment* nouns (*cost containment*), *-al* nouns (*garbage disposal*), *-ure* nouns (*base closure*), and *-ee* nouns (*city employee*). Also possible, although somewhat harder to find, are cases in which the second element is a deverbal adjective, as we find in compounds like *AIDS preventive* or *drug dependent*. The interpretation of the first element of such compounds to a large extent depends on the argument structure of the base of the second element, as well as on the semantic profile of the nominalizing or adjectivalizing affix (see Chapters 10, 11, 12, 14). Nevertheless there is a surprising range of interpretation available depending on context.

The syntactic terminology ('subject, object, prepositional object') we are employing to refer to the different arguments may appear somewhat problematic, as it invites invoking sentential paraphrases for the compounds in question. The methodological or theoretical status of such paraphrases is, however, unclear, and there are certainly additional complexities involved in the mapping of semantic argument structure onto phrasal syntactic representations. These complexities are outside the scope of our treatment since we are dealing with compounds and do not claim that there is any direct relationship between a given compound and a putatively corresponding sentence. For example, *heart* in *heart attack* can be conceived as an object argument of *attack* in spite of the fact that one might not be able to find an acceptable or convincing sentential paraphrase ('something attacks the heart').

As we saw in Chapter 11, the affix *-er* most frequently forms agent/instrument nouns. When *-er* derivatives with this interpretation constitute the second element of an argumental compound, the first element of the compound is typically object or prepositional object referencing, depending on the diathesis of the base verb.

(1)   a.   *object referencing*: air heater, alcohol abuser, antelope hunter, asphalt spreader

      b.   *prepositional object referencing*: adoption worker, asthma sufferer, army deserter, apartment dweller

So with a verb like *heat*, which can take a subject and object, *air* as the first element of the compound *air heater* receives the object interpretation. With a verb like *suffer* that takes a subject and a prepositional object (someone suffers from something), the *-er* form is agentive and the first element of the compound is interpreted as the prepositional object.

The affix *-ee* typically forms patient nouns, as we saw in Chapter 11, and when used as the second element of the compound, the first element is frequently subject referencing, as the examples in (2a) illustrate. But with *-ee* forms that are more agentive in flavour, like the *-er* forms discussed immediately above, the first element of the compound can receive an object or prepositional object interpretation, as the examples in (2b, c) show.

(2)   a. *subject referencing:* Bush appointee, Delta acquiree, army detainee, Ford nominee

b. *object referencing:* conference attendee

c. *prepositional object referencing:* army retiree, catalogue devotee, band escapee

So a *Bush appointee* is someone who Bush has appointed (subject referencing), a *conference attendee* someone who attends a conference (object referencing), and an *army retiree* someone who retires from the army (prepositional object referencing).

With nominalizing affixes like *-ing*, *-ation*, *-ment*, *-al*, and *-ure* we find argumental compounds where the interpretation of the first compound element expresses one of the arguments of the second (deverbal) element. As with the readings exhibited by nominalizations themselves (see Chapter 10), the readings exhibited by compounds of which they form the second element are highly context-dependent. We illustrate this with compounds whose second elements are nominalizations in *-ation*, *-al*, or *-ing*, but comparable examples can be found for items formed with the other nominalizing and adjectivalizing affixes as well (data from COCA).

(3)   a. *subject referencing:* army investigation, party nomination, airline hiring, administration refusal

New York Times 1996: An **army investigation** later found that most of the Israelis killed were hit by gunfire directed at the armored convoys on their way to and from the tomb.

New York Times 2006: And it was unclear how much political support Mr. McGreevey had among Democrats: even before Mr. Cipel first threatened to sue, Mr. McGreevey's spotty performance and the lingering scandals around his associates had led some party leaders to lobby for Mr. Corzine to get the **party nomination** for governor next year.

Atlanta Journal Constitution 2003: Then terrorism and a recession all but halted major **airline hiring** and put thousands of pilots on furlough.

PBS Newshour 1991: Mr. Veliotes, isn't that one of the other arguments that is behind **administration refusal** to get involved, that success by either the Kurds or the Shiites would mean either an administration by one of them or the dismemberment of Iraq?

b. *object referencing*: abuse investigation, candidate nomination, baby swapping, anger arousal

Atlanta Journal Constitution 2001: After a four-month impasse over an **abuse investigation** at the northwest Atlanta church, state child welfare officials say they're tired of such intransigence.

Arab Studies Quarterly 2006: "Electoral law" stands for the family of rules governing the process of elections from the calling of the election, through the stages of **candidate nomination**, party campaigning and voting, right up to the stage of counting votes and determining the actual election result.

Dateline NBC 2003: The tests are supposed to help circumvent kidnappings and **baby swapping**, but the private investigator says there are ways to get around DNA tests.

Journal of Social Psychology 1997: When experiencing **anger arousal**, isolated people without a support system may suppress their anger simply because no one is present to receive their cathartic expressions.

c. *prepositional object referencing*: Emmy nomination, aid application, activity participation, abortion ruling, ash disposal

Parenting 2007: Mel Brooks copped an **Emmy nomination** for his meaty, bleaty performance in the title segment.

USA Today 2007: Your tax return is not required with an **aid application**, but you do have to provide income and other numbers from your return.

Health & Social Work 2006: Research participants reported their sociodemographic information, physical health status, vision status, subjective experience of agerelated vision loss, functional ability, social support from family and friends, **activity participation**, rehabilitation service use, and coping strategies.

PBS Newshour 1992: The Supreme Court ended its term today with its long-awaited **abortion ruling**.

Boston College Environmental Law Affairs Review 1993: Public opposition usually involves the following: concern with health and environmental risks from air emissions and **ash disposal**; ...

As the examples in (3) illustrate, the interpretation of compounds whose second elements are nominalizations in *-ation*, *-al*, or *-ing* can vary widely. For example, for an *-ation* noun formed on a transitive verb like *investigate* either subject or object may be referenced in the first element of a compound. For a ditransitive verb like *nominate*, it is apparently possible for any of the three arguments—subject (*party nomination*), object (*candidate nomination*), or prepositional object (*Emmy nomination*)—to be referenced by the first element of the compound. This is an important point to note, as there have been claims in the theoretical literature that the subject interpretation is not permitted (see Selkirk 1982: 34; Adams 2001: 78–9, for example). We find to the contrary that the subject interpretation is often available, and indeed occurs with some frequency in journalistic writing. This said, however, we should acknowledge that forms in which the first element is interpreted as object or prepositional object are clearly more frequent in the corpora than forms in which the first element receives a subject interpretation. We note as well that the first element of an affixal compound need not bear an argumental relationship to the second element, a point that we will return to in Section 20.4.

Affixal argumental compounds in which the second element is a past participle are also frequent. The first element may be interpreted as a subject or prepositional object of the second, but cannot receive an object interpretation.

(4)   a. *subject referencing*: teacher written, sun baked

> *Journal of Instructional Psychology 2004*: **Teacher written** tests can be quite valid in testing which cover what was taught.

> *Saturday Evening Post 2001*: their verdure now beautifully shaded the quaint, narrow lanes, and transformed into cool wooded roads what once had been only barren **sun baked** wastes.

   b. *prepositional object referencing*: achievement related, arsenic exposed

> *Journal of Sports Behavior 1994*: Subsequent research investigated causal attributions predominantly within **achievement related** contexts

> *Journal of Environmental Health 2008*: Results We found nine relevant studies within three general domains: 1) four studies begin with **arsenic exposed** populations and seek excess childhood cancer,

As with other argumental compounds, the first element can also be interpreted as something other than an argument, a point to which we will return in Section 20.4.

Let us now turn to non-affixal deverbal compounds, that is to those where the argument-taking head is a noun that can be analysed as being derived from a verb by conversion (e.g. *government claim*). As with the affixal argumental compounds we discussed above, with non-affixal argumental compounds a wide range of interpretations may be found, interpretations again being highly dependent on context.

We give examples of compounds with subject, object, and prepositional object orientation in (5). The examples in (5) and (6) are taken from Lieber (2010: 129–30), which is itself a compilation of examples from Jespersen (1942), Marchand (1969), Bauer and Huddleston (2002), Jackendoff (2009), Plag *et al.* (2008), Bauer and Renouf (2001), the Morbocomp corpus (http://morbocomp.sslmit.unibo.it), and Lieber's own collection from American newspapers. Given the coding available in corpora like COCA and the BNC, it is unfortunately not possible to amass examples of these compounds systematically, as it is with items containing overt affixes.

(5)   a. *subject referencing*: bee sting, bellyache, brain bleed, bus stop, cloud burst, daybreak, dog attack, dogfight, earthquake, eyewink, flea bite, foot step, footfall, frostbite,

government claim, government collapse, ground-swell, headache, heartbeat, heartbreak, heartburn, land slide, moonrise, mouse squeak, nightfall, nosebleed, plane crash, rainfall, sunburn, sunrise, sunset, sunshine, thunderclap, troop advance, waterfall

b. *object referencing*: age limit, air traffic control, ball kick, birth control, blood test, bloodshed, bodyguard, car park, clambake, cost control, court reform, dress design, energy audit, fare increase, fee hike, funding increase, gun control, haircut, handshake, heart attack, manslaughter, rate hike, robot repair, spending cut, sun worship, tax hike, wind break

c. *prepositional object referencing*: baby care, linguistics lecture, peace talks, tax vote

Lieber (2010) claims that it is far easier to find the subject interpretation among non-affixal argumental compounds than it is with affixal argumental compounds. We tested this claim with two different data sets. The first set is 324 argumental compounds taken from CELEX as used in Plag *et al.* (2007). These compounds are largely taken from dictionaries. The second data set consists of the 641 argumental compounds found in the Boston University Radio Speech Corpus as used in Plag *et al.* (2008) and Kunter (2011). The most striking finding is that, with -*er* compounds, subject interpretations are completely absent from either data set (376 -*er* compounds all together). Subject interpretations are, however, not infrequently found with all other types of compounds, with varying proportions across subtypes and data sets. For example, among non-affixal argumental compounds we find 43 per cent subject interpretations in the CELEX data and 14 per cent in the Boston corpus data. Among compounds ending in -*ation* or -*ing* there are 30 per cent and 20 per cent, respectively, with a subject interpretation in the Boston corpus (CELEX has too few of these types of compound to allow for any meaningful quantitative analysis). In sum, the quantitative analysis has shown that subject interpretations can and do arise with all morphological categories whose semantics allows for such interpretations.

It should be noted that for many argumental compounds non-argumental interpretations are also readily available. For example, *government claim* could in principle also refer to a claim sent to the government (non-argumental interpretation) instead of to a claim made by the government (subject argument interpretation). Any of the forms cited in (5) could thus also be cited as an example of non-argumental readings. We cite them as argumental because the argumental interpretation is at least available.

20.2.2 Argumental verbal compounds

We have seen in the previous chapter that in many cases we can analyse verbal compounds as back-formations from compounds whose second elements are either deverbal nouns in -*er* or -*ing*, or participles in -*ed*. In such cases the first element in the verbal compound is interpreted in whatever way the first element would be in the corresponding deverbal compound. So if *to birdwatch* is a back-formation from *birdwatcher* or *birdwatching*, the element *bird* receives the same object interpretation in all cases. If *carbon-date* is a back-formation from *carbon dating*, then the carbon receives the same interpretation in both cases. That is, the verbal compounds can be classed as argumental or non-argumental, just as their sources can. Further, to the extent that we allow for the direct coining of verbs where there does not seem to be an obvious pre-existing *-ing* or *-er* form (for example, *blind bake, sugarcoat, blow-dry*) we can still classify the resulting compounds as argumental or non-argumental on the basis of the relationship displayed between the verbal second element and the first element.

One interesting point might be noted, however. Whereas we have seen that the first elements in typical argumental compounds can express either subject, object, or prepositional object interpretations, we seem not to find subject interpretations in verbal back-formations. That is, although we have found that compounds like *administration refusal* or *army investigation* in which the first element is interpreted as subject do exist, to our knowledge we do not find back-formations like *to administration refuse* or *to army investigate*. It is unclear whether this state of affairs is simply the consequence of the low proportion of subject interpretations among affixal argumental compounds, or whether we are dealing with a true fact that needs explanation.

20.2.3 Argumental compounds with relational nouns and argument-taking adjectives as heads

There is yet another class of argumental compounds that is rarely discussed in the literature but deserves mentioning here. Apart from verbs, there are also nouns and adjectives that can take arguments. Such nouns are also known under the label 'relational' (as against 'sortal' nouns). According to Löbner (1985: 292), sortal nouns classify objects while relational nouns describe objects in their relation to other objects. Examples of relational nouns are *birth, bride, distance, head, status, surface, victim*. Similarly, adjectives can take arguments as exemplified by *free, prone*, or *proud*. Such argument-taking nouns or adjectives freely occur as heads in argumental compounds. Consider, for example, the adjectival compounds *fat-free, freckle-free, toll-free, divorce-prone, drug-prone, storm-prone, America-proud, fraternity-proud, neighborhood-proud*. Analogous formations with relational nouns as heads are *child birth, company birth, galaxy birth, club member, university member, village member, glacier surface, moon surface, pond surface, cancer victim, crime victim, fire victim*.

20.2.4 Non-head is argument-taking

In the preceding sections we dealt with argumental compounds where the first element—the non-head—functions as an argument to the second element—the head. There is also, however, a type of non-affixal argumental compound in which it is the second element that functions as an argument to the first element. As we do not find compound-internal inflection in English, it is usually not possible to determine the categorial status of the first element in this type of non-affixal argumental compounds. In most cases we have first elements that could be analysed equally well as verbs or as (relational) nouns derived from those verbs. In a few cases, we do find first elements for which a nominal conversion form is unattested in the relevant sense (e.g. *go* in *go cart*), but in most cases either analysis seems consistent with the data. We will therefore refrain here from deciding on this matter. What argument is expressed in the compound again depends on context and on the verbal diathesis of the first element. We did not find any prepositional verbs that participate in this type of formation.

(6)   a.   *subject referencing*: attack dog, blowtorch, call bird, clamp screw, cover letter, cry baby, drag man, driftwood, finish coat, flashlight, go cart, jump jet, punch press, rattlesnake, rip saw, screech owl, scrub woman, slide rule, spark plug, stop watch, tow truck, tugboat, watch dog

   b.   *object referencing*: bore hole, call girl, draw string, drawbridge, dropcloth, jump rope (NAmE), kick ball, kickstand, mincemeat, punch card, push boat, push cart, rip cord, row boat, show bread, showplace, skim milk, throw stick, tow net

Note that compounds of this type are easily interpreted as non-argumental, especially when the head is a sortal noun, and as such all the usual interpetations of NN compounds become available. For example, a rattlesnake may be so called because it rattles (subject-referencing argument interpretation), or because it has a rattle (non-argumental interpretation). The same problem holds for some compounds with a base ending in the suffix *-ing* (e.g. *manufacturing plant, ramming device, heating system*, all from the Boston University Radio Speech Corpus).

None of these interpretations is necessarily 'correct', and any of these could also be cited as an example of non-argumental. We put them here because the argumental interpretation is at least available, while for root compounds that have sortal nouns as both heads and non-heads an argumental interpretation is not available. See Section 20.3.1 for a discussion of verb–noun non-argumental compounds.

20.2.5 Exocentric examples

English has only a small cohort of argumental compounds that are exocentric, apparently all of them of the non-affixal variety. Among these are examples like *pickpocket, cutpurse, scarecrow, tattletale, killjoy, scofflaw, know-nothing, turncoat, spoilsport, breakwater, rotgut, turnkey* (with the now archaic meaning of 'jailer'), *shearwater, stopgap*. The majority of them denote types of people, animal, or object. According to Marchand (1969: 380–1), which contains the most exhaustive listing of such compounds in the literature, these were formed on a pattern of French agentive and instrumental compounds that remains productive today in many of the Romance languages. Although Marchand (1969: 382) claims that this pattern 'has proved exceedingly productive in English', this is certainly not true in the contemporary language. It seems doubtful that any new examples are being coined, and indeed, many of the examples that Marchand cites have become archaic or obsolete.

20.3 NON-ARGUMENTAL COMPOUNDS

Non-argumental compounds are those in which neither element of the compound denotes an argument of the other. Among the non-argumental compounds we can make a basic division between ATTRIBUTIVE and COORDINATIVE compounds. The former are compounds in which the relationship between the first and second elements is one of loose modification; this applies both to endocentric attributives, in which the second element is clearly the head and the compound as a whole is a hyponym of the second element, and to exocentrics which may be syntactically headed by their second element, but which are not hyponyms of those elements. In coordinative compounds a more equal relationship between first and second elements obtains, such that one could argue that this type of compound has more than one semantic head (e.g. Haspelmath 2002: 89) or has no semantic head (e.g. Booij 2007: 80). We will examine attributive compounds in Section 20.3.1 and coordinative compounds in Section 20.3.2.

20.3.1 Attributive compounds

20.3.1.1 *Endocentrics*

Quite a few theorists have attempted to catalogue a finite set of relationships that can be expressed in attributive compounds: see Lees (1960), Hatcher (1960), Marchand (1969), Brekle (1970), Levi (1978), Ryder (1994), Jackendoff (2009) for just some of the attempts since the mid-twentieth century. As is widely acknowledged, however, nearly any conceivable relationship can obtain between the first and second elements of attributive compounds. The relationships between the elements are fluid and frequently determined by context, except in compounds that have lexicalized meanings (see for example Downing 1977). Consequently, the fit between any given compound and any gloss from a fixed list is, in context, likely to be approximate; indeed, the same compound in the same context can frequently be read in different ways, so that *police dog* could be interpreted as a dog used by the police or a dog working for the police or a dog trained for police work.

   That said, we should acknowledge that the nature of the compounded elements and especially of the second element does have some effect in circumscribing the range of meanings conceivable for any given attributive compound. If the second element is a relational noun, for example, a body part noun like *leg* or *arm*, or a kinship noun like *mommy* or *father*, the first element of the compound is likely to express the expected argumental relationship 'leg of X', 'mommy of Y' as we see in compounds like *table leg* or *rabbit mommy*, and in the vast majority of other compounds with *leg* or *mommy* that can be found in COCA. But it does not have to express this relationship, as the following *leg* compounds and their meanings in context from COCA illustrate.

(7) aluminum leg   'made of aluminum'
     back leg   'located at the back'
     bench leg   'human leg that is located on bench'
     bow leg   'shaped like bow'
     cigarette leg   'shaped like cigarette'
     fishnet leg   'covered in fishnet'
     polio leg   'affected by polio'
     summer leg   'cosmetically suitable for summer'
     support leg   'intended for support'

Similarly, if the second element is an adjective like *crazy* or *friendly* that can express a relationship ('X is crazy about Y', 'X is friendly to Y'), the first element is likely to express the expected relation, as we find in *trout-crazy* or *beginner-friendly*, although others are conceivable (for instance, compounds like *angry-crazy* or *goofy-crazy* that can be found in COCA).

The less relational the second element, the wider the range of meanings conceivable between the first and second elements of the compound. For example, with a sortal count noun like *bed* in its central meaning as a piece of furniture in which one sleeps, we find the following relationships exhibited by compounds attested in COCA. Alternative paraphrases are of course possible and nothing hinges on any particular paraphrase.

(8) adult bed   'for an adult'
     air bed   'filled with air'
     alcove bed   'located in alcove'
     army bed   'used by the army'
     bamboo bed   'made of bamboo'
     birth bed   'place where birth takes place'
     bunk bed   'with bunks'
     custom bed   'custom made'
     day bed   'for use during the day'
     designer bed   'made by a designer'
     dream bed   'that you dream about'

emergency bed	'for use in an emergency'
fairy-tale bed	'like something in a fairy-tale'
foldout bed	'that folds out'
heirloom bed	'that is an heirloom'
marshmallow bed	'that is soft like a marshmallow'
observation bed	'where one undergoes observation'
sex bed	'in which one has sex'
Shaker bed	'from a Shaker design, in the Shaker style'
sofa bed	'that is also a sofa'
tanning bed	'designed to allow the tanning of skin'
travel bed	'intended to be used while traveling'

It seems safe to say that given an appropriate context just about any relationship is conceivable. However, some relationships between the first and second elements are more predictable or pragmatically more likely (see Štekauer 2005). In particular, it has been shown in psycholinguistic experiments that new compounds tend to be interpreted with the same meaning relationship as other compounds with the same head or non-head (Gagné and Shoben 1997 and Gagné 2001, see also Chapter 23).

Basically the same general principles of interpretation apply to endocentric adjective–noun compounds. Thus we find very straightforward cases of adjectival modification, as in *sweetcorn*, which is a sweet-flavoured kind of corn, or *brownstone*, which denotes a darkbrown sandstone. But other adjective–noun compounds show that less straightforward relationships are also readily available, as in *silly-season*, which is the name of a period of a time when newspapers publish articles on trivial, silly matters due to the scarcity of real news.

A special case of adjective–noun compounds are those in which the adjective is relational in nature, as in *medical school, social worker, solar system*. Here the head of the compound is semantically associated with the base noun of the adjectival modifier, and many readings become available in principle. The correct interpretation requires world knowledge, which again stresses the similarity of adjective–noun compounds and noun–noun compounds.

A final group of non-argumental nominal compounds are those that can be analysed as having a verb in the first position. As already discussed in Section 20.2.4 above the categorial status of the first element as either verb or noun is often impossible to decide, but at least in some cases the pertinent noun is unattested in the relevant sense (e.g. *surf* in *surf lesson, board* in *board pass*), which rules out a consistent treatment of this pattern as noun–noun. The pattern is illustrated in (9), with data from Dollinger (2008) and from COCA (not all of these are usual in all varieties of English).

(9) call card, carry bag, disappear act, dive suit, drain board, draw power, dress gown, drill platform, drill rig, drink box, dump truck, finish line, frypan, patch kit, sail boat, ship town, surf lesson, swim meet, wait time

The interpretation of these compounds works along the same lines as that of other nominal non-argumental compounds. Any type of semantic relationship seems possible, based on the meaning of the constituents and pragmatic considerations. A very common interpretation is instrumental, with the head denoting an entity with which the action denoted by the verb is performed (e.g. *carry bag, dive suit, drill rig*), but many other types of interpretation can be found. A disappear act is an act in which someone or something disappears, a finish line is a line where something finishes, and so on. Note that non-argumental compounds with a verbal non-head may sometimes have rival forms with a verb ending in *-ing* as non-head (e.g. *dressing gown, drilling platform*, see Chapter 19). The latter type of compound behaves generally like other noun–noun compounds, as illustrated in (8) above (cf. *tanning bed*), and appears from examples in the BNC to give rise preferentially to a purpose meaning.

With compounds consisting of two verbs, we can get an interpretation in which the first verb denotes the manner in which the second verb is performed. So to *blow-dry* is to dry by blowing, and to *trickle-irrigate* is to irrigate by trickling. Also in this category we might put *dive-bomb, freeze-dry, skim-read*, and *slam-dunk*. As we saw in Chapter 13, we also find verbal compounds in English that are created by conversion of nominal compounds, for example, *blacklist, break dance, carbon-copy, cold shoulder, end-run, lipstick, litmus-test, machine-gun, pitchfork*. If we analyse these as typical cases of noun to verb conversion, we would expect them to display the same wide range of interpretations we find with noun to verb conversion with non-compound nouns (see Chapter 13). This is indeed what we find: so *blacklist* is locative ('to put on a blacklist'), *carbon-copy* is resultative ('to make a carbon copy'), *break dance* or *end-run* performative ('to do a breakdance or endrun'), *lipstick* ornative ('to put lipstick on'), *machine gun* or *pitchfork* instrumental ('to use a machine gun or pitchfork'), and so on.

Let us turn to attributive compounds whose second element is adjectival. When the second element of the compound is a qualitative adjective the relationship between the first and second elements is frequently one of similitude (for example, *butter yellow, blizzard cold*), but it need not be. We find other relationships expressed as well: 'compared to' (*ankle high*), 'composed of' (*cadmium yellow*), 'in relation to' (*color blind*). It appears that the relationship between first and second elements is no more fixed in adjectival compounds than in nominal ones.

It is of course possible in English to find compounds composed of more than two elements, and in such the opportunity arises for multiple interpretations. The semantic interpretation of multi-element compounds depends on the bracketing of the elements. In a compound like *toy poodle groomer manual*, at least four interpretations are possible, corresponding to four different syntactic bracketings.

(10)   a. 'a manual for groomers of toy poodles'
         [[[toy poodle] groomer] manual]

   b. 'a groomer manual for toy poodles'
      [[toy poodle][groomer manual]]

   c. 'a poodle groomer manual that is a toy'
      [toy [[poodle groomer] manual]]

   d. 'a manual for toy groomers of poodles'
      [[toy [poodle groomer]] manual]

Granted that some interpretations are more plausible pragmatically than others, none of these can be ruled out a priori.

20.3.1.2 *Exocentrics*

Exocentric attributives are highly productive in English. The bahuvrihi or 'possessive' type are all metonymic or metaphorical in nature. Typical of such compounds are the examples in (11) with the second element *head*, the majority of them taken from COCA.

(11)   a. *stupid, annoying, or malevolent people*: air head, bastard head, blockhead, bone head, bubble head, dick head, egg head, fuck head, hot head, knuckle head, meat head, penis head, pin head, poop head, shit head

   b. *people addicted to various substances*: acid head, crack head, dope head, hash head, helium head, java head, pot head, smack head

   c. *people with obsessive interest in something*: football head, baseball head, cheesehead, gear head, granola head, muscle head, petrol head (*BrE*), radio head

   d. *offensive terms for minorities*: handkerchief head, towel head

   e. *animal or plant name*: steel head (trout), fiddle head (fern), butter head (lettuce)

   f. *inanimate object*: bobble head (figurine)

   g. *miscellaneous others*: redhead, bedhead, blackhead

So, a *meat head* is someone 'having a head like meat', a *gear head* someone 'whose head is full of gear' (that is, in colloquial NAmE, someone with obsessive interest in equipment or gear connected with a particular sport or hobby), a *fiddle head* a kind of fern whose emerging shoot looks like the top of a fiddle, and so on. The main difference between these and the endocentric attributive compounds is simply that the characterization of their referents is figurative, often being metaphorical or metonymic. Thus, an analysis is possible that treats them as regular endocentric compounds with a metonymic or metaphorical reading of the head noun. Many compounds are not to be taken literally, and appear to fit the definition of an exocentric as a result: *elbow grease, mind fuck, rug rat.*

A different kind of exocentricity can be found in cases of ellipsis. There are, for example, binary compounds that have originated through ellipsis of a final third base, as in *roll-neck* for *roll-neck sweater/shirt/jersey/pullover,* as shown in (12), from the BNC.

(12)   *CDX W_biography 1991*: I knew she didn't like my **roll-neck pullover**.

  BMW W_fict_prose 1991: she recognised the slight figure in black **roll-neck sweater** and skin tight pants.

  AMU W_fict_prose 1992: spare combat jacket and two pairs of jungle trousers; for night work, black cotton **roll-neck**, black tracksuit bottoms and black cotton gloves; slacks and a light jumper for Mariana.

  BMW W_fict_prose 1991: Never a big man, overnight his frame seemed to have become almost frail and the sinews in his neck were raised and stringy above the cotton **roll-neck**.

Other examples are *hardtop* (a car), *house-warming* (a party), *turtleneck* (a garment, NAmE), or *underground* (a railway). It seems that this kind of exocentricity is a special case of a much wider pattern of metonymy that affects both complex and simplex lexical items. Many two-member compounds also lose their final element and thus become metonymic expressions, as in *business* for *business class, chair* for *chairperson, Northwestern* for *Northwestern University, the Tate* for *the Tate Gallery, Tasman* for *Tasman Sea, vacuum* for *vacuum cleaner.* The semantic consequences of these kinds of ellipsis in compounds seem no different than the metonymy that arises from syntactic ellipsis (as in *the House* for *the House of Representatives*) or even without ellipsis, as in *Washington* for the government residing in Washington.

20.3.2 Coordinative compounds

Coordinative compounds are ones in which the relationship between the first and second elements is not one of hyponymy but rather one in which the two elements bear equal semantic weight. As with the other major categories of compounds coordinative compounds may be either endocentric or exocentric. As Bauer (2008) argues, within each of these sub-classes a number of different equative relationships can obtain. Coordinative compounds can be appositional, additive, or compromise, and we will discuss each type in turn. Examples in this section are taken from Olsen (2001) and Bauer (2008), and from the internet.

APPOSITIONAL compounds, as given in (13), are compounds which refer to a single individual or object that represents the intersection of two sets: a *singer-songwriter* is a person who is both a singer and a songwriter, a *scholar-athlete* someone who is at the same time a scholar and an athlete. Appositional compounds are not limited to two nouns, as compounds like *actor-producer-director* are entirely conceivable.

(13)   singer-songwriter, scholar-athlete, advertiser publisher, tent-office, comedy-drama, nerd-genius

The second type of coordinative compound that is highly productive in contemporary English is what we might call ADDITIVE, again following Bauer (2008). Among these are many that consist of proper nouns, including coordinated place and company names.

(14)   Austro-Hungary, Alsace-Lorraine, Hewlett-Packard

Such names denote a merger of territory or business, and to them we might add the hyphenated surnames, as for example, the name *Koslosky-Pappafilovich* that the couple might adopt when Ms Koslosky marries Mr Pappafilovich. Additive compounds of this sort are of course not limited to two proper nouns. Especially with company names we find coordinations of more than two names, as for example in the corporate name *AOL Time Warner*.

Additive compounds are also possible with common nouns or adjectives, although our impression is that such compounds are less frequent in English than appositional compounds or additive compounds formed on the basis of proper nouns.

(15)   angry-crazy, cough-laugh, deaf-mute, historical-philosophical, goofy-crazy, murder-suicide

The distinction between these and the appositional compounds is delicate, and sometimes not entirely clear. Our instinct is that in the additive type we have two events, objects, or qualities bundled or conceptualized together whereas in the appositional type we are thinking of a single item with two distinct labels. So a *murder-suicide* is a murder closely followed by a suicide, a *cough-laugh* could probably be interpreted as a noise that muffles a laugh with a cough, *deaf-mute* a state of being both unable to hear and unable to speak.

To the extent that we find verbal compounds in the native speaker's mental lexicon, we can offer a semantic analysis. In the few cases where the compound verb is made up of two verbs (for example, *blow-dry*, *dive-bomb*, *shrink-wrap*), we find at least two sorts of interpretation, one of which is a coordinative interpretation in which two actions are performed simultaneously or sequentially (cf. *drink-drive*, *stir-fry*, *sleep-walk*), the other being resultative, as in *blow-dry*. The borderline between the two types is often unclear: is *freeze-dry* 'to dry by freezing' or 'simultaneously to freeze and to dry'? Pragmatically there is little difference, and both classifications are found (see Renner 2008; Bauer 2010b).

A final type of coordinative compound is what Bauer (2008) terms COMPROMISE coordinatives. These are the type represented by adjectival compounds like *blue-green*, and nominal compounds like *northeast*, which designate an intermediate property, for example, between blue and green or between north and east. This type of compound is limited pragmatically by the nature of objects, qualities, and events: there are ontological limits to what can be blended or seen as a compromise between two entities. But where pragmatic considerations allow, we do find such compounds formed rather productively, as might be evidenced by names for mixed breed (or 'designer') dogs such as *Afghan spaniel, Akita shepherd, Cocker pug*, and the like (although the vast majority of these seem to be blends, see Section 20.5.1 below).

There are also exocentric coordinative compounds, which denote a relationship between the elements. This can be seen most clearly in compounds like *Arab-Israeli (conflict)* where the compound as a whole does not denote a merger or aggregate of Arabs and Israelis, or some sort of mixture of the two, but rather a relationship between two separate entitities. Such compounds can consist of two adjectives, as with *Arab–Israeli (conflict)* or *Dutch–English (dictionary)*, or of two nouns (*father–daughter [dance]*, *Boston–Philadelphia [flight]*) or even two verbs (*pass–fail [test]*). In the latter cases the compounds are functionally as well as semantically exocentric: the majority of exocentric coordinative compounds, regardless of categorial composition, function as premodifiers of nouns.

The precise relationship expressed between the two compounded elements depends to some extent on the noun that they are predicated of. We might distinguish three types of relationship. In the CONJUNCTIVE type, the relationship between the first and second elements of the compounds is one of aggregation, for example, both father and daughter participate in a *father–daughter dance*; this type includes what Bauer (2008) calls 'co-participant' coordinative compounds. In the TRANSLATIVE type, the relationship between the first and second elements is one of 'between-ness': a *Boston–Philadelphia flight* is one between Boston and Philadelphia, a *mother–daughter conversation* is one between mother and daughter. The final type is one that we might call DISJUNCTIVE (this is one not mentioned by Bauer 2008) in which the relationship between the first and second elements of the compounds is one of mutual exclusivity; we have in mind here compounds like *pass–fail (test)* or *true–false (question)*.

(16) a. *conjunctive*: father–daughter (dance), brother–sister (duet), fall–winter (collection), Pitt–Aniston (wedding), love–hate (feelings)

  b. *translative*: Arab–Israeli (conflict), Dutch–English (dictionary), Boston–Philadelphia (flight), mind–brain (connection), mother–daughter (conversation), Utah–Arizona (border), subject–verb (agreement), hand–eye (coordination)

  c. *disjunctive*: pass–fail (test), true–false (question), push–pull (gizmo)

Above we said that the majority of exocentric coordinative compounds function as premodifiers, but not all do. Consider, for example, the compound *push–pull* as it is used in (17).

(17)   *People 2007*: What Wife gets right is the **push–pull** of marriage, the way the comfort of the familiar can butt up against the siren call of the new.

Here, the coordinative compound is both semantically and categorially exocentric, but does not function as a premodifier. It is reminiscent of the sort of dvandva compounds more frequently found in other languages (see for example, Wälchli 2005).

20.4 THE BORDER BETWEEN ARGUMENTAL AND NON-ARGUMENTAL COMPOUNDS

The classificatory schema that we have followed in the previous two sections covers the majority of compound types to be found in contemporary English. As with most classificatory systems, however, there are potential problems.

One problem may be the boundary between arguments and adjuncts. In our discussion we have treated compounds as argumental if the first element is interpreted as a core argument of the verb, that is, as subject, object, or prepositional object. In those cases where the first element would be considered an adjunct, we treat the compounds as non-argumental. We list some of those cases in (18). In all of these examples the first element receives an interpretation that would be expressed syntactically by an adjunct phrase rather than a core argument. Note that we intend the labels 'location', 'time' etc. to refer to possible but not necessary readings.

(18)   a. *location*: aerial observer, airport parking, alley fighter, backyard gardener, bakery worker, vine-ripened

   b. *time*: advance preparation, after-hours trading, afternoon trainer

   c. *status*: absentee landowner

   d. *concerned with*: account officer, AIDS meeting

   e. *purpose*: acne medication, asthma inhaler, backup singer

   f. *instrument*: air popper, arsenic poisoning, hand-washed

   g. *containing*: action thriller, adventure education

   h. *made of*: adobe construction, almond filling, bamboo steamer

   i. *caused by*: acid indigestion

   j. *comprised of*: activist organization

Just about any relationship between first and second elements is conceivable when the first element is not interpreted as a core argument, and the relationship is largely determined by context. Indeed, the range of interpretations available for such compounds is unlimited, just as we find with attributive non-argumental compounds. We take the position here that a compound should be considered argumental only if one element may be interpreted as a core argument of the other. Certain borderline cases may exist, but this is unavoidable in any classificatory system.

Another problem arises with compounds that have relational nouns as heads. Although we have used a seemingly clear definition of how argument-taking nouns, that is relational nouns, can be distinguished from non-argument-taking nouns, that is sortal nouns, we acknowledge the existence of cases where the boundary is not so clear.

20.5 THE SEMANTICS OF BLENDS AND NEOCLASSICAL COMPOUNDS

In Chapter 19 we treated the formal characteristics of blends and neoclassical compounds. Here, we look at their semantic characteristics, which are to a large extent similar to those of compounds, especially of non-argumental compounds. We begin with blends and proceed to neoclassical compounds, keeping in mind that the dividing line between the two types is sometimes not entirely clear.

20.5.1 The semantics of blends

The vast majority of blends in English display the semantics of non-argumental compounds, with both attributive and coordinative types amply attested. Attributives are illustrated in (19). All examples of blends in this section are taken from Wordspy (www.wordspy.com).

(19) *attributive blends*
agritourist	◆	(agriculture + tourist)
beersicle	◆	(beer + popsicle)
carbage	◆	(car + garbage)
daycation	◆	(day + vacation)
dormcest	◆	(dorm + incest)
foodoir	◆	(food + memoir)
menoporsche	◆	(menopause + Porsche)

In semantically attributive blends, as in attributive compounds, the blend as a whole is a hyponym of the second blended element, and the first element bears some contextually plausible relationship to the second. So a *beersicle* is a popsicle made of beer, *carbage* is garbage located in one's car, and a *daycation* is a one-day holiday.

For blends that have coordinative interpretations, we find both appositive and compromise types. Note that for some of these an endocentric reading is also possible.

(20)   a. *appositive coordinative blends*

    actorvist   •   (actor + activist)

    aireoke   •   (air guitar + karaoke)

    celesbian   •   (celebrity + lesbian)

    fictomercial   •   (fiction + commercial)

    b. *compromise coordinative blends*

    avoision   •   (avoidance + evasion)

    broccoflower   •   (broccoli + cauliflower)

    chofa   •   (chair + sofa)

    freshmore   •   (freshman + sophomore)

    puggle   •   (pug + beagle)

As with compounds of this sort, the appositives denote the intersection of two types of entity or action. So an *actorvist* is both an actor and an activist, and *aireoke* is the simultaneous action of playing air guitar and singing karaoke. The compromise coordinatives denote hybrid entities or concepts. A *chofa* is a piece of furniture somewhere between a chair and a sofa, a *puggle* a cross between a pug and a beagle. The creation of names for new mixed breed dogs through blending is in fact highly productive (see, for example, http://www.dogbreedinfo. com/hybriddogs.htm), but blending can also be found with other kinds of hybrids in the animal kingdom (e.g. *jagupard, liguar, tigon, zebrule, zorse*). There seems to exist also a convention to place the dam's name in final position in such blends (see, for example, the *Wikipedia* entries *Panthera hybrid* and *Zebra*). If people do this, or to the extent they do this, such formations may be considered no longer strictly coordinative.

Only rarely do we find argumental compounds among blends, although there does not seem to be any principled reason why this should be the case. In the Wordspy corpus, we find a few examples, among them the ones in (21).

(21)   *argumental blends*

    agrimation   •   (agriculture + automation)   'automation of agriculture'

    bitlegging   •   (bit + bootlegging)   'bootlegging of software'

    buttlegging   •   (butt + bootlegging)   'bootlegging of cigarettes'

    Coca Colonization   •   (Coca Cola + colonization)   'colonization by Coca Cola and similar companies'

    kidfluence   •   (kid + influence)   'influence by kids'

    spamdexing   •   (spam + indexing)   'indexing spam'

As these examples illustrate, argumental blends are frequently affixal (*agrimation, Coca Colonization, spamdexing*), and can be either object-referencing (*agrimation, bitlegging, buttlegging, spamdexing*) or subject-referencing (*Coca Colonization, kidfluence*).

There is a small residue of blends that is difficult to characterize. Some blends can be rather opaque, as we find with the blend *Boyzilian* (• boy + Brazilian), which is the name for a bikini-wax for men. A few blends seem to be examples of idiosyncratic word play as much as they are blends, for example *Internot* (• internet + not) which denotes a person who refuses to use the internet or *transwestite* (• west + transvestite), which denotes a person who likes to dress up as a cowboy. In such cases, some semantic element needs to be added to arrive at the appropriate interpretation, in other cases, the intended meaning is clear. Nevertheless, it seems safe to say that blends generally are interpreted in the same way that compounds are, though not necessarily in the same proportions.

20.5.2 The semantics of neoclassical compounds

The interpretation of neoclassical compounds raises special issues. For one thing, in the case of conventional compounds and the sorts of blends illustrated above, there is no particular question as to the semantic status of the individual elements that make up the complex word: they mean what they mean. For neoclassical combining forms, however, the question may always be raised to what extent the individual elements are meaningful to native speakers. Second, it is sometimes difficult to distinguish the elements that make up neoclassical compounds from derivational affixes. Finally, as neoclassical combining forms have no clear categorial status, they present problems for our classificatory scheme, at least for the distinction between argumental and non-argumental compounds. We will take up each of these issues in turn.

As to the first, we might say that the forms that make up neoclassical compounds are meaningful to at least some speakers of English. Indeed, some of them are quite common and probably known to most speakers of English. Many speakers of English know that *-osis* has something to do with disease or illness and *neuro-* to do with the nervous system or the brain, for example. Other combining forms constitute part of the learned vocabulary of the language and are often specific to particular scholarly disciplines. For those conversant in the relevant disciplines such elements have as much meaning as free forms. For example, while many English speakers know the meaning of the combining form *neuro-*, far fewer know that *sarco-* means 'flesh' or that *-odynia* means 'pain', but this is knowledge that we might expect from doctors or biologists.

Nevertheless, neoclassical combining forms do sometimes present special semantic challenges, as McCray *et al.* (1988: 166) note. They cite the example of the initial combining form *leuko-*, which literally means 'white', and occurs in such neoclassical compounds as *leukocyte*, *leukotomy*, and *leukopathy*. The issue here is that in each case what is modified by *leuko-* is left implicit: in *leukocyte*, *leuko-* implicitly modifies 'blood' (*leukocyte* = white [blood] + cell), in *leukotomy* it modifies part of the brain (*leukotomy* = white [part of brain] + cutting), and in *leukopathy*, it implicitly modifies skin pigmentation (*leukotomy* = white [skin pigmentation]

+ disease). What we have here appears to be a sort of semantic ellipsis that is not predictable. This kind of ellipsis can be found even with combining forms that are quite well-known, as with the compound *cardiophobia*, which, as McCray *et al.* point out, means not 'fear of hearts' but 'fear of heart disease'.

As for the dividing line between neoclassical combining forms and derivational affixes, it must be acknowledged that no firm distinction may be drawn. As Bauer (1998b) has pointed out, there is a cline from most semantically contentful to least semantically contentful bound morphemes (see also Prćić 2005, 2008; Amiot and Dal 2007). At the more contentful end we have what we would call neoclassical combining elements; these are the forms that are most like independent lexical morphemes in meaning, having what Bauer (1983: 215) refers to as 'a higher density of lexical information'. At the less contentful end we have what we would tend to call affixes. But there are many forms that fall somewhere between the two extremes.

Probably the thorniest issue for our purposes is whether it makes sense to fit neoclassical compounds into the classificatory system we have used here, given that neoclassical combining forms have no syntactic category and therefore cannot be said to have arguments (or to not have them) in the same way that free forms do. This is an open issue. If we argue purely on the basis of semantics, as opposed to categorial status, it is possible to classify neoclassical compounds according to the same schema we used for other compounds. But this analysis comes with some cost.

Neoclassical compounds are typically right-headed, as other compounds and blends are; that is, the compound as a whole is a hyponym of the second element. For the most part they are endocentric. So far, our comparison is unproblematic. If we wish to further classify neoclassical compounds, however, we must proceed strictly on the basis of 'translation'. This translation sometimes ends up with argument-taking deverbal nouns, as in (22a), and sometimes with sortal nouns, as in (22b).

(22)   a. gastrostomy   ◆ (gastro/stomach + stomy/opening)
           neurogenic   ◆ (neuro/brain + gen-ic/producing)
           neurology   ◆ (neuro/brain + ology/study of)
           bibliocide   ◆ (biblio/book + cide/killing)
           omnicide   ◆ (omni/all + cide/killing)

       b. gastrodynia   ◆ (gastro/stomach + dynia/pain)
           keratosis   ◆ (kerato/cornea + osis/disease)
           mycosis   ◆ (myco/fungus + osis/disease)

The compounds in (22a) might be considered argumental insofar as we consider the translation of their second elements to be verbal or deverbal in nature, and the first element seems to bear a relation like that of object to the second. So in *omnicide*, the second element translates as a deverbal noun 'killing', and the first element as the erstwhile object of the verb. The neoclassical compounds in (22b), on the other hand, have a relational noun as the second element and can thus also be classified as argumental. Still, as McCray *et al.* (1988) point out, with neoclassical compounds, as with other attributive compounds, it is frequently not predictable how the relationship between the first and second elements should be construed.

Following our classificatory schema, we find that some neoclassical compounds can have coordinative interpretations, as we find, for example, in a compound like *alveo-palatal*, which designates a point mid-way between the alveolar ridge and the palate, and therefore constitutes a COMPROMISE coordinative. Or we can have an ADDITIVE interpretation, as we find in the compound *laryngeotracheobronchitis*, cited by McCray *et al.* (1988: 167) as meaning 'an inflamation of the larynx, trachea, and bronchi'. Indeed, as McCray *et al.* point out, parts of neoclassical compounds can be coordinated in quite complicated ways. In *acrocephalosyndactyly*, *acrocephaly* 'high skull' is coordinated with *syndactyly* 'together (i.e. fused), digit' which denotes a condition characterized by both a high skull and fused digits, whereas in *myoendocarditis*, the elements *myo* and *endo* are coordinated with each other and modify *carditis*, so the whole denotes 'inflamation of the muscle and membrane of the heart'.

So far, we have looked at neoclassical compounds that are composed entirely of neoclassical combining forms, but of course, combining forms can be compounded with free morphemes, as we find in the examples in (23).

(23) a. gastropub   (gastro/stomach + pub)
          gastro-porn   (gastro/stomach + porn)
          neuro-chip   (neuro/brain + chip)
          neuro-jargon   (neuro/brain + jargon)
          assholiosis   (asshole + osis/disease)

      b. bitchicide   (bitch + cide/killing)
          roboticide   (robot + cide/killing)
          oceanaut   (ocean + naut/traveler)
          neuro-numbing   (neuro/brain + numbing)
          neuroadaptations   (neuro/brain + adaptations)

Semantically, these behave much the same as both pure neoclassical compounds and compounds composed entirely of free morphemes. They are largely right-headed and endocentric, and can be classified as argumental or non-argumental in the same way that we classified the purely neoclassical compounds above.

20.6 MISCELLANEOUS COMPOUNDS

There are a number of types of compound or compound-like phenomena that we have not yet discussed, either because they are of only marginal productivity, or because their status as compounds has been disputed. We take up those types here (see again Chapter 19 for discussion of their morphological status).

20.6.1 Phrasal compounds

Phrasal compounds are highly productive in contemporary English, as the examples in (24) from COCA suggest.

(24)   anybody-but-Bush syndrome
        black-hole-in-a-bag syndrome
        boy-on-a-bike syndrome
        breaking-out-in-song syndrome
        catch-as-catch-can syndrome
        dad-needs-a-sports-car syndrome
        failed-back-surgery syndrome
        fear-of-failure syndrome
        first-to-know syndrome
        get-rich-quick syndrome
        grass-is-greener syndrome
        guilt-gets-grants syndrome
        guitar-as-phallus syndrome
        holier-than-thou syndrome
        I'm-OK-you're-not syndrome
        it-wasn't-me syndrome
        look-at-me syndrome
        not-in-my-backyard syndrome
        out-of-the-nest syndrome
        sheriff-of-Nottingham syndrome
        staying-young syndrome
        too-much-of-a-good-thing syndrome
        tortoise-and-hare syndrome
        use-it-or-lose-it syndrome
        woman-behind-the-man syndrome

Although rarely, if ever, recorded in dictionaries (because their token-frequency is generally low), such compounds can be frequently found in informal writing, as in the following examples from a novel.

(25) He was the groundsman, handyman, **if-there's-any-sort-of-difficulty-ask-William-and-he'll-fix-it-for-you person** about the place. (*Meynell 1978*, p. 10)

We've got a **what-the-unions-will-allow-us-to-print press**. (p. 80)

The old **manage-somehow-on-a-shoestring days** were definitely gone (p. 125)

The examples in (24) and (25) illustrate two important semantic properties of phrasal compounds. First, the phrasal part of the compound is not in any way restricted to lexicalized, institutionalized, or idiomatic phrases (although such phrases are of course not ruled out), contrary to claims in the literature (see, for example, Bresnan and Mchombo 1995). Second, although in some examples, the phrasal element has a clear quotative flavour (*anybody-but-Bush syndrome, it wasn't me syndrome*), more often than not there is no real justification for calling this element quotative, as both Bresnan and Mchombo (1995) and Wiese (1996a) do.

The interpretation of phrasal compounds is in most cases that of endocentric attributive compounds. The initial phrasal element bears some plausible relationship to the second element, with the relationship often being obvious only in context.

(26) hour-by-hour gossip   (time)
      quick-to-spread gossip   (manner)
      below-the-stairs gossip   (location)
      hide-and-seek house   (function)
      stone-and-redwood home   (material)

In other words we expect to find the same range of interpretations in phrasal compounds that we find in non-phrasal endocentric attributive compounds.

Phrasal compounds with argumental interpretations are harder to find, but they do seem to exist. Consider the examples in (27), again from COCA.

(27) limits-and-consequences conversation
      burned-rope-and-sugar taste
      letters-to-the-editor writer

In the first example, we might say that the phrase *limits-and-consequences* bears the prepositional object relation to the deverbal noun *conversation*; similarly for the second example. The phrase in the third example seems clearly to be interpreted as object of the verb *write*.

We do not, however, seem to find phrasal compounds with a coordinative interpretation, but that should not be surprising. Coordinative compounds are characterized by the juxtaposition of the same kinds of formal entity, that is nouns, or verbs, or adjectives. For phrasal compounds this would mean that both compound constituents be phrases. However, as discussed in Chapter 19, phrases are generally ruled out in morphosyntactic head position.

20.6.2 Reduplicative compounds

Reduplicative compounds are frequently found in colloquial spoken English, and in more informal genres of writing, and only infrequently in formal writing. Examples like the following from COCA are typical.

(28) *Sports Illustrated 1992*: John then fires another of his surprise questions: "When was the last time you read a book?" She pauses in mid-grip to reply, "You mean a **book book**? Not having anything to do with sports? In college, I guess. That was three years ago."

Triquarterly 1990: "I have to go home," I said when she woke up. She thought I meant home to her house in the Canyon, and I had to say No, **home home**.

New England Review 2002: I asked her if she wanted to go have a drink afterwards and she said Drink! and I said it didn't have to be a **drink drink** (I swear people who overheard us sometimes must have thought we were retarded) and she said Sorry?

Lawrence Block 2000: "Mine is green." "**Green green**? Or more like an olive green?"

Tamara Leigh 2008: "Yes, hot!" The "ruched" young woman jabs the air again, looks around, and startles. "Er, not **hot hot**. Hot, as in under the collar. "Ticked off." // That's my cue to appear relieved that she didn't mean hot as in carnal, as she's obviously connected to this company – at least to the receptionist.

To the extent that we consider reduplicative compounds to be compounds, we must acknowledge that their semantic properties are a bit different than the compounds we have looked at thus far. They appear to be endocentric, with the compound as a whole being a hyponym of the head. However, as pointed out by Hohenhaus (2004) and Ghomeshi *et al.* (2004), for the most part, such compounds have a standard interpretation in that they serve to pick out or identify a prototypical exemplar of the second element of the compound. So a *book book* would be something with more pages than a pamphlet or a magazine, and probably with paper and hard or soft cover, as opposed to, say, an e-book. *Green green* would be a color like kelly green or apple green, as opposed to olive or chartreuse.

PART V
....

Interaction

....

CHAPTER 21

Combination of affixes

21.1 Prospectus

In this chapter we will discuss complex words that have more than one affix. This topic has been of considerable theoretical interest and there are different approaches that try to account for the existence or non-existence of given affix combinations. One of these approaches focuses on lexical strata, with the native versus non-native distinction at its centre. This distinction played a role in our treatments of various morphological categories throughout this volume and is investigated at a more general level and in considerable detail in Chapter 27. The present chapter is concerned with all issues of affix combinations beyond the native/non-native issue, focusing on derivational affixes, but also taking a look at inflectional suffixes.

In the next section we will look at combinations of suffixes and combinations of prefixes, the areas which research on affix combination has traditionally focused on. Section 21.3 will then be devoted to types of derivative that have received hardly any attention so far, those in which a prefix and a suffix are found in a single word. For the sake of simplicity, in Sections 21.2 and 21.3 we will restrict discussion to formations that feature only two affixes at a time. We will also take up the intersection of conversion with affixation (Section 21.4). Section 21.5 will deal with inflection, and Section 21.6 with affixation involving more than two affixes.

21.2 Suffix combinations and prefix combinations in derivation

2.1 Suffix combinations

With the rise of lexical phonology and morphology the question of affix combinations started receiving a lot of attention, see Chapter 27). Beginning with Fabb's (1988) influential paper, a number of publications (e.g. Plag 1996; Hay and Plag 2004) showed that the stratal approach is not well-suited to account for the empirically attested patterns of prefix combinations and suffix combinations. The rather comprehensive new investigation of the assumed stratal division in English morphology presented in Chapter 27 further supports this. Given the empirical and theoretical inadequacy of the stratal approach (see also Plag and Baayen 2009 for a summary), the intriguing question remains what is responsible for the occurrence or non-occurrence of a particular combination of affixes.

The most successful approach to this question is to predict combinations of prefixes and of suffixes on the basis of the selectional restrictions of the affixes (and bases) involved (e.g. Fabb 1988; Plag 1996, 1999, 2002; Hay and Plag 2004). These restrictions are structural in nature and may refer to various properties of the elements involved: phonological (segmental or prosodic), semantic, syntactic, or morphological. For example, the suffix *-ify* is restricted to bases ending in a stressed syllable, the suffix *-ess* is restricted to nominal bases that denote higher sentient beings, and the suffix *-ation* attaches productively only to the verbal suffixes *-ize*, *-ify*, and *-ate*. Apart from the morphological restrictions, selectional restrictions are not specifically geared towards other affixes but are general selectional preferences that can be conceptualized as being part of the lexical entry of the affixes in question. In the preceding chapters such preferences or restrictions have been described for each of the morphological processes under investigation.

Crucially and inevitably, such preferences have important repercussions for the combination of affixes, namely in those cases where the base is already affixed. To give a simple example, if a suffix attaches only to adjectives and nouns, all combinations of that suffix with bases that contain an outermost verbal suffix are ruled out. Or consider again the suffix *-ify*, which strongly tends to attach only to bases ending in a stressed syllable. This restriction has the consequence that *-ify* may not attach to very many already suffixed bases since English suffixes that create final syllables in their derivatives are mostly unstressed (e.g. *-able*, *-age*, *-al*, *-ant*, *-ary*, *-er*, *-ery*, *-ful*, *-ic*, *-ish*, *-ism*, *-ist*, *-ive*, *-less*, *-ly*, *-ness*, *-ous*, *-ure*, *-y*; these are suffixes which are neither consonantal nor auto-stressed). The selectional restrictions still allow a great number of combinations, long lists of which can be found in Chapter 27, or, for example, in the appendices of Plag and Baayen (2009, for suffixes), and Zirkel (2010, for prefixes).

On the basis of the affix-specific restrictions it becomes possible to predict possible and impossible combinations of affixes quite successfully. For example, Hay and Plag (2004) investigate 15 suffixes with 210 theoretically possible combinations (excluding combinations of two identical suffixes). Of these, only 36 (i.e. 17 per cent) are actually attested in their large database. It turns out that all attested combinations are also structurally possible, that is allowed by the selectional restrictions of the suffixes involved and the vast majority of unattested combinations are actually ruled out by the selectional restrictions. There are only six additional combinations that are structurally clearly possible but that are not attested in Hay and Plag's database. Apparently, their large database was not large enough, since attestations of all six expected but missing combinations can be found in COCA, on the internet, or in other linguistic works. Example (1) lists some of the pertinent forms.

(1)   a. *-ling-ly*

      USA Today 1993: Elegant women wearing evening gowns—a few in **darlingly** short chemises layered with fringe—lace shawls draped over their shoulders, jewels flashing, sat back in the velvet-covered easy chairs, sipping cocktails. (COCA)

   b. *-ling-dom*

      Anyways, screw this weak attempt at **weaklingdom**, and check out the real deal at www.theweaklings.com. (http://www.amazon.co.uk/review/R16DF1MLUJAH7W)

   c. *-ling-ish*

      Philip Leverington took this of the Lilac Muscovy ducklings at the weekend (yes, I know, there's nothing very **ducklingish** about them any more ....!) (http://www.facebook.com/pages/Gillamoorganics/146169232118586)

   d. *-ness-less* (from Plag and Baayen 2009: 115, who give more examples)

      Eight Deadly Sins Of Web 2.0 Start-Ups. [...] **Happinessless**: Your start-up has no future if you are not happy. (http://www.slideshare.net/imootee/eight-deadly-sins-of-web-20-startups/)

   e. *-ee-less*

      employeeless (not comparable) Having no employees. (http://en.wiktionary.org/wiki/employeeless)

   f. *-ee-ness*

      Theological Studies 2010: If the incarnation reveals that the Divine is not averse to the conditions of human existence (sickness, **refugeeness**, and impoverishment), it also sets a standard for the community that claims to be the concrete manifestation of the 'glory, grace and truth' of God in human history. (COCA)

Two important points emerge here. First, the suffix-particular restrictions that are needed independently to account for the behaviour of a suffix straightforwardly account also for the existing and the non-existing combinations of that suffix with suffixed bases, that is with other suffixes. Second, very large databases are needed to find certain affix combinations due to the fact that the co-occurrence of two affixes in one word is generally not particularly common. This has been noted before by Hay and Plag (2004), who calculate, for example, that the probability of finding a combination of *-ee* and *-hood* among any set of words (i.e. types), based on CELEX type frequencies, is 0.0000006.

Hay and Plag (2004) further observe that suffixes form a hierarchy, such that a suffix occurring inside another suffix cannot occur outside that suffix. Given a suffix sequence A–B and another B–C, we can expect to find A–C, but not C–A. We will see in Section 21.5 that this is overly simple for English, where there are some strings that operate against such presuppositions. Nevertheless, it is largely true, especially with two-suffix sequences: that is the presence of A–B and B–C largely excludes B–A or C–A. Crucially, the position of a given suffix in the hierarchy is largely determined by the separability of that suffix. What exactly does 'separability' refer to?

The underlying idea is that the morphological segmentability or separability of affixes is a gradient phenomenon. Some words are clearly composed of more than one morpheme (e.g. *clueless, concreteness, unhelpful, dethrone*), other words are clearly monomorphemic (e.g. *fish*), and there are words whose status as complex words may be not so clear (e.g. *analyze, business, interview, listless, perceive, rehearse*). In most current models of morphological processing, access to morphologically complex words in the mental lexicon works by direct access to the whole word representation ('whole word route') or by access to the segmented elements ('decomposed route'). The separability of an affix therefore depends on which route is more prominent for derivatives with this affix. This in turn depends on various properties, for example the frequency, phonotactics, and semantics of derivatives with the given affix (see, for example, Plag 2003: 175–8 for an introductory treatment).

From what we have said so far, interesting insights follow. The same suffix will be differently separable in different words depending on the respective properties of the words in question. For example, *discernment* is more decomposable than *government*. The derived word *government* is much more frequent than its base *govern*, which induces as a whole-word bias for *government*. This whole-word bias is reflected in the non-transparent phonology and semantics of *government*. The form is pronounced with either assimilation of base-final /n/ to the suffix-initial /m/, or even with the complete loss of the last syllable of the base, and semantically *government* does not show the expected event meaning 'action of governing', but the extended meaning 'people who govern'. In contrast, *discernment* is rather infrequent and much less frequent than its base *discern*, which leads to a strong bias towards decomposed processing for *discernment*.

The more low frequency forms we find with a given affix, the more separable that affix will appear. For example, *-ish* has many derivatives with low frequencies (such as *housewifish, out-of-the-way-ish*, or *soupish* whereas *-ic* has few low-frequency words but many derivatives with higher frequencies (e.g. *democratic, fantastic, terrific*) so that *-ish* tends to be more separable than *-ic*.

Now, returning to the problem of affix ordering, we can use this notion of separability to predict that more separable affixes will occur outside less separable affixes (cf. also Burzio 1994: 354). This is because an easily decomposable suffix inside a non-decomposable suffix would lead to difficulties in processing, whereas a less easily decomposable inside a more easily decomposable suffix is easy to process. Based in this reasoning, Hay (2000: 23, 240) sets up the hypothesis that 'an affix which can be easily parsed out should not occur inside an affix which can not'. This mechanism leads to the kind of hierarchy observed in Hay and Plag's study, which has earned it the name of 'complexity-based ordering' (Plag 2002).

This implies a measure of separability. One simple measure of separability is productivity. Productive processes are characterized by a large proportion of low frequency, that is easily separable, forms, while unproductive morphological categories show a low proportion of rare words. Thus, following Hay's hypothesis, and confirmed by the empirical findings in Hay and Plag (2004), suffixes that are closer to the base in the hierarchy (e.g. nominal *-th*, verbal *-en* in Hay and Plag's suffix set) are less productive, that is less easily segmented, and suffixes that are further away from the base in the hierarchy (e.g. *-ness, -ful* in Hay and Plag's suffix set) tend to be more productive, that is more easily segmented.

In a follow-up study, Plag and Baayen (2009) tested a larger set of suffixes (N=31) and their potential 930 combinations against behavioural data (lexical decision and naming latencies) to get a better idea of the processing issues involved. Again a similar hierarchy was found and a similar (though weaker) correlation between a suffix's productivity and its position in the hierarchy. But the behavioural data do not fully support the idea of complexity-based ordering. The processing costs of a given word with a particular suffix are not related to the rank of that suffix in the hierarchy. However, the average processing costs of a given suffix (i.e. across all words with that suffix) and its rank in the hierarchy are correlated. Suffixes at both ends of the hierarchy enjoy a processing advantage, either through easy memory retrieval (the innermost suffixes), or through easy parsing (the outermost suffixes). Overall, it seems, however, that the individual selectional restrictions are the mechanism that decides about the possibility of coining a particular word with two given suffixes (see Plag and Baayen 2009: 142–4 for more detailed discussion).

We have given a lot of space to this processing account of suffix-ordering because it seems to us to be a very explanatory approach. Others have considered, in general terms, rather than related specifically to English, semantic explanations for ordering, either in terms of relevance (Bybee 1985) or in terms of semantic scope (Rice 2000). While these factors appear relevant in the ordering of English derivational suffixes, they cannot explain which of several synonymous adjectival suffixes will be used in an individual position after a given nominal suffix, for instance. That is, purely semantic explanations could not rule out a sequence of *-ess-ic* (not attested in COCA) while allowing *-ess-y* (attested in COCA in *actressy, mistressy, waitressy*).

21.2.2 Prefix combinations

A similar picture emerges with prefixes. In Zirkel's (2010) study of 15 prefixes and their combinations, of the 225 potential prefix combinations (including repeated prefixes) 35 per cent were actually attested. A closer analysis reveals the existence of a hierarchy, similar to that of suffixes, such that more productive prefixes attach quite freely to less productive prefixes and more productive prefixes tend not to occur inside less productive prefixes.

With regard to their combinatorial properties, prefixes are generally less restricted than suffixes. They normally do not impose phonological restrictions on potential bases, and they are on average more flexible with regard to the syntactic categories they may attach to (Plag 2004: 201). Given this higher flexibility of prefixes in general, the larger proportion of 35 per cent attested combinations as against 17 per cent for suffixes in Hay and Plag (2004), is not surprising. In fact, 81 per cent of all 225 potential prefix combinations are permissible in terms of the selectional restrictions of the prefixes involved, according to Zirkel (2010: 253). So for prefixes, selectional restrictions do not nearly constrain their combinations as severely as they do for suffixes. Why less than half of the structurally possible prefix combinations are attested is unclear, however.

One possibility is that they are ruled out by processing considerations, since many of them would violate the Zirkel's (2010) prefix hierarchy. Another possibility is that the lack of pertinent forms is simply a matter of restricted corpus size. To test these two possibilities in a preliminary fashion, we checked 18 randomly picked combinations that violate the hierarchy, and that are nevertheless structurally possible, but are not attested in Zirkel's (2010) version of COCA (February 2008 version, 360 million words). These 18 combinations (involving the prefixes *inter-*, *sub-*, and *pre-* in first position) were checked against the COCA version of April 2012, which, containing 425 million words, is almost 20 per cent larger than Zirkel's COCA version. Of the 18 formerly unattested combinations we actually found four newly attested ones using this larger database.

The results for prefixes and suffixes thus point in the same direction, with complexity-based orderings the norm and violations of the prefix and suffix hierarchies being dispreferred. For sequences of native and non-native in regard to prefixes, see Chapter 27.

It appears to be relatively easy to add prefixes to etymological prefixes (that is, of Latin or Greek origin) whose semantic value has become lost. Examples such as *disconnect, ex-researcher*, for instance show bases (*connect, researcher*) where no prefix can be analysed in English, even though there was one in the donor languages. Even instances like *disavow, unrefined*, where we can analyse a prefix in English, have bases which are item-familiar and well-established. This is, of course, in line with the generalizations made above about ease of processing. Also in line with these generalizations are cases of prefixes whose selectional restrictions would allow for either ordering and where in fact both orderings can be found. In such cases, we often find that the inner prefix is less separable than the outer prefix, as we see in examples like *underrepresented* versus *re-understand, inter-react* versus *re-interview, unpolychrome* versus *polyunsaturated*.

Non-native prefixes, both learned and very productive recent forms like *mini-*, co-occur, with the main factor determining order apparently being semantic scope: the outermost prefix has scope over not only the base, but the combination of base and innermost prefix. Examples from the corpora are given in (2).

(2)   anti-postmodern, ex-nonentity, ex-superstar, hypermultilateralist, mega-supermarket, micro-cogeneration, micronanosecond, mini-pseudo-Medici, mini-submarine, multimegabyte, multitransnational, nanotransformer, neo-antibiotics, neo-metaphysical, non-hyperactive, nonmicroporous, nonperinatal, nonpoststructural

Note that alongside *anti-postmodern* (cited above) we find *postantibiotic*, illustrating that the order is not fixed by grammar or phonology. From a descriptive point of view, however, it is difficult to say whether this is true of all such pairs, since combinations are rare in texts. While COCA provides *ex-co-presidency*, even Google fails to find a hit for 🖐 *co-ex-wives*, which one might expect to be possible.

21.2.3 Recursion

Although it is possible to find sequences of two homophonous affixes in English (as in *friendlily*), and sequences where an affix is found on a base which ends with a string homophonous with the suffix (as with *adulterer*), it does not seem to be the case that words in standard English end freely with a repetition of the same suffix. The nearest we get to this is those instances where the affix is redundantly repeated to guarantee that it occurs on the right edge of the word: the BNC provides *asphalterer-over*, but more generally words like *fixer-upperer* occur (see Chapter 11). An example such as that in (3) (from COCA) may or may not count as real recursion, since *-ation* is added to a verb made of a converted noun.

(3)   *MAG_ScienceNews 2011*: Elements undergo what's called physical and chemical **fractionation** during processes such as going from liquid to solid.

Prefixes can be used recursively, though such uses are not particularly common. The prefix *re-* usually alternates with *again* to avoid meaningful sequences of *re-re-* (see (4) below from COCA), though *re-* on a word beginning with non-morphemic <re> is relatively common (*re-record*, *re-review*) and COCA provides the recursive example *re-re-revised*. Recursive examples with other prefixes are provided in (5).

(4)   *ACAD_Africa_Today 1993*: separatist tendencies **re-emerged once again**

      SPOK_NPR-Talk_Nation 2002: the people of Newark, who are ready to **re-elect him again**

(5)   *NEWS_SanFrancisco 1997*: We're in the **pre-prelaunch** stage

      NEWS_Atlanta 1991: They've got all these **post-post-post-feminist** things at their fingertips.

      NEWS_Denver 2009: with mandatory prison sentences on any individual, company, subcontractor, **sub-subcontractor** or **sub-sub-subcontractor** or corporation that receives taxpayer money and hires illegal aliens

      MAG_NatlReview 1994: why should the existing information superhighways be upgraded to **super-superhighways**?

      FIC_Bk;HabeasCorpses 2005: she seemed content: being "**un-undead**" suited her just fine.

> *MAG_RollingStone 2000*: "It was a coming-of-age film, shot entirely in India—very, very ambitious.— # Very, very is an **under-understatement**.

> *FIC_IowaRev 2004*: there's nothing in the world I want more than to have her as my **ex-ex-wife**, to try again

Prefixes showing size seem to be particularly prone to recursion, with some examples from COCA in (6), but even then, the additional use of quasi-synonymous prefixes may be preferred (see (7)).

(6)   *MAG_ScienceNews 1991*: A "**hyper-hyperparasite**," known more simply as the "cheater," sneaks into the placid community

   SPOK_MSNBC_Cosby 2006: They are becoming **mega-mega-stars.**

   MAG_Bicycling 2004: What with CO_2 cartridges and those nifty **mini-minipumps**, the traditional, super-effective frame pump has become a sign of retrohood.

   NEWS_CSMonitor 1994: One self-described "**ultra-ultraconservative** Democrat" defected

(7)   *MAG_PopMech 2007*: It's like a hip **micro-minivan**.

   CNN_Showbiz 2009: And its also scary to see how isolated these **mega-superstars** are.

   FantasySciFic 1994: he was making time payments on one colossal, outsize, **super-mega-omniprayer** of his own asking being answered some day.

21.3 COMBINATIONS OF PREFIXES WITH SUFFIXES IN DERIVATION

In this section we will look at a phenomenon that has received very little attention in the literature, namely the combination of a prefix and a suffix in the same word. There are four types of formation that one could distinguish based on which affix is the outermost one. In (8), the four possibilities are illustrated with data from COCA. In (8a) the prefix is attached to an existing suffixed derivative, in (8b) a suffix is attached to an existing prefixed word, and in (8c) either of the previous analyses is synchronically possible. Finally, (8d) gives examples of parasynthetic formations, which are defined as derivatives that come about through the simultaneous prefixation and suffixation to a base. The attachment of prefix and suffix is 'simultaneous' in the sense that neither a suffixed base nor a prefixed base is attested before the emergence of the prefixed and suffixed form, which differentiates parasynthetic formations from the cases of multiple hierarchical formations as shown in (8a) to (8c). We will deal with clearly hierarchical multiple pre- and suffixation in the next subsection and with parasynthetic formations in Section 21.3.2.

(8) a. *Prefix as outermost affix (right-branching)*

after-retirement, dedogmatize, meta-learning, non-additive, semi-attractive, vice-president

b. *Suffix as outermost affix (left-branching)*

embodiment, interviewer, midcontinental

c. *Ambiguous cases (right-branching or left-branching)*

semi-blindness, mistreatment, unhumanize

d. *Parasynthetic formations*

deasbestocize, decaffeinate, embolden, enliven

Combinations of these patterns are also possible, as in [[micro[dis[continu-iti]]]es], [non[anti[bacteri-al]]], [[non[intervent-ion]]ist] (where *discontinuity* provides a possible instance of ambiguity).

21.3.1 Multiple hierarchical affixation

The cases (8a) to (8c) are usually considered unproblematic as they follow straightforwardly from the selectional restrictions of the affixes involved, and such words are also quite common in English. Exactly how common has rarely been investigated (but see Berg 2003), and it is also unclear whether the combination of a prefix and a suffix in a single word is principally constrained beyond what we would expect on the basis of the selectional restrictions involved.

In order to take a closer look at this, we investigated left- and right-branching structures in more detail. For the study of right-branching structures we randomly picked five prefixes with different degrees of productivity (*de-*, *mid-*, *non-*, *semi-*, and *vice-*) and checked for each prefix a random sample of 50 derivatives from the unlemmatized COCA word lists we had generated as part of the research for this volume. These word lists contain derivatives in which the affix in question can be analysed as the outermost suffix, thus including also the ambiguous cases shown in (8c). We ended up with an average proportion of 47 per cent of the derivatives in the samples from the five lists having at least one derivational suffix in addition to the prefix, with the individual percentages ranging between 34 per cent for *mid-* and 70 per cent for *semi-*. This means that the prefixes in question are quite likely to attach to already suffixed words, forming right-branching structures as in (8a).

We then applied an analogous procedure to left-branching structures. For this we took our word lists with the randomly picked suffixes *-ize*, *-ness*, *-age*, *-able*, and *-some* as the outermost affix to see how many of their bases are prefixed. In this sample, only 5 per cent of the pertinent derivatives were found to be based on prefixed words (on average, the suffixes ranged between zero per cent prefixed bases for *-some* and 12 per cent prefixed bases for *-able*). In other words, these suffixes are rather unlikely to attach to prefixed words.

Assuming that these exploratory results are representative, how can this asymmetry between prefixes and suffixes be explained? Why would prefixes attach more happily to already suffixed words while suffixes are much less prone to attach to already prefixed words? Interestingly, this asymmetry in our two samples is predicted by complexity-based ordering. In general, prefixes tend to be more easily separable than suffixes due to the left-to-right nature of the speech signal. Prefixes enter the processor before the base, whereas the base comes first with suffixed words. In either case, the leftmost morpheme has an advantage in lexical access and representation (see, for example, Plag 2002, for more detailed discussion). With regard to multiple affixation this means that under the assumption of complexity-based ordering the average prefix should be outside the average suffix, which is equivalent to saying that, given a word with a prefix and a suffix, we expect the structure of this word to be right-branching rather than left-branching. This expectation fits nicely with our finding that among the words with an outermost prefix, we find very many bases that are suffixed.

And complexity-based ordering would also predict that in those cases where we deal with a left-branching structure (as in *embodiment*) we expect the prefix to be less easily segmentable than in the average right-branching case (e.g. *semi-attractive*). This prediction seems to be borne out by the facts: Berg (2003) finds that in his data set left-branching is generally uncommon among productive prefixes, but is highly frequent with unproductive prefixes. Recall that unproductive prefixes are less easily segmentable and thus have a greater chance of occurring inside suffixation, as part of a left-branching structure.

Overall, these exploratory investigations into the combination of prefixes and suffixes in the same words present a picture similar to that of prefix combinations and suffix combinations. The prefix hierarchy and the suffix hierarchy interact in ways predicted by complexity-based ordering, with unproductive prefixes being located at one end of the hierarchy (perhaps together with certain unproductive suffixes), and productive prefixes being located at the other end of the affixal hierarchy. More research is obviously called for to further study the interaction of prefixes and suffixes and to test the tentative claims put forward here on the basis of an investigation of a small sample of affixes.

21.3.2 Parasynthetic affixation

Parasynthetic formations as defined above are rare in English, but they raise a number of theoretical problems, the most prominent of which is branching. For illustration, we show in (9) three potential analyses of *decaffeinate*, with three kinds of constituent structure and branching.

(9) a. [[de-caffein]-ate]   b.   [de-[caffein-ate]]   c.   [de-[caffeine]-ate]

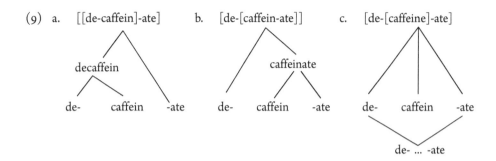

In some theories, morphological branching is strictly binary (e.g. Aronoff 1976), which would rule out a representation like (9c). We do not want to discuss here all the theoretical and empirical problems related to the binary branching hypothesis, but it seems that with regard to parasynthetic formations, there is a problem for this approach. With our example *decaffein-ate*, there was no verb *caffeinate* at the time of creation to which the reversative prefix *de-* might have attached. There was also no potential base *decaffein* for the attachment of the suffix *-ate* (Plag 1999: 101). This means that the meaning 'remove X' is expressed through both the prefix and the suffix, with the suffix contributing the verbal semantics and the prefix the privative meaning. It might seem that we would be forced to posit a circumfix *de-ate* with that meaning, as shown in the lower part of the tree in (9c), but both *de-* and *-ate* occur independently elsewhere with the relevant meanings, which is not typical of a circumfix. The alternative is to assume, as in (9b), the existence of a putative verb *caffeinate* 'provide (with) caffeine' (such a solution is sometimes termed an 'overgenerating morphology'—Allen 1978). This putative verb is then prefixed with the reversative prefix *de-* (see e.g. Guevara 2007 for a general discussion of this kind of solution). The same kind of analyses and problems apply to the other forms cited in (8d).

None of these analytical possibilities seems particularly attractive from a rule-based or generative perspective, but there is yet another approach possible, one that is based on analogy or constructional schemata. There are quite a number of derivatives that feature both the prefix *de-* and the suffix *-ate* on a nominal base with the meaning 'remove X' (where X is the denotation of the base), such as *deacylate, decapacitate, dechlorinate, dehyphenate*. The parasynthetic form may be analysed as simply following this pattern (or schema, in constructionist terms).

21.4 Conversion and affixation

In principle it might be expected that conversion would interact with suffixation in the same kind of way that affixation processes interact with each other. The reality is rather more difficult to establish than this would suggest.

There seems to be no particular reason why a converted word could not act as a base for subsequent affixation. Once the verb *empty* has been created by conversion from the adjective *empty*, it can inflect as a verb (*empties, emptied, emptying*), and we might expect it to be used as a derivational base as well, as it is in (11). However, there do not appear to be any established derivatives from the verb *empty*, and the question is whether this is typical or just happenstance.

There are so many cases of conversion in English that there are times when it is difficult to decide which member of the pair of converted forms is involved in a derivation. Our data sets are full of such instances. For example, the derivatives *designer, flapper, harpooner, peeper, plasterer, scorer, toner, trooper, whisperer* might all be derived from either a noun or a verb base. We would probably decide that all of them are derived from verbs since *-er* appears to attach more frequently to verbs than to nouns and since the semantics is consistent with the base being a verb. If that is the case, though, it seems that at least *harpooner* and *plasterer* must be formed on the basis of nouns used as the base for conversion. Thus there is no barrier in principle to derivational affixation applying to instances of conversion. In the very nature of things, however, it is difficult to quantify how often this occurs.

Conversion of affixed forms is slightly easier, at least where suffixes are concerned. Marchand (1969: 372–3) claims that derived nouns rarely undergo conversion. He argues that this is because of blocking (although he does not use the term): the converted verb would have the same meaning as that of the base verb. However, it is shown in many chapters in this book that blocking is never a strong force, and an argument based on it is correspondingly weak. In (10) we provide some examples of words whose derivational morphology suggests that they are not verbs and yet which can be found inflected as verbs.

(10)   adventure, bandage, blinker, cashier, champion, commission, condition, disadvantage, function, package, pilgrimage, pressure, provision, sanction, scooter, section, signal, streamer, stopper, tenant, tension, waitress

We have drawn attention elsewhere to forms such as *intellectual* and *disposable* (Chapter 25) which are marked as adjectives and yet which can be marked for plural and head noun phrases. Similarly we have drawn attention to forms in *-an* and *-ist* (Chapter 14) which regularly provide both adjectives and nouns. All of this suggests that conversion of affixally derived bases is quite normal. The examples in (11) all illustrate established nouns being used as bases.

(11)   *ACAD_Symposium 1993*: In this dynamic, space is always convertible, **emptiable** or fillable.

   FIC_IowaRev 2012: she can go back to doing her job, which is **princessing**, which delights Audrey Hepburn

Psychology Today 2011: Researchers also identified two other categories of nonerotic thoughts—"**spectatoring**," or stepping outside your body to judge your own performance, and body image concerns

21.5 INFLECTION

Although English inflection is exclusively suffixal and also rather impoverished, two questions still deserve answers: What is the ordering of inflectional versus derivational suffixes, and what is the ordering of inflectional suffixes if more than one suffix ends up on the same base? We will deal with each question separately.

21.5.1 Inflection in interaction with derivation

It is generally agreed that in English (as in many other languages), inflection is outside derivation. This is illustrated in (12), with adverb formation given in parentheses due to its debated status as an inflectional process (see Chapter 15 for discussion).

(12)   *Nouns: plural and genitive*
       curiosities, princesses; discussant's, manager's

       Verbs: tense, person, and aspect
       hyphenated, personifies, verbalizing

       Adjectives: gradation (and adverb formation)
       unofficialer, winningest (adaptively, aimlessly)

Apparent exceptions to this general rule can be found when the inflection is irregular and not clearly affixal, but even then only a few examples of a few types are found, as shown in (13).

(13)   a. better]$_A$]$_V$ ment, lessen, moreish, mostly, worsen

       b. *feetage, *geesish, *menly, *micelings, *womenize; *ateing, *caughtment, *dranker, *grewage

Another set of apparent exceptions occurs when things which might be analysed as inflectional affixes (and in particular, *-s*, *-ed*, and *-ing*) are found inside one of a very few extremely productive derivational affixes. Examples are given in (14). Note that in (14) adverbial *-ly* is treated as derivational; if it is inflectional, these examples belong elsewhere.

(14)   folk-s-y, interest-ed-ly, interest-ed-ness, interest-ing-ly, interest-ing-ness, sud-s-y, wedd-ing-ish

There are also a few examples of other irregular plurals occurring inside derivational affixes, but the clearest example we have found of this, *mediawise*, has the base *media*, which may no longer be perceived as a plural noun.

Although it is strictly irrelevant, in that there is no interaction between inflection and derivation, it is perhaps worth noting here that plurals are often found internal to compounds, as illustrated with examples from COCA in (15) (see also Chapter 19.3.1).

(15)   alumni relations, arms embargo, books editor, criteria levels, feet movement, grounds maintenance, mice feces, universities consortium

Finally, there are also cases where it is not so clear that the inflectional suffix is the outermost suffix; these cases concern parasynthetic formations, in which a derivational prefix and an inflectional suffix come together. This is quite common with verbal participles. For example, we have noted in Chapter 13 that ornative verbs with the suffix *be-* are often coined as past participles, that is with the simultaneous attachment of the prefix *be-* and the suffix *-ed* to a nominal base (e.g. *bedenimed, bejowled, besmogged, bestuccoed*, all from COCA, see also Marchand 1969: 148, and the *OED* s.v. *be-*[7] for discussion). Note that such formations do not pose a problem for a binary-branching approach to word-formation since these forms, in contrast to the parasynthetic formations discussed in Section 21.3.2, can be analysed straightforwardly as left-branching, that is as a prefixed form with a suffix, as in, for example, [[*bedenim*]-*ed*]. In other words, with regard to these formations, the term 'simultaneous' refers to the speaker's act of coining the word, and not to a theoretical notion of derivationally simultaneous attachment (e.g. via ternary structures). However, because the *-ed* in these formations could be interpreted as an ornative *-ed* (see Chapter 14), and thus derivational, it is not clear how far these examples are relevant here.

21.5.2 Inflection interacting with inflection

We now turn to the ordering of multiple inflectional endings. Such multiple inflectional endings cannot be found with verbs due to the non-agglutinative nature of the English verbal inflectional system, but they may appear, at least theoretically, with nouns and adjectives. Nouns may be inflected for genitive and plural at the same time, in which case the genitive marker follows the plural marker (as in *brethren's, oxen's*). The picture is of course more complicated than that since the combination of the regular plural marker *-s* with the genitive marker *-'s* triggers haplology in rather intricate ways (e.g. genitive plural *boys'*). The details of this conflation of plural and genitive marking are discussed in Chapter 7 and need not be repeated here.

With adjectival inflection, we can have the stacking of gradation and adverb formation, but of course only under the premise that we consider adverb formation as inflection. If we do so, it seems that the two kinds of suffix may simply not combine. With *-ly* adverbs, the periphrastic comparative (e.g. *more boldly*) is obligatory, with only very few variant exceptions (e.g. archaic *quicklier*). If these exceptions are taken as sufficient evidence, it seems that gradation is outside adverb formation.

Finally, we note in Chapter 24 that there are some processes which might be considered inflectional, but are not usually taken to be inflectional, particularly formations involving numbers. Examples like *fif-th-s* and *fif-teen-th-s* show that these processes are less peripheral than the clearly inflectional plural. Examples in (14) are relevant here if adverbial *-ly* is assumed to be inflectional.

Overall, English is very poor when it comes to the stacking of inflectional suffixes. Where it would be possible at all, it is highly restricted and occurs only with morphologically irregular or otherwise exceptional forms (*oxen's* and the examples in (13a)).

21.6 Derivatives with more than two affixes

So far, we have limited the discussion to words with no more than two derivational affixes. Needless to say, these words may take inflectional endings, to the effect that the combination of one or more derivational affixes with an inflectional suffix is unproblematic (e.g. *decontextualizations, disauthenticated, semi-customized*). The number of derivational affixes that can be found in a single word seems in principle unlimited, but processing becomes difficult with longer forms. This is probably the reason why finding derivatives with four affixes is still quite possible, but finding words with five or more derivational affixes becomes increasingly hard, even though the attested forms could even be further expanded by additional suffixation or prefixation. In (16) we list some pertinent examples from COCA. For the reader's convenience, we provide hyphens to separate the affixes. A particularly instructive example is the recursive prefix *great-*, which is attested in COCA a number of times with four instantiations in one word, but never with more (see (16b) for one example). Note that while we list forms in (16) in terms of the number of affixes overall, if we look at the number of prefixes or the number of suffixes it is, in most cases, even more constrained in actual use.

(16) a. *Four affixes*:

neo-en-light-en-ment, counter-re-form-ation-al, anti-americ-an-iz-ation, anti-constitut-ion-al-ist, epi-phenomen-al-iz-ation, institut-ion-al-iz-ation

b. *Five affixes*:

great-great-great-great-grand-parents, anti-inter-nat-ion-al-ism, (*cf.* ✋anti-inter-nat-ion-al-ist-ic, *which would have one more affix and is not attested*), neo-retro-maxi-minim-al-ist (cf. ✋neo-retro-maxi-minim-al-ist-ic)

508 *Combination of affixes*

One of the differences between looking at sequences of just two affixes and looking at longer sequences is that we can see recursion over longer sequences that are not easily observable over just two. English does allow sequences such as *-ation-al-ize* and *al-ist-ic* (Bauer 1983: 69). We find words like *sens-ation-al-ize, compartment-al-iz-ation, organ-iz-ation-al* which show that the order between the three affixes, while fixed, is recursive. Examples with the same affix twice are rare, though COCA provides *sens-ation-al-iz-ation*, and *nat-ion-al-iz-ation* (and derivatives of that). Equally we find *individ-ual-ist-ic, ego-ist-ic-al, theatr-ic-al-ist* which indicate that recursion with certain constellations of *-ic*, *-ist*, and *-al* should be possible, and COCA provides us with *phys-ic-al-ist-ic* and *form-al-ist-ic-al-ly* which illustrate actual recursion. That recursion of this type appears to be restricted to the sets *-ation-al-ize* and *-al-ist-ic* is of some interest; on the other hand, the presence of recursion at all is a point of theoretical importance.

....

CHAPTER 22

Affixation on compounds
and phrases

22.1 Prospectus

In this chapter we address the issue of derivation on bases that are compounds or phrases. It
is normally assumed that derivation applies either to simplex bases (bound or free), or to
already affixed forms (see Chapter 21). Compounds can themselves be formed from derived
bases (*knowledge economy*), and phrases can certainly contain derived bases (*knowledge of
linguistics*), but general wisdom suggests that the opposite is only rarely the case. Theoretical
constructs such as Level-Ordering (regarding compounds) (e.g. Siegel 1978; Kiparsky 1982a),
and the Lexical Integrity Hypothesis (regarding phrasal bases) (e.g. Lapointe 1981) are
grounded in these assumptions. We will show below, however, that it is not at all rare to find
derivational affixes in English appearing on compound bases, and that phrasal bases are perhaps not as rare as our intuitions might suggest. We will first review the data here, much of
which can be found in previous chapters treating specific types of derivation, and then consider the factors that might contribute to the ability of an affix to take a compound or phrasal
base. Finally, we will raise the issue of the nature of the compounds and phrases to which
affixes attach, that is, whether affixation is restricted to compounds and phrases which are
highly lexicalized.

22.2 Data

22.2.1 Affixes on compound bases

We divide affixes into three categories according to the frequency with which they attach to
compounds: those that frequently allow compound bases (more than ten types found in
COCA), those that occasionally allow compound bases (one to nine types), and those that
never allow compounds as bases. In (1) we list those affixes which are not found on compound bases.

(1)   a. *Suffixes*: -acy, -age, -al$_A$, -al$_N$, -ian, -ance, -ant, -ary, -ate, -eer, -en, -ese, -ess, -ette, -ful$_A$, -ic, -ical, -ify, -ine, -ation, -ite, -ity, -ive, -ize, -ling, -ly, -ment, -ory, -ous, -some, -ure

       b. *Prefixes*: a-, ante-, back-, be-, by-, circum-, cis-, contra-, counter-, demi-, dis-, down-, en-, hemi-, hypo-, $_{LOC}$in-, $_{NEG}$in-, mal-, meta-, mis-, mono-, nano-, off-, on-, para-, peri-, pico-, poly-, supra-, uni-

There may be instances where it is not clear whether the base should be interpreted as a compound or a phrase. Although we have tried to be accurate and consistent here, the point of the chapter is not affected if individual examples are mis-classified.

It is perhaps somewhat surprising that there are so many prefixes and suffixes that do take compound bases. Table 22.1 lists examples.

Table 22.1 Suffixes that frequently take compounds as bases

Suffix	Examples
-dom	automobiledom, bestsellerdom, blockbusterdom, breakfastdom, bubblegumdom, couch-potato-dom, crackpotdom, highwaydom, newspaperdom, stakeholderdom, statepriesterdom, teenagerdom
-er	babysitter, backloader, bagpiper, basketballer, beachcomber, bedsitter, bellyacher, curbstoner, footballer, gen-exer, grade-schooler, grandstander, jitterbugger, keelhauler, keynoter, kneecapper, landscaper, mainlander, motocrosser, motowner
-ery	ass-kickery, blacksmithery, crackpottery, dogoodery, dumbassery, folk-freudery, gasbaggery, head-squishery, henpeckery, hornswogglery, housewifery, ironmongery, jackassery, knickknackery, peacockery, pudfootery, ragtaggery, slapdashery, sleazebaggery, tightwaddery, tomcattery, tomfoolery, wedding-cakery, werewolfery, whizbangery
-esque	all-terrain-esque, appleseed-esque, broadway-esque, disneylandesque, horror-movie-esque, hummingbirdesque, merchant-ivoryesque, prom-queenesque, snowbirdesque, snowboard-esque, strobe-lightesque, thanksgivingesque
-ish	art-nouveauish, backcountryish, bargain-basement-ish, bedfellowish, bedroomslipperish, block-busterish, blue-greenish, boy-scoutish, bulldoggish, cheerleaderish, comicbookish, cookie-cutterish, cowboyish, curtain-roddish, daredevilish, doomsdayish, eggplantish, everyman-ish, fairy-taleish, farmhand-ish, film-scorish, fire-escape-ish, french-fryish, hay-feverish, hefnerpaddish, hip-hoppish, homeboyish, *and many others*
-ism	bandwagonism, big-shotism, blue-bloodism, copycatism, deaf-mutism, foot-ballism, front-runnerism, fuddy-duddyism, he-manism, highbrowism, hotshitism, lame-duckism, meatballism, policemanism, red-tapism, short-termism, stakeholderism, thirdworldism, trickle-downism, turntablism, watchdogism
-ist	automobilist, avantgardist, bagpipist, dotcomist, fluegelhornist, folklorist, keyboardist, landscapist, storyboardist, third-worldist, turntablist, watercolorist
-less	air-conditionless, airportless, backboneless, breakfastless, box-scoreless, cocktailless, earbobless, eyebrowless, footnoteless, girlfriendless, grandchildless, hairdresserless, keyboardless, lifestyleless, lipstickless, makeupless, mass-transitless, newspaperless, nicknameless, octoberfestless, roommateless, shoelaceless, sidewalkless, suitcaseless, sunspotless, swordfishless

Suffix	Examples
-ness	absent-mindedness, accident-proneness, air-headedness, airportness, airworthiness, babyfacedness, baseballness, bigheartedness, bond-indebtedness, bone-tiredness, bushman-ness, butterflyness, checkmateness, childfriendliness, church-relatedness, class-consciousness, cocksureness, colorblindness, commonplaceness, costeffectiveness, couch-potato-ness, crazy-busyness, cross-borderness, down-homeness, earth-embeddedness, everlastingness, hanky-pankiness, headstrongness, hip-hopness *and many more*
-ship	caretakership, headmastership, role-modelship, roommateship, uptownship; *lots of examples in* x-manship, x-personship
-y$_A$	asskissy, backwoodsy, cardboardy, headachy, hot-tubby, hound-doggy, householdy, kiss-assy, knick-knacky, name-droppy, networky, new-agey, old-maidy, oldtimey, pepperminty, pin-cushiony, pine-woodsy, pipsqueaky, piss-stinky, red-necky, red-peppery, sandpapery, secret-agenty, singsongy, stand-offy, sunshiny, woodworky

Table 22.2 Prefixes that frequently take compounds as bases

Prefix	Examples
anti-	anti-age-discrimination, antibackflow, anti-blacklist, anti-breast-cancer, anti-car-theft, anti-comic-book, anti-cookie-baking, anti-direct-lending, anti-drug-abuse, anti-hair-mussing, anti-home-birth, anti-kidney-stone, anti-land-reform, anti-meat-eating, *and many more*
co-	co-anchorman, co-babymaker, co-boat-owner, co-chairman, co-concertmaster, co-decision-making, co-filmmakers, co-headlines, co-leaseholders, co-scriptwriter, co-songwriters
ex-	ex-alcohol-addict, ex-ballplayer, ex-bandmates, ex-boomtown, ex-bus-driver, ex-case-worker, ex-cheerleader, ex-churchgoers, ex-councilwoman, ex-farmhand, ex-fisherman, ex-grad-student, ex-hothead, ex-jailbird, ex-love-parade, ex-newscaster, ex-redneck, ex-schoolteacher, ex-sidekick, ex-skinhead, *and many more*
mega-	mega-bailouts, mega-best-seller, megablockbuster, mega-bookstore, mega-boxoffice, mega-crayfish, megadatabase, mega-earthquakes, mega-feedlot, mega-girl-group, mega-hardware, megahorsepower, megajackpots, megalandfills, mega-landlord, megalawsuit, megamainframe, mega-man-hours, mega-mastermind, mega-meltdowns, mega-network, megatracksites, mega-wildfire
micro-	micro-bloodvessels, microbroadcasters, micro-buzzbaits, microcornrows, micro-cowlicked, micro-earthquake, micro-hula-hoops, microkeyboard, microlandscape, microlivestock, microtiddlywinks, microwarehouse, microwatershed
mid-	midafternoon, mid-backstroke, midbroadcast, mid-cockpit, mid-dogfight, mid-driveway, mid-photo-spread, mid-price-point, mid-running-step, midsidewalk, mid-single-digit, mid-treetop, midwatercourse
mini-	mini-aircraft, mini-backpack, mini-battlewagon, mini-bloodbath, minibugsucker, mini-cheeseburgers, mini-comeback, mini-crossbow, minidesktop, mini-firestorm, mini-food-processor, minigreenhouse, mini-guitar-case, mini-jumpsuit, mini-landslide, mini-meatballs, mini-nutcracker, mini-playgrounds, mini-spreadsheet
multi-	multibedroom, multi-cactus-plant, multi-care-level, multi-decisionmaker, multi-earth-mass, multi-fall-lined, multihousehold, multinetwork, multiseafood, multi-snow-sport, multispacecraft, multistakeholder, multi-touchdown, multiwarhead, multiwavelength
neo-	neococktail, neo-gentleman, neo-glam-rock, neo-hunter-gatherer, neo-icehouse, neo-loungeheads, neo-main-street, neo-norsemen, neo-slapstick, neo-zenbohemian

Prefix	Examples
non-	nonabstinence-based, nonadhesive-backed, non-African-born, non-airmen, non-art-world, non-barrier-island, nonbedridden, non-bullet-proof, noncheesy-looking, non-college-track, non-control-top, non-credit-card, nondatabase, non-drug-using, non-empty-net, non-elf-sized, non-fairtrade, non-full-face, non-grade-level, *and many more*
post-	post-affirmative-action, post-babyboom, postbaseball, post-blacklist, post-bluegrass, post-childbirth, post-classroom, post-closing-bell, post-cough-syrup, post-digital-camera, post-foster-care, post-goal-scoring, posthomework, post-knee-injury, post-lovemaking, post-phone-number, *and many more*
pre-	pre-air-conditioned, prebaseball, pre-birthday, pre-bodice-ripping, pre-book-tour, prebullfight, pre-ceasefire, pre-computer-literate, precowboy, pre-cram-school, pre-dogfighting, pre-drywall, pre-fieldwork, pre-freeze-frame, pre-heart-attack, pre-homeroom, pre-job-offer, *and many others*
semi-	semibackbreaking, semi-bandwidth, semi-baseball, semi-beavertail, semihardshell, semi-homemade, semi-landlocked, semilowland, semi-open-stance, semisidelined, semi-sideways, semi-star-crossed, semi-supply-sider, semi-tractor-trailer, semi-warehouse, semi-widetake, semi-work-related
sub-	sub-cabinet-level, subfootnotes, sub-freshman, sub-golfsize, sub-hide-outs, sub-lightspeed, sub-lightyear, submachinegun, submainstream, sub-medium-grade, subnetwork, sub-notebook, sub-passageway, sub-record-breaking, sub-room-temperature, sub-watershed, sub-wave-length
super-	super-airliner, super-bookstores, superboomtown, super-bottom-heavy, super-broadband, superchecklist, super-featherweight, super-first-class, superflywheel, supergirlfriend, superguardsmen, superheavyweight, super-high-end, super-landfills, super-leftwing, super-mudroom, super-muscle-car, superpipelining, supersalesman, supershareholder, super-stonewashed, super-sunflowers, super-side-angle
ultra-	ultrababyfat, ultrabroadband, ultra-cold-hardy, ultra-deadpan, ultra-deep-field, ultra-deepwater, ultra-fast-acting, ultrafine-grained, ultra-free-market, ultra-fuel-efficient, ultra-hands-on, ultra-heat-resistant, ultra-heavy-duty, ultrahigh-capacity, ultra-left-wing, ultralightweight, ultra-thinwall, ultra-underdog, ultrawideband
un-	unairbrushed, unairconditioned, unbackcountry, un-blindfold, unbulldozed, un-chain-store-afflicted, uncomputer-savvy, undinosaur-looking, undoublespace, un-dye-packed, unflightworthy, unfloorplanned, unfootnoted, ungridlocked, unhandcuff, unhousebroken, unloveworthy, unmakeshift, un-model-perfect, un-nerve-wracking, un-Paris-Hilton-looking, unsolaraided, unstreamlined, un-Texas-size, un-user-friendly

Table 22.3 Suffixes that only occasionally attach to compounds

Suffix	Examples
-able	backpackable, bushwhackable, copyrightable
-ee	blackmailee
-ful$_N$	classroomful, hatboxful, mailboxful, papercupful, shoeboxful, tablespoonsful, trash-canful, windshieldful
-hood	beach-bunnyhood, jackasshood, statesmanhood, wallflowerhood
-let	bookmarklet
-ward	northeastward, northwestward, southeastward, southwestward

Table 22.4 Prefixes that only occasionally attach to compounds

Prefix	Examples
after-	after-bedtime, after-breakfast, after-federal-tax, after-lovemaking, after-math-time, after-thanksgiving, after-workout
arch-	arch-dipshit
auto-	auto-treadmill
crypto-	crypto-deadhead, crypto-right-winger
de-	debottlenecking, de-mothballed
extra-	extra-bubble-butt, extra-classroom, extrahousehold, extra-lightweight, extra-sure-footed
fore-	fore-topmast
hyper-	hyper-health-conscious, hyper-rapid-fire, hyper-sports-utilities, hyper-weight-conscious
inter-	intergenebank, interhousehold, interjumppoint, interkeystroke, inter-landau-level, internecktie
intra-	intra-beltway, intrahousehold, intra-landau-level, intra-network, intra-working-class
over-	over-air-conditioned, overautomobiled, over-lifesize, over-lip-synced, overpipelined, overstreamlined, overwallpapered
out-	out-back-stabbed, out-cheap-shot, out-comeback, out-french-horn, out-horsepower, out-redneck, out-swashbuckle, out-tailgate, out-tax-cut
proto-	proto-bluegrass, proto-daily-paper, proto-dipstick, protodownscale, proto-highlands, proto-hip-hop, proto-jumpsuit, proto-performance-art, proto-punk-rock
re-	rebabyproof, rebroadcast, relandscaped, rewaterproofing
retro-	retroopensource, retro-roadside
tera-	teraelectronvolt
trans-	transboundary-scale, trans-lightspeed, trans-windshield
under-	under-fingernail, under-gunwale, under-tablecloth
up-	up-full-court

22.2.2 Affixes on phrasal bases

It is much rarer to find affixes on phrasal bases. The examples in Table 22.5 can be found in COCA.

Table 22.5 Affixes on phrasal bases

Affix	Examples
-dom	low-carbdom, middleclassdom, wife-and-motherdom
-er	back-bencher, bottom liner, do-gooder, do-it-yourself-er, down-easter, fifth-grader, first-rounder, free-trader, hall-of-famer, in-and-outer, in-towner, left-hander, no-brainer, one-liner, out-of-towner, threewheeler, *and others*
-ery	old-fartery, white-trashery
-hood	above-averagehood, one-step-behindhood, senior-skier-hood
-ish	dark-reddish, dog-in-the-mangerish, feelgoodish, fox-in-the-henhouseish, girl-next-doorish, last-mannish, low-keyish, metal-lumpish, up-your-buttish

Affix	Examples
-ism	can-doism, do-goodism, donothingism, don't-give-a-damnism, don't-rock-the-boatism, feel-goodism, get-even-with-themism, holier-than-thouism, know-nothingism, me-firstism, me-tooism, not-in-my-backyardism, old-fartism, old-fogeyism, one-worldism, over-the-topism, stand-patism
-ness	all-over-ness, at-homeness, at-largeness, at-oneness, day-to-dayness, does-nothingness, do-it-yourselfness, down-and-outness, down-to-earthness, every-girlness, feel-goodness, fifth-wheelness, getting-on-ness, here-and-now-ness, high-and-mightiness, hot-button-ness, I-can-do-it-too-ness, ill-at-easeness, in-loveness, in-placeness, in-shapeness, just-so-ness, larger-than-lifeness, know-nothingness, letting-in-ness
-ward	down-and-southward
after-	after-initial-sale, after-real-life
anti-	anti-big-business, anti-big-government, anti-business-as-usual, anti-free-speech, anti-global-capitalism, anti-poor-women, anti-reproductive-rights
co-	co-first-place
ex-	ex-friends-with-benefits, ex-man-of-steel, ex-olympian-turned-pro
extra-	extra-longrange
out-	out-crash'n'burn
post-	postbaby-on-board, post-connery-as-bond, post-death-of-god, post-fall-of-Baghdad, post-hunter-and-gatherer, post-Pearl-and-Jacob, post-state-of-nature, post-two-year-college
pre-	pre-cold-war, pre-end-of-world, pre-fifth-century, pre-Redford-and-Hoffman, pre-shock-and-awe
semi-	semi-fast-pitch
ultra-	ultra-low-cal, ultra-right-wing

22.3 FACTORS INFLUENCING AFFIXATION ON COMPOUNDS AND PHRASES

It is clear from the data presented in Section 22.2 that it is not at all unusual for affixes to attach to compounds, and that even on phrasal bases, affixation is less unusual than intuition might suggest. The obvious question to ask is what the factors are that influence the ability of affixes to take compounds and phrases, and whether there is anything systematic to be said about the phenomenon. In what follows, we will look at possible factors influencing the ability of affixes to attach to compounds and phrases.

Etymological origin seems only to be of minor significance in determining the propensity of an affix to attach to compounds and phrases. Suffixes of native origin (*-dom, -ish, -less, -ness, -ship*) do seem to be more likely than non-native suffixes to attach to compounds and phrases, although some non-native suffixes are quite productive on compounds and phrases (*-ery, -esque, -ism, -ist*). Among prefixes, however, the opposite seems to be the case: it is the non-native ones (*anti-, mega-, mid-, non-, post-, sub-*) that show somewhat more of a tendency to accept compounds and phrases. But again, we can find productive use of native prefixes (*after-, over-, out-, under-*) as well.

Etymological origin is sometimes seen as a proxy for phonological structure in some way. By denying an absolute correlation between etymological origin and affixation on compounds and phrases, we are also implicitly denying a clear correlation between phonological behaviour and such affixation. This is illustrated in (2) and (3), with all sorts of affixes (native or non-native, auto-stressed or not, stress-neutral or stress-shifting) showing either behaviour.

(2) *affixes that do not appear on compounds and phrases*

   -al, -ance, -ant, -ation, -eer, -ful$_A$, -ic, -ical, -ify, -ity, -ive, -ize, -ment, -ory, a-, counter-, dis-, en-, in-, mal-, meta-, supra-

(3) *affixes that do appear on compounds and phrases*

   -able, -dom, -er, -ery, -esque, -ful$_N$, -hood, -ish, -ism, -ist, -ness, -ship, -y, co-, de-, mega-, multi-, non-, post-, proto-, re-, sub-, un-, up-

The phonotactics of the base–affix boundary is equally not an influencing factor. Among the affixes that do not attach to compounds and phrases, the preponderance have a vocalic boundary segment, but there are also some where the boundary segment is consonantal. And there is no particular bias towards consonantal boundary segments in the affixes that do attach to compounds and phrases; among the suffixes, for example, *-less, -ness*, and *-ship* have consonantal boundary segments, but *-ery, -ish, -esque, -ism, -ist,* and *-y* do not. We must therefore look elsewhere for factors influencing the combination of affixes with compounds and phrases.

Another factor that might be thought to influence the ability of affixes to attach to compounds and phrases is categorial selection. Since the majority of compounds formed in English are nominal or adjectival and verbal compounding is significantly less productive, we might expect that affixes that attach exclusively or primarily to verbal bases would be the least inclined to accept compounds and phrases as bases. This is true to some extent, as we find that affixes like *-al$_N$, -ful$_A$, -ation, -ive, -ment, -ory, -ance, -ant*, and *-ure* do not appear at all on such bases. But some affixes (*-able, -ee, -er*, reversative *un-*, and *re-*) do appear on compound verbs. So it is not clear that categorial selection figures in a major way in the ability of affixes to appear on compounds and phrases. While the category of the base is only one of a host of potential restrictions on the base that might be relevant, and it may in principle be impossible to check them all, we can find no such constraint which appears relevant in our data.

Perhaps the clearest and most significant factor in determining whether affixes will accept compounds and phrases is the extent to which those affixes are otherwise productive. We stress otherwise here to eliminate the risk of circularity. What we mean to say, then, is that the closer an affix is to being fully productive on non-compounds and phrases, the more likely it is to accept compounds and phrases as well. For example, the suffix *-ness* comes as close as any derivational affix in English to being fully productive, and it is also perhaps the one most frequently found on compounds and phrases. Similarly with *-dom, -er, -esque, -ish*, and the other suffixes shown in Table 22.1. This is not to say, of course, that all productive affixes take such bases; the affixes *-age, -an, -ify, -ation, -ize, a-, counter-, dis-,* and *mis-,* for example, do not. Whether it is a matter of their lesser degree of productivity, or other restrictions that prevent them from attaching to compounds and phrases is unclear at this point. But what is clear is that high productivity in other respects is correlated with high productivity on compounds and phrases.

22.4 The role of lexicalization

So far we have concentrated on trying to determine the kinds of affixes that can attach to compounds and phrases. In this section we will look at the question from the opposite direction: that is, it is also worth considering whether there are any restrictions on the types of compounds and phrases to which affixes can attach. Specifically, we should consider whether affixes can attach only to compounds or phrases which display some degree of lexicalization (or at least item-familiarity), or whether the affixes that attach to compounds and/or phrases attach freely to any sort of compound and/or phrase.

The data given in the tables above does suggest prima facie that item-familiar or lexicalized compounds and phrases more frequently serve as bases for derivational affixation than item-unfamiliar or non-lexicalized ones. However, we should not be too quick to jump to the conclusion that derivation is restricted to item-familiar or lexicalized compounds and phrases. For one thing, we do find a significant number of derived forms on compounds or phrases that are not item-familiar or lexicalized, among them: *ass-kickery, folk-freudery, head-squishery, pud-footery, merchant-ivoryesque, crazy-busyness, earth-embeddedness, pine-woodsy, piss-stinky, anti-cookie-baking, ex-love-parade, micro-buzzbaits, mid-running-step, mini-bugsucker, multi-fall-lined, neo-loungeheads, neo-zenbohemian, non-empty-net, non-elf-sized, semi-open-stance, sub-golfsize, super-side-angle, ultre-deep-field, ultra-thinwall, un-chain-store-afflicted, un-dinosaur-looking, un-dye-packed, unloveworthy, un-model-perfect, un-Paris-Hilton-looking, un-Texas-size, senior-skier-hood, dark-reddish, metal-lumpish, ex-olympian-turned-pro,* and so on.

For another, as pointed out in Chapter 19, the more item-familiar or lexicalized a compound is, the likelier it is to be written as one word or with a hyphen. This leaves open the possibility that the high ratio of item-familiar to item-unfamiliar compounds might be due to the way we have extracted data from COCA and other corpora. Orthographically spaced compounds would not show up in the sort of string search that we are limited to. String searches for affixes only work on strings that are uninterrupted by spaces. For example, with the search string 'ex*' we might extract *ex-baseball-player* (on the item-familiar hyphenated base *baseball-player*), but not *ex-kazoo player* (on the non-item-familiar *kazoo player* spelled with a space between the two words). Both examples are compound bases, but the unlexicalized one would simply not show up in our searches. This methodological difficulty leads to an over-representation of item-familiar and lexicalized forms and an under-representation of item-unfamiliar forms.

22.5 CONCLUSION

We conclude that derivation is not infrequent in English on compounds and phrases and that few generalizations can be drawn about the conditions that favour such derivation. The strongest generalization that emerges from our scrutiny of corpus data is that affixes that are highly productive in other ways are also likely to be highly productive in this way, a conclusion which should not come as a surprise to us. Productive affixes are more easily segmented, that is have stronger morphological boundaries (see Chapter 21.2.1) and thus seem to be able to also accommodate bases with stronger morphological boundaries.

CHAPTER 23

....

Paradigmatic processes

23.1 PROSPECTUS

In general, most phenomena of English morphology can be described in either a syntagmatic or paradigmatic way, that is, either in terms of concatenation or in terms of a set or grid of related words. Which of the two analyses is to be preferred for the majority of inflectional, derivational, or compounding processes may depend on the researcher's theoretical preference. However, there are also a number of phenomena described in the previous chapters for which a syntagmatic approach seems very hard to implement and which strongly suggest an analysis in terms of paradigmatic structure or analogy.

Recent psycholinguistic research has also substantiated the important role of paradigmatic relationships for lexical access and processing, but it is far from clear how linguistic modelling and theorizing can deal with the wealth of paradigmatic relationships that seem to play a role in the processing of complex words and in the emergence of the diverse properties such words can have in a language. In this chapter we will take a closer and more systematic look at the pertinent phenomena and describe them in more detail. The more general implications of the data for morphological theory will then be discussed in Chapter 29.

23.2 TERMINOLOGICAL PRELIMINARIES

In the chapters on inflection, derivation, and compounding we mention a number of cases where the data do not lend themselves to a straightforward analysis in terms of the concatenation of established morphemes into a larger string. Instead, it seems that in such cases the resulting complex word with its specific properties can only have arisen through some mechanism (or mechanisms) that involves other, often morphologically complex, words. Before discussing these cases in more detail in Section 23.3, some terminological clarifications seem necessary.

In this chapter we use the term 'paradigm' in a wide sense to refer not only to sets of inflectionally related word-forms of the same lexeme, but also to the morphological relatedness of derived words and compounds. Thus, any complex word stands in a paradigmatic morphological relationship to those words that contain the same base or the same suffix.

Throughout this volume we have referred to sets of words with the same affix, such as *leader, reader, singer, walker,* etc. as 'morphological categories'. Sets of words with the same base, for example *impress, impression, impressive,* are known as 'morphological families'. The psycholinguistic reality of such paradigmatic relationships has been shown in many studies. For example, reaction times in lexical decision tasks vary significantly across morphological categories (Plag and Baayen 2009) and are dependent on the size of the morphological family of a given complex word (Schreuder and Baayen 1997).

Morphological relatedness is part of an even larger web of lexical relationships. Lexical relatedness may be based on a wide range of lexical properties, including orthographic, phonological, syntactic, semantic, or pragmatic ones. These kinds of relatedness may interact with morphological relatedness in intricate ways. As an illustration, consider rival morphological processes. Different suffixes such as *-er, -ant,* and *-ist* may all be used to derive agent nouns (as in *writer, discussant, artist*). As these derivatives belong to the same semantic class (that of agent nouns), they are all lexically related even though they might not share either the same base or the same affix. Nevertheless, this relatedness may have repercussions for the morphology since the existence of sets of lexically related forms in the lexicons of individual speakers may influence the choice of a particular affix to form a new word in a given situation. On a larger scale, the result of many such choices is known as morphological productivity.

Another instance of a relationship between semantic lexical relatedness and morphological relatedness can be found with verbal inflection. As discussed in Chapter 5.3.2, irregular verbs differ from regular verbs not only in how they inflect, but also in their degree of semantic relatedness to each other and to other words in the lexicon. Irregular verbs tend to have more semantic relations to other words, and are semantically more similar to each other than regulars are.

In the discussion that follows we include cases where the evidence strongly suggests an analysis that makes reference to morphological or lexical relatedness, and we will refer to such cases loosely as 'paradigmatic morphology'. In general, paradigmatic morphology is based on some sort of resonance or similarity between words in the lexicon (e.g. semantic, phonological, orthographic, etc.).

To account for such similarity-based paradigmatic effects, the notion of analogy is often invoked, although it is rarely spelled out in detail how exactly this mechanism would work, either in general, or in a given case. In those cases where it is, proportional relationships are sometimes appealed to, in which the comparison of three forms leads to the computation of the fourth form; see, for example, Becker (1993), Arndt-Lappe (2013) for discussion. Becker (1993: 3) gives the example repeated in (1).

(1)   deceive   :   deceivable
    =   syntagmatize   :   X   (= syntagmatizable)

Apart from 'analogy' at least two other concepts are currently used in referring to phenomena that imply the existence of paradigmatic effects in the make-up of complex words. The first of these concepts is back-formation, or 'back-derivation' as Marchand (1969) also terms it. Back-formation is traditionally defined as the deletion of an affix or affix-like sequence of segments on analogy to pairs of base and derivative that feature the affix in question (see also Chapters 2 and 13). A standard example is *edit* • *editor* on the basis of pairs such as *credit* • *creditor* or *exhibit* • *exhibitor*. In spite of the common conception of back-formation as the deletion of an affix (or something that appears to be an affix), however, back-formation is not actually a strictly syntagmatic process. Rather, back-formation critically depends on an analogical pairing of forms with and without the suffix:

> (2)   exhibitor   :   exhibit
>   =   editor   :   X (= edit)

Therefore, back-formation is at least partially paradigmatic in nature and can even be viewed as a special kind of analogy (see again Becker 1993 for discussion).

The second concept is variably known under the names of 'paradigm uniformity' (Steriade 2000), 'multiple correspondence' (e.g. Burzio 1998), 'stem selection' (Raffelsiefen 2004), or the 'split-base' effect (Steriade 1999) (see also Chapter 9.4.2 for discussion). The variation in the terminology reflects the range of theories in which the pertinent phenomena are treated, but these theoretical differences need not concern us here. All four terms refer to the fact that complex words often show phonological properties that strongly suggest influences not only from a single base, but from other words, or even a whole network of related words, that is from a word's paradigm. For example, *humídify* has the stress pattern of *humídity*, not of *húmid*, and *predáte* (that is, 'act as a predator') has inherited the stress pattern of *predátion*.

The notion of paradigm here again refers to sets of words that may share either the same base or the same affix, as described above, so that there are two kinds of paradigm. What is important in this particular context is that these two kinds of paradigm may impose conflicting requirements on a given derivative. Thus, all derivatives with a given base ideally have the same formally and semantically recognizable base, as in, for example, *crystal, crystalize, crystalline*. If they do not, we refer to the relationship between the bases as allomorphy if the difference concerns their phonological shape, as in, *produce, production, productive*, or as semantic opacity if apparent bases do not share the same meaning, as in, for example *list* and *listless*. At the same time, each of the different derivatives with that base has to conform to the formal and semantic requirements of its particular morphological category. This may result in conflicts between the two paradigmatic dimensions, for example, if a particular morphological category imposes a prosodic restriction on its derivatives that would involve some adjustment of the phonological shape of a given base, thus leading to base allomorphy. The base EXPLAIN is a case in point, as it appears as [ɪksˈpleɪn] in *explain, explains, explaining, explained, explainer, explainable*, but it has different allomorphs in *explanatory* or *explanation* due to the phonological requirements imposed by the morphological categories of *-ory* and *-ation*. Such conflicts often lead to non-uniform paradigms (from the perspective of the morphological family of the base, as with EXPLAIN), or to the exceptional behaviour of individual derivatives (from the perspective of a particular morphological category, as with, for example, *predáte*, which does not conform to the regular stress pattern of verbs in *-ate*).

It will become clear along the way that some pertinent phenomena can be subjected to equally convincing analyses in terms of either multiple correspondence or back-formation, and, furthermore, that analogy is such a wide notion that it can practically be applied to any case of back-formation and multiple correspondence. In the next sections we give an overview of paradigmatic effects in English morphology, with many of them having already been mentioned in previous chapters. In this overview we will use the terms 'analogy', 'back-formation', and 'multiple correspondence' to informally label and classify different kinds of phenomena in a preliminary fashion. In the following subsections we will remain largely agnostic as to what kind of mechanism might be best suited to formalize and explain the pertinent cases. This problem will be taken up in Chapter 29.

23.3 INFLECTION

We saw in Chapter 5 that the patterning of regular and irregular verb-forms in the different ablaut classes and the behaviour of nonce verbs in experiments suggests that irregular verbal inflection is best accounted for by some kind of analogical mechanism, according to which verbs of a particular phonological make-up tend to show similar inflectional behaviour. For example, the variation patterns found with verbal lexemes that have variable preterite forms and past participles suggests that the preferential a–b–b variant ablaut pattern (e.g. *keep, kept, kept*) attracts verbs on the basis of phonological similarities. In the same vein, ablaut forms in general are most likely with monosyllabic bases that also share some segmental characteristics (such as /s/-initial onset, /ɪ/ as their base vowel, or a final velar nasal, in various combinations).

In noun inflection, the variation in the pluralization of foreign loan words, but also occasionally of native words, suggests the work of analogy, too, as shown in the forms in (3). The variant *-i* plural of *octopus* is non-etymological and apparently coined on the basis of similar-sounding pluralized words of Latin origin. The variant plural *sistren* is found as a correspondent to the male *brethren*.

(3) alumni • octopi • octopuses
     brethren • sistren • sisters

With regard to genitive marking, there is a priming effect in the choice of synthetic marking with *-'s* and periphrastic marking with *of*. Given a particular noun in a genitive choice context, the presence of a particular genitive variant in the preceding discourse influences the choice of the variant with the given noun (see Chapter 7). This means that the exponent of the genitive depends not only on the properties of the noun phrase in question but also on other exponents of the same morphosyntactic category that happen to be co-activated at the moment of production. A similar online priming effect can be found in adjectival inflection, that is with the synthetic versus periphrastic encoding of the comparative and superlative (-*er* versus *more*, -*est* versus *most*, see Chapter 6).

23.4 DERIVATION

In derivation, we find many cases of back-formation into verbs. A large number of verbs in -*ate* are back-formed from diverse kinds of complex noun. The evidence for this kind of analysis comes mainly from their semantic or phonological properties, which clearly relate them to their complex bases (see Chapter 13 for detailed discussion). Where available, the earliest dates of attestation often support a back-formation analysis. The forms in (4) illustrate some uncontroversial cases of back-formation. Those in (5) are cases of multiple correspondence with derivatives from various categories.

(4)   advection ◆ advect, escalator ◆ escalate, escalation ◆ escalate, fabrication ◆ nano-fabrication ◆ nano-fabricate, optimized ◆ nano-optimized ◆ nano-optimize

(5)   húmid ◆ humídity ◆ humídify, cátholic ◆ cathólicism ◆ cathólicize, confér ◆ cónference ◆ cònferée, remedy$_{N/V}$ ◆ remédial ◆ remédiable

The forms in (6) seem especially interesting as, depending on the theoretical background, they can be analysed with equal justification as being back-formations, cases of multiple correspondence, and analogical formations.

(6)   formátion ◆ formáte 'fly in formation', gelátion ◆ geláte, lenátion ◆ lènáte, notátion ◆ notáte (~ nótate), olátion ◆ oláte, predátion ◆ predáte, solátion ◆ soláte, solvátion ◆ solváte

They may be seen as back-formations as they are based on corresponding complex nouns, they may be analysed as cases of multiple correspondence as their morphosyntax is that of other -*ate* formations, but their stress pattern is not in accordance with the regular pattern of -*ate* verbs. Instead, it is faithful to the complex base from which the verb is derived. And, since the creation of the forms in (5) involves patterns of similarity that could be expressed in terms of proportional analogy, all these forms can be classified as analogical formations, too.

The items in (7) are -*ate* formations that are also based on individual (sets of) model words, but do not involve back-formation (all twentieth-century neologisms from the *OED*).

(7) active • activate • inactive • inactivate

active • radioactive • activate • radioactivate

regular • regulate • stereoregular • stereoregulate

plasticate • masticate

Finally, (8) presents a similar case of analogy based on a single model word, but outside the verbal domain, and also without the paradigmatic support of a morphological category. Thus, before the coinage of the new words, *singleton* was the only established word with the suffix *-ton*.

(8) singleton • doubleton • tripleton

We also count as paradigmatic morphology sets of words with related suffixes in which every word of one morphological category has a potential correspondent in another category. Sometimes all derivatives with the same base are attested, sometimes not. Consider, for example, the suffixes *-ism*, *-ist*, and the combination *-ist-ic*. For each abstract noun in *-ism* there is a potential personal noun in *-ist* denoting the follower of the theory or framework denoted by the corresponding form in *-ism*, and a potential adjective in *-ist-ic* (for example, *communist • communism • communistic; anarchist • anarchism • anarchistic*). We are faced in such cases with the curious situation that the meaning of the personal noun in *-ist* and the adjective in *-ist-ic* incorporate the meaning of the abstract noun in *-ism*, although the abstract-noun-forming suffix is no longer present in the personal noun or adjective.

This is illustrated with two pertinent forms in (9), from COCA. The derivative *boycottist* in (9a) is not synonymous with the agent noun *boycotter* 'someone who boycotts' but means something like 'someone supporting boycottism', with *boycottism* referring to the 'use of boycotts as a form of protest or punishment' (*OED*). Similarly, as shown in (9b), an *abstractionist* is someone who is part of the artistic school of abstractionism, as implicitly indicated by the adjective *major* preceding the derivative in question.

(9) a. *Africa Today 1990*: The ANC itself, as well as the CP and the COD, supported candidates for parliamentary elections in the 1950s and only moved gradually to a totally **boycottist** position (and had cordial relations with Buthelezi until 1979).

b. *American Craft 2003*: Marvin Lipofsky explored many forms in his artistic development, achieving a style that defines him as a major **abstractionist**.

There are other examples of morphological categories that appear to participate in paradigmatic relationships. One of these is the set *-ate*, *-ant*, and *-ance* (e.g. *hesitate • hesitant • hesitancy, alternate • alternant • alternance, participate • participant • participance*) discussed in Chapter 10. In a case like this, it is impossible to decide whether the base of the *-ance* nominal is a verb in *-ate* or an adjective in *-ant*. Other cases of paradigmatic morphology that have been mentioned in earlier chapters are the corresponding forms in *-ive* and *-ify* (*subjective • subjectify*) and those in *-ize* and *-ism* (*baptize • baptism*) (see Chapter 13).

From the point of view of paradigmatic relatedness, it is quite striking that new words of a particular morphological category are often coined in the textual neighbourhood of morphologically related forms with the same base, but a different suffix. This is illustrated in (10) (see also (21)). Examples (10b) to (10e) are from COCA.

(10) a. The fact is, saying Yes hadn't been a **pointless** exercise at all. It had been **point*ful*** (*Wallace 2008:394*, italics in the original)

b. *Parenting 2001*: Both the **haircutter** and the **haircuttee** will need a little psychological preparation.

c. *Today's Parent 2000*: Whether your child is the **snubber** or the "**snubbee**," your discreet guidance now is going to go a long way toward laying the groundwork for the turbulent teens.

d. *Outdoor Life 2007*: For the observer, it may seem as if the **falling** person arrives at his landing spot in a mere fraction of a second. For the **fallee**, however, there is a great deal of time to think.

e. *Atlanta Journal Constitution 2005*: Compared to my colleagues who struggle with more challenging **commutes**, I'm a lucky man.... Trim 8-hour **commute**, then let's talk # You can learn a lot being a "**commutant**."

23.5 COMPOUNDING

In compounding, there are many forms that are modelled on particular existing compounds, with the new compound inheriting crucial components of the institutionalized meaning of the model compound. A selection of such compounds is given in (11).

(11) aftermath • beforemath (*Wordspy*)

carpooling • cowpooling 'Purchasing a whole cow or side of beef from a local farmer and sharing the cost among multiple families' (*Wordspy*)

earthquake • seaquake 'a submarine eruption or earthquake' (*OED*)

hangover • hangunder 'the funny feeling you get when you wake up after a night of not drinking and you're not hungover like usual' (*Urban Dictionary*)

honeymoon • babymoon 'romantic vacation during a pregnancy' (COCA)

horse whisperer • dog whisperer 'A person who has, or claims to have, a natural ability to relate to or connect with dogs' (*Wordspy*)

housewife • househusband 'male partner who carries out the household role and duties traditionally associated with a housewife' (*OED*)

rat race • mouse race 'lower-stress life-style' (*Wordspy*)

strawman • straw poll 'an apparent but not real poll, a test poll' (COCA)

Back-formation also frequently leads to non-canonical compounds, as is frequently the case with verbal compounds, illustrated in (12).

(12)   a. *denominal:* babysitter ◆ babysit, brainwashing ◆ brainwash, chainsmoker ◆ chain-smoke, crash-landing ◆ crash-land, ghetto-blaster ◆ ghetto-blast

      b. *de-adjectival:* horror-struck ◆ horror-strike, tailor-made ◆ tailor-make

There are also some general effects of morphological families with compounds. As discussed in more detail in Chapter 19, there is very good evidence that stress-assignment to NN compounds is largely predictable from the stress-behaviour of related compounds that have the same left or right constituent (e.g. Plag *et al.* 2007; Plag 2010; Arndt-Lappe 2011). Such constituent families are also predictive of compound stress in a different way. The smaller the constituent family of the second constituent of a given compound, the more likely it is that the NN compound will be right-stressed (Bell and Plag 2012).

Similar paradigmatic effects can be found with compound interpretation. Psycholinguistic experiments have shown that the semantic interpretation of new compounds heavily relies on the distribution of pertinent meanings in the pertinent constituent families (Gagné and Shoben 1997; Gagné 2001). Consider, for example, the right constituent family of *mountain magazine*, which in the majority contains compounds for which the semantic interpretation is one in which the left constituent denotes something that is the main topic of the press organ denoted by the second constituent.

23.6 SPLINTERS

Another pertinent phenomenon, which shows a mixture of syntagmatic and paradigmatic traits, is the emergence of splinters, which were defined in Chapter 2 as originally (mostly) non-morphemic portions of a word that have been split off and used in the formation of new words with a specific new meaning. The use, recognition, and interpretation of a splinter as found in a new word thus necessarily requires a paradigmatic relationship. Interestingly, the new morpheme, that is the splinter, receives its new meaning only through that paradigmatic relationship. An oft-cited example of a splinter which still yields the occasional neologism (e.g. *Breastgate* in 2010, COCA) is -*gate* 'scandal, disaster', based on Nixon's *Watergate* scandal. The meaning assigned to the string -*gate* only emerged when the first new word containing it was coined on the basis of a semantic and formal similarity to the well-known existing word. The birth of splinters is thus a paradigmatic process itself, and so is the coinage of further similar words, at least until the new formative is established with that meaning in the lexicon. Given that splinters seem to be only moderately productive, it may even be the case that most of them are never firmly established as bound morphemes. But when they do become more productive, they may even start a life as a free form, as in the case of *burger* 'patty served on a bun'.

In (13) to (30) we present some more splinters with their meaning paraphrased, their presumed model word(s), some of their derivatives, and one example in context. Examples are from COCA, unless otherwise specified; the orthography found in COCA is preserved:

(13) *-ati* 'elite or would-be elite group related to base word': literati ◆ arterati ◆ chatterati ◆ designerati ◆ glitterati ◆ hip-erati ◆ hipsterati ◆ jazzerati ◆ Niggerati ◆ Twitterati

U.S. News & World Report 2000: Both Burns and Ward see their work as an attempt to reach beyond the factional discord of the "**jazzerati**" to introduce nonaficionados, and particularly younger Americans, to the story of one of the nation's most distinctive musical traditions.

(14) *-bot* 'robot': Cajunbot ◆ Hotbot ◆ Frankenbot ◆ Spybot ◆ Stickybot

National Geographic 2009: Engineers studied these terrific toes to make a robot called **Stickybot**. Stickybot uses a material like the hairs on the gecko's toes.

(15) *-burger* 'patty served on a bun': hamburger ◆ bambiburger ◆ beanburger ◆ beefburger ◆ bisonburger ◆ buffaloburger ◆ cheeseburger ◆ fishburger ◆ nutburger ◆ pauaburger (*found on the menu of a New Zealand restaurant*) ◆ peaburger ◆ quailburger ◆ shrimpburger ◆ slugburger ◆ tofuburger ◆ steakburger ◆ kosherburger ◆ kiwiburger (*Note that in the last two examples, the first element is not an ingredient. A kosherburger is just a burger that is kosher, and a kiwiburger a kind of burger advertised in New Zealand, rather than a patty made of kiwi.*)

Southern Living 2003: There are as many stories in Corinth surrounding the history of the **slugburger** as there are places serving them (and that's a lot).

(16) *-delic* 'wild, mind-altering': echodelic ◆ folkadelic ◆ funkadelic ◆ plaque-adelic ◆ psychedelic ◆ sample-delic ◆ scallydelic ◆ shagadelic ◆ shankadelic ◆ slumadelic

Rolling Stone 2003: "We call it **slumadelic**," said Big Boi of OutKast's far-reaching blend of hip-hop, funk, rock and otherworldly sounds.

(17) *-holic* 'person addicted to': bagoholic ◆ beanoholic ◆ chocoholic ◆ dealaholic ◆ eventaholic ◆ fishaholic ◆ hoardaholic ◆ playaholic ◆ sexoholic ◆ workaholic ◆ yogaholic

Prevention 1990: If today Bob is a "**yogaholic**," it has a lot to do with the fact that up until four years ago he was a workaholic.

(18) *-illion* 'a very large number': million ◆ billion ◆ trillion ◆ zillion ◆ bazillion ◆ bajillion ◆ frillion ◆ jillion ◆ gajillion ◆ gazillion ◆ kajillion ◆ kazillion

Scholastic Scope 2007: I mean, like I was going to give myself a facial, touch up my highlights, pick out an outfit, and about a **gajillion** other things.

(19) *-tarian* 'someone with a diet restriction': vegetarian ◆ eggitarian ◆ flexitarian ◆ fruitarian ◆ pescetarian ◆ pollotarian ◆ value-tarian

USA Today 1997: Parnevik first tried volcanic sand after meeting a Swedish "**fruitarian**" who sold him on the benefits of an all-fruit diet, which purports to clean the toxic waste from your system.

(20) *-licious* 'appealing': delicious ♦ bagelicious ♦ barfalicious ♦ bootielicious ♦ diva-licious ♦ goodielicious ♦ lowcarbolicious ♦ pig-a-licious ♦ snugglelicious ♦ thug-a-licious ♦ weavealicious

So not the drama 2007: Cool, laid-back Sarah was the cream, light cocoa-complexioned, thick curly hair to her ears, to Jessica's coffee-bean skin, broad nose, thick lips, and extremely straight **weavealicious** hair down past her shoulders.

(21) *-matic* 'automatic (device)': automatic ♦ airmatic ♦ bowlamatic ♦ chop-o-matic ♦ dripomatic ♦ futurmatic ♦ inflatomatic ♦ mince-o-matic ♦ randomatic ♦ sculpt-o-matic ♦ towelmatic ♦ vote-o-matic

ABC_20/20 1993: How many of those did you sell? Mr. POPEIL: Oh, hundreds of thousands. Hundreds of thousands of the **Chop-O-Matic**, **Dial-A-Matic**, **Veg-A-Matic**, **Mince-O-Matic**, the smokeless ashtray, Miracle Broom, the Ronco Clean Air Machine.

(22) *-o* 'language production error': typo ♦ speako (*Wordspy*)

Speech recognition systems are seeing increased use in warehouses, although users must avoid substituting '**speakos**' for 'typos' when designing the system. (2001 cited in *Wordspy*)

(23) *-orama* 'event or display of considerable size': panorama ♦ Adorama ♦ Audiorama ♦ Astrorama ♦ cashorama ♦ Censorama ♦ Clitorama ♦ comporama ♦ fawnorama ♦ Junk-o-rama ♦ Motorama ♦ Pianorama ♦ Pornorama ♦ Sensorama ♦ spin-orama ♦ Sponge-o-rama ♦ Teaserama ♦ Striporama ♦ tack-orama ♦ voodoorama

Christian Science Monitor 2007: I wrote about the sport in the 1960s and 1970s, which was the medieval age compared with today's big-bucks **cashorama**. The players then uniformly were underpaid.

(24) *-rific* 'extremely (good), characterized by': terrific ♦ ballerific ♦ calorific ♦ cheeserific ♦ moisturific ♦ slow-jammerific ♦ splatterific ♦ stuporific ♦ terrorific ♦ Tiggerific ♦ Twitterific

Entertainment Weekly 2007: The "Run It" singer has love—or at least lust—on his mind with songs like the T-Pain-featuring "Kiss Kiss," and the **slow-jammerific** "Take You Down."

(25) *-scape* 'view or picture of a scene or scenery': landscape ♦ Aquascape ♦ cityscape ♦ dreamscape ♦ hardscape ♦ Netscape ♦ memoryscape ♦ moonscape ♦ manscape ♦ nightmarescape ♦ streetscape ♦ soundscape ♦ townscape ♦ tablescape ♦ Xeriscape

Studies in the Novel 2008: These representations associate images of the slave trade with typical post-traumatic responses in characters who live hundreds of years after that era of violence and loss that marred the African **memoryscape**.

(26)   *-stan* 'country': Afghanistan ◆ Pakistan ◆ Bin Ladenstan ◆ divorcistan ◆ Londonistan ◆ Islamistan ◆ New Yorkistan ◆ Refugeestan ◆ Richistan ◆ skate-istan ◆ Youngistan

   The song is you 2009: Julian Donahue married in optimistic confusion, separated in pessimistic confusion, and now was wandering toward a mistrustful **divorcistan**, a coolly celibate land.

(27)   *-tainment* 'entertainment': entertainment ◆ advertainment ◆ agritainment ◆ asthetainment ◆ autotainment ◆ charitainment ◆ communitatinment ◆ dinotainment ◆ edutainment ◆ eatertainment ◆ exertainment ◆ infotainment ◆ infomerciatainment ◆ intertainment ◆ kid-ertainment ◆ newsy-tainment ◆ psychotainment ◆ shoppertainment ◆ shop-o-tainment ◆ skankertainment ◆ retailtainment ◆ technotainment

   Denver Post 2002: The Mills Corp. and developer Greg Stevinson are spending $ 300 million to build the '**shoppertainment**' mecca, anchored by discount outlets of Neiman Marcus and Saks Fifth Avenue, SuperTarget and Gart Sports.

(28)   *-tronic* 'electronic, futuristic': electronic ◆ animatronic ◆ conceptronic ◆ daytronic ◆ easytronic ◆ ethnotronic ◆ geartronic ◆ mediatronic ◆ parktronic ◆ psychotronic

   Futurist 2000: Using credit-card databases, the companies develop profiles of road users and adjust their **mediatronic** and other outdoor displays to offer products and services of interest to drivers with these profiles.

(29)   *-ware* 'software': software ◆ crimeware ◆ eduware ◆ freeware ◆ malware ◆ netware ◆ spyware ◆ trialware ◆ CaptureWare

   PC World 2007: Then there's **trialware**, or preloaded software that functions only for a set period, generally 30 to 90 days.

(30)   *-zilla* 'overbearing exemplar': Godzilla ◆ bridezilla ◆ Babyzilla ◆ Clonezilla ◆ Cordzilla ◆ cowzilla ◆ Dogzilla ◆ ErrorZilla ◆ groomzilla ◆ Hogzilla ◆ Nunzilla ◆ Ringzilla ◆ Rockzilla ◆ Shopzilla ◆ Stopzilla ◆ teenzilla

   Money 2006: I'm fairly certain that I'm not the only parent who doesn't want a **teenzilla** living in the upstairs bedroom –

There are a number of interesting observations to be made. First, some of the splinters have the same meaning as the full forms on which they are originally based. This is, for example, the case with *-bot*, *-tainment*, and *-ware* (in computer terminology), perhaps even with *-stan*. This being the case, the pertinent new derivatives could also be analysed as blends, as we will discuss below. What may speak against such an analysis, however, is the general structure of blends. Thus, in their vast majority, the first elements of blends lose some of their phonological material (see Chapter 19), whereas the forms in (14), (26), (27), and (29) do not show such a clear patterning. Nevertheless, those forms that do feature phonological loss in the first part, such as *intertainment* 'internet entertainment' or *exertainment* 'exercise entertainment', seem to lend themselves to a straightforward analysis in terms of blending. In general, a blend analysis is impossible in those cases where the splinter carries a meaning that is different from that of the original word. This is actually the case for the majority of splinters shown in (13) to (30), that is for *-ati, -illion, -tarian, -o, -orama, -rific, -scape, -zilla*. In sum, only a small minority of potential splinter derivatives lend themselves to a convincing analysis as blends.

Second, some cases in (13) to (30) lend themselves more than others to an analysis as compounds instead of derivatives involving splinters. Formations with *-burger*, for example, are clearly more on the side of compounding than *-tarian*, as *burger* is also used as a free form by now, but with *bot* it is perhaps unclear whether it is a free form for speakers outside the robotics scene, in spite of its being attested as a free form in COCA. With most other splinters a compound analysis is certainly not convincing. For instance, although *ware* is a free form and can be found in many compounds (such as *glassware, hardware, silverware, stoneware*, or *warehouse*) the splinter *-ware* has a distinct meaning 'software' and seems not to be usable as free form with that meaning. Again, all other splinters are clearly bound morphs, which speaks against a compound analysis.

Third, splinters may easily become polysemous, as for example, with *value-tarian*, in which the object of the restriction is extended to non-food consumables, as shown in (31). Another case in point may be *-gate*, whose meaning oscillates between 'scandal' and 'disaster', illustrated in (32).

(31)   *Money 1995*: Bob Rodriguez, 46, who has led $181 million FPA Capital since 1984, is a devout **value-tarian**. He buys only small-cap stocks that look cheap on the basis of their earnings or book value (the per-share worth of the company's assets).

(32)   *San Francisco Chronicle 1992*: Perhaps eventually we will look back on our government's performance at the Earth Summit as an aberration, an environmental **Riogate** or Bay of Pigs, a lapse that woke us up to the need for our country once again to become the leader of the Environmental Revolution that is sweeping the globe.

Fourth, as indicated by the many forms in the corpus that are found with capitalization of the first letter, a large number of words with splinters are proper nouns, often referring to brand names or names of specific products. This suggests that coinages using splinters are perceived as rather unusual and are seen as linguistic forms that attract more attention than many other words would. Such a view seems justified on psycholinguistic grounds since the online recognition and interpretation of pertinent forms seems to require more processing effort than simple lexical access to a memorized form would.

Fifth, as splinters heavily rely on analogy it is not surprising that we find variability in the possible phonological shape of formations. In other words, the degree of phonological similarity to the model word may not be uniform across formations, as can be seen with *retailtainment* versus *shop-o-tainment* versus *kid-ertainment*, or *eggitarian* versus *fruitarian*.

It is also worth mentioning that splinters seem to have a strong tendency to emerge from nouns and to derive nouns. Although there are several splinters that derive from adjectives (*-delic, -holic, -licious, -matic, -rific, -tronic*), even among these the new formations are often nouns (especially proper nouns) rather than the expected adjectives.

Finally, a closer look at the various sets of forms shows that the initial elements often share certain semantic features. This may be due to the meaning of splinter, as in the case of *-tarian*, which, due to its own semantics, primarily takes bases that denote food items. However, even when the meaning of the splinter is not so restrictive, we still find rather coherent sets of bases. For example, *-zilla* derivatives seem to be primarily based on animate bases, and *-ati* derivatives have bases denoting concepts related to art, music, and culture. Note also the choice of *speak* as a base for *-o*, which is semantically closely related to *type*, which in turn leads the highly specific meaning of the splinter *-o* assumed here. All of this suggests that not just any form is selected by speakers to participate in analogical processes, but that these forms are selected on the basis of already existing, more or less salient similarities.

23.7 Conclusion

In this chapter we have looked at morphological processes that seem to necessitate an analysis in terms of paradigmatic structure and analogy. We have seen that such processes are too numerous to be dismissed as isolated exceptions in an otherwise well-behaved system. Paradigmatic morphology can be found in any subdomain, that is in inflection, derivation, and compounding, and paradigmatic processes are based on orthographic, phonological, morphological, semantic, and syntactic similarities between related forms. Furthermore it can be observed that the computations leading to new word-forms or new lexemes seem generally to suggest an analysis that makes use of proportional analogy. Notably, we often find a web of words contributing to the emergence of a new word, instead of only a single model word. Any theory of morphology, or of analogy, would need to be able to account for these phenomena. We will return to this subject in Chapter 29, where we will consider how paradigmatic facts can best be accounted for, how general a mechanism of analogy might be needed, and how the difference between regular and idiosyncratic cases might be dealt with.

PART VI

Themes

CHAPTER 24

....

Inflection versus derivation

24.1 PROSPECTUS

In this chapter we take up the vexed question of the difference between inflection and derivation as it applies to English. We consider the kinds of criteria that might distinguish between
the two, the value of the distinction where English is concerned, and features of English that
make applying the distinction awkward.

24.2 THE BASIS OF INFLECTION AND DERIVATION

The distinction between inflectional morphology and derivational morphology is an ancient
one. Fundamentally, it is a matter of the means used to create new lexemes (derivational affixes
among other processes) and those used to mark the role of the lexeme in a particular sentence
(accidence, inflectional morphology). In the description of many languages, including most
obviously the so-called inflected (flectional, fusional) languages, the distinction is clear and
uncontroversial in the vast majority of instances. The problem with the distinction has come,
historically, in giving a definition to the two types of morphology, particularly a definition
based on necessary and sufficient criteria. Part of the difficulty here arises because the distinction seems to depend on a recognition of the distinction between lexemes and word-forms of
lexemes, yet that distinction is defined in terms of the distinction between inflection and derivation, so that there is a constant danger of having a circularity built into the definitions. In
Chapter 2 we attempted to avoid this particular problem by providing an ostensive definition
of inflection for English, and allowing everything else to be derivation by default.

The literature provides us with at least two ways of dealing with this awkwardness. The first
is to define inflectional and derivational morphology as canonical categories rather than as
classical categories. This approach is taken by a number of scholars, including Scalise (1988),
Dressler (1989), Plank (1994), Stump (1998), Bauer (2003b). These scholars prioritize different features of inflection or derivation in their discussions, and Plank (1994) gives a lengthy
list of possible features of one or the other prototypical category. This includes features such
as the following.

- Inflection is typically formally regular; derivation may not be.
- Inflection is typically semantically regular; derivation may not be.
- Inflection is typically fully productive; derivation typically shows (unmotivated) gaps in productivity.
- Inflection does not add significantly to the meaning of the base, but contextualizes that meaning; derivation adds to the meaning of the base.
- Inflection allows the prediction that a form will exist to cover some notion; derivation does not allow the same security of prediction.
- Inflection does not change the major category (noun, verb, etc.), but derivation may.
- Inflection is what is relevant to the syntax; derivation is not syntactically relevant.
- You cannot replace an inflected form with an uninflected form in a sentence, but you can replace an inflectional base (which may have been created by derivational morphology) with a morphologically simple form (that is, one belonging to a different lexeme).
- Where both occur in the same word-form, derivational affixes are typically closer to the root than inflectional ones.

These features are an attempt to get at the canonical characteristics of inflection and derivation, but none of them quite gets to the heart of the distinction. Inflection must be available to be added to words which the speaker has never encountered before, its meaning and form must thus be regular, and the precise form is by the syntactic structure in which it occurs. Derivation changes lexemes, which may mean changing word class, but provides the input to inflection, on a par with morphologically simple bases. Some fusional languages provide challenges for the individual criteria or the distinction as a whole, but do not invalidate the basic division. They may, for instance, have lexemes which do not inflect, they may have defective paradigms, in which certain expected forms do not occur, they may order some affixes in unexpected ways, they may have very regular derivation, particular semantic categories may belong to an unexpected morphological category. The existence of such instances does not upset the canonical distinction. Neither does the fact that the application of individual features may be difficult to determine in particular instances.

Particularly important among these criteria has been the notion that inflection is what is relevant to the syntax (Anderson 1992). But this criterion presupposes that we are clear on what we mean by 'relevant to the syntax'. The problem is that the decision as to what is relevant to syntax is at least in part theory bound, so that adherents of one theory might be inclined to see as inflectional what in another theory might be deemed derivational.

A second (and not necessarily mutually exclusive) way to deal with the awkwardness of the inflection–derivation distinction might be to break inflection and derivation down further into subcategories. However, the only further division which has become generally accepted is that between inherent and contextual inflection (Booij 1996a). Inherent inflection is that inflection which is meaningful for the sentence, representing distinctions that are semantically intrinsic to specific syntactic categories—the expression of tense on the verb, for example, the expression of person and number on nouns, or the expression of degree (comparative and superlative) on adjectives. Inherent inflection is thus conceptually closer to derivation, in the sense that choice of a particular form (say a first person singular noun) affects the semantic interpretation of the sentence. Contextual inflection, on the other hand, is entirely driven by syntactic environment: for example, the expression of subject person and number on the verb, or the expression of case on the noun are all instances of contextual inflection.

Subdivisions of the category of derivation are not widely accepted, and yet it is well-known that in some languages evaluative affixation (diminutive and augmentative affixes) often behaves as a rather unusual instance of derivation: it may re-apply to its own output; the order of diminutive affix and plural affix may not be as predicted by general rules (see Bauer 1997a); and evaluative affixes may occur in paradigmatic relationships with more canonically inflectional categories like singular and plural. Accordingly, it seems reasonable to assume that the category of derivation is not monolithic either, even if the divisions within it are not so well established.

In principle, at least, it might be open to an investigator to claim that there is, in a given language, no distinction to be drawn between inflection and derivation. To our knowledge no such claim has ever been made about English, but various points have been made about English which indicate that it is not necessarily clear where to draw the line between the two categories in English.

24.3 SOME PROBLEM CASES

In this section we examine some of the problem cases that have been raised in the literature or where we are aware that evidence for a particular affix's being either inflectional or derivational is compromised.

24.3.1 The nominal plural

In Chapter 7 we defined the plural as part of inflection in English. On the other hand, Beard (1982), within a framework in which derivation (in his terms, the process of changing the semantic or morphosyntactic content of a lexeme) is distinguished from affixation (the actual process of adding phonological material to a base), argues that the plural, across Indo-European languages, is a derivational category.

First, he argues that plural marking in English, like derivational marking, is formally irregular. The existence of plurals such as *alumni, children, deer, feet, matrices, mice, oxen, wives* and so on illustrates this. The problem with this claim is that it is formulated as a claim about classical categories: if something does not fit into category C, it must fit into category not-C. If, on the other hand, we look at our categories as being prototypes, then a few examples that fail to show the feature of formal regularity do not discredit the notion that the prototype is still relevant. Of course, we may then get into an argument as to how many irregular forms there are and how many there need to be for the feature not to hold, an argument which, it seems to us, would be unfruitful. But we note that in Chapter 7 we pointed out that Latin plurals are usually not obligatory, and that Italian plurals are really cases of code-switching and not cases of English inflection. In other words, the number of irregular forms that are obligatorily part of the English system is considerably smaller than Beard would imply.

The next argument for considering plural-marking in English as derivational is that there are a number of nouns marked with the plural morph which fail to behave like plurals: *blues, greens, measles, oats, scissors, shorts* and so on. However the semantics of such forms is to be represented, grammatically most of them are treated as plurals by the grammar. *Your greens/ oats/scissors/shorts are/*is on the table. Measles* is treated variably by speakers of English (possibly on a geographical basis). Some words like *draughts, fives, ninepins* are either singular by elision—*(a game of) draughts*—or by metonymy.

A further argument is that many nouns do not have plural forms, so that the plural is not fully productive. It is certainly true that some nouns such as *knowledge, mahogany, peace, pork, waving* are unusual in the plural form, but we argue elsewhere (Chapter 25) that nouns that normally lack plural forms are almost always subject to coercion (Jackendoff 1991; Pustejovsky 1995), such that given the right context they are quite naturally inflected for the plural. The example in (1) from COCA is illustrative.

(1)   *Chicago Sun-Times 1996*: Armour now has a line of seasoned and marinated **porks.**

To summarize, although an argument can be made that the plural sporadically fails to exhibit a number of the features of inflection, for the most part plural marking is consistent with a canonical notion of what inflection is.

24.3.2 Adverbial marking with *-ly*

Traditionally, because *-ly* produces adverbs from adjectives and so brings about a change in word class it has been treated as derivational. However, several theorists, among them Haspelmath (1996) and Giegerich (2012) have argued that it is inflectional. We have considered the status of this suffix at length in Chapter 15, concluding that the evidence is inconclusive, and we have been very tentative in our classification elsewhere as a result. We will not reiterate those arguments here, but refer the reader to Chapter 15, where they may be found.

24.3.3 Ordinal *-th*

Ordinal *-th* is rarely discussed in the literature on inflection and derivation, perhaps because its status is not clear. First we have to recognize that there is considerable suppletion in the derivation of ordinals, with *first, second,* and *third* replacing **oneth, *twoth, *threeth.* Suppletion, except in the case of proper names, is probably more usual in inflection than in derivation in English (see Chapter 2). However, it is not clear that this argument is helpful: unless we can prove in some independent and non-circular way that suppletion is unique to inflection, the fact that there is suppletion in these forms cannot be taken conclusively to prove their status as inflectional. The suffix *-th* is formally regular (apart from the suppletion), semantically regular, productive (see below), and obligatory. Whether or not the change from cardinal to ordinal number involves a word class change is perhaps controversial. Yet the change from *five* to *fifth* is probably felt as being lexical rather than grammatical: standard dictionaries tend to treat these words as separate lemmas and as independent lexical items linked by their meanings.

The criterion of productivity is also problematic since the productivity of *-th* can be viewed two ways (Bauer 2001: 148). Either there is no productivity, because *-th* is already listed in virtually every possible environment, and *32,300,426th* simply illustrates a new occurrence of *sixth,* or *32,300,426th* is a new application of *-th.* The application of *-th* to words like *zillion* and *squillion* and its application to non-numerals like *n* and *umpteen* argue for a limited degree of productivity, even if the first of these two solutions is adopted. However, the first solution suggests that we are dealing with derivation rather than with inflection.

As with other suffixes dealt with here, the features of *-th* split between inflection and derivation.

24.3.4 Other numerical formatives: *-teen* and *-ty*

Both *-teen* and *-ty* have things in common with ordinal *-th.* The question of their productivity is dubious, for the same reasons as were presented above (although, again there are occasional productive uses as in *umpteen, umpty*). They can be followed by *-th,* which gives ambiguous information as to whether they are inflectional or derivational, as was seen in Section 24.3.3. They can be followed by *-fold,* whose semantics suggest that it is a derivational affix rather than a compound element. Both *-teen* and *-ty* are formally and semantically regular, though with suppletion for *eleven* and *twelve.* They both seem to be treated by standard dictionaries as lexical affixes. Overall, they both look rather more derivational than ordinal *-th,* but they do not precisely match the canonical pattern.

24.3.5 The participles

When forms ending in *-ing* and *-ed* (or one of its irregular congeners) are used in the creation of complex verb groups there is no doubt as to their status as inflectional affixes. So the instances in (2) illustrate inflectional *-ing* and *-ed.* However, when the same forms are used to create words used as premodifiers (3) or when *-ing* is used to create more nominal forms (4), there is doubt as to their status in the inflection/derivation categorization.

(2) He is driving to Cologne today.

　　She has implicated one of her colleagues.

(3) It's the driving dynamics that make the Toyota appealing. (*adapted from a COCA example, Popular Mechanics 2009*)

　　The implicated students deny any involvement.

(4) The driving of speedboats requires immense concentration.

　　His driving is atrocious.

We have the option, of course, of viewing the *-ing* in (2) as being a different affix from the *-ing* in (3) and (4), or of seeing the examples in (3) and (4) as some form of conversion or zero-derivation (though see Chapter 25). It is also possible to see the examples in (3) and (4) as instances of class-changing inflection as suggested by Haspelmath (1996). These examples will be taken up in more detail in Chapter 25, where we suggest that any decision as to whether the participles should be treated as instances of derivation or inflection is an intricate matter that, like so many of the examples discussed in this chapter, is intimately dependent on one's theoretical framework.

24.3.6 Summary

In short, English has several borderline examples which seem to throw the distinction between inflection and derivation into doubt. However, where we have borderline cases for canonical categories, they do not invalidate the basic distinction, as long as there are clear-cut examples at both ends, and as long as the distinction is useful where it can be applied. It is to those examples that we now turn.

24.4 Clear-cut distinctions

In this section we will consider the difference between the nominal plural (regularly of the form <(e)s>) compared with the nominal collective (the affix *-ery*) (following Plank 1994), and the present participle *-ing* compared with the deverbal nominalization *-ation*. The point is to show that these relatively similar processes can be appropriately divided into inflectional and derivational along the expected lines, and that the division can be drawn in English.

Formally, most of these affixes seem to be regular. The <(e)s> marking the regular plural covers, as is well-known, three distinct pronunciations (/z/, /ɪz/ and /s/), each of which occurs in a well-defined environment. The *-ery* affix usually has only the single form *-ery* (and where that occurs following a base spelled with a final <e>, there is elision of one of the <e>s, as in *tracery*). The *-ing* affix also has a single form. Only *-ation* shows a range of forms whose distribution might be unpredictable: *competition, compulsion, definition, hospitalization, inhibition, resolution, starvation* (see Chapter 10). The suffix *-ation* is also attached to unpredictable base allomorphs in *compulsion, consumption, perception, redemption, reduction*, and so on. So *-ation* is clearly less regular than the other affixes.

Although there are instances where we might have the <(e)s> form with no clear plural meaning (see Chapter 7), in general the meaning of this affix is regular. While it arguably has a different meaning when added to non-count nouns as in *breads, toothpastes* from what it has when added to count nouns such as *heads, tastes*, the meaning is predictable from the countable or uncountable nature of the noun phrase as a whole.

The *-ing* suffix is again entirely semantically regular, both when used for strictly inflectional purposes as part of a verb group, and also when used as a nominalization (see Chapter 10).

The suffixes *-ery* and *-ation* are not semantically regular. In *cookery* the suffix can be interpreted as an event or product, in *fernery* as a location or a collective, in *baffoonery* as a noun denoting a type of behaviour, in *snuggery* as a location on an adjectival base. We suggested in Chapter 12 that this range of polysemy is not unexpected, although the reading we get for any given form derived in *-ery* is highly dependent on the nature of the base and the context in which the form is found (see also Lieber 2004). Like *-ery*, the suffix *-ation* has a range of readings depending on the base verb and the syntactic context in which the derived form is found, including event, state, location, product, and means (see the discussions in Chapter 12).

Since it is quite possible to have plural locations, forms like *rookeries* are totally legitimate and show inflectional *-s* further from the root than derivational *-ery*. Similarly with plurals like *vacations* or *transmissions*, the plural occurs outside of *-ation*. COCA gives the example of *transformationing* from the spoken part of the corpus. So these suffixes seem to show canonical behaviour of derivational and inflectional affixes. However, in order to make the observation, we have to know that they are, indeed, derivational and inflectional, so this observation risks being circular.

On the whole, plural marking is not obligatory, since the choice between singular and plural marking on nouns is meaningful: this is inherent, not contextual inflection. However, we can construct environments in which a plural noun is required: *a pair of ~, between the ~, both ~* (e.g. *a pair of feet, between the feet, both feet*). We cannot construct an environment where we must have an *-ery* derivative: *amongst the jewellery, amongst the detritus; we will meet in the fernery, we will meet in the house*. Similarly, *-ing* is obligatory in *They are ~ the food* (*eating, over-salting, preparing*—at least, the only things that might fit in there with no *-ing* are prepositions like *on*), but there is no position in which an *-ation* word is required: *Their ~ of the food* (*preparation, characterization*; but also *cooking, love*).

While *-ery* or *-ation* always add lexical meaning, *-s* might be argued to do so in a minority of cases (see Section 24.3.1 above) and *-ing* may do so on some occasions, all of which are quite lexicalized (e.g. *boring, building, interesting, railing, smashing* ('excellent' BrEsl.), *warning*). So while this criterion is not necessarily clear-cut, at least the tendency is in the expected direction.

Number and tense/aspect are among the semantic categories which tend to be inflectional, while collectives and nominalizations are among the semantic categories which tend to be represented by derivational morphology. Since we recognize that these are no more than cross-linguistic tendencies (although fairly robust ones), this cannot be strong confirmation, but fits with the expected findings.

Plurality can affect most nouns in English (see Section 24.3.1 above) and *-ing* can be applied to any non-modal verb in English. They are as productive as anything gets in English. The suffix *-ation* has a rather restricted productivity; *-ation* is productively added mainly to verbs ending in *-ize* or *-ify* (see Chapter 10). As we have shown in Chapter 12, *-ery* is surprisingly productive in contemporary English, but still not comparable to the plural or *-ing* in productivity.

Finally, as it happens both *-ery* and *-ation* are borrowed affixes, while both *-s* and *-ing* are native. This is relevant insofar as inflectional affixes are only rarely borrowed, but derivational affixes often are.

So although we might not want to say that any of these four affixes is totally canonical in its behaviour, it is clear that we can draw a firm line between them in terms of the kinds of distinction that were made earlier in this chapter. The implication of Plank (1994) is that this is an expected and generalizable result. But we do have to stop and ask ourselves how much this helps.

24.5 WHY MIGHT WE NEED TO KNOW?

It is one thing to say that, in general terms, we can distinguish between instances of inflectional morphology and derivational morphology in English, but a more important question is why this distinction is likely to be useful. There seem to be at least three points for discussion here: the question of productivity, the question of affix ordering and the question of headedness, and these will be treated in turn below.

24.5.1 Productivity

One of the big differences between inflection and derivation is, as we have seen, the degree of productivity of the affixes. It is certainly true that in English we see a huge range of levels of productivity, from third-person singular *-s* or *-ing* on all non-modal verbs to the suffix *-red* which appears only in the word *hatred* with no apparent tendency to move beyond that word. But to what extent full productivity correlates with inflectionality is a different question.

If we move from third-singular *-s* and *-ing*, and look at past tense and past participle inflection in English, we start to get a slightly different picture of what is happening. There are many verbs in English which do not have a past-tense form in *-ed*. These verbs have alternative past tense forms which, it is frequently claimed, block the regular form. So the particular affix is not fully productive, but the morphological category of past tense probably is.

At this point we start to get into impossible questions such as whether the pattern of ablaut in *give/gave*, the irregular suffixation in *spent* and the regular suffixation in *wandered* are all different renditions of 'the same morpheme' {past tense}. But we have to take care that the argument does not become circular. If we define all these things as allomorphs rather than, say, as synonymous morphemes (Bloch 1947; Hockett 1947), we cannot then claim that {past tense} is fully productive, because it has become so totally circularly by way of our definition. In any case, we need to take a wider look. While, as we have shown in Chapter 10, not all English verbs have a nominalization other than with *-ing*, the productivity of a putative category {nominalization}, which includes the affixes *-ation*, *-ment*, *-al*, and so on, as well as conversion, is far higher than the productivity of any one of the individual processes involved. If we are going to consider the productivity of {past tense} rather than the productivity of {-ed}, why would we not also consider the productivity of {nominalization}? There are answers to this question: the obvious one is that the various ways of creating nominalizations are not strictly in complementary distribution, and may occasionally contrast on a given base, while the various markers of the past tense, while they are not strictly in complementary distribution in the wider speech community, do not seem to provide any semantic contrast. Nevertheless, the point we wish to make here is that the difference in productivity between a so-called inflectional category and a so-called derivational one may be less clear-cut than appears on a superficial consideration of the data.

If we look at past participles, the situation is slightly worse. Although English does not have as many defective verbs as we might find for more highly inflected languages, it does have verbs whose past participle is either missing or at least subject to great variation in the community, with a consequential lack of confidence about the form of the participle and a tendency to avoid it. Perhaps the best-known such example is the case of STRIDE, although the participle(s) of the verbs CLEAVE and TREAD are also instructive. With STRIDE the past participle is used occasionally, but varies between *strided*, *strid*, *strode*, and *stridden*. With CLEAVE, which of course historically is two separate verbs, the past participle not only varies between *cleaved*, *clove*, *cloven*, and *cleft*, but some of these forms are required in specific uses: *cleft palate* but *cloven hoof*, for example. Such specialization suggests that there is some level of contrast between the various patterns. In NAmE, TREAD comes close to being an example of defective verb: except in fixed phrases (*a well-trodden path*), speakers are often reluctant to use any past participle.

Plurals have already been discussed in this chapter, and they are less obviously fully productive than past participles, but the arguments are very similar. Note, though, that there may be semantic distinctions between *appendixes* and *appendices*, for instance.

At the other end of the scale, we need to discuss a suffix like *-able*. This suffix is often believed to be restricted to transitive verbs, though as we saw in Chapter 14, its use is wider than that. However, there is nothing to compete with *-able*, and on transitive verbs it seems to be absolutely productive. Even though *hospitalizable* was not attested in COCA or the BNC at the time this chapter was written, we cannot say that it would be an impossible formation. So we have a derivational affix like *-able* which may be more productive within its domain than inflectional affixes like the markers of the past participle. Perhaps the domain is what is crucial here: but even with third-person singular *-s* we had to restrict its domain to non-modal verbs rather than all verbs, so it is not clear that reduced domains should make a difference to our argument.

In other words, productivity is a feature of the individual affix, varies according to the individual affix, but does not necessarily correlate in any straightforward way with the categories of inflection and derivation.

24.5.2 Affix ordering

A distinction between inflectional and derivational affixes allows a simple statement of some instances of affixal ordering. Other things being equal, inflectional affixes will occur further from the root than derivational affixes.

One of the difficulties with such a statement is that it requires a certain amount of ad hoc modification because it is not absolutely true. Some counterexamples (many of which stand for classes of words rather than being isolated instances) are given in (5).

(5)   gutsy, interestedly, interestingly, looksism (COCA), lovingness, moreish, mostly, outdoorsy, prohibitedism (COCA)

Of course, if *-ly* is inflectional, examples of this sort would not be problematic, but as we have argued in Chapter 15, we do not find the arguments for the inflectional status of this affix completely convincing.

The examples in (5) fall into a few recurrent classes and there are no doubt good reasons for the exceptions. Nevertheless, the overall generalization does not hold.

An alternative approach would be to consider the ordering of affixes as subject to semantic scope (see, for example, Rice 2000). This generalization appears to hold over the examples in (5), as well as over more canonical examples such as *entrained, fantasizing, hospitalizes, kingdoms*, and so on. That being the case, the generalization about inflection and derivation is not only partly misleading, but unnecessary.

24.5.3 Headedness

Theoretically, the inflection/derivation distinction might be of use in clarifying the notion of 'headedness'. Using the most simplistic notion of 'head' (the head of the word is the single morpheme that determines the syntactic category and morphosyntactic properties of the word), we might hope to find a clear correlation: derivational affixes would always behave as heads and inflectional affixes would never behave as heads. The reality is not nearly so simple, however. For one thing, the data of English do not support this simplistic dichotomy and in any case, it is not clear that any current theorist actually subscribes to this simplistic definition. It emerges that a consideration of headedness sheds little light on the status of affixes as inflectional or derivational.

The facts about headedness in English morphology are well-known, so we only review them briefly here. While it is usually the case that derivational suffixes act as heads, prefixes are typically not heads (category-changing prefixes like *de-* do exist, though). Further, it is clear that inflections, while they typically do not change syntactic category (but see the discussion of participles above), do add or change morphosyntactic features. So the correlation between headedness and the inflection/derivation divide is murky to begin with.

Further, headedness in words has been a controversial topic for discussion for some time now. It is in Marchand (1969), where the terms 'determinans' and 'determinatum' are used and it was brought into the generative literature by Williams (1981). Part of the difficulty is that there is no agreement about the relative importance of criteria for headedness, or what criteria are being used. Thus Bauer (1990) argues that criteria for headedness do not pick out a coherent element in the word for the head, while Lieber (1992) shows what can be achieved by using a much more restricted definition of headedness.

In all of this discussion, the position of inflectional endings has been a particular problem. Bauer (1990) argues that inflectional and derivational affixes do not provide a coherent picture of what the head must be; Lieber (1992) argues that inflectional affixes need special treatment in terms of headedness; Di Sciullo and Williams (1987) argue that we need a notion of 'relativized head' to deal with inflection—though not only with inflection. It seems that however we try to define the head of a word, the definition does not apply easily to inflection.

It is hard to know what point the discussion on headedness has reached. Many scholars argue that at least for derivational morphology, it is possible to point to a morph which is the head of the word. Di Sciullo and Williams (1987) do not accept that the word necessarily has a single head; it may have many of them. Di Sciullo and Williams (1987: 27) also say that their approach allows them 'to maintain that inflectional affixes are not separated from derivational morphology in any way', and this is consistent with the view from many scholars that there is no split morphology (see Haspelmath 2002 for a neat summary). Those who see a distinction between the headedness of inflection and derivation are consistent with the scholars who see morphology as split.

Overall, the confusion about the headedness of inflectionally-marked words not only detracts from the theoretical standing of the notion of head of a word, but also undermines the distinction between inflection and derivation, particularly in a language which, like English, has cases which seem to lie close to the inflection–derivation divide.

24.5.4 Conclusion

It seems that although we probably can maintain a distinction between inflectional and derivational morphology relatively well in English—albeit with certain problematical cases which do not invalidate the fundamental notion—the distinction is not helpful to us in understanding any other aspects of the morphology of English. The classification might be useful in terms of typology, but does not throw much light on the behaviour of English morphological processes. On the other hand, the distinction between inflection and derivation in English might be necessary for syntacticians, and indeed, as we suggested above, particular syntactic frameworks might be forced to draw the line between inflection and derivation in different places.

CHAPTER 25

The analysis and limits of conversion

25.1 PROSPECTUS

In this chapter we review the notion of conversion and its correlates. As noted in Chapter 2 we consider conversion to be a directional process which links an input and an output form that are formally but not semantically identical. Since it is definitional that the output of this process is formally but not semantically identical to the input, it is what Bauer calls an identity operation (Bauer 1983: 32). It is a part of morphology by virtue of being an operation— or, more accurately, a set of operations (there are different patterns of conversion)—which is parallel to operations of affixation.

In this chapter we will principally be concerned with two points. The first is to investigate which of the various types of systematic homonymy or polysemy that can be found in English are instances of conversion. We approach this by considering the extent to which they match the canonical pattern of conversion in English. The second point is to consider and evaluate the various theoretical approaches to conversion (frequently called something other than 'conversion') which can be found in the literature. The various types of conversion in English are dealt with in this volume where they correspond to various types of affixal derivation (e.g. in deverbal nominalizations, in denominal verbs, and so on). Here we stand back and take an overview.

25.2 THE ISSUES

The main issue raised here concerns which forms should be said to be linked by the process(es) of conversion. English is full of homophonous forms which perform functions that range from slightly different to extremely different. We use HOMOPHONY here in its most literal sense of 'any two grammatically or semantically distinct forms that sound the same'. At one end of a scale, we find forms that are accidentally homophonous, and therefore clearly synchronically unrelated. The insect a *cricket* and the game have no obvious semantic relationship, although they may go back to the same French word. Similarly, *port* 'harbour' and *port* 'fortified wine' are semantically unrelated, and apparently homophonous by chance. At the other end of the scale, *beaten* the participle as used in the passive voice, as in *Chelsea were beaten in the semi-final*, and *beaten* the participle as used, for example, in the present perfect, as in *Chelsea have beaten Manchester City*, are systematically homophonous, and there is little reason even to assume that there are two different morphosyntactic words in English.

In between we find a range of different types of homophony, treated in a range of different ways by linguists and lexicographers. The most lexical of these are of little relevance here: these are examples like *cricket* and *port* above. There are many other types, however, which are potentially relevant to the study of morphology.

As a first example, consider homophonous affixal morphs. English is full of these. A few examples are given in (1) for illustration.

(1)	decency	fatty		<y>, /i/
	friendly	stupidly		<ly>, /li/
	killer	smaller		<er>, /ə ‖ ər/
	teachers	provides	towards	<s>, /z/
	warmth	tenth		<th>, /θ/
	vicarage	coverage		<age>, /ɪdʒ/
	wisdom	kingdom		<dom>, /dəm/

Most of the examples in (1) are probably uncontroversial instances of homophonous but distinct affixes (for example *-er, -ly, -s, -th, -y*): cases of affixal homonymy. Some of them are more often viewed as instances of polysemy (*-age, -dom*). We have already noted in several places in this volume that where there is doubt, we prefer the polysemy solution, but there are places where polysemy is simply not tenable. The difficulty is in stating the conditions under which homonymy has to be preferred to polysemy (see Bauer 2003b; Lieber 2004). It may be that, rather than there being a set of necessary and sufficient criteria, each case has to be treated on its merit—which may also be true with lexical morphemes.

Somewhere in the range between homonymy and polysemy is a set of homophonous words which are generally taken to be derivationally related. The base forms or citation forms of two lexemes are homophonous, but the two lexemes belong to different word classes (and thus form parts of different inflectional paradigms where this is relevant), despite being semantically related. We will take the examples in (2) as being clear-cut instances of what we would consider to be conversion:

(2)	a leaflet	to leaflet
	dirty	to dirty
	to spy	a spy

There are a number of reasons why examples like these are seen as a definable type of homophony between homonymy and polysemy, and why the relationship between them is seen as being derivational.

The first of these is that such examples fit into parallel sets where a similar relationship between lexemes is marked by a derivational affix. This seems to imply that the relationship in this type should also be considered derivational. Examples are given in (3).

(3) a. leaflet   to leaflet
        fluoride   to fluoridate
        patina   to patinize
        beauty   to beautify

     b. dirty   to dirty
        legal   to legalize
        pretty   to prettify
        flat   to flatten
        rich   to enrich

     c. to spy   a spy
        to kill   a killer
        to reside a resident
        to inhabit an inhabitant

This link with overt derivational affixes has led to analyses in which there is said to be an affix linking these words, but it is an affix of zero form. This analysis will be taken up below (Section 25.4.2).

In cases like those in (2) and (3) as well as in the overtly derived examples, there is also a semantic relationship between base and derivative that can be teased apart into two factors. First, there is semantic dependency, where an explanation of the meaning of the derivative naturally uses the base lexeme, but not vice versa. Thus *resident* might be defined as 'person who resides', and *legalize* as 'make legal'. *Legal*, on the other hand, would not naturally or usefully be defined as 'what something becomes once it is legalized' nor would *reside* be defined as 'to act as a resident'. Semantic dependency of this sort normally leads to lower frequency for the derived word, as the added complexity of meaning narrows down the versatility of the word in discourse.

Second, the derivative frequently has a less broad semantic scope than the base. For example, the base *rich* can refer to something that causes indignation (as in *It was a bit rich of her to suggest that she was entirely innocent*), but you cannot *enrich* a conversation by putting into it comments which are seen as being *rich* in this sense. In other words, some semantic nuances of the base are not carried over to the derivative. Or the opposite may occur, where the derivative has nuances that could not be predicted from the semantics of the base; for example, the noun *fluoride* simply refers to a particular chemical substance, but the derived verb *fluoridate* is used exclusively for the addition of fluorides to consumables for the purpose of improving dental health, not just any addition of fluorides to anything. The result of the reduced semantic scope of derivatives is again that text frequency of the derived lexeme tends to be lower than the text frequency of the base lexeme.

Note that semantic dependency may not always correlate with the relative age of the base and the derivative (Bram 2011). That is, although typically, the base is older than the derivative and the derivative also depends semantically on the base, this is not necessarily the case. Where this situation is reversed, we typically have cases of back-formation. For example, *babysitter* can be defined as 'one who babysits', with the noun being semantically dependent on the verb. The verb *babysit*, however, is not attested until nine years after *babysitter* (1946 versus 1937, according to the *OED*), thus pointing to this as a clear case of back-formation (see also Chapter 23). However, the expected norm is that order of coining in English correlates with semantic dependency, semantic scope, and text frequency.

In all of these ways, therefore, we have pairs where it seems we can see a base and a corresponding derivative, and that the derivative behaves in ways consistent with those derivatives that are overtly marked.

Moreover, the productivity of such cases appears to work like the productivity of other lexical derivations: there are apparently unmotivated gaps in the paradigm, there is competition with other affixal forms, the existence of a particular form to fill a slot in the semantic paradigm is not entirely predictable, and there can be doublets (for example, *teaser* and *tease*). Cases which meet these criteria we term instances of 'conversion', a term which we here intend to be theory-neutral. Consider the list of agentive nouns from monosyllabic verbs presented in (4).

(4)   a.   *affixation*
             bake ♦ baker
             hunt ♦ hunter
             serve ♦ servant
             stand ♦ standee

      b.   *conversion*
             flirt ♦ flirt
             guide ♦ guide
             judge ♦ judge
             spy ♦ spy

However, our working definition is not sufficient to delimit cases of conversion completely. There are many instances of pairs of words in English which are close to conversion, but which might not meet the definition entirely, and we consider some of these in the next section. There are also theoretical objections to the picture we have painted thus far, which will be taken up later.

25.3 Cases for further consideration

Less central cases are less central for a number of reasons. In this section, a number of different types will be considered, and the extent to which they might be considered to belong with the canonical cases of conversion.

25.3.1 Adjective to noun cases

Adjective to noun conversion was not included in the examples in (2) because there is more than one type, and the status of some of the types is controversial. We review three cases in this section: de-adjectival definite nouns, de-adjectival concretes, and plural nouns from adjectives.

25.3.1.1 *De-adjectival nouns preceded by* the: the rich, the ridiculous

Here we consider a type where a word with the same form as an adjective can occur in the position of a head noun in a definite phrase preceded by *the*. The specificity of the environment is part of the argument for this not being straightforward conversion.

The productivity of this type is not usually fully recognized. Any pragmatically appropriate adjective may be used in this way. However, there is a difference between the case where the phrase is understood as singular (whether or not singular concord is overtly used) (5) and where it is understood as plural (6). The examples in (5) and (6) are from the BNC.

(5) *New Statesman and Society 1985–1994:* **The old** is dead. Where is **the new**?

Today 1985–1994: Now, however, **the outrageous** is expected.

Ring of Fire 1988: Neither **the demonic** nor **the angelic** is suppressed.

New Musical Express 1992:…we had grown to expect **the remarkable** as a matter of course

London School of Economics lecture 1993: **The good** has to be imposed from outside, it's not, it's not in human nature.

(6) *The Daily Mirror:*…a stone's throw from the marina in Puerto Banus where **the rich and famous** moor their luxury yachts.

Radical Approaches to Adult Education 1988: Thus, as we have argued at length in a recent book, "doubly disadvantaged" sections of the working class—**the unemployed**, women, black people, **the retired**, and **the disabled**—have especially acute educational needs.

Introduction to Social Administration in Britain 1990: **the old** are more frequently ill than the rest of the population

The Daily Mirror 1992: only **the strong** survive.

The Redundancy of Courage 1992: And so they processed, **the defiant** and **the hopeless**, **the resigned** and those who pleaded with a silent desperation…

Where the phrase is understood as singular, it denotes something non-human, whereas when it is understood as plural, it denotes something human. In neither case, note, is there any feeling that a noun has been omitted (or is 'understood' in the terminology of traditional grammar), as is the case in the examples in (7), also from the BNC.

(7)   *Still Life 1988*: A pinker skin-tone under **the brown**…

Bible study group meeting 1993: The old nature has been crucified, **the new** has come.

The productivity of the construction under discussion is masked by the fact that tokens of the relevant construction types are rare, and where they do occur are often not in a syntactic context where number is apparent. It is also masked by the de-adjectival concrete type discussed in Section 25.3.1.2, which may sometimes provide tokens which appear to be counterexamples to the generalization stated here. There are occasional other apparent counterexamples, like *the accused*, which is like the examples from Section 25.3.1.2 in that it can occur in a full range of phrase types, but unlike it in that it takes no plural marking.

This type of formation is almost certainly syntactic rather than lexical: it is extremely productive, the output forms are not full nouns in that they do not inflect as nouns (they do not show plural forms, for instance), and the syntactic context is a crucial part of the construction. These instances are not usually treated as conversion, and it is no doubt for these reasons.

25.3.1.2 *De-adjectival nouns that take any determiner:* an intellectual

Unlike the previous case, the nouns created by this process take part in the full inflection of nouns and may occur in a full range of noun phrases (with all relevant determiners). Also there are unpredictable gaps in the paradigm: there is no obvious reason why *intellectual* has become a full noun meaning 'intellectual person' but *poor* has not become a full noun meaning 'poor person', but belongs to the category described in Section 25.3.1.1. Some established examples of conversion are presented in (8).

(8)   Arctic, Australian, bilingual, composite, daily, digestive, empty, executive, favourite, green, imponderable, intellectual, interrogative, mural, parliamentarian, round, simian, variable

25.3.1.3 *Adjectives with plural noun counterparts:* news, burnables

We consider next examples in which we have nouns that appear to be derived from adjectives, but with the addition of a plural *-s*. This is a particularly murky area, as it is not clear that we are dealing with a single, unified phenomenon. In a few cases there is no singular noun corresponding to the plural. For example, although there is an adjective *new* and a noun *news*, there is no intermediate noun *new*; the form *news*, furthermore, is semantically singular. In other cases, we do have a corresponding singular. The noun *good* exists as a technical term in the field of economics, alongside *goods*, and *goods* is treated as a plural noun. Perhaps most perplexing is that we are not necessarily dealing here with a small number of discrete or marginal examples. Consider the examples in (9):

(9)   adjustables, allowables, affordables, burnables, buyables, chewables, drinkables, durables, freezables, hand-washables

The formation of de-adjectival nouns in *-ables* is quite productive in contemporary English as the examples above from COCA suggest, but it is far from obvious whether we should treat them as examples of conversion. Indeed, in some or all of these cases we might be tempted to treat the plural marker as a derivational suffix, which would rule these words out as potential instances of conversion. In Chapter 7.2.1 we left this possibility open, without pursuing it, and we will continue to leave it open here.

25.3.2 Mention versus use: '*but me no buts*'

Any word which is mentioned can appear as a noun and be inflected as such. Proverbial sayings are full of admonitions such as

> If **ifs** and **buts** were apples and nuts
> all the wee laddies would fill their guts
> If **ifs** and **ands** were pots and pans
> there'd be no trade for tinkers

Google gives almost 2.5 million hits for the expression *no more thank yous*. In principle, even whole sentences could be used this way: ☜*Don't give me any of your 'I can't do it's.*

The use of such items as verbs is rather less usual, but still not unusual. *Effing and blinding* (BrE 'using swear words') has become a fixed phrase, where the *-ing* seems to indicate a verbal usage. Again, a phrase could provide the input to this process: ☜*Stop your I-can't-ing.*

The fact that this is possible with virtually any base suggests that it is syntactic rather than lexical, and thus should not count as conversion.

25.3.3 Formations related to prepositions: *a down, to down, the down train*

Prepositions are rare as bases in derivation, and where they do occur tend to be sporadic: for example, we can have a *downer*, but there are no established words *overer, paster, througher, underer*, and so on.

With the case of *the down train* (also *the up train, a through train*) there is no particular reason to believe that the relevant items have 'become' adjectives. Many things other than adjectives can appear in attributive position in English, and these could simply be prepositions (or prepositional adverbs, or particles) in attributive position.

With other cases, it is noteworthy that the noun and the verb seem to be independent derivatives from the preposition: *to have a down on somebody* ('to be ill-disposed towards someone' chiefly BrE, AusE, or NZE) has nothing to do semantically with *to down a drink* or *to down tools* (BrE 'to go on strike') except the independent relationship with *down*.

Nevertheless, this process is clearly lexical and not syntactic. It shows semantic dependency and the expected difference of semantic scope, with the lower frequencies in the derivatives. It therefore seems that the examples where a preposition becomes a noun or a verb could reasonably come under the heading of conversion, albeit as a minor type.

25.3.4 Minor phonological modification

25.3.4.1 *Devoicing of final obstruent:* believe ◆ belief

This seems to be a non-productive class of related words, where the difference, synchronically, between the two words lies in the final obstruent. In (10) there are examples of verbs and nouns linked by the voicing of a final fricative.

(10)   *verb*   *noun*

abuse /z/   abuse /s/

advise   advice

believe   belief

calve   calf

devise   device

excuse /z/   excuse /s/

grieve   grief

halve   half

house /z/   house /s/

mouth /ð/   mouth /θ/

prove   proof

relieve   relief

sheathe	sheath
sheave	sheaf
shelve	shelf
strive	strife
teethe	teeth
thieve	thief
use /z/	use /s/
wive	wife
wreathe	wreath

In (11) the relationship is again one of voicing contrast between final fricatives, but this time the pairs are verb and adjective.

(11) *verb*   *adjective*

        loathe   loath ~ loth

        save   safe

In (12) there is a difference in voicing in the final obstruent, but this time the sounds are alveolar plosives.

(12) *verb*   *noun*

        ascend   ascent

        bend   bent

        descend   descent

        extend   extent

        gild   gilt

        portend   portent

Finally, in (13) there is a set which are linked by the final fricative, like those in (10), but there is a concomitant vowel difference, which is synchronically unpredictable (though in many instances it derives from the fact that one of the vowels was long, the other short, in Middle English).

(13) *verb*   *noun*

        bathe   bath

        braze   brass

        breathe   breath

        choose   choice

clothe	cloth
glaze	glass
graze	grass
live	life
lose	loss

In these pairs of words there is not necessarily a consistent directionality: semantically, it would seem that *belief* depends upon *believe*, but that *sheathe* depends upon *sheath*. In some cases, such as *clothe* and *cloth*, the precise relationship at the time of formation is masked by subsequent semantic changes. Nevertheless, these pairs are clearly more related than chance near-homonyms.

Some authors (Bauer 1983; Štekauer 1996 by implication) include such cases among instances of conversion. Others (Bauer and Huddleston 2002) do not. Since one of the central defining features of conversion is that the form remains constant, it seems that these formations must be excluded from the domain of conversion.

25.3.4.2 *Stress shift:* frágment ♦ fragmént

Pairs of this type have been discussed elsewhere (see Chapter 10), and full exemplification will not be provided here. The important point is that the noun and verb differ in stress: sometimes this leads to differences in vowel quality (as in /ˈfrægmənt/ versus /frægˈment/), sometimes it does not (as in /ˈdaɪdʒest/ versus /daɪˈdʒest/).

On the basis of the discussion in Section 25.3.4.1, it might appear that these cannot be instances of conversion (pace Bauer 1983; Štekauer 1996) because there is a difference in form. However, there are differing theoretical interpretations of the facts which can lead to diametrically opposed conclusions.

The first theoretical position looks at the surface forms of the nouns and the verbs related in this way, and sees a difference in phonological form which is a concomitant of the change of word class. Since the change of word class is marked by that difference in form, this fails one of the crucial tests for conversion, and so must be some other kind of word-formation—some kind of internal modification (Bauer 2003b).

An alternative view might consider the production of such forms as a linear process. For example, in various generative models ranging from Chomsky and Halle (1968) to Distributed Morphology (see, for example, Harley and Noyer 1999), there is a lexical entry in which there is no stress marked. In Distributed Morphology the word class is attributed to the word by virtue of its position in a syntactic tree. Once the morphosyntactic process has determined whether the relevant phonological string is to be considered a noun or a verb (that is, once the conversion process, however that is to be understood, has taken place), the phonology assigns a stress pattern to the string, using its word class designation as part of the input. Once the stress is determined, the precise nature of the vowels is determined by general reduction rules. In such a model, the difference in stress is a result of the marking of word class, not an element which in itself forces the interpretation of the derivative as a noun or a verb. At the point at which word class is determined (Distributed Morphology) or the change from one word class to another takes place (Chomsky and Halle 1968), there is no marker of the changed status, and so this can be seen as conversion on a par with words such as *control* where there is no stress difference and no segmental difference between the noun and the verb.

Despite the possibility of this sort of theoretical treatment, it seems that for the hearer, stress must act as part of the signal that a verb or a noun is present, in more or less the same way that an affix does. In other words, from the listener's point of view, stress does function as the marker of the changed status. That being the case, it seems that the conservative option is not to treat stress shift as being in the same category as conversion.

25.3.5 Participles: *his shooting, an interested party*

The theoretical treatment of participial forms has always been a contentious matter. Solutions from the literature include a conversion analysis, of course, as well as the postulation of homophonous affixes (Allen 1978), the treatment of the categorial status of participles purely as a matter of syntactic structure, as for example in Distributed Morphology, or as an example of category-changing inflection (Haspelmath 1996). It is not our purpose here to review all of the many theoretical approaches to participles, much less to decide among them; we merely point out here that the problem has been dealt with in many ways in the literature. It should also be noted that the processes dealt with here look more like conversion under some theoretical approaches to conversion than under others. The question of theoretical approaches will be taken up again in Section 25.4.

The *-ing* form appears as an inflectional affix (by definition—see Chapters 2 and 5) on verbal bases in the progressive forms of the verb (14a). It may also occur in attributive position before a noun, where it may be sub-modified by *so, very,* and so on (14b). It may also be used as the base for *-ly* adverbial suffixation (14c) and in various constructions in which it has some nominal and some verbal features (14d, e). Morphologically, it is possible for such forms to take a plural *-s* (14f).

(14) a. They were smiling at the camera.

  b. They had a very convincing argument.

  c. 'How nice,' she added smilingly.

  d. Shooting elephants is not politically correct.

  e. Their shooting of the elephants caused international headlines.

  f. The recordings are archived on hard disk.

As the examples in (14) illustrate, the suffix *-ing* occurs in a range of places from those in which it looks entirely verbal to those where it looks entirely nominal. There is no allomorphy of this form, and it is as close to fully productive as any English morphology, so that all non-modal verbs have an *-ing* form. While not all *-ing* forms are equally readily found in all of these uses, it is not clear to what extent that is a syntactic matter, and to what extent it is a pragmatic matter.

The thing that makes this look like a lexical process is the fact that different forms seem to become integrated into the new word class in idiosyncratic ways. For example, *interesting* is clearly an adjective, with a full range of adjectival uses and a meaning which is no longer compositional, but it does not become so much of a noun that it takes a plural *-s*. *Leaning*, on the other hand, can be used attributively as in *the leaning tower*, and has also become a noun which can be pluralized: *leanings*.

The issues concerning past participial *-ed* (and its irregular congeners) are similar to those concerning *-ing*. The *-ed* suffix is used inflectionally to mark past participles (15a). It can also be used attributively before a noun, in which position it can be sub-modified (15b). Forms in *-ly* and *-ness* can be derived from such *-ed* forms (15c). Following the pattern discussed in Section 25.3.1.1, such words can also surface as nouns (15d), and can also form plurals, although far less easily than *-ing* forms (15e).

		regular	*irregular*
(15)			
	a.	He has visited the castle already.	He has seen us.
	b.	a very isolated community	a well trodden path
	c.	excitedly	brokenness
	d.	help for the afflicted	whiteness […] ironically becomes the hidden (*BNC*)
	e.	the undecideds (*COCA*)	the assimilateds (*COCA*)

As is clear from (15), there is variation in the past participial forms, and the form of the more adjectival or nominal uses is typically the same as for the inflectional verbal uses. There are instances like *drunken* and *sunken* which have become fixed as adjectives and no longer have verbal use in standard varieties, and these do complicate the issue, since the old forms may usurp some of the functions that are normally held by the past participle form, but even then the current past participle form may sometimes be used in the ways indicated: *the sunk foundations* (BNC).

The problems with including such historical developments as cases of conversion are first that in the clear-cut cases conversion involves the transfer of a base belonging to a lexeme of one word class to the base of a lexeme of a different word class. Here, it is arguable that the word classes differ, but it is not an unmarked base which is adopted, but an overtly inflected form. Semantically, the effects of that inflection have to be ignored, but the form remains as the word moves to a different word class. Second, it is not always clearly the case that all the expected features of the new word class are achieved: there seem to be degrees of verbiness and nouniness in different constructions with the *-ing* forms, for example, as illustrated in (14).

In looking at both types of participle, we must distinguish between those processes which are genuinely automatic and those which are much more clearly idiosyncratic. The gerund usage illustrated in (14) seems totally productive, and should probably be seen as syntactic in some way. Perhaps the gerund could be considered a construction which uses the present participle, a form generated inflectionally. Or the inflection could be seen as using a derived *-ing* form. The morphological extensions of *-ing* and *-ed* may behave like *-ly*, *-ness*, and the plural markers. On this account, the lack of a word like *connivingness* in our corpora is simply a gap. However, why *drunk* becomes a pluralizable noun while *woken* does not is left unexplained: at a guess, it is something to do with the frequency of *drunk* in nominal environments which leads speakers to expect full nominal behaviour. If this is true, there is no morphological principle as such involved. The same principle could account for the fact that some *-ing* and *-ed* forms feel like better adjectives than others. It is not a matter of grammar, but a matter of semantics and frequency in particular environments, which allows extensions into other adjectival environments by analogy.

There are instances of participles also appearing in environments that suggest that they are prepositions: *concerning, excepted, excepting, given, including, regarding,* and so on. It is nevertheless not clear that there is a process deriving prepositions from verbs: rather verbal constructions become used so often that they become perceived as chunks which have the same function as prepositions (Kortmann and König 1992).

25.3.6 Type coercion

In the discussion of derivational processes in this book we have frequently made use of the notion of TYPE COERCION, or simply COERCION (Pustejovsky 1995). This is a semantic process by which a lexical item of one semantic type, say a count noun or an intransitive verb, is forced by the syntactic context in which it is used into an interpretation as another semantic type, say a non-count noun or a transitive verb. Since the input and output of type coercion are semantically distinct but formally identical, the question arises whether they should be seen as related by conversion.

25.3.6.1 *Mass versus count:* a cake • some cake

The majority of common nouns in English can be used as either count nouns or as non-count nouns. While there are a few like *knowledge* which seem extremely awkward in count environments, on the whole the shift between count and non-count uses is automatic. Even count/non-count pairs like *bread* and *loaf* are subject to type coercion, as in advertisements for *Reizenstein's breads* or the phrase *some loaf of bread* (BNC). Here there is an argument (Jackendoff 1990; Pustejovsky 1995) that it is not strictly the noun which is count or non-count but the noun phrase in which it occurs: the reading is count or non-count because of the syntactic context, not because of the particular noun chosen. If this argument is accepted, the distinction between count and non-count nouns per se is purely a syntactic matter and not a matter of lexis at all. That being the case, this is not a matter of conversion or of morphology; it may not even be a matter of polysemy.

25.3.6.2 *Transitive versus intransitive:* to walk ◆ to walk the dog

While there are instances in English where the difference between a transitive and an intransitive usage is marked, this is not the norm. Some examples of the marking are provided in (16). The processes illustrated in (16) are not readily available to speakers of contemporary English for new coinages.

> (16) *intransitive*   *transitive*
>
>   sit   set
>   moan   bemoan

As in the case of count versus non-count nouns considered in Section 25.3.6.1, it can be argued that the verbs take on the requisite meaning from the syntactic constructions in which they occur, and that this polysemy is thus a matter of type coercion.

There is also the question of semantic dependency. With *smell*, the intransitive seems to depend on the transitive; with *walk*, transitive senses seem to derive from and postdate intransitive senses. The lack of consistent semantic dependency also seems to suggest that we are not dealing here with a derivational matter. We will therefore not include this type of relationship under the heading of conversion.

25.3.6.3 *Proper versus common nouns:* Mary ◆ the four Marys

It seems that all proper nouns can be used as common nouns with the meaning 'entities which bear this name'. This is not only true of given names like *Mary*, but also of family names (*the Joneses, the Smiths*—usually meaning the plural members of a single family) and place names (*there's a Cambridge in Massachusetts and another one in New Zealand; the river Avon I'm talking about is in Christchurch*). Even where the name denotes a unique entity, a plural common noun may occur either by ellipsis (17) or by virtue of a figurative splitting of the original entity (18), as these examples from the BNC illustrate:

> (17) *Country Living 1991*: the Russells also breed Berkshires, Saddlebacks, Lops, Middle Whites, Large Blacks and Tamworths

> (18) *The Savage and the City in the Work of T.S. Eliot 1991*: Dawson emphasized the "two Englands" created in the nineteenth century...

The change of grammatical category here seems to be a matter of type coercion, and does not appear to be a derivational relationship. We will not include it as conversion.

25.3.6.4 *Non-gradable versus gradable:* English • very English

Given the right syntactic context, almost any non-gradable adjective can be made gradable (examples from the BNC, see also Chapter 6):

(19)   *Central television news scripts*: It's **more English** than anywhere else.

   New Statesman and Society 1992: The Frigido deep-freeze has **an indefinably Antarctic quality** (unlike the more Arctic Norfrigge).

   Adam's Paradise 1989: Ruth rose too, suddenly held by **a despair more absolute** than any she'd yet felt.

This seems to be rather like the changes between count and non-count nouns: a polysemy which is forced by the syntactic context. That being the case, this is not conversion.

25.3.7 Adverb formation: *real ale* • *real good*

There are a number of forms in English which are found functioning both as adjectives and as adverbs (see Chapter 15). The number of forms concerned differs from variety to variety, so that some speakers allow *She ate her meal leisurely*, while others require *She ate her meal in a leisurely manner*. There are also differences between words that have an overtly distinct adverbial form like *late* and *lately*, or *real* and *really* from those which have no such distinctions. As is clear from the examples, the overtly marked adverbs may be synonymous with the unmarked adverbs, or semantically distinct from them. Finally, using *real* as an intensifier carries clear social messages, being overtly proscribed by purists, while the dual use of *leisurely* (for those speakers who use it) appears to be socially neutral.

There are many forms which can be adjectival which are also used as intensifiers for adjectives. Some are listed in (20). Most of these are considered non-standard by purists, but are extremely common in speech, where *very* (itself originally an adjective) is now rare in the vernacular (see e.g. Bauer and Bauer 2002).

(20)   blind, bloody (*and euphemisms*), dead, deadly, fucking (*and euphemisms*), jolly, mighty, pretty, real, right, wicked

In (21) we list some of the forms which can be used as either adjectives or adverbs in standard English. Those forms in (21b) avoid the repetition of adjectival *-ly* followed by adverbial *-ly*, which is less and less acceptable in modern English. Some comparative forms such as *better* (the comparative of both *good* and *well*) also fall into the category illustrated in (21a).

(21)   a.   early, fair, fast, hard, loud

   b.   daily, deadly, fortnightly (*BrE*), friendly (*NAmE*), kindly, leisurely, monthly, nightly, quarterly, weekly, yearly

Others of this type are rather less clearly acceptable in formal language, and have overt adverbial alternatives, but are widely found. Examples are given in (22).

(22)   Kiss me quick.   Kiss me quickly.

       Go/drive slow.   Go/drive slowly.

       He did it wrong.   He did it wrongly.

In (23) there are some examples where the meanings of the adjectival forms and the adverbial forms are so different that it is probably safer to view the two as separate lexemes, whatever the etymology.

(23)   *adjectival function*   *adverbial function*

       I'm ill.   We can ill afford the ticket.
                              (now old fashioned)

       an even distribution   She even ate it.

       his late father   He arrived late.

       the round table   We wandered round.

       the very person   a very interesting book

Part of the difficulty in discussing this type of relation is that many adverbs can be used in attributive position, where they might be considered to be partly adjectival. We take the view that use in attributive position is not sufficient to illustrate a recategorization of these words. Some examples are given in (24).

(24)   the off switch, the overnight parcel rate, overseas mail, the then king, a through train, an upward(s) movement

For a fuller discussion of this area of grammar, see Valera Hernández (1996).

Most of these types appear not to be productive, or only marginally so. Which words are found with both functions and which are not seems to be a matter of lexis, and therefore this is a reasonable area for word-formation, even if not productive word-formation. If we take the point of view that adjectives and adverbs in English are distinct categories (Payne *et al.* 2010), then the change of category criterion is met. Directionality seems to go from the adjective to the adverb, since the forms are nearly always clearly adjectival. All of this seems to be compatible with there being conversion here, albeit limited and non-productive conversion.

25.3.8 Compounds and phrases

It is not unusual in contemporary English to find cases in which a compound of one word class can be found without modification in the syntactic context of another word class. For example, where *stir-fry* would usually be assumed to be a verbal compound, it can be found in a context which is clearly nominal.

(25) *Washington Post 2004*: I've also used the leaves in **a stir-fry** with broad bean sauce

Similarly, although *seatbelt* and *blowtorch* are typically nominal compounds, they can appear in verbal contexts as well, as the following examples from COCA suggest:

(26) *Virginia Quarterly Review 2004*: Graves was **seatbelted** in the shotgun position next to Ahktar, jostling in the inert manner of a crash-test dummy.

 Best Friends for Never 2004: What are you going to do tomorrow when I forget about you again? **Blowtorch** my bedroom?

Such examples fairly straightforwardly meet the criteria for conversion set out in Section 25.2: the verbal and nominal forms are homophonous, they clearly belong to distinct word classes, they are semantically related, and their semantic relationships are similar to those found between bases and overtly affixed forms derived from them. Some examples of conversion from compounds are clearly lexicalized (*to day dream, to pickpocket, to blackmail*), but the examples in (26) show that the process is productive. Examples of this sort are discussed in more detail in the relevant chapters.

The same argument can be made for phrasal elements of certain sorts. For example, we frequently find that phrasal verbs like *blow up, break down, call back, give away, hang out, put down* can appear in nominal contexts. Idiomatic nominal phrases of certain sorts can also appear in obviously verbal environments, as the examples in (27), from COCA, show.

(27) *Fantasy and Science Fiction 1995*: Behind Zane Gerard, Tyque Raymond was **thumb-upping** me.

 Fantasy and Science Fiction 2002: The cameras were all installed to monitor the reactor, so they faced the center of the room. Most of them **close-upped** on specific pieces of equipment.

So from (*give someone*) *a thumbs up* we get the clearly verbal form *thumb-upping* (interestingly, with loss of the plural *-s*). The second example is more intricate: what we apparently have here is a verb *to close-up* corresponding to a noun *a close up* (a kind of photograph) from an adjective (*we saw it close up*). Again, although forms of this sort may be less frequent than the compound cases in (25)–(26), they still appear to have some productivity in the contemporary language (see also the examples in (27) discussed in Section 25.4.2).

25.4 Modelling conversion

The label 'conversion' has been used at least since Sweet (1891). In part it has remained a useful label because it does not make many theoretical claims. One claim that it does seem to make is that there is a process linking the words involved: conversion turns one thing into another. What is more, if a word is the output of conversion, it would seem to imply that it has all the relevant functions of the type to which it has been converted. Even these implications might be controversial.

A number of different terminologies and approaches to conversion can be found in the literature. To a large extent, it is not clear that they are much more than alternative nomenclatures for the same idea. But some of them have different implications for how conversion should be dealt with in a grammar, including whether they are a part of morphology at all. In what follows we consider some of these alternative approaches, and ask whether there is any evidence to support their predictions.

25.4.1 Conversion, narrowly defined

Thus far, 'conversion' has been used as a cover-term for the process under review. But we can specify it more closely within the theoretical literature, as hinted above. Conversion is a process which links an input form to an output form: it is directional. Since it is definitional that the output of this process is formally (but not semantically) identical to the input, it is an identity operation (Bauer 1983). It is a part of morphology by virtue of being an operation—or, more accurately, a set of operations (there are different patterns of conversion)—which is parallel to operations of affixation. Because it is a morphological operation, we expect it to show productivity (availability and profitability) in the same way as other morphological operations. Because it is a derivational process, we expect to find gaps in the established outputs of the process, and places where the process is in competition with other morphological processes.

All of this provides a coherent picture in line with what has been illustrated so far. The productivity of conversion is illustrated elsewhere in this book (see Chapters 10, 11, 13, 14, 15) and the issue of competition was outlined in Section 25.2, example (3)). Nevertheless, it is controversial, as will become clear when we consider alternative points of view.

25.4.2 Zero-derivation

The zero-derivation approach takes the parallelism between conversion and other affixed forms illustrated in (3) seriously. If we are dealing with a derivational process, and it is parallel to instances of affixation, then perhaps we should say that it is another kind of affixation, one where the form of the affix is zero. Just as *legalize* is made up of *legal+ize*, so *empty* (the verb) is made up of *empty+∅*.

There are various standard objections to this analysis. The first is to question the proliferation of zeroes this gives rise to. If *empty* (adjective) has no affix on it, but *empty* (noun) has a zero on it, *empty* (verb) must contain a different zero, since it is a non-synonymous affix. We find, therefore, not only various zeroes contrasting with each other, but contrasting with the lack of zero, that is with nothing at all. While this may give rise to a system which could be run on a computer, it is hard to see how it could be a learnable system for real speakers.

Next, it is queried how we know that there is only one zero-affix in all cases of, say, verb to noun derivation. Given the parallelism with affixed forms like *amendment, closure, confusion, dismissal, hatred, laughter, marriage,* and so on, why should we expect *change, freeze, influence, recompense, remark,* and others to have the same affix? At the same time, if they do not have the same affix, how can we tell which base has which affix? The obvious riposte to this argument is that we assume a single zero because of Ockham's razor, but it remains true that it is hard to prove that a single zero is involved, or even that the zero is a suffix and not a prefix.

The third objection considers the nature of the output. If we consider the nouns *oil, package, landmine* we assume that these are simple, derivationally complex, and compound respectively. What then about the corresponding verbs *oil, package, landmine*? If they have a zero-affix, they should all have exactly the same status, they should all be derivatives, and the different statuses of their bases should be irrelevant. But it is not clear that we have any real reason to say that the verbs are anything other than simple, derivationally complex, and compound, and if this is true, the use of the zero-affix is masking something. Consider the two examples below.

(28)   Then he called me a week later and said never mind, so I **never minded** (*Parker 2000: 65*)

(29)   Writing the soundtrack of /Crazy Heart/ with his Fort Worth childhood friend T Bone Burnett gave Bruton the national profile in contemporary Americana that he'd earned decades previously by **right-hand-manning** it with Kris Kristofferson and Bonnie Raitt (http://www.austinchronicle. com/music/2010-02-19/967813).

In each case, an apparent phrase is turned into an inflected verb. We would presumably not wish to say that the verbs *never mind* and *right-hand-man* are phrases, and yet the bases look like phrases. So the application of the zero-affix could be analysed here as having the effect of making the word-formation process a morphological one. This seems to contradict the argument just above about *oil, package,* and *landmine* (that is, that we have no reason to believe that the status of the base has changed under zero-affixation), because if the verb does not always retain the nature of its base, it is not clear that it does in any of these instances.

None of these arguments against zero-derivation is completely convincing—and accordingly there are a number of scholars who use the zero-derivation analysis (see Bauer and Valera 2005). If we reject it here it is largely because it seems to make assumptions that are not necessary.

There is an alternative view of the zero-affix hypothesis, deriving from the notion propounded by Beard (1995) that derivation and affixation are two separate processes. According to this view there is a semantic derivation that, for instance, makes a verb into a noun, but no affixal material to realize that semantic derivation. This view has the option of making the parallel with other cases of affixation overt (they all take part in the same semantic process) while at the same time not requiring a zero form to be part of the derived string: the semantic process is just given no realization. Both Plag (1999: ch. 8) and Lieber (2004: ch. 3) point out the pitfalls of this sort of analysis, however: noun to verb conversion in English actually forms a wider variety of verb-types than any of the overt verbalizing affixes do and shows a much wider variety of meanings than any of the overt affixes, so considering verbalization as a single process seems like an incorrect move.

25.4.3 Relisting

Another way of considering conversion is that the input word is simply relisted in the lexicon with a new word class. Some scholars (e.g. Strauss 1982) see this as a rebracketing, so that the verb *empty* has the structure $[[\text{empty}]_A]_V$. Others (e.g. Lieber 1980) do not use this formulation, and it is not clear whether this is or is not theoretically significant.

Unlike the Beardian analysis described in the previous subsection, the relisting option seems to suggest that the semantic effects of conversion should be less constrained than those of any overt affix, although they should not be entirely random. Since this sort of analysis assumes that one entry is the basis for another, we would expect at least some minimal content from one entry to be transferred to the new entry. Some scholars (e.g. Adams 1973) comment on the semantic regularity of the conversion process, and give quite constrained lists of potential meanings for conversion. Lieber (2004), however, finds a wider range of meanings than can be found with, say, *-ize* or *-ify*, and concludes that the relisting analysis has at least some advantage over a zero-affixation analysis.

25.4.4 Underspecification/multifunctionality

Some scholars deny that there is any process of conversion at all, but rather argue that roots in English are underspecified or completely unspecified for word class. In this sort of analysis, there is no derivational process relating a noun like *hammer* to the verb *hammer*. Instead, there is simply a single lexical item *hammer* whose category is determined by syntactic context. Similar analyses have been put forward both in generative frameworks (Hale and Keyser 1993) and in Cognitive Grammar (Farrell 2001).

Various versions of the underspecification analysis have in common the difficulty of explaining intuitions that the relationship between noun and verb is often felt to be directional. Generally this problem is approached by appeal to semantic idiosyncrasies of the underspecified bases: although bases may lack syntactic category, they do have semantic information that accounts for the intuition that, say, *hammer* is more fundamentally an entity than an event, and *kiss* the opposite. It is unclear whether the need to appeal to semantic representation undermines the basic claims of this sort of analysis.

Also problematic within underspecification analyses is the failure of many roots to appear in a full range of word classes. Although such analyses tend to focus on noun–verb pairs, there is no reason why truly categoryless roots should not occur in adjectival contexts as well. Indeed, the root *calm* can appear in adjectival environments (*a calm disposition*), nominal environments (*a calm*), and verbal environments (*to calm*). The problem is that true multi-functionality of this sort is too rare in English to attribute to accidental gaps.

25.4.5 The influence of pragmatics: contextuals

Clark and Clark (1979) argue that in many cases a new instance of conversion cannot be understood without reference to the pragmatic environment in which the word is coined. For example, in the example in (30), we need to understand what Groucho Marx typically does with his eyebrows in order to be able to understand the conversion.

(30) Lisa popped a cherry tomato leftover from her salad in her mouth and *Groucho Marxed* her blonde eyebrows. (http://1000days.douglasblaine. com/20110420/the-sex-is-still-always-just-fine/)

In *He telegraphed his intention* we have to work out pragmatically what the relationship is between what he does to his intentions and telegraphy. Clark and Clark call these CONTEX-TUALS (see also Aronoff 1980), because they become meaningless outside of a particular context.

It is not clear that the requirement of pragmatic interpretation of new words is confined to contextuals in general or instances of conversion in particular. Phrased differently, it may be the case that all neologisms are, to some extent, contextual. Given the expression *big benefactors receive no tax breaks in Britain; nor are they lionised at cocktail parties* (BNC) we must, if the item is not already item-familiar, determine the connection between lions and what happens at cocktail parties. In the case of the BNC example *auditionee* in (31), context may leave less room for choice, but the fundamental principles seem to be the same.

(31)   *So you want to be an actor 1991*: As an **auditionee**, I knew I worked best if I attempted something outrageous (BNC)

The requirement for some pragmatic help in the interpretation of neologisms is not controversial. In this context, the question becomes whether instances of conversion require particularly high levels of pragmatic information to be interpreted. Phrased this way, it is not clear that the question is answerable. It seems likely that there is a cline of the amount of pragmatic information required, since a synthetic compound like *parrot smuggler*, if literal, requires relatively little information beyond what is present in the construction, for its interpretation. *Parrot smuggler* is invented (but see NZPA 2007); *budgie smugglers*, on the other hand, is an AusE expression for a pair of skimpy men's swimming trunks. In such cases, a great deal of pragmatic information is required to arrive at the correct interpretation. The example makes the point that even here, whether a smuggler is or is not human is a matter of pragmatics.

Nevertheless, designating a particular subset of neologisms as contextuals, does not seem to be particularly insightful; rather, to the extent that it makes sense to designate an entire construction in this way, it denotes some vaguely determined point on a scale. Instances of conversion such as *to crimson* from *crimson* or *to carpet* from *carpet* (at least in the sense 'to cover with carpet') seem to require relatively little pragmatic information, and are on a different point of the cline. Not all cases of conversion are the same in this regard, and we therefore do not view this as a feature which is distinctive in conversion.

25.4.6 Conversion as inflectional

Myers (1984) argues that conversion is not derivational but inflectional. The argument is placed within a specific generative model, and it is not clear how far it can be separated from that theory.

Like the analyses discussed in Section 25.4.4, Myers' analysis assumes that lexemes have no word class until they are entered into a syntactic tree, at which point they gain the word class from the syntactic structure and may be obliged to take on a specific morphological form to reflect that word class. Given an underlying form which we can characterize as *hate* in a syntactic structure $[DP_{[+genitive]}$ hate $PP_{[+of]}]$ (leading to surface structures like *their hatred of the United States* (COCA)), the underlying element *hate* must take on the surface form *hatred* because it is in a nominal position. *Hatred* is clearly an unpredictable form, and so must be a listed variant for *hate* as a base form that occurs under just such circumstances.

In instances like *I hunger for your touch*, on the other hand, *hunger* and *touch* require no morphological modification, but pass straight into the appropriate form. Their verbal or nominal character (respectively) is guaranteed by a zero-affix which carries a word class marking and the required inflectional categories (in the case of *hunger*, 1st person, non-past tense). Had the sentence been *I hungered for your touches*, there would be overt suffixation rather than the zeros required in the original version of the example. The benefit of this procedure, according to Myers, is that it keeps the righthand head rule intact, and allows headedness to apply to inflectional as well as to derivational morphology in English. These are not clearly benefits, however: it is clear that the righthand head rule does not work for English (cf. cexceptions such as the category-changing prefix *de-*), and there are many issues with allowing inflectional affixes to be heads (see Chapter 24). Further, this analysis appears to combine the underspecification analysis (Section 25.4.4) with a variant of the zero-affixation analysis (Section 25.4.2), and therefore carries with it the problematic elements of both.

25.4.7 Conversion as metonymy

If conversion is a case of metonymy (Schönefeld 2005), it is a very special case. Most instances of metonymy maintain word class, so that *the crown* means 'the monarch' by metonymy, not 'to rule'. But even if we relax the term metonymy, or simply say that pairs of words that are linked by conversion are linked by a figure of speech and not by a morphological relationship, we would have to explain why the relationship is so like derivational relationships, as well as so unlike other figurative relationships.

25.4.8 Various other nomenclatures

Various other terms are suggested in the literature as a way of avoiding the term conversion. These include 'transposition' and 'functional shift'. As far as we are aware, all of these can be reduced to one of the other options we have already mentioned. The terms may focus on one aspect of the process or downplay some aspect of the process, but none adds anything new.

The same is true of the periphrasis that 'word W is used as an item of word class Z' ('*empty* is used as a noun', for example). While this mode of expression is often tempting, it is not clear what it means 'to use something as Z' if it doesn't mean that the form has taken on the functions typically associated with class Z. If that is an accurate gloss, then it is not distinct from the other views which have been discussed above.

25.5 Summary

Conversion in English is defined as what we find when a cluster of canonical conditions are met, and as we move away from those canonical conditions, we move more into lexical or syntactic processes rather than strictly morphological ones. Although there are various approaches to conversion, we prefer one which flows naturally from this cluster of conditions, and this is captured by the nomenclature of conversion rather than any of the other terminologies that have been suggested.

CHAPTER 26

....

Blocking, competition, and productivity

26.1 PROSPECTUS

In this chapter we consider the three interlinked topics of competition, blocking, and productivity. We define morphological processes as being in COMPETITION when they share some domain between them, producing outputs which, if acceptable, might fill the same functional slot in a paradigm (derivational or inflectional). So, for instance *-ness* and *-ity* may be in competition with the result that in some cases only an *-ity* word is attested, in others only a *-ness* word, and in yet others the two co-exist. One way to prevent competition at the level of the individual word would be through blocking. Aronoff (1976: 43) defines blocking as 'the nonoccurrence of one form due to the simple existence of another'. Unfortunately, such a definition raises as many questions as it resolves. Can *thief* block *stealer* (Bolinger 1975: 109), or does blocking affect only words created from the same base by competing morphological processes? How is 'simple existence' to be understood in this context? Similarly, what does 'nonoccurrence' mean, given that we now have ready access through the world-wide web to billions of words of text from a wider range of writers than was available when Aronoff wrote this definition? We will need to consider such questions.

Bauer (2001: 211) says that "'productivity' deals with the number of new words that can be coined using a particular morphological process, and is ambiguous between the sense 'availability' and the sense 'profitability'." Not only does such a definition require the isolation of 'a particular morphological process' and further definitions of 'availability' and 'profitability', but it also requires that it should be possible to count neologisms and it requires a notion of a new word.

None of our fundamental topics for this chapter is thus straightforward, and their interaction is correspondingly less straightforward. Some of these matters have already been traversed relatively superficially in Chapter 2. Here we wish to focus on the theoretical constructs that are the foundations of dealing with these aspects of the morphology of English. In some places, this will involve moving away from our general synchronic approach to morphological matters, and viewing things in a more diachronic way.

26.2 NEW WORDS AND OLD

Although there are many estimates of a speaker's vocabulary size in the literature, they are not reliable (see Nation 1993 on some of the reasons for this). Often there is not even agreement on what kind of 'word' is being counted or what it means to 'know' a vocabulary item. One of the fundamental assumptions of any such measure is that individual speakers do 'know' a number of 'words'. Since the numbers cited in any of the experiments on the numbers of words speakers 'know' is considerably smaller than the number of words in the largest dictionaries of English, there must be a number of words of English which individual speakers do not 'know'. Beyond that, there are items which are not known to individuals, are not in the largest dictionaries, but have the potential to be words.

The words known to an individual speaker are, presumably, of no particular interest to the linguist except insofar as large numbers of speakers share the same words, and there is a social contract on what those words mean and how they are used. However, there are certainly many words that only a minority of speakers share, and that are unfamiliar to most other speakers.

The set of words listed in dictionaries is always slightly out-of-date, chosen to meet criteria which are irrelevant to the linguist (such as having a fixed number of attestations in written English), and often underrepresents the most productive morphological processes. For instance, at the time of writing, the *OED* does not have a listing for *fashion crime*, for *ginga* (/gɪŋə/ 'red-headed person') or a *-ly* adverb corresponding to *hippopotamic*.

(1)   The Fat Man yawned widely. Indeed **hippopotamicly**, thought Pascoe. If such a word existed. (*Hill 2001: 335*)

Potential words are of interest to the linguist. As Aronoff (1976: 19) points out, it is 'the task of a morphology to tell us what sort of new words a speaker can form'. The difficulty is that the main evidence the linguist has as to what is a potential word is the set of actually observed words. Since productivity involves previously non-actual words that were nevertheless potential words becoming actual, the distinction is vital to studies of productivity: vital, but possibly not directly measurable, especially if we take into account that speakers may vary a great deal in their knowledge of words.

The real problem is the gap between what dictionaries register and what is merely non-actualized potential. In this book, we have filled that gap by looking at corpus examples. But any corpus example could be innovative, coining a new form, or could be repeating a form which is already item-familiar to some speaker or writer. All we can assume is that attested words in this in-between stage are recently coined and relatively recent innovations. The word 'relatively' here hides a potential problem that, again, comes in through between-speaker variation.

Speakers are aware of some innovations (if not all), and occasionally draw attention to them in their speech, as in example (1) above, and as in the examples in (2).

(2)   a. Could that polish have been **tainted** with cyanide? Could Susan have been the **tainterer**? Was there such a word a **tainterer**? Maybe she was a tainteress? (*Strohmeyer 2004: 73*)

     b. The houses on Devonshire Close weren't castles...but there was nevertheless something distinctly **castleish**—**castlesque**? **castleine**? **castilian**?—about them. (*Block 2004: 36*)

     c. It was a low-maintenance farm, ... some fields rented out to the '**horsiculture**'—the riding fraternity—and some set aside (*Lovesey 1997: 244*)

     d. Do you use "cinnamony" to describe something with cinnamon? If not, what do you use? (http://www.answerbag.com/q_view/1306672#ixzz1zPuSJ5cO)

While such examples may be indicative, they provide poor evidence as to the actual state of the language. The form *tainterer* ought to be ungrammatical as it has two agentive suffixes *-er*, where one is usually enough; *castlesque* gets only one hit on Google, and that's a name—the *OED* lists only *castle-like*; *cinnamony* gets hundreds of thousands of hits on Google. So we know that there are new words, but we cannot be sure at any given time whether a word is or is not new. In principle it is new or not new only with respect to a given speaker at a given time. Accordingly, there can be no direct measure of new words being used in the language, but we know there must be new words.

A distinct question is whether we can be sure about newly established words in the speech community. Here we are on a slightly firmer footing. Large dictionaries such as the *OED* provide a continually up-dated list of established words, and the internet allows us to see how widespread a given word is. By comparing corpus data with a source such as the *OED* we can see whether a particular morphological process continues to be productive, though it is doubtful that we can turn that into any specific measure. To illustrate this point, consider the suffix *-fold* (see Chapter 18.4.3). The *OED* provides a handful of examples, not in its lemmas but in its explanation of the history of the form. COCA provides hundreds of forms. Yet many of the forms found in COCA must have been used many times in the past; it is simply that the *OED* does not note the most productive uses, because there is no lexicographical benefit to doing so.

Given this state of affairs, it is sometimes an open question how far unique forms can be trusted as good data (see Bauer 2001: 57–8 for some discussion). We have generally trusted our corpus data, and where individual examples fit into widespread patterns there seems to be little reason to doubt it (see Chapter 3 for more discussion). Rarer patterns always have to be treated with a little more care. At the same time, we must be careful not to dismiss forms on the basis of our own prejudices.

26.3 Competition

26.3.1 Competition in inflection

The traditional point of view is that there is no competition in inflection: *oxen* blocks a potential **oxes*, *stood* blocks a potential **standed*, and so on. Thus it is that the standard view of level-ordered morphology puts these irregular forms at level I and then assumes that they block the regular morphology at level II (e.g. Kiparsky 1982a).

We have seen that this is true only to a certain extent. Not only do forms like *oxes* and *standed* arise in child-language (where we might be tempted to dismiss them as incompetent formations), but they arise also where we are not dealing with literal uses or where we are dealing with compounds, especially compounds which are not literal endocentric compounds. To cite a well-known example, the preterite of the verb *grandstand* is *grandstanded*, not **grandstood* in standard varieties of English. Not only is the number of incompetent regular formations greater than is usually assumed, but variation with regular forms (and with competing irregular forms) is also found in instances where the incompetence excuse does not seem to be available. If this were not the case, the well-attested movement of irregular forms to regular forms over time could not arise; the diachronic processes of *holp* > *helped* and *shoon* > *shoes* depend upon variability between regular and irregular forms.

Accordingly, we must allow for competition in inflectional morphology, and we must allow for competition between irregular forms as well as competition between regular and irregular forms. We have distinctions such as *spit* and *spat* as the preterite of *spit* (this may depend on dialect to a very large extent), between *come* and *came* as the preterite of *come*, between *forgot* and *forgotten* as the past participle of *forget*, between *tread* and *trod* as the preterite of *tread*, between *proved* and *proven* as the past participle of *prove*, between *swam* and *swum* as the preterite of *swim*, and so on (see Chapter 5). If we do not include Latin plurals for nouns as part of English here, it is only because there is an argument that they involve code-switching rather than genuinely alternative English inflections.

Standard stories are that frequency protects irregularity in morphology, so that an infrequent irregular form tends to become regularized (e.g. Bybee 1985), while words with a particular pattern tend to create a template which can attract more words—whether this involves movement to regular or irregular morphology (Bybee and Moder 1983). At the same time, denominal verbs tend to be regular, even when homophonous with irregular verbs (the *grandstanded* case and also *He ringed/*rang the pigeon*).

We do not attempt to apply these general formulations systematically to our data to predict outcomes, but we do need to consider what kinds of pattern might be attracting new forms. Anderwald (2009) suggests that the homophony of the preterite and the past participle might be a principled pattern in modern English. This principle supports the non-standard patterns in which *come* is the preterite of *come* and *swum* is the preterite of *swim*, for example. It does not explain why *spit* • *spat* • *spat* should alternate with or turn into *spit* • *spit* • *spit*. It might explain a paradigm of *tread • trod • trod*, but not one of *tread • tread • trod*. Bybee and Moder (1983) propose that a general template illustrated in (3) means that verbs like *swim* are changing to the pattern of verbs like *sink*.

(3)   …∧ C~nasal-or-velar~]~VERB + PAST~

While we have evidence of the power of such a template, its precise status is in question given that we have words like *junk* and, despite the spelling, *monk*, which are not (primarily) verbs, and words like *flunk* which are not past tense (but see Albright and Hayes 2003 or Keuleers 2008 for discussion).

Another pattern which might be added to the list is a preference for monosyllabic verbs with a final alveolar plosive to have the same form in all three parts of the verb (Bauer 1997b). Again, we could set out a template, like that in (3), which might be something like (4) (see Bauer 1997b on the vowels involved).

(4)   [Onset V C~alveolar plosive~]~VERB (ALL FORMS)~

This generalization covers standard and fixed forms like *cut, hit, put*, but also forms with variation like *fit, knit, rid, shit, spit, tread*.

Part of the difficulty with such views of what is happening in competition between morphological processes is that they seem to be teleological: they seem to assume a motivated movement in a particular direction towards a more regular distribution of the processes involved. In many instances, all we can see is that there is variation, not which direction we are moving in. For example, the use of *dove* as the preterite of *dive* started in the USA and is a more recent innovation in CanE, AusE, and NZE, but appears to be gaining ground there, even though having *dive • dove • dived* not only breaks Anderwald's predictions on patterning, but it also mixes regular and irregular forms in the same paradigm, and having *dive • dove • dove* does not fit with any other general pattern of vowel alternation. In instances like *shit*, we know what the variation is (preterite *shat ~ shit*), but we do not, at the moment, know which form is likely to become the new standard (if either). Templates like (3) or (4) might have to be reinterpreted as templates about domains where there is variation, rather than as patterns promoting change.

From this brief discussion, we can abstract the following points:

- There can be competition between formal ways of filling the same inflectional slot in the paradigm.
- Competition is seen in variable forms for the inflected word-form.
- Competition may indicate static variation, or a gradual acceptance of one of the variants at the expense of the other(s).
- Individual instances of variation may be part of a general pattern of variation or may be isolated.

- Change based on such variation may lead to greater regularity (analogical levelling) or may not; where there is regularity this may be defined in terms of predictability of paradigms or in terms of more widespread use of the default variant ('the regular past tense ending') and the two may contrast.

26.3.2 Competition in derivation

Competition in derivation looks rather different in that the sources of competitors tend to be rather different. Nevertheless, the same fundamental principles seem to apply.

There can be variation in the ways of filling the same slot in a derivational paradigm. In most cases, though this is not variation in the particular derivative formed (there is some of that, too), it is a matter of having two or more synonymous affixes. Thus *-ness* and *-ity* are typically cited as affixes which both have the function of deriving abstract nouns from adjectives, and as such are in competition (Chapter 12). Similarly *-ify* and *-ize* (and possibly other processes) compete in creating new verbs (Chapter 13), *-ly*, *-ish*, and *-esque* compete in producing adjectives of similarity from nouns (Chapter 14), *-er* and *-ist* compete in producing words denoting people in a particular profession or people who (habitually) perform certain actions (Chapter 11).

Some of this variation seems to be static, some of it is variation involved in change. The variability between *-ify* and *-ize* is identified by Plag (1999) as being largely determined by the phonology of the base (or the phonology of the output word). The suffix *-ize* requires an unstressed syllable preceding it, whereas *-ify* requires a syllable with some degree of stress preceding it (see Chapter 13). On the other hand, the variation we find between nominalization affixes in words like *closure, laughter, marriage, texturization* seems to have diminished with time, so that now we can still use *-ation*, but rarely use the others to create new forms (see Chapter 10).

Variation may be part of a general pattern or be limited to a particular set of lexemes. The prefixes *mono-* and *uni-* are rarely established on the same base, but the *Concise Oxford Dictionary* lists both *monocycle* and *unicycle* and *monopod* and *unipod*. On the other hand, there is regular alternation between negative prefixes so that we find pairs like those in (5), with or without meaning differences (see Chapter 14 for discussion).

(5) amoral   immoral
     apolitical   unpolitical
     astable   instable
     athematic   unthematic
     atypical   untypical
     incomputable   uncomputable
     inconspicuous   unconspicuous

indecisive   undecisive

inessential   unessential

intestate   untestate (*marked as obsolete in the OED*)

In derivation, it can be difficult to decide whether there is a default affix for a particular meaning, although where there is competition between a non-native affix and a native affix it is often the case that the native one has the wider distribution. Nevertheless, there are instances of competition in derivation leading to greater paradigm uniformity and instances where uniformity seems to be less of a driving force. For example, over the past two hundred years, *-ity* has gained ground vis-à-vis its rival *-ness* with bases ending in the suffix *-al*, making it practically obligatory in this morphological context, while overall *-ity* has lost ground to *-ness* in the formation of new words (Arndt-Lappe 2012, based on *OED* data). Sometimes any uniformity is masked by the fact that words containing affixes which are no longer productive (or whose productivity is marginal) tend to persist in the vocabulary of the speech community.

An example of this point is the history of nominalization markers in English (see Bauer 2006a). Despite the existence of hundreds of nominalization words with a host of different affixes, only *-ation*, *-ing*, and conversion are reliably productive today (and then in very restricted domains, see Chapter 10). There is, in one sense, regularization, but no regularity can be determined by looking at a list of established words.

26.3.3 A diachronic view of competition

In principle, competition can be absolutely stable, even over a long period of time. More often, though, at least one of the processes is gaining or losing productivity. Again in principle, we can have any combination of stability and gaining productivity or losing productivity. The stability can be a lack of productivity or can be at some level of productivity. The stability of *laughter*, *hatred*, or *length* is due to lack of productivity. The current stability of *-ify* and *-ize* is based on the productivity of both.

Perhaps the expected picture is that a given morphological process with a certain function is replaced with another process with the same meaning. Thus *-ster* with the meaning 'feminine' was replaced by *-ess* in Middle English (Bauer 2006a). The suffix *-ster* has persisted to the present day, and is still productive, just not with that meaning. Words still in use that were formed with the original *-ster* (*baxter, seamster, songster, webster*, some now only used as names) no longer have the meaning 'feminine'.

There are many other possibilities, though. Among others, there are instances where two affixes are in competition only in a small part of their domain. The suffixes *-ness* and *-ity* appear to be in particular competition following the suffixes *-ive* and *-ous* (Aronoff 1976: 37–45; Arndt-Lappe 2012) and barely in competition following *-able*, with only 69 types attested in COCA for forms in -*ableness* and more than 1000 for forms in -*ability*.

The results of diachronic competition are also unpredictable. As we have just seen, the feminine meaning of the suffix -*ster* has vanished, even though the affix has survived with other meanings. The suffix -*th*, which once created de-adjectival or deverbal nominalizations (*warmth*, *birth*), has left many words behind which still have their original meaning. Words like *to-stand* (Anshen and Aronoff 1997) have vanished completely with the construction that licensed them. The suffix -*(e)rel* mentioned by Marchand (1969) (see Chapter 18) in words like *mackerel* and *wastrel* is no longer recognized as an affix.

Where there is stable variation or variation leading to change, it would be expected that variationist studies of morphology would indicate the different options being preferred by different parts of the population. We know only of studies that involved inflectional forms, such as past tense -*ed* (e.g. Labov 1972; Cheshire 1982). The difficulty for such studies is that often the variation is spread over large periods of time, typically with insufficient textual material to allow good conclusions to be drawn.

26.4 BLOCKING

If there can be competition between morphological processes on the same base, there can be no blocking. The two notions are mutually incompatible. It might be possible to say no more than that, and to refer to the many examples of failed blocking that appear elsewhere in this book for support. The notion of blocking is, though, widespread, and there may be value in attempting to deconstruct it a little.

Blocking can be divided into two parts: blocking by synonymy and blocking by homonymy. Blocking by synonymy is a generalization of an older notion that there can be no synonyms (Bloomfield 1935: 145), or that one of a pair of synonyms tends to be 'lost' (Sturtevant 1917: 99; Ullmann 1957: 112 and works cited there; Paul 1995 [1920]: 251).

Blocking by homonymy is occasionally used in historical linguistics to explain the disappearance of one term in favour of another. The best examples involve some kind of embarrassment for speakers: the replacement of *ass* by *donkey*, the replacement of *coney* (pronounced /kʌni/ and thus having obscene connotations) by *rabbit*, the replacement of *cock* by *rooster*. Unfortunately there are other examples where potentially embarrassing homonymy has not led to the abandonment of a word. *Hookers* in rugby have not been renamed because of street-walker *hookers*. And there are many expressions including *cock* which have not been changed, including *cock-a-doodle-do, cockatoo, cockeyed, cockpit, cock of the walk*. The embarrassment need not be on grounds of obscenity, but on grounds of conflicting usage: French examples of verbs for 'milk' and 'mill' collapsing as *moudre* or for 'cat' and 'rooster' collapsing as *gat* in Gascony are widely cited (Orr 1962) as instances of homonymy which have had to be repaired after the fact. Parallel examples are rarely cited in the history of English, which seems to accept homonymy. Indeed, non-embarrassing homonymy is so widespread that its value as an explanation for 'non-occurrence' must be called into question (see Nevalainen 1999: 453). Obvious homonymy cases are words such as *funny, hot, jolly, light, mash, mass, mast, retort,* or *liver* (as in *The Verne-Smiths were not long livers. Lewis's father had died at sixty and his grandfather at sixty-two.* w_fict_prose 1987, from COCA). In extreme cases, we find that forms like *cleave* and *let* can survive for many years with two diametrically opposed meanings: 'stick together' and 'split apart', and 'allow' and 'prevent' (as in *without let or hindrance*), respectively. To the extent that there are good examples of homonymy being a factor in preventing the acceptance of a particular word, it must be a weak one.

Blocking by synonymy is thus potentially a much more powerful explanation than blocking by homonymy. There are at least two ways in which this synonymy can arise (as mentioned above). Either the supposed blocker can be a morphologically unrelated word, or the supposed blocker can be a word based on the same root (perhaps even the same base) as the supposed blockee.

In order to test either of these hypotheses, we have to know what will be taken as evidence of blocking functioning. It seems that blocking fails systematically in a number of places. These include the following.

- Instances where the expected blockee is formed with an extremely productive process. Thus Aronoff (1976: 45) claims that *-ness* affixation is not blocked because derivatives in *-ness* are never listed in the lexicon. The implication is that it is not formations which are blocked, but listing in the lexicon which is blocked.
- Instances where the expected blockee is used in a way which is not synonymous with the blocker or where the connotations are markedly different from those of the blocker. This allows, for example, *committal* and *commitment* to be used to mean something other than *commission*. Such deliberate use of competing affixes is relatively common. *Denseness* and *density* can mean the same thing, but the *OED* suggests that *denseness*, when it occurs, is used mainly in non-technical areas, while *density* is mainly a technical term. COCA and the BNC support this interpretation. Such subtle differences in meaning arise in individual pairs in specific contexts, as shown in Chapter 12.
- Instances where the speaker, either temporarily or permanently, is unaware of the earlier usage. Failure of memory is often a factor here, but so too is the necessity for sophisticated vocabulary from someone who is not used to producing this level of language. This also applies to some children's utterances.

These conditions can be summarized by saying that blocking does not prevent the production of a word, it prevents the institutionalization of a word, and by saying that blocking does not work unless the blocker and blockee are not only synonymous but also stylistically equivalent (see also Aronoff 1976: 56; Rainer 1988).

Rainer (1988) distinguishes between token-blocking, of the type discussed above, and type-blocking where affixes are used within different domains, and the domain for affix *x* is not available for affix *y* and vice versa. An example from English would be nominalizations of verbs in *-ation* as opposed to nominalizations using conversion. If *-ation* suffixation in the contemporary language is restricted or virtually restricted to verbs ending in *-ify* and *-ize*, and conversion to nouns does not apply to this set of verbs, then there is type-blocking between the two. While we accept this general point, it seems to us that the mechanisms are so different that the use of the term 'blocking' in the type-blocking sense is misleading. Accordingly, we focus on token-blocking here.

Even in the reduced sense of 'blocking' to which this leads, it is our view that we have found too many examples of the failure of any such principle for us to be able to give it much credence. Our evidence might appear in many instances to come from ad hoc neologisms rather than from institutionalized words, but some of these apparent neologisms can be used fairly widely and a clear-cut distinction between what is and what is not institutionalized can be hard to establish.

Some instances are given below to illustrate our point (not, it must be stressed, an exhaustive coverage). Many others can be found in the pages of this book.

Orientate has replaced (or largely replaced) the verb *orient* in the sense of 'position oneself or an object in respect of the compass or some other object'. The verb *orient* still remains, but typically with more abstract types of location, as suggested by the examples from corpora (e.g. *it has been oriented towards an academic hermit's life*, American Studies International 2003, COCA).

As was shown in (5), various negative prefixes, even the less productive ones, may be used with a certain degree of variability. While these sometimes show (or are said to show) a difference in meaning (*amoral* versus *immoral*, for example), this is not always the case, as illustrated in (6) with examples from COCA (see Chapter 17 for more examples and discussion).

(6) *Esquire 2010*: Spitzer was every bit as dishonest and **amoral** and greedy as the worst of his enemies

   NPR_TalkNation 2008: But when I do mention it to them, they assume that we're **immoral**, that we don't have a moral code.

The various prefixes glossed as 'to remove ~ from' such as *de-*, *dis-*, and *un-* in *denature, dismast, uncap* show some diachronic patterning among themselves, but in some instances are found on the same base with the same meaning (e.g. *dethrone, disthrone, unthrone*; see Bauer 2006a).

Various adjective-forming suffixes may be found on the same base apparently without semantic distinction: *barbaric, barbarous; gigantean, gigantic; Greenlandic, Greenlandish; womanish, womanly*. This is not to deny that the same pairs of suffixes have, on occasions, become lexicalized with distinct meanings: *cupric, cuprous; mannish, manly; official, officious*.

Regular plurals are used for nouns which normally have irregular forms when they are (a) parts of names or (b) non-literal. This gives us *Mickey Mouses*, *Mapleleafs*, and *their gooses are cooked* (non-standard) (see Chapter 7 for more discussion).

None of this provides a picture of blocking functioning as expected. That being the case, the question of whether blocking involves *thief* and *stealer* or only examples like *bequeathal* and *bequeathement* becomes moot, and need not be taken seriously.

26.5 PRODUCTIVITY

It appears to be uncontroversial to say that some morphological processes can be used in the creation of new words while others are rarely or never used in this way. In recent years, following Corbin (1987) it seems to have become generally accepted that questions about productivity can be split into two: can a given process be used at all, and if so, to what extent is it used? These are distinguished as 'availability' and 'profitability', though as we mentioned in Chapter 2.6 we do not use the terminology unless potential ambiguity forces us to.

Even at this point we may have strayed beyond the boundaries of the uncontroversial: although we can say at a given point that we lack evidence of the productivity of a given morphological process, this cannot be interpreted as meaning that it could not be resurrected at some point. Only those processes which leave no traces in the vocabulary can be safely assumed to be dead.

The discussion of productivity (sensu profitability) has been carried out in two distinct terminological frameworks. On the one hand, there is current usage of questions of 'constraints' on productivity. In this framework, the nominalizing suffix *-al* has as a constraint that it must be added to a verb which carries stress on the final syllable. The alternative terminology—one we have employed freely in other places in the book—is in terms of domains of productivity. In these terms, the nominalizing *-al* suffix is productive only in the phonological domain which has stress on the final syllable of the base (or, equivalently, on the penult of the derivative). We take it that these two views are equivalent, though one focuses on the exclusion of impossible forms and the other focuses on potential sites of inclusion. It is for this reason that the 'domain' metaphor seems to be preferable in general. Nevertheless, there are places (such as the reduced use of adverbial *-ly* after an adjective which ends in *-ly*) where the constraint terminology seems reasonable, since the limitations are more neatly expressible in such terms.

Some types of domain are well-established in the literature, others are less well developed. Domains may be established in phonological terms, in morphological terms (the affix *y* may be added to a word which ends in affix *x*), in terms of word class (the affix *x* may be added only to bases of word class *y*), in terms of semantics (the affix *x* may be added to a word which bears the semantic specification [y]), in terms of pragmatics (the affix *x* may be added only to bases to which the speaker wishes to express a particular attitude or when a word expressing a particular attitude is required); the affix *x* may be added only to create a word in some technical area) or in terms of etymology (the affix *x* may added only to bases with a certain etymology—though we have suggested that such domains are likely to be weak in contemporary English). In principle a domain could be established by the intersection of any set of these.

A full discussion of domains is still required (though see van Marle 1985). It seems that some domain types are, if not impossible, then not found in English. We do not have a domain for a particular suffix which demands a prefixed base, for instance, or a domain for a particular prefix that demands a suffixed base. While we have some affixes whose domains seem to be monomorphemic bases, it is not clear that we have any whose domains are specifically and exclusively morphologically complex bases, or which attach only to compounds. Similarly, there are domains referring to prosodic categories or structures, but it is unclear whether there are any principled restrictions as to which types of prosodic domain would not be be able to play a role. While we do not find in English affixes which attach only to words denoting animals or trees (for example), there seems to be no reason why such processes would not be possible (and some occur in other languages). The best constraint seems to be that the same category is not marked tautologically twice on the same base, but even that is not always true, for example with diminutives (see Chapter 18), agentive nominalizations (Chapter 11), or historically as in *children* when an earlier marker loses its force. Arguably, multiple prefixation of the type *sub-sub-prime* is not tautological.

It is not always clear at what level domains should be stated. If, for example, *-ity* attaches to words ending in *-al* (and allomorphs), *-able*, *-ic*, and also *-ive* (see Chapter 12.2.1), it may be that there is a point at which it should be determined that the domain of this suffix is non-native adjectival bases. The fact that other non-native affixes such as *-ous* and *-ian* can be added to the list makes this seem reasonable. It is, however, not clear to what extent the lack of words in *-esquity*, *-istity*, *-entity*, or *-antity* disproves the wider claim. The more specific claims seem less contentious.

Not only may various different affixes share domains, even contrasting affixes can share domains. Thus, *-ee* and *-able* may both be added to transitive verbs (so they share a domain, but do not compete), and *-ness* and *-ity* may both be added to adjectives in *-ive* (where they do compete). So the core cases of competition are instances where synonymous affixes (or, more generally, morphological processes) share domains. Again, there is some question as to how the various domains are best formalized. If it is the case that *-ness* has any adjective as its domain, the fact that it competes with *-ity* on adjectives in *-ive* is more or less accidental. Nevertheless, the basic point holds.

Some more general constraints on productivity have been proposed in the literature. These include the word base hypothesis (Aronoff 1976: 21), The Unitary Base Hypothesis (Aronoff 1976: 48), the Unitary Output Hypothesis (Scalise 1984: 137), level ordering constraints (starting with Bloomfield 1935, but see also Kiparsky 1982a, and Plag 1999: 45, Bauer 2001: 128 for critical discussion). We mostly deal with these elsewhere in this book (see Chapter 29), but here simply need to repeat that where it is clear how such constraints are to be interpreted, they do not appear to be strongly supported by our data.

If affixes can compete in the same domain, we can imagine various possible outcomes. One is that all bases in the domain can be used with either affix. Another is that the affixes are distributed more or less randomly among the bases, perhaps with some duplication. This is what appears to happen with *-ness* and *-ity* on bases in *-ive*. We can have *expensiveness* but ?*expensivity* seems odd (despite *expansivity*); ?*evasivity* seems not to be used (and is not in COCA at the time of writing). The implication is that the affixes in such instances are not of equal productivity in particular domains. A more general conclusion is that even in domains, there are degrees of productivity, it is not simply a matter of availability or non-availability within a domain.

Another factor which can make productivity appear to be scalar in this way is the number of bases that are available for a particular morphological process to act upon. In Chapter 18.4.6 the example of the suffix *-ton* is given, which appears to occur only on one base in the established lexicon (*singleton*) but which can be attested on two other bases. It is an open question as to whether ☜ *quintupleton* is a possible word of English or not, but even if it is, there are only a handful of possible bases for formations with this suffix. There are more potential bases for the prefixation of *step-* (see Chapter 11.2.5 and 11.3.2), but not huge numbers. On the other hand, the bases for *-er* suffixation or *un-* prefixation are legion. It is not clear how the productivity of *-er* and *-ton* can be compared. It seems that the number of formations produced is one factor in determining productivity, so that even if *-ton* is found on all of the words to which it can in principle attach, and *-er* is found on not quite all of the words to which it can in principle attach, *-er* will be viewed as more productive. This is contrary to the claim made by Aronoff (1976).

This example makes it clear that, even in simple cases, it can be difficult to determine the productivity of individual morphological processes. The actual productivity of morphological processes is no less fraught. Although we can do calculations over established words from a source such as the *OED* (Plag 1999), and this will give some kind of impression of productivity, or deduce productivity from the number of hapaxes in a corpus (Baayen and Lieber 1991; Baayen 1992, 1993) in ways which give intuitively plausible results, we do not appear to be able to give reliable and repeatable measures of productivity that allow cross-linguistic comparisons to be made or even that allow comparisons between different corpora (see Baayen 1993 and for some discussion, Bauer 2001). Moreover, dictionary counts and corpus counts tend to provide quite distinct results, in many instances.

That is not to say that we do not have any clues. Following the work by Baayen (1992, 1993) it is generally accepted that the more productive a particular morphological process is, the more it will have outputs which are of low token frequency, while the products of non-productive morphology will tend to have high token frequency. In a large enough corpus, all the examples of an unproductive morphological process repeat words from a closed list of established words. With productive morphological processes, in contrast, at least some of the words found in a corpus are likely to be neologisms or relatively recent formations, which will have low token frequency. While it is by no means the case that all hapaxes in a corpus like the BNC will illustrate productive morphological processes at work, nevertheless, the hapaxes will provide a proxy measure for the number of words of low frequency which are being formed by the relevant morphological process. This correlation has been used in other chapters in this book to deduce productivity in various morphological processes.

Accordingly, we have not attempted in this book to give accurate measures of productivity, but have restricted ourselves to rather impressionistic statements of degree of productivity. From a practical point of view, it is not entirely clear how accurate measures would be of value. It is clear that, for instance, EFL learners and teachers need to be most aware of the most productive morphological processes, and can ignore those processes which are of very low productivity, at least as far as the productive skills of speaking and writing are concerned. From a theoretical point of view, it is not clear how productivity should be seen as part of the language system, or even whether it should be (Bauer 2001 provides some discussion and references). It has been claimed that productive morphology is stored differently in the brain from unproductive morphology and if this is true, then some linguists will want to model the two in different ways (e.g. Pinker and Prince 1994; Pinker 1999); others, however, want to model them in precisely the same way (Rumelhart & McClelland 1986; Skousen *et al.* 2002; Keuleers 2008). We can observe different behaviours on the part of different morphological processes, but the interpretation of those behaviours is still controversial.

One of the possibilities is that productivity is not a cause of morphological distinctions, but the result of morphological distinctions (Hay 2003). It may be that differences in productivity are caused by differentials in phonological and semantic transparency, parsability or naturalness (see, e.g. Mayerthaler 1981) between affixes, and that affixes which are easier for the speaker/listener to isolate because their meaning is clearer, because their form is more consistent, and because they comply with general cognitive principles and expectations of language structure are more productive than those which are more difficult to isolate. Tempting though this hypothesis may be, there are some features of English morphology that tend to cast it into doubt. One of those features is the productivity of conversion in English, which is not easily accounted for given the assumptions of theorists of naturalness. Second, we have seen that affixes are productive in particular domains, some of which force lack of transparency (for example, the use of velar softening) at morpheme boundaries, without apparently losing productivity. Again, what we see is that the morphological facts are open to several theoretical interpretations.

26.6 CONCLUSION

Competition, blocking, and productivity are interlocking concepts in the study of morphology. Our data shows so much competition in domains of productivity that we cannot find strong support for any strong notion of blocking, even if we try to restrict the notion. The notion of productivity is important in morphological description, but its theoretical importance is open to interpretation and controversial. As a result we describe some of the phenomena we observe in this area, but do not attempt to provide a theoretical interpretation of these phenomena.

....

CHAPTER 27

The nature of stratification

27.1 PROSPECTUS

Although the primary subject of this volume has been the contemporary state of English morphology, we cannot completely ignore the historical circumstances that have given rise to the exceptional richness and intricacy of present-day English. Marchand (1969) of course provides us with details of the origins and development of particular affixes and types of compounding and conversion, and the *OED* supplements this with etymological information about affixes, but neither gives a complete overview. Further, theoretical developments in the last forty years have drawn us to look at the intertwined strands of English morphology in new ways, and our current study of contemporary corpora can be used to shed further light on theoretical issues that arise with regard to the interaction of different strata in English morphology: those aspects of morphology that are native to the language and those aspects that come into English as a result of wholesale borrowing from French and the classical languages Latin and Greek.

The theoretical issues have hinged for the most part on the extent to which and the specific ways in which these strata can interact with each other. What we will suggest in the following is that theoretical claims have largely been based on an incomplete picture, and that there is less in the way of stratification in English derivation than has been assumed. This is in fact a good result: as Aronoff and Fuhrhop (2002: 469) have pointed out, it is unclear 'how the etymological distinction is reflected in the synchronic grammar of a naïve speaker of English, who cannot be expected to know the origins of words'. The conclusion that we come to is that the etymological distinction is only a faint one, if it exists at all in the mental lexicons of contemporary native speakers of English.

In Section 27.2 we will summarize in tabular fashion a very large amount of data on the combinatorial properties of both suffixes and prefixes. Some of this data can be found piecemeal in previous chapters, but the bulk of it is drawn from a careful search of COCA. In Section 27.3 we will assess what a close look at the data can tell us about the interactions of native and foreign strands of morphology in contemporary English. Specifically, concentrating on combinations of suffixes, we will examine the extent to which contemporary English can really be said to have separate strata, and the ways in which the strata behave differently. In Section 27.4 we consider the theoretical consequences of stratification (or the lack thereof).

27.2 DATA

Although a fully general discussion of stratification in English morphology might logically include the behaviour of compounds—for example, the extent to which neoclassical combining forms have come to combine with native bases (e.g. *forkology, cardioglider, psychobabble*)—in this chapter we will confine ourselves to a discussion of the extent of stratification in affixation. In what follows, we will refer to *native* and *non-native* affixes (see the discussion in Chapter 2.7). The reader is referred to the individual chapters for more detail on the formal behaviour and semantics of individual affixes. In the tables below we consider most of the productive affixes of English, but the reader should note that they are not absolutely exhaustive. If an affix appears in one of the tables, but fails to occur in others this absence is significant, as it indicates that pertinent combinations are not attested in our data.

As can be seen from Table 27.1, all native affixes with even marginal productivity in the contemporary language can attach to either native or non-native bases. In Table 27.1 and the following tables, the symbol '✓' indicates that a particular form or combination is attested in our data, the symbol '!' indicates that a particular form or combination appears in very few types, and a blank indicates that we have not found the form or combination attested.

As Tables 27.2 and 27.3 suggest, non-native affixes vary in their ability to take native bases; nevertheless many prefixes and also quite a few suffixes can be found on both non-native and native bases:

It is fairly clear from Tables 27.2 and 27.3 that non-native suffixes are generally more inclined to be selective in their bases than non-native prefixes are, but perhaps less so than earlier literature suggests (cf. Giegerich 1999, for example).

We must also ask to what extent we find both native affixes attached to non-native affixes and non-native attached to native ones. In a derivational system without stratification, we might expect the two orderings to be equally likely, all other things being equal (that is, as long as each affix can fulfil its other selectional requirements). Of course, all things are never equal: as we have seen in Chapter 21 (and references cited there), accounting for the ordering of affixes in English is quite a difficult issue as there are many factors that seem to be involved in determining what can attach to what. Nevertheless, we might expect to find at least a fair amount of interleaving of native and non-native affixes.

In Tables 27.4–27.7 we have put together examples of combinations of suffixes that we have found attested. Many of these are taken from Plag and Baayen (2009) (marked with 'p' in the Source column), who themselves have gathered examples from Hay and Plag (2004) and from the *OED*. To these we have added our own examples of combinations we find attested in COCA, and very occasionally from Google (marked with 'g' in the Source column).

Tables 27.8–27.11 show combinations of prefixes. Searching for combinations of prefixes presents a problem that generally does not occur in searching for combinations of suffixes,

Table 27.1 Native affixes and the bases they select

Affix	Native bases	Examples	Non-native bases	Examples
after-	✓	afterbirth, afterchurch, afternoon	✓	aftercourse, after-effect, after-image
back-	✓	backboard, backflow, backland	✓	back-country, back-focus, back-office
be-	✓	befall, befriend, behead	✓	becalm, beglamored, besport
by-	✓	by-blow, by-catch, byway	✓	by-effect, by-election, bypass
-dom	✓	beardom, kingdom, wisdom	✓	pariahdom, entreedom, marveldom
down-	✓	down-beat, downbound, downfall	✓	down-ballot, downcity, downcycle
-er	✓	writer, thinker, sleeper	✓	employer, attacker, defaulter
-fold	✓	sevenfold, twofold	✓	billion-fold
fore-	✓	forearm, forebode, foresee	✓	forecourt, foremastered, fore-thorax
-ful$_A$	✓	slothful, wakeful, rightful	✓	deceitful, resentful, purposeful
-hood	✓	babehood, thinghood, fatherhood	✓	geniushood, mountainhood, gorillahood
-ish	✓	babyish, goodish, doomish	✓	iconish, modernish, caricaturish
-less	✓	eyeless, fatherless, houndless	✓	ageless, captionless, roseless
-let	✓	eyelet, leaflet, ringlet	✓	chainlet, coverlet, statelet
-ling	✓	darkling, earthling, lordling	✓	changeling, princeling, sharkling
-ly	✓	nightly, fleshly, readerly	✓	actorly, comradely, musicianly
mid-	✓	mid-answer, midbreath, mid-glide	✓	midargument, midcareer, midevent
mis-	✓	mishit, misbelieve, misbirth	✓	misact, misdefine, mispredict
-ness	✓	afraidness, awakeness, bigness	✓	abjectness, benignness, obtuseness
off-	✓	off-black, off-board, off-earth	✓	off-angle, off-campus, off-license
on-	✓	ongoing, onload, onset	✓	onmarch, onmoving, on-passing
out-	✓	out-bid, outbreak, outflow	✓	out-anticipate, outbalance, outdistance
over-	✓	overall, overanswer, overbid	✓	overabrade, overattend, overcapture
-ship	✓	queenship, hateship, fathership	✓	consulship, tenureship, carpetship
-some	✓	healthsome, darksome, mirthsome	✓	adventuresome, frolicsome, fruitsome
-ster	✓	oldster, youngster, spinster	✓	fraudster, strumster, scenester
un-	✓	unfair, unlearn, undeath	✓	unable, undevout, unmanifest

(continued)

Table 27.1 Native affixes and the bases they select (continued)

Affix	Native bases	Examples	Non-native bases	Examples
under-	✓	underarm, underdrive, undereat	✓	underachieve, underclass, underemploy
up-	✓	upbound, upflow, uphold	✓	upcycle, upgrade, upmountain
-ward	✓	deathward, downward, godward	✓	cityward, equatorward, mirrorward
-wise	✓	babywise, drinkwise, healthwise	✓	agewise, caloriewise, fashionwise
-y_A	✓	houndy, choosey, dreary	✓	arty, moderny, perfumey

Table 27.2 Non-native suffixes and the bases they select

Affix	Native bases	Examples	Non-native bases	Examples
-able	✓	bakeable, bearable, doable	✓	admirable, cherishable, imaginable
-acy	!		✓	advocacy, conspiracy, determinacy
-age	✓	footage, gooseage, readage	✓	baronage, brokerage, symbolage
$-al_N$	!	upheaval	✓	acquittal, disbursal, recital
$-al_A$	!	bridal, tidal	✓	aerial, bronchial, electoral
$-an_N$	!	Roughian	✓	centenarian, grammarian, musician
$-an_A$	!	elvan	✓	apian, brontosaurian, carnivoran
-ance	!	riddance, hindrance	✓	abettance, conductance, utterance
-ancy	!		✓	claimancy, hesitancy, occupancy
$-ant_{A/N}$	!	heatant, coolant, floatant	✓	accelerant, refrigerant, accountant
-ary	!		✓	deputary, expansionary, sectary
$-ate_V$	!		✓	alienate, capsulate, assassinate
-ation	!	botheration, flirtation, starvation	✓	abbreviation, insinuation, revolution
-ee	✓	askee, callee, helpee	✓	contactee, expellee, interpretee
-ery	✓	cheesery, grainery, wifery	✓	museumery, riflery, distillery
-ese	!	motherese	✓	dissertationese, funeralese, computerese
-esque	✓	girlesque, hell-esque, island-esque	✓	bordello-esque, divaesque, humanesque
-ess	✓	witchess, falconress, folkstress	✓	composeress, mentoress, hauntress
-ette	✓	wenchette, wifette, yeomanette	✓	conductorette, reporterette, chefette
-ic	!	folkloric, runic	✓	aquatic, iconic, synaptic
-ical	!	churchical, folklorical, raspberrical	✓	physical, exegetical, meteorological
-ify	!	churchify, mouse-ify, prettify	✓	electrify, liquify, purify
-ine	!		✓	adamantine, estuarine, pantherine
-ism	✓	motherism, foodism, leftyism	✓	ageism, careerism, abnegationism
-ist	✓	leftist, hornist, womanist	✓	absolutist, biologist, colonist
-ite	!	foamite	✓	aluminite, calcite, dendrite
-ity	!	oddity	✓	absurdity, binarity, density

(continued)

Table 27.2 Non-native suffixes and the bases they select (continued)

Affix	Native bases	Examples	Non-native bases	Examples
-ive	!	talkative, walkative	✓	adaptive, captive, substantive
-ize	!	ironize, leatherize, weaponize	✓	analogize, crystallize, unionize
-ment	!	unfoldment, upliftment, wonderment	✓	advisement, bombardment, incitement
-or	!	sailor	✓	abductor, counselor, descriptor
-ory			✓	commendatory, divinitory, modulatory
-ous	!	heathenous, lumpous, righteous	✓	amorous, cancerous, frivolous
-trix			✓	adminstratrix, coredemptrix, generatrix
-ure			✓	accenture, exposure, procedure

Table 27.3 Non-native prefixes and the bases they select

Affix	Native bases	Examples	Non-native bases	Examples
a-			✓	acultural, asemantic, acephalous
ante-	!	ante-buildings, anteroom	✓	antebellum, antecedent, antenatal
anti-	✓	anti-day, anti-bone, antichoice	✓	anti-abrasion, antichemistry, antinatural
arch-	!	archdeacon, archbishop, archfriend	✓	arch-conservative, archheresy, archvillain
circum-			✓	circumambient, circumcontinental, circumlocution
cis-			✓	cisalpine, cislunar, cisplatinum
co-	✓	co-band, co-believer, co-father	✓	co-adapted, co-composer, co-suspect
contra-	!	contraflow	✓	contra-causal, contradistinction, contrafactual
counter-	✓	counterblow, counter-death, counter-flow	✓	counteract, countereffect, countertheory
crypto-	!	cryptochurches, crypto-free, cryptokeys	✓	crypto-analysis, cryptologic, crypto-racist
de-	✓	dehorn, debone, deice	✓	deautomate, decharge, deidealize
demi-	!	demi-cheese, demigod, demi-island	✓	demi-celebrity, demifigure, demisphere
dis-	!	disbelief, disband, dislike	✓	disaffect, disconfirm, disfunction
en-	✓	endear, enroll, enshroud	✓	enact, encapsulate, enchain
ex-	✓	ex-baker, ex-band, ex-boyfriend	✓	ex-assistant, ex-beauty, ex-chief
extra-	✓	extra-cold, extra-deep, extra-kin	✓	extraabdominal, extracreative, extradense
hemi-	!	hemi-field	✓	hemicycle, hemiparasite, hemithyroid
hyper-	✓	hyperflow, hypercool, hyperbright	✓	hyperactive, hyper-complex, hyperplastic
hypo-	!	hypospray, hypostick	✓	hypoacoustic, hypodermal, hypothermic
in_{NEG}-			✓	immortal, inactive, infertile
inter-	✓	interarm, interband, interbreed	✓	interaction, intercept, interpsychic
intra-	✓	intraisland, intraday, intra-earth	✓	intracerebral, intragranular, intra-item
mal-	!	mal-feeling	✓	malaligned, malfunction, malpractice
mega-	✓	megabad, megacool, megadrive	✓	megachain, megamachine, megapopular
meta-	✓	meta-awareness, meta-beliefs, metaman	✓	meta-analysis, metalinguistic, metastructure
micro-	✓	microbeam, microcraft, microdrive	✓	microabrasion, microbiology, microunit
mini-	✓	minibreak, mini-foot, miniloaf	✓	mini-capital, mini-environment, mini-interval

(continued)

Table 27.3 Non-native prefixes and the bases they select (continued)

Affix	Native bases	Examples	Non-native bases	Examples
mono-	✓	monoband, monobrow, monoman	✓	monocausal, monopedal, monotheism
multi-	✓	mulit-field, multi-board, multifight	✓	multi-agent, multicavity, multi-family
nano-	✓	nano-boat, nano-death, nanogear	✓	nanoarray, nanocycle, nanomagnet
neo-	✓	neo-cool, neodeath, neofold	✓	neoantique, neofeudal, neoliterate
non-	✓	non-arm, nonbedridden, nonchosen	✓	nonadept, noncapital, non-comic
para-	✓	parachurch, paraglide, parasail	✓	para-capitalist, paranationalist, paraphysical
peri-	!	peri-workout	✓	periapical, perinatal, periurban
pico-	!	picofast	✓	picogram, picoplankton, picowatt
poly-	✓	polywater, polybands, polycold	✓	polycarbon, polynuclear, polyvapor
post-	✓	post-afternoon, post-awakening, postbath	✓	post-acquittal, post-devolution, postmodern
pre-	✓	pre-answer, prebake, pre-cold	✓	pre-activity, precombat, prefuneral
proto-	✓	proto-board, proto-earth, protoheart	✓	proto-adult, protohuman, protomodern
pseudo-	✓	pseudo-cool, pseudo-friend, pseudo-men	✓	pseudo-abstract, pseudodistance, pseudo-legal
re-	✓	reheat, rewash, rewrite	✓	reaccept, reignite, repollute
retro-	✓	retrobreeding, retrocool, retroglide	✓	retrocession, retrosexual, retrovirus
semi-	✓	semi-clean, semi-death, semi-float	✓	semi-assault, semi-deviant, semiformal
sub-	✓	subband, sub-breed, subdeal	✓	subacute, subcategory, subdomain
super-	✓	superchild, superbright, superclean	✓	superabundant, supergenerous, superintense
supra-	!	supra-church, supralife, supra-neighborhood	✓	supraannual, supraethnic, supra-state
tera-	!	terabeam	✓	terascale, terameter, terabase
trans-	!	transcool, transearth, trans-light	✓	trans-bay, transcanal, transcontext
ultra-	✓	ultraaware, ultraclean, ultradark	✓	ultra-accurate, ultrafilter, ultrapure
uni-	!	unibrow, unicorn, uni-tree	✓	uniblock, unilateral, uniport

Table 27.4 Non-native suffixes followed by native suffixes

	Affixes	Source	Examples
-able	able+ness		admirableness
-age	age+er		packager
	age+ful	p	carriageful
	age+less	p	carriageless
	age+ness	p	foolageness
	age+wise	p	percentagewise
	age+y		cleavage-y
-al$_A$	al+dom		intellectualdom
	al+er		trialer
	al+hood		tribalhood
	al+ish		normalish
	al+less		institutionalless
	al+ship		gubernatorialship
-al$_N$	al+wise		arousal-wise
-ance	ance+er		remembrancer
	ance+less		distanceless
	ance+ship		acquaintanceship
	ance+wise		appearance-wise
	ance+y		Renaissancy
-ancy	ancy+wise		consistency-wise
-ant$_N$	ant+hood		servanthood
	ant+less		servantless
	ant+ship		assistantship
-ary	ary+hood	p	secretaryhood
	ary+less	p	dictionaryless
	ary+ness	p	elementariness
	ary+ship	p	judiciaryship
	ary+wise		culinary-wise
-ation	ation+er		vacationer
	ation+ful		actionful
	ation+hood		nationhood
	ation+less		affectionless
	ation+ship		relationship
	ation+wise		admiration-wise
	ation+y		suctiony
-ee	ee+dom		refugee-dom
	ee+hood	p	employeehood
	ee+ship	p	assigneeship
-ery	ery+dom	p	nurserydom
	ery+less		batteryless
	ery+ship	p	ministryship
	ery+wise		jewelry-wise
-ese	ese+er		Portugueser
	ese+y		Chinese-y

(continued)

Table 27.4 Non-native suffixes followed by native suffixes (continued)

	Affixes	Source	Examples
-esque	esque+ness		Freudianesqueness
-ess	ess+dom	p	princessdom
	ess+hood	p	priestesshood
	ess+less	p	governessless
	ess+ly	p	princessly
	ess+ship	p	governessship
	ess+wise	p	huntresswise
	ess+y		princess-y
-ette	ette+ish	p	noveletteish
-an	ian+dom	p	Christiandom
	ian+er	p	musicianer
	ian+hood	p	roughianhood
	ian+ish	p	christianish
	ian+less	p	guardianless
	ian+ly	p	guardianly
	ian+ness	p	Victorianness
	ian+ship	p	musicianship
	ian+wise	p	Christianwise
-ic	ic+ish		cinematic-ish
	ic+ness		democraticness
	ic+wise		economic-wise
-ical	ical+ness		clericalness
	ical+wise		political-wise
-ify	ify+er		acidifier
-ine	ine+er		mariner
-ist	ist+dom	p	artistdom
	ist+er	p	alchemister
	ist+ly	p	artistly
	ist+ship	p	evangelistship
	ist+y		dentist-y
-ite	ite+ish		Israelitish
	ite+ship		Naziriteship
	ite+wise		favorite-wise
-ity	ity+dom		celebritydom
	ity+less		gravityless
	ity+wise		coachability-wise
-ive	ive+ly	p	adaptively
	ive+ness	p	addictiveness
	ive+wise		defensive-wise
-ize	ize+er		neutralizer
-ment	ment+ee	p	experimentee
	ment+er	p	documenter
	ment+ful		apartmentful
	ment+ship	p	governmentship
	ment+ward		apartmentward
	ment+wise		assignment-wise

	Affixes	Source	Examples
	ment+y		testament-y
-or	or+dom	p	protectordom
	or+ful	p	traitorful
	or+hood	p	traitorhood
	or+ish	p	administratorish
	or+less	p	connectorless
	or+ling	p	professorling
	or+ly	p	sailorly
	or+ship	p	administratorship
-ory	ory+ness		obligatoriness
	ory+wise		laboratory-wise
-ous	ous+ly	p	adventurously
	ous+ness		ambiguousness
-ure	ure+er		sculpturer
	ure+ful		pleasureful
	ure+hood		creaturehood
	ure+less		pressureless
	ure+ly		creaturely
	ure+ship		tenureship
	ure+some		adventuresome
	ure+wise		disclosure-wise

so a word is in order about our data. For the reasons noted in Chapter 21, it is more likely for prefixes to occur on already suffixed bases than for suffixes to occur on already prefixed bases. Therefore, in looking at combinations of prefixes, care must be taken to examine the likely bracketings of a complex word to determine whether a prefix is attached directly outside another prefix, or outside a suffix that is itself outside a prefix. That is, strictly speaking prefix combinations should show a structure like (1a), rather than (1b):

(1) a. prefix [prefix [base-suffix]]

     b. prefix [[prefix-base] suffix]

In the examples in Tables 27.8–27.11 we have confined ourselves to the bracketing in (1a), where possible, and have marked cases where the bracketing is in doubt or is likely to be that in (1b) with a following *. Especially problematic are forms in which a prefix is attached to a deverbal form in -*ing* or -*ed*, as the analysis of such forms is highly theory dependent. We have included such cases.

Table 27.5 Native suffixes followed by non-native suffixes

	Affixes	Source	Examples
-en	en+able		resharpenable
	en+ee	p	flattenee
	en+ment	p	lengthenment
	en+ize		blackenize
-er	er+age	p	farmerage
	er+ese		computerese
	er+esque		painteresque
	er+ess	p	breweress
	er+ette	p	sleeperette
	er+ial		managerial
	er+ian	g	Quakerian
	er+ism	p	boxerism
	er+ist	p	consumerist
	er+ite		bleacherite
	er+ous		debaucherous
	er+ize		blenderize
-ful$_A$	ful+ize		awfulize
-hood	hood+ism	p	neighbourhoodism
-ish	ish+ian	p	Irishian
	ish+ism	p	Britishism
	ish+ist	p	Yiddishist
	ish+ment	p	foolishment
	ish+ery	p	Scottishry
-let	let+ist	p	novelettist
-ly	ly+ism	p	orderlyism
-ship	ship+ment	p	courtshipment
-ster	ster+age	p	hucksterage
	ster+ess	p	hucksteress
	ster+ette	p	rhymsterette
	ster+ian	p	spinsterian
	ster+ism	p	hucksterism
	ster+ous	p	spinsterous
-y$_A$	y+esque		hippyesque
	y+ism		anti-smoochyism

Table 27.6 Native suffixes followed by native suffixes

	Affixes	Source	Examples
-dom	dom+ful	p	kingdomful
	dom+less	p	kingdomless
-en	en+er	p	flattener
-er	er+dom	p	printerdom
	er+ful	p	tumblerful
	er+hood	p	loverhood
	er+ish	p	robberish
	er+less	p	leaderless
	er+ling	p	preacherling
	er+ly	p	loverly
	er+ship	p	controllership
	er+wise	p	loverwise
	er+y		slacker-y
-fold	fold+ness	p	tenfoldness
	fold+wise	p	manifoldwise
-ful$_A$	ful+ness	p	carefulness
	ful+wise	p	despiteful-wise
-hood	hood+er		neighborhooder
	hood+less	p	childhoodless
	hood+ly		neighborhoodly
	hood+wise		sisterhood-wise
	hood+y		neighborhoody
-ish	ish+ly	p	babyishly
	ish+ness	p	amateurishness
	ish+wise	g	Englishwise
	ish+y		Englishy
-less	less+ness	p	aimlessness
	less+wise	p	carelesswise
-let	let+hood		triplethood
	let+wise		couplet-wise
-ling	ling+less	p	seedlingless
	ling+ship	p	ducklingship
-ly	ly+hood	p	knightlihood
	ly+ness	p	courtliness
	ly+wise	p	beastlywise
-ness	ness+wise	p	businesswise
	ness+y		business-y
-ship	ship+er		townshipper
	ship+ful	p	kingshipful
	ship+less	p	censorshipless
	ship+wise		citizenship-wise
	ship+y		hero worshipy
-some	some+ness		fearsomeness
-ster	ster+dom	p	gangsterdom
	ster+hood	p	spinsterhood

(continued)

Table 27.6 Native suffixes followed by native suffixes (continued)

	Affixes	Source	Examples
	ster+ish	p	spinsterish
	ster+ly	p	spinsterly
	ster+ship	p	tapstership
	ster+y		gangster-y
-th	th+en	p	lengthen
	th+less	p	depthless
	th+wise	p	depthwise
-ward	ward+ness		inwardness
	ward+wise		backward-wise
-wise	wise+ness	p	otherwiseness
-y$_A$	y+ish	p	woollyish
	y+ness		airiness

Table 27.7 Non-native suffixes followed by non-native suffixes

	Affixes	Source	Examples
-able	able+ism		probabilism
	able+ist		compatibilist
	able+ity		absorbability
	able+ize		tangibilize
-age	age+able		packageable
	age+ery	p	plumagery
	age+ette		suffragette
	age+ism		suffragism
	age+ist		assemblagist
-al$_A$	al+ese		legalese
	al+esque		industrialesque
	al+ian		sesquipedalian
	al+ic		vocalic
	al+ism		behavioralism
	al+ist		environmentalist
	al+ite		socialite
	al+ity		eventuality
	al+ize		actualize
	al+ous		triumphalous
-an	an+age	p	guardianage
	an+ary	p	physicianary
	an+ate		Americanate
	an+ese		lesbianese
	an+esque		Italianesque
	an+ic		Romanic
	an+ism	p	Europeanism
	an+ist	p	Europeanist

	Affixes	Source	Examples
	an+ous	p	ruffianous
	an+ize		Africanize
-ant_N	ent+al		presidential
	ant+ery		tenantry
	ant+ese		consultantese
	ant+ic		cartomantic
	ant+ism		protestantism
	ant+ist		obscurantist
	ent+ize		immanentize
-ary	ary+ian	p	librarian
	ary+ism	p	secretaryism
	ary+ist	p	voluntaryist
	ary+ize		sedentarize
	ary+ous		alimentarious
-ate_V	ate+able		activatable
	ate+al		striatal
	ate+ant		hydratant
	ate+ation		activation
	ate+ee		allegatee
	ate+ese		administratese
	ate+ic		automatic
	ate+ism		privatism
	ate+ive		adulterative
	ate+or		activator
	ate+ory		assimilatory
	ate+ous		coruscatious
	ate+ure		implicature
-ation	ation+able		actionable
	ation+al		educational
	ation+ary		inflationary
	ation+esque		blaxploitationesque
	ation+ese		educationese
	ation+ette		recessionette
	ation+ism		assimilationism
	ation+ist		abortionist
	ation+ize		televisionize
-ee	ee+ess	p	refugee-ess
	ee+ism	p	absenteeism
-ery	ery+al		cemeterial
	ery+ian		cemeterian
	ery+ic		imageric
	ery-ist	p	effronterist
	ery+ize		batteryize
-ess	ess+ery		witchessery
-ette	ette+age	p	briquettage
	ette+ism	p	suffragettism

(*continued*)

Table 27.7   Non-native suffixes followed by non-native suffixes   (continued)

	Affixes	Source	Examples
-ic	ic+ate		authenticate
	ic+ian		statistician
	ic+ism		aestheticism
	ic+ist		geneticist
	ic+ity		electricity
	ic+ize		academicize
-ical	ical+ism		biblicalism
	ical+ist		theatricalist
	ical+ity		cyclicality
	ical+ize		theatricalize
-ify	ify+able		identifiable
	ify+ance		significance
	ify+ant		significant
	ify+ate		unificate
	ify+ation		electrification
	ify+ee		justifiee
	ify+ic		beatific
	ify+ive		significative
	ify+ory		amplificatory
-ine	ine+age		libertinage
	ine+al		doctrinal
	ine+ate		glycerinate
	ine+ic		alkalinic
	ine+ism		alpinism
	ine+ist		alpinist
-ism	ism+al		baptismal
	ism+ic		monopolismic
-ist	ist+ery	p	dentistry
	ist+ess	p	artistess
	ist+ette		columnistette
	ist+ic		artistic
	ist+ical		egotistical
-ite	ite+ess		Moabitess
	ite+ic		anchoritic
	ite+ical		cenobitical
	ite+ism		Jacobitism
	ite+ist		Maronitist
-ity	ity+ate		debilitate
	ity+ive		capacitive
	ity+ism		ability-ism
	ity+ist		complicitist
	ity+ize		securitize
-ive	ive+al		perspectival
	ive+ate		activate
	ive+ism	p	activism
	ive+ist	p	activist

	Affixes	Source	Examples
	ive+ity		activity
	ive+ize		activize
-ize	ize+able		actualizable
	ize+ance		cognizance
	ize+ant		cognizant
	ize+ation		actualization
	ize+ee		socializee
	ize+ment		aggrandizement
	ize+or		destabilizor
-ment	ment+al		argumental
	ment+ary		testamentary
	ment+ee		experimentee
	ment+ical		testamentical
	ment+ism		good-governmentism
	ment+ist	p	developmentist
	ment+ive		argumentative
	ment+ite		transvestmentite
	ment+ous	p	medicamentous
-or	or+age	p	tutorage
	or+ance		doctorance
	or+esque		survivor-esque
	or+ess	p	editoress
	or+ette		conductorette
	or+ial		editorial
	or+ian	p	protectorian
	or+ical		oratorical
	or+ism	p	actorism
	or+ist	p	detectorist
	or+ous	p	traitorous
	or+ize		factorize
-ory	ory+ial		accusatorial
	ory+ize		accessorize
-ous	ous+ist		seriousist
	ous+ity		pomposity
-ure	ure+able		pleasurable
	ure+al		closural
	ure+ess		adventuress
	ure+ous		moisturous

Table 27.8 Non-native prefixes preceding native prefixes

	Prefix combination	Example
anti-	anti+back	antibackflow
	anti+mis	antimiscarriage*
	anti+out	anti-outsourcing
	anti+over	anti-overrun
	anti+up	antiuplander*
co-	co+be	co-belonging
	co+under	co-underwriter
counter-	counter+out	counter-outrage
ex-	ex+be	ex-betrothed
	ex+fore	ex-forehead
	ex+mid	ex-midshipman
	ex+out	ex-outlaw
	ex+un	ex-untouchable
hyper-	hyper+be	hyper-bedecked
	hyper+over	hyper-overarching
	hyper+un	hyper-unemployment
mega-	mega+off	mega-offspring
	mega+out	megaoutlet
	mega+up	megaupload
meta-	meta+after	metaafterphysics
micro-	micro+mis	micromismanagement*
mini-	mini+down	mini-downtown
	mini+out	mini-outbreak
	mini+up	mini-uproar
mono-	mono+un	mono-unsaturated
multi-	multi+out	multioutlet
	multi+un	multi-untalented
neo-	neo+out	neo-outlaw
non-	non+after	nonafterburning
	non+be	nonbelonging
	non+by	nonbypassable*
	non+down	nondowntown
	non+fore	non-foreclosed
	non+mid	non-midday
	non+mis	non-misleading
	non+out	non-outgassing
	non+over	nonoverweight
	non+under	non-underserved
	non+up	non-updatable*
para-	para+mid	paramidline
poly-	poly+un	polyunsaturated
post-	post+be	post-bewitched
	post+down	postdownsizing
	post+fore	post-foreclosure
	post+mid	postmidnight
	post+out	postoutbreak

	Prefix combination	Example
	post+up	post-uprising
pre-	pre+down	pre-downfall
	pre+fore	pre-foreclosure
	pre+mid	pre-midsentence
	pre+on	pre-onset
	pre+out	pre-outburst
	pre+over	pre-overhead
	pre+under	pre-understanding
	pre+up	pre-update
proto-	proto+up	proto-uproar
pseudo-	pseudo+out	pseudo-outcome
re-	re+fore	reforecast
	re+out	reoutline
	re+over	reoverlaying
	re+un	reunveil
	re+under	re-underwriting
	re+up	reuptake
semi-	semi+out	semi-outlaws
	semi+un	semi-unknown
	semi+under	semi-underground
	semi+up	semi-upscale
sub-	sub+fore	sub-foreman
super-	super+out	superoutburst
	super+over	super-overheated
	super+un	super-unfunny
	super+under	super-underdog
	super+up	super-upset
ultra-	ultra+under	ultra-underdog
	ultra+up	ultra-upscale

Table 27.9 Native prefixes preceding non–native prefixes

	Combination	Example
back-	back+re	back-reaction
	back+trans	back-translated
down-	down+dis	down-dislocation
mid-	mid+inter	mid-interview
	mid+para	midparagraph
	mid+peri	midperiphery
	mid+pre	mid-preview
	mid+re	mid-rewind
	mid+sub	mid-suburban
mis-	mis+co	miscoordination

(continued)

Table 27.9   Native prefixes preceding non-native prefixes (continued)

	Combination	Example
	mis+dis	misdisunderstanding
	mis+en	misencoded
	mis+inter	misinterpret
	mis+pre	mispredict
	mis+re	misrepresent
	mis+trans	mistranslated
off-	off+dis	off-dissonant
	off+micro	off-microphone
out-	out+mega	out-megaphoned
	out+re	outrebounded
	out+trans	out-transmutation
over-	over+co	over-coordinated
	over+de	over-decentralized
	over+dis	overdiscounted
	over+en	overentangled
	over+extra	overextrapolate
	over+inter	over-interactive
	over+meta	over-metaphysical*
	over+pre	over-predict
	over+re	overreaction
	over+sub	oversubscribed
	over+super	oversupervise
un-	un+circum	uncircumscribed
	un+co	uncooperative*
	un+dis	undisguised
	un+en	unenlightened
	un+ex	unexcommunicated
	un+extra	unextraordinary
	un+hypo	unhypocritical
	un+inter	un-international
	un+meta	unmetaphysical
	un+para	unparagraphed
	un+poly	unpolychrome
	un+post	un-post-modern
	un+pre	unpredictable*
	un+re	unreburied
	un+sub	unsubtitled
	un+super	un-supervised
	un+trans	untransformed
under-	under+dis	underdisclosure
	under+inter	under-interpretation
	under+micro	undermicrowaved
	under+pre	underprescribed
	under+re	underrepresented
	under+sub	under-subscribed
	under+super	undersupervisor*
	under+trans	undertransmission

Table 27.10 Native prefixes preceding native prefixes

	Prefix combination	Example
after-	after+mid	after-midnight
	after+un	after-unfolding
mid-	mid+after	midafternoon
	mid+fore	mid-forearm
mis-	mis+over	mis-overheard
	mis+under	misunderattributed
over-	over+out	over-outrage
	over+under	over-underachiever
un-	un+back	unbackcountry
	un+be	unbewitch
	un+down	undowntrodden
	un+fore	unforetellable*
	un+mid	un-Midwest
	un+up	unuphold

Table 27.11 Non-native prefixes preceding non-native prefixes

	Prefix combination	Example
a-	a+meta	a-metaphysical
ante-	ante+post	ante-postmodern
	ante+retro	anteretrograde
anti-	anti+ante	anti-ante-bellum
	anti+crypto	anticryptography
	anti+de	anti-deforestation*
	anti+dis	antidisclosure
	anti+en	antientitlement*
	anti+ex	anti-ex-combatant
	anti+hyper	anti-hypertension
	anti+in	anti-independent
	anti+inter	anti-intercellular
	anti+meta	antimetaphysical
	anti+micro	antimicrobacterial
	anti+multi	anti-multicultural
	anti+neo	anti-neo-colonialist
	anti+non	anti-non-Anglo
	anti+poly	antipolygamy
	anti+pre	anti-premarital
	anti+proto	antiprotozoal
	anti+pseudo	anti-pseudojournalists
	anti+re	anti-replay
	anti+sub	anti-submissive
	anti+trans	anti-transplant
co-	co+dis	codiscoverer
	co+en	coenrollment

(continued)

Table 27.11 Non-native prefixes preceding non-native prefixes   (continued)

	Prefix combination	Example
	co+inter	co-interventions
	co+poly	copolymer
	co+re	co-represent
	co+sub	co-sub-halos
	co+super	co-supervisor
counter-	counter+dis	counterdiscursive
	counter+en	counterenactment
	counter+hemi	counter-hemisphere
	counter+inter	counter-intervention
	counter+mono	countermonologue
	counter+para	counterparadigm
	counter+pre	counter-preemption
	counter+re	counterreactions
	counter+sub	countersubversive
	counter+super	counter-superpower
crypto-	crypto+a	crypto-atheistic
de-	de+en	de-entitle
	de+inter	de-interlacing
	de+mono	demonopolization
	de+multi	demultiplexing
	de+poly	depolymerized*
	de+re	derearrange
	de+sub	desublimate
	de+super	desuperheater
	de+uni	deunification
demi-	demi+semi	demi-semi-democratic
dis-	dis+co	discoordinated
	dis+en	disentangle
	dis+in	disinhibition
	dis+inter	disintermediate
ex-	ex+anti	ex-anti-kid
	ex+counter	ex-counterterror
	ex+crypto	excryptographer
	ex+in	ex-independent
	ex+inter	ex-intercontinental
	ex+neo	ex-Neo-Destour
	ex+non	ex-non-entity
	ex+para	ex-paracommando
	ex+poly	ex-polytechnics
	ex+re	ex-replacement
	ex+semi	ex-semi-permanent
	ex+super	ex-supermodel
extra-	extra+anti	extra-antiwear
	extra+hemi	extrahemispheric
	extra+hypo	extrahypopharyngeal

	Prefix combination	Example
	extra+sub	extra-subcutaneous
	extra+super	extra-super-sensitive
hemi-	hemi+a	hemianopia
	hemi+crypto	hemicryptophytes
	hemi+demi	hemidemisemiquaver
	hemi+trans	hemitransfixion*
hyper-	hyper+circum	hyper-circumspect
	hyper+de	hyperdeformed
	hyper+en	hyperenriched
	hyper+in	hyperinsecurity
	hyper+inter	hyperintervention*
	hyper+meta	hypermetabolic
	hyper+multi	hypermultilateral
	hyper+para	hyper-parathyroidism*
	hyper+pre	hyper-preparedness
	hyper+re	hyperreactive
	hyper+sub	hyper-suburban
	hyper+uni	hyper-unilateralism
hypo-	hypo+para	hypoparathyroid
	hypo+re	hyporeactivity
NEG*in-*	in+co	incoordination
	in+de	indecomposable*
	in+dis	indissoluble*
	in+pre	inprescribable*
	in+sub	insubordination
	in+trans	intransmutable*
inter-	inter+co	intercooperation
	inter+hemi	interhemisphere
	inter+in	interindependent
	inter+intra	inter-intragroup
	inter+meta	intermetamorphosis
	inter+micro	intermicrotubule
	inter+re	inter-react
	inter+sub	intersuburban
	inter+trans	intertransverse
intra-	intra+peri	intrapericardial*
mega-	mega+re	megarenovation*
	mega+sub	megasubdivision*
	mega+super	megasuperstar
meta-	meta+re	metarepresentational
	meta+sub	meta-subtext
micro-	micro+co	micro-cogeneration
	micro+dis	microdisarmament
	micro+en	microencapsulated
	micro+meta	micrometastases
	micro+mini	microminidress

(continued)

Table 27.11   Non–native prefixes preceding non–native prefixes   (continued)

	Prefix combination	Example
	micro+nano	micronanosecond
	micro+para	micro-parameters
	micro+re	microreform
	micro+sub	microsubmersibles*
	micro+trans	microtransactions*
mini-	mini+de	mini-defibrillator*
	mini+dis	mini-discovery*
	mini+en	mini-enclosure*
	mini+micro	mini-microwave
	mini+mono	mini-monograph
	mini+pre	mini-preview
	mini+pseudo	mini-pseudo-Medici
	mini+re	minireunion
	mini+retro	miniretrospectives*
	mini+sub	minisubmarine
	mini+trans	minitransmitters*
mono-	mono+anti	monoantiplatelet
multi-	multi+anti	multiantibiotic
	multi+dis	multidisabled
	multi+inter	multi-interdisciplinary
	multi+mega	multimegawatt
	multi+para	multiparagraph
	multi+re	multi-representational*
	multi+tera	multi-terawatt
	multi+trans	multi-transnational
nano-	nano+en	nano-enabled
	nano+inter	nano-interrogation
	nano+re	nano-reinforced
	nano+trans	nanotransformers
neo-	neo+a	neoatheistic
	neo+counter	neo-countercultural
	neo+crypto	neocryptopygus
	neo+dis	neodissociation*
	neo+en	neoenlightenment*
	neo+inter	neointerventionism*
	neo+meta	neometaphysical
	neo+post	neo-post-Marxists
	neo+pre	neopremodern
	neo+re	neo-restructuring
	neo+retro	neoretromaximinimalist
	neo+ultra	neo-ultramontanist
non-	non+anti	nonantisocial
	non+circum	noncircumstantial*
	non+co	noncooperation*

(*continued*)

	Prefix combination	Example
	non+contra	noncontraceptive*
	non+counter	noncounterfeit
	non+de	nondecodable*
	non+dis	nondisordered
	non+en	non-entitlement*
	non+hyper	nonhyperactive
	non+hypo	non-hypoallergenic
	non+in	nonindependence
	non+inter	noninteractive*
	non+intra	non-intracranial
	non+mal	nonmalware
	non+mega	nonmegapixel
	non+meta	nonmetaphysical
	non+micro	nonmicrogravity
	non+multi	nonmultimedia
	non+neo	nonneoplastic
	non+para	nonparametric*
	non+peri	nonperinatal
	non+poly	non-polycarbonate
	non+post	nonpostdoctoral
	non+pre	non-pre-emptible*
	non+proto	nonprototypical
	non+re	nonrenewable*
	non+sub	nonsuburban
	non+super	nonsupernatural
	non+trans	nontransplanted
	non+ultra	non-ultra-orthodox
	non+uni	nonunidimensional
para-	para+neo	paraneoplastic
peri-	peri+sub	perisubmandibular
post-	post+anti	post-antibiotic
	post+de	post-deregulation*
	post+dis	post-discharge
	post+en	postenlightenment*
	post+hemi	post-hemiabdominal
	post+inter	post-interview
	post+meta	postmetamorphic*
	post+mono	post-monopolization*
	post+multi	post-multicultural
	post+neo	postneonatal
	post+para	post-paracentesis
	post+re	postrestructuring
	post+retro	post-retrofit
	post+sub	post-suburban
	post+super	post-superpower

(continued)

Table 27.11 Non-native prefixes preceding non-native prefixes   (continued)

	Prefix combination	Example
	post+trans	post-transplant
pre-	pre+ante	preantepenultimate
	pre+anti	pre-antibiotic
	pre+co	pre-coordination
	pre+contra	precontraception
	pre+counter	pre-counterculture
	pre+de	predecode
	pre+dis	predischarge
	pre+en	pre-enlistment
	pre+in	preindependence
	pre+inter	preinterview
	pre+meta	premetamorphosis
	pre+micro	pre-microchip
	pre+mono	pre-monotheistic
	pre+neo	pre-neoclassical
	pre+para	preparadigmatic*
	pre+post	prepostmodernists
	pre+proto	preprototype
	pre+retro	preretrofit
	pre+trans	pretransplant
proto-	proto+de	proto-deconstruction*
	proto+demi	proto-demi-Celts
	proto+in	proto-indeterminacy*
	proto+inter	proto-internet
	proto+meta	proto-metaphysical*
	proto+post	proto-postmodern
	proto+pre	proto-preservationist*
	proto+sub	protosuburban
	proto+super	proto-superstate
pseudo-	pseudo+dis	pseudo-disclosure
	pseudo+en	pseudo-enchantment*
	pseudo+in	pseudoindependents
	pseudo+inter	pseudo-interview
	pseudo+meta	pseudo-metathesis
	pseudo+multi	pseudo-multimedia
	pseudo+neo	pseudoneointima
	pseudo+poly	pseudo-polymaths
	pseudo+re	pseudo-review
	pseudo+super	pseudo-superheroes
re-	re+co	recoordinated
	re+de	redefruition
	re+dis	redislocation
	re+en	re-enforce
	re+inter	reinterview
	re+meta	re-metamorphizes
	re+mono	remonopolization*

	Prefix combination	Example
	re+sub	resubjugate
	re+trans	retransmit
retro-	retro+trans	retrotransposable
semi-	semi+co	semi-cooperative
	semi+crypto	semi-crypto-necrophiliac
	semi+de	semi-defrost
	semi+dis	semi-disassemble
	semi+en	semi-enclosed
	semi+ex	semi-ex-baseball fan
	semi+hypo	semi-hypochondriac
	semi+in	semi-invisible
	semi+mono	semi-monopoly
	semi+non	semi-nonsense
	semi+para	semi-parametric
	semi+peri	semi-peripheral
	semi+pre	semi-premeditated
	semi+re	semi-rebuilding
	semi+sub	semi-submarine
	semi+super	semi-superpower
	semi+trans	semi-transparent
sub-	sub+anti	sub-antarctic
	sub+hyper	sub-hypersonic
	sub+nano	sub-nanometer
	sub+para	sub-paragraph
	sub+re	sub-replacement*
	sub+trans	sub-transfer
	sub+uni	sub-universities*
super-	super+anti	super-antioxident
	super+de	super-dehydrated
	super+dis	super-discharge
	super+en	super-entrenched
	super+hyper	super-hyper-regional
	super+micro	super-microdots
	super+mini	superminimalists
	super+mono	super-monopolists
	super+para	superparamagnetic
	super+poly	super-polymer
	super+post	superpost-panamax
	super+re	super-reinforced
	super+sub	super-subsonic
	super+extra	superextraordinary
	super+inter	superinternational
	super+multi	supermultivitamins
	super+trans	supertransport
supra-	supra+re	supra-representational*

(*continued*)

Table 27.11 Non–native prefixes preceding non–native prefixes   (continued)

	Prefix combination	Example
	supra+sub	supra–subsonic
	supra+uni	supra–universal*
trans-	trans+anti	trans–antarctic
	trans+peri	transpericardial*
	trans+sub	trans–substantiate
ultra-	ultra+dis	ultradisposable*
	ultra+meta	ultrametabolism*
	ultra+micro	ultra–micro–engraving
	ultra+mini	ultraminiature
	ultra+para	ultra–paradoxical
	ultra+re	ultra–reactionary*
	ultra+sub	ultra–suburban
	ultra+super	ultra–supercritical
	ultra+trans	ultra–transparent
uni-	uni+multi	uni–multipolar

27.3 PATTERNS

If we look at the full range of data, what we see is that English derivational morphology actually displays very little in the way of stratification. We show this first by grouping affixes according to their restrictiveness with regard to bases, that is, showing the extent to which they allow bases that are both simple and already derived, and the extent to which those bases can be both native and non-native. Example (2) ranks the suffixes in the tables from most to least restrictive:

(2) a. Allow only non-native simplex bases; do not allow complex bases at all:
Non-native: *-ancy, -ine*
Native: none

   b. Allow both non-native and native simplex bases; do not allow complex bases at all:
Non-native: none
Native: *-en$_V$, -fold, -let, -ster*

   c. Allow both non-native and native simplex bases; do not attach to complex bases with native affixes:
Non-native: *-ation, -al$_N$, -ance, -ant, -ary, -ate$_V$, -ic, -ical, -ity, -ive, -or, -ory, -ure*
Native: none

   d. Allow both non-native and native simplex bases; allow both non-native and native complex bases

Non-native: *-able, -age, -al*$_A$*, -ee, -ery, -ese, -esque, -ess, -ette, -an, -ism, -ist, -ite, -ize, -ment, -ous*

Native: *-dom, -er, -ful*$_A$*, -hood, -ish, -less, -ling, -ly, -ness, -ship, -some, -ward, -wise, -y*

We note that while there are non-native suffixes that only attach to simplex non-native bases, there are no native suffixes that are restricted with regard to the etymological origin of the simplex bases they attach to, although there are a few that attach only to simplex bases (that is, they are never found attached to already affixed bases). There is a small cohort of non-native suffixes that attach at least sporadically to native simplex bases, but attach only to complex bases ending in non-native suffixes. For native suffixes, on the other hand, if they attach to complex bases at all, they tend to attach freely to those ending in both native and non-native suffixes. The majority of native suffixes fall into this least restrictive of categories. What is perhaps surprising is the number of non-native suffixes that fall into the least restrictive category as well: indeed, there are more non-native suffixes (N = 16) that attach freely in this way than there are ones that fall into the more restrictive category (N = 13).

Prefixes show an even clearer pattern. All of the native prefixes attach indiscriminately to both native and non-native bases, as do the vast majority of non-native prefixes. There are only five non-native prefixes that seem never to attach to native bases (*a-, circum-, cis-,* $_{NEG}$*in-, mal-*) and eight that attach to native bases only rarely (*contra-, hemi-, peri-, pico-, supra-, tera-, trans-, uni-*). It is notable that none of these prefixes is particularly productive in contemporary English. As for attaching to other prefixes, non-native prefixes of course attach freely to other non-native prefixes, but they also seem to attach readily to native prefixes as well. If anything is surprising at all in the data compiled in Tables 27.8–27.11, it is that native prefixes are relatively unlikely to attach to any other prefix, whether native or non-native. We have far more combinations of non-native attaching to native than the reverse.

What the data indicate, then, is that native and non-native affixes in English may not be completely integrated into a single derivational system, but they are far more integrated than might at first be imagined. We find near-complete integration among prefixes, and only a bit less integration among suffixes. We offer this result with some caveats however. First, it must be acknowledged that some of the examples in the tables in this chapter are derived on complex bases that are rather lexicalized (*wizardess, bastardize, courtshipment, dictionaryless, ministry-ship, celebritydom, co-belonging, ex-betrothed, megaoutlet, mini-uproar, pre-onset,* etc.), and therefore arguably are not perceived as complex. Second, some of these forms appear to violate the selectional restrictions of affixes they contain: for example, we find forms like *tribalhood* or *gubernatorialship*, where *-hood* and *-ship* generally attach only to nouns. And most importantly, not all combinations are equally productive. Some are attested multiple times, others a few times, several only once.

It is of course difficult to know what to make of those combinations that occur only once. On the one hand, it is easy enough to dismiss the combinations that occur infrequently or only once; Aronoff and Fuhrhop (2002) tend to dismiss occasional occurrences as not significant, for example. On the other hand, as Hay and Plag (2004) point out, given two low-probability affixes, the probability of their combination becomes extremely low indeed; they calculate that to attest a single example of *-ee-hood* would require nearly 1.7 million types in a corpus. Correspondingly, we cannot exclude the possibility of finding new combinations as the corpus grows larger. Given these comments, the fact that we find even a single example of a particular combination should be taken as significant. We have therefore not dismissed such isolated occurrences.

Taking these caveats into account, we can conclude that native affixes are more productive on non-native bases (both simplex and complex) than non-native affixes are on native bases, but that the latter pattern is not at all rare or anomalous. We might even speculate that the less frequent occurrence of the non-native-on-native ordering is not to be attributed to any vestige of stratification, but rather to the fact that the non-native affixes in question are less generally productive or less separable than native ones. Certainly, in the case of prefixes, where the level of separability is higher (see Chapter 21), we have a higher level of attachment of non-native to native.

This being the case, we have to ask why the myth of stratification is so well-established in the literature on English word-formation. We believe there are several reasons, all of which contribute to some degree.

- *Typology*: It is often the case in other languages that native goes with native and non-native with non-native (see, for example, Fleischer 1975 on German, and Townsend 1975 on Russian). These languages treat stratification rather more restrictively than is the case in English. This may have established expectations about the way in which English was likely to behave.
- *Genesis*: Non-native affixes made their way into English by being borrowed as parts of non-native words, and the best parallels to bases in the non-native words were equally non-native. Thus the earliest English formations using non-native affixes were probably on non-native bases, but as is indicated by our data, that has changed in more modern English.
- *Item-familiarity*: Even in the examples listed above, many of the mixtures of native and non-native occur in words that are not item-familiar. Generalizations over item-familiar words thus exaggerate the influence of stratification.

27.4 THEORETICAL CONSEQUENCES

The patterning of native and non-native affixes is interesting enough on its own, but it is perhaps more interesting when put in the context of theoretical claims about the stratification of English derivation made, for example, by the theory of Lexical Phonology and Morphology (Siegel 1974; Allen 1978; Kiparsky 1982a; Giegerich 1999) or Aronoff and Fuhrhop's (2002) Monosuffix Constraint.

Lexical Phonology and Morphology, at least in its earliest form, is now largely discredited as a theory of the interaction of morphology and phonology, but the notion that there are two classes of affixes or two strata of derivation in English still persists to some extent. It has never been explicitly claimed that the two strata align perfectly with the etymological origins of particular affixes, but scrutiny of the most complete breakdown of affixes, that in Selkirk (1982), suggests that the division falls to a large extent along etymological lines. Note that Selkirk's (1982) list of affixes overlaps to a large extent with those in the tables presented here, but not entirely. For example, she treats *-man* (*postman*) as a suffix, whereas we do not. On the other hand, she does not categorize *-ite* or *-ess* at all.

(3)   Selkirk's breakdown of suffixes:

   a. *Class 1*: -ette, -ity, -th, -ance, -ee, -ation, -al$_A$, -ic, -ary, -ous, -an, -ese, -esque, -ive, -ory, -ify, -ate$_V$, -en$_V$

   b. *Class 2*: -hood, -ship, -dom, -er, -let, -ling, -ful, -age, -ness, -al$_N$, -less, -ly, -y, -ish, -some

   c. *Both*: -ist, -ism, -ment, -able, -ize

What this organization suggests is that with the exception of the suffixes *-age* and *-al$_N$*, all non-native affixes are Class 1, and with the exception of the unproductive native *-th*, all native affixes are Class 2. Selkirk does not explicitly justify this division, referring to previous work on the subject (Allen 1978; Siegel 1978), but some of the reasoning for including *-al$_N$* is theory internal, and would seem to argue for several other Class 1 affixes being Class 2 instead, a conclusion that Giegerich (1999) develops in some detail. Assuming the division in (3), however, Selkirk claims that Class 2 suffixes may follow Class 1 suffixes, but not vice versa. The net effect is that for the most part native suffixes follow non-native, but non-native suffixes usually do not follow native suffixes.

After Selkirk, there is remarkably little attention given to individual English affixes in the literature on Lexical Phonology and Morphology, the assumption presumably having been that once classified as stress-changing (Class 1) and stress-neutral (Class 2), there was little more to be said about particular affixes. As can be seen from our observations in this volume, however, this is by no means a sound assumption. We have seen that when non-native affixes are stress-changing, they are rarely stress-changing in exactly the same way (see especially Chapter 9, as well as Burzio 1995; Raffelsiefen 1999). The data in Section 27.2 suggest further that there is far more interleaving of native and non-native affixes than Lexical Phonology and Morphology would have predicted (see also Chapter 21).

We should point out that the strict stratal division of affixes is a tenet only of classical Lexical Phonology and Morphology. A more recent version of the theory, that of Giegerich (1999), advocates distinct lexical strata, but not on the basis of a division of affixes. Indeed, Giegerich argues that quite a few affixes would have to belong to both Class 1 and Class 2, if the behaviour of affixes were taken seriously. Giegerich instead advocates a model in which bases rather than affixes are assigned to different strata. What is interesting about Giegerich's model for our purposes is that he claims that the native/non-native distinction does have a place in English morphology. Specifically, he argues that non-native affixes (in his terms [+Latinate]) are largely confined to non-native bases, while native affixes ([−Latinate] in his terms) have no such restriction. In other words, he argues that regardless of how our theoretical model is constructed, the distinction between native and non-native affixes is still active in the contemporary language. The data we have gathered here offer little support for Giegerich's claim: while there is a tendency for non-native suffixes to favour non-native bases, there is far more mixing of the two systems of derivation than such theoretical claims might have led us to expect.

As we have mentioned, the classic theory of Lexical Phonology and Morphology has been largely discredited, and therefore our observations might be deemed unnecessary nails in an already sealed coffin. The notion that there is something to be said about the differential behaviour of native and non-native derivation persists, however. A prominent example of this is Aronoff and Fuhrhop's (2002: 473) Monosuffix Constraint, which they state as in (4).

(4)   Suffixes that select Germanic bases select unsuffixed bases.

Indeed, Aronoff and Fuhrhop (2002: 475–6) make the stronger claim that English derivation is strongly stratified on a native/non-native basis.

Furthermore, although Latinate suffixes may disobey the constraint, they attach to unsuffixed words much less commonly than Germanic suffixes do, and they normally attach to suffixes which also carry the feature Latinate, so the picture drawn here is that there are two different word-formation systems, especially within the combination of suffixes, one Germanic and one Latinate.

Aronoff and Fuhrhop's claims seem weak even on the basis of their own evidence, which is largely culled from the *OED*. Although they claim that *-ness* is the only suffix that attaches freely to other Germanic affixes, their own charts show at least twenty other examples of native-on-native suffixed forms. Their reason for dismissing these combinations is that they are infrequent, sometimes attested more than a century ago and therefore not contemporary, and presumably therefore not productive.

We have given good reasons in this chapter and elsewhere in this volume to suggest that examples cannot be dismissed because they are infrequent. And oddly, not all of the combinations that Aronoff and Fuhrhop dismiss really are infrequent. For example, they indicate that there are thirty examples of *er + y* and twenty of *er + ship*. Given that they were working with dictionary data, and that forms with these affixes are likely to be relatively transparent, we find these patterns to be quite robust. If these combinations were semantically transparent, why would we expect them to be recorded in a dictionary at all? In any case, the examples that we have cited above are largely contemporary (the ones we have added from COCA are entirely contemporary), and although some of them are quite infrequent, we still consider them as significant. The conclusion that we draw is that the distinction between native and non-native morphology is not strong in the contemporary language.

27.5 CONCLUSION

The data adduced here thus suggest that stratification is only faintly visible in contemporary English derivation: although there is a tendency for non-native suffixes to be somewhat selective, neither native affixation nor non-native prefixation seem to be stratified. Nevertheless, we might rightly raise the question of how a naïve native speaker of English would be able to maintain even this faint distinction without having any conscious knowledge of the etymology of English morphemes. The best answer still seems to hinge on phonological characteristics of native versus non-native derived words. With respect to bases, Adams (2001) notes the following:

> But the native–foreign distinction does correlate to some extent with differences in the shapes of words. Native words are often monosyllabic, or have two syllables with the accent on the first. Foreign words often have three or more syllables and are typically not accented on the initial syllable (Adams 2001: 12).

Further clues might come from phonological coherence and segmentability. As has been observed in several ways (Raffelsiefen 1999; Hay 2003), native suffixes by and large are more likely to form distinct phonological words, or in psycholinguistic terms to be more easily separable than non-native suffixes. Non-native prefixes often have the characteristics of forming distinct phonological words and being easily separable as well. And affixes that constitute distinct phonological words or are in other ways more separable would be expected to follow those that are phonologically cohering and therefore less separable (see Chapter 21 for discussion). In other words, to the extent that both prefixes and native suffixes are more likely to be less phonologically fused to their bases than non-native suffixes, the distinction between native and non-native continues to maintain a sort of shadow existence psycholinguistically.

....

CHAPTER 28

English morphology in a typological perspective

28.1 PROSPECTUS

It is beyond the scope of the present volume to show where English stands typologically with respect to the myriad types of morphology displayed in the languages of the world. For one thing, such a comparison would require much better knowledge than we have of the cross-linguistic parameters that characterize morphology. In addition, it is not yet clear what sorts of insight are to be gained from such large-scale comparisons. We nevertheless begin with the traditional way of characterizing morphology as isolating, agglutinating, fusional, or polysynthetic that goes back to the work of Humboldt (1836) and Sapir (1921), as well as more modern attempts at large-scale classification, concluding in the end that such schemas do not tell us much that is interesting or useful.

We argue, however, that typological comparisons on a more local level have the potential to be more illuminating, and therefore we opt for a finer-grained comparison of English with Romance morphology on the one hand and Germanic on the other. Specifically we will compare English inflection and word-formation to that of French and German. French of course has had direct historical influence on English, but German has not. Dutch or Frisian might be thought a more accurate point of comparison, or even Danish, as its ancestor Old Norse had some influence up until the Norman invasion. Nevertheless, German provides a familiar and convenient West Germanic language for comparative purposes.

As a Germanic language with a huge non-native vocabulary made up largely of Romance elements, English finds itself torn between Germanic and Romance types of structure. Occasionally there are signs of Greek types, as well. On this more local level of comparison, then, English is typologically heterogenous, having been influenced in different directions by the patterns derived from different parts of its patrimony. This makes it interesting, and also challenging from the point of view of typology.

28.2 BROAD CLASSIFICATORY SCHEMES

28.2.1 The traditional Humboldtian classification

Since the work of Humboldt (1836) and Sapir (1921), it has been traditional to classify morphological systems as belonging to one of four types: isolating, agglutinating, fusional, or polysynthetic. It is well-known, however, that morphological systems as a whole rarely fit squarely into one of the four categories, and even looking at inflection and derivation separately it is sometimes hard to apply a hard and fast classification. Comrie (1981: 51) therefore suggests two intersecting scales, which he calls the index of synthesis and the index of fusion. The index of synthesis gauges how many morphemes there typically are per word, with isolating languages being low on the index and polysynthetic languages high. The index of fusion gauges how many meanings are typically packed into a single morpheme in a language, with fusional languages being higher on the index than agglutinating languages. We will look at English briefly both in terms of the original classification and in terms of Comrie's modification of it.

We begin with English inflection. Old English clearly had fusional inflection, with, for instance, case and number expressed in a single exponent (Kastovsky 2000). Contemporary English, however, has little inflection left to begin with, and in terms of the inflection it does have, very few traces of fusional inflection remain. First, irregular past tenses and past participles like *began* and *begun* show the fusion of the root and grammatical information, as do umlaut plurals like *feet*, *mice*. Second, the third-person non-past singular *-s* in *carrie-s*, *reduce-s*, *understand-s* is fusional to the extent that third-person and singular can be seen as independent grammatical features of English verbs. This is slightly dubious, since apart from the use of this *-s*, the only place where singular and plural are regularly distinguished on verbs is with the verb BE. The verb BE is also the only place where person is regularly marked on verbs apart from the use of this *-s*. In other places, fusion has vanished. Singular on nouns is unmarked. Where plural is marked irregularly, plural and genitive show agglutination, not fusion (as in *ox-en-'s*). In the regular cases we have suggested that there is haplology of one of the markers of plural and genitive (see Chapter 7.3.3). Regular past tenses are agglutinative, too.

We turn now to derivation. Oddly, English is frequently said to be an isolating type of language. Although in less ornate styles English might tend towards simplex words, its morphology nevertheless cannot be said to be isolating. Many English words of more than three syllables turn out to be morphologically complex (*Jansen-ism*, *mater-ial-ism*, *penny-pincher*), although this is certainly not always the case, as examples like *peristroika* or *kangaroo* show. On the other hand, very little derivation in English is fusional, and the fusional derivation we find is lexicalized, for example, the isolated pairs *abide* • *abode*, *sing* • *song*, and the very few causative forms linked by vowel change like *fall* • *fell*, *lie* • *lay*. Of the morphological types suggested by the four-fold classification, derivation in English comes closest to being agglutinative. Even where there are instances like *persuasion* /pəˈsweɪʒən ‖ pərˈsweɪʒən/ where it can be difficult to say precisely where the morpheme boundary runs, there is no doubt as to the fact that there is a string of elements. But calling English agglutinative is at best a broad-brush characterization: English of course has abundant non-agglutinative derivation in the form of conversion (Chapters 10, 11, 14, 25) and clipping (Chapter 18). We will return to this point shortly.

Compounds are, by their very nature, agglutinative, at least those compounds that we have referred to as canonical compounds (Chapter 19). However, non-canonical compounds—those that seem to have been formed by back-formation or conversion—again raise questions for the Humboldtian classification.

We can conclude that in terms of the traditional classification, English morphology fits best overall into the agglutinative type. There are two ways in which this conclusion is unsatisfying, however. First, English morphology is rather different from that of other agglutinative languages like Turkish or Finnish (but see Haspelmath 2009 for a cross-linguistic test of the notion of agglutination). In this regard, we could perhaps look to Comrie's indexes of fusion and synthesis to provide some nuance. We might say, for example, that English would be ranked relatively low on the index of fusion, with few examples where more than one meaning is packed into the same morpheme, and somewhere midway on the index of synthesis, with words—at least multisyllabic ones—frequently having more than one morpheme. Comparatively, Turkish would probably be lower than English in terms of fusion and higher in terms of synthesis.

But even with the more nuanced measure, our classification of English is still unsatisfying. First, it is vexing that the classification as a whole does not tell us what to do about sorts of morphology that are non-concatenative, for example, conversion, back-formation, and clipping. Since these are significant processes in English derivation and compounding, classifying English as agglutinative misses something important. Worse, however, is that we are left with a feeling that this kind of classification does not give us any real insight into English in comparison to other languages. In other words, once we have determined that English belongs to this category or that, what does this lead us to expect in terms of correlated structural properties or historical developments? To our knowledge, nothing follows from these classificatory schemes (see Haspelmath 2009; Bauer 2010a: 136–7 for a similar conclusion).

28.2.2 Head- versus dependent- marking

Nichols (1986) suggests that another way of looking at morphological systems—specifically inflectional systems—is in terms of head- versus dependent-marking. In head-marking languages, relationships between the head of a phrase and its dependents (a term which Nichols uses to cover arguments and modifiers), are signalled by inflection on the head, whereas in dependent-marking languages inflection appears on the arguments or modifiers of the head. In English, for example, possession is marked on the possessor rather than on the possessed noun (*the dog's bed*), which would suggest that English is a dependent-marking language. However, subject person is marked on the verb (at least for third-person singular in the present tense), which might be interpreted as head-marking, similar to plural marking in noun phrases. If this is correct, then English could not be regarded as strictly one or the other type, not even necessarily within the same phrase types. Given the general dearth of inflection in English, it is not clear how useful this distinction is for the typological classification of English, nor again does it allow us to predict other characteristics of English.

28.3 A FINER-GRAINED VIEW

The failure of broad classificatory schemes to tell us anything satisfying about English does not mean, however, that we have given up on typology. It just means that we find a finer-grained approach to cross-linguistic comparison more telling. The strategy we opt for here is to look at English inflection, derivation, and compounding in comparison to our closer neighbours, that is, Germanic and Romance languages. For the reasons indicated in Section 28.1, we focus most closely on a comparison with German and French, although we will have reason to refer to the classical languages on occasion as well.

28.3.1 Inflection

One typological parameter along which languages may differ is the distinction between word-based and stem-based inflection. Inflection in contemporary English is overwhelmingly word-based. That is, the inflectional affixes are attached to morphological entities which can stand alone, at least in the regular instances, as shown in (1).

(1)   cat   cat-s
      walk   walk-s
      walk   walk-ed
      walk   walk-ing
      big   big-ger big-gest

This contrasts with Old English, which had a stem-based verbal system and a heterogeneous nominal system (Kastovsky 2006: 245–6). The status of German is controversial. While Old High German is regarded unanimously as stem-based, the modern language has been analysed as stem-based or word-based by different authors and across verbal, nominal, and adjectival domains (see Harnisch 2001 for discussion). French also invites somewhat inconclusive analyses of this parameter. Its nominal and adjectival inflection are word-based, as shown in (2a) (with the plural /s/ showing up in liaison contexts and in the orthography), but verbal inflection seems unclear in its status, as what can be analysed at the phonological level as a stem, as in (2b) can also appear as a free form, as illustrated in (2c). It is the orthography that still reflects the earlier stem-based nature of the system.

(2)   a.   *French*   *gloss*
              enfant   'child'
              enfant-s   'children'
              petit   'small (sg)'
              petit-s   'small (pl)'

       b.   /ɛm/   'love (*stem*)'
              aim-er   'love (infinitive)'
              aim-e   'love (1sg/3sg/imperative)'
              aimes   'love (2sg)'
              aim-ons   'love (1pl)'

       c.   Tu /ɛm/ tes enfants.
              'You (sg.) love your children'

Overall, it nevertheless seems to be the case that of the three languages, English is most clearly word-based.

The English umlaut plurals (e.g. *feet, geese, lice, men, mice, teeth*) are a Germanic heritage. The system of umlaut is still much more elaborate in modern German than in modern English, and is widely found supporting affixes, as well as being the only marker of plural (compare English *brother • brethr-en*). The English system shows only the remnants of umlaut, most umlaut forms having become regularized (see Chapter 7.2.4). Part of the result of this regularization is that there are no declension classes in English nouns, just a division between regular and irregular forms (Kastovsky 2000: 220–1).

The only case marking that English retains is in the genitive, and as was shown in Chapter 7 this has moved a long way from the genitive marking in English's Germanic neighbours. The periphrastic genitive has parallels in French, and in many of the modern Germanic languages, where they are, however, relatively recent innovations. The English third-person singular non-past tense -*s* is typologically extremely odd. It is odd from a universalist point of view in being the only marking in the present tense paradigm, and yet being on the third-person singular, usually the person which is least likely to be marked. Even within the system of English it is odd, since it means, as pointed out by Kastovsky (2000: 217), that—except in the verb BE—person and number are marked only in the non-past, where tense is not marked, while tense is marked only in the past, where person is not marked.

The lack of a morphological future in English is another Germanic feature, and specifically not Romance. The Germanic languages can all mark future time by using the non-past form of the verb, or by the use of auxiliaries.

Ablaut marking in preterites and past participles (often accompanied by suffixation) is again a Germanic phenomenon. The system seems to have been predictable in the earliest stages of Germanic (Mailhammer 2007), but is unpredictable in all the modern Germanic languages. All the languages have lost verbs of this type to regular paradigms. This has certainly been the case in English, although, it is not always the case: as we have shown in Chapter 5.3.5.2 certain patterns continue to attract new members through the workings of analogy. English no longer has the circumfixes that characterize the other West Germanic past participles, although in earlier stages of English the past participle was frequently circumfixed (for example, Middle English *ydrunken, yhoped* 'drunk', 'hoped' and even Early Modern English *yclept* 'called').

English adjectival inflection shows only marking for comparative and superlative, and not gender (as French and German), number (as French and German), or definiteness (as German). Overall, English inflectional morphology is fundamentally Germanic in nature, albeit much simplified from its West Germanic origins. It has lost declension and conjugation classes, and most of the Germanic case marking (there are a few remnants in the morphology of pronouns). What is perhaps odd typologically, however, is that where English inflection shows variation between analytic and synthetic forms (that is, in the genitive or the comparative and superlative, as illustrated in Chapters 6 and 7), the distribution of the analytic and synthetic forms is probabilistic rather than categorical in nature.

28.3.2 Derivation

Just like English inflection, English derivation is very largely word-based, see (3), where we find obligatorily bound roots, they are virtually always borrowed. This is illustrated in (4), with *unkempt* being a form that is based on a native bound root.

(3)   arriv-al, command-er, em-power, hope-less, hospital-ize, parent-al, pre-arrange, preferment, short-ish

(4)   auth-or, bapt-ism, ed-ible, electr-ify, in-ept, leg-al, psych-ology, regul-ar, scient-ist, un-kempt

There are a few instances of word-formation by internal modification left in the lexicon: *abide* ♦ *abode, believe* ♦ *belief, ímport* ♦ *impórt, rise* ♦ *raise, sing* ♦ *song*, but only those with stress shift show any signs of being productive. Word-formation involving vowel change is far more widespread in German (as, for example, in the noun–verb pairs *Bruch* 'break' ♦ *brechen, Schnitt* 'cut' ♦ *schneiden, Stand* 'stand' ♦ *stehen*, etc., see Fleischer and Barz 2007: 218), but not productive there, either.

Both German and French show both prefixation and suffixation (there is a minimal amount of circumfixation in German and Dutch word-formation), and the English pattern of prefixes looking rather like prepositions is common to all three languages. Both French and German are right-headed in derivation, so the right-headedness of English is unsurprising. One surprising thing, though, is that we find a few cases of left-headedness in English (for example, *de-* and a few other prefixes discussed in Chapter 29.3.1), which are not supported by models from these other languages. Various analyses that attempt to avoid the left-headedness of such formations (e.g. Kastovsky 1999; Nagano 2011) are partly motivated by the awkwardness of marginal left-headedness.

It might be interesting to see how English compares with other languages in terms of the semantic categories of derivation that it exhibits. We expect that all languages will have means for changing items from one lexical category into another (that is, noun to verb, verb to adjective, etc.), as English certainly does. But a broader comparison of the derivational categories that are available cross-linguistically (for example, agentive or instrumental nouns, causative or inchoative verbs, ranges of evaluatives, and the like) is not yet possible. The problem here is that there is as yet no coherent cross-linguistic inventory of derivational categories that might serve to test English against. Beard's (1995) attempt to list possible derivational categories is highly dependent on the range of inflectional categories in Indo-European, and wider typological surveys are not as yet available (but see, for example, Štekauer *et al.* 2012). The notion that there might be a universal paradigm of derivational categories to gauge English against is an intriguing one, but one that will have to await further research.

This said, there are still certain observations that we may make. While English is rich in the means it has to derive agents and instruments, we have observed that it is rather poor in the means of deriving patient nouns, especially inanimate ones. As we saw in Chapter 11, we frequently find affixes whose primary function lies elsewhere being stretched to produce patient nouns when they are needed. And although it is sometimes said that English is poor in evaluative morphology, at least by comparison to German, Dutch, Spanish, or Italian, we have found to the contrary (see Chapter 18) that contemporary English has many ways of forming diminutives and augmentatives.

28.3.3 Conversion

Conversion, as the notion is used in reference to English, is not a universal. In the first instance it has to be distinguished from multifunctionality of the type reported for some Polynesian languages, where virtually any word can be used in any function. Further, the term conversion can be used of rather different types of process in English than can be observed in French and German.

In French, for example, an inflected form can function as a word in a word class not supported by the inflection. This is most obvious with infinitives (which are, of course, very nominal-like parts of verbs), so that we find, for example, *pouvoir* 'to be able' • *pouvoir* 'power'. In French such usage tends to be sporadic, but in German it is systematic, and the infinitive of any verb can function as a neuter noun: *das Bellen* 'barking', *das Essen* 'eating, food', *das Rückwärtsfahren* 'reversing' (Hammer 1983: 263). This is rather similar in some ways to the nominal uses of *-ing* forms in English.

Typically, in German, though, conversion of verb to noun is based on the stem rather than on the inflected verb, so that we get forms like *laufen* 'to run' • *der Lauf* 'the run'. In such instances, no further morphology is required for the nominative singular form of the noun, though further morphology is required for plural forms, for instance. In noun to verb conversion, on the other hand, extra morphology is automatically required—in German or in French. Thus, for the English noun–verb pair *telephone* • *to telephone* we get French *le téléphone* • *téléphoner*, German *das Telefon* • *telefonieren* (see Manova and Dressler 2005 for further discussion). The result is that the paucity of inflectional morphology in English appears to make the process of conversion marginally easier to manage. How significant a factor this is in the growth of conversion in English is hard to determine.

Conversion is an all-pervasive word-formation process in English. However, from the point of view of Natural Morphology (for example, Manova and Dressler 2005), conversion ought to be relatively infrequent, since it is not structurally iconic: 'more meaning' is not reflected by 'more form'. It is also less natural than affixation in a number of ways, including morpho-semantic transparency. Manova and Dressler (2005) admit this, and admit that English shows greater productivity for conversion than would be expected. They suggest that the pattern of conversion was established by the erosion of endings, and that the preference for conversion arises from a language-specific pattern. This seems to imply that there may be some correlation not just between lack of inflection and conversion but specifically between loss of inflection and conversion. Any such correlation remains to be established.

28.3.4 Compounds

It is not clear whether compounding exists in all languages (see Bauer 2009b), but it is certainly an extremely widespread form of word-formation, so that the existence of compounds in English, in other Germanic languages, and in Romance is not surprising. However, the types of compound that are widespread in Germanic and Romance are different, and English appears to have been influenced to some extent by both sides. There is also influence from Greek in neoclassical word-formation.

28.3.4.1 *From Germanic*

Compounding is an active means of word-formation in all Germanic languages, but the rest of Germanic tends to have a far more predictable template for compounds than English does, including lefthand stress and relatively stable orthographic representation. Germanic languages have a compounding pattern where uninflected words are put side-by-side: these are sometimes referred to as *echte* or *eigentliche* 'genuine' compounds in the German literature

(Grimm 1826; Fleischer and Bartz 2007: 136). There are also patterns with linking elements, mostly derived from genitive or plural markers from earlier stages of the languages. English seems to have abandoned linking elements in compounds, except possibly in a very few sets such as *sportsman, swordsman, yachtsman.* The status of the *-s* in compounds of this sort is somewhat controversial, however; although these compounds might be analysed as having a linking element, other forms (for example, *arms trade, drinks cabinet, perennials catalogue,* and *new tastes menu*) appear to have an *-s* that is genuinely interpretable as a plural.

In what follows, we comment on correspondences between English patterns and patterns in other Germanic languages. In some cases, the features discussed here are common to compounding in many languages, and in some cases there seems to have been parallel development across Germanic.

Binary-branching is one of those features that may be a much broader phenomenon. Generally we do find binary-branching in compounding in English, as well as in other kinds of word-formation, but it is also the rule in most other languages that have compounding. Some linguists might even argue that it is a language universal. However, in English, as in German, there are exceptions to the binary-branching rules in coordinate compounds, especially, but not exclusively, the type illustrated by *singer-songwriter-recording artist.* A similar pattern exists in French, with *le bleu-blanc-rouge* ('the blue-white-red', referring to the French flag), but is not widespread there.

Connected with binary-branching is the question of recursion. In English, as in other Germanic languages, compounds have the ability to be embedded in other compounds—a feature so common in German and Danish that it is sometimes mocked by speakers of those languages, with examples like German *Donau-dampf-schiff-fahrts-gesellschafts-unter-offizier* 'Danube steamship line under officer' or Danish *spor-vogns-skinne-skidt-skraber-fag-forenings-magasins-beklædnings-forvalter* 'street car rail dirt scraper trade union storehouse clothing director'. English examples such as *Auckland University Law Library shelving policy* show similar trends. This is not a given, if we look on a wider scale. There are several languages, such as Fongbe (Lefebvre and Brousseau 2002), Ngiti (Lojenga 1994), and Slovak (Pavol Štekauer, p.c.) where compounds are either not recursive or show very limited recursiveness.

As we have shown in Chapter 20 the range of semantic relationships possible between the first and second elements of English compounds is virtually unlimited, when all compound types are taken into account. This is especially true with regard to attributive compounds: although attempts have been made at various times to catalogue a fixed set of semantic relationships, these have invariably proven unsuccessful (see Chapter 20.3.1). Other Germanic languages seem to have equally large sets of relationships. Yet this, again, is not something that can be presupposed. Hup is said (Epps 2008: 216) to encode just three semantic relations in compounds. According to Heath (2008: 191) many compounds in Jamsay are 'equivalent to a possessive construction'—though see Bauer and Tarasova (2010) for an alternative interpretation of such observations. Biber and Gray (2011) also claim that the number of relationships in English has increased since the seventeenth century as the number of different classes of noun used as modifiers has increased. The examples they cite from their earlier period are almost all locatives of some kind (particularly if the modifier in a form like *linen handkerchief* is viewed as a source rather than as a material).

Historically, Germanic compounds are characterized by a specific, that is leftward, stress pattern, and the fact that a language shows a specific stress pattern in its compounds is not unusual, see also Finnish, Hup (Epps 2008: 217), or Lango (Noonan 1992: 115). In English the inherited and rather strict compound-specific stress pattern has given way, however, to a complex and highly variable pattern of leftward and rightward stresses today (see Chapter 19.3.3). Other Germanic languages, for example German, also show some limited degree of stress variation, but English is certainly most advanced in this respect among its relatives.

It may be that English also inherits from Germanic the tendency for words formed by compounding to be nouns. However, there are more compound verbs in other Germanic languages than there are in English, where formation of canonical compound verbs (as opposed to the creation of things that look like compound verbs by back-formation or conversion) seems to be very new (Kastovsky 2000: 216). English shares with other Germanic languages a tendency for coordinate compounding to be a productive type, although less prominent than attributive compounding, for example (Olsen 2001; Bauer 2010b). The low use of coordinate compounds is probably an areal feature (Wälchli 2005), though, that stretches beyond Germanic and Romance.

28.3.4.2 *From Romance*

Despite a somewhat obscure history (see Kastovsky 2009: 336–7), the kind of compound illustrated by *cut-throat, pickpocket, scarecrow* in English is widely considered to be supported in English by parallel types in Romance, and specifically French. Certainly the type is far more productive in French than it is in contemporary English. Though historically there was some marginal productivity of the type in English, the type is likely no longer productive in the contemporary language.

Superficially the prevalence of this type in Romance and its relative absence in English might be said to show that English and Romance are typologically distinct. But this claim of distinctness holds only if the *cut-throat* type compound is seen as an alternative in Romance to the sort of synthetic compound that is typical in Germanic. An alternative analysis counts the *cut-throat* type as the exocentric equivalent to *blow torch, call girl, driftwood, hangman, mincemeat, pay day, plaything, searchlight, washhouse, whetstone,* and so on, where there is a verb in the first element and a head noun which stands in various grammatical and/or semantic relationships to that verb. Indeed, we have analysed the *cutthroat* type in this way as exocentric argumental compounds in Chapter 20.2.3 (see also Lieber 2010).

More interestingly, perhaps, French might be seen as the origin of structures like *canine tooth, domestic goddess, equine anemia, human genome, equinoctial gale, melodic minor, quantitative analysis, spiritual dimension,* and the like that compete with compounds in English; indeed we raised the question in Chapter 19 whether these were to be treated as compounds (see

Chapter 19.2.1.2 for discussion). Since French traditionally avoids nominal modification of nouns but creates derivational adjectives from nouns, it provides a model for such structures, while Germanic frequently uses nouns to modify other nouns, thus creating compounds. By inheriting both systems, English ends up with a mixed system. Having a system that allows both kinds of modification, apparently synonymously, English has the possibility of two routes to express the same fundamental idea. In some cases, as in (5), such pairs differ stylistically, and in others, as in (6), we find semantic distinctions.

(5) atom bomb/atomic bomb, climate change/climatic change, dogtooth/canine tooth, language development/linguistic development, noun compound/nominal compound, sex therapy/sexual therapy, town planning/urban planning, weather map/meteorological map, woman doctor/female doctor

(6) brute strength/brutal strength, country house/rural house/bucolic house, demon lover/ demonic lover, folk music/popular music, health farm/healthy farm, nature strip/natural strip, rhythm section/rhythmical section

Interestingly, it seems to be the case that derived adjectives are not historically parts of adjective–noun compounds (Bauer 2009c: 403–4 and sources there). A few foreign adjectives with foreign affixes are now found in Danish and German in such compounds (Danish *centralvarme*, German *Zentralheizung* 'central heating'), but they are still relatively rare. It seems that for naming, English still prefers noun–noun compounds with Germanic and early Romance vocabulary and adjective–noun phrasal constructions with later Romance vocabulary unless the Romance vocabulary is very recent or is employed mainly or exclusively in scientific domains (see Schlücker and Plag 2011 for the treatment of phrases versus compounds in naming in German). Thus we get *eyebrow* and not **ocular brow*, *table top* not **tabular top* but *descriptive passage* not **description passage* and *parliamentary language* not **parliament language*. There is enough lexicalization in the system to confuse matters from time to time (e.g. *popular* no longer means simply 'of the people', *infantile* is disparaging so that we do not get **infantile school*), and there are also some examples which go against this general trend (such as *pole star* rather than *polar star*). Overall, however, there seems to be an effect of history here which affects the typological appearance of the language. We do not wish to develop this idea here, since it overlaps very largely with the areas of syntax and lexicography or lexicology, and certainly goes beyond morphology, but we point to it as being a factor in the structure of current English.

Another set of constructions that come into English from French and are sometimes classified as compounds, is the set of constructions made up of a noun and a postposed adjective, like *attorney general, blood royal, court martial, governor general, lie direct, notary public, princess royal*. While these persist as lexical items, there is some evidence that they are no longer perceived as being left-headed (as they are in French), as the plural marker is more and more added to the righthand word (where relevant). Here, the English typological pattern appears to have over-ruled the French one, but this has happened as these items have moved from being syntactically created expressions in the original French to fixed lexical expressions in current English.

28.3.4.3 *From Greek*

English of course also has a large and to some extent productive cohort of neoclassical compounds deriving for the most part from Greek. We will not reiterate the characteristics of these compounds here. The reader is referred to Chapter 19.4.5 for detailed discussion of them, as well as comparison of their analysis in contrast to Greek.

28.4 CONCLUSION

What we have suggested here is that English morphology is not homogeneous from a typological point of view, and that some, at least, of that heterogeneity derives from the mixed history of English vocabulary. A typological approach of the kind that has been taken here does not necessarily tell us a great deal about the operation of English morphology, but does raise questions about processes of diachronic development and the way they interact with typological tendencies.

....

CHAPTER 29

English morphology and theories of morphology

29.1 PROSPECTUS

We did not write this book with the primary aim of making a contribution to linguistic theory, but rather with the intention of giving as theory-neutral and as comprehensive as possible a description of the contemporary state of English inflection and word-formation. Our strategy of relying on data from corpora has given us substantial insight into the workings of English morphology though, and we have tried in Part VI to show how those data speak to a number of recurrent themes in morphological theory. In this last chapter we take a broader view of what the English data tell us about morphological theory in general. In Section 29.2 we consider a range of theoretical models, concluding that the facts of English morphology do not allow us to argue strongly for or against most extant frameworks. Section 29.3 looks at a variety of theoretical principles that are relatively independent of broader frameworks; here we argue that the corpus data do provide strong arguments against many of the specific claims that have been made in the literature. In Section 29.4 we turn to what we do know, and how that knowledge should help us to frame new theoretical models.

29.2 BROAD THEORETICAL MODELS

Complex and intricate as it is, English morphology vastly underdetermines several major points in morphological theory. What we mean by this is that the facts of English inflection and word-formation are compatible with many different frameworks that have been proposed. This is not to say that all theoretical models are equal with respect to accounting for all aspects of English morphology, but just that no single existing model seems to make substantially better predictions about English morphology as a whole than any other. We cannot of course look in detail here at every possible theory of inflection and word-formation that has been proposed over the last six or so decades, but we will consider some of the major proposals. Following Stump's (2001) taxonomy of linguistic theories we start with two major issues, the status of the morpheme as a theoretical construct (Section 29.2.1) and the nature of the mechanisms by which morphosyntactic features are mapped onto phonological forms (Section 29.2.2). Finally, we turn to a totally different set of theories, analogical and constructional models.

29.2.1 Are there morphemes? IA, IP, and WP

Perhaps the single most important point at the heart of any morphological theory is the treatment of the morpheme. Starting with the American structuralist tradition and continuing with much of the generative literature from the 1970s on, scholars have been engaged in lively debate as to whether the morpheme is a legitimate unit of analysis, or whether it should be dispensed with entirely as a theoretical construct. On the one hand we have theories in which morphemes are taken to be the basic units of analysis that are put together into hierarchically organized structures, much as syntactic rules generate hierarchically organized structures from words. In the American structuralist tradition, such theories were dubbed Item and Arrangement (IA) models (Hockett 1954, see also Harris 1942; Bloch 1947; Nida 1948). This sort of model continues in the generative tradition in the work of Lieber (1980, 1992), Selkirk (1982), Williams (1981), and Di Sciullo and Williams (1987), and in Distributed Morphology in such works as Halle and Marantz (1993) and Harley and Noyer (1999). On the other hand we have theories that generally eschew the morpheme as a unit of analysis and cast morphology as a set of processes. Two sorts of theory belong to this camp, Item and Process (IP) theories (Hockett 1954; Aronoff 1976 in the generative tradition, Booij 2010 in Construction Morphology) and Word and Paradigm (WP) theories (Robins 1959; Matthews 1972; Anderson 1992; Stump 2001). The differences between IP and WP models will be taken up in the next section; for our purposes it is sufficient to say here that both IP and WP frameworks eschew the morpheme as a theoretical construct. We note, however, that it is not impossible to construct a theory that is basically processual in nature but that nevertheless countenances the morpheme as a theoretical construct. Chomsky and Halle (1968) is a candidate for such a theory.

In analysing affixation in English (both inflectional and derivational), IA, IP, and WP models are more similar to each other than might at first appear. Consider, for example, the formal representations in (1), where (1a) uses an IP format, (1b) an IA format, and (1c) a WP format:

(1) a. *Word-formation Rule from Aronoff (1976: 63) (IP)*
        Rule of negative *un#*
        $[X]_{Adj} \rightarrow [un\#[X]_{Adj}]_{Adj}$
        semantics (roughly) un#X = not X

     b. *Lexical representation from Lieber (1980: 65) (IA)*
        Negative *in-*
        (phonological representation)

semantic representation: negative

category/subcategorication $[_A$ ___ $[_A$

diacritics: Level I

   c. *Blevins (2003: 748) (WP)*

Preterite, Perfect participle, and Passive participle

Operations	$F_d(X) = Xd$
Preterite	$R([\text{PAST}]) = F_d(X)$
Perfect part	$R([\text{PERF}]) = Y: F_d(X)$
Passive part	$R([\text{PASS}]) = Y$

Although the notation and the nature of the operation involved in building or relating words differ from one framework to another, in the end all three in some way relate a shorter form (call it a base) with a longer form which is a base augmented by a string of phonemes (*un-, in-, -d*).

Other formal variations on these rule formats can be found as well. Haspelmath (2002: 50) represents derivational rules as in (2), and Booij (2010: 8) as in (3):

(2) $/X/_V \leftrightarrow /X\text{ə}r/_N$

'do$_x$'   ' a person who (habitually) does$_x$'

(3) $\omega_i \leftrightarrow N_i \leftrightarrow$ [one who PRED$_j$]$_i$

    | | \

  $[\ ]_j[\text{ə}r]_k$ V_j Aff$_k$

Again, the notation differs—Booij's theory separates phonological, morphological, and semantic information into three parts, linked by the double-headed arrow, Haspelmath's notation collapses the phonological and morphological information and seems to lack internal bracketing in the affixed word, but the end result is not all that different. Any one of these approaches can provide an account of the basic facts of English affixational morphology.

Given that affixation per se presents no formal problems for any of these frameworks, arguments over theoretical frameworks have come to hinge on types of morphological phenomena that English lacks (root and pattern morphology, consonant mutation) or is very poor in (infixation, reduplication, ablaut, and other sorts of internal modification). However, with clipping (see Chapter 18) and blend formation (see Chapter 19), even English has some non-concatenative morphology that poses a challenge to certain theories. In particular, the argument is made that non-concatenative morphology is much less suited to formal treatment in IA models. The question is, how much of the morphology of a given language must be non-concatenative to discredit IA models. For English morphology, concatenation is certainly more characteristic than non-concatenation.

To illustrate the potential inadequacy of IA approaches to non-concatenative morphology, consider the ablaut that occurs in the irregular verbal and nominal paradigms (see also Chapters 5 and 7). Ablaut in English at first glance does seem to provide prima facie evidence against an IA model. To defend an IA analysis, Nida (1948), for example, is forced to postulate what he calls a 'replacive morpheme' represented as *eɪ* → *ʊ* in order to derive the past tense *took* from the present tense *take*, an analysis which is not terribly attractive; the sequence *eɪ* → *ʊ* certainly looks more like a rule or process than a morpheme. Blevins (2003: 246–7), in defending a WP analysis of West Germanic verbal inflection, concedes that in English many irregular verbs may be treated as listed patterns, an analytical option that does not favour one framework over another. There are of course a few ablaut patterns in English that still spread (see the discussion in Chapter 5), but these constitute at best weak evidence against IA. It is, however, much less clear how the subtractive patterns we find in hypocoristics, clippings, and blends can be accommodated in an IA approach.

29.2.2 Realizational versus non-realizational models

English does not seem to provide good evidence one way or the other in the debate between realizational and non-realizational theories of morphology. Stump (2001: 2) distinguishes between theories that are non-realizational or 'incremental' as he terms them and realizational theories. Non-realizational theories allow bases to be inherently specified for morphosyntactic features and morphemes or morphological rules to add morphosyntactic features to bases. Realizational theories, on the other hand, conceive of word-forms as being inherently devoid of morphosyntactic features; features and forms are associated to each other by mapping procedures of various sorts where the mapping between features and word-forms need not be (and typically is not) one to one. In the former sort of theory, 'words acquire morphosyntactic properties only as a concomitant of acquiring the inflectional exponents of those properties', and in the latter 'a word's association with a particular set of morphosyntactic properties licenses the introduction of those properties' inflectional exponents...' (Stump 2001: 2) In the literature (Anderson 1992; Stump 2001) realizational theories are almost always supported by appeal to complex inflectional systems, something which English, of course, lacks.

Realizational theories are often said to be superior to non-realizational ones in two respects: they allow more elegant analyses of the phenomena of multiple exponence and of syncretism. In multiple exponence, a morphosyntactic feature in some language may be expressed by more than one form in a word. With syncretism, the same affix or base may be associated with more than one set of morphosyntactic features. Both cases involve mappings between form and meaning that are not one-to-one. It is argued that non-realizational models are well suited to account for morphological phenomena in which the relationship between form and morphosyntactic features is one-to one, but ill-suited to deal with other sorts of mappings.

English inflection is too impoverished to exhibit much, if any, multiple exponence, but it does display at least one prominent case of syncretism. Specifically, the regular past tense, past participle, and passive participle forms are all marked with *-ed*. We argued in Chapter 5 that what some people call the passive participle and the past participle are not two separate forms in English. Rather the passive is a construction that makes use of the past participle. Blevins (2003: 746–7) makes a convincing argument that regular verbal inflection in West Germanic languages is best treated in a realizational framework, as only that framework allows reference to what he calls the dental stem form, a form ending in *d/t* (depending on the language in question) which is inherently meaningless, but is associated with either the preterite or the past participle or passive participle by realizational rules. But Blevins's argument is most convincing for West Germanic languages other than English; he himself notes that,

> If one were to restrict attention to English, it is not obvious what would count as decisive evidence against a morphemic account that was prepared to countenance the affix- and word-level homophony entailed by a 'one meaning-one affix' principle. How precisely does one establish that preterites and participles are marked by the same exponent, and not merely by homophonous suffixes? (Blevins 2003: 246–7)

So although the facts of English are consistent with a realizational model, the real argument for this model comes from West Germanic languages that have more in the way of verbal inflections.

Although realizational theories are primarily thought of in relation to inflectional systems, they need not be. Stump himself (2001: 252) very briefly considers the extent to which derivation can be treated in a realizational framework, and Beard's (1995) Lexeme Morpheme Base Morphology might be said to give a realizational account of derivation and conversion: instead of derivation being a process of adding affixal morphemes with determinate meanings onto bases, for Beard there are two processes, first derivation in his terms, which involves the association of a semantic or grammatical feature with a base, and second the association of that base with a specific derivational exponent (which may be an affix or nothing, in the case of conversion). The separation of the semantic part of the process from the formal part is what makes it possible to construe the theory as realizational.

The problems with Beard's hypothesis are well-known, and here, data from English derivation do provide some insight (see, for example, Booij 1996b; Plag 1999: ch. 8). Generally, it is not clear that the semantic effects of derivation or conversion can be reduced to a small set of semantic functions that are parallel to grammatical or morphosyntactic functions, as Beard suggests. Further, the widespread tendency of affixes to express a number of different related semantic functions is not easily accommodated; for example, in English the polysemy of the *-er* that forms person, instrument, location, and sometimes patient nouns (see Chapter 11) is in principle treated no differently than the homophony of that affix with respect to the comparative *-er*: everything is homophony in such a theory and in effect, we would be forced to postulate five or six different *-er* suffixes. Further, it is also not clear how realization rules effect the association between a form that has undergone derivation in Beard's sense and the affix that expresses that derivation. To mention just one problem, unlike inflection, where each morphosyntactic configuration is normally mapped onto a single form, in derivation a single base marked with a specific semantic/grammatical feature need not be associated with a unique form (take the nominalizations *commission, commital, commitment* from the verb *commit*, for example). We can conclude that to the extent that a realizational model can be extended to word-formation, the English data suggest a number of problematic points.

29.2.3 Analogical models and Construction Morphology

In Chapter 23 we saw that there are phenomena in English derivation, inflection, and compounding that are hard to accommodate in any theory that is restricted to the concatenation of formatives. It was also argued in that chapter that these phenomena can be accounted for if one assumes some kind of analogical mechanism. The status of such a mechanism is, however, largely unclear, as is its relation to the theories and problems discussed in the previous two subsections.

There are two main approaches within this family of models. One is computational, the other theoretical. The theoretical approach has been developed mainly by Booij (e.g. 2010) and is known under the name of Construction Morphology. This model posits form–meaning pairs of various levels of granularity (called 'schemas' and 'subschemas'), which can express different kinds of generalizations across morphologically related items in the lexicon. In this model the existence of local analogical formations is acknowledged, but is not formally integrated into the model architecture itself, which is restricted to schemas and subschemas. Nevertheless, local analogy is seen as something that can gradually turn into a schema (Booij 2010: 88–93). Non-concatenative processes can also be formalized in a way that is consistent with the overall architecture of the model. The flexibility of schemas and subschemas gives Construction Morphology a conceptual and empirical advantage over many other morphological models. However, in addition to schemas and subschemas, analogy is needed as an additional and quite separate mechanism in order to account for the manifold isolated analogical formations that seem to be quite common in English (and other languages).

This brings us to the other family of approaches, those in which analogy is the only morphological mechanism available. In such models, the notion of analogy receives a formal definition in terms of the kinds of features over which similarity is systematically computed over sets of words. This process of similarity computation is implemented in computational algorithms and can be used to predict, generate, or select pertinent complex words as the output of a morphological category. Three well-known such algorithms are the Tilburg Memory Based Learner (TiMBL, Daelemans and van den Bosch 2005; Daelemans *et al.* 2007), Skousen's Analogical Model of Language (AM, Skousen 1989, 1992; Skousen *et al.* 2002, Skousen and Stanford 2007), and the Generalized Context Model (Nosofsky 1986, 1990). Albright and Hayes' (2003) Minimal Generalization Learner may also be subsumed under this label, as there seems to be no principled difference between the 'miminal generalizations' these authors call 'rules' on the one hand, and the analogically derived sets of bases with the same feature values one gets with models that call themselves 'analogical'.

Analogical algorithms create or select new forms on the basis of the similarity of a given base with existing forms in the lexicon. Consequently, analogies are based on sets of words of varying sizes with varying degrees of similarity, where a 'set' may consist of only a single word, or may have dozens, hundreds, or thousands of words, depending on how many words share a given set of features or feature constellations under comparison. The algorithm thus capitalizes on the multiple relationships that words in the lexicon may have. Consider for instance the many different classifications of irregular verbs discussed in Chapter 5. Each of these classifications is based on certain kinds of similarities shared by smaller and larger sets of pertinent verbs, and we argued that the theoretical or practical value of such classifications is questionable. With an analogical algorithm, all kinds of similarities between a given verb and the verbs in the lexicon can be used to predict its inflected forms.

In this way, analogical algorithms can model both rule-like behaviour (based on very large analogical sets) and the rather idiosyncratic local analogies (in which the set of analogues may be as small as only a single item). Furthermore, the often quite variable behaviour that seems characteristic of large parts of the morphology of English emerges naturally through the variable choices that become available by the different kinds of similarities that different analogues or analogical sets may share with a given base. In sum, such algorithms seem theoretically well equipped to deal with the wide range of categorical and variable phenomena we find in English morphology, including especially seemingly problematic phenomena such as regular versus irregular inflection (Chapter 5), split base effects (Chapter 23), the emergence of splinters, or other paradigmatic morphology. But how do they fare empirically?

It has to be stated that both Construction Morphology and analogical approaches to morphology are currently research programmes rather than established theories. Booij's Construction Grammar has been developed mostly with case studies of Dutch morphology, and the above-mentioned analogical algorithms have been applied so far only to a small subset of phenomena of English morphology: verbal inflection (Skousen 1989; Derwing and Skousen 1994; Albright and Hayes 2003; Keuleers 2008), the history of some negative prefixes (Chapman and Skousen 2005), compound stress (Plag *et al.* 2007; Arndt-Lappe 2011; Arndt-Lappe and Bell 2012), the choice between *-ity* and *-ness* (Arndt-Lappe 2012), and adjectival comparison (Elzinga 2006). All of these studies have provided very promising results, some of them actually showing the superiority of analogical models to competing non-analogical models. It remains to be shown how analogical algorithms can deal on a larger scale with the wealth of intricate problems English morphology has in store.

29.3 SPECIFIC CLAIMS

While English morphology provides relatively little fodder for the big-picture differences among frameworks that have dominated theoretical discussions for the last six or seven decades, it does provide clear evidence that bears on some of the more specific theoretical principles that have been formulated at one time or another. It is of course not possible to cover all theoretical proposals that have been made; we limit ourselves to a selection of the most prominent ones here for which English data provide some insight.

29.3.1 The Righthand Head Rule

The Righthand Head Rule (Williams 1981) has been a remarkably influential proposal. Assuming that the notion that words have heads is a coherent one (see Chapter 24), Williams proposes that the rightmost morpheme in a word is its head. In effect this predicts that suffixes should be word class changing but prefixes should not be. It is well-known that while the Righthand Head Rule works for the bulk of English morphology, it fails in a number of cases. Compounds are right-headed, if they are headed at all, and inflection is suffixal (to the extent that inflections are said to have the properties of heads), but derivation deviates from the Righthand Head Rule at least with respect to prefixation. Specifically, English has several prefixes that change category: *be-*, *de-*, *dis-*, *en-*, *out-*, and *un-*. Depending on how we analyse the locative prefixes that make nouns into prenominal modifiers (e.g. *post-war Europe*, see Chapter 16), we might count them among the category-changing prefixes as well. The majority of these affixes display at least some degree of productivity, so it is not possible to dismiss them as relics of some sort. It is of course possible to argue that the prefixes do not themselves change category (Nagano 2011), but this argument is not terribly convincing.

29.3.2 The Unitary Base and Unitary Output Hypotheses

Aronoff (1976: 48) proposes the Unitary Base Hypothesis which states that 'the syntacti-cosemantic specification of the base, though it may be more or less complex, is always unique'. In other words, Aronoff suggests that we should not find an affix that attaches to both verbs and nouns, much less to all lexical categories. Aronoff dismisses potential counterexamples like the suffix *-able* by arguing that *-able* is in fact two suffixes. The argument is not a strong one, Aronoff fails to note cases like *marriageable* where the deverbal and denominal *-ables* make the same semantic contribution to their base. Positing natural classes such as [+ Noun] to cover cases where, for example, adjectives and nouns can be selected as input to a word-formation rule does not help either. As shown in Plag (2004: 201) no feature system is able to cope with the many different constellations of different base categories one finds with the derivational affixes of English. This point is further substantiated by the data presented in this volume. It would seem that it is not at all exceptional for affixes to attach to bases of a number of different word classes—indeed, it seems more to be the norm than the exception.

Scalise (1984: 137) proposes what he calls the Unitary Output Hypothesis which states that a form cannot be analysed as 'a single affix if it produces outputs with different category labels or different semantics'. Under this hypothesis, we would be forced to treat an affix like *-an* in English as two separate affixes, one that produces nouns (*magician*) and another that produces adjectives (*suburban*). The problem with this hypothesis is that many *-an* forms do double duty as nouns and adjectives (*Bolivian* and other inhabitant names, *amphibian*, *egalitarian*, etc.). It would seem odd to maintain that the noun *Bolivian* and the adjective *Bolivian* are derived by distinct affixes, and such data therefore suggest that the Unitary Output Hypothesis is incorrect. The only alternative is to consider such cases as conversion, in which case the hypothesis is unfalsifiable.

29.3.3 Blocking and the Elsewhere Condition

Blocking and the Elsewhere Condition are two theoretical principles that are proposed to explain a purported avoidance of synonymy in the mental lexicon.

We have shown in some detail both in Chapter 26 and in the descriptive chapters of Part III that blocking is at best a tendency and at worst a myth with respect to English morphology. Synonymy in derived forms is not at all unusual. Corpus examples can be found throughout this volume, for example, *display* ◆ *displayal*, *disregard* ◆ *disregardance*, *disruption* ◆ *disrupture*, *omission* ◆ *omitment* (in Chapter 10), *educationalist* ◆ *educationist* (in Chapter 11), *Barbie-ish* ◆ *Barbieesque* ◆ *Barbie-like* (in Chapter 14). Indeed, we agree with Plag (2003: 63–8) that rather than being a theoretical principle, blocking is at most an artefact of lexical retrieval: the more frequent an established form is, the easier it is for speakers to access, and the less likely they are to produce a synonymous derived form.

Blocking is a specific case of the Elsewhere Condition. The Elsewhere Condition (Kiparsky 1982a) has a long history in linguistics, dating back to the Sanskrit grammarian Panini. Roughly, it ensures that when two rules can potentially apply to the same base, the more specific rule preempts the more general one. We do not intend here to consider the merits of the Elsewhere Condition with respect to phonological rules. It has, however, been invoked in the analysis of inflection (see, for example, Xu and Aronoff 2011 for a recent treatment), although here we again find that it cannot be taken as a hard and fast principle. We have seen much more variation in English inflection than the Elsewhere Condition would lead us to expect; example (4), discussed below, is a fairly convincing case in point.

29.3.4 Lexical Phonology and Morphology: Level Ordering and Bracket Erasure

Lexical Phonology and Morphology is a theoretical framework that had its heyday in the early 1980s, and has since been largely discredited. Nevertheless here we mention two of the important theoretical claims of the framework, and the sort of data from English that have been used to call them into question.

Lexical Phonology and Morphology assumes first of all, that morphology may be strati-fied into two or more levels, each of which is associated with a set of morphological rules and an accompanying set of phonological rules. For English, Kiparsky (1982a), for example, pro-poses three levels, roughly a level that contains derivational rules that involve stress shift and allomorphy of base and affixes, a second level that contains derivational rules that do not involve stress shift and allomorphy, and a level for inflection. Lexical Phonology and Morphology therefore assumes that English word-formation is stratified. In Chapter 27 we have shown in some detail that the notion of Level Ordering that is part of Lexical Phonology and Morphology is incorrect for English, and in fact that English displays only the faintest trace of stratification, so we will not repeat those arguments here.

Another prominent tenet of Lexical Phonology and Morphology is the Bracket Erasure Convention, a notion that actually goes back at least as far as Chomsky and Halle (1968). In its most prominent expression Kiparsky (1982d: 140) states that at the end of each level of the phonology and morphology all word-internal structure is eliminated. In effect, Bracket Erasure obliterates the derivational history of a form. Kiparsky argues that this principle allows us to explain why, when a noun is derived from a strong verb, and then undergoes conversion back to a verb, the result is a regular verb (the familiar example is that of *grandstand*, whose past tense is *grandstanded* rather than *grandstood*). The reasoning goes that if internal brackets are erased, it will not be possible to 'see' that the verbal base is strong, and the newly derived verb will of necessity be inflected regularly. The problem is that such internal information is not always eliminated. For example, although the verb to *fly out* ('to hit a fly ball') is usually given a regular past tense (*flied out*) as predicted by the Bracket Erasure Convention, it is neverthe-less possible to find the strong form, as the following example from COCA suggests.

(4) *Chicago Sun-Times 1999*: Mark Grace, with the bases loaded and two out in the ninth, **flew out to** right field and furthered the theory he has lifted many more beer bottles than barbells.

Clearly if such forms are possible, knowledge of derivational history cannot be completely obliterated.

Comparative forms such as *harder-line* or *lower-key* are another problem for level ordering, as discussed in Chapter 6. If, as proposed in stratal approaches, compound-formation
is ordered at a later derivational stage than affixation, the insertion of an affix into a compound is predicted to be impossible. Furthermore, formations such as *bug-friendlier* or
sugar-plummier constitute further instances of level ordering paradoxes, as the semantic
scope of the comparative suffix is the whole compound, while comparative suffixation to
such long polysyllabic adjectives should be impossible for prosodic reasons.

29.3.5 The Monosuffix Constraint

Aronoff and Fuhrhop (2002: 473) state what they call the Monosuffix Constraint for English,
which says that 'Suffixes that select Germanic bases select unsuffixed bases'. This says in effect
that we should never find a native suffix attached outside another native suffix. The sole
exception they allow is the suffix *-ness*. However, as demonstrated by Plag (2002), Hay and
Plag (2004: 592-3) and in Chapter 27 of this book, it is not unusual to find native suffixes
attached outside native suffixes; Table 27.6 shows many such combinations.

29.3.6 The First Sister Principle and related proposals

Proposed by Roeper and Siegel (1978: 208) in an influential analysis of English synthetic compounding in early generative morphology, the First Sister Principle states that 'All verbal compounds are formed by the incorporation of a word in first sister position of the verb'. The first
sister of the verb is generally the verb's object, sometimes what would be considered an adjunct
in contemporary linguistic theory, but never a subject. Compounds like *girl-swimming* would
therefore be ruled out. Selkirk's First Order Projection Condition (1982: 37) and Lieber's
(1983) Argument-Linking Principle differ in detail but have similar effects in that both rule out
compounds in which the first element has a subject-referencing interpretation.

We have shown extensively in Chapter 20, however, that it is not at all unusual to find
English argumental compounds in which either the first or the second element is subject-
referencing. Such readings are sometimes, but not always, context-dependent, but they can
and do occur with some frequency. It must be concluded that the First Sister Principle and
related proposals cannot be correct.

29.3.7 The Lexical Integrity Hypothesis and related proposals

This hypothesis has been framed in a number of ways over the years: the Generalized
Lexicalist Hypothesis (Lapointe 1980), the Word Structure Autonomy condition (Selkirk
1982), the Atomicity Thesis (Di Sciullo and Williams 1987) (see Lieber and Scalise 2006 for
an overview). Bresnan and Mchombo (1995) give this definition:

A fundamental generalization that morphologists have traditionally maintained is the *lexical integrity principle*, which states that words are built out of different structural elements and by different principles of composition than syntactic phrases. Specifically the morphological constituents of words are lexical and sublexical categories—stems and affixes—while the syntactic constituents of phrases have words as the minimal unanalyzable units; and syntactic ordering principles do not apply to morphemic structures. (Bresnan and Mchombo 1995: 181)

As we have shown extensively in the descriptive chapters of Part III, as well as in the general discussion in Chapter 22, the Lexical Integrity Hypothesis (at least in this version) cannot be said to hold of English. English indeed provides two sorts of evidence against the strongest forms of the Lexical Integrity Hypothesis.

First, we have shown that many productive processes of affixation and compounding incorporate phrases, and not just lexicalized phrases. However we are to conceive the relationship between syntax and morphology, there can be no strict prohibition on interaction, as proposed under, for example, Botha's (1983) No-Phrase Constraint. The term itself is a counterexample to its own claim, as has frequently been noticed. Indeed, as we have shown in Chapter 22 the ability to attach to phrases goes hand in hand with high productivity.

One of the consequences of the Lexical Integrity Hypothesis is the prediction that it should be impossible to use a pronoun or reflexive to refer either to the base of a derived word or to the first element of a compound, a phenomenon generally referred to as Anaphoric Islandhood in the literature (Postal 1969). It is well-known, however, that many English speakers allow sublexical reference, and it is not difficult to find evidence for this claim in the corpora, as the example in (5) illustrates:

(5) *USAToday 1993*: The story of Jessie Lee (a highly **Clintonian** figure–as in Eastwood, not Bill–played with steely-eyed grit by Van Peebles) and his wild bunch may be the stuff of pulp fiction.

What we see in example (5) is that the base of *Clintonian* is available for reference, but surprisingly that the complex word is subject to two separate parses: *Clinton* + *ian* for Bill Clinton and *Clint* + *onian* for Clint Eastwood. We do not take a stand on whether this phenomenon is to be treated as a matter of syntax (Lieber 1992) or pragmatics (Sproat and Ward 1987); we merely point out that cases of sublexical reference are not difficult to come by, and as such provide more reason to doubt the Lexical Integrity Hypothesis, at least in any strong form.

29.4 IMPLICATIONS

Thus far, the contents of this chapter might seem disappointing. The facts of English inflection and word-formation do not argue strongly for any particular (current) theoretical framework and are largely compatible with many frameworks. To the extent that English data bear clearly on specific theoretical proposals, in every case we find that English provides strong counter-exemplification.

Still it would be a mistake to conclude that the vast amount we have learned about English morphology is good only for casting doubt on all extant morphological theory, and disastrous to assume that the study of English morphology has little to contribute to theory-construction. While the conclusions we have drawn so far are largely negative, the authors of this book are not merely hunters and gatherers, but also avid theorists; although we have tried to be as theoretically neutral as possible in describing the phenomena of English, that does not mean that we do not see (at least some of) the implications of those data for theory. Our views on morphological theory have inevitably come to be shaped by the knowledge of English we have gained in writing this book. We do not intend to provide an over-arching theory of morphology here (indeed, we doubt that we would ever reach complete agreement on a theoretical framework!). Rather, based on the detailed study of English morphology we have undertaken, we make a number of points that we take to be foundational for any morphological theory.

The following are claims that we take to be uncontroversial, but nevertheless must form critical axioms of a theory of morphology:

(6) a. Morphology is highly computational, but not necessarily computational in the same way as syntax. That is, a theory of syntax must account for both linear order and hierarchical structure, and within most contemporary theoretical frameworks, must allow for some mechanisms (e.g. rules of movement) that account for discontinuous dependencies. Rules of morphology must minimally allow for the generation of an infinite number of new words and therefore must also allow for extensive computation. This must surely involve something that results in synthesis (making longer forms from shorter ones) and possibly also in analysis (in the sense of analysing longer forms into shorter ones). However, there is no convincing evidence that the theoretical correlates of movement rules are needed for morphology.

   b. Morphological computation can involve recursion, but in a more limited way than in syntax. It is an empirical matter whether all languages have recursive morphology, but it is clear that at least some (among them English) do, and morphological theory must allow for that possibility.

   c. Synonymy is rampant in word-formation, and our theory must be able to account for it. We must build theories that do not rule out the generation of potentially synonymous forms.

   d. The mental lexicon is subject to paradigmatic pressure which may result in morphological processes being stretched beyond their usual boundaries. Looked at as an overall system, the morphology of a language makes certain formal means available for inflection and word-formation. Especially with respect to word-formation, if formal means of creating a particular sort of word is lacking, formal means usually used for other purposes can be recruited to cover what's lacking.

e. Models of inflection must be able to deal with variant morphological and periphrastic expression of morphosyntactic categories. Moreover, such models need an architecture that can accommodate the probabilistic distribution of such competing inflectional variants, instead of the apparently more common inflection-class-based or grammatically-governed distribution.

Other assumptions that we make might be more controversial:

(7) a. Morphological rules, however they are formalized, cannot be hard and fast, but rather must in some way be violable. Put in a slightly different fashion, word-formation allows for a particular sort of coercion. This point follows from (6d): if word-formation rules that typically derive one sort of word can nevertheless be deployed to form another sort of word, our theory must have some way of allowing this to happen.

b. Morphology is not syntax or phonology. We must resist the urge to build a theory of morphology on the analogy to models that are created for the phenomena of syntax or phonology. Although morphology interfaces in complex ways with syntax and phonology, it cannot be subsumed under either syntax or phonology.

c. Productivity is uncontroversially a gradient matter, but even minimally productive processes of word-formation may give rise to new forms. We should not be too quick to declare that a process of word-formation is dead. On the other hand, we should probably allow for the possibility that new forms can be influenced by the existence of specific, already established forms, for example, *house husband* on the basis of *housewife*, or *fruitarian* on the basis of *vegetarian*.

d. Whatever our theoretical model, we must have some way of accounting for not only the formal side of morphology, but also the semantic side. Specifically we must be able to account for the substantial evidence that affixes (or morphological processes, if the theorist prefers) are frequently semantically underspecified, and subject to polysemy and meaning extensions of various sorts.

Finally, there is one point that we feel the need to emphasize, even though it does not directly arise out of our study of English.

(8) Storage and computation are not mutually exclusive. That is, even relatively low frequency complex forms can be and often are stored in the mental lexicon. If we take this finding seriously, we must conclude that theories that claim that productively derived words are always created on line cannot be correct.

What does this tell us about the structure of a morphological theory? Given the discussion in Section 29.2, we do not take a stand on whether morphological theory should be morpheme-based or process-based, realizational or non-realizational, although we suspect that the emphasis on these issues over the years has been misguided. Somewhat in the spirit of Optimality Theory, we might think about diverting our attention from the question of how forms get generated and focus instead on how well potential outputs conform to canonical patterns, rules, sets of morphologically related words, or constraints (or whatever we choose to call them). Sometimes the need to find a word in the course of speaking or writing trumps the rules. The best output may not be perfect, but it beats no word at all. And maybe this is the most important theoretical insight we have gained in the process of writing this book. Any theory of morphology worth its salt cannot ignore this fact.

In the end, we come back to a methodological point. Our vision of theory in morphology has been strongly influenced by our initial decision to look at the data available in corpora and to take seriously complex forms that might sometimes rub against the grain of prescriptivist sensibilities. Theory-building would certainly be easier if the data were neater. But English morphology is vastly more complex than we anticipated at the outset of this project and theory must respond by being far more nuanced than it has been thus far. It is our hope that what is to be found in this volume will be instrumental in influencing the next generation of morphological theory.

REFERENCES

Acquaviva, Paolo. 2008. *Lexical plurals: A morphosemantic approach*. Oxford: Oxford University Press.

Adams, Valerie. 1973. *An introduction to modern English word formation*. London: Longman.

Adams, Valerie. 2001. *Complex words in English*. Harlow, Essex: Longman.

Ainsworth, Helen. 1992. The mark of possession or possession's mark? A case study. *New Zealand English Newsletter* 6: 17–20.

Albright, Adam and Bruce Hayes. 2003. Rules vs. analogy in English past tenses: A computational/experimental study. *Cognition* 90: 119–61.

Alexiadou, Artemis. 2001. *Functional structure in nominals*. Amsterdam: John Benjamins.

Algeo, John. 1971. The voguish uses of *non*. *American Speech* 46: 87–105.

Allen, Margaret R. 1978. *Morphological investigations*. Storrs: University of Connecticut dissertation.

Altenberg, Bengt. 1982. *The genitive v. the of-construction: A study of syntactic variation in 17th century English*. Malmö: CWK Gleerup.

Amiot, Dany and Georgette Dal. 2007. Integrating neoclassical combining forms into a lexeme-based morphology. In Geert Booij, Luca Ducceschi, Bernard Fradin, Emiliano Guevara, Angela Ralli, and Sergio Scalise (eds), *Online proceedings of the fifth Mediterranean morphology meeting (MMM5)*, Fréjus, 15–18 September 2005. 323–36.

Anderson, Stephen R. 1992. *A-morphous morphology*. Cambridge: Cambridge University Press.

Anderson, Stephen R. 2005. *Aspects of the theory of clitics*. Oxford: Oxford University Press.

Anderwald, Lieselotte. 2009. *The morphology of English dialects: Verb-formation in non-standard. English*. Cambridge & New York: Cambridge University Press.

Anshen, Frank and Mark Aronoff. 1997. Morphology in real time. *Yearbook of Morphology 1996*: 9–12.

Arndt-Lappe, Sabine. 2011. Towards an exemplar-based model of stress in English noun–noun compounds. *Journal of Linguistics* 47(3): 549–85.

Arndt-Lappe, Sabine. 2012. Regularity and variability in English word-formation: A case study. Ms. Universität Siegen.

Arndt-Lappe, Sabine. 2013. Word-formation and analogy. In Peter O. Müller, Ingeborg Ohnheiser, Susan Olsen, and Franz Rainer (eds), *Word-formation: An international handbook of the languages of Europe*. Berlin: Mouton de Gruyter.

Arndt-Lappe, Sabine and Melanie Bell. 2012. Explaining compound stress analogically. Paper presented at the 15th International Morphology Meeting, Vienna, 9–12 February.

Arndt-Lappe, Sabine and Ingo Plag. 2012. Phonological variability in English blends. In *The twentieth Manchester Phonology Meeting*, Manchester, 24–26 May 2012. 7.

Aronoff, Mark. 1976. *Word formation in generative grammar*. Cambridge, MA: MIT Press.

Aronoff, Mark. 1980. Contextuals. *Language* 56: 744–58.

Aronoff, Mark and Nanna Fuhrhop. 2002. Restricting suffix combinations in German and English: Closing suffixes and the Monosuffix Constraint. *Natural Language and Linguistic Theory* 20(3): 451–90.

Auwera, Johann van der. 1985. Relative *that*—a centennial dispute. *Journal of Linguistics* 21(1): 149–79.

Ayto, John (ed.). 1990. *The Longman register of new words*. London: Longman.

Baayen, R. Harald. 1992. Quantitative aspects of morphological productivity. *Yearbook of Morphology 1991*: 109–49.

Baayen, R. Harald. 1993. On frequency, transparency and productivity. *Yearbook of Morphology 1992*: 181–208.

Baayen, R. Harald and Fermín Moscoso del Prado Martín. 2005. Semantic density and past-tense formation in three Germanic languages. *Language* 81: 666–98.

Baayen, R. Harald and Rochelle Lieber. 1991. Productivity and English word-formation: A corpus-based study. *Linguistics* 29: 801–43.

Baayen, R. Harald, Richard Piepenbrock, and Leon Gulikers. 1995. *The CELEX Lexical Database* (CD-ROM). Philadelphia: Linguistic Data Consortium, University of Pennsylvania.

Baeskow, Heike. 2004. *Lexical properties of selected non-native morphemes of English*. Tübingen: Narr.

Baker, Mark C. 2003. *Lexical categories: Verbs, nouns, and adjectives*. New York: Cambridge University Press.

Bardsley, Dianne and Jane Simpson. 2009. Hypocoristics in New Zealand and Australian English. In Pam Peters, Peter Collins, and Adam Smith (eds), *Comparative studies in Australian and New Zealand English*, 46–69. Amsterdam & Philadelphia: Benjamins.

Barker, Chris. 1998. Episodic *-ee* in English: A thematic role constraint on new word formation. *Language* 74(4): 695–727.

Barnhart, Robert K., Sol Steinmetz, and Clarence L. Barnhart (eds). 1990. *The third Barnhart dictionary of new English*. N.p.: Wilson.

Bat-El, Outi. 2006. Blend. *Encyclopedia of language and linguistics*, 2nd edn, vol. 2, 66–70. Oxford: Elsevier.

Bat-El, Outi and Evan-Gary Cohen. 2012. Stress in English blends: A constraint-based approach. In Vincent Renner, François Maniez and Pierre Arnaud (eds), *Cross-disciplinary perspectives on lexical blending*. Berlin & New York: Mouton de Gruyter.

Bauer, Laurie. 1978. *The grammar of nominal compounding with special reference to Danish, English and French*. Odense: Odense University Press.

Bauer, Laurie. 1983. *English word-formation*. Cambridge: Cambridge University Press.

Bauer, Laurie. 1988. *Introducing linguistic morphology*. Edinburgh: Edinburgh University Press.

Bauer, Laurie. 1990. Be-heading the word. *Journal of Linguistics* 26: 1–31.

Bauer, Laurie. 1993. *Manual of information to accompany the Wellington Corpus of Written New Zealand English*. Wellington: Victoria University, Department of Linguistics.

Bauer, Laurie. 1994. *Watching English change*. London & New York: Longman.

Bauer, Laurie. 1997a. Evaluative morphology: A search for universals. *Studies in Language* 21: 533–75.

Bauer, Laurie 1997b. A class of English irregular verbs. *English Studies* 78: 545–55.

Bauer, Laurie. 1998a. When is a sequence of two nouns a compound in English? *English Language and Linguistics* 2(1): 65–86.

Bauer, Laurie. 1998b. Is there a class of neoclassical compounds, and if so is it productive? *Linguistics* 36(3): 403–22.

Bauer, Laurie. 2000. Word. In Geert Booij, Christian Lehmann and Joachim Mugdan (eds), *Morphology: An international handbook of inflection and word-formation*, 247–57. Berlin & New York: Mouton de Gruyter.

Bauer, Laurie. 2001. *Morphological productivity*. Cambridge: Cambridge University Press.

Bauer, Laurie. 2002. Why are we linguists and not linguisticians? In Katja Lenz and Ruth Möhlig (eds), *Of dyuersitie & chaunge of langage; Essays presented to Manfred Görlach on the occasion of his 65th birthday*, 27–32. Heidelberg: Winter.

Bauer, Laurie. 2003a. English prefixation: A typological shift? *Acta Linguistica Hungarica.* 50(1–2): 33–40.

Bauer, Laurie. 2003b. *Introducing linguistic morphology*, 2nd edn. Edinburgh: Edinburgh University Press.

Bauer, Laurie. 2004a. Adjectives, compounds and words. *Nordic Journal of English Studies* 3(1) (*Worlds of words: A tribute to Arne Zettersten*): 7–22.

Bauer, Laurie. 2004b. *A glossary of morphology*. Edinburgh: Edinburgh University Press.

Bauer, Laurie. 2006a. Competition in English word-formation. In Ans van Kemenade and Bettelou Los (eds), *The handbook of the history of English*, 177–98. Malden, MA: Blackwell.

Bauer, Laurie. 2006b. Compounds and minor word-formation types. In Bas Aarts and April McMahon (eds), *The handbook of English linguistics*, 483–506. Malden, MA: Blackwell.

Bauer, Laurie. 2008. Dvandva. *Word Structure* 1: 1–20.

Bauer, Laurie. 2009a. Facets of English plural morphology. In *The annual of texts by foreign guest professors, vol. 3*. Prague: Univerzita Karlova v Praze & TOGGA.

Bauer, Laurie. 2009b. Typology of compounds. In Rochelle Lieber and Pavol Štekauer (eds), *The Oxford handbook of compounding*, 343–56. Oxford: Oxford University Press.

Bauer, Laurie. 2009c. IE, Germanic: Danish. In Rochelle Lieber and Pavol Štekauer (eds), *The Oxford handbook of compounding*, 400–16. Oxford: Oxford University Press.

Bauer, Laurie. 2010a. An overview of morphological universals. *Word Structure* 3(2): 131–40.

Bauer, Laurie. 2010b. Co-compounds in Germanic. *Journal of Germanic Linguistics* 22(3): 201–19.

Bauer, Laurie. 2010c. The typology of exocentric compounding. In Sergio Scalise and Irene Vogel (eds), *Cross-disciplinary issues in compounding*, 167–76. Amsterdam & Philadelphia: Benjamins.

Bauer, Laurie and Ingrid Bauer. 1996. Word-formation in the playground. *American Speech* 71: 111–12.

Bauer, Laurie and Winifred Bauer. 2002. Adjective boosters in the speech of New Zealand children. *Journal of English Linguistics* 30: 244–57.

Bauer, Laurie and Rodney Huddleston. 2002. Lexical word formation. In Rodney Huddleston and Geoffrey K. Pullum (eds), *The Cambridge grammar of the English language*, 1621–722. Cambridge: Cambridge University Press.

Bauer, Laurie and Antoinette Renouf. 2001. A corpus-based study of compounding in English. *Journal of English Linguistics* 29: 101–23.

Bauer, Laurie and Elizaveta Tarasova. 2010. The meaning link in nominal compounds. Paper presented at Copenhagen Symposium: Approaches to the Lexicon, Copenhagen, 8–10 December.

Bauer, Laurie and Salvador Valera (eds). 2005. *Approaches to conversion/zero-derivation*. Münster: Waxmann.

Beard, Robert. 1982. The plural as a lexical derivation. *Glossa* 16: 133–48.

Beard, Robert. 1995. *Lexeme morpheme base morphology: A general theory of inflection and word.* Albany: State University of New York Press.

Becker, Thomas. 1993. Back-formation, cross-formation and 'bracketing paradoxes' in paradigmatic morphology. *Yearbook of Morphology* 1993:1–25.

Bell, Melanie. 2011. At the boundary of morphology and syntax: Noun noun constructions in English. In Alexandra Galani, Glynn Hicks, and George Tsoulos (eds), *Morphology and its interfaces*, 137–68. Amsterdam & Philadelphia: Benjamins.

Bell, Melanie and Ingo Plag. 2012. Informativeness is a determinant of compound stress in English. *Journal of Linguistics* 48(3): 485–520.

Berg, Thomas. 1998. The (in)compatibility of morpheme orders and lexical categories and its historical implications. *English Language and Linguistics* 2; 245–62.

Berg, Thomas. 2003. Right-branching in English derivational morphology. *English Language and Linguistics* 7(2): 279–307.

Berg, Thomas. 2011. The clipping of common and proper nouns. *Word Structure* 4: 1–19.

Bergen, Benjamin K. 2004. The psychological reality of phonaesthemes. *Language* 80(2): 291–311.

Biber, Douglas and Bethany Gray. 2011. Grammatical change in the noun phrase: The influence of written language use. *English Language and Linguistics* 15(2): 223–50.

Bierwisch, Manfred. 1988a. Tools and explanations of comparison: Part 1. *Journal of Semantics* 6(1): 57–93.

Bierwisch, Manfred. 1988b. Tools and explanations of comparison: Part 2. *Journal of Semantics* 6(1): 101–46.

Bierwisch, Manfred. 1989. The semantics of gradation. In Manfred Bierwisch and Ewald Lang (eds), *Dimensional adjectives* 71–261. Berlin: Springer-Verlag.

Bisetto, Antoinetta and Sergio Scalise. 2005. The classification of compounds. *Lingue e linguaggio* 4(2): 319–32.

Blevins, James P. 2003. Stems and paradigms. *Language* 79(4): 737–67.

Bloch, Bernard. 1947. English verb inflection. *Language* 23(4): 399–418.

Bloomfield, Leonard. 1935. *Language.* London: Allen & Unwin.

Bock, Kathryn, Sally Butterfield, Anne Cutler, J. Cooper Cutting, Kathleen M. Eberhard, and Karin R. Humphreys. 2006. Number agreement in British and American English: Disagreeing to agree collectively. *Language* 82(1): 64–113.

Bolinger, Dwight. 1968. *Aspects of language.* New York: Harcourt.

Bolinger, Dwight. 1975. *Aspects of language.* 2nd edn. New York: Harcourt.

Booij, Geert. 1986. Form and meaning in morphology: The case of Dutch 'agent' nouns. *Linguistics* 24: 503–17.

Booij, Geert. 1993. Against split morphology. *Yearbook of Morphology 1993*: 27–49.

Booij, Geert. 1996a. Inherent versus contextual inflection and the split morphology hypothesis. *Yearbook of Morphology 1995*: 1–16.

Booij, Geert. 1996b. Review of Beard (1995). *Language* 72(4): 812–16.

Booij, Geert. 2007. *Grammar of words: An introduction to linguistic morphology.* 2nd edn. Oxford & New York: Oxford University Press.

Booij, Geert. 2010. *Construction morphology.* Oxford: Oxford University Press.

Booij, Geert and Jerzy Rubach. 1984. Morphological and prosodic domains in lexical phonology. *Phonology Yearbook* 1: 1–27.

Börger, Claudia. 2007. *Word-formation processes from a cognitive perspective: An analysis of complex prepositional lexemes.* Hamburg: Kovač.

Botha, Rudolf P. 1983. *Morphological mechanisms.* Oxford: Pergamon Press.

Boyé, Gilles. 2006. Suppletion. In Keith Brown (ed.), *Encyclopedia of language and linguistics* 2nd edn, vol 12, 297–99. Oxford: Elsevier.

Bram, Barli. 2011. *Major total conversion in English: The question of directionality.* Wellington: Victoria University of Wellington thesis.

Brekle, Herbert E. 1970. *Generative Satzsemantik und transformationelle Syntax im System der englishen Nominalkomposition.* Munich: Fink.

Bresnan, Joan. 1982. Polyadicity. In Joan Bresnan (ed.), *The mental representation of grammatical relations*, 149–72. Cambridge, MA: MIT Press.

Bresnan, Joan and Sam Mchombo. 1995. The Lexical Integrity Principle: Evidence from Bantu. *Natural Language and Linguistic Theory* 13: 181–254.

British National Corpus, The, version 3 (BNC XML Edition). 2007. Distributed by Oxford University Computing Services on behalf of the BNC Consortium. <http://www.natcorp.ox.ac.uk/>, accessed 1 November 2012.

Bulloch, John Malcolm. 1924. The delight of the Doric in the diminutive. In William A. Craigie, John Buchan, Peter Giles, John Malcolm Bulloch, and Burns Club of London. *The Scottish tongue; A series of lectures on the vernacular language of Lowland Scotland delivered to the members of the Vernacular Circle of the Burns Club of London*, 125–51. London & New York: Cassell.

Burnard, Lou (ed.). 2007. *Reference guide for the British National Corpus (XML Edition)* <http://www.natcorp.ox.ac.uk/XMLedition/URG/> (1 February, 2007.)

Burzio, Luigi. 1994. *Principles of English stress.* Cambridge: Cambridge University Press.

Burzio, Luigi. 1995. On the metrical unity of Latinate affixes. In Héctor Campos and Paula Marie Kempchinsky (eds), *Evolution and revolution in linguistic theory*, 1–24. Washington, DC: Georgetown University Press.

Burzio, Luigi. 1998. Multiple correspondence. *Lingua* 104(1): 79–109.

Bybee, Joan. 1985. *Morphology: A study of the relation between meaning and form.* Amsterdam & Philadelphia: Benjamins.

Bybee, Joan and Carol L. Moder. 1983. Morphological classes as natural categories. *Language* 59: 251–70.

Bybee, Joan and Dan I. Slobin. 1982. Rules and schemas in the development and use of the English past tense. *Language* 58: 265–89.

Cannon, Garland. 1986. Blends in English word formation. *Linguistics* 24: 725–53.

Cannon, Garland. 1987. *Historical change and English word-formation.* New York: Lang.

Carney, Edward. 1994. *A survey of English spelling.* London & New York: Routledge.

Carnie, Andrew. 2006. *Syntax: A generative introduction.* Oxford: Blackwell.

Carstairs-McCarthy, Andrew. 2002. *An introduction to English morphology.* Edinburgh: Edinburgh University Press.

Chambers dictionary, The. 2008. 11th edition. Vivian Marr (ed.). Edinburgh: Chambers Harrap.

Chapman, Don and Royal Skousen. 2005. Analogical modeling and morphological change: The case of the adjectival negative prefix in English. *English Language and Linguistics* 9(2): 333–57.

Cheshire, Jenny. 1982. *Variation in an English dialect: A sociolinguistic study.* Cambridge: Cambridge University Press.

Chomsky, Noam. 1970. Remarks on nominalization. In Roderick A. Jacobs and Peter S. Rosenbaum (eds), *Readings in English Transformational Grammar.* 184–221. Waltham, MA: Ginn.

Chomsky, Noam and Morris Halle. 1968. *The sound pattern of English.* New York: Harper & Row.

Clark, Eve V. and Herbert H. Clark. 1979. When nouns surface as verbs. *Language* 55. 767–811.

Coates, Jennifer. 1983. *The semantics of the modal auxiliaries.* London: Croom Helm.

Collie, Sarah. 2008. English stress preservation: The case for 'fake cyclicity'. *English Language and Linguistics* 12(3): 505–32.

Collins English dictionary, 8th edition. 2006. Glasgow: HarperCollins.

Comrie, Bernard. 1981. *Language universals and linguistic typology.* Chicago: University of Chicago Press.

Concise Oxford English dictionary. 2001. 10th edition. Judy Pearsall (ed.). Oxford: Oxford University Press.

Cook, Paul and Suzanne Stevenson. 2010. Automatically identifying the source words of lexical blends in English. *Computational Linguistics* 36(1): 129–49.

Corbin, Danielle. 1987. *Morphologie dérivationelle et structuration du lexique*, 2 vols. Tübingen: Niemeyer.

Covington, Michael A. 1981. *Evidence for lexicalism: A critical review*. Bloomington: Indiana University Linguistics Club.

Croft, William. 1991. *Syntactic categories and grammatical relations: The cognitive organization of information*. Chicago, IL: The University of Chicago Press.

Daelemans, Walter and Antal van den Bosch. 2005. *Memory-based language processing*. Cambridge: Cambridge University Press.

Daelemans, Walter, Jakub Zavrel, Ko van der Sloot, and Antal van den Bosch. 2007. *TiMBL: Tilburg Memory Based Learner, version 6.0, Reference Guide* (LK Technical Report 04-02). Tilburg: ILK.

Dalton-Puffer, Christiane and Ingo Plag. 2000. Categorywise, some compound type morphemes seem to be rather suffix-like: On the status of *-ful, -type*, and *-wise* in Present Day English. *Folia Linguistica* 34(3–4): 225–45.

Davies, Mark. 2008. *The Corpus of Contemporary American English (COCA)*: 400+ million words, 1990–present. <http://www.americancorpus.org/>, accessed 1 November 2012.

Davies, Mark. 2010. *The Corpus of Historical American English (COHA)*: 400+ million words, 1810–2009. <http://corpus.byu.edu/coha/>, accessed 1 November 2012.

Davies, Mark. 2011. *Google Books (American English) Corpus*: 155 billion words, 1810–2009. <http://googlebooks.byu.edu/>, accessed 1 November 2012.

Davis, Stuart. 1988. *Topics in syllable geometry*. New York: Garland Press.

Derwing, Bruce I. and Royal Skousen. 1994. Productivity and the English past tense: Testing Skousen's analogical model. In Susan D. Lima, Roberta Corrigan, and Gregory K. Iverson (eds), *The reality of linguistic rules*, 193–218. Amsterdam & Philadelphia: Benjamins.

Di Sciullo, Anna Maria. 2005. *Asymmetry in morphology*. Cambridge, MA: MIT Press.

Di Sciullo, Anna-Maria and Edwin Williams. 1987. *On the definition of word*. Cambridge, MA: MIT Press.

Dixon, Robert M. W. 1977. *A grammar of Yidiny*. Cambridge: Cambridge University Press.

Dixon, Robert M. W. 2005. *A semantic approach to English grammar*. 2nd edn. Oxford: Oxford University Press.

Dixon, Robert M. W. 2010. *Basic linguistic theory: Methodology*. Oxford: Oxford University Press.

Dixon, Robert M. W. and Alexandra Y. Aikhenvald. 2002. Word: A typological framework. In Robert M. W. Dixon and Alexandra Y. Aikhenvald (eds), *Word: A cross-linguistic typology*, 1–40. Cambridge: Cambridge University Press.

Dollinger, Stefan. 2008. N/V(ing) + N compounds in North American English: On the trail of the S-curve? Paper presented at the *1st Triennial Conference of the International Society for the Linguistics of English*, Freiburg, 8–11 October 2008.

Downing, Pamela. 1977. On the creation and use of English compound nouns. *Language* 77: 810–42.

Dressler, Wolfgang U. 1985. Suppletion in word-formation. In Jacek Fisiak (ed.), *Historical semantics— historical word-formation*, 97–112. Berlin: Mouton de Gruyter.

Dressler, Wolfgang U. 1989. Prototypical differences between inflection and derivation. *Zeitschrift für Phonetik, Sprachwissenschaft und Kommunikationsforschungen* 42: 3–10.

Dressler, Wolfgang U. 2000. Extragrammatical vs. marginal morphology. In Ursula Doleschal and Anna M. Thornton (eds), *Extragrammatical and marginal morphology*, 1–10. Munich: Lincom.

Dressler, Wolfgang U. and Lavinia Merlini Barbaresi. 1994. *Morphopragmatics. Diminutives and intensifiers in Italian, German, and other languages*. Berlin: Mouton de Gruyter.

Earle, John. 1890. *English prose*. London: Smith, Elder.

Elzinga, Dirk. 2006. English adjective comparison and analogy. *Lingua* 116(6): 757–70.

Embick, David. 2007. Blocking effects and analytic/synthetic alternations. *Natural Language and Linguistic Theory* 25(1): 1–37.

Emonds, Joseph. 1976. *A transformational approach to English syntax*. New York: Academic Press.

Epps, Patience. 2008. *A grammar of Hup*. Berlin & New York: Mouton de Gruyter.

Erdmann, Peter. 1999. Compound verbs in English: Are they pseudo? In Guy A. J. Tops, Betty Devriendt and Steven Geukens (eds), *Thinking English grammar*, 239–52. Leuven: Peeters.

Fabb, Nigel. 1988. English suffixation is constrained only by selectional restrictions. *Natural Language and Linguistic Theory* 6: 527–39.

Faiss, Klaus. 1981. Compound, pseudo-compound and syntactic group especially in English. In Peter Kunsmann and Ortwin Kuhn (eds), *Weltsprache Englisch in Forschung und Lehre: Festschrift für Kurt Wächtler*, 132–50. Berlin: Schmidt.

Farnetani, Edda, Carol Taylor Torsello, and Piero Cosi. 1988. English compound versus non-compound noun phrases in discourse: An acoustic and perceptual study. *Language and Speech* 31: 157–80.

Farrell, Patrick. 2001. Functional shift as category underspecification. *English Language and Linguistics* 5: 109–30.

Filppula, Markku. 2004. Irish English: Morphology and syntax. In Bernd Kortmann, Kate Burridge, Rajend Mesthrie, Edgar W. Schneider, and Clive Upton (eds), *A handbook of varieties of English, vol. 2: Morphology and syntax*, 73–102. Berlin & New York: Mouton de Gruyter.

Firth, John Rupert. 1964. *The tongues of men, and speech*. Oxford: Oxford University Press.

Fischer, Olga. 1992. Syntax. In Norman Blake (ed.), *The Cambridge history of the English language, vol. 2: 1066–1476*, 207–408. Cambridge: Cambridge University Press.

Fischer, Olga and Wim van der Wurff. 2006. Syntax. In Richard Hogg and David Denison (eds), *A history of the English language*, 109–98. Cambridge: Cambridge University Press.

Fleischer, Wolfgang. 1975. *Wortbildung der deutschen Gegenwartssprache*. Tübingen: Niemeyer.

Fleischer, Wolfgang and Irmhild Barz. 2007. *Wortbildung der deutschen Gegenwartssprache*. Tübingen: Niemeyer.

Fraser, Bruce. 1974. *The verb–particle construction in English*. New York: Academic Press.

Fudge, Erik. 1984. *English word-stress*. London: Allen & Unwin.

Funk, Wolf-Peter. 1986. Towards a definition of semantic constraints on negative prefixation in English and German. In Dieter Kastovsky and Aleksander Szwedek (eds), *Linguistics across historical and geographical boundaries: In honour of Jacek Fisiak on the occasion of his fiftieth birthday*, 877–89. Berlin: Mouton de Gruyter.

Gagné, Christina. 2001. Relation and lexical priming during the interpretation of noun–noun combinations. *Journal of Experimental Psychology: Learning, Memory, and Cognition* 27: 236–54.

Gagné, Christina and Edward J. Shoben. 1997. The influence of thematic relations on the comprehension of non-predicating conceptual combinations. *Journal of Experimental Psychology: Learning, Memory, and Cognition* 23: 71–87.

Ghomeshi, Jila, Ray Jackendoff, Nicole Rosen, and Kevin Russell. 2004. Contrastive focus reduplication in English (the salad-salad paper). *Natural Language and Linguistic Theory* 22: 307–57.

Giegerich, Heinz J. 1999. *Lexical strata in English: Morphological causes, phonological effects.* Cambridge: Cambridge University Press.

Giegerich, Heinz J. 2004. Compound or phrase? English noun plus noun constructions and the stress criterion. *English Language and Linguistics* 8(1): 1–24.

Giegerich, Heinz J. 2005. Associative adjectives in English and the lexicon–syntax interface. *Journal of Linguistics* 41(3): 571–91.

Giegerich, Heinz J. 2006. Attribution in English and the distinction between phrases and compounds. In Petr Rösel (ed.), *Englisch in Zeit und Raum—English in time and space: Forschungsbericht für Klaus Faiss*, 10–27. Trier: Wissenschaftlicher Verlag Trier.

Giegerich, Heinz J. 2009a. The English compound stress myth. *Word Structure* 2: 1–17.

Giegerich, Heinz J. 2009b. Compounding and lexicalism. In Rochelle Lieber and Pavol Štekauer (eds), *The Oxford handbook of compounding*, 178–200. Oxford: Oxford University Press.

Giegerich, Heinz J. 2012. The morphology of *-ly* and the categorial status of 'adverbs' in English. *English Language and Linguistics* 16(3): 341–59.

Glowka, A. Wayne. 1985. The continuing story of *-ola*. *American Speech* 60(2): 150–6.

Gnutzmann, Claus, Robert Ilson, and Joy Webster. 1973. Comparative constructions in contemporary English. *English Studies* 54(5): 417–38.

Goldsmith, John A. 1990. *Autosegmental and metrical phonology.* Oxford & Cambridge, MA: Blackwell.

Górska, Elzbieta. 1994. Moonless nights and smoke-free cities, or what can be without what? A cognitive study of privative adjectives in English. *Folia Linguistica* 28: 413–45.

Green, Jonathon (ed.). 1991. *Neologisms.* London: Bloomsbury.

Green, Lisa. 1998. ApSec and predicate phrases in African-American vernacular English. In Salikoko S. Mufwene, John R. Rickford, Guy Bailey, and John Baugh (eds), *African-American English: Structure, history and use*, 37–68. London: Routledge.

Gries, Stefan Th. 2001. A corpus-linguistic analysis of English *-ic* vs *-ical* adjectives. *ICAME Journal* 25: 65–107.

Gries, Stefan Th. 2003. Testing the sub-test: A collocational-overlap analysis of English *-ic* and *-ical* adjectives. *International Journal of Corpus Linguistics* 8(1): 31–61.

Gries, Stefan Th. 2004a. Shouldn't it be *breakfunch*? A quantitative analysis of the structure of blends. *Linguistics* 42(3): 639–67.

Gries, Stefan Th. 2004b. Isn't that fantabulous? How similarity motivates intentional morphological blends in English. In Michel Achard and Suzanne Kemmer (eds), *Language, culture, and mind*, 415–28. Stanford, CA: CSLI.

Gries, Stefan Th. 2004c. Some characteristics of English morphological blends. In Mary A. Andronis, Erin Debenport, Anne Pycha, and Keiko Yoshimura (eds), *Papers from the 38th Regional Meeting of the Chicago Linguistics Society. Vol. II: The Panels*, 201–16. Chicago: Chicago Linguistics Society.

Gries, Stefan Th. 2006. Cognitive determinants of subtractive wordformation processes: A corpus-based perspective. *Linguistics* 17(4): 535–58.

Gries, Stefan Th. 2011. Phonological similarity in multi-word symbolic units. *Cognitive Linguistics* 22(3): 491–510.

Grimm, Jacob. 1826. *Deutsche Grammatik*, vol. 2. Göttingen: Theil.

Grimshaw, Jane B. 1990. *Argument structure.* Cambridge, MA: MIT Press.

Guevara, Emiliano. 2007. Binary branching and linguistic theory: Morphological arguments. In M. Cecilia Picchi and Alan Pona (eds), *Proceedings of the XXXII Incontro di Grammatica Generativa, Firenze, 2–4 March 2006*, 93–106. Alessandria: Edizione dell' Orso.

Gussenhoven, Carlos. 2004. *The phonology of tone and intonation.* Cambridge: Cambridge University Press.

Gussenhoven, Carlos and A. Broeders. 1981. *English pronunciation for student teachers.* Groningen: Wolters-Noordhoff-Longman.

Gussmann, Edmund. 1987. The lexicon of English de-adjectival verbs. In Edmund Gussmann (ed.), *Rules and the lexicon,* 79–101. Lublin: Catholic University.

Hale, Kenneth and Samuel Jay Keyser. 1993. On argument structure and the lexical expression of syntactic relations. In Kenneth Hale and Samuel Jay Keyser (eds), *The view from building 20: Essays in linguistics in honor of Sylvain Bromberger,* 53–109. Cambridge, MA: MIT Press.

Halle, Morris and Alec Marantz. 1993. Distributed morphology and the pieces of inflection. In Kenneth Hale and S. Jay Keyser (eds), *The view from building 20,* 111–76. Cambridge, MA: MIT Press.

Halliday, Michael A. K. 1966. The concept of rank: A reply. *Journal of Linguistics* 2(1); 110–18.

Hamawand, Zeki. 2007. *Suffix rivalry in adjective formation.* London: Equinox.

Hamawand, Zeki. 2009. *The semantics of English negative prefixes.* London: Equinox.

Hammer, Alfred Edward. 1983. *German grammar and usage,* 2nd edn, revised by Martin Durrell. London: Arnold.

Hammond, Michael. 1999. *The phonology of English.* Oxford: Oxford University Press.

Hanssen, Esther, Arina Banga, Robert Schreuder, and Anneke Neijt. To appear. Semantic and prosodic effects of Dutch linking elements. *Morphology.*

Harley, Heidi. 2006. *English words: A linguistic introduction.* Malden, MA & Oxford: Blackwell.

Harley, Heidi and Rolf Noyer. 1999. Distributed morphology. *Glot International* 4(4): 3–9.

Harnisch, Rüdiger. 2001. *Grundform- und Stamm-Prinzip in der Substantivmorphologie des Deutschen. Synchronische und diachronische Untersuchung eines typologischen Parameters.* Heidelberg: Winter.

Harris, Zellig S. 1942. Morpheme alternants in linguistic analysis. *Language* 18: 169–80.

Haspelmath, Martin. 1996. Word-class-changing inflection and morphological theory. *Yearbook of Morphology 1995:* 43–66.

Haspelmath, Martin. 2002. *Understanding morphology.* London: Arnold & New York: Oxford University Press.

Haspelmath, Martin. 2007. Coordination. In Timothy Shopen (ed.), *Language typology and syntactic description. Vol. II: Complex Constructions,* 2nd edition, 1–51. Cambridge: Cambridge University Press.

Haspelmath, Martin. 2009. An empirical test of the Agglutination Hypothesis. In Sergio Scalise, Elisabetta Magni, and Antonietta Bisetto (eds), *Universals of language today,* 13–29. Dordrecht: Springer.

Hatcher, Anna G. 1960. An introduction to the analysis of English noun compounds. *Word* 16: 356–73.

Hawkins, John. 1994. *A performance theory of order and constituency.* Cambridge: Cambridge University Press.

Hay, Jennifer. 2000. *Causes and consequences of word structure.* Evanston, IL: Northwestern University dissertation.

Hay, Jennifer B. 2002. From speech perception to morphology: Affix-ordering revisited. *Language* 78(3): 527–55.

Hay, Jennifer. 2003. *Causes and consequences of word structure.* London: Routledge.

Hay, Jennifer and Ingo Plag. 2004. What constrains possible suffix combinations? On the interaction of grammatical and processing restrictions in derivational morphology. *Natural Language and Linguistic Theory* 22(3): 565–96.

Hayes, Bruce. 1982. Extrametricality and English stress. *Linguistic Inquiry* 13(2): 227–76.

Heath, Jeffrey. 2008. *A grammar of Jamsay*. Berlin & New York: Mouton de Gruyter.

Heyvaert, Liesbet 2003. *A cognitive-functional approach to nominalization in English*. Berlin: Mouton de Gruyter.

Hilpert, Martin. 2008. The English comparative—language structure and language use. *English Language and Linguistics* 12(3): 395–417.

Hinrichs, Lars and Benedikt Szmrecsanyi. 2007. Recent changes in the function and frequency of Standard English genitive constructions: A multivariate analysis of tagged corpora. *English Language and Linguistics* 11(3): 437–74.

Hockett, Charles Francis. 1947. Problems of morphemic analysis. *Language* 21(4): 321–43.

Hockett, Charles Francis. 1954. Two models of grammatical description. *Word* 10: 210–31.

Hockett, Charles Francis. 1987. *Refurbishing our foundations: Elementary linguistics from an advanced point of view*. Amsterdam & Philadelphia: Benjamins.

Hohenhaus, Peter. 2004. Identical constituent compounding—a corpus-based study. *Folia Linguistica* 38(3–4): 297–331.

Holmes, Janet, Bernadette Vine, and Gary Johnson. 1994. *The Wellington Corpus of Spoken New Zealand English (WSC): 1 million words, 1988–1994*. Wellington: Victoria University of Wellington.

Horn, Laurence R. 1989. *A natural history of negation*. Chicago: University of Chicago Press. [Reissued: Stanford: CSLI, 2001].

Horn, Laurence R. 2002. Uncovering the un-word: A study in lexical pragmatics. *Sophia Linguistica* 49: 1–64.

Huddleston, Rodney. 2002a. The clause: Complements. In Rodney Huddleston and Geoffrey K. Pullum (eds), *The Cambridge grammar of the English language*, 213–321. Cambridge: Cambridge University Press.

Huddleston, Rodney. 2002b. The verb. In Rodney Huddleston and Geoffrey K. Pullum (eds), *The Cambridge grammar of the English language*, 71–212. Cambridge: Cambridge University Press.

Huddleston, Rodney and Geoffrey K. Pullum (eds). 2002. *The Cambridge grammar of the English language*. Cambridge: Cambridge University Press.

Huddleston, Rodney, Geoffrey K. Pullum, and Peter Peterson. 2002. Relative constructions and unbounded dependencies. In Rodney Huddleston and Geoffrey K. Pullum (eds), *The Cambridge grammar of the English language*, 1031–96. Cambridge: Cambridge University Press.

Hudson, Richard. 1995. Does English really have case? *Journal of Linguistics* 31: 375–92.

Hudson, Richard. 2006. *Wanna* revisited. *Language* 82: 604–27.

Humboldt, Wilhelm von. 1836. *Über die Verschiedenheit des menschlichen Sprachbaues und ihren Einfluss auf die geistige Entwicklung des Menschengeschlechts*. Berlin: Königliche Akademie der Wissenschaften.

Jackendoff, Ray. 1975. Morphological and semantic regularities in the lexicon. *Language* 51: 639–71.

Jackendoff, Ray. 1977. Constraints on phrase structure rules. In Peter Culicover, Thomas Wasow and Adrian Akmajian (eds), *Formal syntax*, 249–83. New York: Academic Press.

Jackendoff, Ray. 1990. *Semantic structures*. Cambridge, MA: MIT Press.

Jackendoff, Ray. 1991. Parts and boundaries. *Cognition* 41(1–3): 9–45.

Jackendoff, Ray. 2009. Compounding in the parallel architecture and conceptual semantics. In Rochelle Lieber and Pavol Štekauer (eds), *The Oxford handbook of compounding*, 105–28. Oxford: Oxford University Press.

Jakobson, Roman, C. Gunnar M. Fant, and Morris Halle. 1951. *Preliminaries to speech analysis: The distinctive features and their correlates*. Cambridge, MA: MIT Press.

Jespersen, Otto. 1914. *A modern English grammar on historical principles. Volume II: Syntax*. London: George Allen & Unwin & Copenhagen: Munksgaard.

Jespersen, Otto. 1917. *Negation in English and other languages*. Copenhagen: Bianco Lunos Bogtrykkeri.

Jespersen, Otto. 1942. *A modern English grammar on historical principles. Part VI: Morphology*. London: George Allen & Unwin & Copenhagen: Munksgaard.

Johansson, Stig. 1979. American and British English grammar: An elicitation experiment. *English Studies* 60: 195–215.

Jones, Daniel. 2003. *Cambridge English pronouncing dictionary*, 16th edn. Cambridge: Cambridge University Press.

Jurafsky, Daniel. 1996. Universal tendencies in the semantics of the diminutive. *Language* 72(3): 533–78.

Kaisse, Ellen M. 1983. The syntax of auxiliary reduction in English. *Language* 59: 93–122.

Kaisse, Ellen M. 2005. The interface between morphology and phonology. In Pavol Štekauer and Rochelle Lieber (eds), *Handbook of English word-formation*, 25–47. Dordrecht: Springer.

Kastovsky, Dieter. 1999. English and German morphology: A typological comparison. In Wolfgang Falkner and Hans-Jörg Schmidt (eds), *Words, lexemes, concepts—approaches to the lexicon*, 39–51. Tübingen: Niemeyer.

Kastovsky, Dieter. 2000. English morphology: A typological reappraisal. In Chris Schaner-Wolles, John Rennison, and Friedrich Neubarth (eds), *Naturally! Linguistic studies in honour of Wolfgang Ulrich Dressler presented on the occasion of his 60th birthday*, 215–24. Torino: Rosenberg & Sellier.

Kastovsky, Dieter. 2006. Vocabulary. In Richard Hogg and David Denison (eds), *A history of the English languages*, 199–270. Cambridge. Cambridge University Press.

Kastovsky, Dieter. 2009. Diachronic perspectives. In Rochelle Lieber and Pavol Štekauer (eds), *The Oxford handbook of compounding*, 323–40. Oxford: Oxford University Press.

Katamba, Francis. 1993. *Morphology*. London: Macmillan.

Katamba, Francis and John Stonham. 2006. *Morphology*. 2nd edn. London: Macmillan & New York: St. Martin's Press.

Kaunisto, Mark. 2007. *Variation and change in the lexicon: A corpus-based analysis of adjectives in English ending in -ic and -ical*. Amsterdam: Rodopi.

Kettemann, Bernhard. 1988. *Die Phonologie Morphologischer Prozesse im Amerikanischen Englisch*. Tübingen: Narr.

Keuleers, Emmanuel. 2008. *Memory-based learning of inflectional morphology*. Antwerpen: University of Antwerpen dissertation.

Killgariff, Adam. 2006. *BNC data base and word frequency lists*. <http://www.kilgarriff.co.uk/bnc-readme.html>, 15 November 2011.

Kim, John J., Steven Pinker, Alan Prince, and Sandeep Prasada. 1991. Why no mere mortal has ever flown out to center field. *Cognitive Science* 15: 173–218.

Kingdon, Roger. 1958. *The groundwork of English stress*. London: Longman.

Kiparsky, Paul. 1982a. Lexical phonology and morphology. In The Linguistic Society of Korea (eds), *Linguistics in the morning calm: Selected papers from SICOL-1981*, 3–91. Seoul: Hanshin.

Kiparsky, Paul. 1982b. Word formation and the lexicon. In Frances Ingemann (ed.), *Proceedings of the 1982 Mid-America Linguistics Conference, Lawrence, University of Kansas*, 3–29. Lawrence: Department of Linguistics, University of Kansas.

Kiparsky, Paul. 1982c. Word formation and the lexicon. In Frances Ingemann (ed.), *Proceedings of the 1982 Mid-America Linguistics Conference, Lawrence, University of Kansas*, 3–29. Lawrence: Department of Linguistics, University of Kansas.

Kiparsky, Paul. 1982d. From cyclic phonology to lexical phonology. In Harry van der Hulst and Norval Smith (eds), *The structure of phonological representations*, vol. I, 131–75. Dordrecht: Foris.

Kiparsky, Paul. 2005. Blocking and periphrasis in inflectional paradigms. *Yearbook of Morphology 2004*: 113–35.

Kjellmer, Göran. 2005. Negated adjectives in Modern English: A corpus-based study. *Studia Neophilologica* 77(2): 156–70.

Klinge, Alex. 2005a. The origin of *Weapons of Mass Destruction*. Investigating traces of lexical formation patterns in the (linguistic) history of Europe. In Henning Nølke, Irene Baron, Hanne Korzen, Iørn Korzen, and Henrik Høeg-Müller (eds), *Grammatica. Festschrift in Honour of Michael Herslund*, 233–247. Pieterlen: Lang.

Klinge, Alex. 2005b. *The structure of English nominals*. Copenhagen: Copenhagen Business School dissertation.

Knowles, Elizabeth (ed.). 1997. *The Oxford dictionary of new words*. Oxford & New York: Oxford University Press.

Kortmann, Bernd and Ekkehard König. 1992. Categorial reanalysis: The case of deverbal prepositions. *Linguistics* 30: 671–97.

Kortmann, Bernd, Edgar W. Schneider, Kate Burridge, Rajend Mesthrie, and Clive Upton (eds). 2004. *A handbook of varieties of English, vol. 2. Morphology and syntax*. Berlin: Mouton de Gruyter.

Koshiishi, Tetsuya. 2002. Collateral adjectives, Latinate vocabulary, and English morphology. *Studia Anglica Posnaniensia* 37: 49–88.

Kösling, Kristina. 2011. *Stress assignment in triconstituent compounds*. Siegen: University of Siegen dissertation.

Kösling, Kristina and Ingo Plag. 2009. Does branching direction determine prominence assignment? An empirical investigation of triconstituent compounds in English. *Corpus Linguistics and Linguistic Theory* 5(2): 205–43.

Kreyer, Rolf. 2003. Genitive and of-construction in modern written English. Processability and human involvement. *International Journal of Corpus Linguistics* 8: 169–207.

Kruisinga, Etsko 1932 [1911]. *A handbook of present-day English. Part II*, 5th edn. Groningen: Noordhoff.

Kubozono, Haruo. 1990. Phonological constraints on blending in English as a case for phonology–morphology interface. *Yearbook of Morphology* 1990: 1–20.

Kunter, Gero. 2011. *Compound stress in English. The phonetics and phonology of prosodic prominence*. Tübingen: Niemeyer.

Kunter, Gero and Ingo Plag. 2007. What is compound stress? In *Proceedings of the International Congress of Phonetic Sciences, University of Saarbrücken, 6–10 August 2007*. Saarbrücken: Universität Saarbrücken.

Kuryłowicz, Jerzy. 1936. Dérivation lexicale et dérivation sémantique. *Bulletin de la Société de Linguistique de Paris* 27: 79–92.

Kuryłowicz, Jerzy. 1964. *The inflectional categories of Indo-European*. Heidelberg: Winter.

Kytö, Merja and Suzanne Romaine. 1997. Competing forms of adjective comparison in Modern English: What could be more quicker and easier and more effective? In Terttu Nevalainen and Leena Kahlas-Tarkka (eds), *To explain the present: Studies in the changing English language in honour of Matti Rissanen*, 329–352. Helsinki: Société Néophilologique.

Kytö, Merja and Suzanne Romaine. 2000. Adjective comparison and standardization processes in American and British English from 1620 to the present. In Laura Wright (ed.), *The development of standard English 1300–1800: Theories, descriptions, conflicts*, 171–94. Cambridge: Cambridge University Press.

Labov, William. 1972. *Sociolinguistic patterns*. Philadelphia: University of Pennsylvania Press.

Lapointe, Steven G. 1980. *A theory of grammatical agreement*. Amherst: University of Massachusetts dissertation.

Lapointe, Steven G. 1981. A lexical analysis of the English auxiliary verb system. In Michael Moortgat, Harry van der Hulst, and Teun Hoekstra (eds), *The scope of lexical rules*, 1–78. Dordrecht: Foris.

Lappe, Sabine. 2007. *English prosodic morphology*. Dordrecht: Springer.

Lass, Roger. 1976. *English phonology and phonological theory*. Cambridge: Cambridge University Press.

Leech, Geoffrey N. and Jonathan Culpeper. 1997. The comparison of adjectives in recent British English. In Terttu Nevalainen and Leena Kahlas-Tarkka (eds), *To explain the present: Studies in the changing English language in honour of Matti Rissanen*, 353–74. Helsinki: Société Néophilologique.

Lees, Robert 1960. *The grammar of English nominalizations*. Bloomington: Indiana University.

Lefebvre, Claire and Anne-Marie Brousseau. 2002. *A grammar of Fongbe*. Berlin & New York: Mouton de Gruyter.

Lehnert, Martin. 1971. *Rücklaufiges Wörterbuch der englischen Gegenwartssprache*. Leipzig: VEB.

Lehrer, Adrienne. 1995. Prefixes in English word formation. *Folia Linguistica* 29(1–2): 133–48.

Levi, Judith N. 1978. *The syntax and semantics of complex nominals*. New York: Academic Press.

Liberman, Mark and Alan Prince. 1977. On stress and linguistic rhythm. *Linguistic Inquiry* 8: 249–336.

Liberman, Mark and Richard Sproat. 1992. The stress and structure of modified noun phrases in English. In Ivan A. Sag and Anna Szabolcsi (eds), *Lexical matters*, 131–81. Stanford: CSLI.

Lieber, Rochelle. 1980. *On the organization of the lexicon*. Cambridge, MA: MIT dissertation.

Lieber, Rochelle. 1983. Argument linking and compounding in English. *Linguistic Inquiry* 14: 251–86.

Lieber, Rochelle. 1992. *Deconstructing morphology*. Chicago & London: University of Chicago Press.

Lieber, Rochelle. 1998. The suffix *-ize* in English: Implications for morphology. In Steven G. Lapointe, Diane K. Brentari, and Patrick M. Farrell (eds), *Morphology and its relation to phonology and syntax*, 12–34. Stanford, CA: CSLI.

Lieber, Rochelle. 2004. *Morphology and lexical semantics*. Cambridge: Cambridge University Press.

Lieber, Rochelle. 2009. *Introducing morphology*. Cambridge: Cambridge University Press.

Lieber, Rochelle. 2010. On the lexical semantics of compounds: Non-affixal (de)verbal compounds. In Sergio Scalise and Irene Vogel (eds), *Cross-disciplinary issues in compounding*, 127–144. Amsterdam & Philadelphia: Benjamins.

Lieber, Rochelle and Sergio Scalise. 2006. The Lexical Integrity Hypothesis in a new theoretical universe. *Lingue e Linguaggio* 5: 7–32.

Lieber, Rochelle and Pavol Štekauer. 2009. Introduction. In Rochelle Lieber and Pavol Štekauer (eds), *The Oxford handbook of compounding*, 3–18. Oxford: Oxford University Press.

Lindquist, Hans. 1998. The comparison of English disyllabic adjectives in -*y* and -*ly* in present-day British and American English. In Hans Lindquist, Staffan Klintborg, Magnus Levin, and Maria Estling (eds), *The major varieties of English. Papers from MAVEN (The international conference The Major Varieties of English)* 97, 205–12. Växjö: Acta Wexionensia.

Ljung, Magnus. 1970. *English denominal adjectives: A generative study of the semantics of group of high-frequency denominal adjectives in English*. Lund: Studentliteratur.

Löbner, Sebastian. 1985. Definites. *Journal of Semantics* 4: 279–326.

Lojenga, Constance K. 1994. *Ngiti*. Cologne: Köppe.

Longman dictionary of contemporary English. 1978. Paul Procter (ed.). Harlow, Essex: Longman.

Lowth, Robert. 1762. *A short introduction to English grammar*. London: Hughes [Reprinted 1967, Menston: Scolar Press].

Lyons, John. 1966. Toward a notional theory of the parts of speech. *Journal of Linguistics* 2: 209–36.

Lyons, John. 1968. *Introduction to theoretical linguistics*. Cambridge: Cambridge University Press.

Lyons, John. 1977. *Semantics*. Cambridge: Cambridge University Press.

McCray, Alexa T., Allen C. Browne, and Dorothy L. Moore. 1988. The semantic structure of neo-classical compounds. In Robert A. Greenes (ed.), *SCAMC'88—Proceedings of the 12th Annual Symposium on Computer Applications in Medical Care*, 165–8. Washington & New York: EEE Computer Society Press.

McMillan, James B. 1980. Infixing and interposing in English. *American Speech* 55: 163–83.

Macquarie Dictionary, The. 1997. 3rd edn. Sydney: Macquarie Library.

Mailhammer, Robert. 2007. *The Germanic strong verbs: Foundations and development of a new system*. Berlin & New York: Mouton de Gruyter.

Manova, Stela and Wolfgang U. Dressler. 2005. The morphological technique of conversion in the inflecting-fusional type. In Laurie Bauer and Salvador Valera (eds), *Approaches to conversion/ zero-derivation*, 67–101. Münster: Waxmann.

Marchand, Hans. 1960. *The categories and types of present-day English word-formation: A synchronic–diachronic approach*. Wiesbaden: Otto Harrasowitz.

Marchand, Hans. 1969. *The categories and types of present-day English word-formation*, 2nd edn. Munich: Beck.

Marcus, Gary F. 1995. The acquisition of the English past tense in children and multilayered connectionist networks. *Cognition* 56; 271–9.

Marcus, Gary F. 1999. Do infants learn grammar with algebra or statistics? Response to Seidenberg & Elman, Eimas, and Negishi. *Science* 284: 436–37.

Marle, Jaap van. 1985. *On the paradigmatic dimension of morphological creativity*. Dordrecht: Foris.

Marsden, Peter H. 1985. Adjective pairs in -*ic* and -*ical*. *Lebende Sprachen* 1: 26–33.

Matthews, Peter Hugoe. 1972. *Inflectional morphology*. Cambridge: Cambridge University Press.

Matthews, Peter Hugoe. 2007. *Syntactic relations: A critical survey*. Cambridge & New York: Cambridge University Press.

Matthewson, Lisa C. 1991. *An application of autosegmental morphology to some nonconcatenative phenomena in the Germanic languages*. Wellington: Victoria University of Wellington MA thesis.

Mayerthaler, Willi. 1981. *Morphologische Natürlichkeit*. Wiesbaden: Athenaion.

Melloni, Chiara. 2007. *Polysemy in word formation: The case of deverbal nominals*. Verona: University of Verona dissertation.

Meys, Willem J. 1975. *Compound adjectives in English and the ideal speaker-listener*. Amsterdam: North Holland.

Miner, Kenneth L. 1975. English inflectional endings and unordered rules. *Foundations of Language* 12: 339–65.

Mish, Frederick C. 1983. *9,000 words*. Springfield MA: Merriam-Webster.

Mohanan, Karuvannur Puthanveettil. 1982. *Lexical phonology*. Cambridge, MA: MIT dissertation.

Mohanan, Karuvannur Puthanveettil. 1986. *The theory of lexical phonology*. Dordrecht: Reidel.

Mondorf, Britta. 2000. Wider-ranging vs. more old-fashioned views on comparative formation in adjectival compounds/derivatives. In Bernhard Reitz and Sigrid Rieuwerts (eds), *Anglistentag 1999 Mainz proceedings*, 35–44. Trier: Wissenschaftlicher Verlag Trier.

Mondorf, Britta. 2003. Support for more-support. In Günter Rohdenburg and Britta Mondorf (eds), *Determinants of grammatical variation in English*, 251–304. Berlin: Mouton de Gruyter.

Mondorf, Britta. 2006. Rewriting English grammar books: Factors constraining the choice between synthetic and analytic comparative forms. In Christoph Houswitschka, Gabriele Knappe, and Anja Müller (eds), *Proceedings of the Anglistentag 2005, Bamberg (Proceedings of the Conference of the German Association of University Teachers of English)*, 587–607. Trier: Wissenschaftlicher Verlag Trier.

Mondorf, Britta. 2009a. *More support for more-support: The role of processing constraints on the choice between synthetic and analytic comparative forms*. Amsterdam: Benjamins.

Mondorf, Britta. 2009b. How lexicalization reflected in hyphenation affects variation and word-formation. In Andreas Dufter, Jürg Fleischer, and Guido Seiler (eds), *Describing and modeling variation in grammar*, 361–88. Berlin: Mouton de Gruyter.

Montgomery, Michael. 1999. A superlative complex in Appalachian English. *Southeastern Journal of Linguistics* 23: 1–14.

Myers, Scott. 1984. Zero-derivation and inflection. *MIT working papers in linguistics* 7: 53–69.

Nagano, Akiko. 2008. *Conversion and back-formation in English: Toward a theory of morpheme-based morphology*. Tokyo: Kaitakusha.

Nagano, Akiko. 2011. The right-headedness of morphology and the status and development of category-determining prefixes in English. *English Language and Linguistics* 15(1): 61–83.

Nation, I. S. Paul. 1993. Using dictionaries to estimate vocabulary size: Essential, but rarely followed, procedures. *Language Testing* 10(1): 27–40.

Nelson, Nicole. 1998. Mixed anchoring in French hypocoristic formation. *RuLing Papers* 1: 185–99.

Nevalainen, Terttu. 1999. Early Modern English lexis and semantics. In Roger Lass (ed.), *The Cambridge history of the English language: Vol. III—1476 to 1776*, 332–458. Cambridge: Cambridge University Press.

Nguyên, T. Anh-Thu', C. L. John Ingram, and J. Rob Pensalfini. 2008. Prosodic transfer in Vietnamese acquisition of English contrastive stress patterns. *Journal of Phonetics* 36: 158–90.

Nichols, Johanna. 1986. Head-marking and dependent-marking in grammar. *Language* 62(1): 56–119.

Nida, Eugene A. 1948. The identification of morphemes. *Language* 24: 414–41.

Noonan, Michael. 1992. *A grammar of Lango*. Berlin & New York: Mouton de Gruyter.

Nosofsky, Robert M. 1986. Attention, similarity, and the identification-categorization relationship. *Journal of Experimental Psychology: General* 115: 39–57.

Nosofsky, Robert M. 1990. Relations between exemplar similarity and likelihood models of classification. *Journal of Mathematical Psychology* 34: 393–418.

OED Online. Oxford University Press. <http://www.oed.com/>, accessed 1 November 2012.

Ohala, John J. 1974. Experimental historical phonology. In John M. Anderson and Carles Jones (eds), *Historical linguistics*, vol. 2, 353–89. Amsterdam & Oxford: North Holland.

Olsen, Susan. 2001. Copulative compounds: A closer look at the distinction between morphology and syntax. *Yearbook of Morphology 2000*: 279–320.

Orr, John. 1962. *Three studies on homonymics*. Edinburgh: University Press.

Orton, Harold, Stewart Sanderson, and John Widdowson (eds). 1978. *The linguistic atlas of England*. London: Croom Helm & Atlantic Highlands NJ: Humanities Press.

Ostendorf, Mari, Patti Price, and Stefanie Shattuck-Hufnagel. 1996. *Boston University Radio Speech Corpus*. Philadelphia: Linguistic Data Consortium, University of Pennsylvania.

Oxford advanced learner's dictionary of current English. 1974. A. S. Hornby (ed.). Oxford: Oxford University Press.

Oxford English dictionary, The. 1933. James Augustus Henry Murray, Henry Bradley, William A. Craigie, and Charles Talbut Onions (eds). Oxford: Clarendon Press.

Oxford English dictionary, The. 1989. 2nd edn. Robert William Burchfield (ed). Oxford: Oxford University Press.

Palmer, Frank. R. 1974. *The English verb*. London: Longman.

Palmer, Frank R. 1990. *Modality and the English modals*, 2nd edn. London & New York: Longman.

Palmer, Frank R. 2001. *Mood and modality*, 2nd edn. Cambridge: Cambridge University Press.

Palmer, Frank, Rodney Huddleston, and Geoffrey K. Pullum. 2002. Inflectional morphology and related matters. In Rodney Huddleston and Geoffrey K. Pullum (eds), *The Cambridge grammar of the English language*, 1565–1620. Cambridge: Cambridge University Press.

Pater, Joe. 2000. Non-uniformity in English secondary stress: The role of ranked and lexically specific constraints. *Phonology* 17(2): 237–74.

Pater, Joe. 2004. Bridging the gap between receptive and productive development with minimally violable constraints. In René Kager, Joe Pater, and Wim Zonneveld (eds), *Constraints in phonological acquisition*, 219–44. Cambridge: Cambridge University Press.

Paul, Hermann. 1995 [1920]. *Prinzipien der Sprachgeschichte*. 5th edn. Tübingen: Niemeyer.

Pawley, Andrew. 2002. Using *he* and *she* for inanimate objects in English: Questions of grammar and world view. In Nick Enfield (ed.), *Ethnosyntax: Explorations in language and culture*, 110–37. Oxford: Oxford University Press.

Pawley, Andrew. 2008. Australian vernacular English: some grammatical characteristics. In Kate Burridge and Berndt Kortmann (eds), *Varieties of English 3: The Pacific and Australasia*, 362–97. Berlin & New York: Mouton de Gruyter.

Payne, John. 2011. Genitive coordinations with personal pronouns. *English Language and Linguistics* 15(2): 363–85.

Payne, John and Rodney Huddleston. 2002. Nouns and noun phrases. In Rodney Huddleston and Geoffrey K. Pullum (eds), *The Cambridge grammar of the English language*, 323–524. Cambridge: Cambridge University Press.

Payne, John, Rodney Huddleston, and Geoffrey K. Pullum. 2010. The distribution and category status of adjectives and adverbs. *Word Structure* 3: 31–81.

Peters, Pam. 1999. Paradigm split. In Christian Mair and Marianne Hundt (eds), *Corpus linguistics and linguistic theory: Papers from the Twentieth International Conference on English Language Research on Computerized Corpora (ICAME 20)*, 301–12. Amsterdam: Rodopi.

Pietsch, Lukas. 2005. *Variable grammars: Verbal agreement in northern dialects of English*. Tübingen: Niemeyer.

Piñeros, Carlos Eduardo. 1998. *Prosodic morphology in Spanish: Constraint interaction in word formation*. Columbus: Ohio State University dissertation.

Pinker, Steven. 1999. *Words and rules*. London: Weidenfeld & Nicolson.

Pinker, Steven and Alan Prince. 1994. Regular and irregular morphology and the psychological status of rules of grammar. In Susan D. Lima, Roberta L. Corrigan, and Gregory K. Iverson (eds), *The reality of linguistic rules*. Amsterdam & Philadelphia: Benjamins.

Plag, Ingo. 1996. Selectional restrictions in English suffixation revisited. A reply to Fabb (1988). *Linguistics* 34(4): 769–98.

Plag Ingo. 1998. Morphological haplology in a constraint-based morpho-phonology. In Wolfgang Kehrein and Richard Wiese (eds), *Phonology and morphology of the Germanic languages*, 199–215. Tübingen: Niemeyer.

Plag, Ingo. 1999. *Morphological productivity: Structural constraints in English derivation*. Berlin & New York: Mouton de Gruyter.

Plag, Ingo. 2002. The role of selectional restrictions, phonotactics and parsing in constraining suffix ordering in English. *Yearbook of Morphology 2001*: 285–314.

Plag, Ingo. 2003. *Word-formation in English*. Cambridge: Cambridge University Press.

Plag, Ingo. 2004. Syntactic category information and the semantics of derivational morphological rules. *Folia Linguistica* 38(3–4): 193–225.

Plag, Ingo. 2006. The variability of compound stress in English: Structural, semantic and analogical factors. *English Language and Linguistics* 10(1): 143–72.

Plag, Ingo. 2010. Compound stress assignment by analogy: The constituent family bias. *Zeitschrift für Sprachwissenschaft* 29(2): 243–82.

Plag, Ingo and R. Harald Baayen. 2009. Suffix ordering and morphological processing. *Language* 85(1): 109–52.

Plag, Ingo, Gero Kunter, and Sabine Lappe. 2007. Testing hypotheses about compound stress assignment in English: A corpus-based investigation. *Corpus Linguistics and Linguistic Theory* 3(2): 199–233.

Plag, Ingo, Gero Kunter, Sabine Lappe, and Maria Braun. 2008. The role of semantics, argument structure, and lexicalization in compound stress assignment in English. *Language* 84(4): 760–94.

Plank, Frans. 1981. *Morphologische (Ir-)Regularitäten*. Tübingen: Narr.

Plank, Frans. 1994. Inflection and derivation. In Ron E. Asher (ed.), *The encyclopedia of language and linguistics*, 1671–8. Oxford: Pergamon.

Poser, William J. 1992. Blocking of phrasal constructions by lexical items. In Ivan Sag and Anna Szabolsci (eds), *Lexical matters*, 111–30. Stanford: CSLI Publications.

Postal, Paul M. 1969. Anaphoric islands. In Rob I. Binnick, Alice Davison, Georgia M. Green, and Jerry L. Morgan (eds), *Papers from the 5th regional meeting of the Chicago Linguistic Society*, 209–39. Chicago: Chicago Linguistic Society.

Poutsma, Hendrik. 1916. *A grammar of late modern English*. Groningen: Noordhoff.

Prasada, Sandeep and Steven Pinker. 1993. Generalization of regular and irregular morphological patterns. *Language and Cognitive Processes* 8: 1–56.

Prćić, Tvrtko. 2005. Prefixes vs. initial combining forms in English: A lexicographic perspective. *International Journal of Lexicography* 18(3): 313–35.

Prćić, Tvrtko. 2008. Suffixes vs. final combining forms in English: A lexicographic perspective. *International Journal of Lexicography* 21: 1–22.

Pullum, Geoffrey K. 1982. Syncategorematicity and English infinitival *to*. *Glossa* 16: 181–215.

Pullum, Geoffrey 1991. English nominal gerund phrases as noun phrases with verb-phrase heads, *Linguistics* 29(5): 763–99.

Pullum, Geoffrey K. 1997. The morpholexical nature of English to-contraction. *Language* 73: 79–102.

Pullum, Geoffrey K. and Rodney Huddleston. 2002. Adjectives and adverbs. In Rodney Huddleston and Geoffrey K. Pullum (eds), *The Cambridge grammar of the English language*, 525–95. Cambridge: Cambridge University Press.

Pustejovsky, James. 1995. *The generative lexicon*. Cambridge, MA: MIT Press.

Quinn, Heidi. 2005. *The distribution of pronoun case forms in English*. Amsterdam & Philadelphia: Benjamins.

Quirk, Randolph, Sidney Greenbaum, Geoffrey Leech, and Jan Svartvik. 1985. *A comprehensive grammar of the English language*. London & New York: Longman.

Radford, Andrew. 1988. *Transformational grammar: A first course*. Cambridge: Cambridge University Press.

Raffelsiefen, Renate. 1993. Relating words: A model of base recognition. *Linguistic Analysis* 23(1–2): 3–159.

Raffelsiefen, Renate. 1999. Phonological constraints on English word formation. *Yearbook of Morphology 1998*: 225–87.

Raffelsiefen, Renate. 2004. Absolute ill-formedness and other morphophonological effects. *Phonology* 21: 91–142.

Rainer, Franz. 1988. Towards a theory of blocking: The case of Italian and German quality nouns. *Yearbook of Morphology 1988*: 155–85.

Ramscar, Michael J. A. 2002. The role of meaning in inflection: Why the past tense doesn't require a rule. *Cognitive Psychology* 45: 45–94.

Ramson, William Stanley (Bill). (ed.). 1988. *The Australian national dictionary*. Melbourne: Oxford University Press.

Randle, William. 1961. Payola. *American Speech* 36(2): 104–16.

Rappaport Hovav, Malka and Beth Levin. 1992. -*er* nominals: Implications for a theory of argument structure. In Tim Stowell and Eric Wehrli (eds), *Syntax and Semantics 26: Syntax and the Lexicon*, 127–53. New York: Academic Press.

Reischer, Jürgen. 2005. WordNexus—Ein Datenretrieval-System für Blends und Kontaminationen mit umfangreichem deutschen und englischen Korpus. <http://www.lingua-ex-machina.de/>, accessed 5 February 2011.

Reischer, Jürgen. 2008. *Die Wortkreuzung und verwandte Verfahren der Wortbildung: eine korpusbasierte Analyse des Phänomens 'Blending' am Beispiel des Deutschen und Englischen*. Hamburg: Kovač.

Renner, Vincent. 2008. On the semantics of English coordinate compounds. *English Studies* 89: 606–13.

Renner, Vincent. To appear. English *cum*, a borrowed coordinator turned complex-compound marker. *Morphology*.

Rice, Keren. 2000. *Morpheme order and semantic scope: Word formation in the Athapaskan verb*. Cambridge: Cambridge University Press.

Rickford, John. 1986. Social contact and linguistic diffusion: Hiberno-English and New World Black English. *Language* 62: 245–89.

Riddle, Elizabeth. 1985. A historical perspective on the productivity of the suffixes -*ness* and -*ity*. In Jacek Fisiak (ed.), *Historical semantics, historical word-formation*, 435–61. New York: Mouton de Gruyter.

Robins, Robert H. 1959. In defense of WP. *Transactions of the Philological Society* 58.1, 116–44.

Roeper, Thomas. 1988. Compound syntax and head movement. *Yearbook of Morphology 1988*: 187–228.

Roeper, Thomas and Muffy E. A. Siegel. 1978. A lexical transformation for verbal compounds. *Linguistic Inquiry* 9: 199–260.

Rohdenburg, Günter. 1996. Cognitive complexity and increased grammatical explicitness in English. *Cognitive Lingustics* 7: 149–82.

Rosenbach, Anette. 2002. *Genitive variation in English: Conceptual factors in synchronic and dia-chronic studies*. Berlin: Mouton de Gruyter.

Rosenbach, Anette. 2005. Animacy versus weight as determinants of grammatical variation in English. *Language* 81(3): 613–44.

Rosenbach, Anette. 2006. Descriptive genitives in English: A case study on constructional gradi-ence. *English Language and Linguistics* 10(1): 77–118.

Rumelhart, David E. and James L. McClelland. 1986. On learning the past tenses of English verbs. In David E. Rumelhart, James L. McClelland, and the PDP research group (eds), *Parallel distributed processing: Explorations in the microstructure of cognition*, 216–71. Cambridge, MA: MIT Press.

Rusiecki, Jan. 1985. *Adjectives and comparison in English: A semantic study*. London: Longman.

Ryder, Mary Ellen. 1994. *Ordered chaos: The interpretation of English noun–noun compounds*. Berkeley, Los Angeles & London: University of California Press.

Ryder, Mary Ellen. 1999. Bankers and blue-chippers: An account of *-er* formations in present-day English. *English Language and Linguistics* 3(2): 269–97.

Sapir, Edward. 1921. *Language*. New York: Harcourt, Brace & Jovanovich.

Scalise, Sergio. 1984. *Generative morphology*. Dordrecht: Foris.

Scalise, Sergio. 1988. Inflection and derivation, *Linguistics* 26: 561–81.

Scalise, Sergio and Antoinetta Bisetto. 2009. Classification of compounds. In Rochelle Lieber and Pavol Štekauer (eds), *The Oxford handbook of compounding*, 49–82. Oxford: Oxford University Press.

Scalise, Sergio and Antoinetta Bisetto. 2012. *Morbo-Comp*. <http://morbocomp.sslmit.unibo.it>, accessed 1 November 2012.

Schlücker, Barbara and Ingo Plag. 2011. Compound or phrase? Analogy in naming. *Lingua* 121: 1539–51.

Schneider, Klaus P. 2003. *Diminutives in English*. Tübingen: Niemeyer.

Schönefeld, Doris. 2005. Zero-derivation—functional change—metonymy. In Laurie Bauer and Salvador Valera (eds), *Approaches to conversion/zero-derivation*, 131–59. Münster: Waxmann.

Schreuder, Robert and R. Harald Baayen. 1997. How complex simplex words can be. *Journal of Memory and Language* 37: 118–39.

Selkirk, Elisabeth O. 1982. *The syntax of words*. Cambridge. MA: MIT Press.

Sepp, Mary. 2006. *Phonological constraints and free variation in compounding: A corpus study of English and Estonian noun compounds*. New York: New York City University dissertaion.

Shannon, Claude E. 1948. A mathematical theory of communication. *The Bell System Technical Journal*, 27: 379–423 & 623–56. <http://cm.bell-labs. com/cm/ms/what/shannonday/shan-non1948.pdf>, accessed 3 November 2010.

Siegel, Dorothy C. 1974. *Topics in English morphology*. Cambridge, MA: MIT dissertation.

Siegel, Dorothy C. 1978. The adjacency constraint and the theory of morphology. In Mark Stein (ed.), *Proceedings of the North Eastern Linguistic Society, 1977*: 189–97. Amherst: University of Massachusetts.

Siemund, Peter. 2007. *Pronominal gender in English: A study of English varieties from a cross-linguistic perspective*. London: Routledge.

Silva, Penny (ed.). 1996. *A dictionary of South African English*. New York: Oxford University Press.

Sinclair, John M. (ed.). 1987. *Looking up. An account of the Cobuild Project in lexical computing.* London: Collins.

Skousen, Royal. 1989. *Analogical modeling of language.* Dordrecht: Kluwer.

Skousen, Royal. 1992. *Analogy and structure.* Dordrecht: Kluwer.

Skousen, Royal and Thereon Stanford. 2007. *AM: Parallel.* Provo, UT: Brigham Young University.

Skousen, Royal, Deryle Lonsdale, and Dilworth B. Parkinson (eds). 2002. *Analogical modeling.* Amsterdam & Philadelphia: Benjamins.

Slotkin, Alan R. 1990. Adjectival *-less* and *-free*: A case of shifting institutional currency. *American Speech* 65(1): 33–49.

Smith, Carlotta. 1997. *The parameter of aspect*, 2nd edn. Dordrecht: Kluwer.

Southerland, Ronald H. 1994. Derivatives in *pre-*: A persuasive morphological resource? *American Speech* 69(2): 168–76.

Spencer, Andrew. 2003. Does English have productive compounding? In Geert E. Booij, Janet DeCesaris, Angela Ralli, and Sergio Scalise (eds), *Topics in morphology. Selected papers from the Third Mediterranean morphology meeting*, Barcelona, 20–22 September 2001, 329–41. Barcelona: Institut Universitari de Lingüística applicada, Universitat Pompeu Fadra.

Sproat, Richard and Gregory Ward. 1987. Pragmatic considerations in anaphoric island phenomena. In Barbara Need, Eric Schiller, and Anna Bosch (eds), *Papers from the 23rd Annual Regional Meeting of the Chicago Linguistic Society*, 321–35. Chicago: Chicago Linguistic Society.

Štekauer, Pavol. 1996. *A theory of conversion in English.* Frankfurt-am-Main: Lang.

Štekauer, Pavol. 2005. *Meaning predictability in word-formation. Novel, context-free naming units.* Amsterdam & Philadelphia: Benjamins.

Štekauer, Pavol, Salvador Valera & Lívia Körtvélyessy. 2012. *Word-formation in the world's languages: A typological survey.* Cambridge: Cambridge University Press.

Stemberger, Joseph Paul. 1981. Morphological haplology. *Language* 57(4): 791–817.

Steriade, Donca. 1999. Lexical conservatism in French adjectival liaison. In Barbara E. Bullock, Jean-Marc Authier, and Lisa A. Reed (eds), *Formal perspectives in Romance linguistics*, 243–70. Amsterdam & Philadelphia: Benjamins.

Steriade, Donca. 2000. Paradigm uniformity and the phonetics–phonology boundary. In Michael Broe and Janet Pierrehumbert (eds), *Papers in laboratory phonology V: Acquisition and the lexicon*, 313–34. Cambridge: Cambridge University Press.

Strang, Barbara M. H. 1968. *Modern English structure.* 2nd edn. London: Arnold.

Strauss, Steven. 1982. On 'relatedness paradoxes' and related paradoxes. *Linguistic Inquiry* 13: 694–700.

Stump, Gregory T. 1998. Inflection. In Andrew Spencer and Arnold M. Zwicky (eds), *The handbook of morphology*, 13–43. Oxford: Blackwell.

Stump, Gregory T. 2001. *Inflectional morphology.* Cambridge: Cambridge University Press.

Sturtevant Edgar H. 1917. *Linguistic change.* Chicago & London: University of Chicago Press.

Sussex, Roland. 2004. Abstand, Ausbau, creativity and ludicity in Australian English. *Australian Journal of Linguistics* 24: 3–19.

Swart, Henriëtte de. 2011. Mismatches and coercion. In Claudia Maienborn, Klaus von Heusinger, and Paul Portner (eds), *Semantics*, 574–97. Berlin & Boston: Mouton de Gruyter.

Sweet, Henry. 1891. *A new English grammar: Logical and historical.* Oxford: Clarendon Press.

Sweet, Henry. 1892. *A short historical English grammar.* Oxford: Clarendon Press.

Sweet, Henry. 1898. *A new English grammar. Part II: Syntax.* Oxford: Clarendon Press.

Szmrecsanyi, Benedikt. 2005. Language users as creatures of habit: A corpus-based analysis of persistence in spoken English. *Corpus Linguistics and Linguistic Theory* 1(1): 113–50.

Szmrecsanyi, Benedikt. 2006. *Morphosyntactic persistence in spoken English: A corpus study at the intersection of variationist sociolinguistics, psycholinguistics, and discourse analysis.* Berlin: Walter de Gruyter.

Szymanek, Bogdan. 1985. On intermorphic extensions in English and Polish. In Edmund Gussmann (ed.), *Phono-morphology. Studies in the interaction of phonology and morphology,* 177–91. Lublin: Catholic University.

Thomas, Macklin. 1983. Interchangeable pairs in *un-*, *in-* and *en-*, etc. *American Speech* 58: 78–80.

Townsend, Charles E. 1975. *Russian word-formation.* Columbus, OH: Slavica.

Trips, Carola. 2009. *Lexical semantics and diachronic morphology: The development of* -hood, -dom *and* -ship *in the history of English.* Tübingen: Niemeyer.

Trudgill, Peter. 1974. *The social differentiation of English in Norwich.* Cambridge: Cambridge University Press.

Tulloch, Sarah (ed.). 1991. *The Oxford dictionary of new words.* Oxford & New York: Oxford University Press.

Ullmann, Stephen. 1957. *Principles of semantics.* Glasgow: Jackson & Oxford: Blackwell.

Urban dictionary. <http://www.urbandictionary.com/>, accessed 1 November 2012.

Urdang, Laurence, Anne Ryle, and Tanya H. Lee. 1986. *Ologies and isms.* 3rd edn. New York: Gale.

Vaan, Laura de, Robert Schreuder, and R. Harald Baayen. 2007. Regular morphologically complex neologisms leave detectable traces in the mental lexicon. *The Mental Lexicon* 2: 1–23.

Valera Hernández, Salvador. 1996. *Adjetivos y adverbios en inglés. La relación de homomorfia.* Granada: Servicio de Publicaciones de la Universidad de Granada.

Vogel, Irene. 2006. Phonological words. In Keith Brown (ed.), *Encyclopedia of language and linguistics.* Vol. 9: 531–34. Oxford: Elsevier.

Wagner, Thomas. 2010. *Interlanguage morphology: Irregular verbs in the mental lexicon of German-English interlanguage speakers.* Tübingen: Narr.

Wälchli, Bernard. 2005. *Co-compounds and natural coordination.* Oxford: Oxford University Press.

Wales, Katie. 1996. *Personal pronouns in present-day English.* Cambridge: Cambridge University Press.

Ward, Gregory, Richard Sproat, and Gail McKoon. 1991. A pragmatic analysis of so-called anaphoric islands. *Language* 67: 439–74.

Ward, Gregory, Betty Birner, and Rodney Huddleston. 2002. Information packaging. In Rodney Huddleston and Geoffrey K. Pullum (eds), *The Cambridge grammar of the English language,* 1363–447. Cambridge: Cambridge University Press.

Weber, Andrea. 2002. Assimilation violation and spoken-language processing. *Language and Speech* 45(1): 37–46.

Webster's new international dictionary of the English language. 1957. 2nd edn. Springfield, MA: Merriam-Webster.

Webster's third new international dictionary of the English language, unabridged. 1993. Springfield, MA: Merriam-Webster.

Wells, John C. 2008. *Longman pronunciation dictionary,* 3rd edn. Harlow: Longman.

Wentworth, Harold. 1941. The allegedly dead suffix -DOM in modern English. *Publications of the Modern Language Association* 56: 280–306.

Wentworth, Harold. 1944. *American dialect dictionary.* London: Constable.

Wiese, Richard. 1996a. Phrasal compounds and the theory of word syntax. *Linguistic Inquiry* 27: 183–93.

Wiese, Richard. 1996b. Prosodic alternations in English morphophonology: A constraint-based account of Morpheme Integrity. In Jacques Durand and Bernard Laks (eds), *Current trends in phonology: Models and methods*, vol. 2, 731–56. Salford: European Studies Research Institute, University of Salford.

Williams, Darrell. 1992. English comparative compounds with OVER, UNDER and OUT. In Michael Bernstein (ed.), *Proceedings of the Ninth Eastern States Conference of Linguistics (ESCOL) 1992*: 272–81. Ithaca, NY: Cornell University.

Williams, Edwin. 1981. On the notions 'lexically related' and 'head of a word'. *Linguistic Inquiry* 12: 245–74.

Williams, Theodore. 1965. On the *ness* peril. *American Speech* 40: 279–86.

Wordspy. The word lover's guide to new words. <http://wordspy.com/>, accessed 1 November 2012.

Wright, Joseph. 1905. *The English dialect grammar*. Oxford: Frowde.

Xu, Fei and Steven Pinker. 1995. *Weird* past tense forms. *Journal of Child Language* 22: 531–56.

Xu, Zheng and Mark Aronoff. 2011. A Realization Optimality Theory approach to blocking and extended morphological exponence. *Journal of Linguistics* 47: 673–707.

Yoon, James Hye Suk 1996. Nominal gerund phrases in English as phrasal zero derivations. *Linguistics* 34(2): 329–56.

Zamma, Hideki. 2003. Suffixes and stress/accent assignment in English and Japanese: A survey. In Takeru Honma, Masao Okazaki, Toshiyuki Tabata, and Shin-ichi Tanaka (eds), *A new century of phonology and phonological theory: A Festschrift for Professor Shosuke Haraguchi on the occasion of his sixtieth birthday*, 456–69. Tokyo: Kaitakusha.

Zandvoort, R. W. 1962. *A handbook of English Grammar*. 2nd edn. London: Longmans.

Zimmer, Karl E. 1964. Affixal negation in English and other languages. An investigation of restricted productivity. *Word* 20(5): 21–45.

Zirkel, Linda. 2010. Prefix combinations in English: Structural and processing factors. *Morphology* 20(1): 239–66.

Zwicky, Arnold. 1985. Heads. *Journal of Linguistics* 21(1): 1–29.

Zwicky, Arnold. 1989. Quicker, more quickly, *quicklier. *Yearbook of Morphology 1988*: 139–73.

Zwicky, Arnold. 1995. Why English adverbial *ly* is not inflectional. *Papers from the 31st regional meeting of the Chicago Linguistic Society* 31(1): 523–25.

SOURCES OF DATA

Amman, George A. 1944. Determining the age of pinnated and sharp-tailed grouses. *Journal of Wildlife Management* 8: 170–71.

Anderson, Kevin J. and Doug Benson. 1995. *Ill wind*. New York: Tom Doherty.

Baum, Frank L. 1900. *The wizard of Oz*. Chicago: George M. Hill.

Block, Lawrence. 2004. *The burglar on the prowl*. Harpenden: No Exit Press.

Cannell, Stephen J. 2003. *Hollywood tough*. New York: St Martin's.

Dekker, Diana. 2007. Obituary for Margaret Neave. *New Zealand Medical Journal* 23 March 2007, 120(1251), <http://www.nzma.org.nz/journal/120-1251/2475/>, accessed 3 February 2010.

Eskin, Frada. 1995. Values and ideals, isms and ologies: Making contact across a desert of differences. *Public Health* 109: 1–5.

Hill, Reginald. 2001. *Dialogues of the dead*. London: HarperCollins.

Kernick, Simon. 2003. *The murder exchange*. London: Bantam.

Lodge, David. 2001. *Thinks*. London: Secker & Warburg.

Lovesey, Peter. 1997. *Upon a dark night*. London: Little, Brown.

McClister, Michael. 1999. *Victim's choice*. New York: St Martin's.

McNab, Andy 2008. *Cross Fire*. London: Corgi.

Men's Health. 2001. Foods that you must must eat before you die. <http://thebestlist.menshealth. com/list/3787>, accessed 23 February 2012.

Meynell, Laurence. 1978. *Papersnake*. London: Macmillan.

Middleton, Sue. 2006. Research Assessment as a pedagogical device: A Bernsteinian exploration of its impact on New Zealand's subject/s of Education. Paper presented at the Australian Association for Research in Education Conference, Adelaide, 27–29 November 2006 <http://www.aare.edu.au/06pap/mid06131.pdf>, accessed 1 November 2012.

Newbie. 2001. *A painless transition, please*. <http://www.mail-archive.com/newbie@linux-man-drake.com/msg58073.html>, accessed 23 September 2011.

NZPA. 2007. Parrot smuggler fined $20, 000. New Zealand Herald, 9 November 2007. <http://www.nzherald.co.nz/nz/news/article.cfm?c_id=1&objectid=10475065>, accessed 7 January 2011.

Parker, Barbara. 2000. *Suspicion of malice*. New York: Dutton.

Rathbone, Julian. 2001. *Homage*. London: Allison & Busby.

Sandford, John. 2001. *Chosen Prey*. London: Simon & Schuster.

Strohmeyer, Sarah. 2004. *Bubbles a broad*. New York: Dutton.

Tolkien, John R. R. 1954. *The lord of the rings*. Part I: *The fellowship of the ring*. London: George Allen & Unwin.

Trevanian. 1998. *Incident at Twenty Mile*. New York: St Martin.

Vittachi, Nury. 2008. *Mr Wong goes west*. Crows Nest, NSW: Allen & Unwin.

Wallace, Danny. 2008. *Yes man*. N.p.: Ebury Press.

Waugh, Alexander. 2008. *The house of Wittgenstein*. New York: Doubleday. Excerpt from <http://www.amazon.com/House-Wittgenstein-Family-War/dp/product-description/0385520603>, accessed 3 February 2010.

White, Stephen. 2002. *Warning signs*. London: Little, Brown.

INDEX OF AFFIXES AND OTHER FORMATIVES

INDEX OF NAMES

INDEX OF SUBJECTS

head 141; nested 149; oblique 142; of 142,
146–9, 521; partitive 123, 146; phrasal 141;
<'s> 141, 146–9, 521; semantics of 142–3
German 140, 165, 389, 612, 619, 620, 621, 622, 624,
625, 626; Old High 619
Germanic 35, 131, 388, 434, 435, 456, 614, 616, 619,
620, 622–3, 623–5, 631; North 35; West 35,
616, 621, 632
Google 499, 551, 570, 584
Google Book Corpus 40, 132, 135
gradability 103–5, 365, 368, 378
grammar; generative 565; traditional 550
grammaticalization 259, 440
Greek 35, 48, 136–7, 177, 182, 256, 295, 357, 397,
426, 441, 456, 498, 583, 616, 627

habitual 62
hapax 580, 581
haplology 112–13, 145, 189–90, 197, 230, 251, 273,
326, 396, 456, 506, 617
head 28, 437, 442, 443, 453, 454, 465, 472, 474,
476, 540, 542–3; left-hand 344, 434, 439, 622,
626; right-hand 442, 443, 464, 486, 487, 567,
622; relativized 543
head-marking languages 618–9
heavy syllable 296, 298, 301
Hebrew 139
homography 54
homonymy 17, 545, 546, 575
homophony 66, 82, 279, 288, 289, 340, 412, 425,
545, 571; of affixes 42, 216, 323, 344, 347, 391,
399, 499, 546, 555, 633
Hup 624, 625
hyphen and hyphenation 10, 54–7, 337, 342,
396, 407, 419, 420, 423, 432, 438, 449–51, 452,
516
hypocoristic 134, 144, 191, 389, 394, 631
hyponymy 464, 465, 474, 483, 486

IA *see* Item and Arrangement
iamb 186, 198, 271, 297, 301
iconicity 623
idiom 12, 64, 89, 124, 489, 561
idiomatization 30, 259

imperative 62, 64, 79
Indo-European 535
infinitival *to* 88–90
infinitive 62, 64, 79
infix 630
inflection 59–158, 436, 493, 505–7, 519, 521–2, 566,
619–21; class-changing 555; contextual 534–5,
539; inherent 103, 534–5, 539; semantics
in 68; stem-based 619; vs. derivation 8, 28–9,
322–3, 440, 505–6, 533–44; word-based 619; *et
passim*
inflectional; base 19, 29; language *see* fusion
informativity 445, 447, 448
initialism 25, 396
institutionalization 30, 437, 489, 576, 577
internal modification 621, 630 *see* ablaut,
apophony, consonant-alternation, stress-shift,
vowel-alternation, umlaut
interrogativity 156
intransitivity 36–7
inversion 442, 452, 453
IP *see* Item and Process
irregularity *see* regularity
isolating 616, 617–8
Italian 128, 139–40, 536, 622
item and arrangement (IA) 629–31
item and process (IP) 629–31
item-familiarity 12, 30, 202, 306, 319, 344, 368,
394, 396, 464, 516, 565, 569, 612

Jamsay 624

Lango 625
Latin 15, 35, 136–7, 176, 180, 182, 206, 256, 297,
409, 418, 426, 438, 441, 498, 521, 571, 583;
Latin plurals in English 137–9, 536
Latinate 614 *see* non-native
lax 166
learned *see* non-native
lemma 537
level ordering 164, 493–508, 509, 571, 579, 637–8;
see also stratification
lexeme 8, 533, 560
Lexeme Morpheme Base Morphology 632–3